Sustainable Economic Development and the Influence of Information Technologies:
Dynamics of Knowledge Society Transformation

Muhammed Karatas
Mugla University, Turkey

Mustafa Zihni Tunca
Suleyman Demirel University, Turkey

Information Science REFERENCE

INFORMATION SCIENCE REFERENCE

Hershey · New York

Director of Editorial Content: Kristin Klinger
Director of Book Publications: Julia Mosemann
Acquisitions Editor: Beth Ardner
Development Editor: Joel Gamon
Publishing Assistant: Kurt Smith
Typesetter: Devvin Earnest
Quality Control: Jamie Snavely
Cover Design: Lisa Tosheff
Printed at: Yurchak Printing Inc.

Published in the United States of America by
Information Science Reference (an imprint of IGI Global)
701 E. Chocolate Avenue
Hershey PA 17033
Tel: 717-533-8845
Fax: 717-533-8661
E-mail: cust@igi-global.com
Web site: http://www.igi-global.com/reference

Library of Congress Cataloging-in-Publication Data

Sustainable economic development and the influence of information technologies : dynamics of knowledge society transformation / Muhammed Karatas and Mustafa Zihni Tunca, editors.

p. cm.

Includes bibliographical references and index.

Summary: "This book provides relevant theoretical frameworks and the latest empirical research findings in the area of information technology as it relates to sustainable economic development and the development of knowledge societies"--Provided by publisher.

ISBN 978-1-61520-709-1 (hardcover) -- ISBN 978-1-61520-710-7 (ebook) 1. Sustainable development--Developing countries. 2. Information technology--Developing countries. I. Karatas, Muhammed, 1972- II. Tunca, Mustafa Zihni, 1972-

HC59.72.E5S883 2010

338.9'270285--dc22

2009046555

British Cataloguing in Publication Data

A Cataloguing in Publication record for this book is available from the British Library.

Editorial Advisory Board

Table of Contents

Detailed Table of Contents

This chapter is a brief account of what we now observe in the growth literature in light of the developments in the voluminous empirical works on economic growth. It is argued that while the empirical knowledge has advanced adequately, little progress has been made in the growth theory since the classic works of Solow. Therefore it can be said that growth economist and policy makers are still confused on how to raise the steady state growth rate of output and some of these confusions are due to our own experiments.

Sustainable social development cannot be fully understood apart from its cultural, moral, political, and educational foundations; and philosophy helps us to see it as a whole and to clearly comprehend its foundations. The main assumption behind that claim is that we can know what to do for realizing sustainable development if we actually know about specific or internal reasons for the fall of the societies and civilizations. This chapter begins with such an assumption and asserts that there must be four integrated foundations for any sustainable social development by benefiting from the views of Max Weber, Ibn Khaldun, Aristotle, John Dewey and some Ottoman Turkish philosophers: among those foundations are

This book chapter re-conceptualises the relationships between technology and development. It focuses on rural economic development and examines how water- and energy-related technologies interact with human-nature relationships. Drawing on case studies in Rajasthan, India, this chapter argues that people's preferences for livelihoods can be incompatible with technological design. The unintended consequences of water and energy interventions can bring uncertainty to policy-making which affects long-term economic development and ecological sustainability. Changing governance structures in challenging caste and gender inequalities also require strong leadership. It proposes a 'people-centred' technological intervention framework which links the macro technical system and the micro process of people's daily practices and subjectivities. In achieving this, it calls for a different approach to understanding human motivations, power dynamics and gender politics.

Section 3
Savings and Investments

Chapter 6
The Influences of Savings and Investments on Sustainable Development and the Role of Information Technology 66
Leonardo Baggiani, Independent Researcher, Italy

This chapter wants to investigates how the combination of savings and investments affects economic development and sustainability. This discussion aims to help to understand the role of savings as a support to growth, and how biasing individual decisions on consumption and debt via monetary policies can be a source of economic growth un-sustainability. Information technology helps to optimise the use of resources, but it even makes dangerous policies easier to implement. Section 1 shows theoretical insights into the contribution of savings to growth, and the concept of sustainability; section 2 focuses on the theories that better deal with the sustainability concern and investigates the role of information technology in monetary policy; section 3 shows the growing, positive contribution of e-money to growth and sustainability, and it suggests a new role for the government as advisor within an information-enhanced economy where information technology can play a prominent role; section 4 concludes.

Chapter 7
Developing the Financial Infrastructure in an Emerging Market Economy: The Role of Credit Rating Agencies 87
Michael G. Papaioannou, International Monetary Fund, USA
George P. Tsetsekos, Drexel University, USA

This chapter examines the role of rating agencies in capital-market development and on the conduct of monetary policy. Rating agencies in developed capital markets provide quality certification to issuers. For emerging capital markets, the role of a rating agency is crucial in enhancing informational efficiency in the marketplace. The authors highlight the indirect macroeconomics consequences from the presence of a rating agency, including its monetary surveillance role of such agency and the positive implications for foreign investments. The chapter outlines the conditions for an effective rating agency in an emerging market economy, discusses the benefits of security ratings to constituencies, and proposes a scenario

for a rating agency's design. The collaboration of regulators, central bankers, and issuers is especially critical to the success of the rating agency.

This chapter examines the hypotheses that trade liberalization and financial liberalization jointly enhances economic growth in the four South Asian countries including Bangladesh, India, Pakistan and Sri Lanka for the period 1970-2007 using bounds testing approach to cointegration. The results suggest that in the long-run except for Bangladesh, financial development plays no role in promoting economic growth in these countries. Furthermore, the results suggest that trade openness plays a significant role in promoting economic growth in Bangladesh and India, while exerts negative effect on Pakistan and no effect on Sri Lanka. The share of domestic investment influences real output significantly in Bangladesh, India and Pakistan. In the long- as well as short-run two-way causality between real output, trade openness, share of investment and inflation rate exists for the case of Bangladesh and India. For the case of India two-way causality between finance and growth exists in the short-run. For the case of Pakistan, there is an evidence of long-run causality between real output, finance, trade openness, share of investment and inflation rate. However, in the short-run, two-way causality between real output, trade openness and share of investment is existed and one-way causality between inflation rate, trade openness and share of investment is also observed. No evidence of short-run causality between finance and growth and vice versa for Pakistan has been seen. Finally, for Sri Lanka, an evidence of long-run causality between real output, finance, trade openness and investment share has been found. In the short-run one-way causality between finance-growth, trade-finance, trade-growth and trade-investment has been obtained. These mixed results suggest that the authorities may focuses more and more on the trade liberalization. In addition, there is a need to further deepen the banking and stock markets and provide investment friendly environment to enhance domestic investment which, in turn, promotes economic growth.

Emerging growth dynamism of Indian economy in rapidly globalising world is highly recognised and commented by a large body of researchers during the recent period. In fact, the Indian planning has made long concerted effort to develop strategic and competitive capabilities in the agents of production. During the recent periods, these capabilities have started paying. Such trends became more lucid with the strengthening of Indian capital especially abroad as the Indian capital has initiated collaborations and mergers with the global players. This chapter provides insights into such achievement of the Indian economy. Besides providing a review of theory and practice of emerging multinationals from developing countries, this chapter examines India's outward foreign direct investment in an evolutionary perspective. In its endeavor the study, besides tracing the emerging pattern of India's outward foreign direct investment, hints at the facilitating role of state policy to encourage the outflow of foreign direct investment.

This chapter explores the link between telecommunications capital intensity and aggregate production efficiency in the framework of meta-frontier analysis. The latter makes it possible to compare technical efficiency levels between countries operating under different technological frontiers. The author's analysis suggests that increasing per capita levels of telecommunication capital will push a country towards its local frontier, but it will not decrease much the technological gap with the global meta-frontier. In Africa policies providing incentives for firms and households to purchase more telecommunications equipment appear to be most justified in terms of efficiency gains, while this does not appear to be the case for the OECD countries. The author's general conjecture is, in order to avoid wasting productive resources on increasing the level of telecommunications capital intensity, it is advisable to keep a close eye on the location of a country's aggregate output with respect to both local and meta-frontiers.

Over the past five years the Philippine IT-enabled services industry has grown tremendously, fuelled primarily by strong global demand. The main competitiveness drivers of the Philippines as an attractive location for offshore IT-enabled services are well documented: highly skilled, English proficient workforce; low labour costs; cultural affinity towards the United States; reliable telecommunications infrastructure; and business-friendly policies. It is this rare combination of resources that has attracted many FDIs to locate their outsourcing operations in the Philippines which has made the country a prime location for customer contact service centres and business process outsourcing. This chapter examines the internal capabilities and external linkages of the Philippine ITES industry based on an empirical study. It focuses on how these various capabilities and linkages play a significant role in facilitating the ITES industry's growth and long term sustainability.

This chapter aims to assess policies regarding information and communication technologies (ICTs) in Turkey within the last five years. The focus of the chapter will be on digital divide: Although, ICTs in general, and the Internet in particular, have become an essential part of everyday life in Turkey, the access to the opportunities provided by these technologies has not been distributed equally. The divides with respect to social class, geographic location, gender and age cripple the potential benefits of these policies. In addition, the programs implemented so far have been highly influenced by the global policy agenda; in a sense, adapting the "information society" vision advanced globally to the local context. In order to actualize an equitable and sustainable transformation process, there is further need to understand the nuanced picture Turkey's social conditions present. This chapter will examine the ways in which information society project has been modelled in Turkey, the policy paradigms that shaped its direction and finally, where they fell short and where they offer potentials.

Undoubtedly, digital technology (DT) has revolutionalised information and communications technology (ICT) base of the global economy, which has impacted tremendously the socio-economic, political, cultural and scientific development in the majority of the world's economies. The chapter examines "digital divide" in a broader perspective of information and communications technologies (ICTs) that encompass not only computers, but also telephone (line and cellular), television (TV), radio etc. It is an open secret that ICTs have played and will continue to play a pivotal role in sustaining economic development in the developed countries. Through ICTs, creating, storing and sharing enormous volume of information with relative ease in almost all the spheres of human endeavour have been made possible. The power inherent in ICT that can break up barriers and boundaries holding countries, continents and businesses miles apart can never be over-emphasized. Despite the attendant benefits of ICTs, there are still deep-seated ICT inequalities both within and among the Organization of the Islamic Conference (OIC) member countries. This chapter investigates the depth of the existing digital divide among the OIC member countries and to unearth the possible obstacles. Finally, some policy recommendations have been offered towards the end of the chapter.

Regional innovation strategies which emerged during the mid 90s and were implemented especially in the developing regions of the world are significant for the transformation of both the knowledge produced in the regional scale and the added value it created into competitive power in the national and global scale. These strategies which have successfully been implemented in different parts of the world are a great opportunity for a country like Turkey which has a large young population and stands out among the other developing countries with her strategic location and potentials for human resources, agriculture and commerce. Focusing on these strategies and exploring national and regional innovation systems, this chapter both investigates the leader implementations in Europe and examines the first implementations of regional innovation strategies in Turkey. This chapter suggests that by transforming her regional innovation skills into products and services that have added value, Turkey will have a potential to achieve rapid social and economic development and therefore increase her significance for the national and international innovative investors.

The notion of new regional development is built on the model of governance in Turkey. E-government has some serious potential of contributing to the implementation of this new notion of regional development. In this context, the aim of this chapter is to discuss the current state of the concept of regional development in Turkey and to analyze the contributions of e-government to the notion and applications of new regional development. Within this framework, initially, paradigmatic shift in regional development is analyzed. And then, the role and effect of e-government is explicated within the triangular relationship between development, good governance and e-government in socio-economic development. Subsequently, the notion of regional development in Turkey and its application is introduced from a historical perspective and the very recently adopted notion of new regional development is explained. Finally, the potential contributions of the e-government applications to this new notion of regional development in Turkey are analyzed.

Foreword

Technology, particularly IT in these days, acts as a great catalyst for economic development. On the other hand, new technologies and innovations do not make any sense unless an important percentage of individuals in a society benefit from them. We all believe that the knowledge society transformation process requires enormous effort and a vast amount of resources. Yet it is the only way to assure the existence of the magic word, sustainability. The editors, Dr. Karatas and Dr. Tunca give us an opportunity to get the whole picture of the influence of ICTs on sustainable economic development in this book. This edited book represents a unique contribution to the literature as the contributors from different countries deeply investigate a variety of highly interesting topics from different perspectives. I hope this book will serve as a useful reference for all those interested in sustainable economic development, and a better understanding of the influence of ICTs and knowledge society transformation process.

Prof.Dr.İsrafil Kurtcephe
Rector
University of Akdeniz, Turkey

Preface

The history of mankind is full of innovation, research, discovery, war, and conquest for the sake of social welfare. Although one can call this complex and endless process as the *meaning of life*, according to economists, it is just the way to improve the quality of life. While countries seek for social welfare at the macro level, human beings try to improve the quality of their lifestyle at the micro level.

Scholars agree that welfare is critically important for economic development. Since welfare is mainly an outcome of the positive change in income level, dramatic growth in developed countries following World War II has attracted much attention. Nevertheless, the distinctive characteristics of wealth and poverty have led economists to seek for dynamics of economic development. Direct and indirect connections among the dynamics of economic development have always been an issue. For instance, productivity is known as the engine of economic development. Then again, education and technology are key elements of productivity. While education is important to improve human-related factors, advanced technology is necessary for technical improvements. No need to mention the importance of education for the technology development process. At this point, it is necessary to highlight the significant role of individuals on economic development. Every human being is a temporary member of the development process. Unlikely, societies are permanent elements of this process as they are responsible for providing human capital to keep the system running.

Apart from Western Europe, North America, Oceania, and Japan, all other regions of the world consist of developing or less developed countries. Considering the fact that most of the developing countries have already completed the development process, it is necessary to understand how did they succeed in sustainable development? A close look at socio-economic, technological, and political changes in those countries can help us for a better understanding of the dynamics of sustainable development.

In the 21st century, size, form and the direction of development primarily affect the transformation process of a nation into a knowledge society. While some countries quickly complete this process, the digital divide between these rapidly advancing countries and the rest of the world has become increasingly wider. By examining the factors which significantly affect the digital divide, we can address the dynamics and the effects of change, which include the acquisition of new knowledge, industrial development, economic development, technological development, migration, differences in religions and ideologies, organizational changes and so on.

Information technology is the key concept for sustainable economic development within both macro and micro perspectives as it can assist in addressing individual, organizational, regional, and global development. Hence, there is an imperative need for an in-depth, systematical investigation of the dynamics and effects of the knowledge society transformation process in order to address the influence of information technologies on sustainable economic development in the 21st century.

Sustainable Economic Development And The Influence Of Information Technologies: Dynamics of Knowledge Society Transformation provides relevant theoretical frameworks and the latest empirical research findings in the area of information technology as it relates to sustainable economic development and the development of knowledge societies. It consists of chapters in wide range of topics, written by a variety of scholars and professionals in various disciplines from different countries.

The book is organized into five sections with 17 chapters. Section 1 addresses some theoretical discussions about sustainable economic development. Section 1 includes three chapters:

> Chapter 1, "*Why The Already Difficult Task of Identifying Sources of Growth has Become even more Challenging?*" provides a summary of some of the useful issues in analyzing and understanding the growth process. It briefly explains how the empirical literature on growth has made identifying sources of growth even more challenging.
> Chapter 2, "*Some Philosophical Reflections on Foundations of Sustainable Social Development,*" provides a discussion of sustainable social development process to achieve sustainable economic development.
> Chapter 3, "*Lessons for Development Economists from the Shanghai Experience, 1842-2008,*" provides a discussion on the financial conjunctures and institutional patterns that had the most lasting impact on how business was carried through in Shanghai before the Pacific War, and compares them with the city's growth dynamic and new knowledge base under the current reform thrust.

Section 2 addresses the importance of natural resources for sustainable economic development. Section 2 includes two chapters:

> Chapter 4, "*Natural Resources Accounting for Sustainable Development: Approaches and Some Applications,*" highlights the potential of using natural resources accounting for making decisions for sustainable development through policies for conservation, management and development of natural resources.
> Chapter 5, "*Re-Conceptualising the 'Technology-Development' Nexus: Linking Water, Energy, People and Governance in India,*" focuses on rural economic development and examines how water- and energy-related technologies interact with human-nature relationships.

Section 3 addresses the significance of savings and investments. Section 3 includes four chapters:

> Chapter 6, "*The Influences of Savings and Investments on Sustainable Development and the Role of Information Technology,*" aims to investigate how the combination of savings and investments affects economic development and sustainability.
> Chapter 7, "*Developing the Financial Infrastructure in an Emerging Market Economy: The Role of Credit Rating Agencies,*" examines the role of rating agencies in capital-market development and on the conduct of monetary policy.
> Chapter 8, "*Does Financial Liberalization and Trade Openness Promote Growth in South Asia,*" analyzes the role of finance, trade and information technology and seeks the possible answer that does financial development, trade openness and information technology promotes economic growth?

Chapter 9, "*Changing Contours of Indian Investment Abroad: Evolution, Diagnosis and Public Policy*," examines India's outward foreign direct investment in an evolutionary perspective by tracing the emerging pattern of India's outward foreign direct investment, hints at the facilitating role of state policy to encourage the outflow of foreign direct investment.

Section 4 addresses the influence of information and communication technologies. Section 4 includes four chapters:

Chapter 10, "*Does Information and Communication Technologies Sustain Economic Growth? The Underdeveloped and Developing Countries Case*," works out theoretically and econometrically whether ICT investment has a positive impact on the long-run growth performance of underdeveloped and developing countries.
Chapter 11, "*An Empirical Analysis of Indices and Factors of ICT Use by Small- and Medium-sized Enterprises in Japan*," attempts to extract factors which promote the introduction and usage of ICT by small- and medium-sized enterprises in Japan.
Chapter 12, "*Telecommunications Capital Intensity and Aggregate Production Efficiency: A Meta-Frontier Analysis*," attempts to estimate the effects of telecommunications capital intensity on the levels of aggregate production efficiency in a broad range of countries around the world, putting a specific emphasis on the difference between country group and global stochastic production frontiers.
Chapter 13, "*Evaluating the Internal Capabilities and External Linkages of the Philippine IT-Enabled Services (ITES) Industry*," examines how internal capabilities and external linkages of the Philippine ITES industry play a significant role in facilitating growth and long term sustainability.

Section 5 addresses the issues about knowledge society transformation and digital divide. Section 5 includes four chapters:

Chapter 14, "*The Potentials and Pitfalls of the Information Society Project in Turkey: A Critical Assessment of Policy Paradigms Regarding E-Transformation and Digital Divide*," examines policies regarding information and communication technologies in Turkey with a special references to Turkey's Information Society Project.
Chapter 15, "*Sustainable Development and the Digital Divide Among OIC Countries: Towards A Collaborative Digital Approach*," examines the digital divide in a broader perspective of information and communications technologies, and investigates the depth of the existing digital divide among the OIC member countries.
Chapter 16, "*Regional Innovation Strategies: Europe and Turkey*," explores the development of regional innovation strategies in Turkey in relation to the relevant EU policies.
Chapter 17, "*Governance-Based Regional Development and E-Government: The Turkish Case*," analyzes the current state of the concept of regional development in Turkey, and examines the contributions of e-government to the notion and applications of new regional development.

Editors
Dr. Muhammed Karatas
Dr. Mustafa Zihni Tunca

Acknowledgment

We would like to thank the contributors of this book. Without their dedication, the book would not have been possible. We express our special thanks to the editorial advisory board of the book. Their constructive suggestions were valuable to quality of this book. We are indebted to Joel Gamon and Rebecca Beistline of IGI, whose support and cooperation have been invaluable. Last but certainly not least, our deepest appreciation goes to our families for their endless support and patience throughout this project.

June 2009
Dr. Muhammed Karatas, Mugla University, Turkey
Dr. Mustafa Zihni Tunca, Suleyman Demirel University, Turkey

Section 1
Towards Sustainable Economic Development

Chapter 1
Why the Already Difficult Task of Identifying Sources of Growth has Become even more Challenging

Rup Singh
The University of the South Pacific, Suva (Fiji)

ABSTRACT

This chapter is a brief account of what we now observe in the growth literature in light of the developments in the voluminous empirical works on economic growth. It is argued that while the empirical knowledge has advanced adequately, little progress has been made in the growth theory since the classic works of Solow. Therefore it can be said that growth economist and policy makers are still confused on how to raise the steady state growth rate of output and some of these confusions are due to our own experiments.

INTRODUCTION

In a survey chapter as this, it is hard to detail all the important issues that growth and development economists face in their daily professional routine. Nonetheless, we summarize some important points that might be of interest to those working on growth topics, particularly for growth and development policy. It is noted that in light of the confusion in the empirical growth literature, growth economists and policy makers alike are unclear about the specific growth enhancing factors that might increase the steady-state growth rate of output. This is because, a clear explanation to the sources of growth is yet to be forthcoming. Factors such as trade openness, human capital and R&D, amongst others, have been identified to be growth enhancing. Recently, contribution from information and communications technology (ITC) seems to be significant for developed and some developing economies (see Keely and Quah, 1998). However, the empirics of growth has either supported or rejected these factors on the basis of personal proliferation, (un)complicated econometric techniques and the use of right or wrong specifications, in time series and cross-sectional studies alike. Consequently a non-exhaustive list of growth enhancing factors has been proposed, most of which have led to further confusion than

DOI: 10.4018/978-1-61520-709-1.ch001

answers to the century-old question in the growth theory - the sources of economic growth.

Recall the well-known Sala-I-Martin's (1997) experiment with two million regressions - the conclusions of which surprised many. A summary of the top ten growth factors in his work is in Berg (2001). In a recent survey of cross-country studies Durlauf, Johnson and Temple (2005) indicate that in various empirical works, the potential growth factors total one hundred and forty five. More recently, Durlauf, Kourtellos, and Tan (2008) have summarised them into six broad categories, viz, (i) economic institutions (ii) legal and political systems (iii) climate (iv) geographical isolation (v) ethnic fractionalization and (vi) culture. It is not surprising that there are endless debates on growth policy; see for example, Bosworth and Collins (2003) and Durlauf, Johnson and Temple (2005). Pritchett (2006) evaluates the usefulness of growth models for policy, particularly for developing countries. He argues that the first generation endogenous models which propagate incentives for innovative technology and are based on the long run (which in calendar years could be close to a generation's lifespan) are of little use for policy in economies whose main interest is to manage the short-to-medium term fluctuations in their growth rates. Rao and Cooray (2008a) provide some guidelines on how to narrow the gap between the implications of growth models and the need to develop practical policies for developing economies. They take the view that the potential of the Solow (1956) model and its variants such as the Mankiw, Romer and Weil (1992) has not been explored adequately to capture the effects of factors on varying time horizons that might be of use for policy in these economies[1].

This chapter briefly explains how the empirical literature on growth has made identifying sources of growth even more challenging. It is organized as follows: In the next section, we discuss the lessons learnt over the last 50 years or so in growth theory and identify the recent additions to growth literature. Section 3 summarizes issues in empirical growth literature while in section 4, we discuss why Solow is correct in saying that the growth theory has not advanced much since his own contributions despite the new insights obtained from both theoretical and empirical research. Section 5 concludes.

LESSONS LEARNT

In a summary, it can be said that although much was said about growth and its sources, the analysis on growth was unsystematic before the works of Solow (1956, 1957). Although useful for short-term policy, see Berg (2001), the famous Harrod-Domer model of the mid-1940s is today more or less ignored because Solow showed the limitations in its assumptions, see Solow (2008) for his brief comments. Another line of exposition, the endogenous models, starting from the works of Romer (1986) created a series of interesting research where innovation, knowledge capital and R&D etc were tested mainly for developed countries. Meanwhile a wave of works largely based on cross-sectional data flooded the literature where the effects of any possibly quantifiable growth factors were tested mainly with ad-hoc specifications. Easterly, Levine and Roodman (2004) argue that most of these models can hardly be justified by the theory and more seriously often imply that there are more possible specifications than the data points in their sample. Unfortunately, these works are just too many to list. Also apparent are works that did not fail to wrongly implement the famous test of Granger (1988), with some exceptions, leading to casual interpretation for growth policy[2]. Solow (2008) thinks that increasing the steady-state growth rate (SSGR) even by 1% is a huge challenge. This is because if for the last 50 years or so, the SSGR has been 2%, one must be able to justify the policies or the sources of growth that have been unveiled that would raise the SSGR from 2% to say 3%. Unless the justifications are forthcoming in the correct magnitudes, it is hard to believe the causal relationships often made in these studies.

Empirical experts following time series methods rallied heavily behind the cointegration techniques without proper specifications. Recently, a similar trend is being noted in studies based on panel data methods. We avoid listing them for the criticisms of polarity. Recently, studies on the 'New Economy" argue that technological break-through explain could why in the face of productivity slowdown, the US economy did not fail to perform badly in the 1990s. The recent growth trends in USA postulate the increasing role for the ICT sector. Harchaoui et. al (2002) use the standard growth accounting framework and comment that both in USA and Canada, the ITC has been the largest contributor to growth via its contribution to capital services during the late 1990s. Saxton (2001) attribute ITC's contribution to labour productivity growth in the USA to be between 60%-90% during this decade. It is agreed that ITC is a modernizing influence leading to capital deepening which in turn can increase a country's overall productivity and output per capita. Thus recent evidence points to the role of innovative technology both in its production and use that can possibly lead to an enhancement in growth rates and economics development. While one may read this as a conclusion of endogenous models, this was also obvious in the Solow (1956) exposition.

ISSUES IN EMPIRICAL MODELS

Some serious issues relating to the empirical growth literature are discussed below. Unfortunately, it is noted that this literature is filled with ad-hoc regressions of country-specific growth rates during some medium-long period on a potentially long list of country characteristics. However, it is logical to think that the SSGR is unobserved in data and short panels (in panel data methods) or average and annual average growth rates (in cross- sectional and time series estimates, respectively) do not replicate the SSGR adequately. At best, one can estimate an augmented production function and derive the growth effects based on the steady state conditions, see Rao and Singh (2007) for a discussion of this approach. A useful time series method (if one is interested in country specific policies) is LSE-Hendry's GETS because of the conflict between the nature of SSGR and the inadequacy of data to replicate it.[3]

However, what we now see are more methodological conflicts than the forthcoming answers to the important questions for policy. Support for this is in Bosworth and Collins (2003) whose assertion on empirical growth literature fuels our doubts even further. They argue that the empirical growth economics is filled with conflicting claims and strong disagreements on the methodology, conclusions on growth factors, measurement errors and variable selection biases. Although some generalizations can be made regarding the growth factors, often those that top the list are policy invariants, like climate, distance, culture etc[4]. This is close to saying that more or less economies that weigh heavily along these factors have their fates sealed and that there is little scope for policy to maneuver their growth trajectory. Note if this is really the case, it would be hard to ensure a sustained increase in human welfare in these economies regardless of our understanding of the growth factors.

Further, Solow (2008) argues that the proper left-hand-side variable should be the growth of TFP rather than that of output because that is what the right-hand-side variables are likely to affect. This justifies the endogenous TFP which is modeled in Rao and Singh (2007). They argue that the exogenous TFP of Solow could be made a function of the possible growth enhancing factors without having to divert from the Solow framework. Senhadji's (2000) work is similar in spirit. Following the growth accounting exercise (merely to estimate the share of capital on output) he regressed a plausible list of growth factors on the estimated growth rate of TFP[5]. However, the array of influences on TFP is certainly large and inter-related. Thus although there might be an identifiable subset of factors which may individually or in combination affect TFP, modeling them is a daunting task. For empirical wizards, the growth effect of factors in econometric models with correct signs are just relieving. However, it should be noted that the estimated coefficients also imply the rate at which policies based on these factors could be used to maneuver the economy and one must be able to justify this plausibility.

Moreover, Solow (2008) thinks that cross country regressions and ad-hoc time series estimates, at best, can only provide interesting descriptive statistics. This is partly because, often the search of proper proxy variables is difficult or debatable and surely mis-specification and multi-colinearity in variables will make estimation complicated. Further the literature is unclear on how one can introduce many of these variables of interest simultaneously in growth models. We are of the view that variables that generate externalities and require no additional resources can still be modeled within an extended framework of Solow, an area of research that is worth exploring. However, those that are not freely available would require multi-equation endogenous models in the spirit of Grainer, Semler and Gong (2004). These factors require additional investment by firms and may have externalities. Endogenous models are computationally demanding in light of the available data for developing countries.

Another limitation in growth empirics based on cross-country regressions is the assumption that aggregate technology is same for all countries in the sample. Similar issues arise in panel regressions where the pooled sample of countries is heterogeneous in economic, social and technological characteristics. Caution is required when we decide which countries should make the sample. For example, there is no point in pooling USA with Kiribati – two varied economies in all respects and making a recommendation that hardly fits any. Furthermore, it is hard to derive country specify growth policies from such studies and for this reason, studies that propagate "one size fits all" are highly criticized. We are thus inclined to argue that there are some merits in country specific time series estimates as opposed to cross sectional or panel regressions if the main objective is to develop country specific growth policies, but with proper specifications.

GROWTH THEORY TODAY

Despite the popularity of endogenous models, Solow still believes that this area of research has added very little to the growth theory. According to Solow (2008), the real contribution of endogenous models has been in the stimulus that they have provided in thinking about the actual production of TFP because these models claim to "endogenise" the growth rate of output. Speaking of the first generation AK type endogenous models, Solow (2008) argues that they were *neither right nor plausible* in their claims to endogenise the growth rate. He states that this required a linear differential equation of output which should be a function of things that one knew how to determine (or manipulate by policy) and surely this dynamic equation is hard to justify. Solow states that the plausibility of the "growth models" depends on the possibility of this assumption, which according to Durlauf, Johnson and Temple (2005) is hard to defend in light of the long list of growth factors – one runs the risk of omitted variable bias. Rao et. al[6] imply that behind every growth equation, there is ought to be a steady-state output equation which can be possibly estimated because it makes little sense to estimate the growth equation directly with data that hardly reflects SSGR.

Endogenous models are complementary to Solow's because they explain (or attempts to) what determines Solow's exogenous productivity. Therefore, disregarding the controversial empirical findings, we have not seen much advancement in the growth theory following the classic works of Solow. However, endogenous models have offered some policy guidelines for increasing the growth rate of output mainly for developed countries. Discussing polices for enhancing TFP in developing countries through R&D, innovation etc does not make sense because (i) the infrastructure and resources for R&D are limited in these economies and (ii) TFP's role on growth rates in these economies is minimal - this is a well known result from many growth accounting exercises, see for example Senhadji (2000), amongst others.

Solow's conjecture on endogenous models is supported in Jones (1995) who argues with time series data that there is no evidence of scale affects (the crucial assumption of endogenous models) in R&D and investment ratios in USA and OECD countries. Others like Hao-His Huang (2002) did not find support for endogenous models in the East Asian Economies and the recent evidence obtained by Lau (2008), although indirectly, fails to support endogenous models. Kohcerlakota and Yi (1996) also do not find much support for endogenous growth by analyzing various types of investment in the USA.

However, the problem still persists for policy. Some recent works show pragmatic compromises, where the TFP that grows at an exogenous rate in the Solow model is endogenised to factors that may affect TFP. Some of these are openness to trade, financial innovation and learning by doing type externalities, but other alternatives methods of testing are also possible. However, the usual practice is fitting data to specifications. New evidences on growth factors do emerge and most of these forces work in some combination - which is the right one, we still can only modestly speculate.

CONCLUDING COMMENTS

This chapter provides a summary of some of the useful issues in analyzing and understanding the growth process. It is suggested that applied growth economists and policy makers ought to pay adequate attention to those emphasized in order to avoid the usual limitations as noted in many of the works from empirical growth literature.

It has been noted that our understanding of the sources of growth is limited, although the empirical literature has provided justifications for many growth enhancing variables. With wrong or right approach, we have at our disposal a host of growth factors which could be relevant for policy, but which one(s), for certainty and in what combination, we do not know. Part of this puzzle is due to our own creation through over-stretching on the empirical front. However, having said that, economists tend to agree that some factors like human capital, R&D, trade openness and now the ITC innovation could lead to sustained growth rate of output and consequently promote economic development.

REFERENCES

Berg, V. (2001). *Economic Growth and Development.* New York: Mc-Graw-Hill.

Bosworth, B., & Collins, S. (2003). The empirics of growth: An update. *Brookings Papers on Economic Activity, 2*(xx), 113–206. doi:10.1353/eca.2004.0002

Durlauf, S., Johnson, P., & Temple, J. (2005). Empirics of growth and development. In P. Aghion & S. N. Durlauf (Eds.), *Handbook of Economic Growth.* Amsterdam: North-Holland.

Durlauf, S., Kourtellos, A., & Tan, C. (2008). Are Any Growth Theories Robust? *The Economic Journal, 118*(527), 329–346. doi:10.1111/j.1468-0297.2007.02123.x

Easterly, W., Levine, R., & Roodman, D. (2004). Aid, policies and growth [Comment]. *The American Economic Review, 94*(3), 774–780. doi:10.1257/0002828041464560

Granger, C. (1988). Some recent developments in a concept of causality. *Journal of Econometrics, 39*(2), 199–211. doi:10.1016/0304-4076(88)90045-0

Greiner, A., Semler, W., & Gong, G. (2004). *The Forces of Economic Growth: A Time Series Perspective.* Princeton, NJ: Princeton University Press.

Harchaoui, T., Tarkhani, F., Jackson, C., & Armstrong, P. (2002). Information technology and economic growth in Canada & the US. *Monthly Labour Review*. Retrieved from http://www.bls.gov/opub/mlr/2002

Hendry, D., & Krolxig, H. (2005). The properties of automatic GETS modeling. *The Economic Journal, 115*(20), C32–C31. doi:10.1111/j.0013-0133.2005.00979.x

Hendry, D., Pagan, A., & Saragan, J. (1984). Dynamic Specification In Z. Grilliches & M. D. Intriligator (Eds.), *Handbook of Econometrics* (Vol. 2, pp. 1023-1100). Amsterdam: North-Holland.

Huang, C. (2002). *How do endogenous models explain the Asian growth experience? A time series study of eleven Asian economies* (Working paper 2002). Department of Economics, National Tsing Hua University.

Jones, C. (1995). Time series tests of endogenous growth models. *The Quarterly Journal of Economics, 110*(2), 495–525. doi:10.2307/2118448

Keely, C., & Quah, T. (1998). *Technology in Growth* (CEP discussion paper no. 391).

Kohcerlakota, N., & Yi, K. (1996). A simple time series test of endogenous vs. exogenous growth models: An application to the United States. *The Review of Economics and Statistics, 78*(1), 126–134. doi:10.2307/2109852

Lau, S. (2008). Using an error correction model to test whether endogenous long run growth exists. *Journal of Economic Dynamics & Control, 32*(10), 648–676. doi:10.1016/j.jedc.2007.06.004

Mankiw, N., Romer, D., & Weil, D. (1992). A contribution to the empirics of economic growth. *The Quarterly Journal of Economics, 107*(2), 407–437. doi:10.2307/2118477

Pritchett, L. (2006). The Quest Continues. *Finance and Development, 43*(1). Retrieved from http//www.imf.org/external/pubs/ft/fandd/2006/03/pritchet.htm

Rao, B., & Cooray, A. (2008a). *How useful is the theoretical and the empirical growth literature for policies in the developing countries.* EERI Research paper Series (9/2008), Belgium.

Rao, B., & Singh, R. (2007). *Effects of trade openness on the steady state growth rates of selected Asian countries with an extended exogenous growth model* (MPRA Paper 8605). University Library of Munich, Germany.

Rao, B., & Tamazian, A. (2008b). A model of growth and finance: FIML estimates for India (MPRA Paper 8763). University Library of Munich, Germany.

Romer, P. (1986). Increasing returns and long run growth. *The Journal of Political Economy, 94*(October), 1002–1037. doi:10.1086/261420

Sala-i-Martin, X. (1997). I just ran two million regressions. *The American Economic Review, 87*(2), 178–183.

Saxton, J. (2001). Information technology and the new economy. A Joint Economic Committee Study, United States Congress, Washington.

Senhadji, A. (2000). Sources of economic growth: An extensive growth accounting exercise. *IMF Staff Papers, 47*(1).

Solow, R. (1956). A contribution to the theory of economic growth. *The Quarterly Journal of Economics*, *71*(1), 65–94. doi:10.2307/1884513

Solow, R. (1957). Technical Change and Aggregate Production Function. *The Review of Economics and Statistics*, *39*(August), 312–320. doi:10.2307/1926047

Solow, R. (2008). The last 50 years in growth theory and the next 10. *Oxford Review of Economic Policy*, *23*(1), 3–14. doi:10.1093/oxrep/grm004

ENDNOTES

1 Rao and Cooray (2008a) show investment ratio has larger short-medium term effects in a number of East Asian Economies. They argue that investment policy can be a useful growth driver in these economies in transition. .

2 Rao and Tamazian (2008b) provide a useful discussion of the Granger's test and how it is mis-conceived

3 Details of this procedure are in Hendry, Pagan, Saragan (1984) and a discussion of its automatic version is in Hendry and Krolzig (2005).

4 Even in Sala-I-Martin (1997), religion (types) and latitude made a few of the top 10 list.

5 Rao and Cooray (2008a) show an improvement over Senhadji's procedure. See details in their paper.

6 ibid

Chapter 2
Some Philosophical Reflections on Foundations of Sustainable Social Development

Hakan Gundogdu
Gazi University, Turkey

ABSTRACT

Sustainable social development cannot be fully understood apart from its cultural, moral, political, and educational foundations; and philosophy helps us to see it as a whole and to clearly comprehend its foundations. The main assumption behind that claim is that we can know what to do for realizing sustainable development if we actually know about specific or internal reasons for the fall of the societies and civilizations. This chapter begins with such an assumption and asserts that there must be four integrated foundations for any sustainable social development by benefiting from the views of Max Weber, Ibn Khaldun, Aristotle, John Dewey and some Ottoman Turkish philosophers: among those foundations are (1) effective working mentality grounded on culture, (2) strong ethical perspective including the virtues of moderation, friendship and sympathy, (3) flexible but stable social stratification which is based on middle class and positive competition, (4) effective state composed of solidarity, democracy and education of critical thinking. All those can, the author thinks, can be seen as parts of a sort of social liberalism rather than classical or neo-liberalism.

INTRODUCTION

As the title shows clearly, special concern in this chapter is not only social development; but "sustainable social development". Put differently, the most and foremost question is, not about how we can start a social development, but how we can have a "sustainable" social development. For, it may be easy to start a socio-economic development and obtain some achievements within particular conditions of any given society. But what will happen after those available conditions disappear due to external -or internal- reasons? Such a point of view, of course, does not mean that I am not interested in social development. Rather, this just means that I regard it merely a step for sustainable social development.

DOI: 10.4018/978-1-61520-709-1.ch002

The former can neither have a real sense nor any serious use without the latter. In absence of the latter, any society, state or civilization will certainly fall down sooner or later. The former is logically a necessary condition for the latter; but is not the sufficient condition of it. It can be therefore asserted that sustainable social development is a whole, and hence its realization needs a holistic approach which appreciates its all necessary components or foundations. Accordingly in this paper I argue that there are four necessary foundations for a sustainable social development, and that its sufficient condition emerges only when they can keep together within a holistic social policy. My position here is, as will be seen further, much more closer to a sort of social liberalism than a classical or neo-liberalism since social liberalism includes such notions like solidarity, common good, positive individual competence, flexible social stratification and effective state.

However, before proceeding to my basic and subsidiary claims on the foundations, first, I should, being a person studying philosophy, briefly say some things about the relation between philosophy and socio-economic development. Why is a philosopher interested with it? Is this a good job for a philosopher? And if it is, why is it so? First of all, this is a good and even necessary job for the philosopher: Many philosophers as J. Bentham, J. S. Mill, John Dewey and Ziya Gokalp always consider the social philosophy and/or philosophy of economy as one of the most important issues of philosophy (Bentham, 1843, p. 117; Mill, 1967, p. 312; Heyd, 1950, p. 43-44). Moreover, it is an undeniable fact that we sometimes have experienced the socio-economic crises as is happening today. People always suffer from great social crises leading to the collapse of economic order. In that case, if we really care happiness of people and survival of our societies, we cannot but think upon social order required for sustainable social development.

While one way for finding necessary foundations of the sustainable social development is to look at Ibn Khaldun's philosophy of history and civilization in his *Mukaddimah*, another way is to benefit from Max Weber's thesis in *Protestant Ethics and the Spirit of Capitalism*. The reason why I care Khaldun's ideas for the purposes mentioned above is that Khaldun's philosophy gives us the reasons for the rise and fall of societies and civilizations. If we know the reasons for the rise and fall of societies, we can promote our society in favour of a sustainable social development. And Weber helps us in understanding cultural and ethical reasons or -more clearly speaking- working and ethical mentality behind the social development in opposition to Marx's view that the economic base of society *fully* determines all other aspects of it. For that reason, my main claim in this paper is similar to those of Weber and Gokalp rather than that of Marx: Social development is exerted by ideals (Heyd, 1950, p. 51). Notwithstanding, more things about this similarity should be said for further clarity. Weber's thesis has, as far as I understand, two parts being general and special: Its first and general part suggests that culture and religion may have a strong operational force upon the social, economic, and political structure. Its second and special part puts forward that only the protestant culture has a motivating force on social development and that other cultures have no actual or potential force on it. My point is that I agree with the first part, but disagree with the second.

I agree with its first part; because socio-economic activities are, I think, not totally value-free, but more or less a part of the cultural and ethical life. The fact that all economic actors hold values which shape their behaviors constitutes an empirical evidence for my judgment. If it is the case, then every theory of socio-economic development focusing on only the "rigid self-interest" and "profit motive", has ignored that the preferences of sellers, consumers, and policy makers are formed by their mentalities stemming from their values while also by other needs. I disagree with second part of Weber's thesis; because it is neither realistic nor logical. I'll talk about them later. But, before that it is better to consider the reasons for the fall of the societies.

Special or Internal Reasons for the Fall of the Societies

Ibn Khaldun asserts that every society, state and civilization has a natural life-time and dies when it is exhausted (Khaldun, 1989, II, p. 431-436; Rosenthal, 1968, p. 90). It is only a "*general reason* for the decline of the societies, states, and civilizations" (Arslan, 2002, p. 136). Yet, what concerns me here is not that, but what he calls the *special or internal reasons* for the decline. I think that the decline can be canceled or even entirely stopped or actually transformed into another survivable structure and through of it a sustainable social development can be created if special reasons of the decline are well known. If citizens are aware of the political weakness of the state, as Aristotle indicates in his *Politics*, they can have a chance to control the situation. The logic in this idea lies in the fact that the special reasons are related to human free-will, not to hard social determinism.

If we are to sum up the special reasons of decline, we can make a short list of them as follows: (1) weaking of solidarity both among the governing and the governed; (2) the decline of the state, (3) collapse of the economy or imbalance among the social classes, (4) degeneration in morality and mentality (Khaldun, 1989, I, p. 425-430, 447, 476). In Khaldun's understanding, all those reasons are largely connected to each other; whenever one of them happens in the society, others follow it. To Khaldun, economic, social, moral and political developments go well together. In other words, there are dialectical relations among them. Nevertheless, it can be asserted that the degeneration in mentality and morality is the real -or as a matter of fact- necessitating reason behind the others. Therefore any attempt to cancel the decline or realize a sustainable social development should begin first with the relation between the culture and the working mentality and then go on with moral values. From that point, I will initially try to show how important the mentality is and then deal with other foundations which are connected thereto.

CULTURE AND WORKING MENTALITY AS A MOTIVATING FACTOR

High rates of development are associated with high levels of success mentality. Thus, any social development move requires, as a precondition to its realization, individuals who have a mentality focused on success. And culture somewhat shapes human mentality and through of it the social substructure, social accumulation and human capital required for social development as seen in the example of some old Turkish Proverbs in *Oguzname* which condemned unemployment and idleness while praised working (Oguzname, 2009, leaf:18b, 27a, 36b). Hence, any theory of social development should first never overlook society's internal, cultural dynamics and next must keep away itself from what I call Weberian reductionism *-whether Weber himself recognized such a thing or not-* meaning that only one unique culture is eligible for social development and that all others must be abandoned for the purposes of realizing the social development. This has two reasons: One is that Weberian reductionism is actually wrong; and second is that cultural identity essentially generates a part of one's self-respect and self-confidence as well as forming one's mentality.

Let's start with the first reason in brief and then talk about the second reason in more details for my specific purposes in this section. Having regarded other world religions and cultures as inconvenient for development unlike Protestantism, Weber, if even in a different way from Marx, repeats the same eurocentrism or orientalism by means of his interpretive understanding. Weberian reductionism that only his own culture (p) is eligible for social development (q) has some logical fallacies. (1) First fallacy confounding the sufficient and necessary conditions for anything goes like this: If p then q, but not p; therefore not q. Now this reasoning confuses that p is a sufficient condition of q with that p is a necessary condition of q since it falsely identifies that if p then q with that "if and only if" p then q. (2) Second logical fallacy is its "rash generalization" derived from a few particular cases in the history. Contrary to his rash generalization, the present empirical findings over the Muslim and Confucian societies show on one hand that it is not true such ideas as free market, equality, liberty and democracy have a little effect in these societies due to their respective cultures, and on the other hand that the Buddhist, Shintoist and Islamic cultures have a motivating role on social wealth and productivity (Imai, 2006; Schwentker, 2005, p. 86; Hayami and Godo, 2005, p. 357-358). (3) There is a third and more misleading point in Weberian reductionism as well. It is, for me, what's called Newspeak Fallacy. It is related to Weber's eurocentric or orientalist point of view which redefines the basic notions and concepts of Islam in regardless of how Muslims understand them. Although Weber has stated that he would not discuss the essential value of cultures during his study (Weber, 2008, p. 25), he has indirectly done it. (4) This fallacy is also related to a fourth flaw, namely to a methodological self-contradiction: Weber breaks his own methodological principle where observer must never impose his subjective understanding on social reality and should essentially try to understand the reality through actor's own perspective.

Actor's own perspective as a person living within the cultural reality is very significant for accurately understanding and interpreting the cultural foundations of social development. Therefore, it is now time to mention the second reason of refraining from Weberian reductionism: Cultural identity essentially generates a part of one's self-respect and self-confidence as well as forming one's mentality. For example, Ottoman intellectuals were certainly aware of that fact: They knew well that societies could never survive with the sense of self-unconfidence. So, their ideal of development, progress and modernization relied on the self-confidence of their own cultural roots. Having known Khaldun's theory which describes the reasons of decay, they were also aware that they couldn't get along more in social and economic life without having a new mentality and working ethic. Ottoman intellectuals thought that the core of Islam as the prominent factor in formation of culture would motivate rather than prevent the social progress and development. Muslim culture had produced great civilizations in the long past from the early years of Islam to the last period of the Ottoman Empire; and therefore could make the same again. What it needed is to pull the ignorance and bigotism down and try to realize the material and mental conditions of social development which leads modern civilization. Modern civilization along with its products and tools should be borrowed from wherever it is found in regardless of its source by making no rigid conservatism (Frasheri, 2002, p. 150-151; Cevdet, 2002, p. 173-174; Gokalp, 2002, p. 193-197). The crucial point was their harmonization to the core Muslim culture.

For Ziya Gokalp, it is not very difficult because he thinks that West's social development has started only when the Protestant mentality became dominant in the west; and then, this kind of motivating mentality for social development has rooted, unlike Catholism, in Protestant culture through interactions between Christians and Muslims in various ways (2002, p. 193-197). Primary point in Gokalp's inference is his emphasize not on identity but similarity between protestant mentality and that of Islam. Whether Protestantism be effected by some basic principles of Islam or not is just a secondary point in his reasoning. Otherwise, Gokalp's reasoning would become a Genetic Fallacy implying if A evolved from B, then A must always be B. But

Gokalp definitely doesn't make such a Genetic Fallacy. His intention is essentially to make the Muslims remember that they can realize a social development inasfar as they embrace forgotten basic principles of their own cultural dynamics. Needless to say, there have always been a great number of advices regarding the role of working and labor within both individual and social life in religious and cultural texts: On the importance of working and labor in individual life, for instance, God himself says so: "that man can have nothing, but what he strives for". (Qur'an; 53:39-40). Akpınar, referring to Salih Akdemir, informs us that fifth verse of Surah al-Fatiha (The Opening) can be read as follows: "Thee do we worship (or/and in Thine name we strive for), and so Thine aid we seek" (Akpınar, 2008, p. 23, 32). In order to notice the importance of working and labor in social life, on the other hand, both Kınalızade Ali Celebi, an Ottoman moral philosopher, and Yusuf Has Hacib, the wise writer of *Kutadgu Bilig (Wisdom to Happiness)* which is known as an old and eminent work of Turkish political philosophy, condemn the religious in private but useless in social life by saying that best of men is one who is the most useful to men (Has Hacib, 2006, couplet: 5723-5731, 5736-5740, p. 953-955; Okumus, 2008, p. 71).

These examples are very similar to Weber's notion of working as a moral and religious duty (Weber, 2008, p. 69, 47, 105): The main idea here is that individual and society cannot be isolated from each other. This, I think, helps people in avoiding what Kılıc called "moral misconception" meaning that one ignores the close relation between one's private religious practices and one's moral life within society (Kılıc, 2008, p. 365). It is not possible to achieve any social development in any society which aims at performing only religious practices and disregards their essential moral ends in social life. This is to say that both a sound ethical insight and a moderate understanding of wealth are necessary for sustainable social development. So, it is this question which now must be asked: What kind of an ethical foundation should we have for sustainable social development? The answer of this question will be the theme of the next section.

MODERATION, FRIENDSHIP AND SYMPATHY ETHICS: WEALTH AS AN END IN ITSELF VERSUS WEALTH AS A MEANS OF HAPPINESS FOR ALL

The end of ethics is both individual and social happiness. Any theory of social development seeking wealth should then serve a goal of public as well as individual welfare by the means of ethics. It should serve neither some small rich groups nor something else but the happiness of all society members. Let's explicate it a little by benefiting from Aristotle's ideas in his *Nicomachean Ethics*: Just as health is the end of medicine, so wealth is the end of economic activities. But is wealth an end in itself? Or is it an end for the sake of something else? It must be overtly clear, as Aristotle said, wealth is not an end in itself (Aristotle, 2007, 1094a: 5-25). Just wealth is not an end in itself, so it is not a good in itself. It has only an instrumental value (1095a:15; Weber, 2008, p. 15, 61; Mevlana, 1960, I, couplet: 980; *Oguzname* 2009, couplet: 27a). So, many thinkers all have censured seeking wealth for wealth itself on the grounds of ethical (Plato, 1961, 422a, p. 663; Weber, 2008, p. 135-136, 151, 157; Veblen, 2007, p. 43-45; Khaldun, 1989, I, p. 427-429), religious (Ghazzali, 1921, p. 91-94; 1873, p. 68; Weber, 2008, p. 140, 151) or social reasons (Plato, 1961, 422e-423b, p. 663-664; Campanella, 2003, p. 50-51). Of course, this condemnation is not totally wrong.

Yet, what is wrong is to make a generalization that wealth is bad by its nature and that it must be completely condemned in any way. These generalizations in fact contradict to having attributed wealth an instrumental value: Just a knife can be used for murdering so it can be used for saving the life of patient by surgical operation. Or as mystic Mevlana said in his *Mesnevi*, water inside the ship causes the ship to sink; but the water under the ship helps it to proceed on voyage (1960, I, couplet: 985). Not having private property says Aristotle, deprives us of fulfillment of some ethical virtues like generosity and temperance (1941, 1263b: 5-15, p.1151-1152). Culture is, I think, of great importance at that point. Muslim culture, for instance, has concurrently attached importance to both possession of private property by work and labor, and its usage for the benefit of society. The model of honest, enterprising, productive and benevolent merchant which the Prophet himself as a moral person represents is the best and striking sample of this approach. Still, it is not the unique example within the culture: Other prominent examples regarding the relation of wealth to the moral conduct are Ghazali's view that wealth is condemnable only if it leads to greed (Ghazanfar, 2003, p. 202) and Yusuf Has Hacib's condemnation of greedy people because that they can never be satisfied even if they have gained all the world (2006, couplet: 2001-2004, 2200, p. 407-409, 435). In his analysis of the words "rich" and "poor", Yusuf Has Hacib also gives a more interesting example of that relationship: For him, greedy people should not be called "rich", but they are in principle to be named "poor" since his possession of wealth does not help him in achieving happiness (2006, couplet: 5384-5390, p. 903). Moreover, culture also enables us making distinctions between the leisured rich class and the productive, benevolent rich class: It is very useful to remember here that both Weber's maxim that even the rich should not eat without working (2008, p. 137) and the Qur'anic principle that man can have nothing, but what he strives for (53: 39-40).

What all these show us is that wealth should not be seen as an end in itself if we target a sustainable social development in a society. Surely, this is a coherent approach with Aristotelian claim that men want the wealth for something else what's called happiness (Aristotle, 2007, 1094a: 5-25; 1095a: 15). Good and happy life is the most important and common goal for all of us living within the society. However, what is "good and happy life"? It may change in relation to what men attach importance to (Aristotle, 1095a: 20). Here I would like to take Khaldun's understanding of happiness as a starting point for sustainable social development. Apart from the material ones, the psychological, ethical and rational needs such as freedom, self-realization, self-respect -and caring for others-, for Khaldun, are the necessary elements of human happiness (Kozak, 1984, p. 123). So, the desire for wealth is useful for sustainable social development as long as it helps the rational policy as a means of individual and social happiness.

Otherwise, such a desire lacking a rational and ethical policy may cause devastating effects on sub-and-super structures of society when individuals come to consume without producing, pursue only material, even non-natural, condemned pleasures, and become unsatisfied with what's in their hands and fight each other for more wealth, and consequently apply to non-natural or illegitimate ways towards wealth. At this stage of society, men, according to Khaldun, more and more weaken in terms of physical and ethical life; and consequently, human nature comes to be distorted, people become insatiable but lazy, each member of the society turns into extreme individualist and subsequently the society entirely collapses (Khaldun, 1989, II, p. 297-304; Arslan, 2002, p. 152-154). And this is an obstacle for human happiness at the last point. For men are social beings, they can achieve self-realization and happiness only as long as they live within a society in which they can develop themselves by keep in touch with others.

So, it must be avoided to ground ethics required for sustainable social development on "rigid self-interest" and on "individual hedonism" because they harm the feeling of mutual trust and the virtue of moderation in social and individual life. As

Khaldun indicates, social dissolution occurs to a great extent first in the social and individual ethics and then in economy, state, and society. Here it is vital to indicate that by the term "rigid self-interest" I don't mean the simple "self-interestedness". Self-interest is not bad in itself. All of us, as Adam Smith reminds, owe our providing what we actually need in our daily life to such those who work for their self-interest as baker and butcher (Smith, 1981, I, p. 26-27). What might make it harmful to social ethics is the possibility of its turning into selfishness or egotism. Selfishness or egotism destroys the moral values, moderation and mutual trust which can all be seen as the social capital behind sustainable social development.

There are various ways to avoid from its devastating effect on this social capital required for sustainable social development. One way is to apply to the sympathy feeling toward others' interest and happiness which is rooted in our human nature. We can learn to care others by placing ourselves in their situation with the help of that sympathy feeling (Smith, 1984, p. 9-11). To David Hume as to Adam Smith, human nature, as empirically observed, has sentiments and dispositions showing that we care others. From the notion that it is contrary to our common sense and experience, Hume objects selfish hypothesis that every action of man including charity and affection is derived from one's seeking self-interest (Hume, 1960, p. 140). Selfish hypothesis is also pragmatically invalid in addition to Hume and Smith's arguments of common sense and sympathy: If each person in the society seeks only one's own self-interest and disregards all others in cases of conflict, or attributes others merely an instrumental value as an aid in pursuit of one's own interests, this certainly destructs human relationship among people. Whereas, sympathy ethics ensures for one to recognize the reality of others and consider them as oneself by helping him or her having the notion of "non-personal self" in contrast to the notion of "closed-self to others" in selfish hypothesis.

With sympathy ethics, thus, we can refrain from both egotism and cold calculations of simple hedonistic utilitarianism which makes it difficult to establish close relationships among members of society (for importance of sympathy in ethics, see Dewey and Tufts, 1959, p. 297-298). Individual hedonism as well as rigid self-interest is not enough to unify the members of the society around an idea of common good. For, it cannot produce an objective end or good shared by others because every man's end will be his or her own pleasure. Thus, to make individual hedonism an organizing principle of social development is to transform life into an exclusive struggle for controlling the means of individual pleasure. This creates only a mass not a public associated around a common good. And this, as Dewey rightly indicates (Dewey, 1957, p. 51-52), means to set up a society in which Hobbesian maxim that the war of all against all is dominant, but non-useful for sustainable social development.

Hobbesian maxim is useless; because, it creates among human groups only associations of power, based on utility. But, it cannot create friendship ties among them. Non-Hobbesian approaches have generally focused on law and justice for stable social order and development. They are of course important and necessary for every stable social order and development; but they are not the sufficient conditions in order to establish it. As Aristotle reminds us in his *Nicomachean Ethics*, we need two more things for it: friendship and sympathy towards our fellowship. Friendship keeps states and societies alive (1155a: 15-25) because first it is helpful for both the rich and the poor as well as the young and the old (1155a: 5-15), and second it constructs a common good among people -regardless of whether they are rich or poor-. Friendship is the most important thing underlying even law and justice (1155a: 25-30). Needless to say, the notion of friendship implied here is valuable if and only if it can be understood a kind of friendship relying on virtue not merely a simple material utility and pleasure.

We call it "true friendship" referring to the analyses of friendship by Aristotle (1157a: 30, 1157b: 5, 1166a: 30), Defterdar Sarı Mehmet Pasha (1969, p. 106) and Yusuf Has Hacib (2006, couplet: 924, 4202-4217, 4233, 4274): True friendship is, in their mind, the friendship of good-people who act with justice, do not perform vices and see friend as a second self.

Now then, it can be claimed that sympathy ethics may be the most effective factor on the sustainable social development provided that it is supported by the virtues of friendship and moderation. What brings me to give it importance is the significance of "human psychology" on social relations. Unlike simple utilitarianism, hedonism and egotism, such a cultivated sympathy ethics ensures all members of the society to deeply feel the sincerity of human relations and have both virtues of friendship, moderation and solidarity in their individual and social lives. Further, it also helps to resolve the class conflicts in the society and to create an understanding of positive competition on the base of individuality and solidarity. I will briefly explicate how it is possible in the following section.

FLEXIBLE BUT STABLE SOCIAL STRATIFICATION: MIDDLE CLASS AND POSITIVE COMPETITION

Different cultures produce different perceptions of class and class relations. Whatever they are, however, almost any culture has produced a dream of classless society in order to defend itself against the dangers of the negative competition based on a rigid self-interest not caring others at all. Being aware of differences between social strata, intellectuals from Thomas More (*Utopia,* 1515) and Campanella (*City of Son*, 1623) to Marx (*Das Capital,* 1867) have dreamt of the same. But Utopian –or sometimes procrustean- systems totally rejecting the market principle of competition in favour of the principle of equality of outcome have always failed up to now. The dream has not become true in practice. Despite this fact, social stratification has been transformed but not canceled. Because, just as sociality is rooted in human nature, so social stratification and division of labour are, as Khaldun and Aristotle indicate, rooted in society (Khaldun, 1989, I, p. 100-101; Rosenthal, 1968, p. 86; Aristotle, 1941, Politics: 1261a: 5-35, p. 1146-1147). The Soviets, for instance, have tried to terminate class-society and create a classless-society in modern times; but what they could achieve was to build only a new social stratification. A new social hierarchy took the place of the old one and afterwards completely collapsed. In that case, what is important for social development is not the absence of social stratification, but the characteristics of the social stratification. Any healthy social stratification must have at least three basic features for the sustainable social development:

(1) Sympathy ethics must primarily prevail among the social strata so that the rich and the poor classes do not hate from each other. Following Dewey's ideas in his *Ethics*, it can be claimed that even charity should not be seen as only a means by which the rich class achieves merit when they make good things for the poor. Charity actions of the rich should not, in other words, be used to cover their probable selfish greed and to keep the poor dependent (Dewey and Tufts, 1959, p. 334). Instead, what ought to be done by the rich is to have an intelligent regard for the welfare of others. To state differently, they must consider the poor's need for freedom and self-realization as a moral -and existential- ideal (Dewey and Tufts, 1959, p. 335). This is possible if and only if each person can put himself or herself in the place of other in order to genuinely understand the other from the sympathy ethics perspective. The person who is able to do so, whether the rich or the poor, in principle, will not make something which he would not like if others did that to him.

(2) Social stratification must be also flexible but stable so that it can be possible to make

transition among different social strata. This is very crucial in terms of both occupational and economic classes within the society.For, in both cases, fixed social stratification indicates an oligarchic society in which lines among the social strata are very divisive. However, the members of an oligarchic society can't concurrently obtain the competitive and cooperative impulses which directly urge them to positive action towards a social development aiming at the happiness of the entire society. Yet, what we primarily need for such a social development is to simultaneously have a competitive and cooperative social structure. There are generally four basic occupational classes or strata in the society: scholars, soldiers, traders -including industrialists in modern times- and agriculturists. None of them, as Ottoman Turkish philosopher Kınalızade says, should suppress others at all: If soldiers intrude in the affairs of traders or vice versa, this disturbs the social stability and integrity (Okumus, 2008, p. 74). In addition to that, neither the superior nor the inferior economic classes should suppress other classes. The best is the political dominance of middle class in the society because it may mirror both the superior and inferior classes, while also enabling the protection of the social stability and the development of democracy. In order for that, as is emphasized in *Kutadgu Bilig*, a method and process like this should be followed: Neither the middle class should be burdened with problems of the rich nor the poor be burdened with problems of the middle class. Instead, the poor should be protected and supported so that they can become a member of the middle class through their zeal. If poor become middle, middle would turn into rich with a little effort; and consequently nation and state come to get more and more rich with peace and harmony among the members of the society (Has Hacib, 2006, couplet: 5561-5568, p. 929). Of course, this is a relative case. There will always be more or less rich people than others in the society. But the richest will have no repressive authority upon the political preferences and conducts of others because the middle class shall prevail over the society. This needs a specific point of view going beyond self-interest and caring about social wealth and justice as a whole.

(3) Accordingly, social stratification must be based on an understanding of positive competition which does require individuality and positive freedom. It is significant here to separate at one side individuality from individualism and on the other positive freedom from the negative. Because, unlike individuality, individualism does demolish the sense of unity and solidarity: Individualism has a conception of "finished and self-sufficient self" aiming merely the rigid self-interest while individuality has a conception of "self" growing and developing within the society (see Dewey, 1920, p.193-196, 207). And these two distinct conceptions of "self" have different notions of freedom. Classical liberalism, which is rooted in the conception of finished and self-sufficient self, as Dewey rightly indicates, wants to destroy external obstacles before the actions preferred by atomic individuals isolated from the society. This is an insight of negative freedom, and assumes the existence of individual prior to the society. But the idea of individual apart from the society in the state of nature is, as Khaldun (Arslan, 2002, p. 88, 95) and Dewey accept, only a fiction: "Men", says Dewey, "are not isolated non-social atoms but are men only when in intrinsic relations to men" (1969, p. 231). In other words, what is individual and social are the two complementary dimensions of man in his tangible existence and unable to separate from each other in any way (Dewey, 1945, p. 2; Dewey, 1920, p. 191, 193). Negative freedom in the sense of absence of external limitations on the individual is, therefore, not enough to realize a sustainable social development.

What we need to realize sustainable social development is positive freedom included in the notion of individuality. Since positive freedom "is not a state but an act which involves methods and instrumentalities for control of conditions" (Dewey, 1967, p. 340), it will be more operational than negative freedom in the process of any sustainable social development. Positive freedom has two functions here: It helps create socialized individuals and realize a positive competition among them. Competition is, as J. S. Mill contends in his *Principles of Political Economy*, necessary for sustainable development although it can be the source of some moral evils like jealousy and hostility among men. First of all, no society can prosper without competition among its members. And then, competition also prevents greater evils like inactiveness, indolence even if it has some evils by its nature (Mill, 1965, p. 795). Hence, what ought to be done is to transform the negative competition into positive one, rather than to completely remove the competition as a stimulus behind social development. When Khaldun talks about morals of trader (1989, II, p. 357; see again Kozak 1984, p. 114-115, 211) and Locke notices on the rights of property and labour (1824, p. 357), they indirectly point to the need for such a transformation by having insisted upon that one must neither hope to make use of other's pain nor intrude what others have improved by their labour. This approach is similar to Dewey's one; and, as he clearly stated, enables us to avoid from extreme individualist and socialist theories: Neither the society exists for the individual, nor the individual exists for the society. Conversely, both are complementary to each other. Otherwise, their conflicts would surely damage individual and social development (Dewey, 1920, p. 187). In order to be able to prevent the probable conflicts between individual and social as well as among individuals themselves and to build a common good to be accepted by all members of society, societies generally need a notion of effective and democratic state. Without having such a state, there is no possibility for having flexible but stable social stratification based on a common good, and consequently for achieving sustainable social development.

EFFECTIVE STATE: SOLIDARITY, DEMOCRACY AND EDUCATION OF CRITICAL THINKING

If we remember what has been said in previous sections as to the reasons for the rise and the fall of the societies with reference to Khaldun's philosophy of history, we can easily see that the rational, strong and effective state is always a requirement or a necessity for civilization and social development. A developed society or civilization is, as Khaldun reminds, like a garden full of flowers and roses; and the state is the wall of this garden which protects it against the invaders (1989, I, p. 94). Once the state collapses, society and civilization can no longer go on to exist along time. The state is to society as form. Just a form by its nature preserves the matter, so the state enables to establish, preserve and improve the society (Khaldun, 1950, p. 101; 1989, II, p. 80). Social development and civilization stemming from the rational demands of men can come into existence only in a rational state as an effective political organization. Following Khaldun's thought that the form, force and efficiency of the state determine the strength and weakness of social life, it can be contended that public welfare and social development require a right kind of state or government.

If the state unjustly interferes with the economic life of its citizens by engaging in trade, monopolizing certain trade goods, seizing private, or setting high taxes, this harms both the state and social development. For, in such a case, citizens will either lose their capability of free enterprise and desire for hardworking, production and trade or migrate to other states in which they can freely perform socio-economic activities which are the means of their own private ends (Khaldun, 1989, II, p. 60, 63, 66, 76-80, 83-85; I, p. 377, 386-387). But if the state begins to move in the opposite direction, and for example sets low taxes, does not interfere with free trade among its citizens, then this naturally increases their working motivation and production desire at a great extent (Khaldun, 1989, II, p. 59, 114). And this fact itself causes citizens to become rich. Once the people become rich, the state becomes even richer. In that case, the welfare of the state and of its citizens are correlative; and so social development actually depends on the good relationship between state and its citizens (Khaldun, 1989, II, p. 66; Rosenthal, 1968, p. 93).

This good relation shows itself not only in the performances mentioned above but also in the social responsibilities and duties of the state for its citizens. This actually explicates the reason why I prefer to refer to Khaldun's views by indicating the role of the state in socio-economic development as well: Khaldun's understanding of the state is not the same with the classical liberal -or libertarian- notions of state despite his apparently liberal views about the relation between the state and free trade. In my opinion, Khaldun's views in his *Mukaddimah* can be read as a close example of social liberalism rather than of classical liberalism. As he suggests in his *Mukaddimah* the state must take care of the poor, orphans, indigents; and make expenditure for such public services as medical care, external and internal security and judicial system. The state must use its revenues in order to build hospitals, and then to assign doctors, nurses, civil servants for public health (Khaldun, 1989, II, p. 126, 129, 133-134). What is more, if it is really desired that the country should develop and flourish, then the state must undertake to make things which ought to be absolutely done in any way but cannot be done by private enterprise (Khaldun, 1989, II, p. 224).

One of the most practical advantages of this undertaking in Khaldun's understanding is that it stimulates economic activities in the society (Arslan, 2002, p. 106); and this is vital for sustainability of development when the society particularly faces socio-economic crises. It is useful also when there are not enough private entrepreneurs as an initiating factor for development in the society. On that point, Gokalp's views about the duty and responsibility of the state is a good example: Being aware of the absence of qualified private entrepreneur of great capital in the last period of the Ottoman Empire as well as the early days of the Turkish Republic, he as a social philosopher, actually defends that the state undertakes to create private entrepreneurs and strong middle class in the society and protect local industry against unbalanced foreign competition. To him, if it is really desired that Turkish society should gradually develop and flourish on its own local human resources, then what ought to be done is nothing, but that (for Gokalp's ideas at the issue see Heyd, 1950, p. 146-148). Yet, the point is that we have been living in a different world from theirs with its peculiar conditions.

However, when we think over our today's globalized world from their perspectives, we can maintain that in our present conditions any effective state, as Muter and Gokbunar utter, must perform such basic duties as protecting and supporting its own citizens, entrepreneurs and local economy against the dangers of an unstable global competition by making infrastructure investments and establishing research-development centers as well as essential auditing mechanisms that all reinforce the competitive capacity of its private sector (Muter and Gokbunar, 2003, p. 67-68). My understanding here depends on two assumptions: One is about the Deweyian maxim that interests of the state and the individual cannot be really in conflict with each other. Since the state, individual and society are the complimentary parts of the same reality, it cannot be thought that the interest of individuals can "conflict with those of the state to which they belong" (Dewey, 1920, p. 191). As related to the first, other is about the necessity of solidarity. Having remembered that one of the most important reasons in fall of societies and states is, as was already emphasized in the second section, the weakening of the solidarity among the ruled and the ruler, we can surely understand the following: What we need for sustainable social development is first of all to reinforce the solidarity between the individual and state. By benefiting Khaldun's notion of solidarity, it can be said that solidarity has two basic types: One is based on ideal, reason and common good; the other relies on ancestry. Former is stronger than the latter (Kozak, 1984, p. 59; Okumus, 2008, p. 44-45). The wider the former is, the stronger and wealthier the state and individual are.

I think that such solidarity between the individual and state can exist only through democracy and education of critical thinking in present conditions of our global world wherever people demand more freedom, respect and right on one hand and compete with each other in all matters including economic, political and cultural issues at a global scale on the other. Democracy is necessary; because it establishes both mutual trust and the sense of common good among all members of the society by guaranteeing that each individual equally joins in the political decision-making process. Some have often argued that democratic policies in particularly underdeveloped countries slow down socio-economic development as compared to autocratic regimes in terms of their powers of planning and practicing development projects. Again they draw attention to the polarizing results of democratic policies on different groups in any state and to its negative effects of rapid economic development. But, they, in my opinion, ignore the close relation between democracy and social development: First of all, their approach within time may make irresponsible rulers or elites without any accountability reside over the state. Lack of accountability leads both the state and society to uncertainty and instability in the long term when, in particular, some wrong policies must be replaced by the right ones. Second, some tangible wealth of autocratic or elitist regimes comes from abundant natural sources of the state; but what will happen when those sources will have been exhausted? What must be done, then, is very obvious: Sustainable social development should ultimately be settled on a rational development policy which primarily depends on human resources before the natural ones. In the third place, since democracy provides their noticeable participation in the government, it promotes the sense of responsibility in citizens and encourages their desire to cope with problems.

From all things that I have so far said, it must be so clear that by the term of democracy as a propulsive force behind social development; here I do mean neither only a political regime nor a mass democracy. Rather, I mean democracy as a way of life which is based on critical thinking. In fact, any survivable democracy can exist merely with individuals having the competence and disposition of critical thinking. Critical thinking is the best tool capable of constructing sustainable democracy and through of it sustainable social development. Indeed, it is even necessary for both social development and democracy to survive. For, it helps men on the one hand to make distinction between the right and wrong information, to know right and false reasoning and to adapt to rapid change in information on the other, and finally strengthens their capability to give right decisions. It also, by means of its self-corrective nature, facilitates the capacity of making changes in their thought upon need. Individuals who can think critically will create a critical public unlike the uncritical masses which is the most indispensible factor behind the sustainable democracy as well as the sustainable social development. Therefore, in any case, states and societies should try to establish and improve the education of critical thinking if they really want to actualize a sustainable social development.

CONCLUSION

Just as socio-economic development cannot be reduced to economic growth since the latter is only a part of the former, so sustainable socio-economic development cannot be grounded on only one factor. We must consider these four reasons for the realization of it in any society:

(1) sound working mentality relied on culture, (2) strong ethical perspective including the virtues of moderation, friendship and sympathy, (3) flexible but stable social stratification which is based on middle class and the notion of positive competition, and finally (4) effective state composed of solidarity, sustainable democracy and education of critical thinking. They all together constitute a sort of social liberalism, which combines the individual and social while also connecting the ethical and economic, rather than the classical or neo-liberalism separating the individual from both the society and the state while depending on the principle of solely rigid self-interest. Consequently, for a sustainable development, we need a sustainable healthy working mentality, a sustainable sympathy ethics, and a sustainable democracy as a way of life; but at first we need a sustainable education of ethics and critical thinking.

REFERENCES

Akpınar, A. (2008). Kur'an'a Gore Calısmanın Cok Yonlulugu ve Ibadet Boyutu. In *Islam ve Calısma Hayatı Ulusal Sempozyumu* (pp. 23-37). Izmir, Turkey: Faculty of Divinity Publishing.

Aristotle. (1941). Politics. In R. McKeon (Ed.), *The Basic Works of Aristotle* (pp. 1127-1325). New York: Random House.

Aristotle. (2007). *Nikomakhos'a Etik* (S. Babur, Trans.). Ankara, Turkey: BilgeSu Press.

Arslan, A. (2002). *Ibni Haldun'un Ilim ve Fikir Dunyası*. Ankara, Turkey: Vadi Publishing.

Bentham, J. (1843). Of the Mode of Warming the Building. In J. Bowring (Ed.), *The Works of Jeremy Bentham* (Vol. 4). Edinburgh, UK: W. Tait.

Campanella, T. (2003). The City of the Sun. In *The New Atlantis and the City of Sun: Two Classic Utopias*. New York: Dower Publications.

Cevdet, A. (2002). Preface by the Translator (M. Sukru Hanioglu, Trans.). In C. Kurzman (Ed.), *Modernist Islam, 1840-1940: A Sourcebook* (pp. 172-175). New York: Oxford University Press.

Dewey, J. (1920). *Reconstruction in Philosophy*. New York: Henry Holt and Company.

Dewey, J. (1957). *Outlines of A Critical Theory of Ethics*. New York: Hillary House.

Dewey, J. (1967). The Public and Its Problems. In J. Boydston (Ed.), *The Early Works, 1882-1898* (Vol. 2). Carbondale, IL: Southern Illinois University Press.

Dewey, J. (1969). The Ethics of Democracy, In J. Boydston (Ed.), *The Early Works, 1882-1898* (Vol. 1). Carbondale, IL: Southern Illinois University Press.

Dewey, J., & Tufts, J. H. (1959). *Ethics*. New York: Henry Holt and Company.

Frasheri, S. S. (2002). Transferring the New Civilization to the Islamic Peoples (M. Sukru Hanioğlu, Trans.). In C. Kurzman (Ed.), *Modernist Islam, 1840-1940: A Sourcebook* (pp. 149-151). New York: Oxford University Press.

Ghazanfar, S. M. (2003). The Economic Thought of Abu Hamid Al-Ghazali and St. Thomas Aquinas: Some comparative parallels and links. In S. M. Ghazanfar (Ed.), *Medieval Islamic Economic Thought: Filling the Great Gap in European Economics* (pp. 184-208). New York: Routledge, Curzon.

Ghazzali, A. H. (1873). *The Alchemy of Happiness* (Henry A. Homes, Trans.). Albany, New York: Munsell.

Ghazzali, A. H. (1921). *Some Religious and Moral Teachings of Al-Ghazzali* (S. N. Ali, Trans.). Baroda, India: Lakshmi Vilas P. Press.

Gokalp, Z. (2002). Islam and Modern Civilization (N. Berkes, Trans.). In C. Kurzman (Ed.), *Modernist Islam, 1840-1940: A Sourcebook* (pp. 192-197). New York: Oxford University Press.

Has Hacib, Y. (2006). *Kutadgu Bilig* (R. R. Arat, Trans.). Istanbul, Turkey: Kabalcı Publishing.

Hayami, Y., & Godo, Y. (2005). *Development Economics: From the Poverty to the Wealth of Nations*. Oxford, UK: Oxford University Press.

Heyd, U. (1950). *Foundations of Turkish Nationalism: The Life and Teachings of Ziya Gokalp*. London: Luzac.

Hume, D. (1960). *An Enquiry Concerning the Principles of Morals*. La Salle, IL: Open Court Publishing.

Ibn Haldun. (1989). *Mukaddime (volume I-III)* (Z. K. Ugan, Trans.). Istanbul, Turkey: Milli Egitim Bakanlıgı Press.

Ibn Khaldun. (1950). *An Arab Philosophy of History: Selections from the Prolegomena of Ibn Khaldun of Tunis (1332-1406)* (C. Issawi, Trans.) (1st ed.). London: John Murray.

Imai, K. (2006). Culture, Civilization or Economy? Test of the Clash of Civilizations Thesis. *International Journal on World Peace, 23*(3). Retrieved January 1, 2009, from http://findarticles.com/p/articles/mi_hb6428/is_3_23/ai_n29321324

Kılıc, R. (2008). Calısma Hayatımızın Problemleri Uzerine. In *Islam ve Calısma Hayatı Ulusal Sempozyumu* (pp. 360-366). Izmir, Turkey: Faculty of Divinity Publishing.

Kozak, I. E. (1984). *Ibn Haldun'a Gore Insan-Toplum-Iktisat*. Istanbul, Turkey: Pınar Publishing.

Locke, J. (1824). Of Civil Government. In *The Works of John Locke* (Vol. 4) (12th ed.). London: C. Baldwin, Printer.

Mevlana, C. R. (1960). *Mesnevi* (V. Izbudak, Trans.). Istanbul, Turkey: Milli Egitim Press.

Mill, J. S. (1965). Principles of Political Economy. In J.M. Robson (Ed.), *The Collected Works of John Stuart Mill* (Vol. 3). Canada: University of Toronto Press.

Mill, J. S. (1967). Essays on Economics and Society: 1824-1845. In J.M. Robson (Ed.), *The Collected Works of John Stuart Mill* (Vol. 4). Canada: University of Toronto Press.

Muter, N. B., & Gokbunar, R. (2003). Devletin Etkinligi ile Ilgili Ekonomik, Politik, Kulturel Teoriler. *Celal Bayar Universitesi Sosyal Bilimler Dergisi, 1*(1), 53–70.

Oguzname. (2009). (critical ed. Ali Haydar Bayat). Ankara, Turkey: Ataturk Kultur, Dil ve Tarih Yuksek Kurumu Press.

Okumus, E. (2008). *Osmanlı'nın Gozuyle Ibn Haldun*. Istanbul, Turkey: Iz Publishing.

Plato. (1961). Republic. In E. Hamilton & H. Cairns (Ed.), *The Collected Dialogues of Plato, Including the Letters* (pp. 575-844). New York: Pantheon Books.

Rosenthal, E. I. J. (1968). *Political Thought in Medieval Islam: An Introductory Outline*. Cambridge, UK: Cambridge University Press.

Sarı Mehmet Pasha, D. (1969). *Devlet Adamlarına Ogutler* (H. R. Ugural, Trans.). Ankara, Turkey: Turk Tarih Kurumu Press.

Schwentker, W. (2005). The Spirit of Modernity: Max Weber's Protestant Ethics and Japanese Social Sciences. *Journal of Classical Sociology, 5*(1), 73–92. doi:10.1177/1468795X05050039

Smith, A. (1981). *An Inquiry into the Nature and Causes of the Wealth of Nations* (Volume I & II). Indianapolis, IN: Liberty Press.

Smith, A. (1984). *The Theory of Moral Sentiments*. (Ed. D.D. Raphael & A.L. Macfie). Indianapolis, IN: Liberty Press.

Suikidi. (2006). Max Weber's Remarks on Islam: The Protestant Ethic Among Muslim Puritans. *Islam and Christian Muslim Relations, 17*(2), 195-205.

Veblen, T. (2007). *The Theory of the Leisure Class*. New York: Cosimo, Inc.

Weber, M. (2008). *Protestan Ahlakı ve Kapitalizmin Ruhu* (Z. Gurata, Trans.). Ankara, Turkey: Ayrac Kitabevi Publishing.

ADDITIONAL READING

Baali, F. (1988). *Society, State, and Urbanism: Ibn Khaldun's Sociological Thought*. Albany, New York: State University of New York Press.

Baum, M. A., & Lake, D. A. (2003). The Political Economy of Growth: Democracy and Human Capital. *American Journal of Political Science, 20*(3), 333–347. doi:10.1111/1540-5907.00023

Bonar, J. (1992). *Philosophy and Political Economy (with a New Introduction by Warren J. Samuels)*. New Brunswick, NJ: Transaction Publishers.

Brack, D., Grayson, R., & Howarth, D. (Eds.). (2007). *Reinventing the State: Social Liberalism for 21st Century*. London: Politicos Publishing.

Bulgakov, S. (2000). *Philosophy of Economy*. New Haven, CT, USA: Yale University Press.

Dewey, J. (1935). The Future of Liberalism. *The Journal of Philosophy, 32*(9), 225–230. doi:10.2307/2015856

Dewey, J. (2000). *Liberalism and Social Action*. New York: Prometheus Books.

Finn, D. (2006). *The Moral Ecology of Markets: Assessing Claims About Markets and Justice*. Cambridge, UK: Cambridge University Press.

Karpat, K. H. (2002). *Studies on Ottoman Social and Political History: Selected Articles and Essays*. Boston: Brill Academic Publishers.

Kung, H. (1998). *A Global Ethic for Global Politics and Economics*. New York: Oxford University Press.

Merquior, J. G. (1991). *Liberalism Old and New*. Boston: Twayne Publishers.

Midgley, J. (1995). *Social Development: The Developmental Perspective in Social Welfare*. London: Sage Publications.

Midgley, J., Hall, A., Hardiman, M., & Narine, D. (1986). *Community Participation, Social Development, and the State*. London: Methuen.

Mill, J. S. (1977). On Liberty. In J.M. Robson (Ed.), *The Collected Works of John Stuart Mill* (Vol. 18) (pp. 213-310). Canada: University of Toronto Press.

Olson, M. (1993). Dictatorship, Democracy, and Development. *The American Political Science Review, 87*(3), 567–576. doi:10.2307/2938736

Paxton, P. (2002). Social Capital and Democracy: An Interdependent Relationship. *American Sociological Review, 67*(2), 254–277. doi:10.2307/3088895

Rajaee, F. (2000). *Globalization on Trial: The Human Condition and the Information Civilization*. CT: Kumarian Press.

Rawls, J. (1971). *A Theory of Justice*. Cambridge, MA: Harvard University Press.

Rawls, J. (2005). *Political Liberalism*. New York: Columbia University Press.

Ryan, W. F. (1995). *Culture, Spirituality, and Economic Development: Opening a Dialogue*. Ottawa, Canada: International Development Research Centre.

Sedgwick, P. H. (1999). *The Market Economy and Christian Ethics*. Cambridge, UK: Cambridge University Press.

Sen, A. (1987). *On Ethics and Economics*. Oxford, UK: Blackwell Publishing.

Smith, A. (1981). *An Inquiry into the Nature and Causes of the Wealth of Nations*,(Vol. I). Indianapolis, IN: Liberty Press.

Ulrich, P. (2008). *Integrative Economic Ethics: Foundations of a Civilized Market Economy* (J. Fearns, Trans.). Cambridge, UK: Cambridge University Press.

Weber, M. (1981). *General Economic History*. New Brunswick, NJ: Transaction Publishers.

KEY TERMS AND DEFINITIONS

Critical Thinking: A way of thinking that distinguishes right reasoning from wrong reasoning by concentrating on evidence, argument, inquiry through some criteria and methods like clearness-distinctness, consistency, skepticism, and rationality. It thus aims at reaching not any result but consistent and reasonable results about any fact, idea or subject. Critical thinking as an upper thinking also requires problem-discovering abilities as well as problem-solving ones; and this makes it a self-correcting thinking which includes reflective thinking dispositions.

Effective State: A state that performs main duties of protecting and supporting cultural, democratic, economic rights of its own citizens against excessive inequalities in local and global society by reinforcing and improving the democratic, educational and economic capacities of its citizens. An effective state considers the state and individual as complimentary parts of the same social reality, and so it neglects neither the interests of the state nor interests of the individual.

Flexible but Stable Social Stratification: The social Structure in which those who belong to an occupational and economic class or stratum can easily enter into another class or stratum without making society instable. Such a social stratification is the contrary to fixed social stratification that constitutes an oligarchic society.

Ibn Khaldun: The fourteenth-century Muslim philosopher of history, civilization and society. In his famous work called *Mukaddimah*, he explains and analyses the external and internal reasons for the rise and fall of the states, societies and civilizations.

John Dewey: The leading American philosopher of democracy in the 20th century who adopts a social liberal philosophy against classical liberalism. He argues that neither the society exists for the individual, nor the individual exists for the society. Conversely, both are complementary to each other. Otherwise, their conflicts would surely harm individual and social development. For him, one way to overcome the conflicts among them is to see democracy as a way of life.

Max Weber: One of the influential Protestant thinkers in cultural, sociological, economical and political studies of 20th century. Weber argues that there are certainly cultural and ethical reasons behind the socio-economic development in opposition to Marx's view that the economical base of society *fully* determines all other aspects of it.

Social Development: The process of social change concurrently aiming at the well-being of individuals and society as a whole by improving their democratic, ethical and economic capacities. But every discipline and system of thought have defined the term 'social development' in different ways as depending on how they understand 'well-being'.

Social Liberalism: A liberalism that moves beyond classical and neo liberalism which is based on the concept of self-sufficient self isolated from the society and the notion of negative freedom; and which argues that individual, society, and state are complementary to each other. A social liberal considers the role of the state as providing positive freedom to individuals, ands thinks that accumulation of power and wealth by few or elite groups is always unacceptable.

Sympathy Ethics: The moral philosophy that accepts sympathy or fellow-feeling is the source of moral value. Because it holds that sympathy feeling towards other's interest and happiness is deeply rooted in human nature. From the perspective of sympathy ethics, one may put himself or herself in other's shoes and can learn having a notion of non-personal self which makes it easy to establish close and sincere relationships among people in contrast to the notion of closed-self to the others which leads people to selfishness and cold calculations of simple hedonistic utilitarianism.

Working Mentality: A characteristic mental attitude that shapes one's approach towards working and determines how one should act at work as depending on cultural, moral or personal points of views. As a mental attitude, it has been seen as a precondition to any social development by some scholars as Max Weber, Ziya Gokalp and Ibn Khaldun.

Chapter 3
Lessons for Development Economists from the Shanghai Experience, 1842-2008

Niv Horesh
University of New South Wales, Australia

ABSTRACT

This chapter compares the contours of Shanghai's economy in the pre-war era (1842-1937) with its breakneck reform thrust following the 1990 designation of the city's Pudong precinct as China's primary financial centre. It will seek to explore why the city was a magnet for so many Chinese entrepreneurs and intellectuals before World War II, and whether the reformed societal and physical infrastructure of Shanghai in the 21st century can bring about similar entrepreneurial dynamism, that might help shake off the legacy of state dirigisme and create a truly global innovation hub.

INTRODUCTION

To many observers Shanghai seemed "incomparable" before the World War II. Once foreigners had been allowed to settle there, soon after the Nanjing Treaty of 1842, the city developed by leaps and bounds. Immune to Chinese sovereignty, and months away from London by sea, the city acquired a reputation for laissez-faire and the mystique of hybridity and vice (Barber, 1979, pp. 144-159; Bergère, 2002, pp. 359-362).

Consider this pithy description from a Western tourist guidebook to the city published in 1936: (*All About Shanghai*, 1936, Chapter 6)

DOI: 10.4018/978-1-61520-709-1.ch003

Cosmopolitan Shanghai, city of amazing paradoxes and fantastic contrasts; Shanghai the beautiful, bawdy, and gaudy, contradiction of manners and morals; a vast brilliantly-hued cycloramic, panoramic mural of the best and the worst of Orient and Occident. Shanghai, with its modern skyscrapers, the highest buildings in the world outside of the Americas, and its straw huts shoulder high. Modern department stores that pulse with London, Paris, and New York; native emporiums with lacquered ducks and salt eggs, and precious silks and jades, and lingerie and silver, with amazing bursts of advertising colour and more amazing bursts from advertising musicians, compensating with gusto for lack of harmony and rhythm. Modern motors throbbing with the power of eighty horses march abreast with tattered one-man power rickshaws; velveted limousines with silk-clad Chinese multi-millionaires surrounded by Chinese and Russian bodyguards bristling with automatics for protection against the constant menace of kidnapping (foreigners are not molested); Chinese gentlemen in trousers; Chinese gentlemen in satin skirts. Shanghai the bizarre, cinematographic presentation of humanity, its vices and virtues; the City of Blazing Night; cabarets; Russian and Chinese and Japanese complaisant "dance hostesses"; city of missions and hospitals and brothels. Men of title and internationally notorious fugitives tip cocktails in jovial camaraderie; Colonels' Ladies and Judy O'Gradys promenade in peacock alley; social celebrities and convivial cocottes; ladies who work; ladies who shirk: ladies who live to love; ladies who love to live. Behold! "The longest bar in the world!" The shortest street in the world with a blatant cacophony of carnality from a score of dance-halls; scarlet women laughing without mirth; virgins in search of life; suicides; marriages; births; carols of vested choirs; cathedral chimes; Communists plotting; Nationalism in the saddle; war in Manchuria!; it's a great old town, and how we hate it and love it! Vital, vibrant, vivacious; strident, turbulent, glowing-Shanghai is the Big Parade of Life of every colour, race, tempo; the bitter end of the long trail for many wastrel souls; the dawn after the dark for others.

This Chapter compares the contours of Shanghai's economy in the pre-war era (1842-1937) with its breakneck reform thrust following the 1990 designation of the city's Pudong precinct as China's primary financial centre. The aim of the comparative perspective offered here is to highlight the ways in which the city's pre and post-war institutional settings differ, and whether they might yield dissimilar outcomes insofar as innovation and entrepreneurship are concerned.

Building on the very latest literature in urban development, management and economic history, the study will focus on three elements that are conventionally seen as vital to sustaining technological innovation: well-functioning capital markets, respect for property rights, free information flow and a quality education system (Belke & Fehn, 2001; Feng, Froud & Johal, 2001; Houben & Kakes, 2002; Warschauer, 2003). Inevitably, it will leave other important areas of exploration to future research, because these are only associated with the contemporary Chinese economy, e.g. research clustering or fiscal federalism (Qian, 2002; Huang, 2008).

In recent years, Western media has highlighted in various ways the staggering makeover of China's economy, culminating with the coverage of the Beijing 2008 Olympic Games. However, with the notable exception of Godø (2008), there seems to be relatively little in the English-language academic literature to put this makeover in historic perspective. Nor is there much literature to help draw out the possible limitations of China's state-led economic makeover based on our understanding of the roots of innovation; of the process of industrialisation in developed countries, or of the long-haul transition from a mass-production "Old Economy" to hi-tech services-based "New Economy" (Madrick, 1995; Waller, 2000). This Chapter is designed as a first tentative step toward elucidating Shanghai's changing role in propelling China's economy, and its prospects as a moot hi-tech hub in light of that historic experience.

SHANGHAI'S POSITION IN THE CHINESE PRE-WAR ECONOMY

Assessment of pre-war Shanghai's contribution to the economic modernization of China is a complex task: the jury, in many ways, is still out. The rapidly changing political and social circumstances in the PRC quite often call for a review of past performance in view of present achievements and failures. In the field of Shanghai Studies, such major scholarly reviews can occur every two decades or so.

For example, in 1981 Marie-Claire Bergère, soon to become the doyenne of Shanghai Development Studies in the West, critiqued Roahds Murphey whose work had represented conventional wisdom in the field in the 1950s. In his *Shanghai: Key to Modern China* (1953), Murphey cast pre-war Shanghai as an all-important bridgehead of Western innovation in East Asia against the backdrop of the Communist takeover of the Mainland. By 1977, however, Murphey had come to view pre-war Shanghai's role within the Mainland as a 'fly on an elephant's back'. In other words, Murphey re-cast pre-war Shanghai as a small enclave of modernity that was ultimately insignificant to the lives of most ordinary Chinese.

Bergère (1981), on the other hand, identified valuable sprouts of civil society, innovation and free enterprise in "golden-age" Shanghai (1920s), when Chinese state power was in decline, but pointed to the resurgence of dirigisme and the stifling of free-markets in the 1930s, after the Nationalists (KMT) had come to power. She suggested that the 1920s saw the birth of a new bolder breed of Chinese businessmen, steeped in the internal dynamics of China's rural hinterland, but equally conversant with market conditions around the world (pp. 32-34).

Chinese intellectuals influenced by radical Western ideology flocked to Shanghai in their thousands in the 1920s. As part of this ferment, the city came to host the founding of the Chinese Communist Party (CCP) in 1921, and was to play a role in the KMT's rise to power nationally in 1927. But ironically, both these rival parties were averse to the free-wheeling nature of the city in the 1920s because precisely because both were autocratic.

KMT founder, Sun Yat-sen, had dreamt of "reforming" Shanghai's wayward character; of subjecting the city's foreign-run precincts straddling Puxi (west of the Huangpu river) to Chinese government control. To that end, he envisioned the boggy and sparsely-populated Pudong district (East of the Huangpu river) as the seat of a new Chinese municipality with strong central powers. After Sun's death, and following its unification of China in 1928, the KMT appointed Wu Tiecheng to accomplish this mission. Wu, who had been educated in Japan, envisioned grand architectural projects in the 1930s but, overall, KMT municipal authorities failed to demonstrate that they were able to manage the Chinese precincts as efficiently as the foreign concession areas because of rampant corruption in their ranks (Wakeman, 1995; MacPherson, 1996, pp.502-514).

The success of foreign-run Shanghai cannot be understood accurately enough without considering the plight of the surrounding Chinese pre-war economy as a whole. Economist such as Rawski (1989) and Brandt (1989) tend to revise conventional Western views of China's pre-war economy as stagnant, tradition-bound and politically-repressed. Rawski and Brandt argue that net annual GDP growth was at approximately 1% between 1842-1937, and that Shanghai's modern economy had had a pronounced positive spill-over effect in the hinterland.

Nonetheless, more recent work by younger scholars contends with one of the two main arguments underpinning this revisionist posture, providing a more balanced picture. It calls into question the notion that China's pre-war economy enjoyed a higher degree of financial integration than previously thought. Ma (2008), in particular, alludes to the fact that much of Rawski's upbeat assessment of China's overall economic performance hinges on the misapplication of Shanghai's vigorous urban growth dynamic and cosmopolitan flair to the rest of the country. The exuberance, entrepreneurship and dynamism of the Shanghainese economy did spill over to the outlying provinces of Jiangsu and Zhejiang but were virtually absent elsewhere in this vast country.

Scholars today seem to agree that pre-war Shanghai, with its semi-colonial setting and its advantageous location as a gateway to the fertile Yangzi Delta, served as an important catalyst for the modernization of the Chinese economy since 1842. Yet more work is needed to explain differences between Western firms and Chinese businesses in other cities where semi-colonial privileges did not clearly obtain and Western financiers were few and far between. Needless to say, variegated climates, production relations, geography and factor endowment all significantly account for the dichotomy between Shanghai and China's vast and predominantly rural hinterland. What seems to be lacking in much of the pertinent literature, however, is the epistemology of economic development.

As a rule of thumb, it would make sense to stylise cities like littoral Tianjin or riverside Guangzhou as an extension of Shanghai's pre-war vibrant economy despite obvious differences in climate and factor endowment with the Yangzi Delta; with it large British-administered concession area and foreign financial institutions, Hankou was perhaps integrated into the very same economic system despite being situated much further inland. But nominal and fairly remote treaty-ports like Mengzi (Yunnan), or Chongqing (Sichuan) may provide instructive contrasts to the rapidly industrializing Yangzi Delta economy. In other words, the demarcation between the Chinese "hinterland" and "littoral" economies should be understood not purely in terms of rural backwardness vs. urban sophistication, or in terms of distance from the coast, but also as the degree to which local peasants produced agricultural commodities for world markets (the Yangzi Delta being a case in point), and as the degree to which factor agents had recourse to treaty-port finance and extra-territorial protection.

Settlement size also explains part why Shanghai was more vital than other treaty-ports that the European powers had carved up, and sent settlers to, along the China coast. By the 1930s, no less that 150,000 expatriates resided in the city side by side with some 4 million Chinese, bringing with them a plethora of cultures and ideas. They made up about half of the foreign community in China. Notably, the Chinese community itself was highly heterogeneous, with over half relocating from other parts of the country in search of menial employment or opportunity.

This distinctive population makeup was administered by an equally unique tripartite municipal structure: the Chinese precincts ('Native City') strove to catch up with the efficiently-run Anglo-American (or 'International') concession area, while the more "straightforwardly colonialist" French concession area vied with the other two to attract Chinese investment. (Wasserstrom, 2000, p.193)

Governed by a partly-elected and highly autonomous body called the Shanghai Municipal Council (SMC), the International concession area was more cosmopolitan in nature though it was devoid of meaningful Chinese representation at the helm. Britons accounted for the majority of SMC executives; it also employed American administrators, Sikh policemen, and had Jews, Germans and Japanese represented on the board. Members of the *Municipalité de la Concession Française de Changhai* were, on the other hand, handpicked by Paris. This administrative multiplicity supported the free flow of information, and exchange of ideas including radical left-wing ideologies imported from Europe by fringe expatriates.

At its pre-war peak, Shanghai's foreign population numbered approximately 150,000 people, of whom there were about 50,000 Europeans (including White Russians) and the rest predominantly Japanese. Foreigners accounted for about 4% of the total population. Today, unofficial estimates put the number of foreigners residing in Shanghai at about 150,000 out of a total of 15 million – the overwhelming majority being overseas Chinese rather than western expatriates. Proportionately, then, pre-war Shanghai could be said to have been four times more cosmopolitan than early 21st century Shanghai (Ma, 2001).

Newspapers appeared in a host of languages: English, French, German, Yiddish, Russian and Japanese. Magazines appeared in dozens of other European languages (King, 1965; Reed, 2004;

Mittler, 2004). Yet it is also important to note the limits of free speech in Shanghai. The foreign-run SMC did partly resist Chinese government pressure to crack down on dissenting Chinese publications. Nonetheless, on some occasions, the SMC preferred to appease the government in Beijing by bringing Chinese dissidents before a Mixed Court on sedition charges (Bergère, 1981, p.12).

This degree of freedom was enough to attract scores of university teachers and intellectuals to the city during the early-Republican era (1912-1927); they escaped the repression, incompetence and arbitrary violence of warlord-ravaged China for the *relative* freedom of Shanghai, notwithstanding its association with European imperialism and expatriate snobbery. Chinese intellectuals working from Shanghai came to be known as the *haipai* ('Worldly School'), which contrasted with the traditionalists or *jingpai* ('Capital School'). Whilst *jingpai* education clung to Cofucian classics, *haipai* education encouraged the acquisition of vocational and English-language skills. With only 1.5% of China's population at any one time, Shanghai accounted for no less than 41 of the 205 institutions of higher education in China in 1949 (Mak & Lo, 1996, pp.377-378). It boasted some of the country's best universities such as Fudan and Jiaotong, as well as prestigious colleges run by missionaries such as Aurora and St John's.

The exchange of ideas and intellectual ferment were facilitated by the most modern infrastructure at the time. Shanghai was one of the first cities in China to develop telecommunications services. In 1871, for example, the Great Northern Telegraph Company of Denmark laid an underwater telegraph cable from Hong Kong to Shanghai, giving the country its first submerged international communications system. In 1907, a local telephone service was introduced and a long-distance service followed in 1923. By 1949, Shanghai had some 85,000 phone lines installed for about 55,000 subscribers. Although subscription was small compared with cities like London, it made up a third of all telephone lines in China at the time (Harwit, 2005, p.1840).

Similarly, the city's financial sector was one of the most competitive in Asia with domestic institutions gradually matching foreign ones in size and efficiency. By 1934, no less then 33 foreign banks had operated in the city, whilst in colonial Hong Kong there were only 17 at the time. In colonial Singapore, there were 21 banks in all. Moreover, in the pre-war era, Shanghai's securities markets far outweighed Hong Kong's (Kuilman, 2007, p.28).

In fact, as Wong Siu-lun (1996) has observed, Shanghai was "head and shoulder" above Hong Kong as a metropolis in many other respects during the pre-war era. The tripartite municipal setting in Shanghai yielded quite a different brand of entrepreneurship than the one prevalent in the full-fledged Crown Colony. In Hong Kong, exclusion of Chinese from civil service fostered grass-roots idealization of small-business ownership (*dang laoban*), resulting in a two-tier economy with diffuse family-based firms and subcontracting networks running side by side with British multinationals. In Shanghai, on the other hand, the Nationalist takeover of Chinese precincts in 1927, meant that Chinese businesses became increasingly enmeshed with government bureaucracy to the extent that corporatism and salaried employment were the grass-root ideal, and Chinese –run firms could eventually rival the size and scope of multinationals with state backing (Wong, 1996, pp. 26, 33-4; Horesh, 2007).

Arguably, the visible hand of KMT government, its autocratic usurpation of venture capital and co-optation of successful Chinese businesses explains why, despite Shanghai' preeminence as China's financial center in the pre-war era, its stock market remained largely confined to the foreign concession areas. There, independent shareholder rights where much more clearly framed than in the city's Chinese precincts. Yet consular regulators were suspicious of Chinese-owned businesses wishing to incorporate under foreign company law and issue stock. Consequently, the stock market was dominated by foreign-run municipal utilities, trading companies and banks like HSBC. It listed very few Chinese industrial ventures. The parallel Chinese-run securities market was, on the other hand, dominated by KMT-issue bonds, effectively crowding out private equity.

There was, in that sense, a striking difference between the Japanese and Chinese securities markets before the turn of the last century. Whereas Japanese securities markets helped finance the buildup of a nationwide railway network and seminal industry, China's was heavily weighted toward foreign banking and insurance companies, as well as municipal utilities with little interest in expanding their cervices outside the city perimeters. In the 1870s, railways were being built in both China and Japan, but Japan achieved a commanding lead within three decades in absolute railway mileage and, of course, in terms of the ratio of mileage to population. Until 1890, two systems of railways operated in Japan side by side: a government-owned one and, equally importantly, one operated by joint-stock companies able to mobilize funds on domestic securities markets. For the impoverished early-Meiji government to defray the construction of the whole railway network would have been fiscally prohibitive. In that sense, joint-stock finance was crucial to Japan's early modernization effort.

The late-imperial Chinese court preferred, on balance, to borrow overseas at a higher cost, and contract railway construction out to foreign firms if only to avert the onset of a strong domestic private sector. Later, the KMT republican government spurned overseas credit in favour of floating public debt domestically, but was equally suspicious of non-aligned private enterprises. It was also embroiled in campaigns against the CCP and skirmishes with the Japanese Kanto army which invaded Manchuria in 1931. Thus, on the eve of World War II, China's railway network as a whole was woefully inadequate, while Shanghai boasted one of the most advanced tramline systems in the world (Minami, 1994; Nobutaka, 1954; Noda, 1980).

In conclusion, Shanghai in the pre-war era seemed to have attracted Westerners because it provided easy and secure access to China's wealthiest provinces, while retaining a distinct *laissez-faire* environment. Chinese intellectuals and investors, for their part, appear to have continually converged on Shanghai *not* because the semi-colonial legal system necessarily protected civil liberties or press freedom, but because its *laissez-faire* environment probably minimised the perceived risks of Chinese government usurpation. That said, the city's competitive tripartite structure allowed some Chinese firms that enjoyed state backing in KMT-run precincts to grow in size and eventually rival multinationals.

POST-WAR SHANGHAI: CENTRAL PLANNING AND REFORM

The Communist unification of Mainland China in 1949 foreboded a drastic makeover of Shanghai's role as an Asian if not global financial hub. The city had been cast as a mainspring of KMT corruption and bourgeois degradation in CCP propaganda but, nonetheless, it still harboured China's industrial base and a wealth of intellectual resources, and could not be easily dispensed with. In its first three years in power, the CCP wisely adopted a moderate platform that allowed for the retention of some private enterprise and a deliberate transfer of urban management skills to Party bureaucrats, who were mostly of rural backgrounds.

The city had been affected by an exodus of wealthy industrialists on the eve of KMT retreat in 1948. Most chose to move to Hong Kong in fear of communist reprisal. This was compounded in the early 1950s by the CCP's decision to relocate many factories further inland as part of a strategy to make China less vulnerable to coastal invasion. Then during the 1960s and 1970s, Shanghai's image as a bastion of bourgeois liberalism became a rallying point for Maoist zealotry. But, contrary to popular perceptions, the city's share of the national economy actually rebounded from the industrial dispersion of the 1950s (Cheung, 1996, pp.56-58).

Inherently prone to manipulation, Chinese government statistics can nevertheless draw out the complex post-war trend: Shanghai's annual industrial output grew by no less than 24.9% on average during the transition period to communist central planning (1949-52). This was lower rate that the national average (34.81%) at the time, reflecting the CCP's massive industrial build-up in, and factory relocation to, the hinterland. Notably, during much of Mao's febrile Cultural Revolution era (1965-1970), the gap between annual industrial output growth in Shanghai and the rest of China actually narrowed down to 10% vs. 11.7% (Howe, 1981, pp.157,-159). More counter-intuitive still is the fact that through much of the Great Leap Forward (1957-1965), an era associated with anti-urban rhetoric and dislocation of production, Shanghai's annual industrial output growth (9.84%) actually exceeded the rest of China (8.9%).

The post-war era also ushered in much tighter population control measures in the city. Before the current reform thrust began, namely, when Mao was in one way or another the arbiter of policy (1949-1976), the CCP implemented a number of large-scale outward migration programmes. These compounded the already acute shortages of skilled laborers and technicians than ensued from the exodus of Chinese businessmen to Hong Kong, the departure of the city's foreign community, and the dispersion of industry across the hinterland in the early 1950s (Wong, 1996, pp.37-40).

These figures, however, tell only part of the CCP agenda. The Party did not seek to eliminate Shanghai's economy but to "socialize" it. In other words, the CCP had attempted at first to extract whatever it could from whatever private wealth that remained there in 1949. It then gingerly nationalized private enterprise, and as of 1952, relocated much of the city's manufacturing base elsewhere. Whilst Shanghai's industry in the pre-war era was overwhelming light in nature (mainly textiles), the city was to become during the first five-year plan (1952-1957) a center for heavy industry in line with the Party's overall emphasis on metallurgy and petrochemicals at the expense of consumer goods. The result was that by 1977 Shanghai accounted for only 14% of China's industrial output, compared with almost 33% in the pre-war era (Ma, 2008; Howe, 1981, pp.167-168, 175-7).

Chinese light industry as a whole recovered only in the late 1970s, as Deng Xiaoping – China's new helmsman – re-opened the country to foreign investment, and as scores of labour-intensive assembly lines were set up by offshore firms across the border from Hong Kong. Arguably because of its pre-war legacy, Deng was reluctant to open Shanghai up for foreign investment during the first decade of the reform era (1978-1988), preferring instead the more peripheral city of Shenzhen and promoting the privatization of Township and Village Enterprises (TVEs) (Mao & Higano, 1996, p.157).

In 1991, Deng Xiaoping changed course. Keen to demonstrate to the rest of the world that China could avert pressure by CCP conservatives to hold back economic reform following the Tianan'men student movement, Deng visited Shenzhen to embolden local cadres. Equally important, he approved new preferential-tax development zones for foreign investment in Greater Shanghai, and allowed the redevelopment of Pudong – first envisioned by Sun yat-sen in the 1921 – to go ahead.

Shanghai has since attracted key foreign manufacturing plants including that of German automaker Volkswagen, but its share of China's GDP has not significantly rebounded because development zones are now spread more evenly across China's eastern seaboard. Whilst its share of China's population has remained fairly stable since the late 1970s (around 1.2%), its share of

China's GDP had actually dropped from 6.91% in 1978 to 4.38% in 1994 (Yeung, 1996, p.15). The government-led redevelopment of Pudong had immediately transformed the city's skyline in the early 1990s, but commensurate structural change to the economy did not seem to follow. In 1994, for example, the private sector accounted for only 2.8% of the city's workforce compared with 9.8% in Guangzhou (Cheung, 1996, pp.50-54).

Official PRC statistics for the 2000s suggest that the Yangzi Delta is gradually catching up with the Pearl River Delta, the region in Guangdong province neigbouring Hong Kong where Shenzhen and Guangzhou are situated, and where Deng's reforms started in 1979. However, in contrast with the pre-war ear, growth in the Yangzi Delta spreads right across the much larger provinces of Jiangsu and Zhejiang. While the self-governing Municipality of Greater Shanghai has become an important node of finance to this region – it accounted for only 4.5% of China's GDP in 2006. As a whole, the Yangzi Delta accounted for 38.7% of China's exports, and 38.9% of total foreign direct investment (FDI), compared with 31.2%, and 20.3% respectively for Guangdong province that borders Hong Kong (*Economist Intelligence Unit*, 2008, pp.37-38).

Since Shanghai staked its claim to fame in both the pre-war and through the current reform eras primarily as a financial hub, it is crucial for scholars to understand the structural differences that set these eras apart if they are to venture a guess about China's future. As indicated above, before the World War II, China's main securities market was run by expatriates and governed by British corporate law. It was mainly geared toward foreign-run financial institutions, offshore mining ventures, shipping and insurance companies, and municipal utilities.

A significant departure from the pre-war pattern is the fact that China's securities markets are no longer concentrated in Shanghai alone. Symbolically, the first stock exchange to be opened in the reform era was set up in Shenzhen in June 1990. To be sure, in November that year, the Shanghai stock exchange was re-established after a 38-year hiatus. Today, China's securities market is fairly evenly divided between Shanghai and Shenzhen, and is invariably geared toward state-owned industrial behemoths. Realistically capitalizeded at US$ 0.5 trillion, this securities market is nominally the third-largest in Asia (after Tokyo and Hong Kong), but only about a third of its listed equity is publicly tradable, and merely a fourth of the firms listed are privately-run (Chen, 2006, pp.21-22).

The relative paucity of privately-run publicly-listed firms is a red thread linking the pre and post-war periods; it is an issue that is clearly relevant to the nature of China's modernization effort in the long-haul, as Bowen and Rose (1998) have argued. After almost three decades of reform in the PRC, private enterprise and private property rights are still lamely-framed within the legal system. Re-established with much fanfare in 1990, the Shanghai and Shenzhen domestic bourses rarely float private firms; PRC taxation policy and the predominantly state-owned banking system similarly disadvantage private SMEs lacking in political connections in favour of well-networked government-backed ventures (Huang, 2008).

Courts in the PRC are reluctant to adjudicate litigation arising from corporate accounting fraud, enforce minority shareholder rights, or promote transparency. This is because the government is often a majority stakeholder. Provincial authorities similarly exert pressure on its judiciary when investors from other parts of China bring charges against local firms. But arguably most pernicious is the Chinese securities market stochastic nature. In 1996, for example, 57% of US corporate stock moved in the same direction. In post-Communist Poland the figure was 82%. In China, virtually the entire market (91.3%) moved along to the same beat. This suggest cycles rather than specific company performance inform share prices, and betrays the skepticism with which investors view the data Chinese listed companies put out (Chen, 2006, pp.33-38).

Another stark difference between the pre and post war periods lies in the area of logistics and infrastructure. Once strung along the silted Bund, Shanghai's port nevertheless handled almost half of Mainland China's maritime traffic and foreign trade. Container facilities have since been expanded and moved closer ashore, but the city's port often came under fire in the 1990s for falling well short of Hong Kong and Singapore. Today, China boasts no less than 200 seaports, which handled together 3.4 billion tones of goods in 2006, up from just 483 million in 1990. Shanghai's newly-developed port, while still one of the largest in China, is relatively shallow and therefore inaccessible to super-size freighters (*Economist Intelligence Unit*, 2008, p.27).

Since 1990, capital works included far more than port facilities. By 1995, a new water plant, gas works, power plant, sewage facilities and an advanced telecommunications network had been installed in Pudong. The second phase of this build-up began in 1996 to the tune of billions of RMB. It saw the construction of the city's second international airport, new subway lines, and a ring-road to alleviate traffic congestion (Lai, Chiu & Leu, 2005, p.305). In 1985, there was only 1 telephone for every 70 people in Shanghai; 15 years later, more than 97 per cent of the city's residents had a telephone installed in their home. By the beginning of 2004, the city had more than 11 million mobile phone subscribers, and 4.3 million internet users. Foreign firms such as Alcatel, McCaw and AT&T were persuaded to enter the market with promises of local-government protection. These companies brought valuable know-how that helped the municipal authorities tout Shanghai as 21st century cyber-hub (Harwit, 2005, pp.1837-845).

Yet today, in contrast to what one might expect in any Western metropolis, the municipal authorities are not only regulating the telecommunications industry or maintaining infrastructure, but also own the largest ISP and local-content portal (Eastday.com) as well as a string of browser cafes. This degree of local-government permeation of the hi-tech sector seems unique even compared to other PRC cities. Beijing and Guangzhou, for example, have not sought to steer residents to municipally-owned websites in quite the same way (Harwit, 2005, pp.1853-5).

During Jiang Zemin's decade in power (1993-2003), Shanghai was often seen as the subject of favourable discrimination by the central government, because Jiang and many of his protégés had held posts in the municipal bureaucracy prior to their elevation to the national arena. A number of development zones and R&D clusters were demarcated within the city's environs since 1990 with a view to attracting foreign hi-tech companies. The best known of these are perhaps the Zizhu Science Park, Waigaoqiao Tax-Free Zone, the Jinqiao Export Processing Zone and the Zhangjiang Hightech Park. The central and local governments provided tax incentives, research funding and venture capital for entrepreneurs willing to bring their expertise to these zones. These efforts were made in conjunction with the local prestigious universities of Fudan and Jiaotong. They have yielded many hardware, software, security, biotech and pharmaceutical ventures, and attracted considerable investment from the likes of Intel, Microsoft and Dell – companies which rarely invest in R&D outside their US home base. Yet anecdotal evidence suggests that the great bulk of R&D activity and start-up initiatives in Shanghai still stem from public funding, and it is unclear how much of it has become self-sustaining. (Lai et al., 2005, p.279). What is more, none of the best known homegrown hi-tech companies that have emerged in the PRC to date – Lenovo (Shenzhen), Huawei (Shenzhen), Galanz (Shenzhen), Haier (Qingdao), Baidu (Beijing) - are headquartered in Shanghai or the Yangzi Delta for that matter.

CONCLUSION

Can the foregoing overview of Shanghai development history be of any interest to contemporary China watchers? With so much attention devoted to themes of Asian economic and political submission in the postcolonial discourse, it is hardly surprising that few attempts have been made to uncover the vibrant legacy of Shanghainese entrepreneurship in the pre-war era, and how it may have presaged China's resurgence in the 21st century. Yet, the resemblance between Shanghai's pre-war economy and the Deng- inspired Special Economic Zone model of the 1990s cannot be lost on anyone but the most imperceptive. Both were heavily dependent on external capital flow, preferential treatment of foreign firms and a degree of municipal immunity to central-government directives.

How sustainable is this formula? Little systematic research has been done to that effect, but suggestive comparisons between the past and present cannot be completely avoided. Following China's entry to the WTO in 2001, some of the very same foreign banks, which had flourished on the Bund before World War II, have once again been authorised to operate in local currency. There are now over 108 foreign banks operating in Shanghai, but unlike the pre-war era, foreign financial institutions play a very small role in the domestic economy (approx. 1.2% in 2002) (Kuilman, 2007, pp.21, 31-33). The old stock exchanges had been shut down decisively in 1952 after a transitional period in which the CCP was tolerant of private enterprise. The have re-opened in the 1990s, and placed under strict state tutelage. What remains to be seen is how this *démarche* will project on China's historically ramshackle securities markets and on its brittle private sector. Sociologists might also add the question whether a civil society will emerge in China along western lines, but this question is beyond our scope.

If history is anything to go by, we can expect tough competition as well as convergence between local and foreign banks. As re-entrants to a long-lost market, foreign financial institutions may now be keener than ever to bankroll promising Chinese private ventures that state-controlled banks and securities markets routinely shut out; but whether in the absence of pervasive political reform Shanghai's stock exchange can grow out of its current doldrums, or eventually outshine that of Hong Kong, is doubtful. A counterintuitive (read: ahistorical) solution to this question may ultimately force theorists to consider the emergence of a new 'Capitalism with Chinese characteristics'.

What this overview does bear out quite concretely is the fact that pre-war Shanghai accounted for a much bigger share of China's economy that present-day Shanghai does. Though replete with semi-colonial racialism, and circumscribed to a much smaller area, pre-war Shanghai was arguably more cosmopolitan, individualistic and entrepreneurial urban space. It was arguably where a Chinese public sphere of sorts was beginning to emerge before 1928. Corporatism has since been the rule, be it under KMT or CCP aegis. It is state-led development and bureaucratic co-optation of private enterprise that has spawned Pudong's impressive (yet somewhat anodyne) skyline.

In her critique of neo-liberal marketplace homogeneity, Godø (2008, p. 32) has posited that *"...organizations outside the markets have the capability of creating innovation regimes, if and when they want to. Their ability to succeed is, of course, a different matter..."*; Markets "...do not possess the type of imagination or creativity that would foster heterogeneity, which is another way of stating that if society wants to be creative and imaginative, it has to muster the political will for this – innovation and heterogeneity are a matter for policy and associated agency." Godø's analysis might, in that sense, partly vindicate the purposeful, relentless makeover of Shanghai as a future hub of technological innovation by the municipal authorities. Nevertheless, most observers of the innovative ICT-based "New Economy" that has emerged in parts of the developed world point to free-access capital markets, to political and educational pluralism, and to the unhindered flow of information as underpinning success. These factors still seem absent from Shanghai's current development prescripts.

REFERENCES

All about Shanghai and environs: A standard guide book. (1936). Shanghai: University Press.

Barber, N. (1979). *The fall of Shanghai*. New York: Coward, McCann and Geoghegan.

Belke, A., & Fehn, R. (2001). *Institutions and structural unemployment: Do capital-market imperfections matter?* (CESifo Working Paper, 504).

Bergère, M. (1981). The other China: Shanghai from 1919 to 1949. In C. Howe (Ed.), *Shanghai: revolution and development in an Asian metropolis* (pp. 1-34). New York: Cambridge University Press.

Bergère, M. (2002). *Histoire de Shanghai*. Paris: Fayard.

Bowen, J. R., & Rose, D. C. (1998). On the absence of privately owned, publicly traded corporations in China: The Kirby Puzzle. *The Journal of Asian Studies*, *57*(2), 442–452. doi:10.2307/2658832

Brandt, L. (1989). *Commercialization and agricultural development: Central and eastern China, 1870–1937*. New York: Cambridge University Press.

Chen, Z. W. (2006). *The stock market in China's modernization process: Its past, present and future prospects*. Yale School of Management - Unpublished Paper Working Paper.

Cheung, P. T. Y. *(1996). The political context of Shanghai's economic development. In Y. M. Yeung & Y. W. Sung (Eds.),* Shanghai: Transformation and modernization under China's open door *(pp. 49-92). Hong Kong: Chinese University Press.*

Economist intelligence unit. (2008). Country profile – China. London: The Economist.

Feng, H. Y., Froud, J., & Johal, S. (2001, November). A new business model? The capital market and the new economy. *Economy and Society*, *30*(4), 467–503. doi:10.1080/03085140120089063

Godø, H. (2008). Technological evolution, innovation and human agency. In E. G. Carayannis, A. Kaloudis, & A. Mariussen (Eds.), *Diversity in the knowledge economy and society* (pp. 18-34). Cheltenham, UK: Edward Elgar.

Harwit, E. (2005). Telecommunications and the internet in Shanghai: Political and economic factors shaping the network in a Chinese city. *Urban Studies (Edinburgh, Scotland)*, *42*(10), 1837–1858. doi:10.1080/00420980500231738

Horesh, N. (2007). The bund and beyond: Rethinking the sino-foreign financial grid in pre-war Shanghai. *China Review*, *7*(1), 1–26.

Houben, A., & Kakes, J. (2002). ICT innovation and economic performance: The role of financial intermediation. *Kyklos*, *55*(4), 543–562. doi:10.1111/1467-6435.00201

Howe, C. (1981). Industrialization under conditions of long-run population stability: Shanghai's achievement and prospect. In C. Howe (Ed.), *Shanghai: Revolution and development in an Asian metropolis* (pp. 153-187). Cambridge, UK: Cambridge University Press.

Huang, Y. S. (2008). *Capitalism with Chinese characteristics: Entrepreneurship and the state.* Cambridge, UK: Cambridge University Press.

King, F. H. H. (1965). *Research guide to China-coast newspapers, 1822-1911.* Cambridge, MA: Harvard University Press.

Kuilman, J. *(2007). Institutional change, diversity and competition: foreign banks in Shanghai, 1847-2004. In B. Krug & H. Hans (Eds.),* The Chinese economy in the 21st century: Enterprise and business behaviour *(pp. 21-41). Cheltenham, UK: Edward Elgar.*

Lai, H. C., Chiu, Y. C., & Leu, H. D. (2005). Innovation capacity comparison of China's information technology industrial clusters: The case of Shanghai, Kunshan, Shenzhen and Dongguan. *Technology Analysis and Strategic Management*, *17*(3), 293–315. doi:10.1080/09537320500211284

Ma, D. B. (2008). Economic growth in the lower Yangzi region of China in 1911–1937: A quantitative and historical analysis. *The Journal of Economic History*, *68*(2), 355–392. doi:10.1017/S002205070800034X

Ma, Z. D. (2001). Shanghai guoji qianyi biandong chutan (Preliminary survey of Shanghai international arrivals and departures). *Journal of Shanghai Public Security Academy*, *11*(3), 42–45.

MacPherson, K. L. (1996). The Shanghai model in historical perspective. In Y.M. Yeung & Y.W. Sung (Eds.), *Shanghai: Transformation and modernization under China's open door* (pp. 493-527). Hong Kong: Chinese University Press.

Madrick, J. G. (1995). *The end of affluence*. New York: Random House.

Mak, G. C. L., & Lo, L. N. K. (1996). Education. In Y.M. Yeung & Y.W. Sung (Eds.), *Shanghai: Transformation and modernization under China's open door* (pp. 375-398). Hong Kong: The Chinese University Press.

Mao, G. P., & Higano, Y. (1996). A Study of the labor input in Shanghai: Effects of information development and employment policy. *Hitotsubashi Journal of Economics*, (37): 155–173.

Minami, R. (1994). *The economic development of China: A comparison with the Japanese experience*. London: Macmillan.

Mittler, B. (2004). *A newspaper for China?: Power, identity, and change in Shanghai's news media, 1872-1912*. Cambridge, MA: Harvard University Press.

Murphey, R. (1953). *Shanghai: Key to modern China*. Cambridge, MA: Harvard University Press.

Murphey, R. (1977). *The outsiders: The western experience in India and China*. Ann Arbor, MI: Michigan University Press.

Nobutaka, I. (1954). The pattern of railway development in Japan. *The Far Eastern Quarterly*, *14*(1), 217–229.

Noda Masaho. (1980). *Nihon shōken shijō seiritsu* [History of the Japanese securities markets]. Tokyo: Yūhikaku.

Qian, Y. Y. (2002). *How the reform worked in China* (William Davidson Institute Working Paper, 473).

Rawski, T. G. (1989). *Economic growth in prewar China*. Berkeley, CA: University of California Press.

Reed, C. (2004). *Gutenberg in Shanghai: Chinese print capitalism, 1876-1937*. Honolulu, HI: University of Hawai'i Press.

Wakeman, F. J. (1995). *Policing Shanghai, 1927-1937*. Berkeley, CA: University of California Press.

Waller, S. A. (2000). *Theories of economic growth and the new economy*. University of Missouri Working paper.

Warschauer, M. (2003). *Technology and social inclusion: Rethinking the digital divide*. Cambridge, MA: MIT Press.

Wasserstrom, J. (2000). Locating old Shanghai: Having fits about where it fits. In J. W. Esherick (Ed.), *Remaking the Chinese city: Modernity and national identity, 1900-1950*. Honolulu, HI: University of Hawai'i Press.

Wong, S. L. (1996). The entrepreneurial spirit: Shanghai and Hong Kong compared. In Y.M. Yeung & Y. W. Sung (Eds.), *Shanghai: Transformation and modernization under China's open door* (pp. 25-48). Hong Kong: Chinese University Press.

Yeung, Y. M. (1996). Introduction. In Y. M. Yeung and Y. W. Sung (Eds.), *Shanghai: transformation and modernization under China's open door* (pp. 1-23). Hong Kong: Chinese University Press.

Section 2

Natural Resources

Chapter 4
Natural Resources Accounting for Sustainable Development:
Approaches and Some Applications

Ramakrishna Nallathiga
Centre for Good Governance, India

ABSTRACT

Economic growth has been conventionally looked upon as the measure for the development of society, while ignoring the other aspects viz., human development, natural resources, environment and ecology. In the conventional accounting of economic development, the value of services and goods provided by natural resources like air, water, land and biota are ignored; neither any attempts are made to monitor and account for the changes in natural resources and environment. For the economic development to be sustainable, the environmental costs have to be limited and to be growing at slower pace than the economic gains. In this chapter, an attempt is made to outline the importance of using Natural Resource Accounting (NRA) for sustainable development through an attempt to estimate the environmental costs and benefits, and also to compare with economic growth in the case of India. This chapter highlights the potential of using NRA to make decisions for sustainable development through policies for conservation, management and development of natural resources.

INTRODUCTION

Sustainable development is now accepted as an important goal of the development of human society, which requires the development to pass on the same benefits from current generation to future generation and which requires sustainable utilization of natural resources like air, water, land mass, biota and other ecological resources (WCED 1987). Natural resources like air, water, land and biota provide material and non-material inputs to the economic development of a country or region, but traditionally they do not enter the conventional national/ regional income accounts, which capture only value addition from economic activities within the country/ region. Natural Resources Accounting (NRA) is an alternative approach, which essentially involves the accounting of material and non-material services

DOI: 10.4018/978-1-61520-709-1.ch004

Figure 1. The UN system of environmental economic accounting (Adapted from Ahmed et al. (1989))

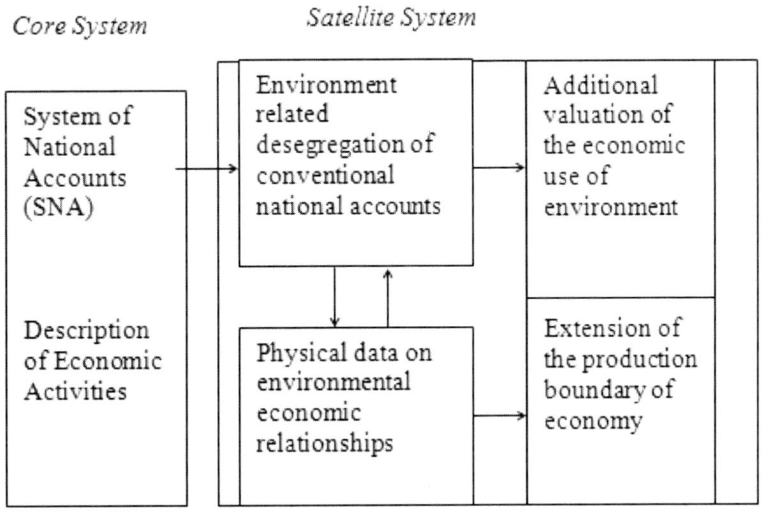

rendered by natural resources viz., air, water, land and biota (El Sarafy 1989). An important utility of NRA is that the national income accounts can be revalued after adjusting for changes in the economic values of natural resources utilized in the past fiscal year (Pearce et al., 1989).

To some extent, NRA can play a major role in the planning of development of existing resource base, as it provides the estimates of economic values as well as the costs associated with the utilization of natural resources, upon which the country/ region's economy is critically dependent. Therefore, NRA provides an opportunity to integrate environmental changes into economic planning. Towards this end, the United Nations pronounced on the need for creating a System of Environmental and Economic Accounting (SEEA), comprising 'Satellite Accounts' of environmental changes that are based on NRA framework (see Figure 1)1. Such system of accounting leads to the development of Integrated Environmental Economic Accounting (IEEA) to serve the purpose of aiding decision and policy making.

NRA framework provides a system of collecting, organizing and analyzing environmental and natural resources data to policy planners and decision makers so that the information can be utilized in decision making. However, it requires standardization; also, it needs to cover information exhaustively in physical and monetary terms that is comparable over time and space. When integrated into the conventional system of economic accounts, these accounts would yield Integrated Environmental Economic Accounts (IEEA), which are useful for the prudent management of economy with ecological harmony, as (United Nations 1993):

- they are potentially very useful in decision making from policy to management level, because, environmentally corrected national accounts provide correct information directly useful to resource conservation/ management
- they are not an end in themselves but a means to decision-making

Resource accounting methods vary widely with the nations/regions in their form as well as structure because of the differences in the frameworks adopted. They vary from the satellite accounts to flow resource accounting of natural resources that consists of inflows and outflows of products and services e.g., Hannon (1991). The United Nations has suggested that the nations should attempt to prepare satellite accounts at least, as a beginning, and then move on to other forms of integrated economic and environmental accounts. Figure 1 shows the broad framework of SEEA, in which the methodology essentially follows physical accounts, economic valuation and monetized accounts of resources vis-à-vis economic accounts (national income) captured in the sectoral economic accounting.

BACKGROUND

Economic growth has for long been considered as a measure of the society's progress and a measure of its development. Most of the countries plan for and lay down target for achieving a certain level of economic growth every year and quarter, thereby, making it central to their policies, investments and development priorities. In the economic growth calculus, natural resources like air, water, land and biota have only the role of providing inputs to the country's economic activities, while ignoring the inherent value of natural resources and that of the services rendered by them. The decline and degradation of natural resources and its concomitant effect on the welfare of population is an important but negative outcome of economic growth (Repetto et al., 1991). Yet, several nations continue to ignore the potential value of natural resources and environment, which results in the pursuit of unsustainable development patterns (Ahmed et al., 1989). Such losses to natural resources and environment were not considered as serious until the concept of "Sustainable Development" was mooted by the Brundtland Report, which defined it as: "*the development that constitutes meeting needs of the current generation without compromising the ability of meeting needs of future generations*" (WCED, 1987, p. 43).

The means of attaining sustainable development involve (Pearce et al., 1989): (a) valuing of environment (natural, built, and cultural) for its various goods and services, (b) extending the time horizon of planning, ensuring equity (inter- and intra-generational). Sustainable development draws upon environmental economics to substantiate itself in designing development policies adopted by the society (Ahmed et al., 1989). Here, environmental economics deals with the study of interaction between economic activities and environment. It essentially comes into picture because of (a) the non-existence of markets and, thus, the lack of value for environmental goods and services; (b) the distorted nature of markets where they exist; (c) behavioral problems with individuals ignoring their actions causing damages (tragedy of commons). It, thereby, helps in policy formulation, either anticipatory or preventive, while also acknowledging the problems of reactive policy. Sustainable development is also elaborated theoretically and, to some extent philosophically, in terms of non-declining wealth (net income), non-declining natural wealth (net natural capital) and resilience (of system) (Pearce et al., 1989).

Although India has been growing fast, the environmental costs of economic growth have not caught the attention of economic policy and decision makers for a long time. Brandon and Hommann (1995) study was the first attempt to make an accounting of environmental costs/benefits vis-à-vis economic growth in India, which provided some stimulus to the thinking about the environmental degradation and its costs inflicted on the Indian society. Parikh et al. (1992) provided a framework for resource accounting in India for a research project covering India. Parikh and Parikh (1997 a & b) provide, respectively, a framework for preparing natural resource accounts at country level and some case studies from Asia Pacific region. Murty (2001) and Haripriya (2000) are only some of the few attempts made in India to outline the importance of making an assessment of water and forest resources, respectively, within the economic accounting framework. Recently,

Figure 2. Framework of economic and environmental accounting

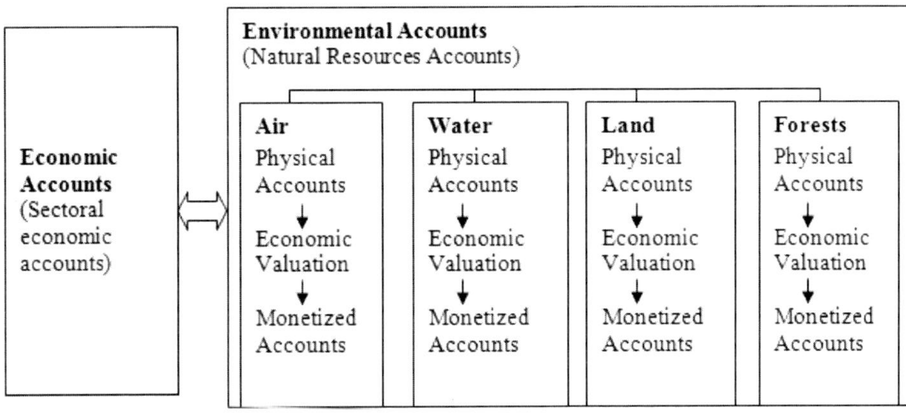

TERI (2006) has made a comprehensive attempt to monitor the resource changes over the last 50 years and set out a vision for the green development of India for next 50 years.

This chapter features a comparison of how economic and environmental accounts have fared over a period of ten years during 1980-90 in India to find whether economic development trajectory has followed a sustainable development path or not. Here, the emphasis is made on applying the principles and methods of environmental economics to come out with economic valuation of environmental resources – air, water, land and forests – so as to show how much they are - both in absolute and relative terms (in relation to the economic accounts). It is hoped to be a beginning towards further research of a comprehensive valuation of environmental resources. The broad framework of the study is shown in figure 2. The methodology essentially follows the sequential preparation of physical accounts, economic valuation and monetized accounts of resources vis-à-vis economic accounts (national income) captured in the sectoral economic accounting.

ECONOMIC GROWTH AND ENVIRONMENTAL DEGRADATION IN INDIA

Economic Growth

Economic activities are driven by the production and consumption of various goods and services under various sectors of the economy. Economic accounts in India are prepared every year by the Central Statistical Organisation under National Accounts Statistics, which present national income from the value additions of various sectors. The data provided therein is used in the study. Table 1 presents the national income accounts of India for the years 1980 and 1990. It clearly shows that the income generated under sectors such industries, transport, and energy, which intake the bulk of natural resources and which contribute significantly to the GDP growth. The services sector has also begun to contribute significantly but much of it has happened after the 1990s. Also, the income accounts do not make any provision for accounting the contribution of household services, which is mostly non-remunerative. Importantly, the aggregate of the income i.e., the GDP, is shown for both years 1980 and 1990 (at constant prices of 1990). This is an important measure of the level of economic activity and its growth.

Table 1. Income accounts of Indian economy (Rs in Crores)

Sector of Economy	1,980	1,990
Agriculture, Forestry and Fishing	104,960	148,001
Mining and Quarrying	4,245	11,785
Manufacturing	48,700	89,160
Electricity, Fuel and Water Supply	4,657	10,464
Construction	13,756	28,616
Trade, Hotels and Restaurants	33,104	61,883
Transport, Storage and Communication	12,880	33,913
Financing, Insurance, Real estate and Business Services	24,280	38,902
Community and Personnel Services	28,878	55,090
GDP at factor Cost	275,460	477,814

Source: (Adapted from Central Statistical Organisation, 1997)

Natural Resources Accounts

Natural resource accounts for India are prepared for all four major resource components of natural environment – air, water, land and forests. The estimation processes as well as its results are explained in the following sections.

Air Environment

Air is an important resource component of natural environment, which is essential for all major life forms. However, air pollution is increasingly becoming a threat due to rapid population growth, increasing urbanization, increasing energy consumption and increasing demand for transport and other services.

i. Air Emissions

Air environment is increasingly becoming polluted due to the emissions coming from various economic activities – industries, household, transport and electricity generation - and the emissions from them depend upon fuel ingredients as well as consumption. The air emissions of important pollutants viz., Suspended Particulate Matter (SPM), Hydro-carbons (HC), Sulphur, Carbon and Nitrogen Oxides (SO2, CO and NOx), are calculated for the dominant economic sectors - Industry, Households, Power plants and Transport, using the consumption figures of various fuels and after making allowance for the emission factors2 developed by National Environmental Engineering Research Institute (NEERI) and Tata Energy Research Institute (TERI). The pollutant-wise emission loads are shown in tables 2 to 5. Here, it was not possible to strictly delineate the contribution of each of the sectors but the aggregates alone were estimated so as to reflect the aggregate loads.

ii. Valuation

Air pollution from various types of fuels gives rise to several health damages (primarily pulmonary health damages) to human beings; it also affects the health and growth of vegetation. The damages arising from air pollution are estimated based on (a) the emission loads estimated above and (b) the unit damage costs of ambient air quality levels on population and vegetation distribution. The unit damage costs to health and ecological functions are estimated based on the studies in NCT-Delhi and Yamuna river sub-basin (NEERI 1997)3. The results show that in 1980-81, total health damage costs in terms of possible rise in mortality and morbidity were estimated at Rs 9.05

Table 2. Emission loads from household sector (in tonnes/year)

Emissions	TSP/SPM		SO2		NOX		CO		HC	
Fuel type	1980	1990	1980	1990	1980	1990	1980	1990	1980	1990
Coal	7,667	9,136	-	-	-	-	92,956	110,618		-
Oil	11,524	14,789	-	-	-	-	194,509	248,971	-	-
Firewood	242,163	261,536	-	-	24,858	26,487	2165,022	2338,224	-	-
Cow dung	145,741	205,495	-	-	-	-	926,285	1306,062		-

Table 3. Emission loads from Transportation sector (in tonnes/year)

Emissions	TSP/SPM		SO2		NOX		CO		HC	
Fuel type	1980	1990	1980	1990	1980	1990	1980	1990	1980	1990
Coal	92,570	43,120	-	-	-	-	78,590	36,610	-	-
Oil	40,615	92,570	15,810	32,200	219,750	447,530	548,195	116,420	250,675	510,510

billion and vegetative damage costs in terms of production and ecological costs were estimated at Rs 440.49 billion. The corresponding figures in 1990-91 were Rs 18.25 billion and Rs 888.10 billion respectively. The details of estimation (in NCT-Delhi) are shown in Ramakrishna *et al.* (2007). From the damage costs of air pollution estimated above, the net increase in the value of air pollution damage costs in money terms over a period of ten years during 1980-90 is Rs 452.99 billion.

Water Environment

Water is an important and integral part of human life that provides drinking, irrigation, domestic, industrial and other service benefits. Water resources are increasingly becoming vulnerable to over-exploitation that is leading to resource depletion and degradation problems in various parts of the country. Ground water, in particular, has witnessed a great pressure that has been resulting in the depletion of aquifers and the pollution of ground water, making it one of the severely abused resources. Surface water, such as in rivers, lakes

Table 4. Emission loads from Thermal Power Plants (in tonnes/year)

Emissions	TSP/SPM		SO2		NOX		CO		HC	
Fuel type	1980	1990	1980	1990	1980	1990	1980	1990	1980	1990
Coal	96,333	243,750	50,000	126,667	16,667	41,883	6,000	15,250	3,000	7,617

Table 5. Emission loads from industrial sector (in tonnes/year)

Emissions	TSP/SPM		SO2		NOX		CO		HC	
Fuel type	1980	1990	1980	1990	1980	1990	1980	1990	1980	1990
Coal	841,000	1425,000	437,000	740,000	143,000	243,000	53,000	90000	260000	450000
Gas	-	-	-	-	151,000	230,000	-	-	-	-

and tanks, is also increasingly coming under the risk of diversion and pollution from the domestic and industrial waste water discharges into them. Accounting water resources, herein, consider these important aspects of resource than any other.

i. Physical Accounts

Ground water has been increasingly becoming significant water resource in the country, with the rising demands for water and with the limitation of transporting surface water. Partly, it is also due to (a) decreasing reliability of surface water resources as well as water distribution networks, and (b) impairment of surface water quality as well as absence of treatment systems making them unfit for direct consumption. Owing to an increasing utilization without concern for its sustainability, quantitative decline and qualitative degradation of ground water was observed in various parts of the country particularly in the northern region, wherein the decline is severe and the degradation associated with them is highest. From the Central Ground Water Board (CGWB) report of ground water decline maps in NCT-Delhi, the annual decline of ground water was estimated, which was of the order of 1540 mcm/year during the period of 1976-89. This decline is associated by degradation of ground water, primarily in the form of increased salinity, alkalinity, sodium and potassium and in some cases fluoride and arsenic.

ii. Valuation

With the help of estimates of ground water decline and based on the avoidance costs for unit rate of quantitative decline (mcm/year), the cost of ground water quantity decline was estimated at Rs 96.90 billion. The unit costs used here are based on the estimations carried out for NCT-Delhi, in which the costs of alternative water supply were estimated and the details of estimation are given in Ramakrishna *et al.* (2007). Here, while estimating the total avoidance costs of quantitative decline of ground water in India, necessary corrections for spatial distribution of surface water resources and population across the country was also made. The costs of degradation from such areas shown in the maps prepared by the CGWB were based on the treatment costs to remedy the degradation, which were placed at Rs 1 billion.

In the case of surface water pollution, the avoidance costs of surface water pollution were based on the treatment costs of wastewater generated and based on the estimated unit costs of treatment in NCT-Delhi and other cities, while giving due consideration for existing capacities and excessive volumes of wastewater treatment. Here, only secondary level treatment of waste water was considered appropriate. Table 6 shows such defensive expenditure incurred towards the waste water treatment in those years wherein the waste water generation estimates were made by the Central Pollution Control Board (CPCB) for Class I cities in India.

iii. Monetized Accounts

Economic valuation of water resource gave the estimates of economic value of ground water and surface in India. The monetized accounts in terms of avoidance and replacement costs of ground water stood at Rs 969 billion and Rs 249.85 billion

Table 6. Defensive expenditures on Wastewater treatment (in Rs billion)

Description	1978	1988
Waste water treatment in existing plants	0.875	1.369
Treatment of further waste water generated in new plants	2.337	6.131
Total costs of waste water discharges	3.212	7.500

Source: (Adapted from Central Pollution Control Board, 1992)

respectively and the avoidance costs of surface water pollution stood at Rs 10.14 billion for the period of 1980-90.

Accounting for Land Environment

Land is also an important resource that provides support for human living and organization of various economic activities ranging from agriculture production to industrial production. However, land as resource is susceptible to very intensive use because of the regular interface of human activities like agriculture, livestock farming and aquaculture. All these activities are continuously carried out with more and more land brought under them. This leads to the deterioration of its quality from excessive erosion (due to wind and water) and soil contamination (due to fertilizer and pesticide use), rendering it unproductive for further/future use. The extent of such losses in India has not been captured to the fullest extent by any study but an attempt was made by the National Bureau of Soil Survey and Land Use Planning (NBSSLUP), Nagpur, which were used in the study.

i. Physical Accounts

The landmass resource degradation in the form of soil erosion, salinity and water-logging is widespread across India. The causative factors are of anthropogenic origin and include excessive use of inorganic fertilizers, over-grazing, excessive irrigation, poor tillage practices and degradation of protective vegetative cover. The extent of land degradation under various forms is shown in Table 7. The degradation process, further, constitutes the severity (or, intensity) of degradation expressed in ordinal rankings such as high, medium, low is observed as under in 1985, which is shown in Table 8.

Table 7. Land degradation in India (in million ha)

Degradation	1976	1981	1985
Erosion processes			
- Water Erosion	96.5	99.6	148.9
- Wind erosion	53.5	55.2	13.5
Chemical deterioration			
- Salinity/Alkalinity	7	7.89	13.8
Physical Deterioration			
- Water logging	6	8	11.6

Source: (Adapted from National Bureau of Soil Survey and Land use Planning, 1994)

ii. Valuation

The extent of land degradation in India during the period of 1980-90 due to erosion, salinity or alkalinity, and water logging, was computed as above. The valuation was done by estimating the likely crop yield losses due to degradation, according to the severity of degradation that were estimated for the affected land mass. This is based on the assumption that the cropping pattern in districts would not have changed much during 1980-90 and the prevailing current prices of agricultural produce also remained constant. Table 6 provides a sum-

Table 8. Severity-wise land degradation in India in 1985 (in million ha)

Degradation	Area
Water Erosion	
- Low	5
- Medium	24.3
- High	107.2
- Very high	12.4
Wind Erosion	
- High	13.5
Chemical Deterioration	
- Low	2.8
- Medium	2
- High	9
Water logging	11.8

Source: (Adapted from National Bureau of Soil Survey and Land use Planning, 1994)

mary of the estimated productivity losses in India in the respective years during 1980-90. Further, land rejuvenation costs, which are those that need to be incurred to bring back land to the original state through various interventions, were estimated based on per unit (ha) expenditure on watershed development programmes for the conservation and rejuvenation of land resource estimated from the watershed programmes implemented by the Government of India in different regions of India.

iii. Monetized Accounts

The monetized accounts of land degradation in India in terms of production losses and land rejuvenation costs for the period 1980-90 are Rs 1,387.5 billion and Rs 240 billion respectively, which sum up to Rs 1,627.5 billion.

Accounting for Biological Environment

Biological resources are very important and are more complex, given their support to the existence of whole ecosystems and biosphere. It is difficult to account even to some extent of the goods and services rendered by them, especially when it comes to the services like ecology, biodiversity, livelihoods etc. Here, we attempt that for forest resource and that too we confine to a limited range of services provided by the forests in conserving the ecological balance.

Table 9. Annual productivity losses due to land degradation (in million Rs.)

Description	1976	1981	1985
Erosion Processes			
• Water erosion	541,720	559,120	835,875
• Wind erosion	155,450	160,390	39,225
Chemical Deterioration			
• Salinity/Alkalinity	28,730	32,390	56,648
Physical Deterioration			
• Water logging	8,925	11,900	17,256
	734,825	763,800	949,004

Source: Calculated by Author

i. Physical Accounts

Forest resources are major biological resources, which constitute to the bulk of the biological resources by preserving most of the vegetation and wildlife. Decline in forest crown cover and crown density and degradation of ground flora has been a major concern, but this is reflected to some extent in the production from forests in national accounts. The physical accounts in terms of the geographical area of forest cover in India spread over an area of 6,39,182 sq km in 1991 and 6,39,600 sq km in 1995 (Forest Survey of India 1995).

ii. Valuation

The forest cover decline in India during the decade 1980-90 was considered and the loss of ecological services due to such decline was estimated as per the provisions laid by the Ministry of Environment and Forests for the economic value of forest services per unit area (hectare) in assessing the benefits and costs of projects involving conversion of forest areas. Biodiversity losses and habitat disturbances have been the major areas of attention but difficult to valuate. The decline in forest crown density, degradation of ground and middle level flora, habitat disturbances and losses in bio-diversity are not estimated in this exercise, which can amount to a very large figure given the diversity of forests in terms of both flora and fauna. Nevertheless, it is also important to know the decline in the amount of commercial value of the forests.

iii. Monetized Accounts

The monetized values of forest cover decline in India during the decade, as estimated above in terms of ecological services lost, are Rs 20.04 billion in 1991 and Rs 7 billion in 1995 respectively.

Summary and Recommendations

Economic growth is important for several countries in order to move forward by planning their resource allocation and prioritizing their investments. However, the intensity of resource utilization and the resulting environmental degradation are equally important for long term sustainability of the economic development. In particular, if the quantity of such costs and their growth is faster than economic growth, it can have serious implications to the future growth and environment, unless the gains from growth are invested into environmental improvement. Normally, the environmental costs are given a back seat and are never even considered or compared with economic progress.

Natural resource accounting provides a framework for such estimation of the costs and to draw a comparison in absolute and relative terms. The estimation of environmental costs in India during 1980-90, attempted here, even in a narrow sense laid down and even with several limitations, may give some pointers to planners and decision makers in laying down the priorities. Table 10 provides summary of statutory economic accounts and the estimated environmental accounts, which shows that the absolute size of the costs is much larger. It may be noted that some of the estimates could not be obtained for some years due to data and procedural limitations.

Besides the quantum, even in relative terms, the growth of GDP has been lower when compared to the raise of environmental costs during the period of 1980-90 as implied in table 11. The rising environmental costs in relation to economic growth are some important pointers to prioritizing the environmental protection through various sectoral policies concerning the resources and ensuring some regulatory compliance. The importance of resource accounts to sectoral policy making at regional level has also been outlined in Ramakrishna (2005).

Table 10. Summary of Economic and Environmental Accounts (Rs billion)

Description	1980	1990
Economic growth (GDP at factor cost)	2754.60	4778.14
Total damage costs of air pollution	449.54	906.53
Total costs of ground water mining	96.90	96.90
Total costs of waste water discharges	3.21	7.50
Total costs of land degradation	7638	-
Total costs of forest cover decline	-	20.04

Table 11. Relative trend of economic income & environmental costs (Rs billion)

Description	1980-90
Economic income (GDP at factor cost) during	2023.54
Total damage costs due to air pollution	453
Total Costs of ground water decline & degradation	1218.85
Total Costs of surface water pollution	10.14
Total Productivity losses due to land degradation	1387.5
Total costs of land rejuvenation	240
Total Costs of Forest loss	200.4
Rise of Environmental Costs during 1980-90	3509.88

Conclusion

Economic growth is important for several countries in order to move forward by planning their resource allocation and prioritizing their investments. However, the intensity of resource utilization and the resulting environmental degradation are equally important for the long term sustainability of economic development. In particular, if the quantity of such costs and their growth is faster than economic growth, it can have serious implications to the future growth and environment, unless the gains from economic growth are invested into environmental improvement. Normally, environmental costs are given a back seat and they are never even considered or compared with measures of economic progress. Natural resources accounting framework can be used for estimating the environmental costs and incorporating them into sectoral income accounts or even compare with them so as to take the required policy decision with regard to environmental resource conservation.

REFERENCES

Ahmad, Y. J., et al. (Eds.). (1989). *Environmental Accounting for Sustainable Development*. Washington, DC: World Bank.

Brandon, C., & Hommann, K. (1995). *The cost of inaction: Valuating the economy-wide costs of environmental degradation in India*. Washington, DC: The World Bank, Asia Environment Division.

Central Pollution Control Board. (1992). *Basin/Sub-Basin Inventory of Water Pollution - The Ganga Basin, Part One: The Yamuna sub-basin*. New Delhi, India: Central Pollution Control Board.

Central Statistical Organisation. (1997). *National Accounts Statistics*. New Delhi, India: Government of India.

El Serafy, S. (1989). The proper calculation of income from depletable natural resources. In Y. J. Ahmad et al. (Eds.), *Environmental Accounting for Sustainable Development*. Washington, DC: World Bank.

Hannon, B. M. (1991). Accounting in Ecological Systems. In R. Costanza (Ed.), *Ecological Economics: The Science and Management of Sustainability* (pp. 234-252). New York: Columbia University Press.

Haripriya, G. S. (2000). Integrating forest resources into the system of national accounts in Maharashtra. *Environment and Development Economics*, *5*, 143–156. doi:10.1017/S1355770X00000103

Murty, M. N. (2001). Environmentally Sustainable Income and Shadow Price of Natural Resources. In *Environmentally Corrected GDP: Valuation and Accounting for Industrial Pollution in India*. New Delhi, India: Institute of Economic Growth.

National Bureau of Soil Survey and Land use Planning. (1994). *Soil degradation in India: Status and Impact* (NBSSLUP Publication No. 38). New Delhi, India: Oxford & IBH Publishers.

Parikh, J. K., & Parikh, K. S. (Eds.). (1997a). *Accounting and Valuation of Environment – Volume I: A Primer for Developing Countries*. Bangkok, Thailand: Economic and Social Commission for Asia and Pacific.

Parikh, J. K., & Parikh, K. S. (Eds.). (1997b). *Accounting and Valuation of Environment – Volume II: Case Studies from the ESCAP Region*. Bangkok, Thailand: Economic and Social Commission for Asia and Pacific.

Parikh, K. S., Parikh, J. K., Sharma, V. K., & Painuly, J. P. (1992). *Natural Resource Accounting: A Framework for India*. Report prepared for Ministry of Environment and Forests. Mumbai, India: Indira Gandhi Institute of Development Research.

Pearce, D., Markandya, A., & Barbier, E. B. (1989). *Blueprint for a Green Economy* (A report prepared for the UK Department of Environment). London: Earthscan Publishers Ltd.

Ramakrishna, N. (2005). Resource Accounting for Regional Water Management: A Case Study of Yamuna River Sub-basin. *South Asian Journal of Management*, *11*(2), 95–110.

Ramakrishna, N., Balakameswari, K., Srinivas Rao, M., & Ram Babu, P. (2007). Integrated Environmental Economic Accounting for Sustainable Development: A Case of NCT-Delhi. *ICFAI Journal of Environmental Economics*, *5*(3), 54–68.

Repetto, R., McGrath, W., Wells, M., Beer, C., & Rossini, F. (1991). *Wasting Assets: Natural Resources in the National Income Accounts*. Washington, DC: World Resource Institute.

TERI. (2006). *Looking back to Change Track: Green India 2047*. New Delhi, India: The Energy and Resources Institute (TERI) Press.

United Nations. (1993). *Integrated Environmental and Economic Accounting, Interim version* (Studies in Methods Series (UNSEE) F. No. 61). New York: Department of Economics and Social Information and Policy analysis.

WCED. (1987). *Our Common Future*. New Delhi, India: Oxford University Press.

KEY TERMS AND DEFINITIONS

Environmental Degradation: A change in the natural condition of environment and ecology that lead to their deterioration in terms of both quality as well as quantity. Environmental degradation is primarily caused by human activities either knowingly or unknowingly, but sometimes through natural activities that cause disturbances in the natural systems viz., natural disasters.

Natural Resources Accounting: Accounting (in either money or non-monetary terms) for the natural resources viz., air, water land and biota, in terms of the changes in their stock, condition and quality with reference to their impact on environment. It is the economic development process that exerts these changes in the state of natural resources, which are not adequately reflected in sectoral accounts.

Sectoral Accounting: Accounting with reference to the changes in the sectors of economy measured in money terms. It is also known as Income accounting, which is used widely used by the governments at various levels, particularly national and provincial governments. The Gross Domestic Product (GDP) of a country or a province or a region is estimated from these estimates.

Sustainable Development: Development of the society that is sustainable in terms of utilizing resources to the current and future requirements and across various sections. It is primarily concerned with the development aimed at leaving adequate resources for future generations while ensuring equitable distribution among current generation.

ENDNOTES

1 For a detailed discussion on approaches to environmentally corrected national income measures, see Pearce (1989)

2 Emission factors, which measure emissions per unit fuel consumption, for the above fuel sources are tested, compiled and derived under laboratory and practical conditions.

3 These damages are based on dose-exposure relationships using the toxicological studies undertaken in laboratory conditions.

Chapter 5
Re-Conceptualising the 'Technology-Development' Nexus:
Linking Water, Energy, People and Governance in India

Sam Wong
University of Leeds, UK

ABSTRACT

This book chapter re-conceptualises the relationships between technology and **development**. *It focuses on rural economic development and examines how water- and energy-related technologies interact with human-nature relationships. Drawing on case studies in Rajasthan, India, this chapter argues that people's preferences for livelihoods can be incompatible with technological design. The unintended consequences of water and energy interventions can bring uncertainty to policy-making which affects long-term economic development and ecological* **sustainability**. *Changing governance structures in challenging caste and gender inequalities also require strong leadership. It proposes a 'people-centred' technological intervention framework which links the macro technical system and the micro process of people's daily practices and subjectivities. In achieving this, it calls for a different approach to understanding human motivations, power dynamics and gender politics.*

INTRODUCTION

This book chapter is different from other chapters in is focus. It does not answer the questions about the relationships between information **technology** and economic development directly. Instead, it will take a wider perspective, intending to re-conceptualise the linkages between technology, poverty reduction and human-nature relationships. It will cover a wide range of water- and energy-related technologies, from indigenous methods, such as rain-water harvesting, to cutting-edged innovations, such as reverse osmosis plants (ie. turning grey-water to drinking water by breaking down the membranes of water molecules). While this paper will place more emphasis on rural development, it will expand the concept of sustainable economic development, from simply continuous economic

DOI: 10.4018/978-1-61520-709-1.ch005

growth to a wider socio-political-environmental perspective, including poverty alleviation, empowerment and environmental sustainability. This paper will, therefore, explore the impact of technology, not only on economic well-being, but also on social relations, **governance** structures and ecosystems.

The role of technology in achieving human development is multiple. It helps alleviate poverty by reducing mortality rates, improving hygiene, finding new drugs to tackle previously incurable diseases, and raising agricultural productivities (Chataway and Smith, 2007; Robins, 2005). The current climate change debates have further ascertained the role of technology in offering solutions to environmental changes (Wong, 2009). As the UNEP (2008) suggests:

Mobilizing and re-focusing the global economy towards investments in clean technologies and natural infrastructure such as forests and soils is the best bet for real growth, combating climate change and triggering an employment boom in the 21st century (p.2).

Some evidence has shown that technology can play a significant role in improving the living conditions of a large number of people living in extreme poverty who lack basic services, such as water, health services, housing and energy (Pauli, 1999). The study by de Janvry and Sadoulet (2002) shows that improving agricultural technology is effective in alleviating **poverty** by raising productivity and lowering production costs. Richards (2005) also highlights the usefulness of technology in mitigating the impact of climate change, and helping poor countries adapt to changing rainfall and agricultural patterns (Richards 2005).

The outcomes of the technological interventions are, however, not always positive. The celebratory account of technology can be misplaced. For instance, the research by Wong and Sharp (2009) suggests that the failure of the UK's first combined rain-water and grey-water systems in Liverpool does not simply mean that the innovation needed to be abandoned, but that poor implementation has reinforced the negative stereotypes that the elderly are anti-technology. Schumacher (1974) has long campaigned for the appropriateness of technology. Adger *et al.* (2003) also takes a governance perspective, suggesting that it is crucial to understand the role of public participation in influencing what technologies are seen as 'public-friendly'.

Literature offers a number of explanations for the limited success of some technological interventions. Firstly, there are questions as to whether long-term planning about repair, maintenance and capacity building is adequate and ready to support new technologies (Roy and Venema, 2002). Secondly, some critics argue that the existing (sustainable) technological interventions are not all 'pro-poor' in nature. The distribution of costs and benefits by (sustainable) technology can be so uneven that poor people in many cases often bear disproportionately high costs while local **elites** capture most benefits (Dikito-Wachtmeister, 2000). Thirdly, the interventions tend to underestimate the structural constraints, such as caste, class, gender and race. These factors can hinder poor people from gaining access to technology in their everyday lives (Feenberg, 1999). Fourthly, the discourse of sustainable technology pays insufficient attention to power dynamics within communities which can reinforce social and environmental inequalities (Cleaver and Frank, 2005). Lastly, from a **gender** perspective, Denton (2002) argues that powerful men often control technology, and make decisions for their community members.

This book chapter will build on these critiques, and argue that the success of technological interventions in rural economic development lies in our understanding of the complex interactions between water, energy, technology and human-nature relationships. It will draw upon an Indian project as a case study. The project aims to explore the feasibility of using brackish underground water to grow biomass for energy production in India. Rajasthan was chosen as an area of investigation since some parts of it receive only 300mm rainfall a year. If the technological interventions are proved effective, this would have significant implications for food security and poverty reduction in other drought-prone areas. The researchers conducted an exploratory fieldtrip in March 2008. With the assistance of Indian research partners, three villages in Rajasthan were identified: Kotdi, Manpura, and Bamlas. The researchers have conducted semi-structured interviews with different stakeholders and examined the impact of various (sustainable) technologies on their **livelihoods** and the ecosystems.

Three main arguments will be made in this chapter: firstly, people's preferences for livelihoods can be incompatible with the technological design. Secondly, the unintended consequences of water and energy interventions bring uncertainty to policy-making which affects the long-term economic development and ecological sustainability. Thirdly, changing governance structures in challenging caste and gender inequalities requires strong leadership and favourable social conditions. It calls for a critical examination of the complex linkages between human motivations, individual livelihoods, governance structures, power dynamics and physical environment in the process. The structure of this book chapter is as follows: the research objectives and methodology of the project will first be introduced. Observations and interviews of the three selected villages will be used to make the arguments. This book chapter will be concluded by re-conceptualising the 'technology- development' nexus and offering insights into building a 'people-centred' sustainable technological intervention framework.

BACKGROUND, RESEARCH OBJECTIVES AND METHODS

This chapter is based on a water and energy project in Rajasthan, India. This £1.3m UK's Engineering and Physical Sciences Research Council-funded programme was aimed at finding alternative sources of water in extreme dry regions in developing countries in order to enhance biomass production for energy generation, and then use the energy to promote economic activities in rural areas. The research consortium includes five English universities and one Indian university. It is an inter-disciplinary study, including engineers, physical scientists, geographers and sociologists. Advice from local academics and NGOs has also been sought.

Rajasthan is a huge and diverse region in terms of water availability and land-use cover (Shankarnarayan *et al.* 1987). East and Central Rajasthan were particularly targeted because these areas receive less than 300 mm rainfall a year which matches the criteria of extreme dry conditions in the project (see Figure 1). Furthermore, Birkenholtz (2008) reminds us that Rajasthan still has no regulations for groundwater management.

The research consortium, however, could not agree on how the project should start. There are two explicit assumptions of the research proposal: firstly, there is un-trapped water available in that region, be it underground water or rain-water, and that the quantity of water being collected should be sufficient for some meaningful interventions. Secondly, growing biomass by using the un-trapped water and then burning the biomass to generate energy for promoting economic activities in rural economy is desirable, sustainable and cost-effective in nature. Though well-intended, this research proposal remains top-down and expert-led in nature. Although some of these questions can be answered by reviewing the literature, the problems are context-sensitive and the effectiveness of the interventions is bound by specific socio-political-ecological circumstances. In the process of writing up the research proposal, local people were not engaged, and their everyday livelihoods of people in Rajasthan were not fully understood. It was also not sure if the proposed technologies would meet the actual local needs and social challenges.

Figure 1. Location of Rajasthan in India

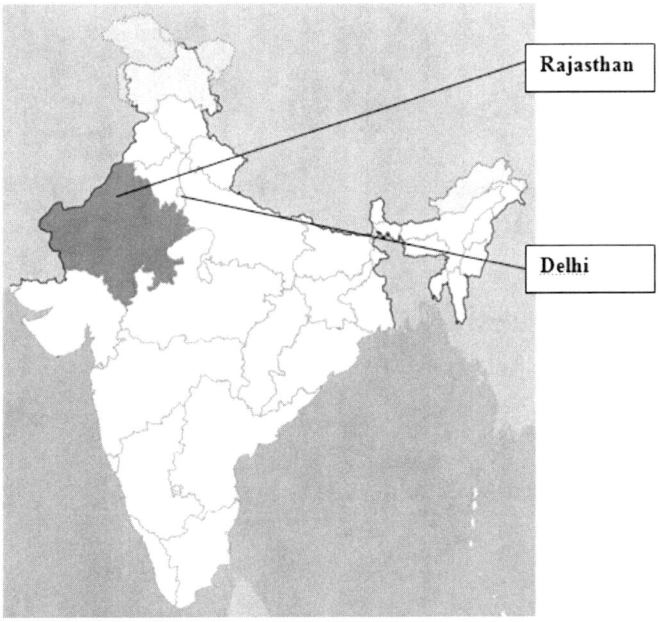

The socio-economic work package leader of the project therefore proposed a deeper understanding of human-nature relationships in the investigated region before any interventions started. Based on this background, an exploratory fieldtrip in Rajasthan was initiated in March 2008. The researchers intended to meet local people and explore the interactions between their livelihoods, physical environments and socio-economic structures of their communities. Special interests were in their agricultural practices and existing technologies, and how they manage water and land resources.

During the fieldtrip, more than 15 academics and NGOs, such as Development Alternatives and Barefoot College, were contacted. Five villages in different parts of East and Central Rajasthan were visited. A case study approach was adopted which helps put the context back into research (Yin, 1994). With the assistance of the Indian research partners, two villages: Manpura and Bamlas, were selected. They both located in North Rajasthan. The former is a very poor village, relying on rain-fed farming whereas the latter is well-connected to the national grid electricity systems and is successful in raising agricultural production by irrigation. Their contrasting socio-economic and physical settings make comparison interesting. The limitations of over-reliance on the Indian research partners' recommendations were recognised because they have had some influence in the villages, such as providing saplings for plantations in Manpura. In addressing this problem, another village, called Kotdi, was introduced by a NGO. It is located in central Rajasthan and has a long history of changing programmes in drinking water supplies. (see Figure 2 for the locations of the three case studies).

A wide range of people in the villages was met, including local leaders, politicians, government officials, poor and rich farmers, and men and women of different castes. The researchers spent some time in the villages and observed people's everyday interactions, social practices and economic activities. They also conducted semi-structured interviews based on four themes: physical environment, economic activities, social arrangements, and technology. In terms of physical environment, the researchers were keen to know

Figure 2. Locations of three villages in Rajasthan

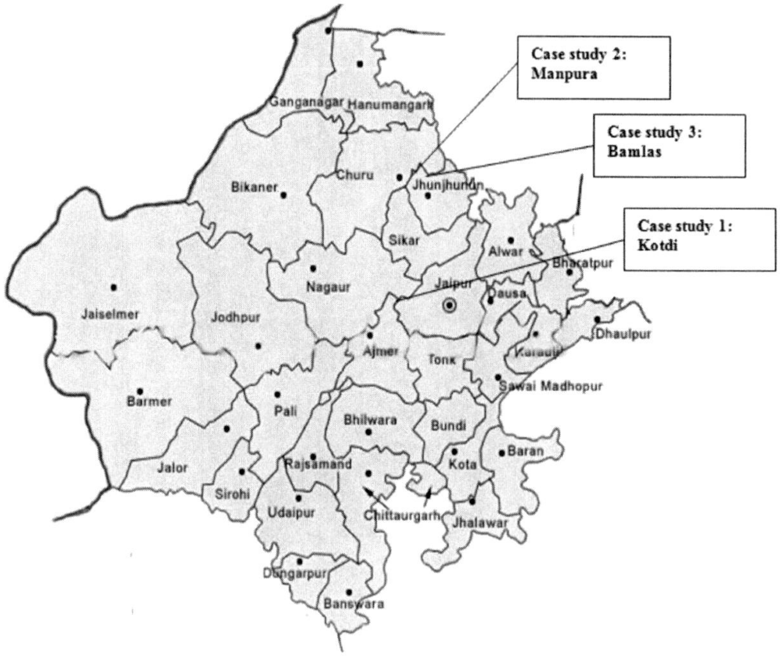

what natural resources were available and how they were managed. In economic activities, the researchers explored what rural industries and agricultural practices existed. In social arrangements, questions as to how governance structures and groups worked in the communities, and how payments for natural resources include some villagers and exclude others, were raised. Concerning technology, the researchers examined what technologies were available, who initiated them, and how costs and benefits were distributed. The research team wrote down the findings in their research diary and critically reflected their assumptions and analysis.

In the following, three case studies will be used to discuss how technology interacts with the 'human-nature' relationships in different aspects.

INDIA'S FIRST 'GREEN' REVERSE OSMOSIS PLANT IN KOTDI

Kotdi is located in central Rajasthan. This village has 300 households and has been practising rain-fed farming. The presence of marble has attracted a few factories to work here. Kotdi constructed India's first 'green' reverse osmosis plant in 2006 which uses solar energy to supplement diesel and converts brackish water to clean drinking water by breaking down the membranes of water molecules (see Photo 1). The water is entirely for human and animal consumption. As the project leader suggested, water produced by the reverse osmosis plant was so expensive and limited that makes irrigation impossible. Before the introduction of the reverse osmosis plant, this village has witnessed a number of changes in drinking water supplies, from using an adjacent lake to pipeline systems. The technical transformations go hand in hand with the changes, not only in water governance structures that manage the water resources, but also in social relations within the community

Figure 3. India's first 'green' reverse osmosis plant in Kotdi

and the perceptions of how the quality of water is associated with social status.

Before 1995, Kotdi relied on an adjacent lake to provide drinking water. Villagers, usually women and their daughters, walked eight kilometres a day to fetch water. The lake, however, gradually dried up owing to successive droughts in the region. The villagers also complained that the water was no longer 'sweet'. Finding an alternative source of water was, therefore, a matter of urgency. In 1995, pipeline systems were introduced and planned to serve all 300 households in the community. Each household would pay 100 rupees a month. The committee paid a local villager monthly 1,500 rupees to look after the systems. The pipeline systems were initially popular, but 90 households from the upper caste decided to quit the project because they preferred constructing individual hand pumps outside their own houses. The withdrawal of these households was a financial blow to the project. Running short of funding, because of the withdrawal, meant that the pipelines could no longer be managed and repaired properly. The gradual break-down of the pipelines caused another 60 households to disconnect from the systems, and most of them came from the lower castes.

A local NGO, called Barefoot College, has been working with the village. It was deeply concerned with the problems of brackish water and the deterioration of the pipeline systems. In 2006, it obtained funding of 2.45 million rupees from the United Nations Development Programme and the Ministry of Non-Conventional Energy to build the reverse osmosis plant. The idea was to use the innovation to reduce pressure on the pipeline systems by providing some drinking water to the existing 150 households who have been connected to the pipeline systems. In order to make the project environmentally sustainable and socially democratic, the funders decided to use solar energy (PV panels), as a supplement to diesel, to generate energy for the reverse osmosis plant which turns brackish underground water to potable water. They also wanted to empower villagers from the lower-castes, especially women, in the governance process. A water committee, composed of six male and four female, was set up. A number of village meetings were called and these elected the committee members. As a result, two male and all four female members came from lower caste background. Each household contributes 10 rupees a month for the reverse osmosis plant, on the top of 100 rupees for the existing pipeline systems. Apart from water brought by the pipelines, each household can collect 20 litres of water daily at the community centre where the reserve osmosis plant is located. The Water Committee leader suggested that the villagers felt that water from the reverse osmosis plant is 'superior, clean and sweet', so they were willing to pay the extra 10 rupees (interview, 25/03/08).

There was initial resistance from the upper castes about the arrangements and the composition of the water committee, but the committee leader told us that, after repeated interactions with lower-caste representatives, the upper caste participants had gradually changed their views and felt less discontent. He argued that: 'breaking the caste system ...... is difficult and challenging because the upper caste used to controlling everything and they do not want to give in or feel threatened' (interview, 25/3/08).

Table 1 summarises the three stages of changing water governance structures. This case study has shown that technology is not merely a physical infrastructure, but it helps re-engineer social relations and power structures. The building of the reverse osmosis plant and the establishment of the water committee is successful in achieving good governance by bringing democracy to the village, advocating women's rights, and challenging the unequal power structures that have been dominated by the upper castes. This case study has indicated that enhancing communication and interactions between the powerful and less powerful, the upper and the lower castes, and men and women, can foster cooperation, but the process is not plain sailing. Strong leadership and favourable social conditions, such as relatively harmonious relationships between the upper and lower castes within the community, help make the changes without creating too much confrontation.

Another water issue in the village is the presence of many marble factories. During the cutting of marble, they use large amounts of water. A strong feeling among villagers is that extraction of water for these industrial uses would negatively

Table 1. Changing water governance structures in Kotdi

Period	Sources of drinking water supplies	Payment	Impact
Before 1995	Adjacent lake, villagers walked 8km to fetch water	Free of charge	The lake was drying up because of reducing rainfall and successive droughts in the region. This has affected the quality of groundwater in the village which has turned water brackish.
1996-2006	Pipeline systems	100 rupees/month	The systems originally served all 300 households, but 90 upper-caste households quit the project because they installed hand-pumps at home. The shortage of funding caused the gradual break-down of the systems. At the end, only 150 households were connected to the pipelines. 60 households from poor and lower caste backgrounds were left out.
2006 – present	Reverse osmosis plant + pipeline systems	110 rupees/month (10R/month for reverse osmosis plant, plus 100R/month for pipeline systems)	The reverse osmosis plant benefits the current 150 households which have already been connected to the pipeline systems. The purpose is to use reverse osmosis plant to reduce the demand on the pipeline systems. A new democratic water governance committee is formed. Among 10 committee members, 2 male and all 4 female came from the lower castes. Initial resistance from upper caste gradually disappeared. No major confrontation emerged.

(source: own research)

affect the availability of water for domestic and agricultural uses in the village, but the villagers also acknowledge that the marble factories provide job opportunities to some villagers, and that helps improve rural economy. A clear priority is needed to resolve the competition over water resources between industry, agriculture and households.

RAIN-WATER HARVESTING IN MANPURA

Manpura is a very poor village which has approximately 400 households and 3,000 populations. There is only one carpenter in the village, and the rest depend on farming for living. Farm size is small, and many households have farmlands of less than a hectare in size. Farmers gather two crops a year: between June and September and between October and March. Poor farmers rely on rain-water for irrigation, and they can only grow less-water demanding crops, such as millet. Less-poor farmers, in contrast, are able to build rain-water harvesting systems or to dig wells, but they are aware that they can only collect 500 litres of water at maximum a day from the well; otherwise the water that comes out has very high salt content. Camels are their only livestock for farming, but 90% of the camels in the village are either sold (because of extreme poverty) or died (because of water scarcity) over the past decade. In terms of energy, more than half of the households are not connected to the grid electricity supplies. They rely on dry wood and kerosene for cooking.

Drinking water is supplied through pipelines. The systems were built by the German government, and the source of the water comes from a canal 200 km away from the village. Similar to Kotdi, the water is not for irrigation. This village, however, is lucky in the sense that it is located in a higher topography, and water is first pumped to their village and then distributed to other villages. But the frequent break-down of the pumping stations has worsen the relationships between Manpura and its neighbouring villages because they accuse Manpura of being selfish for keeping all water for its own use and refusing to share with others.

Apart from the pipeline systems, another government intervention in Manpura is the construction of a 15m long and 15m wide rain-water harvesting system in the early 1970s in order to address persistent droughts (see Photo 2). Villagers told us that when the rain-water harvesting system was built, it was surrounded by forests, and rain-water was collected by gravity. Chronic poverty caused by droughts and crop failure had, however, forced villagers to cut down trees in the forests in order to collect firewood for survival. Villagers also dug up mud to build houses. As a consequence, the forests disappeared, and soil erosion has subsequently led to land degradation. Monsoon rain in summer has stopped running into the rain-water harvesting system because the channels leading rain-water to the harvesting system were all blocked up. The expensive rain-water harvesting project became a white elephant which was finally abandoned.

In 2002-3, the government introduced an individual rain-water harvesting scheme, and assisted individual farmers to build a 3m wide and 5m deep system. In order to attract poor farmers, the government offered subsidies up to 30,000 rupees. This scheme, however, was not popular for two reasons: firstly, each household still need to contribute 20,000 rupees for the construction, but neither can poor farmers afford it, nor think the systems would make any difference to them. Secondly, the government adopted a one-size-fits-all approach and did not allow farmers to choose the types of construction materials or the size of the rain-water harvesting systems. This standardised approach has reduced the flexibility in meeting the needs and circumstances of different farmers in the village.

This case study has demonstrated the importance of villagers' livelihoods in shaping the

Figure 4. The abandoned rain-water harvesting system in Manpura

success of technological innovations. Poverty in Manpura, causing deforestation and land degradation, has had a negative impact on the effectiveness of the old, collective rain-water harvesting systems and the new, individual systems. It is therefore crucial to understand people's changing livelihood priorities in order to devise appropriate technological interventions. It is understood that it is not easy to anticipate people's changing circumstances, but according to Stringer and Reed (2007), using participatory approaches and scenario exercises may help lay people and experts to produce visions for the future, and that can reduce the gaps between current needs and future changes.

IRRIGATED AND INTENSIVE FARMING IN BAMLAS

Compared to Manpura, Bamlas is less-poor and has higher population (2,000 households and 10,000 population). According to local people, Bamlas is high in farm productivity because of good quality water, high soil fertility and hard-working farmers. Another important reason is that nearly all households have been successfully connected to the national electricity grid systems since 1975. Thanks to the electricity supplies and the absence of brackish water problems, large-scale irrigation has been implemented and intensive farming practised (see Photo 3). While farmlands are rain-fed during the monsoon seasons in summer, irrigated water is crucial to the second cropping in winter. Relatively high-water demanding crops, such as wheat and vegetables, are grown. In order to maintain high productivity, farmers use a lot of chemical fertilisers which requires a lot of water to dissolve them. Farmers have also gone deeper and deeper into the ground and built more and more bore-wells in order to obtain sufficient water for irrigation. Compounded with the rising population, the increasing demand for electricity has destabilised the grid systems. As a result, measures, such as rationing the daily supply of electricity to the village, were introduced. Four to five hours electricity are provided a day. This has, undoubtedly, constrained the use of irrigation

Figure 5. Irrigation systems in Bamlas

and has had a negative impact on farm productivity. This case study has shown that technological interventions are inextricably linked to energy and water policies, and they can create unanticipated outcomes which may hinder the economic growth and ecological sustainability of the communities in the long run. The dilemma is that the farmers' goals to continue high-yield agriculture by heavy irrigation may not be a desirable option because the fear that the continuous pumping out of water would lower the water table to an unsustainable level, and that would affect the availability of water to its neighbouring villages.

In contrast to Manpura, Bamlas has high political influence. Local leaders collaborated with adjacent village leaders and formed a Farmers' Committee. It has successfully lobbied the government to provide an extra two hours of electricity supplies a day during the school examinations, so that their children have more time to do the revision. They have also obtained the government's subsidies of 15,000 rupees to install the 'fountain' irrigation systems. These systems help conserve water by controlling the exposure of irrigated water under high evaporation conditions. Despite the subsidies, each household is required to contribute 20,000 rupees to buy the equipment. Poor farmers are excluded from the scheme. This risks deepening the inequalities between the less-poor and the poor, the households with **irrigation** and without, and people from the upper and lower castes.

DISCUSSION

These three case studies have shown intricate and diverse roles of technology in human-nature relationships. A number of lessons can be drawn from this study: firstly, technological interventions are specific and sensitive to local contexts and circumstances. The proximity to water supplies and the availability of underground water affect how water is supplied and whether irrigation is possible. The poor quality of the brackish water in Manpura, for instance, has forced villagers to practise rain-fed farming. The low farming productivity has then perpetuated poverty in Manpura which makes it less able to use technologies to modify the unfavourable physical conditions. In contrast, the availability of water and the presence of marble facilitate mining industry in Kotdi, and job opportunities are created. The competition between industry, agriculture and households over the use of water demands a careful planning about how scarce resources should be managed and allocated.

Social structures and power dynamics are different in villages. They mediate if, and what, technological interventions are welcomed. They also affect what governance structures are suitable to manage technologies, water and land. The setting up of the democratic water committee to include the lower caste members in Kotdi can be seen as an exception, rather than a norm. The relatively harmonious relationships between the upper and the lower castes, and between men and women, have made the re-engineering of social relations less confrontational.

Secondly, the case studies have demonstrated the 'energy-water' paradoxes. The availability of underground water and the electricity supplies in Balmas have facilitated intensive irrigation, but the opening up of more and deeper bore-wells and the higher intensity of farming require continual energy support. The intermittent electricity supplies may help the recovery of the water table level to a sustainable level, but it has become politically unpopular. The solar energy-generated reverse osmosis plant in Kotdi may offer a 'green' solution, but its high initial costs and low production of clean water do not provide a long-term answer to high energy-demanding villages, like Bamlas.

Thirdly, technological interventions can help improve the quantity and quality of water, but whether water being produced and processed is socially acceptable lies in human subjectivity and perception. In Kotdi, villagers are willing to pay extra 10 rupees to obtain water from the reverse osmosis plant because they consider the water as 'superior, clean and sweet'. The embeddedness of social status in the quality of water affects whether water users are willing to switch from one source of water to another. This finding is compatible with Cleaver's water study in Tanzania (2002).

Fourthly, payment for water and water-related facilities is common in the case studies. The range of monetary contributions is wide, from 10 rupees to obtain 20 litres of water by reverse osmosis plant in Kotdi to 20,000 rupees to construct the individual rain-water harvesting systems in Manpura. The user-pay principles have already been widely welcomed in the mainstream economic approach to development. The World Bank, for example, suggests that the principles can foster a sense of ownership and reduce wastage by re-defining water as an economic good (World Bank, 2004). This research is, however, concerned that payment can deepen social inequalities between the rich and the poor by pushing the non-affordable to find alternative water sources which are unhygienic. The serious health implications will further perpetuate poverty and vulnerability. Mehta (2005) argues that if water is a human right, even a voluntary payment or contribution is against this basic principle.

CONCLUSION AND POLICY IMPLICATIONS

This chapter has attempted to re-conceptualise the relationships between technology and development. It has focused on water- and energy-related technologies and explored how water, energy, people, politics and the nature are intertwined. Thefirst case study of Kotdi has demonstrated that the reverse osmosis system is more than a sustainable innovation. It has helped re-engineer social relations and power structures of the community. Setting up the water committee has democraticised the governance of water management by giving power back to women and other lower caste social groups.

The second case study of Manpura has shown that the success of technological interventions lies in our understanding of people's changing livelihoods. The large rain-water harvesting system might be regarded as a solution to poverty since it stored water for irrigation or animal drinking, but it has become a 'victim' of poverty. People cutting down trees and digging up mud for survival has resulted in serious land degradation, and the rain-water harvesting system was left idle. The local government has started a re-forestation programme in the village, and the presence of forest department officers help monitor the re-growth of the forests. One officer, however, warned in interviews that, if chronic poverty persists and when the re-forestation scheme is finished and officers gone by 2013, the forests will return to a piece of barren land (interview, 26/03/08). The third case study in Bamlas has suggested that technological interventions are inextricably linked to energy and water policies, and they can create unanticipated outcomes which may hinder the economic growth and ecological sustainability of the communities in the long run.

This study has indicated that technologies are not necessarily 'pro-poor'. The uneven distribution of costs and benefits of the technological interventions can make the marginalised groups worse off. The impact of technology is so context- and culture-specific that it requires a more flexible approach in the design of the interventions. Institutional building and capacity building are also time-consuming processes, and they need continual support in terms of resources and time.

These observations are useful to develop a 'people-centred' framework for a better understanding of the complex relationships between technology and sustainable economic development. This framework suggests that any sustainable technological interventions need to link the macro water- and energy-related policies and technologies and the micro process, such as users' perception of water quality. It calls for a different approach to conceptualising human motivations (Jackson, 2005). Before any interventions take place, this is important to acquire a deeper understanding of local power and gender dynamics (Chaurey et al. 2004). The 'technology-development' nexus is proved to be complex, but this chapter has shown that making sustainable socio-economic development by considerate technological interventions can achieve equitable outcomes. One of the limitations of this study is that it takes a micro perspective to examine the interactions between the innovations, social norms and governance structures within rural communities. It is equally important to examine how the micro contexts shape, and are shaped by, the meso and regional level of water and energy policies. In addition, the findings of this paper were largely drawn on rural contexts. It is interesting to understand whether, and how, the 'technology-development' nexus can be applicable to urban contexts.

ACKNOWLEDGMENT

Thanks to EPSRC for supporting this study (Grant number: EP/E044360/1). Also thanks to our UK and Indian research partners, NGOs and community members for their comments.

REFERENCES

Adger, W. N., Brown, K., Fairbrass, J., Jordan, A., Paavola, J., Rosendo, S., & Seyfang, G. (2003). Governance for sustainability: towards a 'thick' analysis of environmental decision making. *Environment & Planning A, 35*, 1095–1110. doi:10.1068/a35289

Birkenholtz, T. (2008). Contesting expertise: the politics of environmental knowledge in northern Indian groundwater practices. *Geoforum, 39*, 466–482. doi:10.1016/j.geoforum.2007.09.008

Chataway, J., & Smith, J. (2007). Participation, communication and innovation: thinking about the international AIDS vaccine initiative. *IDS Bulletin, 38*(5), 74–82. doi:10.1111/j.1759-5436.2005.tb00410.x

Chaurey, A., Ranganathan, M., & Mohanty, P. (2004). Electricity access for geographically disadvantaged rural communities – technology and policy insights. *Energy Policy*, *32*, 1693–1705. doi:10.1016/S0301-4215(03)00160-5

Cleaver, F. (2002). Reinventing institutions: bricolage and the social embeddedness of natural resource management. *European Journal of Development Research*, *14*, 11–30. doi:10.1080/714000425

Cleaver, F., & Frank, T. (2005). *Water Governance and Poverty: What Works for the Poor?* Bradford Centre for International Development, University of Bradford.

de Janvry, A., & Sadoulet, E. (2002). World poverty and the role of agricultural technology: direct and indirect effects. *The Journal of Development Studies*, *38*(4), 1–26. doi:10.1080/00220380412331322401

Denton, F. (2002). Climate change vulnerability, impacts, and adaptation: why does gender matter? *Gender and Development*, *10*(2), 10–20. doi:10.1080/13552070215903

Dikito-Wachtmeister, M. (2000). *Women's participation in decision-making processes in rural water projects, Makoni district, Zimbabwe*. Unpublished doctoral dissertation, University of Bradford, UK.

Feenberg, A. (1999). *Questioning technology*. London: Routledge

Jackson, T. (2005). *Motivating sustainable behaviour: a review of evidence on consumer behaviour and behavioural change*. University of Surrey, Centre for Environmental Strategy.

Mehta, L. (2005). *The politics and poetics of water: naturalising scarcity in Western India*. New Delhi, India: Orient Longman.

Pauli, G. (1999). *Towards a technology strategy for sustainable livelihoods*. UNDP programme.

Richards, P. (2005). Plant biotechnology and the rights of the poor: a technographic approach. In M. Leach, I. Scoones, & B. Wynne (Eds.), *Science and Citizens* (pp. 199-214). London: Zed Books.

Robins, S. (2005). AIDS, science and citizenship after apartheid. In M. Leach, I. Scoones, & B. Wynne (Eds.), *Science and citizens* (pp. 113-129). London: Zed Book.

Roy, M., & Venema, H. (2002). Reducing risk and vulnerability to climate change in India: the capabilities approach. *Gender and Development*, *10*(2), 78–83. doi:10.1080/13552070215904

Schumacher, E. F. (1974). *Small is beautiful: a study of economics as if people mattered*. London: Abacus.

Shankarnarayan, K. A., Harsh, L. N., & Kathju, S. (1987). Agroforestry in the arid zones of India. *Agroforestry Systems*, *5*, 66–88. doi:10.1007/BF00046414

Stringer, L., & Reed, M. (2007). Land degradation assessment in Southern Africa: integrating local and scientific knowledge bases. *Land Degradation and Development*, *18*, 99–116. doi:10.1002/ldr.760

UNEP (United Nations Environment Programme). (2008). *Global green new deal – environmentally-focused investment historic opportunity for 21st century prosperity and job generation*.

Wong, S. (2009). Climate change and sustainable technology: re-linking nature, governance and gender. *Gender and Development*, *17*(1), 95–108. doi:10.1080/13552070802696953

Wong, S., & Sharp, L. (2009). Making power explicit in sustainable water innovation: re-thinking subjectivity, institution and structure through environmental citizenship. *Environmental Politics*, *18*(1), 37–57. doi:10.1080/09644010802624785

World Bank. (2004). *Water resources sector strategy. Strategic directions for World Bank engagement*. Washington, DC: World Bank.

Yin, R. (1994). *Case study research: design and methods*. London: Sage.

ADDITIONAL READING

Archer, M. (2000). *Being human: the problem of agency.* Cambridge, UK: Cambridge University Press.

Barnett, J., Doherty, B., Burningham, K., Carr, A., Johnstone, G., & Rootes, C. (2006). *Environmental citizenship: literature review*. UK: Environment Agency.

Bell, D. (2005). Liberal environmental citizenship. *Environmental Politics*, *14*(2), 179–194. doi:10.1080/09644010500054863

Brown, R., & Clarke, J. (2007). *Transition to water sensitive urban design: the story of Melbourne, Australia*. School of Geography and Environmental Science: Monash University, Melbourne.

Carolan, M. (2006). Ecological representation in deliberation: the contribution of tactile spaces. *Environmental Politics*, *15*(3), 345–361. doi:10.1080/09644010600627535

Carter, N., & Huby, M. (2005). Ecological citizenship and ethical investment. *Environmental Politics*, *14*(2), 255–272. doi:10.1080/09644010500055159

Dobson, A. (2003). *Citizenship and the environment.* Oxford, UK: OUP.

Douglas, M. (1987). *How institutions think*. London: Routledge.

Ellis, C., & Flaherty, M. (Eds.). (1992). *Investigating subjectivity: research on lived experience.* London: Sage.

Geels, W., Elzen, B., & Green, K. (Eds.). (2004). *System innovation and the transition to sustainability: theory, evidence and policy.* Cheltenham, UK: Edward Elgar Publishing.

Guy, S., Marvin, S., & Moss, T. (2001). *Infrastructure in transition: urban networks, buildings, plans*. London: Earthscan.

Hayward, T. (2006). Ecological citizenship: a rejoinder. *Environmental Politics*, *15*(3), 452–453. doi:10.1080/09644010600627782

Isin, F. (2002). *Being political: genealogies of citizenship.* Minneapolis, MN: Minnesota University Press.

Jackson, T. (2005). *Motivating sustainable consumption. A review of evidence on consumer behaviour and behavioural change.* Centre for environmental strategy, University of Surrey.

MacGregor, S. (2005). No sustainability without justice; a feminist critique of environmental citizenship. In A. Dobson & D. Bell (Eds.), *Environmental Citizenship* (pp. 101-126). Cambridge, MA: MIT Press.

Maniates, M. (2002). In search of consumptive resistance: the voluntary simplicity movement. In T. Princen, M. Maniates, & K. Conca (Eds.), *Confronting Consumption* (pp. 199-236), Cambridge, MA: MIT Press.

Murphy, J. (Ed.). (2006). *Governing technology for sustainability.* London: Earthscan.

Schlosberg, D. (2004). Reconceiving environmental justice: global movements and political theories. *Environmental Politics*, *13*(3), 517–540. doi:10.1080/0964401042000229025

Schweitzer, L., & Stephenson, M. (2007). Right answers, wrong questions: environmental justice as urban research. *Urban Studies (Edinburgh, Scotland)*, *44*(2), 319–337. doi:10.1080/00420980601074961

Seyfang, G. (2005). Shopping for sustainability: can sustainable consumption promote ecological citizenship. *Environmental Politics*, *14*(2), 290–231. doi:10.1080/09644010500055209

Sharp, L. (2006). Water demand management in the UK: constructions of the domestic water user. *Journal of Environmental Management and Planning*, *49*(6), 51–59.

Shove, E. (2003). *Comfort, cleanliness and convenience*. London: Routledge.

Smith, G. (2005). Green citizenship and the social economy . *Environmental Politics*, *14*(2), 273–289. doi:10.1080/09644010500055175

Valencia, A. (2005). Globalisation, cosmopolitanism and ecological citizenship. *Environmental Politics*, *14*(2), 163–178. doi:10.1080/09644010500054848

Section 3
Savings and Investments

Chapter 6
The Influences of Savings and Investments on Sustainable Development and the Role of Information Technology

Leonardo Baggiani
Independent Researcher, Italy

ABSTRACT

This chapter investigates how the combination of savings and investments affects economic development and sustainability. This discussion aims to help to understand the role of savings as a support to growth, and how biasing individual decisions on consumption and debt via monetary policies can be a source of economic growth un-sustainability. Information technology helps to optimise the use of resources, but it even makes dangerous policies easier to implement. Section 1 shows theoretical insights into the contribution of savings to growth, and the concept of sustainability; section 2 focuses on the theories that better deal with the sustainability concern and investigates the role of information technology in monetary policy; section 3 shows the growing, positive contribution of e-money to growth and sustainability, and it suggests a new role for the government as advisor within an information-enhanced economy where information technology can play a prominent role; section 4 concludes.

INTRODUCTION

This chapter wants to expose the main threads of economic theory analysing the role of savings and investments within the perspective of economic development (which I refer to in terms of GDP growth) and sustainability (which I refer to in terms of GDP variability, including "crisis" phenomena). Information Technology can affect the way savings and investments interact, hence contribute to determine the economic outcome in terms of sustainable development in a way other than the commonly discussed industrial dynamics.

Classical and *Keynesian-like* analyses differ by the value recognised to savings: the former acknowledge the role of savings as funds available to investments, the basis for the future economic development, while the latter stress that savings can work as a brake to economic growth by means of the idle productive capacity. But both threads miss

DOI: 10.4018/978-1-61520-709-1.ch006

the time-frame of production, which lets them lose insight into phenomena such as economic cycles; Austrian economic theories can give a wider perspective on economic cycles, offering a causal link between economic phases. Any different theoretical framework involves a different key to interpret the role of Information Technology. A careful look into the basics of Austrian theories reveals the up-to-datedness of "pure credit" models, which show what part of growth un-sustainability can stem from monetary policy. As Information Technology has made money circulation much faster, it has made monetary policy an even more effective source of cycles.

The chapter aims to introduce the main views on economic growth, to show that economic development and sustainability are problems deeply interconnected, and can be effectively explored thanks to business cycle theories; according to this opinion, savings are much more important than what mainstream economists claim with their imperative attention to consumption, and Information Technology is a very important tool for the underlying mechanisms to be more fluid and effective. These considerations can be used to revise the institutional design of monetary and fiscal interventionism.

BACKGROUND

How savings and investments combine, and what the outcome in terms of economic development and sustainability is, is a topic faced throughout the whole history of economics. Any school, from A. Smith (1776) *Laissez-faire* to C. Marx (1887) *Communism*, through M. Friedman (1968)*Monetarism*, F.A. Von Hayek (1933) *Business Cycle theory*, and J.M. Keynes (1936)*General Theory*, as well as their recent heirs, have either explicitly or implicitly exposed their own ideas and suggested their own policies for the economy to grow in a sustainable way. To simplify the exposition of the chapter, I have chosen to divide the economic knowledge and schooling into two main classes, which I call "*classical*" and "*Keynesian-like*" perspectives, on the basis of the different approaches to "*idle productive capacity*" and "*economic cycles*", concepts that I will explore in the chapter.

The present chapter moves from the basic idea that economic development depends mainly on investments. This causal link is mostly accepted in literature; for instance P. Romer (1994) analysis on the determinants of economic growth has the stock of capital (the sum of previous investments) as an important variable. Another important variable is the "human capital", which can be considered as investments in worker skills. For an economy to grow, it must hold enough instruments to work, and enter them into the productive process for the final goods to get completed.

Beside all the problems involved in the right choice of the investment to do, it is taken for granted that even the mere level of aggregate investment (like in Romer's models) affects how the economy develops; economic development may be considered both *qualitatively*, when the range or quality of "goods" (from here on, I will say "goods" for both goods and services, anything that can be produced or arranged to be exchanged for money) is under scrutiny, and *quantitatively*, when the focus lies on the increasing of economic activity. The latter point of view implies economic development to be intended as "*growth*", so it can be measured via an index such as the (real) Gross Domestic Product (GDP). For the discussion to be led with due simplicity by the use of some macroeconomic aggregates, this chapter will focus on economic development as economic growth.

Investments are therefore necessary for the economy to grow; investments and savings interact to creating a delicate environment, whose weakness shall reflect onto economic growth as *un-sustainability* problems. Here lies the core of the chapter.

Investments and Savings: a Classical Perspective

The framework I consider the most adherent to our reality stems from the basics of *classical* and, to some extent, Wicksell (1965) thought. According to this point of view (see Bordo and Schwartz (2004) as an assessment of its historical relevance, then Nelson & Schwartz (2007) to recognise *Monetarism* as its up-to-date version), savers and investors create a market where they exchange the present availability of funds (to be returned back at a fixed term) for a price, the interest rate . Given these operators to be rational, they must not be affected by money illusion, so they can evaluate the real return of their exchanges; hence, the price they pay attention to is the *real interest rate* (nominal interest rate net of price inflation). Like in any market, prices vary toward equilibrium because of demand and supply forces, the real interest rate shall move this capital (availability) market toward its own equilibrium. We must subsume savers' supply of capitals resulting from a wide range of variables, considerations, and decisional features (e.g. income expectations, decisions persistence and inertia, imitative and "catching up with the Joneses" behaviours, general perspectives), where a great role is played by *inter-temporal consumption preferences* which work as a measure of the cost savers face when postponing their own availability of funds (i.e. their ability to spend). The latter variable tells why savers must pay heed to real interest rates (the real/nominal interest rate distinction is a relevant theme of *classical* legacy, like Woodford (2007) exposes): savers weigh the cost of postponing consumption (a real variable) versus its reward (an interest rate), they must therefore turn both variables into a common measure; as consumption can be described by "goods", interest rates must get "turned" into "goods" too, and this can be done via the real interest rate, the "goods content" of interest rates. As we can consider that the marginal utility of consumption is decreasing, the bigger the amount of funds asked, the higher the real interest rate the savers pretend (see curve S in graph.1, where S is savings and r the real interest rate).

We must also subsume that investors demand for capital results from their will to maximise profits; capitals are needed to buy goods, materials and machinery; the latter factors generate the production process, thence the final goods to be sold and investors' profits, while interests on capital are (at least part of) the cost of production. Production cannot proportionally increase, ceteris paribus, with higher availability of capitals (complementarity constraints, a hint offered by Menger (1871), such as workers availability and organizational problems explain at least part of this decreasing marginal utility of capital), that leads to lower marginal productivity and profitability of capital to reaching the cost of capital as a profitability floor. In analogy to what said before, if we compare production (a real variable) to interest rates, we must consider the real cost of capital i.e. the real interest rate. This makes up a limit to capital investing, which widens (shrinks) with a lower (higher) cost of capital. The lower the real interest rates, the higher the investments (see curve I in graph.1, where I is investments).

The above (brief) analysis of fund supply and demand sums up to the market shown in graph.1, where I and S are linear for simplicity; wherever r may initially be, the usual market process will lead it to its equilibrium level r^* which involves investments and savings equilibrium levels I^* and S^*. Given I^* being stable, the economy can autonomously find its "natural" growth rate; in this sense the economy can permanently exploit its *full potential.*

As investments are the basis of future economic growth, it is up to the market to determine this growth rate. Any attempt to force the interest rate downwards then leads to disequilibrium in the markets of funds, hence price inflation anywhere

Figure 1.

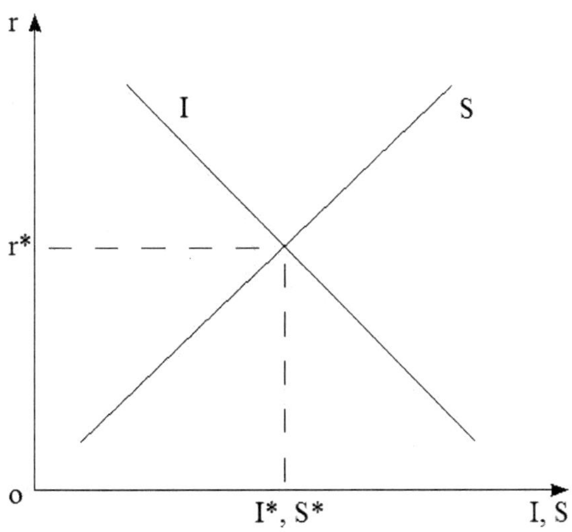

else. Therefore a perfectly competitive market for funds allows the economy to maintain its proper growth pace.

We can get the same result by considering that production (*Y*) goes to satisfy consumption (*C*), investments (*I*), government spending (*G*), and exports (*X*), that is to say

$$Y=C+I+G+X \quad (1)$$

At the same time, income (*Y*), what production constitutes, gets spent into consumption, imports (*H*), taxation (*T*), or gets saved (*S*), that is to say

$$Y=C+S+T+H \quad (2)$$

Combining equations (1) and (2) gains

$$(S-I)+(T-G)=(X-H) \quad (3)$$

Then, net *private savings* (*S-I*) and net *public savings* (public budget surplus *T-G*) is the *Trade Balance* (*X-H*). In a simplified economy with neither government nor external sectors, equation (3) collapses to the equilibrium shown in graph.1 i.e.

$$S=I \quad (4)$$

All this leads to the conclusion that growth, being based on investments, is basically grounded in the economy's saving ability, be it private or public.

State interventions to modify the Trade Balance can affect the investments-savings equilibrium too, which involves consequences onto growth. Referring to equation (3), it is clear that "forcing" Trade Balance to grow (e.g. by fixing a devalued foreign exchange rate, or creating foreign-trade barriers) involves higher net aggregate savings. Unless we believe (I do not) we can exploit some spare productive capacity left "hidden" by mean entrepreneurs as exposed below, if the government cannot squeeze its spending (that would make more goods available) or increases its taxation revenues (that lowers private spending thus making more goods available to foreigners), what we can expect is only higher net private savings (*S-I*). Higher net private savings stem from either higher savings (same effect as higher taxation) or lower investments; and as we cannot say which consequence shall prevail, we must expect sort of a mix of the two, and this means that part of the investments must be dismissed, curtailing part of future economic growth.

A Critic: An Interventionist Perspective

The former conclusion has been getting fought by Keynes and all the economists who still share one fundamental point, which production can permanently run below its potential because of some *spare capacity* due to a lack of either animal spirits in entrepreneurs or aggregate demand (i.e. an excess of savings). The ability of this thread to persist within the economic debate is stated in Forstater & Randall (2007), and its most recent version is *New-Keynesianism* like in Galì (2000). Their recipe to boost growth is straightforward: Government spending and private savings curbing.

Monetary policy can help to reach this aim via lower interest rates, which stimulate investments and discourage savings (as described above). This manoeuvre involves an increase in aggregate demand, which offers an opportunity for entrepreneurs to increase production and subsequent profits; entrepreneurs will in turn boost production thus accelerating economic growth. As this is, at its core, a *short-term perspective* on growth, it cannot properly take into account any relevant discussion on stability but the ability of the government to accumulate debt (which tax-payers will pay in the future, when the economy needs a brake before inflation reaches too high).

It is important, for this chapter's purposes, to highlight the recessive role of savings in this class of theories: savings are resources kept off the market, resources not spent, and hence missing stimuli to growth; right the opposite to the *classical* opinion. For these "disequilibrium" theories there is no need to match savings and investments, as there is already much capital kept "hidden" by entrepreneurs, which a proper policy can surface.

The comprehension of existence or nature of this spare productivity would tell which "school" is the most consistent to reality. By the way, I refer to Hayek (1931) who suggests that this "steady capital" is but the result of wrong expansionary monetary policies, which led entrepreneurs to sort of over-investing or *un-sustainably* investing (this was called "*malinvestment*" by L. von Mises (1934), whose studies lie at the roots of the Austrian *Business Cycle* theories); by this perspective, this capital cannot rapidly get reallocated to meet a "stimulated" aggregate demand (see Monsurrò (2007) for an interpretation of malinvestment as the Keynesian "idle productive capacity"). That erases any real possibility to accelerate growth artificially, unless we are willing to pay in terms of ever-increasing price inflation.

Briefly Defining Sustainability

Before exposing the main thrust of this chapter, I better clarify the concept of "*sustainability*" this chapter discusses. The financial turmoil, which has been shaking economies since mid-2007, has reminded us that growth can be easily hurdled by exploding financial bubbles, rampant inflation, distrust in banks, debt insolvencies, to even recessionary episodes. Economic development usually tracks *peaks* and *troughs* (see graph.2), and seems to unwind along an *upwards trend*, while oscillating there-around (see graph.3), i.e. drawing *cyclic movements*. This seems to tell us that certain growth rates are not sustainable, or that economic policies sometimes fail to sustain growth. No wonder then that, right in periods when economic growth slows, politicians keep on invoking a role for both fiscal and monetary policies, to be led by either local or super-national authorities, to "sustain" the economy; they implicitly tell that at a certain point the economy loses momentum, its previously reached pace cannot be kept, and this weak stance "needs" a help to revert.

The result is a growth path made of peaks and troughs, as graph.2 and graph.3 show. The fact that the overall trend goes upwards probably means that we could do something for the economic path to be *smoother* while maintaining its upward trend, avoiding both positive and negative *excesses*.

If we accept, and somehow explain, the idea that the upward deviations from the main trend (economic upturns) are themselves the cause for the subsequent "crises" (economic downturns), we can grasp the proper meaning of economic sustainability.

The development (growth) sustainability concept I focus on is therefore close to growth variability, whereas it deals with the ups and downs of economic activity and the related opportunity of smoothing the cycle, but it implies also a causal link between these cyclic phases, or even a common cause for the two. The latter interpretation is discussed below.

Figure 2. World GDP – annual percent change. Source: (adapted from IMF public database)

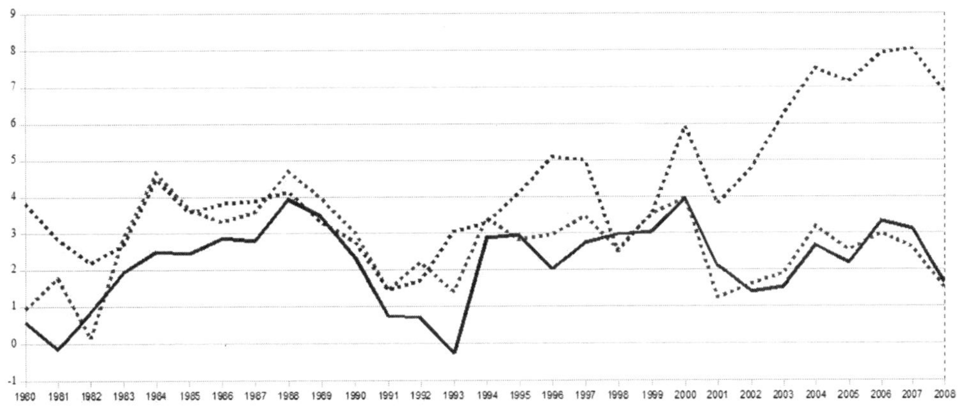

GROWTH SUSTAINABILITY AND E-MONEY GOVERNMENT

Now, I go deeper into the basics of the class of theories I consider the most suitable to explain the relations between savings, investments growth, and sustainability: *Austrian economics*. This will give the necessary theoretical framework for the sequent discussion about how *Information Technology* (IT) has entered the stability discussion, electronic money (e-*money*), and what healthy role the *government* can play in dealing with economic development; a little resume about how to fix sustainability problems follows.

The Sustainability Problem: The Austrian View

Instead of blaming "animal spirits" or mean capitalists who hide their money, I prefer to focus on institutional arrangements in economic governance, especially the *ability to create money* in a wide sense.

In a *classical* analysis, it is clear that forcing interest rates below their equilibrium level involves a general lack of funds, which would impede to sustain the current (higher) level of investments. Should this imbalance persist, the need of funds would require higher interest rates, destroying part of the new investments started in the meanwhile; but this point has not been explored by *classical* economists, as they subsumed a "free" capital market, whose forces would immediately bring interest rates back to equilibrium.

Wicksell gave an important hint on the subject. He theorised a "*pure credit*" economy, where transactions are paid only with the promise of a future exchange of credit for goods, and banks are the operators who can "create" credit. Wicksell showed how, in such an economy, credit (as a payment medium, it must be considered "*money*") can reach any amount, is inversely dependent on bank interest rates (productivity and technology levels are given, and no real increase in production is supposed to occur in the meanwhile), and guides price inflation. In this model we find banks (who create "money"), entrepreneurs (who create production), merchants (who store goods, thus represent savers), and workers (who are employed by entrepreneurs and represent the consumers). Entrepreneurs borrow an amount *K* of money from banks and wage workers before the completion of production; workers in turn spend their wages buying existing goods from the merchants (who bought them at the end of the previous period); merchants then deposit the revenues in the banks,

Figure 3. World GDP trend – annual percent change. Source: (adapted from IMF public database); thin line: trend

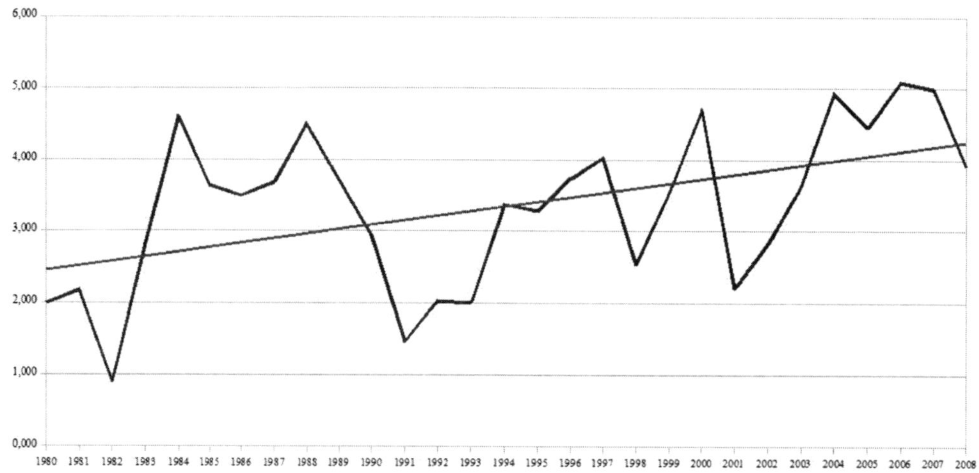

who therefore can create as much money as initially requested, because all created money at last returns to banks themselves. When production is completed, entrepreneurs sell goods to merchants, who pay the amount K plus a margin ρ i.e. $K(1+\rho)$; entrepreneurs use these proceeds to pay back the bank with the sum K plus the interest i i.e. $K(1+i)$, while merchants receive their initial deposit K and the same interest i i.e. $K(1+i)$ from the banks. In this model ρ is the natural rate of interest (NRI), the return of production, and i the market rate of interest (MRI).

If $i=\rho$ the system is price-stationary: entrepreneurs receive $K(1+i)$ from merchants, and pay $K(1+i)$ to banks, who give back $K(1+i)$ to merchants; workers spend the same amount K to buy the same amount of goods, then both prices and real consumption stay idle.

If $i<\rho$ the system is *inflationary*. Entrepreneurs receive $K(1+\rho)$ from merchants, and pay $K(1+i)$ to banks, with a net surplus gain of $K(\rho-i)$; banks return $K(1+i)$ to merchants, who thus are short of $K(\rho-i)$ to rebuild their stock. As entrepreneurs spend their surplus gain to buy goods, merchants will collect the missing $K(\rho-i)$ to complete the payment they due. At this moment the amount $K(1+\rho-i)>K$ gets spent to buy the same amount of goods as before, therefore prices must rise (in this case at the ρ-i rate). In the following period, given the gain entrepreneurs can obtain, we must expect them to hoard workers, which pushes wages up; entrepreneurs can pay workers up to $K(1+\rho-i)$, borrowing this sum from banks, whom they must pay back with $K(1+\rho-i)(1+i)\approx K(1+\rho)$ at the period's end; as entrepreneurs sell their goods to merchant for the sum of $K(1+\rho-i)(1+\rho)\approx K(1+2\rho-i)$, they gather the same $K(\rho-i)$ surplus gain as in the previous period. Now workers can spend $K(1+\rho-i)$, a sum that merchants deposit in banks, who returns them with $K(1+\rho-i)(1+i)\approx K(1+\rho)$ at the period's end; to rebuild their stock, merchants are then still short of $K(1+2\rho-i)-K(1+\rho)=K(\rho-i)$, but as entrepreneurs spend their persistent $K(\rho-i)$ surplus gain to buy goods, merchants can again collect all the money needed to rebuild their stock. The sum $K(1+\rho-i)+K(\rho-i)=K[1+2(\rho-i)]$ is at this moment spent to buy goods with no real increase in production, so prices must rise again (i.e. price inflation persists).

This old model offers a lesson in how to use inflation as a symptom of the liquidity glut caused by interest rates lower than production returns (when MRI<NRI). This lesson is consistent to what the world has been experiencing since mid-2007, when interest rates have been forced down to very low levels, especially in the USA, for a relevantly long period. This model is therefore a first example of economic equilibrium weakened by discretionary economic policies, a first form of *un-sustainability* analysis, while un-hampering the market (i.e. letting interest rates be set to maximise banks profits) would endogenously fix the problem.

The most comprehensive hint on *sustainability* comes from the Nobel Prize Hayek, whose work directly descends from Mises (1931) studies. Conscious of the Wicksell lesson, both Mises and Hayek stressed that lowering interest rates involves a liquidity glut and even (thanks to the insights of Menger and E. von Böhm-Bawerk (1891), who first highlighted the fallacies of a-temporal production functions commonly used by *classical* economists) a lengthening of the production process; this creates a *mismatch* between an increased aggregate demand (see workers wages in Wicksell's model) and production structure, whereas production shall return final goods with an increasing delay. Price inflation is the first symptom of this mismatch (like in Wicksell). Moreover, consumers can force themselves to "save" because the supply does not meet aggregate demand growth; but this cannot last for long, and when consumers cede under the pressure of mounting prices and low interest rates (which disfavour savings), capitals demand shall move to the "short" side of production (the closer to consumers' demand), leaving "longer" investments without funding. The need of capitals to sustain "longer" investments to their completion stresses the capital market, so that (short-term) interest rates rise and provoke failures of part of "longer" investments; that is to say an economic downturn unwinds. This mechanism still lies at the core of the Austrian theories in their most recent versions like in Huerta De Soto (1998) and Garrison (2001).

All the theories related above draw a precise idea of sustainability, depicted as the natural development of economic growth with neither inflationary phenomena nor oscillations in economic activity growth. If we let capital markets work, investments will reach the level permitted by the amount of *real savings* in the economy. In *classical* terms this means reaching an equilibrium level for the real interest rate, the Wicksellian MRI; this must be equal to the Wicksellian NRI, therefore be price-inflation neutral (which avoids a first sustainability problem), even in a system featured with vast credit transactions such as the present one. Such an interest rate would naturally let production structure match people inter-temporal preferences in consumption, which means avoiding tensions on any goods market segment. Deviations from this natural setting of the economy must then lead to some degree of instability or turmoil, which can therefore be traced back to the un-sustainability of any "imposed" growth rate.

A Keynesian-Like View on Sustainability

As reported above, part of economic schools (mainly of *Keynesian* origins, but at varying extent almost all *mainstream* economists) profess an active role of Central Banks and Governments to spur economic activity and sustain it when it lacks momentum.

The basic strategy is simple: assumed that stimulating economy by higher liquidity and (or) lower rates creates price-inflationary tendencies, we can attribute or reckon a certain *utility loss* for the economy running-pace below a certain target, and a *utility loss* for a certain inflation level; the derived *trade-off* would lead the Central Bank decisions. This framework (whose most famous product is the *Taylor Rule*, after J.Taylor (1993), a way to quasi-mechanically determine the interest rates policy by weighing GDP growth and price inflation either present or foreseeable) wants to manage cycle repetitions, considered exogenous, by compensating their upwards or downwards pushes, so to stabilise growth along a determined trend. All this, in these economists' intentions, would solve any sustainability problem: should the targeted growth show sustainability weakness, could we still provide the economy with more money, so banks would get funded at lower rates and could provide additional, cheaper funding to consumers and entrepreneurs; that would boost aggregate demand and economic activity to the desired level. But such a view cannot cope with "sudden" crises such as what has been mounting from mid-2007, as it lacks insight about the very foundations of growth sustainability. No wonder, then, that all recent monetary efforts by Central Banks since mid-2007 have not reversed the current economic stance yet.

Moreover, this point of view implies some abilities in quantifying advantages and losses due to the strategy: while a certain consensus on how to measure the economic activity (GDP) can be reached, we must admit the necessary approximation, or even inability, to measure how the price-inflation level (as well as output and inflation volatility) affects each individual perceptions hence each individual *well-being*. As we tend to enter into evaluating subjective feelings (an individual perception of improvement or loss in living-standard more sophisticated than the mere availability of goods), we progressively get farther from monetary metrics, and pile up layer after layer of simplifications and assumptions, which make this evaluation highly uncertain and, in a sense, even useless.

Money Government, Information Technology, and Growth Sustainability

By what related before, we can tell that exerting government powers onto money market, i.e. managing the liquidity level in the system or the interest rates structure, has got relevant consequences on economic growth. Money is, in facts, the means of *transmission* for both government and private impulses across the economy.

Credit availability, real interest rates, inter-temporal consumption, liquidity preferences, inflation expectations, and productivity conditions, affect savings, consumption, and investment decisions. The ability to "lead" interest rate to a desired level so much as to provide the system with more or less liquidity have then got consequences all across the economy. It is important to stress that a "*means*" needs a "*channel*" to enter or affect the economy; in this case the channel is the banking system.

Providing banks with liquidity has been made easier by IT: nowadays, there is no need to move much paper materially, like funding requests, certificates, approval letters, money itself, and even people; all operations regarding the request of available funds at Central Banks, the exchange of bonds or other securities as collateral, the arrangement of auctions, and the final delivery of sums (and subsequent periodical payments of interests) can all be managed "*on-line*", via information virtually running at the speed of light through various *electronic webs* interconnecting all interested operators. In a sense, there is even no need of money at all, as the Central Bank can simply decide to provide "*electronic*" money i.e. information about a certain sum availability to a bank. Thence money can spread throughout the banking system to the final borrower and forth to its creditors and so on, simply as information jumping from a bank account to another. Money itself can run as information, letting us hold hard cash just for little transactions or precautionary reasons. All this has meant a great spare of time and resources (work, people, and even money itself) in managing money from its "creation" by a Central Bank to any moment of its circulation.

By the side of the single saver/investor, IT has brought important novelties. Market operators (anyone dealing with financial markets, as professionals, savers or private borrowers) have now a wider access to information useful for own purposes, and faster means to implement own decisions. In a sense they can now run at large through the market to find the solution that best fits their needs/wants, with a great spare of time and resources compared to few decades ago. That means also that any manoeuvre and any incentive created by monetary authorities are now almost immediately known and available to anyone; this in turn means that monetary policy can now spread far more faster through the market, with a quick transmission of the authorities' will across the whole economy (e.g. a cut of the Central Bank's official interest rates is almost immediately known by each single operator, who can immediately estimate the consequences in terms of lower market interest rates, then evaluate a new debt and check the opportunities the market offers via electronic webs). Asset management can exploit the same advantages and even the possibility to gather even more and faster information about all that affects both realised and eligible investments.

The banking system as a channel for monetary policy then, thanks to IT, works in two ways: it almost immediately receives stimuli from the authorities, and almost immediately makes its own reactions available to any operator's inquiry. That sums up to an increase in *market efficiency* in Fama (1970) terms: more public information is now rapidly available, with some reduction of room for some information to be kept "private", which enhances the actual market "semi-strong" efficiency features. In this sense we can consider the present economy as sort of "information-based economy".

But all this means also that there are virtually no more limits to money *creation* (we better call it *e-money*), and this possibility becomes even more concrete the further e-money tools evolve and their use spreads. In these facts, and between the lines of my brief summary, we can see the building up of a world much similar to what Wicksell theorised with his "pure credit" economy. The access to "*central money*" from commercial banks has been made easier, safer and faster, while Central Bank maintaining a central power to determine how liquid the market must be and what interest rates must command. The Central Bank can actually either decide at what interest rates it can offer its funds, or guide rates by adjusting funds availability, or even directly operate in the bond markets so to lead rates to the desired levels; Central Banks retain *full powers* on the money market.

What effects on economic growth and sustainability we can expect from these vast and (thanks to IT) effective powers depend on the theoretical framework we consider fit to interpret and describe reality. Briefly, if we consider Monetary Authorities interventions as prejudicial to a "natural" economic equilibrium, then the IT revolution has made the economy likelier to be unstable then growth likelier to prove unsustainable.

Remember This Word: Inflationomics

If we want an example of *growth un-sustainability* due to this human will to "*improve* natural economic mechanisms" via the Monetary Authorities interventionism, we can take a look at the world economy in the last two decades.

It is clear that the main Central Banks, the USA Federal Reserve (Fed) and, from 1998, the European Central Bank (ECB), as well as others who got linked to the former by an exchange rate peg, have led a greatly *expansionary policy*. This was meant to counteract the inevitable downturns that describe the business cycle. As I show in graph.4 (until 1998 the monetary policy has been led by the various European countries' Central Banks with varying degrees of co-ordination and a particularly conservative Bundesbank) and graph.5, Central Banks offered relevant stimuli by either lowering the official interest rates (we can consider the *Fed Funds* interest rate for the Fed, and the main refinancing operations interest rate, or briefly *Refi*, for the ECB) or pumping up monetary aggregates (Central Banks money supplying can be apparent by monitoring the dy-

Figure 4. European monetary policy – annual percent change. Source: (adapted from ECB public database); GDP as GDP at current prices less HICP annual variations

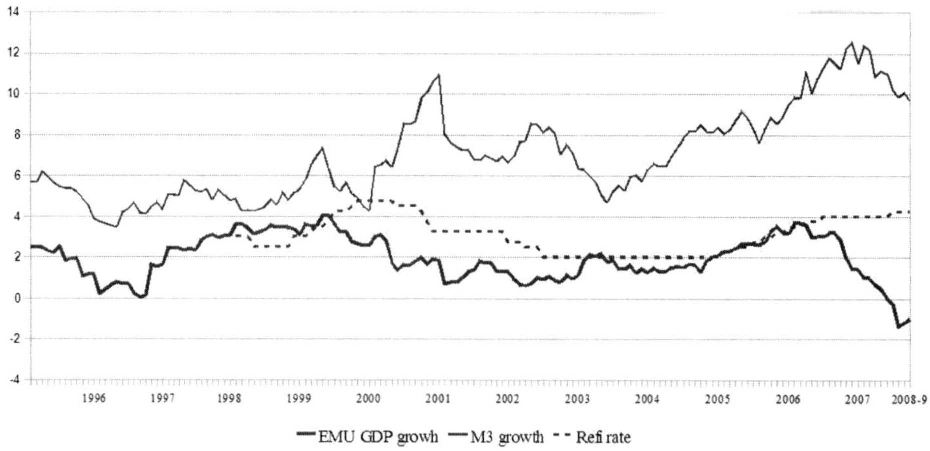

Figure 5. USA monetary policy – annual percent change. Source: (adapted from economagic.com public database)

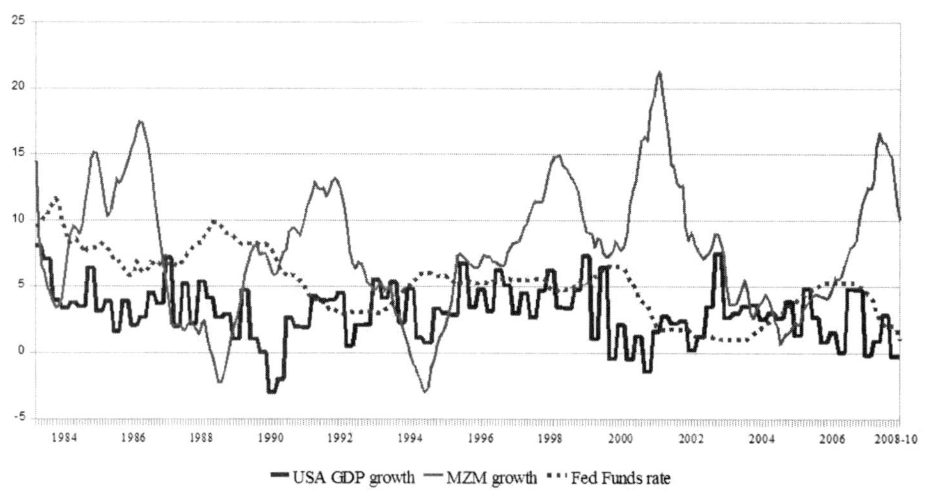

namics of *M3* for the ECB and *MZM* for the Fed) in those moments when growth showed signs of weakness; this policy is far more apparent by the repeated cutting of official rates started in the last quarter of 2008.

This almost "mechanical" policy of inflating economy to deny any tendency to cycles should be called, like the Mises School does, "*inflationomics*" (which means "*theory to govern inflation*"). In a *Keynesian-like* reality, cyclicities involve periods of Central Bank supporting economic growth, and periods of Central Bank braking growth. This is what it seems to have been ruling until early 2008.

We can estimate a world *financial/real economy ratio* in many ways. For the purposes of this paragraph, I consider a gross measure of banks intermediation of international capital flows, the "*locational banking statistics*" provided by the Bank for International Settlement (BIS), comprising 41 countries; this rough, underrating measure of banks' total assets (claims on both banks and non-banks) was about US$ 29.472 billions as of end-2006 and US$ 39.069 billions as of mid-2008, which means more than a 32% growth in two years. In the meanwhile, according to International Monetary Fund (IMF) data, world GDP passed from US$ 60.610 billions as of end-2006 to expected US$ 69.228 billions as of end-2008, which means about a 14% growth. My rough, underrating measure of the world *financial/real economy ratio*, given by the mentioned BIS statistics on IMF world GDP statistics, was about 48,6% in 2006 and is expected to be more than 56% in 2008; beside the magnitude of these statistics, I am interested in their dynamics: should we consider all this intermediated financial wealth as funds available for investment or *money* in a Wicksellian sense (savings deposited in banks, to be directly used for transactions), we should then say that world savings would have tremendously grown in recent years (given the short period considered, I exclude relevant structural changes in the world's bank-intermediation depth); as we know that what it counts, in this chapter perspective, are *real savings* (whose growth cannot actually overwhelm GDP's), we must say that a great part of financial wealth has nothing to do with real savings, and it therefore directly comes from Central Banks "*ex nihilo* created" funds. All this availability of funds has surely stimulated banks to exploit the moment by inflating their "*investment*" branches; IT has surely played an important role in helping banks to build up various financial exoticisms (CDO^2, ABS, derivatives on derivatives, and so on), which must be considered as means to manage or employ the vast mass of money pouring out from Central Banks, a way to exploit an opportunity, not a permanent multiplication of credit.

All this money was intended to sustain growth and avoid any recessive tendencies. Instead, by piling up a mounting distance between investments and savings i.e. fund requests and real savings availability, it led to an increasingly unsustainable growth, to consumption standards well beyond actual possibilities, and an increasing share of even-longer-term investments subject to the risk of non-completion. A great mass of money can lean toward a market or another, and some investment trends may even become *financial bubbles*, which distort agents' habits (e.g. the real-estate bubble has implied an increasing rate of house-collateralised debt, making the system frail to a real-estate bubble bursting). Last decade's world economic growth is therefore an example of what *unsustainable growth* is. This dynamics could not be grasped by an a-temporal theory of production.

Solutions and Recommendations

No solutions can actually be offered to address an economic downturn due to past excesses of monetary policy. When markets start falling and crunching, the economy already finds itself within a *capitals reallocation* process or, we better say, in the first stage of detecting unsustainable branches and markets, forcing them to sort of reveal how much real wealth lies beneath. It is like the economy starts shrieking "*show me the money!*" to discover where money is not available, so to erase credits uncovered by real savings (the trend of *commercial* banks buying *investment* banks, emerged in the second half of 2008, can be a consequence of this automatic/cyclical economic clean-up). Further massive liquidity provisions from Central Banks, the very roots of economic cycles, is not the right answer. Hayek's *Business Cycle* theory can tell us neither a precise break-point nor schedule a timing for crisis developments; his school has not developed an analytical (formal) thread to make any model adhere to reality; it can offer qualitative indications only, because any mathematical/statistical approach can at best capture an instant picture of economic relations and individual valuations lying at the basis of the economy building, and (in this school's credo) can get no clues that these can be treated as quantitatively consistent during time. It cannot be known enough to measure the composition of whole economy's time-to-production, as well as how monetary stimuli (both positive and negative) get spread and distribute across the production structure; individual sensitivity to interest rates can vary amply, because of a not-fully understandable variety of individual logics and complex sensitivities interconnections. The institutional framework can also affect the picture, together with institutional status/reputation features (managing the international reserve currency gives much scope to push the economy beyond any estimated growth path, and this may contribute to explain how the USA succeeded in a 15-year long expansion before the game was over).

In a sense, we should let economy shrink (at worst, collapse), letting it *re-arrange* its real wealth. The freer this process, the faster the crises. Another choice is balancing the social cost (a terrible questions: how can we really weigh individual costs to obtain a valid measure of social cost?) of a fast and deep economic shrinkage with a milder and prolonged slowing down via an ample socialisation of costs (this second option is what governments seem to have chosen, when in October 2008 they decided to cope with the crisis by guaranteeing interbank money exchanges and providing equity to almost any bank). The best solution is anyway straight: *pre-emption*.

Pre-emption means some trust in market mechanisms, which rely on individual correct perceptions of own needs and the general state of the world. As both *classical* and Austrian economics have taught, all needs and goods availability coordinate within a market thanks to spontaneous, *free* price-setting; such a market is the common ground for individual instances to meet and compose orderly.

Pre-emption thus relies on complete and *widespread* information, on the most perfect awareness of state and functioning of the economy, and on the *reliability* of information themselves as the most adherent to reality. Mis-perceptions (due to either incomplete or biased information) are source of actually *inconsistent* behaviours thence *inefficient* capital allocation, which in turn means hindering economic growth or make it unsustainable.

Manoeuvring interest rates and monetary aggregates, the core content of monetary policy, gives biased information to agents. Lowering interest rates by decree tells the market the same signal as more real savings (new wealth) are now available for investments (e.g. because of new natural resources, a technological breakthrough, or higher propensity to save); it means depicting a reality that never was, pushing people to make actions (exploiting the supposed new available savings) which are actually inconsistent to reality.

Avoiding this (un-intended or looked-for) *cheating* erases room for "false" economic boom, erases scope for sudden dramatic cyclical upturns (save true technological advancements), therefore impedes the naturally, inevitably consequent downturn. Economic growth would be led by merely *technological developments* (be they stemming from new production or organisational innovations), thus based on real wealth (and savings) availability, with no perilous myths of *growth from "above"* any longer. Given the firm ground which economic growth would then be anchored to, growth itself would be sustainable, justified by its own wealth-creation. Growth could then be not so fantastically high (but who actually knows?), although its path would surely be smooth with neither excesses nor crises.

Another source of problems can be the role of governments in collecting taxes (or debt) to fund further consumption, investments, or redistribution policies. This affects growth too, as part of the economy's real savings comes from public budget. Whether budget policy is right or wrong, it does not interest this chapter, because it belongs to an inquiry into how politics really matches people wishes and interests (the factual challenge of modern democracies); in this case, government can be seen as an *agent* amongst the others, receiving part of the national income and deciding how to satisfy their own needs, and this decisions become part of the market resuming of all the single wills expressed within the economy. Government contribution to real savings and investments (i.e. bidding and asking for funds) affects the freely set interest rates, which then move to equilibrate the fund balance and make the new growth potential sustainable. Again, whatever the arrangement the economy structure can reach, un-hampering money market (i.e. Central Bank neither creating new credit without real savings to back it, nor forcing interest rates far from their natural level) would make the economic growth-path sustainable.

The simplest way to pre-empt any source of cyclicities, i.e. economic growth un-sustainability, is to abandon any Central Bank temptation to "*help*" the economy. It is not necessary to turn the financial world *upside-down*, abolishing *fractional reserve* banking and arranging a new *gold standard* (or even get back to *gold money*) as Rothbard (2001) and other anarchic-capitalists profess. It is far easier to stabilise the money supply at a certain rate of growth, erasing Central Bank's powers to vary it discreetly and revoking any Central Bank target onto interest rates, so that the market can freely price the *value* of money and time instant by instant, following real economy developments. This rule is, at its core, what *Monetarism* originally professed, with particular regard to the *Friedman k-percent rule* of money supply growing at a steady rate (from 3 to 5%; it is worth noting that gold supply has been estimated to grow at around 4% per year, then, in this sense, a Friedman rule can be seen equivalent to a gold standard regime).

IT advancements give scope to a wider use of credit instead of hard cash, which makes money supply even more *endogenous* during time. The mere fact that there is no external source to affect the amount of credit available in the economy (i.e. no Central Bank interventions), lets markets free to find their monetary equilibrium according to their own *needs* (which are the needs of their participants) and actual production structure (in Wicksellian terms: NRI=MRI). In a sense, inconsistent-to-consumption-and-funding entrepreneurial projects would not be allowed nor even tried.

FUTURE TRENDS

IT has expressed a great potential to change our reality with regard to the economic and financial side of our lives, affecting both our ability to manage money, and our access to information. As to what we can expect in the future, I want to focus first on an even deeper penetration of e-money (credit cards, ATM and so on) and how this enters the growth sustainability discussion, then the role the government can play in spreading new technologies and information to make them known and manageable, instead of biasing individual balances and constraints via old interventionist policies.

E-Money: Vindicating Wicksell

As anticipated before, there is a clear trend of IT affecting the use of money, investigated e.g. in Arnone & Bandiera (2004) and somewhat contrasted in Papadopoulos (2007). Anyway, managing a bank branch via electronic webs has made credit scoring easier, faster, and less prone to errors, while reducing the need of hard cash deposits (which in turn has strengthened bank deposits safety).

An expansionary direction of IT into finance is remote banking. The first gain we can detect is the great spare of time compared to walking to the bank branch holding your account and spending time in a row before you can ask the clerk for your needs. Moreover, the World Wide Web gives you the opportunity to collect various hints, suggestions, and information on a scale which a single clerk (loyal to its bank) cannot reach. Even though all information cannot exactly be complete and fair, and you may not be fully skilled to grasp all information, you have at least got the *opportunity* to improve your awareness of what market offers, and you can spare time in realising the chosen investment or strategy.

Money transfers are now common use; it is just a flow of *information*, with no need of hard cash movements; paying (and providing funds) has thus become easy, fast, and safe, allowing economic agents to expand their activity and manage businesses spread even across different countries. Financial investments have gained a wide range of variety, which helps agents to arrange and manage portfolios the most consistent to available information and agents' appetite for risk. Thanks to IT, finance has been moving toward a tailor-made wealth management, and reducing restraints in realising own decisions have diminished the wasting of resources (such as time, will, and money itself). Having invested in IT has freed new resources for the world to grow and develop in a way not so deeply investigated yet.

From a *Keynesian-like* point of view, IT contribution to growth via the monetary side of the economy resembles a net increase in money supply although actually arising from a reduction of money demand, as represented in graph.6. By this point of view, money demand (L) depends on transaction needs (estimated as a fixed proportion of aggregate income, the vertical dotted line in each L_1 and L_2) and speculative opportunities (decreasing with interest rates, the curved line in each L_1 and L_2). The way this money demand (which in this class of theories signals the amount of savings to employ) combines with money supply (M^s, exogenously pouring from a Central Bank, and playing the role of a means to turn savings into funds available to the economy) sums up to the equilibrium interest rate (i^*), which drives investments (and consumption), then the GDP.

Reducing the need of holding hard cash for transactions (what e-money has been intended for), reduces the amount of money needed and demanded (money demand shifts from L_1 to L_2), leading equilibrium interest rates to a lower level (from i^*_1 to i^*_2). This stimulates economic activity, in other words it boosts economic growth.

According to the *classical* side of economic schooling, creating a net surplus in money supply involves price-inflation pressures. Even a *monetarist-like* analysis can lead to this conclusion: given the *exchange equation* revised by Milton Friedman (1956)

$$MV=PQ \qquad (5)$$

where V is sort of the inverse of *money demand on income* ratio, reducing the money need for transactions implies increasing money velocity, thence nominal income $Y=PQ$; as real income Q is supposed, in the long run, to be driven by technological advancements only, the first effect of *e-money* in a stationary economy must be price inflation.

The former approach rests on the assumption of *idle productive capacity* to be freely stimulated by an increase in aggregate demand. The latter assumes a quite complete rigidity of income in the short run, whereas capacity must already be fully exploited. Both approaches miss a deeper

Figure 6.

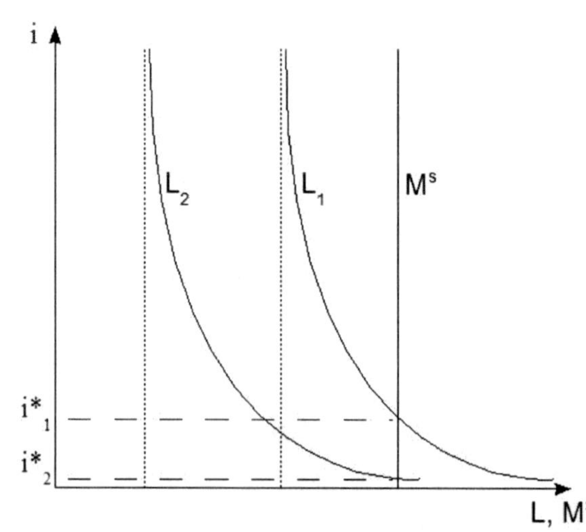

insight into growth sustainability, because they do not pay heed to how savings and investments can naturally coordinate as expressions of individual needs and wants (consumption plans) as well as constraints (ability to save and production opportunities).

Hard cash is held to cope with any sudden unforeseeable need, in order to avoid the cost of liquidating part of own savings e.g. constrained in the form of some security. This money then plays a precise precautionary function; it is actually *employed* for a specific use. Thanks to IT, we can now draw cash from one of the myriad of ATM machines anywhere at an average cost near to zero, while all our savings in form of money can now be deposited in a bank and enter the whole *credit circuit* (although the depth of this entering depends on the specific characteristics of the deposits). All the solutions we have got to leave our money invested by a bank while maintaining a right of immediate liquidation dramatically reduce our need of holding hard cash (the "service" of immediate availability of liquidity gets now satisfied by the bank), and this is a net gain of real savings *availability* (beside new credit "created" by the Central Bank) to be productively employed; as this need is now satisfied by technological advancements, resources can flow to satisfy another. All I said wants to tell you that the effect of e-money spreading is not similar to an expansionary monetary policy, but it is close to the expansion of *real* savings in a *Wicksellian* world (a perspective Baggiani (2007) already tried to expose).

Further researches on the up-to-datedness of Wicksell thought, like in Fontana (2006), would be useful to investigate how endogenous money supply, thanks to IT innovations, actually is, and how e-money will (and did) affect economic development and sustainability. A more general rediscovery of Austrian *Business Cycle* theories, like in Opper (2002), and an improvement of their formal exposure to make them more comparable to mainstream models, would be a relevant help to understand what growth un-sustainability stems from.

A New Role for Governments

Beside what I reported about the perilousness of Central Bank interventionism into the economy, I must finally spend some words on the general role that government policy can play in making growth more or less sustainable. In this regard, I skip all the discussions regarding public order and Rule of Law, as these are the basics of government's role and must be taken for granted; consistently to the chapter's purposes, I focus on public investments and savings.

Like any other economic agents, governments have surely taken advantages from IT. A deeper, wider, and faster access to all needed information has surely improved the way Public Administration works, increasing the *awareness* behind government decisions and allowing relevant resource *saving* (time, money, and workforce); whether the single administration has fully or partially exploited IT potential is a "second level" problem regarding the peculiarities of the bureaucracy under scrutiny. In general terms, the availability of a new, more performing technology can always improve the state of the art; in this sense the wider the government adoption of IT, the greater the State *efficiency*, and some boost to growth must follow.

A wider and timely sight across financial markets has surely helped governments *fund collecting* (in case of budget deficit, when it must be decided what kind of bonds to issue and when to launch them, so to minimise public debt servicing); this has surely avoided unnecessary market stress. The same technology has helped Central Banks to pursue their liquidity and interest rates targets, making their policy far more precise and *effective*, thus permitting a stricter control on all strategic monetary variables (in case you share a *Keynesian-like* view, this is a good thing).

All in all, IT has helped to make production (both public and private) faster and more consistent to the actual features of the economy, thus reducing room for mistakes and resources wasting. Public Administration has gathered so much information, it could even think to be able to extend its operational field, making interventionism more pervasive e.g. to directly leading entrepreneurial choices.

This book is not the right place to explore public choice theories, but we should remind that the best social results come out of all operators being completely aware of the surrounding reality and free to pursue the consequent needs under full conscience of their own constraints.

Given a set of markets (we better say, needs) the society considers best served under a prominent role of the State (e.g., to varying extents, health care, justice, workforce, and infrastructures), governments should keep far from directly intervening in all other markets, and let the latter find their own equilibrium with prices signalling actual scarcity and personal evaluations. Governments should not force operators toward certain actions such as buying certain goods or investing in certain productions, e.g. via fiscal advantages; lowering a price by a fiscal premium means transferring resources form those who do not (or cannot) buy the goods to those who buy, and this means draining purchasing power from one sector to another (a merely discreet reallocation of capitals) or even pushing the aggregate spending beyond its previous level, thus shrinking savings (as I exposed before, this implies weakening the sustainability of growth).

As to the subject of this book, governments should neither stimulate IT implementation by firms and citizens: such a move, implemented via government subsidies, would mean setting "political prices", a market distortion where part of people spending gets biased by non-market prices at the expenses of all other people in the economy. We should at last realise that prices have got a meaning, in that they stem from the cost of their production (the lost opportunity to product something else) and the value acknowledged by buyers (the renunciation to buy something else), therefore any "political price" must be seen as a particular evaluation imposed by an authority.

One thing the government can really do is reasoning on its *own* needs and resources, taking advantages from new tools and new efficiency sources, then being the first *mover* and *implementer*. If the government considers a new technology as a breaking application, then the government itself should adopt it on a large scale and then show the consequent productivity increases. Such behaviour is similar to an *advisory* role, where you give anyone a hint of what it could be done to improve productivity or create new services. If the idea proves good, firms and privates would choose to "invest" in this new technology, *autonomously*, or express a demand for new products more adherent to specific needs. From a wider point of view, the government should promote *workshops* (even one-shot meetings) and let interested operators expose ideas, projects, and insights into the future. Stimulating the spreading of information, as a general advisor, may be the best service such a vast organisation can offer to its citizens; this is something that financial markets authorities already provide via their principle of *level playing field*, corporate information disclosure, and homogeneity of information diffusion across the market (all operators must have the same set of information, and information must be complete, so operators can decide their investment plans in full awareness of reality, and prices can resume as close as possible the actual value of the assets).

The government may be the sole operator in the economy with a statutory aim to work for the interests of all the citizens, not being therefore subject to any incentives to hide information (there is no competitor to defend its own industrial secrets from). It should exploit this role for the sake of the economy, offering the wider set of knowledge, and letting people give them a proper value (i.e. decide what part of production, consumption and savings to be sacrificed because it is worth doing); such a policy does not interfere with budget constraints and personal choices between (real) savings and investments, hence lets the economy itself set a *sustainable* path for its own growth. The outcome of such *information-enhanced economy* (where IT can play a prominent role), with no monetary aim to force its pace, would be the highest degree of economic growth potential *expressed* with the least (or nil) un-sustainability risk.

Further researches to assess each government's ability to lead the technological progress, and the reflections on the whole economy up-to-datedness and productivity, would give new, interesting insights into the public administration contribution to economic development.

CONCLUSION

Investments are an important variable determining economic development, even when we focus on a partial idea of development such as GDP growth. Realising what it makes investments viable, what investments can rely on, is the first step to understand what makes growth sustainable.

A positive role for savings is acknowledged by both *classical* and Austrian analyses, where the real interest rate equilibrates the fund market, making investments, and the subsequent economic growth, sustainable. A negative role for savings is claimed by *Keynesian-like* analyses, which highlight a persistent gap in productive capacity that can be rescued only by stimulating the aggregate demand i.e. curbing savings. But both *classical* (including monetarist) and *Keynesian-like* analyses cannot righteously cope with the sustainability problem, as both of them do not describe a mechanism explaining the "sudden" growth reversals actual economies experience. We must then refer to theories that develop their analyses on a time-frame too, in order to appreciate what links economic upturns to downturns (and vice versa) or a common cause for these cycles episodes: from this point of view, Austrian theories, from Wicksell's "pure-credit" economy to Hayek's *Business Cycle*, give a deeper insight into how savings and investments combine, and how expansionary monetary policies (aiming to stimulate economic growth) actually undermine economic development and lead to un-sustainability problems.

Information Technology enters the growth and sustainability discussion by an industrial perspective as a relevant source of productivity increases, but also in financial terms: it has made information collecting and processing far easier and cheaper with important gains in terms of spared resources. Even financial strategies implementation has become faster, as money itself can be treated as information, but this has even meant that Monetary Authorities can now exert full powers, in terms of both determining interest rates and creating limitless liquidity, to manage financial markets with a faster transmission across the economy; making monetary policy more effective and pervasive has therefore made economies more exposed to sustainability weaknesses. At the same time, the spreading of e-money use is making economies closer to Wicksell's "pure-credit" model, letting more saved capitals free to be used for investments thus increasing the economy growth potential.

In order to strengthen growth sustainability, the economy should be let free to save and invest accordingly, with no monetary interventions to force the pace. Widespread and (as much as possible) complete information is one of the basic conditions for this solution to work properly, and Information Technology is the main tool to realise this project; the economy must turn to an "information-enhanced" system, where governments must not pretend to arrogate individual choices, but play a new "advisory" role helping all relevant information to enter each operator's knowledge, for anyone to be able to set his/her own proper investment or consumption strategy freely.

REFERENCES

Arnone, M., & Bandiera, L. (2004). *Monetary Policy, Monetary Areas, and Financial Development with Electronic Money* (Working Paper, 04/122). International Monetary Fund.

Baggiani, L. (2007). *Il Bene (e il Male) della Moneta Elettronica*. Retrieved April 2, 2007, from http://ideashaveconsequences.org/il-bene-e-il-male-della-moneta-elettronica/jacopo

Bordo, M. D., & Schwartz, A. J. (2004). IS-LM and Monetarism. *History of Political Economy*, *36*(Supplement), 217–239. doi:10.1215/00182702-36-Suppl_1-217

Fama, E. (1970). Efficient Capital Markets: A Review of Theory and Empirical Work. *The Journal of Finance*, *25*, 383–417. doi:10.2307/2325486

Fontana, G. (2006). *The "New Consensus" View of Monetary Policy: A New Wicksellian Connection?* (Working Paper, 476). The Levy Economics Institute.

Forstater, M., & Randall, L. W. (2007). *The General Theory after 70 Years*. Houndsmills, UK: Palgrave Publishing.

Friedman, M. (1956). The Quantity Theory of Money: A Restatement. In M. Friedman (Ed.), *Studies in the Quantity Theory of Money*. Chicago, IL: University of Chicago Press.

Friedman, M. (1968). The Role of Monetary Policy. *The American Economic Review*, *58*, 1–7.

Garrison, R. W. (2005). *Time and Money. The Macroeconomics of Capital Structure*. London, UK: Routledge.

Huerta De Soto, J. (1998). *Dinero, Crédito bancario y Ciclos Económicos*. Madrid, Spain: Unión Editorial. Galì, J. (2000). *New Perspectives on Monetary Policy, Inflation, and the Business Cycle*. Paper presented at the 2000 World Congress of the Econometric Society, Seattle.

Keynes, J. M. (1936). *The General Theory of Employment, Interest, and Money*. London, UK: MacMillan.

Marx, C. (1887). *Capital* (Moore & Aveling, Trans.). London, UK: Engels.

Menger, C. (1871). *The Principles of Economics*. New York, NY: New York University Press.

Monsurrò, P. (2007). *Beni Capitali Submarginali e Non-Neutralità della Moneta*. Retrieved April 24, 2007, from http://ideashaveconsequences.org/beni-capitali-submarginali-e-non-neutralita-della-moneta/jacopo

Nelson, E., & Schwartz, A. J. (2007). *The Impact of Milton Friedman on Modern Monetary Economics: Setting the Record Straight on Paul Krugman's "Who Was Milton Friedman?"* (Working Paper, 2007-048D). Federal Reserve Bank of St. Louis.

Opper, S. E. (2002). *The Austrian Theory of Business Cycle: Old Lessons for Modern Economic Policy?* (Working Paper, 02/2). International Monetary Fund.

Papadopoulos, G. (2007). *Electronic Money and the Possibility of a Cashless Society* (Working Paper, 18.02.2007). EIPE.

Romer, P. M. (1994). The Origins of Endogenous Growth. *The Journal of Economic Perspectives*, *8*(1), 3–22.

Rothbard, M. N. (2001). *The Case for a 100 Percent Golden Dollar*. Auburn, AL: The Ludwig von Mises Institute.

Smith, A. (1776). *An Inquiry into the Nature and Causes of the Wealth of Nations*. New York, NY: Oxford University Press.

Taylor, J. B. (1993). Discretion versus Policy Rules in Practice. *Carnegie-Rochester Conference Series on Public Policy, 39*.

von Böhm-Bawerk, E. (1891). *The Positive Theory of Capital*. London, UK: MacMillan.

von Hayek, F. A. (1931). *Prices and Production*. London, UK: Routledge and Sons.

von Hayek, F. A. (1933). *Monetary Theory and Trade Cycle*. London, UK: Jonathan Crape.

von Mises, L. E. (1931). The Causes of the Economic Crisis. In Greaves B.B. (Ed.), *On the Manipulation of Money and Credit*. Dobbs Ferry, NY: Free Market Books.

von Mises, L. E. (1934). *The Theory of Money and Credit* (Batson, Trans.). Oxford, UK: Alden.

Wicksell, K. (1965). *Interest and Prices: A Study of the Causes Regulating the Value of Money.* London, UK: MacMillan.

Woodford, M. (2007). *How Important is Money in the Conduct of Monetary Policy?* (Manuscript). Columbia University.

ADDITIONAL READING

Arnone, M., & Bandiera, L. (2003). *E-Money: Chances of Success and Consequences for Monetary Policy* (Working Paper, 401). Kiel Institute for World Economics.

Blanchard, O. (1997). Comment on the New Neoclassical Synthesis and the Role of Monetary Policy. In *NBER. Macroeconomics Annual, 1997*, 289–293. doi:10.2307/3585234

Blinder, A. S. (1998). *Central Banking in Theory and Practice.* Boston, MA: MIT Press.

Christiano, L., Eichenbaum, M., & Evans, C. (1996). The Effects of Monetary Policy Shocks: Evidence from the Flow of Funds. *The Review of Economics and Statistics, 10*(1), 16–32. doi:10.2307/2109845

Davidson, P. (1994). *Post Keynesian Macroeconomics Theory*. Northampton, UK: Edward Elgar.

Davis, E. P. (1995). *Debt, Financial Fragility, and Systemic Risk*. Oxford, UK: Clarendon Press.

Ebeling, R. M. (1996). *The Austrian Theory of the Trade Cycle and Other Essays*. Auburn, AL: Ludwig von Mises Institute.

Eichengreen, B., & Mitchener, K. (2003). *The Great Depression as a Credit Boom Gone Wrong* (Working Paper, 137). Bank for International Settlements.

Fisher, S. (1993). The Role of Macroeconomic Factors in Growth. *The Journal of Political Economy*, 32.

Fontana, G. (2006). Hicks on Monetary Theory and History: Money and Endogenous Money. *Cambridge Journal of Economics*, 28.

Friedman, M. (1960). *A Program for Monetary Stability.* New York, NY: Fordham University Press.

Greenspan, A. (1996). *The Challenge of Central Banking in a Democratic Society*. Remarks to the *Annual Dinner and Francis Boyer Lecture of the American Enterprise Institute for Public Policy Research*. Washington, DC.

Hawkings, J. (2001). Electronic Finance and Monetary Policy. In *Electronic Finance: A New Perspective and Challenges* (Working Paper, 7). Bank for International Settlements.

Keynes, J. M. (1930). *A Treatise on Money*. London, UK: Harcourt Brace Jovanovich.

Leontieff, W. W. (1936). The Fundamental Assumption on Mr. Keynes's Monetary Theory of Unemployment. *The Quarterly Journal of Economics, 51*, 192–197. doi:10.2307/1882507

Lindhal, E. (1939). *Studies in the Theory of Money and Capital.* London, UK: George Allen and Unwin.

Miller, M., Weller, P., & Zhang, L. (2002). Moral Hazard and the U.S. Stock Market: Analyzing the "Greenspan Put". *The Economic Journal, 112*(478), 171–186. doi:10.1111/1468-0297.00029

Minsky, H. P. (1986). *Stabilizing an Unstable Economy.* London, UK: Yale University Press.

Mueller, A. P. (2001). Financial Cycles, Business Activity, and the Stock Market. *The Quarterly Journal of Austrian Economics*, *4*(1), 3–21. doi:10.1007/s12113-001-1000-5

O'Driscoll, G. P., Jr., & Rizzo, M. (1985). *The Economics of Time and Ignorance*. Oxford, UK: Basil Blackwell.

Palley, T. (2002). The E-Money Revolution: Challenges and Implications for Monetary Policy. *Journal of Post Keynesian Economics*, *24*(2), 213–233.

Rothbard, M. N. (1978). *Austrian Definitions of the Supply of Money* (Working Paper). Auburn, AL: Ludwig von Mises Institute. Retrieved from http://www.mises.org/rothbard/austrianmoneysupply.pdf

Rothbard, M. N. (1997). *The Logic of Action*. Cheltenham, UK: Edward Elgar.

Sechrest, L. J. (2005). *Two Natural Rates: Friedman and the Austrians* (Working Paper). Auburn, AL: Ludwig von Mises Institute. Retrieved from http://www.mises.org/journals/scholar/sechrest11.pdf

Svensson, L. E. O. (1995). *Optimal Inflation Targets, "Conservative" Central Banks, and Linear Inflation Contracts* (Working Paper, 5251). NBER.

Svensson, L. E. O. (1996). *Inflation Forecasts Targeting: Implementing and Monitoring Inflation Targets* (Working Paper, 5797). NBER.

Von Hayek, F. A. (1937). Investment that Raises the Demand for Capital. *The Review of Economics and Statistics*, *19*(4), 174–177. doi:10.2307/1926358

Von Hayek, F. A. (1941). *The Pure Theory of Capital*. London, UK: Routledge and Sons.

Von Mises, L. E. (1940). *Human Action: a Treatise of Economics.* Auburn, AL: Ludwig von Mises Institute.

White, E. N. (1990). The Stock Market Boom and Crash of 1929 Revisited. *The Journal of Economic Perspectives*, *4*(2), 67–83.

KEY TERMS AND DEFINITIONS

Business Cycle: The structural up-and-down swinging of economic activity expressed in terms of production and employment.

Electronic Money: Any means to manage, transfer, or stock money with the use of electronic tools and webs. Any electronic substitute to the use of hard cash, from ATM cards to credit cards and on-line bank accounts.

Growth: The increase of production and the subsequent improvement in the standard of living in a given economy, apparent beyond the peaks and troughs of its Business Cycle.

Information Technology: Any technology related to the use and circulation, both automatically and on-demand, of electronic information.

Investments: The use and combination of resources (be they money, time, work, or else) to obtain a certain future result in terms of a new products or larger wealth; the resources remain tied up to the end unless incurring in a loss of them.

Savings: The part of (especially monetary) income which does not get spent or consumed, to be stored for future needs.

Sustainability: The economic equilibrium between the magnitude of a certain resource-consuming activity and the ability of the economy to re-create resources which lie at the basis of the activity itself. The lack of this equilibrium generates Business Cycle phenomena.

Chapter 7
Developing the Financial Infrastructure in an Emerging Market Economy:
The Role of Credit Rating Agencies

Michael G. Papaioannou
International Monetary Fund, USA

George P. Tsetsekos
Drexel University, USA

ABSTRACT

This chapter examines the role of credit rating agencies in capital-market development and on the conduct of monetary policy. Rating agencies in developed capital markets provide quality certification to issuers, while their role in emerging capital markets is mainly to enhance informational efficiency in the marketplace. The authors highlight some indirect macroeconomic consequences from the presence of a rating agency, including its monetary surveillance role and the positive implications for foreign investments. The chapter also outlines the conditions for an effective rating agency in an emerging market economy, discusses the benefits of security ratings to constituencies, and proposes a scenario for a rating agency's design. The collaboration of regulators, central bankers, and issuers is especially critical to the success of a rating agency.

INTRODUCTION

A number of Emerging Market (EM) countries have introduced various financial market reforms to attain a more efficient and stable economy in the short-to-medium term and a sustainable economic growth in the longer run. Among these reforms, initiatives for developing the country's broad financial and institutional infrastructure have played a central role in effecting financial deregulation efforts and promoting financial stability. By financial and institutional infrastructure we mean the minimum legal, tax, accounting, and regulatory requirements necessary for the efficient functioning of a country's financial sector.

Deregulation of the financial sector without parallel advancements in the country's broad financial infrastructure, although it provides a fertile envi-

DOI: 10.4018/978-1-61520-709-1.ch007

ronment for developing new financial products, it could nonetheless inhibit the necessary quality differentiation among institutions and instruments. To correct resulting inefficiencies and avoid fraud in the financial sector, government authorities often try to implement disclosure requirements and enforce stricter regulatory guidelines. However, such prescriptions might have short-lived benefits, because they generally have negative effects on financial-sector growth.[1]

Between the two extreme modes of financial-sector development -- namely uncontrollable deregulation of financial services and their government-directed growth, authorities should preferably allow an appropriate mix of government regulatory activity and self-regulatory discipline. Academic research has long suggested that self-regulatory discipline, always under the auspices of the government, is especially desirable for the efficient development of the financial sector in EM economies (Bossone and Promisel, 1999). As such, self-regulation is considered as an integral part of a country's financial infrastructure.

One important element of the self-regulatory financial infrastructure is the development of a rating agency. In an evolving financial sector, lack of quality differentiation among financial institutions and services leads to inefficiencies. In this sense, a rating agency in an EM country may contribute to the speedy development of the financial sector by providing a "discriminating mechanism" for institutions and instruments according to their creditworthiness (Elkhoury, 2008).

The debate on the presence of a credit rating agency in an EM economy is in the domain of both public policy and financial economics. From the public-policy point of view, rating financial institutions and instruments according to their creditworthiness is sometimes perceived as a regulatory barrier restraining speedy development of an emerging financial sector. From the perspective of financial economics, a rating agency enhances conditions of informational efficiency and, by appropriately allocating risks, contributes to the development of capital markets.

In this chapter, we develop the rationale for the presence of a credit rating agency in an EM economy, while we outline conditions for an effective agency and discuss some potential economic benefits to various constituencies. Also, we discuss some macroeconomic implications from the presence of a rating agency and propose steps that regulatory authorities should follow, such as commissioning a feasibility study, on the creation of the agency. Finally, we present some challenges that may be faced in the process (International Monetary Fund, 1999).

The chapter is organized as follows: Section II, provides a background discussion of the evolving development of emerging financial markets, and contrasts their informational efficiency with that of developed capital markets. It also presents the role of a credit rating agency in emerging markets. Section III presents some considerations for creating an effective rating agency within the context of capital-market development. Section IV provides a detailed analysis of the benefits from the presence of a rating agency in an EM economy at both the micro and macro levels and highlights the role of rating agencies in the conduct of a country's monetary policy. Finally, section V proposes a design for a rating agency in an EM country and recommends a close collaboration between regulatory authorities, the central bank, and institutional investors.

FINANCIAL MARKET DEVELOPMENT AND INFORMATIONAL EFFICIENCY

In an EM economy, the full development of the financial market, especially of capital markets, is accomplished through an evolutionary process. Academic research suggests that a country's financial and capital markets evolve in distinct phases. Each phase is characterized by a different level of informational needs for economic agents. Because a rating agency accelerates the evolutionary process of the financial market only if enacted during a specific phase of its development and hampers such development in other phases, it is important to define the phases of financial and capital market development in this connection.[2] In particular, because the need for information to economic agents (household savers, institutional investors, and corporations) varies with each phase of financial-market development, we examine the role of informational efficiency in developing capital markets.

Financial-Market Development and Economic Growth

Financial-market development can be conceptualized as an evolutionary process progressing in distinct phases according to the broad developments in the economy. In the *formative phase* (first phase), the economy is characterized by a traditional society with low productivity, with consumption at subsistence levels. In the *emerging phase* (second phase), assets expand with productivity improvements to promote the emergence of several but limited sectors. In the *growth phase* (third phase), the growth of the economy is poised to increase dramatically. Higher growth with the development of new leading sectors in manufacturing and services and further increases of investment in national income drive the economy toward maturity. Technology and export development have major roles in the *developed phase* (fourth phase), as the economy drives toward maturity. The *mature phase* (final phase) is characterized by additional leading sectors in consumer goods and services, all of which are heavily technology intensive.

In the formative phase of development, the capital market is overshadowed by a strong financing sector concentrating on a few large banks, often state owned, that allocate scarce capital from households to corporations. In an emerging capital market, the role of financial intermediaries is less important than in a developed market, although they are one of the main contributors to the development of a more efficient allocation of capital and risk assessment. In the advanced phases of capital-market development, financial intermediaries specialize in the financing of several developmental and corporate investments. Finally, in a mature capital market, financial intermediaries become separate from the capital market in that they specialize in certain activities.

The primitive phase is characterized by a total absence of a financial sector. With the emergence of dominant sector(s) in the second phase, the economy becomes monetized and better organized. A banking subsector is started, but being still in its infancy, it is accompanied by an informal but active currency market. In the developing (third) phase, as savings and investment increase and social and political institutions proliferate, the banking subsector becomes better organized. With the development of new leading sectors and demand for even higher levels of investments in the fourth phase, the banking sector and the currency markets continue to grow. However, efficiency of financial intermediation through them leaves scope for improvement, and securities markets that provide for the trading of claims issued by economic entities are developed. As development of securities markets progresses, the activities of the informal currency markets diminish. In the final phase, the banking subsector matures with reduced growth, and activities in the secondary securities markets increase dramatically. Financial innovation, in the form of derivative financial instruments based on contingent claims, lends dynamism to the securities markets.

When capital markets move from primitive to more developed phases, institutional infrastructure and supporting services are essential if the issuers of the securities are to disseminate the information to the economic agencies purchasing them. It is well-known that the role of capital markets is to provide mechanisms for 1) allocation efficiency, 2) operational efficiency, and 3) informational efficiency. The allocational role of capital markets implies that the market provides an efficient mechanism for allocating capital from those who save to those willing and able to invest in profitable capital projects. The operational-efficiency aspect of the capital market implies that, for a well-automated microstructure, economic agents are engaged in low-cost transacting. However, the most important element for efficiency is the informational efficiency.

Informational Efficiency

A capital market is said to be informationally efficient if publicly available information is. incorporated into the prices of the securities. In fact, the nature of the information disseminated and the speed of its release play an important role in the market's efficiency. Academic research has invariably reported that the dissemination of information is critical in establishing efficiency in the financial markets (Kumar and Tsetsekos, 1993). If investors have the ability to search and process information without costs, the efficiency in the markets is a foregone conclusion. Because of the costs involved in the search for information and its subsequent processing and dissemination, economies of' scale can be achieved with third-party intermediation in information production.

There are three forms of informational efficiency. The weak form suggests that prices reflect all information contained in the record of past prices. Stock prices reflect past publicly available information. The second form of efficiency, the semi-strong form, posits that prices reflect not only past prices, but also all other published information. According to the semi-strong form of efficiency, a specific unanticipated announcement of earnings, dividends, and mergers is rapidly and accurately impounded into security prices. To the extent that information arrives randomly, so do prices react to the information, hence stock prices follow a random walk. The third form of efficiency is the strong form, which suggests that prices reflect not just public information but all the information that can be acquired by fundamental analysis and inside information. In such a case, the stock market resembles an auction: prices are always fair and no investor would be able to make consistently abnormal returns by having superior information.

Although the efficient-market hypothesis has been frequently misinterpreted, it offers a very strong message to policymakers interested in the development of a country's capital market: Institutional arrangements should be made so that the flow and quality of information to market participants is enhanced to the point that investors and issuers can engage in a fair trading of securities. While this is a precondition for the development of the market, the nature of the information to be disseminated depends not only on atomistic investors but also on credible producers of information.

The Role of a Credit Rating Agency

The role of rating agencies in a well-developed (mature) capital market is twofold: 1) they provide information, which enhances the flow and quality of information regarding the value of securities traded and/or to be issued in the market; and 2) they provide quality certification to issuers.[3] As information intermediaries, rating agencies provide independent opinions as to the quality of securities issued by corporations and governments. This information improves and expands the efficiency in the marketplace and ensures the orderly flow of information from issuers to investors (Moody's Investors Service, 2002).

An additional service offered by a rating agency is quality certification of issuers (U.S. Securities and Exchange Commission, 2003). In markets with considerable asymmetry of information between investors and issuers, good issuers and bad issuers are perceived as the same by investors. However, a good quality issuer may obtain "insurance" from a rating agency, thereby differentiating its quality from that of a bad issuer. The issuer has essentially purchased "insurance" needed for the quality differentiation of its issue.

The output produced from a rating agency is a rating report developed with considerable reputational capital. Bad reports destroy the rating agencies reputational capital and eliminate the future rents associated with services rented. By providing objective reports on worthiness, a rating agency is interested, long term, in building reputational capital in the long term that will be used exclusively to capture rents. Quality certification and reputational capital are interrelated in that reduction of reputational capital is related to reductions in quality certification (Fitch Ratings, 2005).

Who benefits most from the information and assurance provided by published ratings? Investors are not the only beneficiaries of rating services. After all they have access to other more timely sources of information that enable them to price securities without much reliance on current ratings. If the demand for ratings comes from investors, why do issuing companies bear the cost of having their securities rated? Issuers, like many lenders, have incentives to take actions -- after the bonds have been issued -- that would reduce the value of those bonds by transferring wealth to security holders. Because of the possibility of expropriation of wealth, bondholders, unless offered protection from such managerial behavior, will require higher returns for holding these securities.

Kowalski (2003) stresses that ratings help establish the borrowing credibility and credit-worthiness of issuers, which can contribute to the lowering of funding costs and the diversification of funding sources. Bonds with lower ratings indeed pay higher interest costs, but the rating is not to blame (Hand, Holthausen and Leftwich, 1992). A bond rating does not actively determine but simply mirrors the market's assessment of a company's risk. The rating agency initially provides investors with information on company performance especially risk attributes, at very low risk. A rating thus incorporates into a single, easily communicated code all the major ingredients of firm specific risk.[4]

To offer guarantees and protection to investors, issuing firms furnish to the public detailed financial statements and disclosures of indented use of the proceeds. The rating agency then analyzes the company's statements at the time of the issue and offers an independent judgment of the new bond's risk, providing an initial low-cost assessment of the issuing company's credit standing. Furthermore, the rating agency has a comparative advantage in monitoring the changing position of the bond vis-à-vis the company over time. Because these services offer investors both information and greater assurance about future management actions, companies continue to have their bonds rated and to have their performance monitored.

In summary, ratings attest to the relative quality of the issue and the accuracy of the accompanied information about the issuing firm. They further monitor the firm-specific risk over the life of the rated instrument. Extensive academic studies report that ratings and rating changes provide information to capital markets. Unanticipated upgrades result invariably in stock price increases. Conversely, unanticipated announcements of downgrades lead to stock price decreases.

CREDIT RATING AGENCIES AND CAPITAL MARKET EVOLUTION

While the certification feature and the informational enhancement of a rating agency cannot be denied, its role is not always equally important for markets in different phases of development. The following section discusses the role of instruments, information requirements, and the role of rating agencies in each stage of financial-market development. We also enumerate conditions for establishing an effective rating agency.

Phases of Capital-Market Development

Primitive capital and financial markets do not really need a rating agency. In such markets the linking of investors with capital markets and financial intermediaries is just starting. Typically there are a few government instruments with limited maturities. Regulation is in a very formative stage, and the industrial infrastructure is considered fragmented. Only a handful of companies have direct separation of ownership and control.

In the emerging phase of capital markets, corporate debt has been developed and government regulation is well established. There is some secondary market activity and limited participation of institutional investors in trading. Both financial disclosure rules and accounting procedures start to develop and are added to and refined over time.

In a more advanced phase (growth phase), government and corporate securities are traded in the capital markets and all disclosure rules have been developed. Several corporations raise capital through debt or equity securities, and several hybrid securities exist. The secondary market and the swap market have also been developed along with several derivative products (The Securities and Exchange Commission, 1992-1993).

In the developed phase, the capital markets are quite active and trading is considerable. Institutional investors play a prominent role in absorbing, dispensing, and trading securities. The process of securitization enhances liquidity and portfolio investments. The regulatory authorities are dealing with complex cases of insider trading, and the economy consists primarily of companies with distinct separation of ownership from control.

Most likely the role of a rating agency is different in the different phases of capital market development. In the formative phase, the role of the rating agency is to provide information, opinions, and analytical reports on companies. With consistency in reporting, the rating agency assists regulators and accounting organizations interested in the content of those reports. The agency also maintains close communications with the regulatory authorities to ensure that they are aware of the agency's direction.

In the developing phase of capital markets, the credit rating agency begins to build databases on potential issuers and starts preliminary assessment working with issuers, investors, and intermediaries, the agency develops a set of rating criteria and systems. It also maintains close collaboration with an international agency in obtaining technical expertise, support for objectivity and quality control, analytical training and management participation in the organization of the agency.

In the advanced phase of capital-market development, the credit rating agency plays the traditional role as being the evaluator of creditworthiness among a wide range of corporate issues. Important decisions as to the rating scale, along with revisions and additions to the already established criteria, are all important considerations that play a role. The agency creates publications to carry its analyses of issues as well as reviews of ratings. In addition, it should have a system to distribute its ratings to the media. The agency has established a dialogue with regulators and others to share views on accounting and disclosure issues.

In the mature phase, there is competition among rating agencies. Large companies have in-house analytical staff to anticipate rating-agency decisions since these decisions may have an impact on the secondary market. Because the ratings are imbedded in the investment process, all issuers will seek to have their securities rated. Agencies provide the investor with a common language of credit quality across a wide spectrum of debt instrument alternatives. A fully developed securities markets provides better financing costs to issuers. Timely dissemination of ratings is important.

Considerations in Establishing an "Effective" Credit Rating Agency

In principle, in mature capital markets, five conditions make a rating agency creditworthy (Standard and Poor's, 2009b):

Independence. This implies that the rating agency, while maintaining autonomy, should not have conflicts of interest with issuers, investors, financial intermediaries, or other government agencies.

Financial autonomy. Human resources, talent, and required searching expenses are fully covered because of a sound, autonomous financial basis.

Confidentiality of information. Certain information is held in confidence by the rating agency and is disclosed only by the initiative of the issuer.

Acceptability of criteria used in the rating process. The rating agency provides a full disclosure of all criteria applied for the rating of issues; thus, wide acceptability of criteria takes place.

Collaboration with the regulatory authorities. The rating agency has the implicit support of the regulatory authorities, but remains independent of their activities. With a moderate degree of supervision by regulatory authorities, the rating agency can perform a critical role in transmitting information 'to interested parties.

The above conditions have been met in developed markets and have contributed to the development of a flourishing agency-rating industry in the United States and other -developed countries. Currently, there are over 64 credit rating agencies worldwide. The U.S. Securities and Exchange Commission recognizes seven rating agencies, including Moody's Investors Service, Inc., Standard and Poor's Rating Services, and Fitch, Inc.

The sophistication of these agencies analysis parallels the growth and sophistication of capital markets. As markets grow in size and complexity and regulation becomes more important, institutional investors look for objective opinions to assess the quality of issuers. Conversely, corporate issuers are interested in third-party opinions of their securities in order to reduce capital costs. Therefore, on the supply side, quality certification is essential for capital allocation decisions; on the demand side, quality certification is critical to reduce capital-raising costs.

A rating agency in EM and developing countries plays a far more important role than those in developed countries. Because individual investors in emerging capital markets generally lack sophisticated information, rating agencies provide an additional service by making a public good available to all market participants. As such, the rating agency should approach its function from the perspective of an organization that, while profit seeking, is also keen to improve efficiency conditions in the capital markets, especially informational efficiency.

European Union Activities Relating to Credit Rating Agencies

Although it recognized the crucial role of credit rating agencies for both investors and issuers, the European Commission (EC) had not set out specific legislation with respect to rating agencies in European Union (EU) counties until recently. The EC's regulatory approach to rating agencies was last overviewed in its communication of March 11, 2006 (European Union, 2006). In this communication, the EC stated that the three Directives on financial services that are directly or indirectly applicable to credit rating agencies, together with the rating agencies' self-regulation by means of the Code of Conduct of the International Organization of Securities Commissions (IOSCO Code), were sufficient to cover their main activities. This legal framework had to be adopted into national legislation, with the EC monitoring the adoption process very closely. If a member state did not fulfill its obligations, the EC could initiate infringement procedures against it.

The three Directives relevant to credit rating agencies are: (1) the Market Abuse Directive and its implementing Regulation and Directives, which address insider dealing and market manipulation that prevent full market transparency. In general, rating agencies must follow internal policies and procedures designed to ensure objective, independent, and accurate credit ratings; (2) the Capital Requirements Directive, which introduces a capital requirements framework for banks and investment firms. This Directive sets out the main reliability and quality requirements that the rating agencies must meet in order to be recognized as External Credit Assessment Institutions, whose credit assessments are considered essential to the determination of risk weights and consequential capital requirements applied to a bank or investment firm's exposures;[5] and (3) the Markets in Financial Instruments Directive, which is applicable only to rating agencies undertaking investment services and activities over and above their regular credit rating activity. It imposes a number of rules concerning organizational structure and conduct of business.

With respect to the manner in which rating agencies' activities should be conducted, the IOSCO had published its Statement of Principles Regarding the Activities of Credit Rating Agencies in September 2003 (International Organization of Securities Commissions, 2003). This statement aimed at reinforcing investor protection, market fairness, efficiency and transparency in a broader effort to reduce systemic risk. Subsequently, the IOSCO Code of Conduct was created with the intention to apply to rating agencies operating worldwide. The IOSCO Code, as a set of governance rules for rating agencies, aimed at ensuring (1) the quality and integrity of the rating process, including the transparency of used methodologies; (2) the independence of the ratings; and (3) the avoidance of conflict of interest.

On November 12, 2008, the EC proposed a strict regulatory framework for credit rating agencies operating in the EU in response to the ongoing global financial crisis (Commission of the European Communities, 2008).[6] In particular, it proposed a set of rules that aim at closely monitoring rating agencies and avoiding conflicts of interest. Based on the proposed regulation, rating agencies will have to register in a central European database, established by the Committee of European Securities Regulators, so as users of their services to be able to quickly verify the accuracy of their predictions and compare them with competitors.

For increasing the transparency of the rating process, the proposed rules require that rating agencies reveal their methodologies, models, and rating assumptions so that investors have a better understanding of the conclusions reached by the agencies. The supervision of rating agencies remains a national activity, while the EC will ensure that supervisors do not interfere in the content of the ratings to guarantee the independence of ratings. Finally, the EC stated that the proposed rules were based on the IOSCO Code, thus ensuring consistency with international regulation, although it also pointed out that it had proposed stricter rules in those areas where the IOSCO standards were not sufficient to restore market confidence and ensure investor protection.

IMPLICATIONS FROM ESTABLISHING A CREDIT RATING AGENCY IN AN EM COUNTRY

The Benefits of a Credit Rating Agency: Microperspective

The role of a rating agency in an EM economy is important, as its opinions can entail substantial benefits (Papaioannou and Tsetsekos, 1994). In particular, they provide concrete value to the following constituencies in the economy:

- **Investors:** Investors benefit from a rating agency because they obtain an accrued assessment of default risk of certain securities. Ratings provide value principally to institutional investors and pension plans who usually own most of the public funds. All these investors expect the ratings to provide 1) an accurate prediction of the likelihood of default, 2) an assessment of risk premium or added return demanded by investors when purchasing a given security to compensate for the risk that the security will not perform as promised, 3) comparison of risk-adjusted yields over the range of potential purchases or the monitoring of portfolio holdings in comparison with· all other securities available in the market place, and 4) analytical support for decisions on corporate lending, interbank loans, trade finance, swap agreements, and other counterpart risk decisions. Pension investments will be placed in those securities that provide good investment grade and protection for investors.

- **Issuers of financial instruments:** The value of ratings to issuers include: 1) wider access to investor capital, thus furnishing lower-cost borrowing and added, financial flexibility. Substantial savings in funding costs arise from the substitution of bank guarantees for a high rating from a rating agency. Rated issues can come to the market quickly, since the market with many ratings outstanding gives a rated issue a benchmark value against which investor demand for pricing of the issue can be assessed, and 2) rated issues attract more attention from institutional investors since they may be prohibited from purchasing unrated issues.
- **Financial Intermediaries:** Bankers and other intermediaries who underwrite securities find ratings useful in the pricing, marketing, and placing of securities because 1) ratings may help to broaden the investor base and enhance demand, 2) a pool of rated debt securities may help create a risk-based price structure in the market, enhancing underwriters' ability to judge returns that investors are likely to demand on a new issue of a given credit quality, and 3) ratings help intermediaries monitor the risk and pricing of securities held in their own portfolios, either on behalf of clients or for their own accounts.
- **Regulatory organizations:** A rating agency can help regulators promote stability and efficiency in the capital markets by 1) fostering easier communications between issuers and investors, opening up a cost-efficient means of financing to private-sector business and enhancing information dissemination, 2) counteracting rumors and speculation with a rating system that is publicly available and prudently and continuously updated, 3) promoting prudent investment decision making, and 4) allocating resources efficiently, especially scarce capital.

In addition, a rating agency provides the following "invisible" benefits:

- **Protection to investors:** A capital market enables investors to transform passive savings into investments in business enterprises. Inadequate investor protection jeopardizes the supply of much-needed capital to the corporate sector. The existence of ratings contributes to investor confidence, which maintains the flow of capital for economic development.
- **Risk assessment:** The existence of a rating system enables investors to clearly and simply assess the riskiness of an investment and therefore its desirability and suitability. Also, a rating system may help to easier resolve debt restructurings at periods of financial distress (Moody's Investors Service, 2009; Standard and Poor's, 2009a; Fitch Ratings, 2009).

- **Corporate control:** A rating agency indirectly evaluates the quality of a firm's management. A higher rating generally reflects better management of capital resources and real assets. Typically, higher-rated issuers have the ability to attract more capital resources than unrated issuers. This suggests that capital is given to those able to manage it more efficiently. A bypass to a corporate will be the evolution of corporate control and discipline for financing and investment decisions.
- **Capital market development:** High quality credit rating agencies play a key role in developing deep and liquid capital markets, as they reduce the information asymmetry between investors/lenders and issuers about the creditworthiness of institutions and instruments (Asian Development Bank, 2005). To facilitate unbiased and trustworthy rating agencies, appropriate regulation is required to ensure that issuers release correct information. This developmental aspect of rating agencies also underscores the need for their close collaboration with government authorities and regulators.

Macroeconomic Consequences: A Credit Rating Agency and the Conduct of Monetary Policy

Without any doubt, the activities of a rating agency in an EM economy will produce clear benefits at the micro and firm-specific level. However, the function of the rating agency should be viewed in relation to the regulatory activities of the central bank. To the extent that the rating agency is one part of the country's financial infrastructure, it is essential to analyze the interdependencies of a rating agency with other parts of the system and, especially, with the regulatory authorities. An issue requiring systematic analysis is the linkage between the activities of a rating agency and the contact of monetary policy.

The conduct of monetary policy is assisted with the presence of a rating agency because of two considerations: 1) the implicit monetary surveillance role of the rating agency in sector credit and financial conditions; and 2) the international implications of the informational role of a rating agency in attracting foreign investments in an emerging economy. We thus analyze the implications derived from the interplay of a rating agency on the conduct of monetary policy.

The monetary surveillance role of a rating agency. Disclosure of information about ratings is presented with sector analysis and in-depth study of industry conditions, not only at the domestic level but also at the international level. Information derived from the industry sector has feed-back effects on the monetary authorities. First, it allows the central bank to accurately assess credit conditions, profitability, and cash flows in sectors of the economy. The evaluation of sector performance based on the information provided by the rating agency offers monetary authorities additional indications of the state of the economy, thus to appropriate, monetary action. Second, information provided by the central bank about credit conditions in the general economy and industry sector are invaluable to the rating agency information set.

Apparently, the rating agency in collaboration with the central bank offers complementary information about the state of industry sectors. Such information is used for the conduct of monetary policy, in the sense that the monetary authorities also respond to such information by providing corrective actions in the economy. In turn, these actions are interpreted by the rating agency for accurate assessment of industry and firm-specific performance. In very simple terms, the informational role of the rating agency offers central bank regulators an additional surveillance mechanism for the conduct of monetary authorities.

The international implications for foreign investments. To the extent that the country's economy interacts with other economies, the rating agency provides credible information about domestic firms and sector performance. To the extent that there is capital mobility, such information is invaluable to foreign investors for relative comparisons of domestic and foreign industry sectors and firms. Comparisons allow investors to make prudent foreign direct investment decisions in real assets or portfolio investment decisions.

The role of a rating agency in an EM country is thus much more broad in that it provides accurate credible assessment of a country's investment opportunities to foreign investors. Moreover, the rating agency serves as a link between foreign markets and domestic markets, thus reducing any informational gaps among the central bank's authorities and the foreign parties.

Although the implications for attracting foreign direct investment are quite straightforward, the monetary authorities' tasks are much more complex for the following reasons. *First,* foreign direct investments reduce net additional foreign borrowing, .a situation leading to availability of more capital in the economy. All other things being equal, this results in a downward pressure on domestic interest rates and a reduction in the marginal cost of capital for corporations, conditions that enhance domestic economic growth. Therefore, an agency's dissemination of information that leads to foreign direct investments results in a reduction in interest rates an effect having a more profound impact for a more liberalized economy.

Second, additional foreign capital improves the foreign exchange reserves of the central bank. However, increases in foreign exchange reserves inevitably require that the central authorities carry out procedures for managing foreign exchange risk exposure and eventually deal with hedging foreign currencies.

In conclusion, the role of a rating agency in a developing country should be viewed not myopically, but rather on a more integrated basis with special attention to the interactions with the monetary authorities. Information disseminated by the rating agencies has value not only to domestic issuers, but also to international investors whose foreign investment decisions have serious consequences on the central bank's monetary policy. Not only are interest rates affected by such decisions, but there are also clear policy implications for the management of the central bank's foreign exchange reserves.

DESIGNING A CREDIT RATING AGENCY FOR THE FINANCIAL MARKET OF AN EM COUNTRY

Commission of a Feasibility Study

Prior to establishing a rating agency in an emerging financial market, it is necessary to review and catalog all factors contributing to the development of an agency. The analysis should be performed by independent parties having knowledge of the institutional framework in the local economy and abroad. Often, the analysis is conducted within the framework of a feasibility study aiming at identifying policy-induced distortions, regulatory inefficiencies, and informational gaps in the financial markets that may weaken the role of the agency. Results of the feasibility study will uncover areas that need improvement, disclosure requirements that need refinement, and other institutional aspects that the government needs to consider. It is quite possible that the feasibility study may offer a negative recommendation on developing the rating agency.

To avoid issues of subjectivity and lack of credibility, the country's regulatory authority, the central bank or the Ministry of Finance should commission the feasibility study. The study should offer regulators, central bankers, and appropriate government officials clear recommendations for the necessary conditions to be met for developing an institutional infrastructure that allows the rating agency to function appropriately.

Sequencing of Reforms

Subsequent to feasibility study, the regulatory authorities need to add and/or appropriately modify the suggestions provided in the study and develop a timetable for implementing the recommendations. Such a timetable may include legal and regulatory schemes, establishing uniform disclosure rules, and eliminating regulatory inconsistencies and undue duplication. It is also important to prioritize the .reforms and examine consistency and/or deviation of the institutional framework with that of other developed markets and similar emerging-country economies.

Action Program and the Proposed Administrative Structure

The action program encompasses the necessary development of a legal and informational framework through appropriate legislative steps and initiatives. A timetable to be communicated to the institutional constituencies will allow participation and dialogue. In the following discussion, we tentatively present the conditions for an effective administrative structure.

There should be complete separation between decision management and decision control within the rating agency. Such a separation will eliminate possible conflicts of interest between issuers and rating personnel. The board of the rating agency should reflect a broad participation of constituents from the financial and economic sectors.

Representatives from the EM country's committee for the capital market (i.e., the country's SEC), from the country's stock exchange, the association of issuing firms, the banking industry and broker-dealers all should be considered for board membership, and should have only one vote. Assurances should be given that ratings of securities will always be ratified by the board by majority vote.

Collaborative Arrangements and Other Related Issues

As the financial markets become more globalized and international investors and issuers move across borders, the rating agency should establish collaborative arrangements with· other foreign institutions and seek technical expertise for multimarket securities issues. In addition, technical assistance by international rating agencies can improve the quality of the information produced and further refine the scoring mechanism used in assigning credit risk to various firms.

As a *first step,* collaboration must be sought by major banks with considerable investments in corporate and government paper. Participating banks will be informed of the benefits and will be asked to allocate capital for the formation of the agency.

In the *second step,* the agency will build databases on potential issuers and develops preliminary assessment of critical performance characteristics of corporations under consideration. With the assistance of regulators, intermediaries, and issuers, the agency develops a set of rating criteria and systems.

In the *third step,* the agency develops performance-scoring mechanisms and presents rankings of companies based on objective evaluation criteria. The agency creates publications to carry its analyses of issues as well as reviews of performance.

In the *fourth step,* the agency seeks collaboration with an international agency.

Such a collaboration leads to analytical training for staff and assistance in setting up an organizational structure for the newly established agency.

CONCLUDING REMARKS

In this chapter we discuss the role of credit rating agencies in the development of an emerging financial market. We classify the benefits of a rating agency in two categories. At the micro level, rating agencies provide quality certification and improve informational efficiency in the capital markets. In this context, rating agencies play a major role in determining the ability of the institutions that they rate to raise funds and in establishing the rate of interest that these institutions need to pay to obtain credit. At the macro level, rating agencies assist in the contact of an emerging country's economic policy, e.g., for monetary policy by offering a supplementary surveillance mechanism to central bankers, and providing invaluable information (i.e., objective and independent assessment of the credit risk of institutions and instruments) to foreign investors.

We have highlighted several conditions for an effective rating agency in an EM country setting, and outlined its potential benefits to several constituencies. The establishment of a local credit rating system is also an effective process for developing an international investor base for local debt instruments, as local rating agencies are able to maintain frequent contact with local borrowers and thus offer a more timely evaluation of the country's institutions and instruments. Finally, we have tentatively presented a structure for the rating agency and propose that the government authorities commission a more detailed study on the feasibility of establishing a rating agency in an EM country.

REFERENCES

Asian Development Bank. (2005). The Role of Credit Rating Agencies in Asia's Emerging Bond Markets. In *38th Annual Meeting Seminar*, Istanbul, Turkey.

Bossone, B., & Promisel, L. (1999). *The Role of Financial Self-Regulation in Developing Economies, Financial Sector* (Web Note). Washington, DC: The World Bank.

Commission of the European Communities. (2008). *Proposal for a Regulation of the European Parliament and of the Council on Credit Rating Agencies* (COD/2008/0217), Brussels.

Elkhoury, M. (2008). Credit Rating Agencies and Their Potential Impact on Developing Countries. In *United Nations Conference on Trade and Development, Discussion Paper No. 186,* (UNCTAD/OSG/DP/2008/1), United Nations.

Fitch Ratings. (2005, February 8). *Statement of Stephen W. Joynt, President and Chief Executive Officer, Fitch Ratings, in the Hearing of the U.S. Senate Committee on Banking, Housing and Urban Affairs on Examining the Role of Credit Rating Agencies in the Capital Markets*. European Union. (2006, March 11). Communication from the Commission on Credit Rating Agencies (2006/C 59/02). *Official Journal of the European Union, C*(59/02).

Fitch Ratings. (2009, March 3). *Coercive Debt Exchange Criteria.*

Hand, J. R., Holthausen, R. W., & Leftwich, R. W. (1992). The Effect Of Bond Rating Agency Announcements On Bond And Stock Prices. *The Journal of Finance*, *47*(2), 733–752. doi:10.2307/2329121

International Monetary Fund. (1999). Emerging Markets in the New Financial System: Nonstandard Responses to External Pressure and the Role of the Major Credit Rating Agencies in Global Financial Markets. In *World Economic and Financial Surveys, International Capital Markets: Developments, Prospects, and Key Policy Issues*. Washington DC: International Monetary Fund.

International Organization of Securities Commissions. (2003, September 25). *IOSCO Statement of Principles Regarding the Activities of Credit Rating Agencies: A Statement of the Technical Committee of the International Organization of Securities Commissions*.

Kowalski, P. (2003, May 8). *Challenges Facing Rating Agencies In Emerging Markets*. Bucharest: Fitch Ratings.

Kumar, P. C., & Tsetsekos, G. P. (1992). Securities Market Development and Economic Growth. In K. P. Fischer & G. J. Papaioannou (Eds.), *Business Finance In Less Developed Capital Markets* (pp. 55-65). London: Greenwood Press.

Kumar, P. C., & Tsetsekos, G. P. (1993). Managerial Ownership and Stock Price Reaction to Bond Downgrades. *Applied Financial Economics*, *3*(1), 357–364. doi:10.1080/758534950

Moody's Investors Service. (2002, November 21). *Written Statement of Raymond W. McDaniel, President, Moody's Investors Service, Before the United States Securities and Exchange Commission on Credit Rating Agencies*.

Moody's Investors Service. (2009, March). *Approach to Evaluating Distress Exchanges*.

Papaioannou, M. G., & Duke, L. K. (1993). The Internationalization of Emerging Equity Markets. *Finance & Development*, *30*(3), 36–39.

Papaioannou, M. G., & Tsetsekos, G. P. (1994, February 15). *Developing the Financial Infrastructure in Greece: The Role of Rating Agencies* (Drexel University College of Business and Administration Faculty Working Paper Series, WP72-93).

U.S. Securities and Exchange Commission. (2003, January). *Report on the Role and Function of Credit Rating Agencies in the Operation of Securities Markets*.

U.S. Securities and Exchange Commission. (1992-1993). *International Institute of Securities Market Development: Notes On Developing Capital Markets*. Mimeo.

Standard and Poor's. (2009a, January 28). *Ratings Implications of Exchange Offers and Similar Restructurings*.

Standard and Poor's. (2009b, April 10). An Examination of How Investor Needs are Served by Various Ratings Business Models: Ensuring Analytical Independence and Freedom from Conflicts of Interest of Credit Rating Firms [White Paper].

ENDNOTES

1. The liberalization of financial services, especially regulatory changes centered on the liberalization of the banking sector, create the incentives for the development of investment banking and other capital market services.
2. Kumar and Tsetsekos (1992) present a theory linking the evolution of capital market and financial market to the well-known concept of life-cycle. Papaioannou and Duke (1973) argue that effective mobilization of domestic and foreign capital resources occurs at a more advanced phase of development of an emerging equity market.
3. Rating agencies emerged in the United States in the beginning of the 20th century, mainly as providers of information on the financial state of firms. In 1909, John Moody started to publish ratings of US railroad bonds, extending them soon to utility and industrial bonds.
4. In this connection, a crucial question is: If the information provided by bond ratings reflects the firm's characteristics, then what is the value of the credibility established by the rating agency?
5. Basel II has also contributed to the expansion of the role of credit rating agencies by incorporating their ratings into rules for setting weights for credit risk of rated institutions.
6. A European Parliament decision on this proposal is currently anticipated on April 21, 2009.

Chapter 8
Does Financial Liberalization and Trade Openness Promote Growth in South Asia?

Muhammad Arshad Khan
Pakistan Institute of Development Economics, Pakistan

ABSTRACT

This chapter examines the hypotheses that trade liberalization and financial liberalization jointly enhances economic growth in the four South Asian countries including Bangladesh, India, Pakistan and Sri Lanka for the period 1970-2007 using bounds testing approach to cointegration. The results suggest that in the long-run except for Bangladesh, financial development plays no role in promoting economic growth in these countries. Furthermore, the results suggest that trade openness plays a significant role in promoting economic growth in Bangladesh and India, while exerts negative effect on Pakistan and no effect on Sri Lanka. The share of domestic investment influences real output significantly in Bangladesh, India and Pakistan. In the long- as well as short-run two-way causality between real output, trade openness, share of investment and inflation rate exists for the case of Bangladesh and India. For the case of India two-way causality between finance and growth exists in the short-run. For the case of Pakistan, there is an evidence of long-run causality between real output, finance, trade openness, share of investment and inflation rate. However, in the short-run, two-way causality between real output, trade openness and share of investment is existed and one-way causality between inflation rate, trade openness and share of investment is also observed. No evidence of short-run causality between finance and growth and vice versa for Pakistan has been seen. Finally, for Sri Lanka, an evidence of long-run causality between real output, finance, trade openness and investment share has been found. In the short-run one-way causality between finance-growth, trade-finance, trade-growth and trade-investment has been obtained. These mixed results suggest that the authorities may focuses more and more on the trade liberalization. In addition, there is a need to further deepen the banking and stock markets and provide investment friendly environment to enhance domestic investment which, in turn, promotes economic growth.

DOI: 10.4018/978-1-61520-709-1.ch008

INTRODUCTION

Economic growth is one of the major macroeconomic policy objectives of trade liberalization, financial development and information technology (Temple, 1999 and Santos-Paulino and Thirlwall, 2004). Economists are widely accepted the idea that financial repression and trade distortions impedes the process of economic development (Atje and Jovanovic, 1993; King and Levine, 1992, 1993, 1994; Levine and Renelt, 1992; Roubini and Sala-i-Martin, 1991 and Blackburn and Hung, 1998). Literature suggest that trade liberalization and financial development are predominant sources of comparative advantage and both liberalization policies reduces the inefficiencies in the production process and influences economic growth positively through a more efficient allocation of resources; greater competition; increase in the flow of knowledge and investment and foster capital accumulation and technical progress (Santos-Paulino and Thirlwall, 2004 and Hur *et al.*, 2006). The rationale behind this argument is that countries with more open trade and financial policies may grow faster than those with restricted trade and financial policies.[1] The policymakers are now very much convinced that both liberalization policies are expected to exert positive impact on economic growth (Jin, 2000; Fry, 1995, 1997; Darrat, 1999; Levine, 1997, Mckinnon, 1973; Shaw, 1973; World Bank, 1987, 1989; Balassa, 1971, 1985; Bhagwati, 1978; Feder, 1983; Krueger, 1978 and Tyler, 1981).[2] The policymakers also realized that the object of building a powerful and prosperous nation could not be achieved with out the introduction of information technology (IT). Information and Communication Technology (ICT) offer a higher potential for making a positive contribution towards sustainable development by reducing the information and transportation costs, and facilitates cheap, equitable and resource-efficient access to information, accumulated knowledge and learning opportunities for all the citizens of a country.

A large body of literature considers various channels through which financial development, trade openness and information technology affect economic growth (Levine *et al.*, 2000, Feldstein, 2003 and Frankel and Romer, 1999). Kletzer and Bardhan (1987) and Baldwin (1989) argue that countries with relatively well-developed financial system have comparative advantage in industries that relay more on external financial resources. Similarly, Beck (2003) and Svaleryd and Vlachos (2005) find the evidence that countries with a well-developed financial sector enjoys easier access to external finance than those without it, and tend to specialize in industries that are more dependent on external resources (Hur, *et al.*, 2006). Rajan and Zingales (1998) argue that financial development serves as a source of comparative advantage and trade. This means that cheap access to external finance and financial development produces favorable impact on economic growth. Similarly, IT may affect economic activities through improving the quality of existing services, creating new services, raising labour productivity, increasing capital intensity, enhances economies of scale and creating new economic structure.

Over the past few decades researchers have shown that financial sector development plays a significant role in economic growth. In particular, they emphasizes the role of financial development in channeling savings to productive investment, improving corporate governance, reducing transaction and information costs, specialization and innovations and encouraging the adoption of new technology (Bencivenga and Smith, 1999; De Gregorio and Guidotti, 1995; Greenwood and Jovanovic, 1990 and Levine, 2004). Similarly, trade liberalization may helps to produce spillover effects over the rest of the economy through the efficiency, innovations, imitations and promotes overall economic development (Dodaro, 1993 and Deme, 2002).

A wide range of additional growth-inducing benefits have been attributed to trade including capacity utilization, enlarging market size, economies of scale and specialization effects, technological improvements, capital formation, employment creation and efficient management due to greater international competitive pressure (Balassa, 1978, Keesing, 1967, 1979, Krueger, 1988, Bhagwati and Srivasan, 1979, Khalid and Teck-Cheng, 1997 and Dodaro, 1993). These components induce growth of output. In addition, the presence of domestic market constraints impedes growth and trade and provides a "vent-for-surplus" type effects (Dodaro, 1993). Trade opens the possibility for developing countries to earn foreign exchange to import capital goods, raw materials and modern technology for the expansion of domestic production (Dodaro, 1993).

Trade is expected to influence economic growth through a variety of channels. These include: improving resource allocation in line with social marginal costs and benefits, free access to modern technologies, availability of inputs and material, advantage of the economies of scale and scope, favourable environment of growth, transfer of know-how and shakeup of industries that may create conducive environment for growth. Furthermore, trade may affect growth through the deepening of export sector and generate externalities to increase productivity of other sectors of the economy (Dornbusch, 1992 and Lewer and Berg, 2003).

Another factor that may effect economic growth is the suitability of trade and financial policies and reforming the financial and trade sectors may have important implications for economic growth. The effects of trade liberalization may depend on the level of financial development, and economic growth is dependent on both trade and financial factors. Both liberalization policies are expected to increase the productivity through reducing inefficiencies in the investment process.

Many developing countries have undergone extensive trade liberalization since the mid-1970. However, South Asian countries including Bangladesh, India, Pakistan and Sri Lanka have shifted their attention towards free markets and outward-orientation policies since 1990. These policies affect exports and imports and produces positive impact on growth. Thus, an empirical research is needed to determine the effectiveness of financial and trade liberalization policies with regard to growth in South Asian countries. To determine the relative impact of liberalization policies an empirical analysis is needed because these countries followed restrictive policies until early 1990.

Like financial development and trade openness, the availability of ICT accelerates the domestic productivity. However, incentives and institutional structures are critical ingredients for productivity acceleration. Without strong incentives and appropriate institutional arrangements, the development of ICT would not be expected to generate faster productivity growth (Feldstein, 2003). Diffusion of ICT offers a combination of employment opportunities and export revenue from hardware and software. Information technology (IT)-related services enhances economic growth and reduces the balance of payments vulnerability. Developments in IT sector reduce technological and financial barriers to entry of small players in the industry. The liberalization of imports and the relaxation of regulations on foreign firms have increased the share of international players in the domestic PC market.

Existing studies examine the impact of financial and trade liberalization on growth separately despite their shared importance in increasing efficiency of investment and growth. To our best knowledge, only Siddiki (2002), Khan and Qayyum (2006) and Mallick and Agerwal (2007) have examined the joint impact of finance and trade on growth for Bangladesh, India and Pakistan. However, there is need to assess the relative impact of both liberalization policies for major SAARC (South Asian Association for Regional Cooperation) countries on country-by-country basis. The present study is an attempt to fill up this gap.

Given the paramount importance of finance, trade and information technology in the development process, this chapter analyzes the role of finance, trade and information technology and seeks the possible answer that does financial development, trade openness and information technology promotes economic growth? This study focuses only on the role of finance, trade and information technology in the development process. The rest of the chapter is organized as: Section 2 reviews some theoretical and empirical literature. A brief review of policies related to finance; trade and information technology opted by the SAARC countries are also discussed in this section. Model specification, methodology and data related issues are discussed in section 3. Empirical results are interpreted in section 4, while some concluding remarks are given in the final section.

TRADE AND FINANCIAL LIBERALIZATION POLICIES IN SOUTH ASIA

Many economists (Anderson and Tarp, 2003, Khan and Senhadji, 2000, and Levine, 2002, Fase and Abma, 2003, Tadesse, 2002, Iimi, 2004 and Ang, 2008 among others) have argued that financial system plays a crucial role in mobilizing and intermediating savings more efficiently to productive sectors. A healthy financial system is an integral part of the development process in designing policies for economic growth. Inadequately developed financial system may be crisis-prone with potentially adverse effects. Therefore, the important role of financial intermediaries and financial markets merits more attention from researchers and policymakers (Ang, 2008). Market-based financial policies have strengthened the microeconomic foundation of the banking system.

Ansari (1998, 2002) has noted that financial development includes financial broadening and deepening. Financial broadening implies increase in the number of financial instruments and institutions, while financial deepening implies growth of financial services, which are commonly measured by the ratio of monetary aggregates to GDP. Similarly, financial liberalization involves deregulation of interest rates, removal of controls on the capital movements and elimination of other restrictions.

During the1970s and the 1980s many South Asian economies have pursued import substitution industrialization policies to strengthen industrial base, to achieve self reliance, protect infant industries, protect domestic economies from external shocks stemming from international capital markets, reduce the balance of payment deficit and productive use of foreign exchange scarce resources (Siddiki, 2002 and Khan and Qayyum, 2006). To achieve these objectives the authorities have imposed various quantitive and qualitative restrictions on trade and payments system. But these policies do not register any significant impact on the external sector. Restrictive policies results high macroeconomic imbalances, growing inefficiencies and losses in the public sector and eroded the business confidence. To restore the business confidence, South Asian countries implemented a wide range of financial and trade reforms in the early 1990s. This section briefly reviews the financial and trade policies.

Financial Policies

Prior to the 1990s the financial sector of South Asian countries remained heavily controlled. Interest rates were set administratively and were usually negative in real terms. Monetary policy was conducted through the direct allocation of credit. Money markets were under-developed, and bonds and equity markets were almost non-existent. Commercial banks had to lend to priority sectors with little concern for the borrowing firm's profitability (Siddiki, 2002, Khan and Qayyum, 2006, Mallick and Agarwal, 2007, Prasad and Ghosh, 2007, Kabir and Hoque, 2007 and Khan, 2008 among others). These inefficiencies and distortions were exacerbated severe macroeconomic imbalances during the 1980s. To overcome these problems and to enhance economic growth, South Asian countries have implemented a wide range of financial liberalization measures since 1990. The main objectives of these liberalization policies is to make their financial industry more competitive and transparent by privatizing state-owned commercial banks, liberalizing interest rates and credit ceilings, strengthening governance and supervision, standardizing accounting and auditing system, and adopting market-based indirect system of monetary, exchange rate and credit management (Ansari, 1998, Ahluwalia, 2002, Iimi, 2004 and Khan, 2008).

To assess the financial development we have used the ratio of broad money to GDP (M2/GDP) as a measure of financial depth, ratio of private-sector credit to GDP and stock market capitalization to GDP (King and Levine, 1993a, 1993b; Demetriades and Hussein, 1996; Levine, 1997 and Beck *et al.*, 2000). Tables 1-4 present the magnitude of financial development of each country.

It is evident from Tables 1-4 that for each country all the financial development indicators are showing significant growth over the period 1990-2006. It can be seen from Table 1-4 that a steady growth in M2/GDP, showing the deepening of financial sector of each country. The other measure of financial development is the ratio of private-sector credit to GDP which indicates efficient allocation of funds by the banking sector (Beck *et al.*, 2000 and Levine *et al.*, 2000). Furthermore, private-sector credit to GDP is considered more efficient and relevant in making investment decisions. The growth in private- sector credit relative to GDP plays an important role in stimulating the economic activities through the mobilization of financial resources. This ratio has witnessed a substantial rise over the years in each country, showing improvement in the financial deepening

Table 1. Indicators of financial development for Bangladesh

Indicator	1990	1995	2000	2001	2002	2003	2004	2005	2006	2007	
M2/GDP	23.3	28.8	34.6	46.5	49.8	51.4	53.05	56.0	59.22	59.21	
Currency/M2	12.3	14.3	14.0	10.6	9.9	9.1	9.4	9.8	12.0	11.4	
Currency/GDP	2.9	4.1	4.8	4.9	4.8	4.7	5.0	5.5	7.1	6.7	
Private credit/GDP	16.7	20.9	24.7	27.8	30.2	30.2	32.1	34.0	36.15	37.29	
Stock Market											
Capitalization/GDP	1.2	3.5	2.7	2.6	2.5	3.2	5.9	5.1	5.8	-	

Source: calculated using IFS data (CD-ROM, 2008)

Table 2. Indicators of financial development for India

Indicator	1990	1995	2000	2001	2002	2003	2004	2005	2006	2007	
M2/GDP	42.74	44.05	55.62	58.60	63.50	63.80	65.87	66.74	70.20	69.85	
Currency/M2	20.65	21.64	17.43	17.18	16.72	17.03	16.60	16.58	15.95	15.09	
Currency/GDP	8.83	9.53	9.70	10.07	10.62	10.87	10.93	11.06	11.19	12.89	
Private credit/GDP	25.24	22.77	28.85	29.05	32.76	31.94	36.88	40.80	44.99	47.42	
Stock Market											
Capitalization/GDP	12.31	37.65	33.08	23.33	25.44	45.93	55.74	68.64	90.36	-	

See note below table 1

and intermediation. The other indicators of financial deepening include currency to M2 ratio and currency to GDP ratio, reflecting the increase in total deposits relative to currency in circulation and degree of monetization. The decreasing trend in these ratios, showing increased intermediation in the each country. Finally, the increasing behaviour of stock market capitalization relative to GDP favours the increased financial deepening and intermediation. Overall, South Asian countries have made remarkable progress in promoting financial deepening and intermediation over the period 1990-2006.

Trade Policies

Many developing countries have shifted their attention from protection policies to free trade policies (Dornbusch, 1992). Trade liberalization and market-oriented reforms had started in South Asia in the early 1980s and intensified in the 1990s. With the adoption of outward-orientation trade and investment policies during the 1990s, South Asian countries are now more integrated than before the 1990. Globalization and WTO regime enables these economies to reap the benefits from emerging international specialization, obviates the constraints on their development by expansion the size of the markets and enhance the capacity of absorbing spillovers of knowledge creation in different parts of the world (RIS, 2004 and Qayyum and Khan, 2008).

Most of the South Asian countries have adopted import substitution policies for nearly four decades. These policies include high tariffs, different kinds of non-tariff barriers, exchange rate and other

Table 3. Indicators of financial development for Pakistan

Indicator	1990	1995	2000	2001	2002	2003	2004	2005	2006	2007	
M2/GDP	39.24	43.57	38.93	39.64	43.80	46.99	48.42	48.96	48.03 50.05		
Currency/M2	37.56	28.78	27.80	26.02	25.30	25.04	23.99	23.00	23.98 23.14		
Currency/GDP	14.73	12.54	10.82	10.31	11.08	11.77	11.62	11.26	11.52 11.58		
Private credit/GDP	24.22	24.21	22.53	22.02	21.92	24.87	28.74	28.65	28.95 29.42		
Stock Market											
Capitalization/GDP	7.23	17.03	12.05	8.65	16.40	23.68	24.05	30.95	35.33	-	

See note below table 1

Table 4. Indicators of financial development for Sri Lanka

Indicator	1990	1995	2000	2001	2002	2003	2004	2005	2006	2007	
M2/GDP	28.26	38.85	38.44	39.02	38.05	39.44	41.11	41.72	41.04	39.88	
Currency/M2	24.34	16.27	12.96	11.93	12.10	11.91	11.60	11.15	11.20 10.47		
Currency/GDP	6.88	6.32	4.98	4.66	4.60	4.70	4.77	4.65	4.59	4.11	
Private credit/GDP	19.62	31.07	28.83	28.11	27.63	28.92	30.62	32.90	33.97	33.26	
Stock Market											
Capitalization/GDP	11.46	16.00	7.06	8.81	10.27	14.93	18.24	24.3	28.81	-	

See note below table 1

Table 5. Summary of trade policy regime in South Asia

Policy Measures	Bangladesh	India	Pakistan	Sri Lanka
Exchange Rate Policy	Unified Free Float	Unified Free Float	Unified Free Float	Unified Free Float
Payment Convertibility				
Current Account	Yes	Yes	Yes	Yes
Capital Account	No	Yes Limited	No	No
Import Restrictions				
General Import Licensing	No, but some restrictions	No	No	No
Some QRs on imports	Yes	Yes	Yes	Yes, minor
State Import Monopolies	No	Yes	No	No
Tariff Structure on May 2003				
Top normal CD rate	32.5	30	25	25
Average CD rate	16.5	26.8	18.2	9.6
Average CD + other Protective taxes	21.9	32.7	18.2	12.5
No. of normal CD slabs	5	7	4	5
Uses anti-dumping	No	Yes	Yes	No
Export Policies				
Some export QRs	Yes	Yes	No	No
Some export taxes	Yes	Yes	Yes	No
Some direct export subsidies	No	Yes	Yes	No
Fright subsidies for new market and new products.	-	Up to 25%	-	-
Trade Openness (1990)	19.56	15.71	35.12	67.23
Trade Openness (2006)	44.22	48.78	38.61	74.78

Source: Din (2004), World Bank (2003), RIS (2004) and Qayyum and Khan (2008). QRs indicate quota restrictions and CD indicate custom duty.

administrative controls. However, these policies failed to promote import substitution industrialization. The protectionist trade regime has generated anti-export bias, inefficiencies and promoted rent seeking.[3] In 1977 Sri Lanka started liberalizing its external sector. Following Sri Lanka, India and Pakistan started partial liberalization from the mid-1980s. Trade liberalization includes a variety of measures including the reduction of anti-export bias, rationalization of tariff structure and remove of other quantitive restrictions. The main features of trade policy regime in South Asia are depicted in Table 5.

It is evident from Table 5 that all countries in the South Asian region abolished the quantitive restrictions. On May 2003, the maximum custom duty is 25% in Pakistan and Sri Lanka, whereas it is 30% in India and 32.7% in Bangladesh. The average custom duty is 32.7% in India, 18.2% in Pakistan, 21.9% in Bangladesh and 12.5% in Sri Lanka. Trade openness has increased in all countries and higher increase take place in Sri Lanka, followed by India, Bangladesh and Pakistan.

ICT Policies

It is now globally recognized that the development of ICT infrastructure plays a significant role in promoting socio-economic development and modernizing various sectors of the economy. Growth of ICT services provides a cost and time effective mechanism for flow of information, diffusion of knowledge and technology (Ketaja and Jha, 2008). In many developing countries, output and employment growth is increasing faster in high-technology and science-based sectors compared to the manufacturing averages (OECD, 2000, 2003, 2004). This phenomenon has convinced many policy-makers and nations that now-a-days technology plays an important in

Table 6. ICT Indicators for selected countries in Asia-Pacific region (2006-07)

Country	Total Teledensity*	Mobile Density	Internet Subscription	TV Sets	PCs
Bangladesh	15.00	13.25	0.31	10.59	2.42
China	62.62	34.83	10.35	37.99	4.22
Hong Kong	248.15	131.45	64.90	48.79	71.10
India	19.38	14.83	5.44	7.80	1.54
Indonesia	34.87	28.30	7.18	15.16	2.90
Japan	134.12	91.10	86.80	84.26	77.50
Malaysia	92.28	75.45	43.77	21.88	21.54
Pakistan	45.04	40.09	3.50	9.10	2.35
Singapore	151.66	109.34	65.00	20.59	74.00
Sri Lanka	34.89	25.88	2.05	12.47	3.54
Thailand	73.94	63.02	13.07	28.64	15.50

Source: ITU Website/PTA-2006/2007 and www.statpak.gov.pk

*Total teledensity includes fixed, WLL and Cellar mobile teledensities and were surpassing 100 per cent, indicates that some people subscribe to more than one telephone connection.

improving economic performance (Ning, 2007). Developing economies will grow faster as long as they liberalize their trade and invest in modern technology, infrastructure, education, creates market friendly environment. As a result, these countries will not only be able to enjoy welfare gains from trade due to economies of scale, specialization and efficient allocation of resources (Helpman and Krugman, 1985; Krugman, 1990), but would enable to access to the latest knowledge and higher technologies (Atiyas *et al.*, 1992 and Coe and Helpman, 1995), enlarge human capital (Romer, 1990) and create spillover effects on other industries (Sala-i-Martin and Barro, 1995 and Ning, 2007).

Given the importance of ICT in economic development, South Asian counties have experienced a significant rise in the use of PCs in the recent years. However, the degree of expansion has varied between the countries. South Asian countries showed remarkable growth in the ICT sector. Table 6 highlights the indicators of ICT for the year 2006-07.

It can be seen from the Table 6 that Singapore and Hong Kong remained on the top followed by Japan with respect to ICT indicators especially on teledensity and use of PCs and internet. In South Asian countries one can see that there is still a lot of potential for further growth in cellular mobile services when compared to penetration rate in other countries like Hong Kong, Singapore and Japan. However, cellular mobile, telephones, use of PCs and internet and TV set penetration and their coverage is increasing rapidly. It is expected that very soon South Asian countries would catch-up other countries. The number of internet users in Pakistan and other Asian countries are given in Table 7.

Figures reported in Table 7 suggest that penetration rate in South Asian countries is much lower than that of Japan, Malaysia, Singapore, etc.

THEORETICAL AND EMPIRICAL REVIEW OF LITERATURE

Traditional theories of international trade focus mainly on the comparative advantage and factor endowments. Traditional Recardian model states that the technological differences across countries determine the patterns of international trade (Deardroff, 1984, Helpman, 1984). Heckscher-Ohlin-Vanek (HOV) model proposes that relative factor abundance in labour, land and physical capital are

Table 7. Internet usage for selected Asia-Pacific countries (2006-07)

Country	Internet Users million)	Penetration (% population)
Bangladesh	0.4	0.3
China	162	12.3
Hong Kong	4.9	68.2
India	42.0	3.7
Indonesia	20.0	8.9
Japan	68.3	67.1
Malaysia	13.5	47.8
Pakistan	17.0	11
Singapore	2.4	66.3
Sri Lanka	0.3	1.8
Thailand	8.4	12.5

Source: www.statpak.gov.pk/dept/fbs/publications/pakistan_ict/pict_part-2.pdf

the main sources of comparative advantage and trade patterns. However, besides the traditional sources, financial development is another source of comparative advantage. Kletzer and Bardhan (1987) focus on the contribution of credit markets imperfections to inter-country differences to the patterns of specialization and trade. In particular, they show that even when technology and factor endowments are identical between the countries and economies of scale are absent, differences in the level of financial development may lead to higher interest rates and credit rationing in one country compared to other countries. This may led to comparative advantage in industries and sectors that rely more on the external finance. This implies that the level of domestic credit markets development may have important implications for international trade because financial development is an important source of specialization and comparative advantage.

Kletzer and Bardhan (1987) hypothesis is verified by Fanelli and Medhora (2002) that comparative advantage is positively related to financial development. These arguments suggest that financial development and trade liberalization are inter-related and jointly enhances economic growth, while financial repression and trade distortions impedes economic growth (Atje and Jovanovic, 1993, King and Levine, 1992, 1993, 1994, Levine and Renelt, 1992, Roubini and Sala-i-Martin, 1991, Fry, 1982, 1988, Goldsmith, 1969, Mckinnon, 1973, 1982, Shaw, 1973, World Bank, 1989, Balassa, 1971, 1985, Bhagwati, 1978, Feder, 1983, Krueger, 1978, Tyler, 1981 and World Bank, 1987).

Since financial activities and the degree of free trade are the important policy options through which the governments have potential to affect long-term prosperity. However, much of the empirical work favours the opposite direction of causality. Particularly, growth may itself foster the spread and innovations of financial services (Robinson, 1952).

The neoclassical theories of growth highlighted the role of trade and finance in the process of economic development by incorporating the efficiency effects which are resulted from the reduction of rent seeking and gains from internal and external economies of scale (Bhagwati, 1988; Lee 1993; Krueger, 1998; Fry, 1995, 1997 and Siddiki, 2002). Black and Hung (1998) developed a theoretical model that linking economic growth with financial development and international trade. Their model predicts that economic growth is always higher under financial intermediation than direct lending and borrowing. They argued that trade liberalization and financial development accelerates economic growth by reducing the cost of research and development (R&D) and encourages markets for new products and services (Siddiki, 2002).

The endogenous growth theories indicate that knowledge and technology play central role in the development process (Romer, 1993, 1994). Unlike the neoclassical growth theories, the endogenous growth theories focused on the creation of technical knowledge and its transmission. Therefore, R&D, human capital accumulation and externalities generated by ICT could be more valuable in promoting economic growth.

Finance and Economic Growth

The importance of finance in the process of economic growth can be traced back as Bagehot (1873), Schumpeter (1911) and Hicks (1969). More recent studies includes Levine (1998), King and Levine (1993a, 1993b), Rousseau and Wachtel (1998), Rajan and Zingales (1998), and Okedokun (1998). Bagehot (1873) and Hicks (1969) argued that the financial system was an important vehicle in the process of industrialization by facilitating the movement of funds for welfare related works.

Schumpeter contends that a well-functioning financial system would induce technological innovation by identifying, selecting and funding those entrepreneurs that would be expected to successfully implement their products and productive processes. Levine (1997) argued that financial system perform five basic tasks: facilitating the trading, hedging, diversifying and pooling of risk, allocating resources, monitoring performance of managers and exerting corporate control, mobilizing savings and facilitating the exchange of goods and services.

However, there is a considerable debate on the exact channels through which financial development influences economic growth (Gupta, 1984; Spears, 1992). The theories can be subdivided into two broad schools of thoughts: (1) the structuralists and (2) the repressionists. The structuralists contends that the quantity and composition of financial variables induces economic growth by directly increasing saving in the form of financial assets, thereby, encouraging capital formation and hence, economic growth (Goldsmith, 1969; Gurley and Shaw, 1955; Patrick, 1966; Thornton, 1996; Demetriades and Luintel, 1996; Berthelemy and Varoudakis, 1998). Thus financial deepening and the composition of financial variables are important for economic growth.

Kwan and Zhang (1998) show that financial deepening has had a positive impact on output growth (Sinha and Macri, 2001). King and Levine (1993b) found a highly significant relationship between the liquid liabilities-GDP ratio and real per capita income. Lack of financial development could be possibly inducing poverty trap because of the existence of multiple steady state equilibria (Sinha and Macri, 2001). However, the other economists have questioned about the casual relationship established in the empirical studies. For example, Robinson (1952) suggests that financial development responds passively to economic growth as a result of higher demand for financial services. Lucas (1988) has argued that financial development and economic growth are independent and not causally related. Ram (1999) found that empirical evidence does not support the view that financial development promotes economic growth.

Demetrides and Hussein (1996) and Greenwood and Smith (1997) claimed that the two variables are mutually causal and they have a bidirectional causality. However, many theoretical and empirical studies suggest a positive relationship between finance and growth (Levine, 1997). Recent literature has incorporated the role of stock market as a measure of financial development and concludes that stock market liquidity and banking development had a positive effect on economic growth, capital accumulation and productivity (Levine and Zervos, 1998), Sing and Weisse, 1998, Levine, 1998 and Jayaratne and Strahan, 1996).

The financial repressionists, led by McKinnon (1973) and Shaw (1973) believe that financial liberalization in the form of an appropriate rate of return on real cash balances is a vehicle of the rate of capital formation and promoting economic growth. According to this hypothesis, low and negative real interest rates discourage savings. This reduces the availability of loanable funds for investment, which in turn lowers the rate of economic growth. Mckinnon-Shaw model posits that a more liberalized financial system will induce and increase in saving and investment and therefore, promote economic growth. Ahmed and Ansari (1995) found weak support for Mckinnon and Shaw hypothesis for Bangladesh, Khan and Hasan (1998) found strong support for Pakistan.

Greenwood and Jovanovic (1990) conclude that as saver gain confidence in the ability of the financial intermediaries they place an increasing proportion of their savings with their intermediaries. Greenwood and Smith (1997 and King and Levine (1993b) employ an endogenous growth model in which the financial intermediaries obtain information about the quality of individual projects that are not available to private investors and public markets. This information advantage enables financial intermediaries to fund innovative products and productive processes, thereby inducing economic growth (De La Fuente and Marin, 1994).

There is a considerable body of literature that postulates a positive relationship between financial sector development and economic growth using time series analysis. The results have been largely mixed. Jung (1986) and Demetriades and Hussein (1996) found bi-directional causality between financial and real variables. Rousseau and Wachtel (1998) found strong uni-directional link running from finance to growth. Bell and Rousseau (2001) found that financial intermediaries played a more vigorous role in promoting investment than in increasing total factor productivity and interpreted this as evidence for the presence of a factor accumulation. Rousseau and Vuthipadadorn (2005) find strong uin-directional causality from finance to investment and weaker support for a casual link from finance to the level of output.

Sinha and Macri (2001) find a two-way causality between income and financial variables for India and Malaysia, one-way causality from financial variables for Japan and Thailand, and reverse causality for Korea, Pakistan and Philippines. Their results clearly support the general view of a positive relationship between financial development and economic growth. Ghatak (1997) concludes that interest rates and financial deepening increase economic growth.

Demetriades and Hussein (1996) conclude that real per capita income is positively associated with financial deepening and negatively with bank branches. The negative association between per capita income and bank branches reflects inefficiencies in financial intermediation for a given level of financial development. The study also finds that financial repression in the form of selective intervention exerts positive impact on economic growth. Fry (1997) find inverted U-shaped relationship between the growth rate and financial development. The results indicate that economic growth maximized when interest rates are within the range of –5% to +15%. Clark (1996) suggests that the equilibrium real interest rate is undefined and unstable because of its dual role. In one hand, it equilibrates saving and investment, on the other hand, it determines portfolio readjustment and capital inflows. Portfolio adjustment causes fluctuations in interest rates. These fluctuations are intensified by the uncertainty and volatility of expected returns to investment and potential inflows of capital, which may distort the real exchange rate and increase the cost of borrowing.

Arestis *et al.* (2001) find that both stock markets and banks have made important contributions to output growth in Germany, France and Japan, with the stock market's contribution ranging from about one-seventh to one-third of the bank's contribution. A weak link between financial development and economic growth in the UK and the USA is also identified. Furthermore, the results suggest that economic growth is negatively affected by stock market volatility in France and Japan. Khan *et al.* (2005, 2008) suggest that in the long-run financial depth and real interest rate exerted positive impact on economic growth. However, the relationship between growth and financial development is though positive but remained insignificant in the short-run. Their results support the view that growth is an outcome of financial development. Chang and Ho (2000) found the evidence of causality running from financial development to economic growth and not the reverse. The study supports the supply-leading hypothesis for South Korea.

Trade and Economic Growth

The literature on trade liberalization can be grouped into two categories. The first category examines export-growth nexus, while the second relates to the nexus between trade liberalization and growth using with and without and before and after approaches. However, there has been a great deal of controversy. Using cross-section data, Feder (1983); Balassa (1978); Tyler (1981) and Michaely (1977) have finds the evidence of positive association between exports and economic growth. However, these studies involve a spurious correlation due to the fact that exports themselves being a part of national product. This led to a version of cross-sectional studies, which estimate aggregate production function that includes exports as explanatory variable along with other determining fundamentals economic growth such as labour, capital and investment.[4]

The cross-country studies utilize different indicators of trade openness to examine the relationship between trade liberalization and growth. The most important studies include Dollar (1992), Sachs and Warner (1995) and Edward (1998). Dollar (1992) used an index of real exchange rate distortions and an index of real exchange rate volatility as indicators of trade orientation and the results indicate that each indicator is negatively related to growth in a sample of 95 developing countries.

Sachs and Warner (1995) construct a binary index of openness to examine various aspects of trade policies including average tariff rates, non-tariff barriers, and black market premium on exchange rates etc. They find that countries that are more open, enjoys higher growth rates. Yang and Huang (1997) suggest that a decline in the economy-wide tariff leads to more equitable distribution of income in China. Similarly, Edwards (1998) investigated that robustness of the openness-growth nexus by utilizing different indicators of openness. He concluded that there is positive and significant correlation between trade openness and economic growth.

Greenaway *et al.* (2002) analyzed the relationship between trade liberalization and GDP growth rate for 73 developing countries. The empirical results of this study were obtained with three different time period and three different indicators. The short-run results from the first two indicators showed a positive and significant impact of trade liberalization on growth. The last indicator showed insignificant impact of trade liberalization on growth. However, the results from all indicators showed that liberalization affects the GDP growth rate with a lag in the long-run.

Irwin *et al* (2002) examined the relationship between trade liberalization and income growth for countries engaged in bilateral trade for different time periods. The results suggest that more liberal economies enjoy a higher level of per capita income. Yanikkaya (2003) utilized various measures of trade volumes and trade restrictions as alternative indicators of openness in a panel of 100 developed and developing countries. He finds a positive relationship between openness and economic growth when trade volumes are used as an indicator of openness. The study also finds a positive relationship between trade barrier and economic growth.

Khan, *et al.* (1995) suggests that exports promote economic growth. Iqbal and Zahid (1998) suggest that openness has a beneficial impact on economic growth. Mohsin *et al.* (2001) demonstrates that poverty has declined in Pakistan with trade liberalization. Kemal *et al.* (2002) find a positive association between exports and economic growth for all countries. Din *et al* (2003) suggest that there is significant long-run relation between economic growth and openness. However, there is no evidence of short-run causality between economic growth and openness and vice versa. Since Granger causality is based on the statistical property of the data and not on the structural relationships implied by economic theory. Furthermore, there is variety of economic, institutional and political factors influencing economic growth. They recommended that multivariate model might be more appropriate to examine the relationship between economic growth and openness.

Khan and Qayyum (2006) obtain positive relationship between trade openness and real GDP both in the long as well as in the short-run for Pakistan. Their results suggest that trade liberalization allows market forces to channel resources to relatively productive sectors and hence to raise efficiency and economic growth.

ICT and Economic Growth

The major global shift of the last twenty years is technological and this factor has reshaping the global system. The development of Telecom infrastructure, broadband coverage and internet connectivity of households and business establishments contributed to domestic production, imports, exports, employment and investment. Rapid spread of internet and the use of World Wide Web (www) have opening the opportunities to access commercial and political information. The use of computers and software, internet, high speed connections and company data systems allows management to accumulate and process vast amount of information on a timely basis.

ICT has reduced transaction costs of participating sub-contracting (through B2B interaction) and facilitating the operations of IT services suppliers based in developing countries at low-cost (Matambalya and Wolf, 2001). Furthermore, the societies connected with networks provide plentiful information at low costs which, in turn, has significant implications for productivity and economic growth (Quibria et al., 2003). Negroponte (1998) argued that leapfrogging characteristics of ICT enables poor to catch up. With the advent of new ICT, e-commerce has been increased rapidly along with trade in information products. Recent advances in ICT have been an important vehicle in permitting information exchange to develop as a valuable commodity.

Countries and sectors equipped with necessary telecommunications systems have been rapidly moving to post-industrial, growth-orientated information-based economy (Gholami et al., 2003). The primary benefits of modern telecommunication includes the low transport and transaction costs, improved marketing information and increased efficiency of industrial production. Many studies indicate that expanded telecommunications investment is essential for growth (Addison and Hashmati, 2002 and Matambalya and Wolf, 2001).

Hardy (1980) finds that the effect of telecommunications investment on GDP is large in the least development economies and small in the most-developed economies. He concluded that telephone per capita has significant impact on GDP, but spread of radio did not have such impact. Similarly, Norton (1992), Roller and Waverman (2001), Torero et al. (2005) and Mani (2007) have finds that the existence of ICT infrastructure reduces transaction costs and increases domestic output. Particularly, Mani (2007) concluded that to reap the benefits of network externalities and to achieve the high growth rate more and more investment in the ICT sector is needed. Kateja and Jha (2008) examine the casual link between telecommunication and economic growth in India and found that in the short-run growth of telecommunication is influenced by growth in GDP.

Despite the existing literature, the present study receives special attention to have an idea whether the finance-trade-information technology causes economic growth in the context of South Asian countries. It is well-known that South Asian economies have undergone widespread financial and trade liberalization and ICT revolution, especially after the globalization and economic liberalization policies of 1990s. During this period there has been a significant improvement in the growth rate in these economies. These economies are important players in the international market in terms of exports and imports, which significantly affect the economic growth and financial and ICT sectors. Keeping the role of trade, finance and ICT in economic development, it is necessary to study the impact of these variables on the economic growth.

Model, Methodology and Data

To examine the impact of trade, finance and ICT on the level of output, we utilize the theoretical framework developed by Blackburn and Hung (1998) and used by Siddiki (2002), Christopoulos and Tsionas (2004) and Khan and Qayyum (2006):

$$\begin{aligned} Y_t^j &= \beta_0 + \beta_1 FD_t^j + \beta_2 TOP_t^j + \beta_3 IY_t^j \\ &\quad + \beta_4 INF_t^j + \beta_5 IT + u_t^j \qquad (1) \\ &\beta_1 > 0,\ \beta_2 > 0,\quad \beta_3 > 0, \beta >< 0 \end{aligned}$$

where $j = j$ th country (Bangladesh, India, Pakistan and Sri Lanka). Y denotes real GDP used as a proxy for growth, FD is a measure of financial depth, TOP is trade openness, IY is share of investment to GDP and INF is inflation rate. IT is a measure of information technology.[6] All the variables are expressed in logarithmic form. β 's the parameters and u denotes random error term representing the factors that are not accounted for in the model.

To examine the long-run and short-run dynamic relationship between real income, financial development, trade openness, share of domestic investment to GDP, and inflation rate, this study uses autoregressive distributed lag (ARDL) bounds testing approach to cointegration which was developed by Pesaran *et al.* (2001). Unlike residual-based method of cointegration due to Engle-Granger (1987) and maximum likelihood-based approach to cointegration due to Johansen (1988, 1991) and Johansen and Juselius (1990), ARDL approach can be applied regardless of whether the variables are I (0), I (1) or fractionally integrated (Pesaran and Prseran, 1997). This means that ARDL avoiding problems resulting from the non-stationarity of time series data (Laurenceson and Chai, 2003). Furthermore, ARDL approach provides robust results for a small sample size (Majid and Mahrizal, 2007 and Yusof and Majid, 2007).

The dynamic error-correction model (ECM) can be derived from ARDL through a simple linear transformation (Banerjee *et al.*, 1993). The ECM integrates the short-run dynamics with the long-run equilibrium, with out losing long-run information (Yusof and Majid, 2007). The conditional unrestricted equilibrium correction model (UECM) for equation (1) can be written as:

$$\begin{aligned} \Delta Y_t^j &= a_0 + \sum_{i=1}^{p} \alpha_{1i} \Delta Y_{t-i}^j + \sum_{i=0}^{p} \alpha_{2i} \Delta FD_{t-i}^j \\ &\quad + \sum_{i=0}^{p} \alpha_{3i} \Delta TOP_{t-i}^j + \sum_{i=0}^{p} \alpha_{4i} \Delta IY_{t-i}^j \\ &\quad + \sum_{i=0}^{p} \alpha_{5i} \Delta INF_{t-i}^j + a_1 Y_{t-1}^j + a_2 FD_{t-1}^j \\ &\quad + a_3 TOP_{t-1}^j + a_4 IY_{t-1}^j + a_5 INF_{t-1}^j + u_t^j \end{aligned} \qquad (2)$$

where Δ denotes the first difference operator, a_0 is the drift and error terms u 's are assumed to be white noise. The parameters a_i ($i = 1, 2, \ldots\ldots, 5$) are long-run multipliers. Lagged values of ΔY_t^j and current and lagged values of $\Delta FD_t^j, \Delta TOP_t^j, \Delta IY_t^j$ and ΔINF_t^j are used to model the short-run dynamic structure. To test the cointegration relationship between $\Delta Y_t^j, \Delta FD_t^j, \Delta TOP_t^j, \Delta IY_t^j$ and ΔINF_t^j using bounds testing procedure, we examine the joint hypotheses in equation 2. The null hypotheses of no cointegration is defined by $H_1^j : a_1 = \ldots\ldots = a_5 = 0$ is tested against $H_1^j : a_1 \neq \ldots\ldots\ a_5 \neq 0$ by means of F-statistics. The F-statistic is non-standard distribution and depends on the unit root properties of the data, that is, the variables included in the conditional ECM model are I (0) or I (1) and the number of regressors. The critical values for upper and lower bounds are available in Pesaran and Pesaran (1997) and Pesaran *et al.* (1999, 2001). If the calculated F-statistic lies above the upper bound, the hypothesis of no cointegration can be rejected.

Having identified the evidence of cointegration relationship, the next step is to select the optimal ARDL specification of equation (1) on the basis of lag selection criteria such as, Schwartz Bayesian Criterion (SBC). A general representation of $ARDL(p,q,r,s,t)$ model for equation (1) is given by:

$$Y_t^j = b_0 + \sum_{i=0}^{p} b_{1i} Y_{t-i}^j + \sum_{i=0}^{q} b_{2i} FD_{t-i}^j + \sum_{i=0}^{r} b_{3i} TOP_{t-i}^j + \sum_{i=0}^{s} b_{4i} IY_{t-i}^j + \sum_{i=0}^{t} b_{5i} INF_{t-i}^j + \xi_t \qquad (3)$$

The long-run multiplier can be obtained as:

$$\beta_0 = \left(b_0 \Big/ 1 - \sum_{i=1}^{p} b_{1i} \right) \text{ and } \beta_k = \left(b_n \Big/ 1 - \sum_{i=1}^{p} b_{1i} \right)$$

with $k = 1,\ldots,5$ and $n = 2,\ldots,5$

Finally, the short-run dynamic coefficients for the optimal ARDL can be obtained by the estimation of following restricted error-correction model

$$\Delta Y_t^j = c_0 + \sum_{i=1}^{p} c_{1i} \Delta Y_{t-i}^j + \sum_{i=0}^{q} c_{2i} \Delta FD_{t-i}^j + \sum_{i=0}^{r} c_{3i} \Delta TOP_{t-i}^j + \sum_{i=0}^{s} c_{4i} \Delta IY_{t-i}^j + \sum_{i=0}^{t} c_{5i} \Delta INF_{t-i}^j + \lambda ec_{t-1} + \zeta_t^j \qquad (4)$$

such that $\lambda \neq 0$.

Where ec_{t-1} is the error-correction terms and λ is the speed of adjustment towards the long-run equilibrium after a shock.

Data Description

The present study is based on the annual data covering the period from 1970-2006.[5] Several indicators are used in measuring financial development such as M2/GDP, bank deposit liabilities relative to GDP which is equal to the difference between liquid liabilities of the financial system and currency in circulation divided by GDP.[7] This considered the broadest measure of the financial intermediation. However, this variable does not fully reflect the efficiency of the services provided by the financial sector, such as risk management, monitoring and information processing (da Silva, 2002).

The alternative indicator which is frequently used in the literature is the ratio of private-sector credit to GDP, which measures how much intermediation is performed by the banking system and the last indicator is the ratio of stock market capitalization to GDP which measures the size and liquidity of the stock market. However, following King and Levine (1993a, 1993b), Levine (1999), De Gregorio and Guidotti (1995), Ferreira and Silva (2002) and Mallick and Agarwal (2007), we have used the ratio of private sector credit to GDP as a measure of financial development. This measure is closely related to the level and efficiency of investment, and hence to the economic growth.

The main advantage of private sector credit

over indicators is that it excludes credit to the public sector and accurately represents the role of financial intermediation in channeling funds to the private market participants (Mallick and Agarwal, 2007). Real GDP is obtained as a ratio of nominal GDP[8] to consumer price index (CPI 2000=100). The variable TOP is calculated by taking the ratio of the sum of exports and imports to GDP. Data on all the variables are taken from IFS CD-ROM (2008).

EMPIRICAL RESULTS: COINTEGRATION ANALYSIS

Before the implementation of the ARDL bounds test to cointegration, we first determine the order of integration of individual time-series, using Augmented Dickey-Fuller (ADF) test (Dickey and Fuller, 1979, 1981). The bounds test to cointegration does not require any pre-testing of unit roots. However, it is not necessary that all the series are I (0) or I (1). If any of the series are I (2), then the ARDL procedure gives spurious results. Hence, testing of unit root for each series is an important before the implementation of the ARDL cointegration method (Ouattra, 2004 and Khan, 2008). The results are reported in Table 8.

It can be seen from the Table 8 that for Bangladesh, India and Sri Lanka inflation rate (INF_t) is stationary at their level (i.e. I (0)). Real income (Y_t), financial development (FD_t), trade openness (TOP_t) and share of investment to GDP (IY_t) is I (1). In the case of Pakistan, trade openness (TOP_t) and inflation rate (INF_t) are stationary at level (i.e. I (0)), while real income (Y_t), financial development (FD_t) and share of investment to GDP (IY_t) are integrated of order one (i.e. I (1)). These mixed results from unit the root test justify the application of bounds testing approach to cointegration. Table 9 reports the results of the bounds test of cointegration.

Table 9 suggests that the calculated F-statistics is greater than the upper bounds values. It provides the evidence of cointegration between real income, financial development, trade openness, share of investment to GDP and inflation rate for all the countries included in the analysis. It means that in the long-run financial development, trade openness, share of investment to GDP and inflation rate are the important determinants of growth in the South Asian countries.

Given the evidence of cointegration between real income, financial development, trade openness, share of investment to GDP and inflation rate, we now employ ARDL method to estimate the long-run and short-run dynamic relationship between real income, financial development, trade openness, share of investment to GDP and inflation rate by estimating equation (3) and equation (4). The long-run ARDL estimates based on the SBC for South Asian Countries are reported in Table 10.

It is evident from Table 10 that the financial development indicator (i.e. share of private sector credit to GDP) exerts significant and positive impacts on the real output only for Bangladesh. The finding of positive finance-growth relationship verifies the hypothesis that financial development leads economic growth in Bangladesh. This result is consistent with the earlier findings by Siddiki (2002). For India, Pakistan and Sri Lanka, the relationship between financial market indicator and real output remains insignificant and in line with the studies by Khan (2007) and Mallick and Agarwal (2007). This result could be due to the inefficiency of private sector in utilizing loans obtained from the financial institutions. This is little surprising, as financial development is known to help in the growth of the industrial and financial sectors.

A more investigation is required to be able to conclude that increasing financial development insignificantly affects the level of output. One possible reason for this result could be that expanding financial activities are not getting translated to increase economic activities as the funds are not being used for investment purposes. This is true for these countries because in the pre-reform period, the commercial banks have been allocating funds to selective customers and sponsors of leading political parties. Thus, lending to private sector is generally not based on economic consideration.

As a consequence, the vested group has ac-

Table 8. Unit root test

Country	Series	Constant (C) /Trend (T)	Level	First Difference	Decision
Bangladesh	Y_t	T	-1.36 (0)	-8.17 (0)*	I (1)
	FD_t	C	-0.70 (0)	-4.32 (0)*	I (1)
	TOP_t	C	-0.46 (1)	-5.21 (1)	I (1)
	IY_t	C	-1.13 (0)	-4.27 (0)*	I (1)
	INF_t	C	-6.62 (1)*	-12.54 (0)*	I (0)
India	Y_t	T	-2.71(0)	-4.56 (1)*	I (1)
	FD_t	C	-1.66 (1)	-3.65 (1)*	I (1)
	TOP_t	C	-0.25 (0)	-3.83 (0)*	I (1)
	IY_t	T	-1.56 (1)	-4.61 (1)*	I (1)
	INF_t	C	-4.42 (0)*	-7.01 (0)*	I (0)
Pakistan	Y_t	T	-2.78(1)	-4.47 (1)*	I (1)
	FD_t	C	-2.36 (0)	-5.43 (1)*	I (1)
	TOP_t	C	-9.73 (0)*	-7.24 (0)*	I (0)
	IY_t	T	-1.55 (1)	-4.08 (1)*	I (1)
	INF_t	C	-2.83 (0)*	-6.99 (0)*	I (0)
Sri Lanka	Y_t	C	-2.18(1)	-3.19 (1)*	I (1)
	FD_t	C	-1.95 (1)	-3.99 (1)*	I (1)
	TOP_t	C	-2.32 (0)	-4.40 (0)*	I (1)
	IY_t	C	-1.79 (0)	-3.53 (1)*	I (1)
	INF_t	C	-3.61 (1)*	-5.26 (1)*	I (0)
Critical Values	95% = -2.95 with constant		95%= -3.55 with constant and trend		

Number of lags is given in parentheses and Akaike Information Criterion is used for lag selection. * indicate significant at the 1% level. T stands for both intercept and trend.

cumulated a huge amount of money which is termed as non-performing loans (NPLs). The higher NPLs in the banking system are evidence of misallocation of loans and cannot be interpreted by the neoclassical criterion of allocative efficiency. Besides this, these countries are slowly withdrawing from the sphere of production and therefore, the funds are not being utilized for the purpose of investment. Similarly, it is quite possible that financial deepening has only meant an increase in the treasury operations of financial institutions rather than a rise in their lending activities.

Furthermore, the insignificant effect of financial development on growth may be due to a very poor quality of credit disbursal (Khan, 2007 and Mallick and Agarwal, 2007). Two possible explanations for this phenomenon are also offered by Al-Yousif (2002). *First*, the insignificant relationship between the variables is arises from the business cycle effect, rather than a representation of long-run steady-state equilibrium relationship. *Second*, the relationship is due to the inefficiency of the domestic financial system in allocating resources and operating in a weak regulatory en-

Table 9. Results of the bound test to cointegration

Country	Variables Included	Number of Lags	F-Statistic	Decision
Bangladesh	$(Y_t \mid FD_t, TOP_t, IY_t, INF_t)^a$	3	5.59	Cointegration
India	$(Y_t \mid FD_t, TOP_t, IY_t, INF_t)^b$	3	6.19	Cointegration
Pakistan	$(Y_t \mid FD_t, TOP_t, IY_t, INF_t)^c$	2	6.95	Cointegration
Sri Lanka	$(Y_t \mid FD_t, TOP_t, IY_t, INF_t)^d$	2	7.33	Cointegration

Note: The number of lags is selected on the basis of Akaike Information Criterion (AIC). The critical values are given by Pesaran *et al.* (2001).
a= unrestricted constant, no trend and number of regressor k=4.
b= unrestricted intercept, no trend and number of regressor k=4.
c= unrestricted intercept, unrestricted trend and number of regressor k=4.
d= restricted intercept, unrestricted trend and number of regressor k=4.

Table 10. Long-run cointegration results

Country	Bangladesh (1, 1, 2, 2, 3)	India (3, 2, 3, 1, 0)	Pakistan (1, 2, 0, 1, 2)	Sri Lanka (1, 0, 1, 2, 2)
Constant	14.05 (13.88)*	10.96 (14.94)*	9.06 (61.65)*	8.55 (20.37)
FD_t	0.47 (6.92)*	0.25 (0.57)	0.06 (1.12)	0.20 (1.51)
TOP_t	0.57 (2.77)**	0.70 (2.21)**	-0.28 (-2.70)*	-0.36 (-0.98)
IY_t	0.29 (2.50)*	2.13 (2.14)**	0.25 (3.88)*	0.16 (0.49)
INF_t	0.01 (1.50)	-0.07 (-3.33)*	-0.01 (-3.94)*	-0.005 (-1.31)
Trend	-	-	0.06 (63.94)*	0.04 (17.09)*
Short run Diagnostic Tests				
$x^2SC(1)$	0.61 [0.42]	0.57 [0.45]	0.03 [0.863]	0.17 [0.677]
$x^2FF(1)$	3.18 [0.06]	2.90 [0.088]	32 [0.571]	0.16 [0.690]
$x^2NO(2)$	0.12 [0.94]	3.95 [0.139]	2.14 [0.343]	0.38 [0.825]
$x^2HET(1)$	0.37 [0.54]	0.16 [0.693]	0.13 [0722]	3.50 [0.061]

Note: *, ** indicates significant at the 1% and 5% level significantly. The estimated results of equation 3 are available from the author. χ^2_{SC}, χ^2_{FF}, χ^2_{NO} and χ^2_{Het} are Lagrange multiplier statistics for test of residual correlation, functional from mis-specification, non-normal errors and heteorskedasticity, respectively. These statistics are distributed as Chi-square values with degree of freedom in parentheses.

vironment. Because of the inefficiency of financial intermediaries, economic growth is therefore, slowed down. The inefficiency of the domestic financial system in channeling the funds into more productive sectors was one of the main causes of the East Asian financial crisis in mid-1997.[9]

Similarly, Krugman (1998) has pointed out that the domestic financial systems in most of the East Asian countries are weak, due to the poor regulatory framework, and the inconsistent and inappropriate sequencing of liberalization measures. South Asian countries lack investment opportunities and funds were directed towards the property market. As a consequence, the presence of an external shock will easily jeopardize the fundamental strength of the financial sector, as well as the overall economy. All these factors makes financial development indicator insignificant.

Trade liberalization exerts positive impact on real output for Bangladesh and India. The positive and significant link between trade and real output supports the trade-led growth hypothesis for Bangladesh and India. This implies that in these countries an expansion of trade leads to enhances economic growth. This result is consistent with the earlier finding of Siddiki (2002), Mallick and Agarwal (2007) and Kabir and Hoque (2007). This result implies that trade is beneficial to economic growth for Bangladesh and India. For the case of Pakistan trade openness exerts negative impacts on real output, while the impact of this variable remains insignificant for Sri Lanka. This result may be justified on the grounds that trade could generate excess demand for imports, leading to worsen the current account balance.

Furthermore, trade liberalization may promote growth from the supply side but, if the balance of payment worsens, growth may be adversely affected from the demand side because the payment deficits resulting from liberalization are usually unsustainable and not easily rectified by relative prices (real exchange rate) changes (Khan and Zahler, 1985 and Santos-Paulino and Thirlwall, 2004). The second possible reason could be the large proportion of imports in volume of trade that may adversely effect real output. Another possibility may be that the lack of institutional based, governance related issues and political instability have a large contribution in poor export performance (SBP, 2007).

The share of investment to GDP exerts positive and significant influence on real output for Bangladesh, India and Pakistan. This implies that as the share of investment increases, the level of income is also increases through the multiplier effect (Khan, 2008). In the case of Sri Lanka, this variable remains insignificant. One possible reason could be the lack of macroeconomic and political instability, weak institutions, lack of good governance and lack of investment climate makes investment-productivity insignificant. Furthermore, the impact of investment may also be captured by financial development, because it represents the availability of funds (Khan, 2008).

The rate of inflation exerts negative and significant impact on real output in India and Pakistan. This implies that high domestic inflation hinders real output in India and Pakistan. However, the impact of this variable is very weak. This may be due to the proactive macroeconomic policies perused by the government of these countries in the past. In contrast, inflation produces no influence on real output in Bangladesh and Sri Lanka. However, inflation does not seem to be statistically significant for growth in both countries.

In overall term, our results suggest that financial development exerts no effect on real output, while trade liberalization enhances domestic productivity in the case of Bangladesh and India. For Pakistan trade liberalization hinders productivity and it produces no effect on Sri Lankan real output. Thus for the long-run we obtained mixed support for the hypothesis that both trade and finance exerts positive impact on economic growth in the long-run.

To determine the direction of causality between real output, financial development, trade openness, share of investment to GDP and inflation rate we employ multivariate Granger causality test based on vector error-correction model (VECM). Table 11 reports the multivariate Granger causality results. The results suggest that when real GDP growth (ΔY_t) is considered as dependent variable, the error-correction terms (ec_{t-1}) for all countries possesses expected negative signs and are statistically significant. The significance of error-correction terms confirms the existence of long-run causality among the variables included in the equation (1). Particularly, real GDP, trade openness, investment share and inflation rate adjust to correct deviations from the long-run equilibrium for the case of Bangladesh, India and Pakistan, while deviations from the long-run equilibrium for the Sri Lanka are mainly caused by the changes in real GDP, financial development and investment share.

In short-run, the evidence of two-way causality between real GDP, trade openness, investment share and inflation rate exists for the case of Bangladesh. One-way causality running from real GDP to financial development is observed for Bangladesh. An evidence of two-way causality between real GDP, financial development and trade openness exists for the case of India. For Pakistan, an indication of two- way causality is observed between real GDP and trade openness, while no evidence of short-run causality between real output and financial development observed for Pakistan. One-way causality running from financial development to real output and real output to trade openness is existed for Sri Lanka.

The findings of no short-run causality between finance-real output in Bangladesh and Pakistan supports the "neutral hypothesis" because "*importance of financial factor is badly overstressed*" (Lucas, 1988, p. 6) and "*none of the pioneers of development economics .... even list finance as a factor of development*" (Chandavarkar, 1992, p. 134). For India, two-way short-run causality between finance and real output supports "demand-following and supply-leading hypotheses". This means that both financial development and economic growth are interdependent in the Indian context. The short-run causality running from finance to growth supports finance-led growth hypothesis in the Sri Lanka.

The existence of two-way short-run causality between growth and trade openness supports the trade-led growth and growth-led trade hypotheses in the case of Bangladesh, Pakistan and Sri Lanka. This means that in these countries trade and growth are interdependent in the short-run. The higher the volume of trade the higher will be the growth and the higher the growth, the higher will be the trade. On the other hand, the existence of one-way causality running from growth to trade supports the hypothesis of growth-led trade in the Indian case. This implies that the higher the growth in India the higher will be the trade.

CONCLUSION

This study has examined the impact of trade and financial liberalization on real output in four South Asian countries including Bangladesh, India, Pakistan and Sri Lanka over the period 1970-2007 using bounds testing approach to cointegration. Our results show that real GDP, financial development, trade openness, share of investment to GDP and inflation rate are significantly cointegrated, implying stable long-run relationship between these variables. The results show that, in the long-run financial development exerts positive impact on real output only in the case of Bangladesh, while for India, Pakistan and Bangladesh the effect of financial development is insignificant.

Trade openness influences real output positively for Bangladesh and India. For Pakistan, trade openness exerts negative effects on real output. In the case of Sri Lanka trade openness plays no role to influence real output. The share of investment to GDP exerts positive impact on real output for Bangladesh, India and Pakistan, while this variable remains insignificant in the

Table 11. Multivariate vector error correction causality between real output financial development and trade openness

Country	Dependent variable	Independent Variables					
		ΔY_t	ΔFD_t	ΔTOP_t	ΔIY_t	ΔINF_t	ec_{t-1}
Bangladesh	ΔY_t	-	0.001 [0.970]	10.68 [0.005]	9.41 [0.009]	34.93 [0.000]	-0.08 (-2.51)**
	ΔFD_t	4.60*** [0.100]	-	6.15** [0.013]	6.69** [0.035]	12.51* [0.000]	-0.23 (-1.55)
	ΔTOP_t	9.63** [0.002]	4.53 [0.104]	-	0.20 [0.654]	14.39* [0.002]	-0.58 (-3.97)*
	ΔIY_t	13.86** [0.003]	0.93 [0.334]	0.98 [0.328]	-	1.77 [0.184]	-0.27 (-2.83)**
	ΔINF_t	8.36** [0.015]	12.60** [0.006]	2.25 [0.522]	6.14** [0.046]	-	-2.05 (-6.14)*
India	ΔY_t	-	7.23** [0.027]	0.26 [0.611]	46.54* [0.000]	14.31* [0.000]	-0.09 (-3.23)*
	ΔFD_t	9.28** [0.002]	-	19.35* [0.000]	0.02 [0.898]	43.39* [0.000]	0.06 (0.76)
	ΔTOP_t	6.89** [0.009]	12.16** [0.002]	-	5.74** [0.017]	18.12* [0.000]	-0.42 (-3.77)*
	ΔIY_t	8.67** [0.034]	0.99 [0.320]	8.45** [0.038]	-	3.04 [0.219]	-1.13 (-4.37)*
	ΔINF_t						
Pakistan	ΔY_t	-	3.06 [0.216]	8.36** [0.004]	34.50* [0.000]	15.03** [0.001]	-0.69 (-5.66)*
	ΔFD_t	0.03 [0.873]	-	2.09 [0.149]	1.05 [0.304]	8.03** [0.018]	-0.42 (-2.66)**
	ΔTOP_t	6.69** [0.009]	0.72 [0.398]	-	20.99* [0.000]	21.68* [0.000]	-0.77 (-5.75)*
	ΔIY_t	29.12* [0.000]	3.39 [0.184]	17.76* [0.000]	-	17.88* [0.000]	-0.48 (-6.57)*
	ΔINF_t	0.006 [0.938]	0.65 [0.420]	54.38* [0.000]	6.17** [0.046]	-	-0.52 (-3.21)*
Sri Lanka	ΔY_t	-	4.08** [0.043]	1.21 [0.271]	7.02 [0.030]	6.80** [0.033]	-0.21 (-2.10)**
	ΔFD_t	2.66 [0.103]	-	3.79** [0.051]	1.46 [0.227]	1.23 [0.268]	-0.27 (-2.26)**
	ΔTOP_t	4.81*** [0.090]	2.70 [0.259]	-	23.49* [0.000]	30.64* [0.000]	-0.12 (-0.75)
	ΔIY_t	2.03 [0.154]	1.20 [0.273]	32.39* [0.000]	-	7.23** [0.027]	-0.59 (-5.87)*
	ΔINF_t	2.05 [0.152]	1.95 [0.162]	4.34** [0.037]	0.25 [0.619]	-	-1.000 (none)

Note: *, ** and *** represents significant at the 1%, 5% and 10% level of significance. ec_{t-1} is the error- correction terms. By imposing zero restrictions on the coefficients of each variable using Wald F- test for each coefficient in all the equations. Figures in parentheses and squared parentheses represent t-statistics and probabilities for F-statistics respectively.

case of Sri Lanka. Finally, the rate of inflation adversely effect real out put in India and Pakistan in the long-run, while inflation rate produces no significant impact on real output in Bangladesh and Sri Lanka.

In the short-run, the significance of the error-correction terms for ΔY_t, ΔTOP_t, ΔIY_t and ΔINF_t suggests the existence of long-run causality for the case of Bangladesh and India. Furthermore, in the short-run two-way causality exist between ΔTOP and ΔY_t, ΔIY_t and ΔY_t ΔINF_t and ΔY_t, and one-way causality exists between ΔFD_t and ΔY_t in the case of Bangladesh and India. There is an evidence of long-run causality between ΔY_t, ΔFD_t, ΔTOP_t, ΔIY_t and ΔINF_t for the case of Pakistan as indicated by the significance of the respective error-correction terms. In the short-run there is an evidence of short-run causality between ΔTOP and ΔY_t, ΔIY_t and ΔY_t and one-way causality between ΔTOP_t, ΔIY_t and ΔINF_t. For Pakistan there is no evidence of short-run causality between ΔFD_t and ΔY_t. There exists an evidence of long-run causality between ΔY_t, ΔFD_t, ΔTOP_t and ΔIY_t in the context of Sri Lanka as indicated by the significance of their error-correction terms. However, in the short-run there exists two-way causality between ΔTOP and ΔY_t, and one-way causality between ΔTOP and ΔIY_t.

These mixed results for each country suggest significant variations in the structure and degree of the existing financial institutions. This could be possible when countries differ in their level of financial development due to differences in policies, institutional capacity and implementation and sequencing of liberalization policies. The other reason for the insignificance effect of financial factor on economic growth may be due to the structural weaknesses of the banking system in mobilizing financial resources. In these countries banking system suffers from many severe problems such as, adverse selection, moral hazard, political influence to direct credit and huge default loans. These factors may affect the results.

Only trade liberalization pays a significant role in the growth process in these countries in the long as well as in the short-run. This result supports the importance of trade liberalization in enhancing economic growth. This means that financial development and trade openness may be substitute of promoting economic growth and not complementary as suggested by Rajan and Zingales (2003).

Based on these findings, the study suggests that the authorities may focus more on the trade liberalization policies and accelerates domestic investment to boots economic growth. Furthermore, the authorities should take further measures to deepen and modernize existing financial institutions both commercial banks, non-bank financial institutions and stock markets. The authorities may encourage financial institutions and provide enabling environment for investment to allocate their assets in the stock markets. Besides the opening of financial markets, improving institutional infrastructure, good governance and rule of law may encourage the financial development as well as economic development.

ACKNOWLEDGMENT

I am grateful to Dr. Mustafa Zihni TUNCA, Editor of this book for providing an opportunity and encouragement to contribute a chapter. Two anonymous reviewers are also greatly acknowledged for their valuable suggestions and comment on the earlier draft of this chapter. I would also like to thank Mr. Aziz Khan Librarian Pakistan Institute of Development Economics, Islamabad for the proof reading of this manuscript.

REFERENCES

Addison, T., & Heshmati, A. (2002). *Democratization and New Communication Technologies as Determinants of Foreign Direct Investment in Developing Countries*. Paper Presented at the Conference on "New Economy in Development". Helsinki: UNU/WIDER.

Ahluwalia, M. S. (2002). Economic Reforms in India Since 1991: Has Gradualism Worked? *The Journal of Economic Perspectives*, *16*(3), 67–88. doi:10.1257/089533002760278721

Al-Yousif, Y. K. (2002). Financial Development and Economic Growth: Another Look at the Evidence from Developing Countries. *Review of Financial Economics*, *11*, 131–150. doi:10.1016/S1058-3300(02)00039-3

Andersen, T., & Tarp, F. (2003). Financial Liberalization, Financial Development and Economic Growth in LDCs. *Journal of International Development*, *15*, 189–209. doi:10.1002/jid.971

Angus, J. B. (2008). A Survey of Recent Developments in the Literature of Finance and Growth. *Journal of Economic Surveys*, *22*, 536–576. doi:10.1111/j.1467-6419.2007.00542.x

Ansari, M. I. (1998). Financial Development and Economic Growth: The South Asian Experience. *Journal of Asian Economics*, *9*, 503–517. doi:10.1016/S1049-0078(99)80100-6

Ansari, M. I. (2002). The Impact of Financial Development, Money, and Public Spending on Malaysia National Income: An Econometric Study. *Journal of Asian Economics*, *13*, 72–93. doi:10.1016/S1049-0078(01)00113-0

Arestis, P., Demetriades, P. O., & Luintel, K. B. (2001). Financial Development and Economic Growth: The Role of Stock Markets. *Journal of Money . Credit and Banking*, *33*, 16–41. doi:10.2307/2673870

Atiyas, S. W., Dutz, M., & Frischtak, C. (1992). *Fundamental Issues and Policy Approaches in Industrial Restructuring* (Industry and Energy Department Working Paper, World Bank Industry Series Paper, No. 56).

Atje, R., & Jovanovic, B. (1993). *Finance and Development*. Mimeo, New York University.

Bagehot, W. (1783). *Lombard Street*. Homewood, IL: Irwin.

Balassa, B. (1971). *The Structure of Protections in Developing countries*. Baltimore, MD: Johns Hopkins University Press.

Balassa, B. (1978). Exports and Economic Growth: Further Evidence. *Journal of Development Economics*, *5*(2), 181–189. doi:10.1016/0304-3878(78)90006-8

Balassa, B. (1985). Exports, Policy Choices and Economic Growth in Developing Countries after the 1973 Oil Shock. *Journal of Development Economics*, *18*, 23–35. doi:10.1016/0304-3878(85)90004-5

Balassa, B. (1989). Outward Orientation. In H. Chenery & T.N. Srinivasan (Eds.), *Handbook of Development Economics* (pp. 1645-1690). New York: North Holland.

Baldwin, R. (1989). Exporting the Capital Markets: Comparative advantage and Market Imperfections. In D. Audretsch, L. Sleuwaegen, & H. Yamawaki (Eds.), *The Convergence of International and Domestic Markets*. Amsterdam: North-Holland.

Banerjee, A., Dolado, J. J., Galbraith, J. W., & Hendry, D. F. (1993). *Coitegration, Error-Correction and the Econometric Analysis of Non-stationary Data*. Oxford, UK: Oxford University Press.

Beck, T. (2003). Financial Dependence and International Trade. *Review of International Economics*, *11*, 396–316. doi:10.1111/1467-9396.00384

Beck, T., Levine, R., & Loyaza, N. (2000). Finance and the Sources of Growth. *Journal of Financial Economics, 58*, 261–300. doi:10.1016/S0304-405X(00)00072-6

Bencivenga, V. R., & Smith, B. D. (1991). Financial Intermediation and Endogenous Growth. *The Review of Economic Studies, 58*(2), 195–209. doi:10.2307/2297964

Berthelemy, J. C., & Varoudakis, A. (1998). Financial Development, Financial Reforms and Growth: A Panel Data Approach. *Revue-Economique, 49*(1), 195–206. doi:10.2307/3502501

Bhagwati, J. N. (1978). *Foreign Trade Regime and Economic Development: Anatomy and Consequences of Exchange Control Regimes.* Cambridge, UK: Ballinger.

Bhagwati, J. N. (1988). Re-examining Export-Led Growth Hypothesis: A Multivariate Cointegration Analysis. *Applied Economics, 31*, 525–530.

Bhagwati, J. N., & Srinivasan, T. N. (1979). Trade Policy and Development. In R. Dornbusch & J. A. Frenkel (Eds.), *International Economic Policy: Theory and Evidence* (pp. 1-38). Baltimore, MD: John Hopkins University Press. Blackburn, K., & Hung, V. T. Y. (1998). A Theory of Growth, Financial Development and Trade. *Economica, 65*, 107-124.

Chandavarkar, A. (1992). Of Finance and Development: Neglected and Unsettled Questions. *World Development, 22*, 133–142. doi:10.1016/0305-750X(92)90142-I

Chang, T., & Ho, Y.-H. (2002). Financial Development and Economic Growth in South Korea: A Note on Testing Demand-Following or Supply Leading Hypothesis. *The Indian Economic Journal, 77*(2), 153–160.

Christopoulos, D. K., & Tsionas, E. G. (2004). Financial Development and Economic Growth: Evidence from Panel Unit Root and Cointegration Tests. *Journal of Development Economics, 73*, 55–74. doi:10.1016/j.jdeveco.2003.03.002

Clarke, R. (1996). Equilibrium Interest Rates and Financial Liberalization in Developing Countries. *The Journal of Development Studies, 32*(3), 391–413. doi:10.1080/00220389608422421

Coe, D. T., & Helpman, E. (1995). International R&D Spillovers. *European Economic Review, 39*(5), 859–887. doi:10.1016/0014-2921(94)00100-E

Dadaro, S. (1993). Exports and Economic Growth: A Reconsideration of Causality. *Journal of Developing Areas, 27*, 227–244.

Darrat, A. F. (1999). Are Financial Deepening and Economic Growth Causality Related? Another Look at the Evidence. *International Economic Journal, 13*(3), 19–35. doi:10.1080/10168739900080018

Das, R. K., & Kumar, R. (2007). Export-led Growth in South Asia: A Panel Evidence. *The Indian Economic Journal, 55*(3), 132–146.

De Gregorio, J., & Guidotti, P. E. (1995). Financial Development and Economic Growth. *World Development, 23*(3), 433–448. doi:10.1016/0305-750X(94)00132-I

De La Fuente, A., & Marin, J. M. (1994). *Innovations, Bank Monitoring and Endogenous Financial Development* (Universitat Pompeu Fabra Working Paper, No. 59).

Deardorff, A. (1984). The General Validity of the Law of Comparative Advantage. *The Journal of Political Economy, 88*, 941–957. doi:10.1086/260915

Deme, M. (2002). An Examination of the Trade-Led Growth Hypothesis in Nigeria: AS Cointegration, Causality, and Impulse Response Analysis. *Journal of Developing Areas*, *36*(1), 1–15.

Demetriades, P. O., & Hussein, A. K. (1996). Does Financial Development Cause Economic Growth? Time Series Evidence from 16 Countries. *Journal of Development Economics*, *51*, 387–411. doi:10.1016/S0304-3878(96)00421-X

Demetriades, P. O., & Luintel, K. B. (1996). Financial Development, Economic Growth and Banking Sector Controls: Evidence from India. *The Economic Journal*, *106*, 359–374. doi:10.2307/2235252

Din, M.-u. (2004). Exports, Imports, and Economic Growth in South Asia: Evidence Using a Multivariate Time Series Framework. *Pakistan Development Review*, *43*(2), 105–124.

Din, M.-u., Ghani, E., & Siddique, O. (2003). Openness and Economic Growth in Pakistan. *Pakistan Development Review*, *42*(4), 795–807.

Dollar, D. (1992). Outward-Oriented Developing Economies Really Do Grow More Rapidly: Evidence from 95 LDCs, 1976-85. *Economic Development and Cultural Change*, *40*(3), 553–544. doi:10.1086/451959

Dornbusch, R. (1992). The Case for Trade Liberalization in Developing Countries. *The Journal of Economic Perspectives*, *6*(1), 69–85.

Edwards, S. (1992). Trade Orientation, Distortions, and Growth in Developing Countries. *Journal of Development Economics*, *39*, 31–57. doi:10.1016/0304-3878(92)90056-F

Edwards, S. (1998). Openness, Productivity and Growth: What Do we Really Know? *The Economic Journal*, *108*(447), 383–398. doi:10.1111/1468-0297.00293

Engle, R. F., & Granger, C. W. J. (1987). Cointegration and Error Correction: Representation, Estimation and Testing. *Econometrica*, *55*(2), 251–276. doi:10.2307/1913236

Fanelli, J. M., & Medhora, R. (2002). Finance and Competitiveness: Framework and Synthesis. In J. M. Fanelli & R. Medhora (Eds.), *Finance and Competition in Developing Countries* (pp. 1-19). Ottawa, Canada: International Development Research Centre.

Fase, M., & Abma, R. (2003). Financial Environment and Economic Growth in Selected Asian Countries. *Journal of Asian Economics*, *12*, 11–21. doi:10.1016/S1049-0078(02)00237-3

Feder, G. (1983). On Export and Economic Growth. *Journal of Development Economics*, *12*, 59–74. doi:10.1016/0304-3878(83)90031-7

Feldstein, M. (2003). Why is Productivity Growing Faster? *Journal of Policy Modeling*, *25*(5), 445–451. doi:10.1016/S0161-8938(03)00039-5

Ferreira da Silva, G. (2002). The Impact of Financial System Development on Business Cycle Volatility: Cross-Country Evidence. *Journal of Macroeconomics*, *24*, 233–253. doi:10.1016/S0164-0704(02)00021-6

Frankel, J. A., & Romer, D. (1999). Does Trade Causes Growth? *The American Economic Review*, *89*, 379–399.

Fry, M. J. (1988). *Money, Interest, and Banking in Economic Development*. Baltimore, MD: Johns Hopkins University Press.

Fry, M. J. (1995). *Money, Interest Rate, and Banking in Economic Development* (2nd ed.). Baltimore, MD: The Johns Hopkins University Press.

Fry, M. J. (1997). In Favour of Financial Liberalization. *The Economic Journal*, *107*, 754–770. doi:10.1111/1468-0297.00191

Ghatak, S. (1997). Financial Liberalization: The Case of Sri Lanka. *Empirical Economics*, *22*(1), 117–131. doi:10.1007/BF01188173

Golami, R., Sang-Yong, T. L., & Almas, H. (2003). *The Casual Relationship between Information and Communication Technology and Foreign Direct Investment* (WIDER Discussion Paper, No. WDP 2003/30).

Goldsmith, R. W. (1969). *Financial Structure and Development*. New Haven, CT: Yale University Press.

Greenaway, D., Morgan, W., & Wright, P. (2002). Trade Liberalization and Growth in Developing Countries. *Journal of Development Economics*, *67*, 229–244. doi:10.1016/S0304-3878(01)00185-7

Greenwood, J., & Jovanovic, B. (1990). Financial Development, Growth and the Distribution of Income. *The Journal of Political Economy*, *98*(5), 1076–1107. doi:10.1086/261720

Greenwood, J., & Smith, B. (1997). Financial Markets in Development and the Development of Financial Markets. *Journal of Economic Dynamics & Control*, *21*, 145–181. doi:10.1016/0165-1889(95)00928-0

Gupta, K. L. (1984). *Finance and Economic Growth in Developing Countries*. London: Croom Helm.

Hardy, A. (1980). The Role of the Telephone in Economic Development. *Telecommunications Policy*, *4*(4), 278–286. doi:10.1016/0308-5961(80)90044-0

Helpman, E. (1984). The Factor Content of Foreign Trade. *The Economic Journal*, *94*, 84–94. doi:10.2307/2232217

Helpman, E., & Krugman, P. R. (1985). *Market Structure and Foreign Trade: Increasing Returns, Imperfect Competition and the International Economy*. Bridgton, ME: Wheatsheaf Books.

Hicks, J. (1969). *A Theory of Economic History.* Oxford, UK: Clarendon Press.

Hur, J., Raj, M., & Riyanto, Y. E. (2006). Finance and Trade: A Cross-Country Empirical Analysis on the Impact of Financial Development and Asset Tangibility on International Trade. *World Development*, *34*, 1728–1741. doi:10.1016/j.worlddev.2006.02.003

Iimi, A. (2004). Banking Sector Reforms in Pakistan: Economies of Scale and Scope, and Cost Complementarities. *Journal of Asian Economics*, *15*, 507–528.

Iqbal, Z., & Zahid, G. M. (1998). Macroeconomic Determinants of Economic Growth in Pakistan. *Pakistan Development Review*, *37*(2), 125–148.

Irwin, A. D., & Tervio, M. (2002). Does Trade Raise Income? Evidence from the Twentieth Century. *Journal of Development Economics*, *58*(1), 1–18.

Jayaratne, J., & Strahan, P. (1996). The Finance-Growth Nexus: Evidence from Bank Branch Deregulation. *The Quarterly Journal of Economics*, *111*(3), 639–670. doi:10.2307/2946668

Jin, J. C. (2000). Openness and Growth: An Interpretation of Empirical Evidence from East Asian Countries. *The Journal of International Trade & Economic Development*, *9*(1), 5–17. doi:10.1080/096381900362517

Johansen, S. (1988). Statistical Analysis of Cointegrating Vectors. *Journal of Economic Dynamics & Control*, *12*, 231–254. doi:10.1016/0165-1889(88)90041-3

Johansen, S. (1991). Estimation and Hypothesis Testing of Cointegrating Vectors in Gaussian Vector Autoregressive Models. *Econometrics*, *55*, 251–276.

Johansen, S., & Juselius, K. (1990). Maximum Likelihood Estimation and Inference on Cointegration-with Application to the Demand for Money. *Oxford Bulletin of Economics and Statistics*, *52*(2), 169–210.

Kabir, S. H., & Hoque, H. A. A. B. (2007). Financial Liberalization, Financial Development and Economic Growth: Evidence from Bangladesh. *Savings and Development*, *31*, 431–448.

Kateja, A., & Jha, D. (2008). Exploring the Casual Relationship between Telecommunication and GDP Growth in India, 1988-2007. *Artha Vijnana*, *L*(3), 195–208.

Keesing, D. B. (1967). Outward-looking Policies and Economic Development. *The Economic Journal*, *77*(306), 303–320. doi:10.2307/2229306

Keesing, D. B. (1979, August). Trade Policies for Developing Countries (World Bank Staff Working Paper, 353).

Kemal, A. R., Din, M.-u., Qardir, U., Fernando, L., & Colombage, S. (2002). *Exports and Economic Growth in South Asia*. A Study Prepared for the South Asia Network of Economic Research Institutes.

Khalid, A., & Cheng, B. T. (1997). Imports, Exports and Economic Growth: Cointegration and Causality Tests for Singapore. *The Singapore Economic Review*, *42*(2), 32–39.

Khan, A. H., & Hasan, L. (1998). Financial Liberalization, Savings, and Economic Development in Pakistan. *Economic Development and Cultural Change*, *46*(3), 581–597. doi:10.1086/452359

Khan, A. H., Malik, A., & Hasan, L. (1995). Exports, Growth and Causality: An Application of Cointegration and Error-Correction Modelling. *Pakistan Development Review*, *34*(4), 1001–1012.

Khan, M. A. (2007). *Foreign Direct Investment and Economic Growth: The Role of Domestic Financial Sector* (PIDE Working Papers 2007:18).

Khan, M. A. (2008). Financial Development and Economic Growth in Pakistan: Evidence Based on Autoregressive Distributed Lag (ARDL) Approach. *South Asia Economic Journal*, *9*(2), 375–391. doi:10.1177/139156140800900206

Khan, M. A., & Qayyum, A. (2006). Trade Liberalization Financial Sector Reforms, and Growth. *Pakistan Development Review*, *45*(4), 711–731.

Khan, M. A., Qayyum, A., & Sheikh, S. A. (2005). Financial Development and Economic Growth: The Case of Pakistan. *Pakistan Development Review*, *44*(4), 819–837.

Khan, M. S., & Senhadji, A. S. (2000). *Financial Development and Economic Growth: An Overview* (IMF Working Paper 00/209). Washington, DC: International Monetary Fund.

Khan, M. S., & Zahler, R. (1985). Trade and Financial Liberalization Given External Shocks and Inconsistent Domestic Policies. *IMF Staff Papers*, *32*, 22–55.

King, R. G., & Levine, R. (1992). *Financial Indicators and Growth in Cross-Section of Countries* (World Bank Working Paper No. 819).

King, R. G., & Levine, R. (1993a). Finance and Growth: Schumpeter Might be Right. *The Quarterly Journal of Economics*, *108*, 717–737. doi:10.2307/2118406

King, R. G., & Levine, R. (1993b). Finance, Entrepreneurship and Growth. *Journal of Monetary Economics*, *32*, 30–71.

Kletzer, K., & Bardhan, P. (1985). Credit Markets and International Trade. *Journal of Economic Development*, *27*(1-2), 57–70. doi:10.1016/0304-3878(87)90006-X

Krueger, A. O. (1978). *Foreign Trade Regime and Economic Development, Liberalization Attempts and Consequences*. Cambridge, MA: Ballinger.

Krueger, A. O. (1988). *The Experience and Lesson of Asia's Super-Exporters*. In V. Corbo, A. Krueger, & F. Ossa (Eds.), *Export-Oriented Development Strategies: The Success of Five Newly Industrializing Countries*. Boulder, CO: West View Press.

Krueger, A. O. (1998). Why Trade Liberalization is Good for Growth. *The Economic Journal*, *108*, 1513–1522. doi:10.1111/1468-0297.00358

Krugman, P. R. (1990). *Rethinking International Trade*. Cambridge, MA: MIT Press.

Krugman, P. R. (1998). *What Happened in Asia?* (Mimeograph). Cambridge, MA: MIT. Retrieved from http://www.web.mit.edu/krugman/www/DISINTER.html

Kwan, A. C., Wu, Y., & Zhang, J. (1998). An Exogeneity Analysis of Financial Deepening and Economic Growth: Evidence from Hong Kong, South Korea, and Taiwan. *The Journal of International Trade & Economic Development*, *7*(3), 339–354. doi:10.1080/09638199800000018

Laurenceson, J., & Chai, J. C. H. (2003). *Financial Reforms and Economic Development in China*. Cheltenham, UK: Edward Elgar.

Lee, J.-W. (1993). International Trade Distortions and Long-run Economic Growth. *IMF Staff Papers*, 299-328.

Levine, R. (1997). Financial Development and Economic Growth: Views and Agenda. *Journal of Economic Literature*, *35*, 688–726.

Levine, R. (1998). The Legal Environment, Banks, and Long-run Economic Growth. *Journal of Money . Credit and Banking*, *30*, 596–613. doi:10.2307/2601259

Levine, R. (2002). Bank-Based or Market-Based Financial Systems: Which is Better? *Journal of Financial Intermediation*, *11*, 398–428. doi:10.1006/jfin.2002.0341

Levine, R. (2004). *Finance and Growth: Theory and Evidence* (NBER Working Paper No. 10766).

Levine, R., Loayza, N., & Beck, T. (2000). Financial Intermediation and Economic Growth: Causality and Causes. *Journal of Monetary Economics*, *46*, 31–77. doi:10.1016/S0304-3932(00)00017-9

Levine, R., & Renelt, D. (1992). A Sensitivity Analysis of Cross-Country Growth Regressions. *The American Economic Review*, *82*, 942–963.

Levine, R., & Zervos, S. (1998). Stock Markets, Banks, and Economic Growth. *The American Economic Review*, *88*, 537–558.

Lewer, J. J., & Van den Berg, H. (2003). How Large is International Trade's Effect on Economic Growth? *Journal of Economic Surveys*, *17*(3), 363–396. doi:10.1111/1467-6419.00198

Lucas, R. E. Jr. (1988). On the Mechanics of Economic Development. *Journal of Monetary Economics*, *22*, 3–42. doi:10.1016/0304-3932(88)90168-7

Majid, M. S. A., & Mahirizal. (2007). Does Financial Development Cause Economic Growth in the ASEAN-4 Countries? *Savings and Development*, *31*(4), 369–398.

Mallick, H., & Agarwal, S. (2007). Impact of Real Interest rates on Real Output Growth in India: A Long-run Analysis in a Liberalized Financial Regime. *The Singapore Economic Review*, *52*, 215–231. doi:10.1142/S021759080700266X

Mani, S. (2007). Revolution in India's Telecommunication Industry. *Economic and Political Weekly*, *42*(7), 578–580.

Matambalya, F., & Wolf, S. (2001). *Performance of SMEs in East Africa: Case Studies from Kenya and Tanzania*. Bonn, Germany: Centre for Development Research (ZEF).

Mckinnon, R. I. (1973). *Money and Capital in Economic Development*. Washington, DC: Brooking Institution.

Mckinnon, R. I. (1982). The Order of Economic Liberalization: Lessons from Chile and Argentina. In K. Brunner & A. Metzler (Eds.), *Economic Policy in a World of Change: Carnegie-Rochester Conference Series on Public Policy* (Vol. 17). Amsterdam: North Holland

Michaelpoulos, C., & Jay, K. (1973). *Growth of Exports and Income in Developing World: A Neoclassical View* (AID Paper No. 28).

Michaely, M. (1973). Exports and Economic Growth: An Empirical Investigation. *Journal of Development Economics*, *18*, 49–54.

Mohsin, M. H., Kemal, M. A., & Qadir, U. (2001). *Impact of Trade Reforms on Poverty*. Pakistan Institute of Development Economics, 16th Annual General Meeting: Islamabad.

Nair-Reichert, U., & Weinhold, D. (2001). Causality Tests for Cross-Country Panels: A New Look at FDI and Economic Growth in Developing Countries. *Oxford Bulletin of Economics and Statistics*, *63*, 153–171. doi:10.1111/1468-0084.00214

Negroponte, N. (1998). The Third Shall be First: The Net Leverages Latecomers in the Developing Worlds. *Wired Magazine*.

Ning, L. (2007). Economic Liberalization for High-Tech Industry Development? Lesson from China's Response in Developing the ICT Manufacturing Sector Compared with the Strategies of Korea and Taiwan. *The Journal of Development Studies*, *43*(3), 562–587. doi:10.1080/00220380701204547

Norton, S. W. (1992). Transaction Costs, Telecommunications, and the Microeconomics of the Macroeconomics Growth. *Economic Development and Cultural Change*, *41*(1), 175–196. doi:10.1086/452002

Odedokun, M. O. (1998). Financial Intermediation and Economic Growth in Developing Countries. *Journal of Economic Studies (Glasgow, Scotland)*, *25*, 203–224. doi:10.1108/01443589810215351

OECD. (2000). *Policy Brief: Science, Technology and Innovation in the New Economy*. Retrieved from http://www.oecd.org/publication/pol_brief/

OECD. (2003). *OECD Science, Technology and Industry Scoreboard 2003: Towards a Knowledge-Based Economy*. Retrieved from http://www1.oecd.org/publications/e-book/92-2003-04-1-7294/

OECD. (2004). *Science and Innovation Policy: Key Challenges and Opportunities*. Retrieved from http://www.oecd.org/publications/pol-brief/

Ouattara, B. (2004). *Foreign Aid and Fiscal Policy in Senegal*. Mimeo, University of Manchester.

Pesaran, M. H., & Pesaran, B. (1997). *Working with Microfit 4.0: An Interactive Approach*. Oxford, UK: Oxford University Press.

Pesaran, M. H., Shin, Y., & Smith, R. J. (1999, February). *Bounds Testing Approaches to the Analysis of Long Run Relationships* (Working Paper).

Pesaran, M. H., Shin, Y., & Smith, R. J. (2001). Bounds Testing Approaches to the Analysis of Level Relationships. *Journal of Applied Econometrics*, *16*, 289–326. doi:10.1002/jae.616

Prasad, A., & Ghosh, S. (2007). Competition in Indian Banking: An Empirical Evaluation. *South Asia Economic Journal*, *8*, 265–284. doi:10.1177/139156140700800205

Quibria, M. G., Ahmed, S. N., Tschang, T., & Reyes-Macasaquit, M.-L. (2003). Digital Divide: Determinants and Policies with Special Reference to Asia. *Journal of Asian Economics*, *13*, 811–825. doi:10.1016/S1049-0078(02)00186-0

Rajan, R. G., & Zingalas, L. (1998). Financial Dependence and Growth. *The American Economic Review*, *88*, 559–586.

Rajan, R. G., & Zingalas, L. (2003). The Great Reversals: The Politics of Financial Development in the Twentieth Century. *Journal of Financial Economics*, *69*, 5–50. doi:10.1016/S0304-405X(03)00125-9

Ram, R. (1985). Exports and Economic Growth: Some Additional Evidence. *Economic Development and Cultural Change*, *33*, 415–425. doi:10.1086/451468

Ram, R. (1999). Financial Development and Economic Growth: Additional Evidence. *The Journal of Development Studies*, *35*(4), 164–174. doi:10.1080/00220389908422585

Research and Information System (RIS) for the Non-aligned and Other Countries. (2004). *South Asia Development and Cooperation Report 2004*.

Robinson, J. (1952). *The Rate of Interests and Other Easys*. London: Macmillan.

Roller, L.-M., & Waverman, L. (2001). Telecommunication Infrastructure and Economic Development: A Simultaneous Approach. *The American Economic Review*, *91*(4), 909–923.

Romer, P. M. (1990). Endogenous Technological Change. *The Journal of Political Economy*, *98*(5), 71–102. doi:10.1086/261725

Romer, P. M. (1993). Idea Gaps and Object Gaps in Economic Development. *Journal of Monetary Economics*, *32*(3), 543–573. doi:10.1016/0304-3932(93)90029-F

Romer, P. M. (1994). The Origin of Endogenous Growth. *The Journal of Economic Perspectives*, *8*(1), 3–22.

Roubini, N., & Sala-i-Martin, X. (1991). *Financial Development, the Trade Regime and Economic Growth* (NBER Working Paper No. 3876).

Rousseau, P. L., & Vuthipadadorn, D. (2005). Finance, Investment, and Growth: Time Series Evidence from 10 Asian Economies. *Journal of Macroeconomics*, *27*, 87–106. doi:10.1016/j.jmacro.2003.09.004

Rousseau, P. L., & Wachtel, P. (1998). Financial Intermediation and Economic Performance: Historical Evidence from Five Industrialized Countries. *Journal of Money . Credit and Banking*, *30*(4), 657–678. doi:10.2307/2601123

Sachs, J. D., & Warner, A. (1995). Economic Reforms and Process of Global Integration. *Brookings Papers on Economic Activity*, *1*, 1–118. doi:10.2307/2534573

Sala-i-Martin, X., & Barro, R. J. (1995). *Economic Growth*. New York: McGraw-Hill.

Santos-Paulino, A., & Thirwall, A. P. (2004). The Impact of Trade Liberalization on Exports, Imports and the Balance of Payments of Developing Countries. *The Economic Journal*, *114*, F50–F72. doi:10.1111/j.0013-0133.2004.00187.x

Schumpeter, J. A. (1911). *Theorie der Wirtschaftlichen Entwicklung* [The Theory of Economic Development] (Opie, R. Trans.). Leipzig, Germany: Dunker & Humblot.

Shaw, E. S. (1973). *Financial Deepening in Economic Development*. Cambridge, MA: Harvard University Press.

Siddiki, J. U. (2002). Trade and Financial Liberalization and Endogenous Growth in Bangladesh. *International Economic Journal*, *16*, 23–37. doi:10.1080/10168730200080019

Singh, A., & Weisse, B. A. (1998). Emerging Stock Markets, Portfolio Capital Flows and Long-Term Economic Growth: Micro and Macroeconomic Perspectives. *World Development*, *26*(4), 607–622. doi:10.1016/S0305-750X(98)00003-5

Sinha, D., & Macri, J. (2001). Financial Development and Economic Growth: The Case of Eight Asian Countries. *Economia Internazionale*, *54*(2), 218–234.

Spears, A. (1992). The Role of Financial Intermediation in Economic Growth in Sub-Saharan Africa. *Canadian Journal of Development Studies*, *13*(3), 361–380.

State Bank of Pakistan. (2007). *Annual Report for 2006-07* (Vol. 1).

Svaleryd, H., & Vlachos, J. (2005). Financial Markets, the Pattern of Specialization and Comparative Advantage. *European Economic Review*, *49*, 113–144. doi:10.1016/S0014-2921(03)00030-8

Tadesse, S. (2002). Financial Architecture and Economic Performance: International Evidence. *Journal of Financial Intermediation*, *11*, 429–454. doi:10.1006/jfin.2002.0352

Temple, J. (1999). The New Growth Evidence. *Journal of Economic Literature*, *37*, 112–156.

Thornton, J. (1996). Financial Deepening and Economic Growth in Developing Economies. *Applied Economics Letters*, *3*(4), 243–246. doi:10.1080/758520872

Torero, M., Choudhary, S., & Bedi, A. S. (2005). Telecommunication and Economic Growth: Implications for India. In A. Saith & M. Vijayabaskar (Eds.), *ICT's and Indian Economic Development* (pp. 231-264). New Delhi, India: Sage Publications.

Tyler, W. (1981). Growth and Export Expansion in Developing Countries. *Journal of Development Economics*, *9*, 121–130. doi:10.1016/0304-3878(81)90007-9

World Bank. (1987). *World Development Report*. Oxford, UK: Oxford University Press.

World Bank. (1989). *World Development Report 1989*. Oxford, UK: Oxford University Press.

Yang, Y., & Haung, Y. (1997). *Impact of Trade Liberalization on Income Distribution in China* (Economic Division Working Paper No. 1).

Yanikkaya, H. (2003). Trade Openness and Economic Growth: A Cross-Country Empirical Investigation. *Journal of Development Economics*, *72*(1), 57–89. doi:10.1016/S0304-3878(03)00068-3

Yusof, R. M., & Majid, M. S. A. (2007). Macroeconomic Variables and Stock Returns in Malaysia: An Application of the ARDL Bound Testing Approach. *Savings and Development*, *31*(4), 449–469.

ENDNOTES

1. Barriers to trade and anti-export bias will reduce exports growth and imports controls may likely to reduce efficiency (Santos-Paulino and Thirlwall, 2004).
2. However, the presumption that trade liberalization will raises the economic growth is uncertain because this depends on the relative impact of liberalization on export and import growth and the prices of the traded goods. Santos-Paulino and Thirlwall,(2004, p. F50) stated that "trade liberalization may promotes economic growth from the supply side but, if the balance of payments worsens, growth may be adversely affected from the demand side because the payments deficits resulting from liberalization are unsustainable and not easily rectified by relative price (real exchange rate) changes".
3. In the mid-1980s, except Sri Lanka all South Asian economies protected their import competing sectors with very high tariffs (i.e. India and Pakistan had the highest duties). Sri Lanka removed most quantitive restrictions in the 1980s. By the end of 1990s only a few controls remained on selected agricultural

and industrial commodities (Dash and Kumar, 2007).

4 For further detail, see Ram (1985), Balassa (1985), Michaelpoulos and Jay (1973).

5 The sample period for India and Sri Lanka is 1970-2006, for Pakistan the sample span is 1972-2007 and for Bangladesh the sample period consists of 1974-2006.

6 Sufficient data on IT indicators are not available. Therefore, we exclude IT variable from the analysis.

7 The standard measure of financial development is the ratio of M2 to GDP (World Bank, 1989). However, this ratio measures the extent of monetization rather than financial development. In developing countries, monetization can be increasing without financial development; therefore, M2/GDP is not a satisfactory indicator of financial development. Therefore, we define ratio total bank deposit liabilities to GDP as proxy of financial development.

7 Nominal GDP is adjusted for 1999-00 base.

8 It may also be possible that the funds from portfolio investment were diverted to financing long-term loans for productive purposes.

Chapter 9
Changing Contours of Indian Investment Abroad:
Evolution, Diagnosis and Public Policy

Lakhwinder Singh
Punjabi University, India

Varinder Jain
Centre for Development Studies, India

ABSTRACT

Emerging growth dynamism of Indian economy in rapidly globalising world is highly recognised and commented by a large body of researchers during the recent period. In fact, the Indian planning has made long concerted effort to develop strategic and competitive capabilities in the agents of production. During the recent periods, these capabilities have started paying. Such trends became more lucid with the strengthening of Indian capital especially abroad as the Indian capital has initiated collaborations and mergers with the global players. This chapter provides insights into such achievement of the Indian economy. Besides providing a review of theory and practice of emerging multinationals from developing countries, this chapter examines India's outward foreign direct investment in an evolutionary perspective. In its endeavor the study, besides tracing the emerging pattern of India's outward foreign direct investment, hints at the facilitating role of state policy to encourage the outflow of foreign direct investment.

INTRODUCTION

During recent years, the Indian economy has shown high dynamism in its process of structural transformation and economic growth. Such achievement has been the result of long concerted efforts made by the Indian government to develop strategic capabilities in (economic) production agents. It is noteworthy that the innovations system put in place by the Indian development strategy, which itself has undergone unprecedented changes from import substitution to nearly open system, has developed and nurtured some strategic and unique cost reduction capabilities in economic agents of production.

The Indian policy regime, guided by national development priorities, allowed Indian enterprises to invest abroad for attaining not only the economies

DOI: 10.4018/978-1-61520-709-1.ch009

of scale but also to remain competitive vis-à-vis their counterparts in other nations. Earlier phase of Indian economic development, under restrictive policy regime (to invest abroad), aimed at boosting domestic investment, which enabled Indian enterprises to learn adaptive capabilities whereas the second phase of Indian economic development encouraged Indian companies to invest abroad for reducing the deficiency of strategic asset requirements for sustaining domestic development process. Consequently, during the recent phase of fast economic growth, the Indian enterprises have been expanding both in the domestic and international market while competing with the global brands and multinational enterprises. The Indian enterprises have a long experience of investing abroad in technologically low end or equal level countries, which happened to be India's strategic trading partners.

The recent spurt in India's outbound investment in the developed countries needs to be examined seriously. In this line, the present chapter examines, in an evolutionary perspective, India's outward foreign direct investment and in its endeavor, the chapter besides tracing the emerging pattern of India's outward foreign direct investment hints at the facilitating role of state policy to encourage the outflow of Indian foreign direct investment.

The chapter is spread across five sections. Besides this (first) introductory section, second section provides a review of theory and practice of emerging multinational corporations belonging to developing countries. The changing structure of Indian outward foreign investment, both country-wise and industry-wise, is discussed in section three. The facilitating role of Indian state policy, since 1974, to encourage outward foreign direct investment is examined in the fourth section whereas the emerging conclusions are discussed briefly in the last (fifth) section.

MNC'S EMERGENCE FROM DEVELOPING ECONOMIES: THEORY AND EMPIRICS

Recently, international expansion of business has attracted attention of a large number of researchers. The theory of international operation of firm has sought to understand the major determinants influencing 'Outward Foreign Direct Investment' (OFDI, hereafter). The established theories of international investment based on the experience of the firms from the industrially advanced countries suggest that the competitive advantage allows firms to expand business and secure higher returns. The theoretical perspectives on the international operation of firm have evolved from Hymer (1976), Dunning (2000) and several others. The unique competitive advantage possessed by firms is based on innovation activity largely concentrated in the home country. This unique competitive advantage, in the form of ownership, location and internationalization, allows firms to acquire monopolistic or oligopolistic power in the market and expand their businesses internationally through investments, mergers and acquisitions.

It is widely recognized fact that the national innovation system of the emerging developing economies and emerging multinational enterprises of the developing countries do not possess such unique competitive advantage primarily due to the infancy of their national innovation systems. Consequently, the emerging multinational enterprises of these developing economies internationalize businesses mainly to acquire competitive advantage, which they do not possess (Nayyar, 2008). Under such circumstances, the theoretical developments explaining motives behind internationalization of business by firms, based on the experience of industrially advanced country firms, remain inadequate to explain recent spurt in internationalization of firms from developing economies (including India).

Mathews (2006), based on outward foreign direct investment from newly industrializing East

Asian countries, explains that firms of emerging developing countries make overseas investments to secure strategic resource for enhancing their learning capabilities. The emerging multinational firms from developing economies seem to have been using defensive and assertive options leveraging on their unique assets or resources (Dawar and Frost, 1999). Khana and Palepu (2006) has argued that the emerging multinational firms of developing countries possess distinct advantage to deal with institutional voids that can be exploited to counter foreign multinational firms both in the local economies and can be extended to international markets.

Aulakh (2007) has argued that the 'emerging economy multinationals' use the existing ownership advantage to pursue the acquisition of complementary resources and capabilities required to develop potential competitive advantage for survival in more competitive environments. More recently, the rules and regulations governing the international firms have been dramatically altered to facilitate operations of the firms in the international markets (UNCTAD, 2008). Opening up of capital markets have been made easier (than before) for emerging multinational enterprises from developing countries to raise equity capital and debt besides facilitating their listing of shares on foreign stock exchanges. These firms have been encouraged by emerging developing countries as well as they (home countries) have made suitable policy changes to enable their firms raise equity capital and debt from foreign markets (Ramamurti, 2008; RBI, 2009).

Thus, it emerges from above brief review of literature that there are multiple and complex factors, such as market access for exports, horizontal/vertical integration, delivery of services, acquisition of international brand names, access to technology and resources, and to aspiration of global leadership, driving the internationalization of firms.

TREND AND PATTERN OF INDIAN OUTWARD FOREIGN DIRECT INVESTMENT (OFDI)

During the recent phase of globalization, the outward foreign direct investment has dramatically increased (Table 1). The OFDI stock of the world as a whole has increased from US $1,785,267 million in 1990 to US $6,148,211 million in 2000 and further increased to US $15,602,339 million in 2007. The share of the stock of world OFDI in the global gross domestic product increased from 9.10 per cent in 1990 to 18.10 percent in 2000 and further increased to 27.90 per cent in 2007. On the other hand, stock of OFDI of the developing economies was US $144,862 million in the year 1990, which was just 4 per cent of the gross domestic product of the developing economies. During the 1990-2000 period, the stock of OFDI of the developing economies has grown at a fast rate than that of the total world stock of OFDI. The share of stock of OFDI of developing economies increased from 4 per cent in 1990 to 12.90 percent in the year 2000. This rapid rise in magnitude of OFDI stock of developing countries was essentially attributed to the emergence of multinational firms from developing countries.

There is a qualitative change in the pattern of international investment abroad by emerging

Table 1. Global trend of OFDI, 1990-2007 (US $ millions)

Year	World	Developing Economies	Developing Economies' share in World	India
1990	1785267 (09.10)	144862 (04.00)	08.11	124 ---
2000	6148211 (18.10)	861842 (12.90)	14.02	1859 (00.40)
2007	15602339 (27.90)	2288073 (16.50)	14.66	29412 (02.60)

Note: Figures in parentheses are percentage of GDP.
Source: (Adapted from UNCTAD, 2008).

Table 2. India's foreign direct investment inflows and outflows (US $ millions)

Year	Inward FDI	Outward FDI
1995	2125	119
1996	2525	240
1997	3619	113
1998	2633	47
1999	2168	80
2000	3585	509
2001	5472	1397
2002	5627	1669
2003	4323	1879
2004	5771	2179
2005	7606	2978
2006	19622	12842
2007	22950	13649
Total	88052	37711

Source: (Adapted from UNCTAD, 2008).

multinational companies from the developing countries, which has drawn the attention of several scholars interested in understanding this phenomenon (Dunning et al., 1998; Gammeltoft, 2008; UNCTAD, 2006). The noteworthy feature of stock of both global and developing economies' OFDI was that there was slow rise in the stock of OFDI between the period 2000 and 2007. The rise of stock of OFDI from developing countries increased more than two times faster than that of the global stock of OFDI. However, the rise of stock of OFDI from both the developing and global economies was nearly similar. Contrary to this, the stock of OFDI from India increased sixteen times during the 2000-07 period whereas it was just more than two and half times in the case of developing economies.

This dramatic rise in OFDI from India needs an explanation. It is pertinent to notice here that both outward and inward flows of investment in the Indian economies increased quite rapidly with some spurts in some of the years (Table 2). The average foreign direct investment inflows, during the 1995-2007 period, were US $ 6,771.23 millions. Except the years 1998, 1999 and 2003 where investment was below the earlier levels, the foreign direct investment inflows have increased substantially during the period under consideration.

Table 2 reveals that the outward foreign direct investment from India was quite meager during the period 1995 to 1999 whereas, it increased to US $ 243 million in 1996 from US $ 119 million in 1995. It started declining after 1996 and reached to a whopping low of US $ 47 million in the year 1998. But in the next year, that is, 1999 it increased again to US $ 80 million. During the whole period (1995-2007), the average increase in OFDI was US $ 2,900.08 million. However, a consideration of the 2000-2007 period reveals that the average annual rise in the OFDI from India was US $ 4,637.75 million.

Comparative analysis of the flows of FDI and OFDI clearly brings out the fact that FDI inflows continuously remained higher than that of the OFDI flows. However, the gap between the FDI and OFDI flows, which were very wide before the year 2000, has been narrowed down substantially after the year 2001. That is why the period 2001-2007 has been described as the arrival of Indian companies in the developed countries and expanded Indian investment abroad. This spurt of outflows of investment abroad has been taken with surprise. Thus, the scrutiny of such new trends is essentially being done from the point of view of both theory and public policy in understanding the process of the emergence of Indian companies as global players (Aulakh, 2007; Ramamurti, 2008).

The share of OFDI in various sectors (over time) is presented in Table 3 to reveal the sources of OFDI from India. It has been the manufacturing sector that has contributed largely to OFDI from India. The share of the manufacturing sector was 23.84 percent in the year 2000-01. Thereafter the share of manufacturing sector increased to 53.82 percent in 2001-02 and further jumped to 70.69

Table 3. Sectoral distribution of India's OFDI, 2000-01 to 2007-08, (US $ millions)

Year	Manufacturing	Financial Services	Non-financial Services	Trading	Others	Total
2000-01	169 (23.84)	6 (00.85)	470 (66.29)	52 (07.33)	12 (01.69)	709 (100)
2001-02	528 (53.82)	4 (00.41)	350 (35.68)	79 (08.05)	20 (02.04)	981 (100)
2002-03	1271 (70.69)	3 (00.17)	404 (22.47)	82 (04.56)	38 (02.11)	1798 (100)
2003-04	893 (59.77)	1 (00.07)	456 (30.52)	113 (07.56)	31 (02.07)	1494 (100)
2004-05	1170 (65.88)	7 (00.39)	304 (17.12)	192 (10.81)	100 (05.63)	1776 (100)
2005-06	3407 (67.46)	160 (03.17)	895 (17.72)	377 (07.46)	207 (04.10)	5050 (100)
2006-07	3545 (26.34)	28 (00.21)	7486 (55.62)	1739 (12.92)	656 (04.87)	13459 (1000
2007-08	6240 (34.84)	26 (00.14)	1635 (09.13)	8993 (50.21)	1010 (05.64)	17910 (100)

Source: (Adapted from RBI Annual Reports, 2005-06 and 2007-08).

percent in 2002-03, which is the highest relative contribution of the manufacturing sector across sectors and over time. The manufacturing sector's share declined in the year 2003-04, but was of the order of 60 percent. It slightly picked up in the next two years and again its relative contribution started declining substantially and was 26.34 per cent of the total investment abroad during 2006-07. Thereafter, the share of manufacturing sector increased to 34.85 percent during 2007-08. The major manufacturing industrial groups in which Indian investment abroad have been made were chemical and allied products, transport equipment, primary metal and fabricated metal products, electronic and other electrical equipment except computers, measuring analyzing and controlling equipments and pharmaceuticals.

The description of Indian economy as the 'Office of Global Economy' signifies the worldwide recognition of well-developed service sector of its economy. Therefore, the importance of non-financial sector in terms of its contribution to the total investment abroad is but natural. The share of non-financial service in the OFDI from India was 66.29 percent in the year 2000-01. However, the share of non-financial services declined sharply since 2000-01 and the manufacturing sector contributed substantially during the early years of the 21st century.

Among the non-financial sector, the business services dominated in terms of their contribution to India's OFDI. The other services that have contributed substantially to India's OFDI were engineering, accounting, research, management and related services, communication, hotels, security and insurance. The OFDI related to trade, during the 2000-08 period, has assumed third place in terms of its contribution to the total OFDI from India. The share of trade related services in OFDI from India was just 7.33 percent in the year 2000-01 and slowly increased during the period of analysis and was of the order of 50.21 percent in the year 2007-08. It is worth noticing that India's OFDI in financial services remained negligible during the period under consideration (Table 3).

The presence of Indian companies abroad has attracted the attention of both media and academics alike due to reason that the aggressive poster adopted by the Indian companies to purchase companies in the developed countries in the recent past. The evidence of international investment made by Indian companies abroad through mergers and acquisitions is presented in Table 4. It becomes evident from the analysis of sale and purchases of the Indian companies in the form of mergers and acquisitions abroad that the total sales during the period 2000 to 2008 was US $ 22,991 million. Whereas the total purchases were of the order of US $ 56,114 million during the same period. Thus, the aggressive mergers and acquisition strategy of the Indian companies

Table 4. India's Value of Cross-Border Mergers & Acquisitions 2000-08, (US $ Millions)

Year	Sales	Purchases	Sales-Purchases Gap
2000	1219	910	309
2001	1037	2195	-1158
2002	1698	270	1428
2003	949	1362	-413
2004	1760	863	897
2005	3754	4958	-1204
2006	4740	6586	-1846
2007	5580	30414	-24834
2008	2254	8556	-6302
Total	22991	56114	-33123

Source: (Adapted from UNCTAD, 2008).

resulted into purchases larger than the sales of the order of US $ 33,123 million.

Out of the nine years period under consideration, the purchases exceeded sales with substantial margin in six years. The purchases made by the Indian companies abroad between the period 2005 and 2008 were substantially higher than earlier years. The consistent rise in the value of OFDI in mergers and acquisitions by Indian companies has provided the status of 'Global Players' to Indian companies. Available evidence on mergers and acquisitions of Indian companies abroad shows that more than 40 per cent were in manufacturing sector (pharmaceuticals, automotive, consumer goods, chemicals, fertilizers, and metals). However, the 30 percent share of mergers and acquisitions has gone to sectors like IT, software and business process outsourcing (CMIE, 2007).

An interesting feature of Indian companies' strategy of mergers and acquisitions, during 2000-07 period, was that more than 42 mergers and acquisitions were only in the US, 19.52 per cent were in the UK and the Western Europe accounted for 52.19 per cent of the total acquisitions (Bertoni, Elia and Rabbiosi, 2008). Thus, both sectoral and geographical spread lead one to believe that the Indian companies have entered into high value added industries and that too of the developed countries businesses.

Table 5 provides information on top twenty-five foreign acquisitions by Indian firms during the period 2000-07. Out of the top 25 foreign acquisitions by Indian firms, six foreign acquisitions belonged to the Tata group of companies and five belonged to the Indian public sector companies. Two of the foreign acquisition of the Tata Group has been in UK and USA each and two were in East Asia (one each in Singapore and Thailand) whereas out of five foreign acquisitions of Indian public sector companies, four belonged to ONGC Videsh and one belonged to VSNL Ltd. It is important to note that the ONGC Videsh targeted petroleum and the foreign acquisitions were made in the countries other than the developed ones. However, the VSNL Ltd. (targeting telecommunication) has foreign acquisition in the US.

This table further reveals that out of the top 25 foreign acquisitions by the Indian companies, sixteen were in the developed countries and the nine were spread over to various other parts of the globe. The seven foreign acquisitions by Indian firms were in the area of resources such as petroleum, steel and aluminum. The sectoral distribution of top 25 foreign acquisitions by Indian companies shows that the largest number of foreign acquisitions, that is, five belongs to the consumer goods sector, followed by steel and petroleum (four each), pharmaceutical and information technology (three each), telecommunication (two), and each one foreign acquisition in the sectors such as aluminium, medical equipment, energy and paper.

Furthermore, it also reveals the ownership (or effective control) pattern of these foreign acquisitions. It is important to notice that among the top 25 foreign acquisitions, 100 percent ownership were reported in twelve foreign acquisitions, followed by 97 percent to 50 percent in four foreign acquisitions, and one each foreign acquisition has ownership control of 30 percent and 25 per cent, which were the minority joint ventures. However, the rest of the seven foreign acquisitions have not reported equity participation ownership. From the above discussion, it can be concluded that the foreign acquisitions by the Indian companies were targeting to have a complete control over the ownership of these companies.

INDIAN OUTWARD FOREIGN DIRECT INVESTMENT POLICY SINCE 1974

The government of India has shown the need of outward foreign investment by Indian companies to ease foreign exchange constraint through exports of Indian capital goods, technology and consultancy services. It was in the year 1974 when Inter-Ministerial Committee on Joint Ventures Abroad was set up under the Ministry of Commerce by the Government of India to scrutinize the proposals made by Indian companies for overseas investment for granting approvals. The Inter-Ministerial Committee formulated detailed guidelines for approving Indian companies' proposal for overseas investment. These guidelines were prepared with the view to synchronize Indian participation in accordance with the host country regulations. The guidelines encouraged formation of joint ventures with the host economy enterprises and Indian enterprise equity participation should be made in terms of exporting indigenous plant and machinery and also technical know how from the existing Indian joint ventures. Keeping in view the scarcity of foreign exchange, the cash remittances of capital to overseas joint ventures were discouraged but provision was made to allow it in exceptional cases.

This policy has substantially increased Indian investment flows abroad in the second half of the 1970s. By 1980, India emerged as the third largest exporter of industrial OFDI among the developing countries (Lall, 1983). The import substitution regime has enabled Indian companies to learn to adapt technology, capital goods fabrication capability and human resources. This created assets and provided requisite advantages to Indian companies to extend their business abroad, which boosted Indian outward foreign direct investment. The magnitude of Indian investment abroad declined substantially in the early eighties and turnaround in OFDI occurred again towards the mid-eighties. Indian overseas investment largely remained concentrated in the developing countries in the seventies and the eighties. However, some change has been noticed since the mid-eighties, which had witnessed some rise of investment in the advanced industrial countries (Kumar, 1995).

The first phase of India's outward foreign direct investment, which spanned over 1978 to 1992, has been quite restrictive as outward foreign investment was possible only in the form of minority owned joint ventures. The second phase of Indian outward investment started in the year 1992, when an automatic route for Indian investment abroad was adopted and overseas investment up to US $ 2 million were permitted. The restrictions on cash remittances and minority-ownership were removed. The limit on overseas investment through automatic route was increased to US $ 4 million in the year 1995. An important change with regard to the approval of proposals of overseas investment was shifted from the Ministry of Finance to the Reserve Bank of India (RBI). The RBI was vested with approval amount up to US $ 15 million and the approvals beyond US $ 15 million remained under the purview of the Ministry of Finance.

In the year 2000 and 2002, the upper limit for automatic overseas investment approval was raised to US$ 50 million and US$ 100 million respectively. It needs worth mentioning here that the second phase of India's overseas investment coincided with worldwide liberalization of rules and regulations related to foreign direct investment. During the period 1992 to 2007, the number of countries introducing changes in the regulatory mechanism increased from 43 in 1992 to 92 in 2005 (Table 6). The number of regulatory

Table 5. Top 25 foreign acquisitions by Indian firms from 2000 to 2007

Year	Value (US $ million)	Rank	Indian Firm	Target Firm	Country	Industry	Ownership per cent
2007	12100	1	Tata Steel	Corus Steel	UK	Steel	100
2007	6000	2	Hindalco	Novelis	USA	Aluminium	100
2006	1400	3	ONGC Videsh	Petrobas	Brazil	Petroleum	
2002	766.1	4.	ONGC Videsh	Greater Nile Oil Project	Sudan	Petroleum	25
2006	677	5.	Tata Tea and Tata Sons	Glaceau	USA	Health Drinks	30
2004	600	6.	ONGC Videsh	Greater Plutonio Project	Angola	Petroleum	50
2004	600	7.	Opto Circuits India Ltd	Eurocor GmbH	Germany	Medical Equipment	
2006	570.3	8.	Dr. Reddy's	Betapharm Arzneim-ittel GmbH	Germany	Pharmaceuticals and Healthcare	100
2006	565	9.	Suzlon Energy	Hansen Transmis-sions	Belgium	Energy	100
2006	522	10.	Kraft Foods Ltd	United biscuits	UK	Food and Beverages	
2000	431.2	11.	Tata Tea	Tetley Group	UK	Food and Beverages	100
2006	324	12.	Ranbaxy Laborato-ries Ltd	Terapia SA	Romania	Pharmaceuticals and Healthcare	97
2000	323	13.	ONGC Videsh	Sakhalin-I PSA Project	Russia	Petroleum	100
2005	300	14.	Ispat Industries Ltd	Finmetal Holdings	Bulgaria	Steel	
2005	289.2	15.	Videocon Interna-tional	Thomson SA (CRT business)	Europe, china	Consumer Goods	100
2004	283.7	16.	Tata Steel	NatSteel Asia Pte.	Singapore	Steel	100
2005	254.3	17.	VSNL Ltd	Teleglobe Interna-tional Holdings Ltd	USA	Telecom	100
2005	234.7	18.	Mtrix Laboratories	Docpharma NV	Belgium	Pharmaceuticals and Healthcare	95.5
2006	220	19.	Tata Coffee	Eight o' Clock Coffee Co.	USA	Food & Beverages	100
2006	210	20.	Susken Communi-cation Tech Ltd	Bornia Hightec	Finland	Information Tech-nology	
2006	209	21.	Ballarpur Industries Ltd	Sabah Forest Indus-tries	Malyasia	Pulp and Paper	77.8
2003	191.2	22.	Reliance Infocomm	Flag Telecom	USA	Telecom	100
2006	185	23.	Seagate Tech Ltd	Evault Inc.	USA	Information	
2001	184.6	24.	Citrix Software India Pvt. Ltd	Sequoa Software	USA	Information Tech-nology	
2005	175	25	Tata Steel Ltd.	Millenium Steel Plc	Thailand	Steel	100

Source: (Adapted from UNCTAD, 2008).

Table 6. Global trend of regulatory changes relating to international investments from 1992-2007

Items	1992	1995	2000	2005	2006	2007
Number of countries that introduced changes	43	63	70	92	91	58
Number of regulatory changes	77	112	150	203	177	98
More favorable changes	77	106	147	162	142	74
Less favorable changes	0	6	3	41	35	24

Source: (Adapted from UNCTAD, 2008).

changes increased during the same period from 77 to 203 and more favorable changes towards overseas investment also increased from 77 to 162. This shows that global economy has framed rules and regulations to attract foreign investment and India has also framed regulations, which permitted Indian companies to try their metal in the international markets. These relaxed regulations in the global economy were also accompanied with much greater access to financial markets.

The policy changes with regard to Indian overseas investment since the year 2004 have been described as liberal (Nayyar, 2008). The liberal phase of the policy changes are described in the Table 7. A perusal of table 7 reveals that the automatic route was extended up to 100 percent of the firm's net worth and was increased to 200 per cent of the net worth in the year 2005. The prior approval from RBI was dispensed with and firms were also allowed to obtain the remittances through any authorized foreign exchange dealer. In 2005, banks were permitted to lend money to Indian companies for acquisitions of equity in overseas joint ventures, wholly owned subsidiaries or other overseas companies as strategic investment.

In the year 2007, the limit of overseas investment of Indian companies was increased to 300 per cent of net worth in the month of June 2007 and further raised to 400 per cent of the net worth of a company in the month of September 2007. The analysis of the changes related to overseas investment presented in Table 7 clearly brings out the fact that Indian government has eased any difficulty arising on the way of Indian companies undertaking OFDI. The big boost of Indian outbound investment since the year 2000 can essentially be attributed to the policy changes affected by the government of India to encourage Indian companies during the period 2000 to 2008.

CONCLUSION

Indian firms have a long experience of operation and investment in other countries of the world. The overseas investment experience of Indian firms has revealed that they have operated largely in the developing countries possessing technological and other capabilities equal or lower than at home. The recent spurt in expansion of OFDI from India was in sharp contrast of its own earlier OFDI experience as well as from other developing countries. The more than 70 per cent of OFDI from India flowed to industrially advanced countries. The larger proportion of OFDI from India was in the manufacturing activities. The significant proportion (80 per cent) of acquisitions was in the developed countries.

Indian economy has been regarded as the office of the global economy that signifies the importance of information technology and communication services provided to the industrially advanced countries of the world. There has been a gradual shift in the composition of Indian OFDI during the late nineties of the twentieth century and the early years of twenty-first century from manufacturing to more favorable to service sector, which includes information technology and communications.

Among the total value of mergers and acquisitions of Indian companies abroad, 30 percent share of mergers and acquisitions has gone to sectors like IT, software and related services. Out of the top twenty-five acquisitions of Indian companies abroad from the period of 2000 to 2007, the five were from the information technology and communications. These all the five acquisitions were

Table 7. Selected changes in Indian overseas investment policy

1.	Indian companies permitted to undertake overseas investments by market purchases of foreign exchange without prior approval of RBI up to 100.0% of their net worth; up from the previous limit of 50.0%.
2.	An Indian company with a satisfactory track record allowed investing up to 100.0% of its net worth within the overall limit of US$ 100.0 million by way of market purchases for investment in a foreign entity engaged in any bona fide business activity from 2004. The provision restricting overseas investments in the same activity as its core activity at home of the Indian company were removed. Listed Indian companies, residents and mutual funds permitted to invest abroad in companies listed on a recognized stock exchange and in company that has the shareholding of at least 10% in an Indian company listed on a recognized stock exchange in India.
3.	Indian companies in special economic zones permitted to undertake overseas investment up to any amount without the restriction of the US$ 100.0 million ceiling under the automatic route, provided the funding was done out of the Exchange Earners Foreign Currency Account balances.
4.	The three years profitability condition requirement was removed for Indian companies making overseas investments under the automatic route.
5.	Overseas investments were allowed to be funded up to 100.0% by ADR/GDR proceeds up from the previous ceiling of 50.0%. Further an Indian firm that had exhausted the limit of US$ 100.0 million in a year could apply to the RBI for a block allocation of foreign exchange subject to such terms and conditions as may be necessary.
6.	Overseas investments were opened up to registered partnership firms and companies that provided professional services. The minimum net worth requirement of Rs. 150 million for Indian companies engaged in financial sector activities in India was removed for investment abroad in the financial sector.
7.	In 2004, Indian firms allowed to undertake agricultural activities, which were previously restricted, either directly or through an overseas branch; and are now permitted under the automatic route.
8.	In 2004, the RBI further relaxed the monetary ceiling on Indian companies' investment abroad. Indian companies can now invest up to 100.0% of their net worth without any separate ceiling even if the investment exceeds the US$ 100.0 million limit. Furthermore, Indian companies can now invest or make acquisitions abroad even in areas unrelated to their business at home.
9.	In 2005, banks were permitted to lend money to Indian companies for acquisition of equity in overseas joint ventures, wholly owned subsidiaries or in other overseas companies as strategic investment.
10.	In 2006, the automatic route of disinvestments was further liberalized. Indian companies are now permitted to disinvest without prior approval of the RBI in select categories. To encourage large and important exporters, proprietary/unregistered partnership firms have been allowed to set up a JV/WOS outside Indian with the prior approval of RBI.
11.	In 2007, the ceiling of investment by Indian entities was revised from 100 per cent of the net worth to 200 per cent of the net worth of the investing company under the automatic route of overseas investment. The limit of 200 per cent of the net worth of the Indian party was enhanced to 300 per cent of the net worth in June 2007 under automatic route (200 per cent in case of revisited partnership firms). In September 2007, this was further enhanced to 400 per cent of the net worth of the Indian party.
12.	The Liberalized Remittance Scheme (LRS) for Resident individuals was further liberalized by enhancing the existing limit of US$ 100.00 per financial year to US$ 200.00 per financial year (April-March) in September 2007.
13.	The limit of portfolio investment by listed Indian companies in the equity of listed foreign companies was raised in September 2007 from 35 per cent to 50 per cent of the net worth of the investing company as on the date of its last audited balance sheet. Furthermore, the requirement of reciprocal 10 per cent shareholding in Indian companies has been dispensed with.
14.	The aggregate ceiling for overseas investment by mutual funds, registered with SEBI, was enhanced from US$ 4 billion to US$ 5 billion in September 2007. This was further raised to US$ 7 billion in April 2008. The existing facility to allow a limited number of qualified Indian mutual funds to invest cumulatively up to US$ 1 billion in overseas Exchange Traded Funds, as may be permitted by the SEBI would continue. The investments would be subject to the terms and conditions and operational guidelines as issued by SEBI.
15.	Registered Trusts and Societies engaged in manufacturing/educational sector have been allowed in June 2008 to make investment in the same sector(s) in a Joint Venture or Wholly Owned Subsidiary outside India, with the prior approval of the Reserve Bank.
16.	Registered Trusts and Societies which have set up hospital(s) in India have been allowed in August 2008 to make investment in the same sector(s) in a JV/WOS outside India, with the prior approval of the Reserve Bank.

Source: (Adapted from RBI, 2009; Jha, 2006)

in the industrially advanced countries. The IT boom of mergers and acquisitions seems to have worked in the late nineties of the last century and early years of present century. However, recently the structure of Indian OFDI has moved more favorably towards manufacturing sector.

The changing pattern of OFDI from India during the recent past can essentially be attributed to numerous underlying factors. Indian economy has shown high degree of dynamism in the process of structural transformation that has provided dividends in terms of OFDI. This achievement is due to concerted efforts made by the Indian government to develop strategic capabilities in the economic agents of production. The innovations system put in place by the Indian development strategy, which itself has undergone unprecedented changes from import substitution to nearly open system, has developed and nurtured some strategic and unique cost reduction capabilities in the economic agents of production (Nagraj, 2006). Indian policy regime, keeping in view the national development priorities, allowed Indian enterprises to invest abroad to achieve economies of scale and remain competitive with companies of other countries. In the early stage of Indian economic development, the Indian enterprises faced restrictive policy regime (to invest abroad).

Primarily with a concern to boost domestic investment, they were enabled to acquire adaptive capabilities. During the second phase of Indian economic development, the Indian companies were increasingly encouraged to invest abroad to reduce the deficiency of strategic asset requirements for sustaining domestic development process. The liberalization phase boosted OFDI due to increasing domestic competition and suitable policy changes related to encouraging and enabling Indian firms to expand overseas investment. The liberalization policy environment has succeeded more recently due to the systematic development of capabilities, in the form of technology and management, to compete in the international markets. The national innovation system developed during the last five and a half decades has paid high dividends. This is the foremost lesson that can be learned from the experience of the rapid expansion of Indian OFDI to developed countries.

ACKNOWLEDGMENT

The authors are grateful to two anonymous referees for their constructive comments and helpful suggestions on the earlier version of the chapter.

REFERENCES

Aulakh, P. S. (2007). Emerging Multinationals from Developing Economies: Motivations, Paths and Performance. *Journal of International Management*, *13*(3), 235–240. doi:10.1016/j.intman.2007.05.001

Bertoni, F., Elia, S., & Rabbiosi, L. (2008). *Drivers of Acquisitions from BRICs to Advanced Countries: Firm-Level Evidence*. Paper presented in the conference on Emerging Multinationals: Outward FDI from Emerging and Developing Economies, Copenhagen Business School, Copenhagen, Denmark.

CMIE. (2007). *Mergers and Acquisitions*. Mumbai, India: Centre for Monitoring the Indian Economy.

Dawar, N., & Frost, T. (1999). Competing with Giants: Survival Strategies for Local Companies in Emerging Markets. *Harvard Business Review*, *77*(2), 119–129.

Dunning, J. H. (2000). The Eclectic Paradigm as an Envelope for Economic and Business Theories of MNE Activity. *International Business Review*, (2): 163–190. doi:10.1016/S0969-5931(99)00035-9

Dunning, J. H., et al. (1998). Third World Multinationals Revisited: New Developments and Theoretical Implications. In J.H. Dunning (Ed.), *Globalization, Trade and Foreign Direct Investment*. Oxford, UK: Pergamon.

Gammeltoft, P. (2008). Emerging Multinationals: Outward FDI from the BRICS Countries. *International Journal of Technology and Globalisation, 4*(1), 5–22. doi:10.1504/IJTG.2008.016184

Hymer, S. (1976). *The International Operation of National Firms*. Cambridge, MA: MIT Press.

Jha, R. (2006). Outward Foreign Direct Investment from India. In *2006 Global Meeting*. VA: Emerging Markets Forum.

Khana, T., & Palepu, K. (2006). Emerging Giants: Building World-Class Companies in Developing Countries. *Harvard Business Review, 84*(10), 60–70.

Kumar, N. (1995). *Industrialization, Liberalization and Two Way Flows of Foreign Direct Investments: The Case of India* (Discussion Paper No. 9504). Institute for New Technologies, Maastricht: United Nations University.

Lall, S. (1983). *The New Multinationals: the Spread of third World Enterprises*. New York: John Wiley.

Mathews, J. A. (2006). Dragon Multinationals: New Players in 21st Century Globalization. *Asia Pacific Journal of Management, 23*(1), 5–27. doi:10.1007/s10490-006-6113-0

Nagraj, R. (2006). Indian Investments Abroad: What Explains the Boom? *Economic and Political Weekly, 41*(46), 4716–4717.

Nayyar, D. (2008). *Internationalization of Firms From India: Investment, Mergers and Acquisitions. Trade and Globalization*. New Delhi, India: Oxford University Press.

Ramamurti, R. (2008). *What Have We Learned About Emerging-Market MNEs? Insights from a Multi-Country Research Project*. Paper Presented in the Conference on Emerging Multinationals: Outward FDI from Emerging and Developing Economies, Copenhagen Business School, Copenhagen, Denmark.

RBI. (2009, January). Indian Investment Abroad in Joint Ventures and Wholly Owned Subsidiaries: 2008-09. *Monthly Bulletin*. Mumbai, India: Reserve Bank of India.

RBI. (2005-06). *Annual Report*. Mumbai, India: Reserve Bank of India.

RBI. (2007-08). *Annual Report*. Mumbai, India: Reserve Bank of India.

UNCTAD. (2006). FDI from Developing and Transition Countries: Implications for Development. In *World Investment Report 2006*. New York: United Nations.

UNCTAD. (2008). Transnational Corporations and the Infrastructure Challenge. In *World Investment Report 2008*. New York: United Nations.

ADDITIONAL READING

Agarwal, J. P. (1985). *Pros and Cons of Third World Multinationals: A Case Study of India*. J.C.B. Mohr, Tubingen, Kieler Studien.

Indian Investment Centre. (2000). *Guidelines for Indian Joint Ventures and Wholly Owned Subsidiaries Abroad*. New Delhi.

Kumar, N. (1998). Emerging Outward Foreign Direct Investment from Asian Developing Countries: Prospects and Implications, In N. Kumar (Ed.), *Globalization, Foreign Direct Investment and Technology Transfers* (pp. 177-194). London: Routledge.

Lall, R. B. (1986). *Multinationals from the Third World: Indian Firms Investing Abroad*. Delhi, India: Oxford University Press.

Pradhan, J. P. (2003). *Rise of Service Sector Outward Foreign Direct Investment from Indian Economy: Trends, Patterns and Determinants* (RIS Discussion Paper, No. 63/2003). New Delhi.

Pradhan, J. P. (2004). The Determinants of Outward Foreign Direct Investment: A Film-level Analysis of Indian Manufacturing. *Oxford Development Studies*, *32*(4), 619–639. doi:10.1080/1360081042000293371

WTO. (1998). *Trade Policy Review: India*. Geneva, Switzerland.

Section 4
Information and Communication Technologies

Chapter 10
Does Information and Communication Technologies Sustain Economic Growth?
The Underdeveloped and Developing Countries Case

Erkan Erdil
Middle East Technical University, Turkey

İ. Hakan Yetkiner
Izmir University of Economics, Turkey

Burcu Türkcan
Ege University, Turkey

ABSTRACT

This chapter tests the impact of ICT on economic growth for underdeveloped and developing countries by using a panel dataset for the period of 1995-2006. The authors first develop the theory of the relationship between ICT and economic growth. They show that ICT-capital has a positive effect both on long-run and transitional income per capita, if it is considered as a factor of production. Next, the authors estimate a panel data set with 131 underdeveloped and developing countries under the assumption that ICT is one of the determining factors of economic growth. They find that ICT has positive and significant effect on economic growth even after the use of some control variables.

INTRODUCTION

In the mid 1990s and early 2000s, a popular, but unsubstantiated belief was that information and communication technologies (ICT) would change the world so quickly that the world would witness rapid (and perhaps sustainable) growth and productivity gains in the years to come.[1] This belief caused a big bubble in the world economy and especially in the US economy. In 2001, the bubble burst and the world has since returned to a "brick-and-mortar" economy.[2] It was soon realized by many that the

DOI: 10.4018/978-1-61520-709-1.ch010

ICT revolution was just a bubble from the stock market dimension. The negative experience of the stock market, however, stressed only the speculative aspects of the ICT revolution. In fact, the ICT revolution led to positive concrete changes in the real economy. In particular, it created a huge goods and services economy with strong forward and backward linkages. Given its overwhelming impact, the ICT revolution has begun to be classified by many economists as a general-purpose technology, as in the case of steam engine and electricity.[3]

Many economists consider ICT a general-purpose technology due to its pervasive character: it has already become an indispensible part of production of goods and services, irrespective of industry. The literature has identified two important channels by which ICT can have real effects on real economy: production of ICT and the use of ICT (by other industries). Firstly, the ICT sector itself has rapidly become an important industry at global level coinciding with the growth of the service industries. Processors, RAMs, hard disks, motherboards, desktops, notebooks, and super-computers are just few items that ICT industry produces. It is estimated that the global marketplace for ICT will exceed $3.7 trillion in 2008 and $4 trillion by 2011 (WITSA, 2008). In short, the ICT production sector is very important for real economy as this industry (i) nourishes GDP, (ii) increases its share in GDP due to the characteristics of this industry: rapid technological progress, strong and persistent demand, falling (relative) prices, rising quality, and increasing product variety.

Secondly, ICT revolution has contributed significantly to the whole economy by raising productivity. First, ICT increases labor productivity in ICT-using industries by simply making labor more productive (c.f., van Ark *et al.* (2003) and Matteucci (2005)). For example, a secretary can handle the same office tasks in a shorter period due to the ICT revolution. Second, ICT makes physical capital more productive (c.f., Röller and Waverman (2001)). A good example is the computer numerical control (CNC) machine, which has increased productivity of physical capital in all manufacturing industries since its use.[4] All in all, the ICT revolution had led to significant productivity increases in the ICT-using industries.

The discussion presented above however fails to address the issue of how individual economies are affected by the 'ICT revolution'. In particular, we need to know whether developed and developing countries benefit homogenously from the ICT revolution. The curiosity arises from the general observation that underdeveloped and developing countries do not have a sizeable ICT producing industry and may not have the capacity to absorb full benefits of using ICT. Firstly, ICT production is concentrated in few countries (e.g., U.S., Ireland, China, and Taiwan). Much of the rest of the world, including all African, Latin America and many Asian countries, have no physical capacity to produce ICT. In this respect, ICT products are nothing but imported goods for the majority of underdeveloped and developing countries. Secondly, human capital and physical capital is a scarce factor of production for a majority of underdeveloped and developing countries. In this respect, these countries may not able to exploit the full benefits of using ICT as they lack proper and sufficient amount of human and physical capital that complements the ICT revolution. This observation raises curiosity as to the different extents to which underdeveloped and developing benefits from the ICT revolution.

We believe that a good macro variable that may verify whether underdeveloped and developing countries benefit from the ICT revolution is to examine the contribution of ICT to economic growth, which is the precise aim of this study. In particular, this paper aims to investigate whether the ICT stock has had any positive effect on the long-run growth rate of underdeveloped and developing countries between 1995-2006. Figure 1 below is a descriptive representation of the question: it scatter plots the relationship between average growth rate and the ICT index in our sample data.

Figure 1. Average growth rate of GDP per capita versus ICT-index, 1995–2006

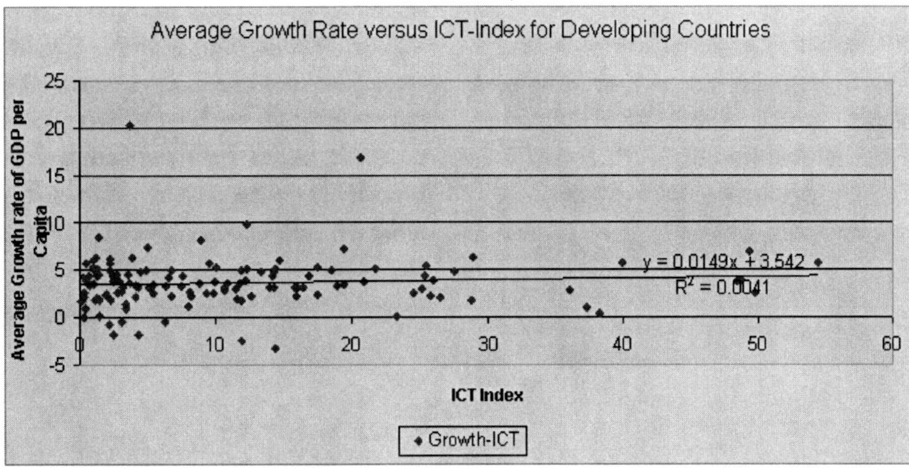

Figure 1 suggests that ICT investment may also be a positive determinant of long-run growth in underdeveloped and developing countries. We believe that the answer to the question of whether ICT enhances economic growth is especially important for policy makers of developing countries. We discussed above that ICT has two channels that enhance productivity (and hence economic growth) and that many underdeveloped and developing countries are solely importers of ICT products. Policy makers of these countries may make the assumption that ICT-use is sufficient to increase productivity. The weak positive correlation illustrated in figure 1 suggests that this idea may be naïve in the sense that investment in ICT may not automatically generate higher productivity and growth. Given that these countries have limited resources, the extent that ICT-use contributes to economic growth becomes more crucial.

This study works out theoretically and econometrically whether ICT investment has a positive impact on the long-run growth performance of underdeveloped and developing countries. In the theoretical part, we augment Solow model à la Mankiw-Romer-Weil (1992), henceforth MRW (1992), and Yoo (2003) by defining ICT capital as factor of production next to from physical and human capital in the production function. We show that the expected sign of ICT investment is theoretically positive. In the empirical part of this study, we undertake a panel data analysis to assess the validity of this argument. Our panel data analysis show that the use of ICT services (generated from the ICT-index) has contributed positively to the long-run growth performance of underdeveloped and developing countries. This finding is also supported by studies such as Hardy (1980), Norton (1992), Avgerou (1998), Röller and Waverman (2001), Bassani and Scarpetta (2002) and Yoo (2003), all of which have shown the positive impact of ICT investment on economic growth.[5]

The organization of the paper is as follows. Section 2 portrays an illustrative theoretical framework. We borrow the framework from Yoo (2003). Our contribution in this part is to extend his work and to suggest some modifications. We show that ICT investment has a positive effect on economic growth for a model economy. Section 3 first describes the data, its limitations, and the panel data model. Next, the findings of the model and its implications are presented. The last section provides some concluding remarks and discusses policy implications of findings.

AN ILLUSTRATIVE FRAMEWORK

This study considers an augmented Solow model, à la MRW (1992). We suppose, as Yoo (2003), that there are three types of capital, namely physical capital, $K(t)$, human capital, $H(t)$, and ICT capital, $Z(t)$. The production technology is a constant-returns-to-scale Cobb-Douglas in the form of

$$Y = K^{\alpha} H^{\beta} Z^{\gamma} \left(AL\right)^{1-\alpha-\beta-\gamma} \quad 0 < \alpha, \beta, \gamma \text{ and } \alpha + \beta + \gamma < 1 \tag{1}$$

where α, β, and γ are production elasticities of physical capital, human capital, and ICT capital, respectively. Following the literature, we assume that labor $L(t)$ and technology $A(t)$ do grow exponentially at the exogenously given rates of n and g: $L(t) = L(0)e^{nt}$ and $A(t) = A(0)e^{gt}$.

Let us assume that output per effective capita is defined as $\tilde{y} \equiv \dfrac{Y(t)}{A(t)L(t)}$. Similarly, we define physical capital per effective labor $\tilde{k} \equiv \dfrac{K(t)}{A(t)L(t)}$ human capital per effective labor $\tilde{h} \equiv \dfrac{H(t)}{A(t)L(t)}$ and ICT capital per effective labor $\tilde{z} \equiv \dfrac{Z(t)}{A(t)L(t)}$

Then, the production function in (1) becomes $\tilde{y} \equiv \tilde{k}^{\alpha} \tilde{h}^{\beta} \tilde{z}^{\gamma}$ in terms of effective capita. Under the assumption that a constant share of output is saved and invested for each type of capital, the following accumulation functions are defined:

$$\dot{\tilde{k}} = s_K \tilde{y} - (n + \delta + g)\tilde{k} \tag{2a}$$

$$\dot{\tilde{h}} = s_H \tilde{y} - (n + \delta + g)\tilde{h} \tag{2b}$$

$$\dot{\tilde{z}} = s_Z \tilde{y} - (n + \delta + g)\tilde{z} \tag{2c}$$

where s_K, s_H, and s_Z represent constant saving rates for physical capital, human capital, and ICT capital accumulation, respectively. For matter of tractability of the model, we assume that the depreciation rates for each type of capital are same.

It can be easily demonstrated that the differential equation system defined in (2) will not generate endogenous growth at the transitional period or at the steady state and $\tilde{k}$, $\tilde{h}$, and $\tilde{z}$ will have the following steady state values[6]:

$$\tilde{k}^* = \left[\frac{s_K^{1-\beta-\gamma} s_H^{\beta} s_Z^{\gamma}}{n + \delta + g}\right]^{\frac{1}{1-\alpha-\beta-\gamma}} \tag{3a}$$

$$\tilde{h}^* = \left[\frac{s_K^{\alpha} s_H^{1-\alpha-\gamma} s_Z^{\gamma}}{n + \delta + g}\right]^{\frac{1}{1-\alpha-\beta-\gamma}} \tag{3b}$$

$$\tilde{z}^* = \left[\frac{s_K^{\alpha} s_H^{\beta} s_Z^{1-\alpha-\beta}}{n + \delta + g}\right]^{\frac{1}{1-\alpha-\beta-\gamma}} \tag{3c}$$

By substituting respective values of $\tilde{k}^*$, $\tilde{h}^*$ and $\tilde{z}^*$ in equation (1), we find the respective steady state value of $\tilde{y}^*$:

$$\tilde{y}^* = \left[\frac{s_K^{\alpha}}{(n + \delta + g)^{\alpha}} \frac{s_H^{\beta}}{(n + \delta + g)^{\beta}} \frac{s_Z^{\gamma}}{(n + \delta + g)^{\gamma}}\right]^{\frac{1}{1-\alpha-\beta-\gamma}} \tag{4}$$

Via taking natural log of equation (4), we can show that

$$\ln \tilde{y}^* = \frac{\alpha}{1 - \alpha - \beta - \gamma}\left[\ln s_K - \ln(n + \delta + g)\right] \tag{5}$$

This is equation (3) in Yoo (2003). However, in contrast to Yoo (2003), we argue that this is not the ultimate form of the equation that should be regressed[7]. Visibly, the variable on the left hand side is output per effective labor, which is immeasurable. In that respect, we need to transform it into output per capita. Using the definition, we get

$$\ln y^* = \ln A(0) + g \cdot t + \frac{\alpha}{1-\alpha-\beta-\gamma}\ln s_K + \frac{\beta}{1-\alpha-\beta-\gamma}\ln s_H + \frac{\gamma}{1-\alpha-\beta-\gamma}\ln s_Z - \frac{\alpha+\beta+\gamma}{1-\alpha-\beta-\gamma}\ln(n+\delta+g) \quad (6)$$

where $y \equiv \frac{Y(t)}{L(t)}$ is output per capita and y^* is the steady state (long-run equilibrium) value of the same variable. This is one of the equations that inspired us in the empirical part of our analysis, à la MRW (1992). The model-economy shows that investment in ICT has a positive impact on real income per capita.

The Speed of Convergence in the Augmented Solow Model

Equation (6) alone may not be sufficient to capture the impact of ICT on economic growth in developing countries. What is measured in (6) is the contribution of ICT on economic growth at steady state. However, ICT is also important on economic growth in the transition to steady state. In particular, it is interesting to find out whether ICT plays any significant role in convergence of developing countries and this extension is missing in Yoo (2003). Below, we drive the convergence equation of ICT-augmented Solow model.

Recall that the production function becomes $\tilde{y} = \tilde{k}^{\alpha}\tilde{h}^{\beta}\tilde{z}^{\gamma}$ in efficiency units. Then the growth rate in income per efficiency units of labor is given by $\hat{\tilde{y}} = \alpha\hat{\tilde{k}} + \beta\hat{\tilde{h}} + \gamma\hat{\tilde{z}}$, where a hat on top of a variable denotes growth rate, i.e., $\hat{\tilde{x}} = \frac{\dot{\tilde{x}}}{\tilde{x}}$ for a variable $\tilde{x}$. Expressing the three-equation differential system in (2) in growth terms and then substituting $\hat{\tilde{y}} = \alpha\hat{\tilde{k}} + \beta\hat{\tilde{h}} + \gamma\hat{\tilde{z}}$ yields:

$$\hat{\tilde{k}} = s_K\tilde{k}^{\alpha-1}\tilde{h}^{\beta}\tilde{z}^{\gamma} - (n+\delta+g) \quad (7a)$$

$$\hat{\tilde{h}} = s_H\tilde{k}^{\alpha}\tilde{h}^{\beta-1}\tilde{z}^{\gamma} - (n+\delta+g) \quad (7b)$$

$$\hat{\tilde{z}} = s_Z\tilde{k}^{\alpha}\tilde{h}^{\beta}\tilde{z}^{\gamma-1} - (n+\delta+g) \quad (7c)$$

Log-linearizing the differential equation system in (7) yields

$$\hat{\tilde{y}} \approx -(1-\alpha-\beta-\gamma)(n+\delta+g)\left[\alpha\left(\ln\tilde{k} - \ln\tilde{k}^*\right) + \beta\left(\ln\tilde{h} - \ln\tilde{h}^*\right) + \gamma\left(\ln\tilde{z} - \ln\tilde{z}^*\right)\right] \quad (8)$$

where a superscript star again indicates steady state value of the respective variable. Note that the growth rate in income per efficiency units involves $\ln\tilde{y} = \alpha\ln\tilde{k} + \beta\ln\tilde{h} + \gamma\ln\tilde{z}$. Hence, $\ln\tilde{y} - \ln\tilde{y}^* = \alpha\left[\ln\tilde{k} - \ln\tilde{k}^*\right] + \beta\left[\ln\tilde{h} - \ln\tilde{h}^*\right] + \gamma\left[\ln\tilde{z} - \ln\tilde{z}^*\right]$
Using this result in (8) yields

$$\hat{\tilde{y}} \approx -\lambda\left[\ln\tilde{y} - \ln\tilde{y}^*\right] \quad (9)$$

where $\lambda = (1-\alpha-\beta-\gamma)(n+\delta+g)$. Consequently, the rate of convergence is $\frac{\partial\hat{\tilde{y}}}{\partial\ln\tilde{y}} = -\lambda$. Equation (9) is a differential equation and its solutionyields $\ln\tilde{y}(t) = e^{-\lambda t}\ln\tilde{y}(0) + (1-e^{-\lambda t})\ln\tilde{y}^*$ Subtracting $\ln\tilde{y}(0)$ from both sides gives

$$\ln\tilde{y}(t) - \ln\tilde{y}(0) = -(1-e^{-\lambda t})\ln\tilde{y}(0) + (1-e^{-\lambda t})\ln\tilde{y}^* \quad (10)$$

Substituting the respective value of $\tilde{y}^*$ from (4) and recalling that $\tilde{y}(t)\cdot A(t) = y(t)$ gives

$$\ln y(t) - \ln y(0) = \left(1-e^{-\lambda t}\right)\ln A(0) + g\cdot t - \left(1-e^{-\lambda t}\right)\ln y(0) + (1-e^{-\lambda t})\left[\frac{\alpha}{1-\alpha-\beta-\gamma}\ln s_K + \frac{\beta}{1-\alpha-\beta-\gamma}\ln s_H + \frac{\gamma}{1-\alpha-\beta-\gamma}\ln s_Z - \frac{\alpha+\beta+\gamma}{1-\alpha-\beta-\gamma}\ln(n+\delta+g)\right] \quad (11)$$

This is the second equation that one may use to measure the impact of ICT on economic growth.

Equation (11) suggests that growth of income is a function of the determinants of the ultimate steady state and the initial level of income, $\ln y(0)$.

DATA, METHOD AND RESULTS

Data

For operational and analytical purposes, we used the World Bank classification, which uses Gross National Income (GNI) per capita as the main criterion for classifying economies. Every economy is classed as either low, middle (subdivided into lower and upper middle), or high income by the World Bank, based on GNI per capita. According to 2007 GNI per capita, the groups are: low income, \$935 or less; lower middle income, \$936 - \$3,705; upper middle income, \$3,706 - \$11,455; and high income, \$11,456 or more. We considered low income and middle income countries of the World Bank classification as underdeveloped and developing countries in our study (the list of countries is given in Annex A).

ICT investment data have been retrieved from World Development Indicators Online Database and is composed of members of fixed line and mobile phone subscribers per 100 people and internet users per 100 people. We are aware of the fact that these two statistics alone cannot to any extent be considered satisfactory in representing the ICT stock. However, there are serious data availability problems for underdeveloped and developing countries and we are forced to use these limited data. We also retrieved growth rates of per capita GDP, human capital, and high technology exports data directly from WDI Online. Our data set consists of 131 underdeveloped and developing countries for the period of 1995 – 2006. It is unbalanced data set because of lack of some data in series, especially for underdeveloped countries.

The economic growth rate is the dependent variable in our model, which is expressed by annual growth rate of GDP per capita. High technology exports (HIGHEXP), the percentage share of the value of high technology exports in manufactured exports, is one of the independent variables used in the empirical analysis to capture the impact of ICT on economic growth indirectly under the assumption that exports of high technology indicate the level of ICT embedded in the production. Another independent variable is ICT stock, the value of which is calculated by the number of fixed line and mobile phone number of subscribers per 100 people and Internet users per 100 people. We are aware of the fact that our definition of ICT can only be considered a first approximation. Given the limited availability of data especially for underdeveloped countries, we are forced to define ICT in this way. We also used one-year lagged value of GDP as independent variable under the expectation that previous GDP is a significant determinant of current GDP. As a proxy for human capital variable, we employed primary school completion rate (PSCR) from the WDI database. Even though there are more suitable candidates such as UNDP data on combined gross enrolment ratio for primary, secondary and tertiary education or UNDP education index, the use of these proxies causes a considerable fall in degrees of freedom because of the lack of availability of data for many of the underdeveloped countries in the data set.

Panel Data Analysis

Panel data analysis has become more popular among researchers due to its advantages. The description of panel data comes from surveys of individuals. In this context, a "panel" is a group of individuals surveyed over time repeatedly (Frees, 2004). Panel data sets have several advantages over cross-section and time-series data sets, such as providing multiple observations on each individual in the relevant sample. It usually gives a wide range of data points to the researchers by increasing the degrees of freedom and reducing the collinearity among explanatory variables. Consequently, it improves the efficiency of econometric estimates. Moreover, panel data analysis allows researchers to analyze important questions that may be overlooked in cases of using cross-sectional or time–series data sets (Hsiao, 2002).

Econometric Analysis

Several studies[8] found that the economic relationships are dynamic and using panel data techniques is the best method of conceptualizing the dynamics of adjustment[9]. For our case, it is an unquestionable fact that current growth of GDP is a function of previous growth rates. Therefore, existence of such a situation permits us to utilize the dynamic panel data model. Moreover, the inclusion of lagged independent variable makes the OLS estimator both biased and inconsistent. Arellano and Bond (1991) proposed an efficient generalized method of moment (GMM) estimator (see Arellano (2003) for a summary of further developments in the method of GMM). Thus, this discussion in the literature led us to select GMM estimation method as the most suitable. Furthermore, the result of Hausman test (that is provided below) rules out the possibility of using fixed effects estimators. Further, we specify the weighting scheme, providing for additional efficiency of GMM estimation, under the assumption of 2SLS instrument weighting matrix (Arellano, 2003). For this reason we utilized the lagged values of independent variables as instruments. Before beginning to any econometric estimation, it is important to test the reliability of series in order to get consistent results. Consequently, first of all, we carried out unit root tests of variables, which revealed that both ICT and human capital variables suffer from the unit root problem. This problem was solved by taking the first difference of the series. Further tests show us that both variables are integrated at order one (unit root test results are available from the authors on request).

Secondly, the Hausman specification test of correlated effects was applied in order to test random effects against fixed effects. According to Hausman specification test of correlated effects shown below, our model would be random effects model.

After determining the true type of the model, the dynamic panel data estimation with GMM is carried out for three alternative models. The results are shown below.

According to our results, ICT investment has a positive and significant impact on the growth rate of underdeveloped and developing countries in models 1 and 2. In particular, we find that one unit increase in ICT usage leads to about 0.1 percentage rise in GDP growth. Yoo (2003) had previously found the value of the coefficient of investment in ICT to be 0.553, which, we believe, is somewhat excessive. Our results indicate a negative and insignificant HIGHEXP. Recall that we

Table 1. Correlated random effects: Hausman test

Test Summary	Chi-Sq. Statistic	Chi-Sq. d.f.	Prob.
Cross-section random	1.475847	3	0.6879

Table 2. Dynamic panel data estimation results

Variable	Model (1)	Model (2)	Model (3)
Δ(ICT)	**0.108***	**0.103***	**0.048**
	(2.076)	(1.992)	(0.744)
HIGHEXP	**-0.010**	**-0.012**	
	(-0.987)	(-1.233)	
GDP_{t-1}	**0.654****	**0.636****	**0.816****
	(8.116)	(8.171)	(14.409)
Δ(PSCR)	**0.198**		**0.004**
	(0.812)		(0.005)
CONSTANT	**1.130***	**1.406****	**0.748**
	(2.362)	(4.070)	(0.909)
Total Observations	**855**	**863**	**1122**
Adj. R^2	**0.101**	**0.152**	**0.034**

Note: t values are in parentheses.
* significant at the 10% level; ** significant at the 5% level; *** significant at the 1% level

used this variable an alternative measure of ICT on economic growth under the assumption that ICT is embodied in high-technology exports. The only explanation we have for this discrepancy is data problem that these countries have. The positive relation between GDP growth and its lagged value is also consistent with the literature. We find positive but insignificant impact of human capital on economic growth. All in all, we show that ICT has a positive and significant impact on economic growth. The main obstacle in researching an economic question for underdeveloped and developing country is the problem of obtaining reliable data. Unfortunately, this study is not an exception to this general rule, and any consideration of our results must also take into account this limitation.

CONCLUDING REMARKS

The positive impact of ICT investment on economic growth has not been sufficiently studied for underdeveloped and developing countries in the literature. In this study, we run three models to test whether ICT investment has a positive impact on economic growth. The results are important for policy makers because in the case of the impact of ICT use having a significant and positive element of economic growth, underdeveloped and developing countries should reserve resources for ICT to achieve sustainable growth. Our results show that this is, in fact, the case: ICT has a positive impact on economic growth. We therefore suggest policy makers that they should continue to invest in ICT.

Nonetheless some reservation is needed when interpreting the results, due to serious data limitations. Our ICT definition depends on data availability. As we discussed at the very beginning, ICT is rather a general-purpose technology with a very high level of pervasiveness. Data restrictions did not allow us to define a better ICT. The proxy for human capital we are forced to use also has serious limitations. Similar problems exist for human capital and even for the share of high-tech exports. Future research must focus on compiling better data for the same analysis.

REFERENCES

Arellano, M. (2003). *Panel data econometrics*. New York: Oxford University Press.

Arellano, M., & Bond, S. (1991). Some tests of specification for panel data: Monte Carlo evidence and an application to employment equations. *The Review of Economic Studies*, *58*, 277–297. doi:10.2307/2297968

Avgerou, C. (1998). How can IT enable economic growth in developing countries? *Information Technology for Development*, *8*(1), 15–29.

Baltagi, B. H. (2008). *Econometric analysis of panel data*. West Sussex, UK: John Wiley&Sons Ltd.

Bassani, A., & Scarpetta, S. (2002). Growth, technological change, and ICT diffusion: Recent evidence from OECD countries. *Oxford Review of Economic Policy*, *18*(3), 324–344. doi:10.1093/oxrep/18.3.324

Bresnahan, T., & Trajtenberg, M. (1995). General purpose technologies. *Journal of Econometrics*, *65*, 83–108. doi:10.1016/0304-4076(94)01598-T

David, P. (1990). The dynamo and the computer: A historical perspective on the modern productivity paradox. *The American Economic Review*, *80*(2), 355–361.

Frees, E. W. (2004). *Longitudinal and Panel Data: Analysis and Applications in the Social Sciences*. West Nyack, NY, USA: Cambridge University Press.

Hardy, A. (1980). The role of the telephone in economic development. *Telecommunications Policy*, *4*(4), 278–286. doi:10.1016/0308-5961(80)90044-0

Helpman, E. (Ed.). (1998). *General purpose technologies and economic growth*. Cambridge, MA: MIT Press

Hsiao, C. (2002). *Analysis of panel data*. Cambridge, UK: Cambridge University Press.

Kleinknecht, A. (1987). *Innovation Patterns in Crisis and Prosperity: Schumpeter's Long Cycle Reconsidered*. London: Macmillan Press.

Kondratieff, N.D. (1926). Die Langen Wellen der Konjunktur. *Archiv fur Sozialwissenschaft und Sozialpolitik*, *56*, 573ff.

Mankiw, N. G., Romer, D., & Weil, D. N. (1992). A contribution to the empirics of economic growth. *The Quarterly Journal of Economics*, *107*(2), 407–437. doi:10.2307/2118477

Mansell, R., & When, U. (Eds.). (1998). *Information technology for sustainable development*. Oxford, UK: Oxford University Press.

Matteucci, N., O'Mahony, M., Robinson, C., & Zwick, T. (2005). Productivity, workplace performance and ICT: Industry and firm-level evidence for Europe and the US. *Scottish Journal of Political Economy*, *521*(3), 359–386. doi:10.1111/j.0036-9292.2005.00349.x

Mensch, G. (1979). *Stalemate in technology: Innovations overcome depression*. Cambridge, MA: Ballinger Publishing Company.

Mokyr, J. (1990). *The lever of riches*. Oxford, UK: Oxford University Press.

Norton, S. W. (1992). Transaction costs, telecommunications, and the microeconomics of macroeconomic growth. *Economic Development and Cultural Change*, *41*(1), 175–196. doi:10.1086/452002

Pohjola, M. (2002). The new economy in growth and development. *Oxford Review of Economic Policy*, *18*(3), 380–396. doi:10.1093/oxrep/18.3.380

Röller, L.-H., & Waverman, L. (2001). Telecommunications infrastructure and economic development: A simultaneous approach. *The American Economic Review*, *91*(4), 909–923.

Schumpeter, J. A. (1939). *Business cycles: A theoretical, historical, and statistical analysis of the capitalist process*. New York: McGraw-Hill.

van Ark, B., Inklaar, R., & McGuckin, R. H. (2003). ICT and productivity in Europe and the United States: Where do the differences come from? *CESifo Economic Studies*, *49*(3), 295–318. doi:10.1093/cesifo/49.3.295

van Duijn, J. J. (1983). *The Long Wave in Economic Life*. London: George Allen & Unwin.

WITSA. (2008). *Digital planet 2008*. Retrieved from http://www.witsa.org/

Yoo, S.-H. (2003). Does information technology contribute to economic growth in developing countries? A cross-country analysis. *Applied Economics Letters*, *10*, 679–682. doi:10.1080/1350485032000138971

ENDNOTES

1 We use Information and Communications Technologies (ICT) as an umbrella term to include all technologies used for the manipulation and communication of information. We believe that ICT encompasses the term Information Technology (IT), though sometimes the two are used interchangeably.

2 The bubble covered approximately 1995–2001 and generally coined 'dot-com bubble', as the newly founded Internet-based companies was the main characteristic of the

period. During the bubble, venture capital was widely available and, in consequence, stock prices increased rapidly.

3 General purpose technologies, also called drastic technologies, describe great leaps of innovation that can affect the global economy. Examples are the steam engine, railroad, and electricity. Since Kondratieff (1926), many researchers, including Schumpeter (1939), Mensch (1979), van Duijn (1983), Kleinknecht (1987), and Mokyr (1990) contributed to the issue by identifying their main characteristic that drastic technological changes generally appear in clusters and leaps. Relatively recently, David (1990) and especially Bresnahan and Trajtenberg (1995) made the term general-purpose technology (GPT) popular again. Many, e.g., Helpman (1998), consider that ICT is the general-purpose technology of modern times.

4 Computer numerical control (CNC) is a computer 'controller' that drives a powered mechanical device typically used to fabricate components.

5 Other studies, such as Pohjola (2002), failed to show any significant relationship between ICT and economic growth.

6 Yoo (2003) defines the solution procedure as "substituting the production function (1) in the differential equations (2), taking logarithms, and solving the resulting linear system". This procedure cannot give the solution he presented in equation (3) in his paper. Firstly, "taking logarithms of equations in (2)" does not lead to a solution. Secondly, "taking logarithms of equations in (2)" does not yield a linear system. The true procedure is as follows. Firstly, we express equation (2) in growth rates by dividing both sides by the respective capital. Next, we jump to steady state. Third, we take time derivatives of both sides of differential equations and recall that all variables grow at constant rates at steady state. Fourth, we prove that variables do not grow at steady state. Finally, using the information that variables do not grow at steady state, we solve the 3-equation non-linear system and find respective steady state values of the three types of capital.

7 Yoo (2003) mis-named variables by calling $\frac{Y(t)}{A(t)L(t)}$ as output per capita and $\frac{X(t)}{A(t)L(t)}$ as capital per capita, for $X = K, H, Z$. Perhaps this was the reason why he disregard transforming per efficient units into per capita and hence missed the opportunity of presenting the ultimate form of solution.

8 Please refer to several studies cited in Baltagi (2008).

9 For a wider discussion on dynamic panel data models see Baltagi (2008) and Arellano (2003).

ANNEX A

1	Albania	South Asia	Low income
2	Algeria	Sub-Saharan Africa	Low income
3	Angola	Sub-Saharan Africa	Low income
4	Antigua and Barbuda	Latin America&Caribbean	Low income
5	Argentina	East Asia & Pacific	Low income
6	Armenia	Sub-Saharan Africa	Low income
7	Azerbaijan	Sub-Saharan Africa	Low income
8	Bangladesh	Sub-Saharan Africa	Low income
9	Barbados	Latin America&Caribbean	Low income
10	Belize	Sub-Saharan Africa	Low income
11	Benin	Sub-Saharan Africa	Low income
12	Bhutan	Sub-Saharan Africa	Low income
13	Bolivia	Sub-Saharan Africa	Low income
14	Bosnia and Herzegovina	Sub-Saharan Africa	Low income
15	Botswana	Sub-Saharan Africa	Low income
16	Brazil	Sub-Saharan Africa	Low income
17	Burkina Faso	Sub-Saharan Africa	Low income
18	Burundi	East Asia & Pacific	Low income
19	Cambodia	Europe & Central Asia	Low income
20	Cameroon	East Asia & Pacific	Low income
21	Cape Verde	Sub-Saharan Africa	Low income
22	Central African Republic	Sub-Saharan Africa	Low income
23	Chad	Sub-Saharan Africa	Low income
24	Chile	Sub-Saharan Africa	Low income
25	China	Sub-Saharan Africa	Low income
26	Colombia	Sub-Saharan Africa	Low income
27	Comoros	East Asia & Pacific	Low income
28	Congo, Rep.	Sub-Saharan Africa	Low income
29	Costa Rica	Sub-Saharan Africa	Low income
30	Côte d'Ivoire	South Asia	Low income
31	Croatia	East Asia & Pacific	Low income
32	Djibouti	Sub-Saharan Africa	Low income
33	Dominica	Sub-Saharan Africa	Low income
34	Dominican Republic	Sub-Saharan Africa	Low income
35	Ecuador	East Asia & Pacific	Low income
36	Egypt, Arab Rep.	Sub-Saharan Africa	Low income
37	El Salvador	Europe & Central Asia	Low income
38	Equatorial Guinea	Central Africa	Low income
39	Eritrea	Sub-Saharan Africa	Low income
40	Ethiopia	Sub-Saharan Africa	Low income

41	Fiji	Sub-Saharan Africa	Low income
42	French Polynesia	Pacific	Low income
43	Gabon	Europe & Central Asia	Low income
44	Gambia, The	East Asia & Pacific	Low income
45	Georgia	Middle East & North Africa	Low income
46	Ghana	Sub-Saharan Africa	Low income
47	Grenada	Sub-Saharan Africa	Low income
48	Guatemala	Europe & Central Asia	Lower middle income
49	Guinea	Middle East & North Africa	Lower middle income
50	Guinea-Bissau	Sub-Saharan Africa	Lower middle income
51	Guyana	Europe & Central Asia	Lower middle income
52	Haiti	Europe & Central Asia	Lower middle income
53	Honduras	South Asia	Lower middle income
54	India	Latin America & Caribbean	Lower middle income
55	Indonesia	Europe & Central Asia	Lower middle income
56	Iran, Islamic Rep.	Sub-Saharan Africa	Lower middle income
57	Jamaica	East Asia & Pacific	Lower middle income
58	Jordan	Latin America & Caribbean	Lower middle income
59	Kazakhstan	Sub-Saharan Africa	Lower middle income
60	Kenya	Middle East & North Africa	Lower middle income
61	Kiribati	Latin America & Caribbean	Lower middle income
62	Korea, Dem. Rep.	Latin America & Caribbean	Lower middle income
63	Kyrgyz Republic	Middle East & North Africa	Lower middle income
64	Lebanon	Latin America & Caribbean	Lower middle income
65	Lesotho	Latin America & Caribbean	Lower middle income
66	Liberia	Latin America & Caribbean	Lower middle income
67	Libya	South Asia	Lower middle income
68	Macao China	Asia	Lower middle income
69	Macedonia, FYR	Middle East & North Africa	Lower middle income
70	Malawi	Middle East & North Africa	Lower middle income
71	Malaysia	East Asia & Pacific	Lower middle income
72	Maldives	Sub-Saharan Africa	Lower middle income
73	Mali	Europe & Central Asia	Lower middle income
74	Mayotte	Indian Ocean	Lower income
75	Marshall Islands	South Asia	Lower middle income
76	Mauritania	East Asia & Pacific	Lower middle income
77	Mauritius	East Asia & Pacific	Lower middle income
78	Mexico	East Asia & Pacific	Lower middle income
79	Micronesia, Fed. Sts.	Middle East & North Africa	Lower middle income
80	Moldova	Sub-Saharan Africa	Lower middle income
81	Mongolia	Latin America & Caribbean	Lower middle income
82	Morocco	Latin America & Caribbean	Lower middle income

83	Mozambique	East Asia & Pacific	Lower middle income
84	Namibia	South Asia	Lower middle income
85	Nepal	Sub-Saharan Africa	Lower middle income
86	New Caledonia	Southwest Pacific	Lower middle income
87	Nicaragua	Sub-Saharan Africa	Lower middle income
88	Niger	Middle East & North Africa	Lower middle income
89	Nigeria	East Asia & Pacific	Lower middle income
90	Oman	Arabia	Lower middle income
91	Pakistan	East Asia & Pacific	Lower middle income
92	Panama	Middle East & North Africa	Lower middle income
93	Papua New Guinea	Europe & Central Asia	Lower middle income
94	Paraguay	Europe & Central Asia	Lower middle income
95	Peru	East Asia & Pacific	Lower middle income
96	Philippines	Middle East & North Africa	Lower middle income
97	Rwanda	Latin America & Caribbean	Upper middle income
98	Samoa	Sub-Saharan Africa	Upper middle income
99	Saudi Arabia	Arabia	Upper middle income
100	Senegal	Europe & Central Asia	Upper middle income
101	Seychelles	Latin America & Caribbean	Upper middle income
102	Sierra Leone	Europe & Central Asia	Upper middle income
103	Slovenia	Europe	Upper middle income
104	Solomon Islands	Latin America & Caribbean	Upper middle income
105	Sri Lanka	Sub-Saharan Africa	Upper middle income
106	St. Kitts and Nevis	Latin America & Caribbean	Upper middle income
107	St. Lucia	Latin America & Caribbean	Upper middle income
108	St. Vincent and the Grenadines	Europe & Central Asia	Upper middle income
109	Sudan	Europe & Central Asia	Upper middle income
110	Suriname	Middle East & North Africa	Upper middle income
111	Swaziland	Middle East & North Africa	Upper middle income
112	Syrian Arab Republic	Europe & Central Asia	Upper middle income
113	Tajikistan	East Asia & Pacific	Upper middle income
114	Tanzania	Sub-Saharan Africa	Upper middle income
115	Thailand	Sub-Saharan Africa	Upper middle income
116	Timor - Leste	East Asia&Pacific	Lower middle income
117	Togo	Europe & Central Asia	Upper middle income
118	Tonga	East Asia & Pacific	Upper middle income
119	Trinidad and Tobago	Latin America&Caribbean	Lower middle income
120	Tunisia	Latin America & Caribbean	Upper middle income
121	Turkey	Europe & Central Asia	Upper middle income
122	Turkmenistan	Europe & Central Asia	Upper middle income
123	Uganda	Europe & Central Asia	Upper middle income
124	Uruguay	Sub-Saharan Africa	Upper middle income

125	Uzbekistan	Sub-Saharan Africa	Upper middle income
126	Vanuatu	Latin America & Caribbean	Upper middle income
127	Venezuela, RB	Latin America & Caribbean	Upper middle income
128	Vietnam	Latin America & Caribbean	Upper middle income
129	Yemen, Rep.	Europe & Central Asia	Upper middle income
130	Zambia	Latin America & Caribbean	Upper middle income
131	Zimbabwe	Latin America & Caribbean	Upper middle income

Chapter 11
An Empirical Analysis of Indices and Factors of ICT Use by Small- and Medium-Sized Enterprises in Japan

Masatsugu Tsuji
University of Hyogo, Japan

Teruyuki Bunno
Kinki University, Japan

Hiroki Idota
Otemon Gakuin University, Japan

Hiroaki Miyoshi
Doshisha University, Japan

Masaru Ogawa
Kobe Gakuin University, Japan

Yasushi Ueki
Bangkok Research Center, Institute of Developing Economies/Japan External Trade Organization, Thailand

ABSTRACT

This chapter attempts to extract factors which promote the introduction and usage of ICT by SMEs (small- and medium-sized enterprises) through the method of mail surveys and in-depth interviews conducted in two of the largest SME clusters in Japan, Higashi-Osaka and Ohta Ward, Tokyo. The questionnaire was sent to more than 6,000 SMEs there, and received nearly 1,200 replies. Questions are related to company characteristics and purposes for ICT use. Moreover, the followings indexes are selected which present the degree of ICT use by SMEs: (i) software that contributes to efficient utilization of managerial

DOI: 10.4018/978-1-61520-709-1.ch011

resources; and (ii) Internet usage. Based on these data, factors are extracted by utilizing the regression methods such as OLS, logit and probit estimation. Among them, the most important elements in promoting ICT use are found to be a future-oriented vision for SMEs such as expectations for restructuring business process through ICT, and managerial orientations.

INTRODUCTION

Background and Objectives of Analysis

Information and Communications Technology (ICT) was introduced in the early 1990s, and since then, it has been transforming the frameworks of not only economies but also business firms. ICT has been creating new businesses such as e-commerce and contributing for economies to become more globalized and more competitive due to easier access to all kinds of information through ICT. The development of business management has also increased greatly due to ICT. Business organizations have also been undergoing rapid transformation; ICT has created new forms of organization by destroying the traditional ones.

SMEs (Small- and medium-sized enterprises) undergird Japan's entire manufacturing sector by supplying it with high-quality parts; it is well known that the unsurpassed quality of Japanese products is largely based on SMEs. In accordance with the above transformation, however, SMEs have been attempting to adapt ICT in their business, but they are not necessarily successful. This chapter examines current ICT use by SMEs, namely, examines empirically what are the factors that promote ICT use by SMEs. The analysis is based on field surveys, a mail survey and in-depth interviews conducted by the authors in two of Japan's most prominent SME clusters, located in Higashi-Osaka city, Osaka Prefecture, and Ohta ward, in the metropolitan area of Tokyo. The questionnaire was sent to more than 6,000 SMEs in two clusters, and received nearly 1,200 replies.

Questions sent to SMEs were related to (i) company characteristics (amount of capital, number of employees, etc); (ii) managerial orientation, which classifies SMEs as the expansion, incentive-providing, adapting, or data-using category; (iii) business environment such as the degree of competition; (iv) purposes of ICT use, such as raising profit and productivity; (v) expectations for ICT use; and (vi) other factors such as ICT investment in the most recent fiscal year and the company's understanding of importance of the ICT in business management. Regarding managerial orientation, a detailed explanation is called for. The questionnaire contains ten questions regarding managers' daily activities. Since there is some overlap between the ten questions, an attempt was made to isolate the variables through component analysis.

In this manner, four variables, which account for 70.1% of the total responses, were isolated. The first of these includes questions to determine to what extent an SME is geared toward expansion. The second category, orientation to incentives, contains questions on management's performance vis-à-vis stakeholders, and on any incentives it gives employees by relinquishing rights and responsibilities to them. The third variable includes questions on the extent to which firms learn from their mistakes, and on whether top management considers employee suggestions. Since such courses of action are indicative of management's responsiveness, this factor is referred to as "orientation to expansion". The last variable, called "orientation to data use," contains questions on how firms make use of data for decision-making.

The followings indexes were selected to represent the degree of ICT use by SMEs: (i) the amount of software that contributes to efficient utilization of managerial resources; and (ii) Internet usage. Based on these data, the factors extracted were extracted by making use of regression methods such as OLS (Ordinal Least Squires), logit and probit estimations. Thus, the result of estimations can be compared.

One of the most important factors found in our research is "expectation from ICT use," such as "restructuring of the whole business process," which is identified as a significant factor in all of our estimations. SMEs with intensive use of ICT believe in its effect and actually invest lots. It follows from this that the most important way to promote ICT use among SMEs is to encourage them to be forward-looking. Once they adapt such an outlook, SMEs can determine the exact ways in which they will introduce and use ICT, according to their specific goals. By the probit analysis, the behaviour of CEO or the top management was also found to be especially important.

Since ICT use is a function of a business's management and strategy, the decisions made by senior managers are crucial. Even if SMEs operated under optimal conditions, they would not be able to use new technologies to their advantage without correct decisions by their managers. Similar conclusions were reached by Tsuji and Choe (2004), who also tried to identify factors that encourage regional information policies by using the same framework. They concluded that the leadership of top local government is the most significant.

Once those factors are grasped correctly, then they are used for establishing suitable policy measures to enhance SMEs. Based on rigorous researches, proper policy measures should be established.

The chapter consists of eight sections. In section 2, the indices of ICT use by SMEs are constructed by focusing the usage of software and the Internet. In section 3, the variables for estimations and the method of estimations are provided, and estimations by OLS, as well as 5 logit and probit estimations are conducted. In section 5, problems and policies for ICT use by SMEs are identified based our survey. Concluding remarks and the future direction of research are given in section 5.

Previous Studies

The authors (Bunno et al (2006), Giovannetti, Kagami and Tsuji (2003), Kuchiki and Tsuji (2005), Tsuji (2005), Tsuji, et al. (2005)) have been analyzing why there is a difference in adaption of ICT by SMEs, that is, some SMEs are successfully adapting ICT and restructuring their businesses and organizations, while some failed. In other words, we attempt to investigate what are the factors to promote ICT use by SMEs by making use of various methodologies such as OLS, probit and logit methods.

Here, on the other hand, we make an attempt to identify what are the bases for SMEs to adapt ICT, or which factors form abilities of adapting, enhancing and utilizing ICT. These abilities are sometimes referred to as the "ICT capability," which is defined as follows: a firm's ICT capability is defined here as its ability to mobilize and deploy IT-based resources in combination or co-present with other resources and capabilities (Bharadwaj, 2000, p. 171). ICT is just technology, but in order to utilize ICT fully, SMEs should have some bases for it. If the e-mail system, for example, is introduced simply to all employees, it does not necessarily increase their productivity. The whole organization or whole business processes must be transformed at the same time. Such ability to transformation in accordance with the introduction of ICT is defined as the ICT capability.

Other views of ICT use can be found in Barney (1991a), Barney (1991b), Barney and Clark (2007), Mata et al. (1995), and so on. Mata et al. (1995), for example, conducted an empirical research from the point of RBV (Resource

Based View) on the relationship between ICT and competitive advantage, and they focused on the following five attributes of skills such as customers' switching costs, access to capital, proprietary technology, technical IT skill and IT managerial skill. They concluded based on empirical studies that only IT managerial skill can be an origin of the sustainable competitive advantage. According to them, IT managerial skill consists of the following abilities: (a) to recognize and understand the business needs of other functional managers, suppliers, and customers; (b) to collaborate with these functional managers, suppliers, and customers to appropriate IT; (c) to coordinate; (d) to forecast the future IT needs; and (e) ability to manage market risk.

These are accumulated inside the firm as tact knowledge through business practices and experiences. The IT managerial skill is firm specific and thus it is difficult for rivals to imitate. It becomes a part of routine works to the particular firm because of its nature, and in addition, its routine works are related to other sections, suppliers, and customers, that is, it has relationships with factors outside of the firm. The managerial ability of business process and the organization by ICT use is the source of sustainable competitive advantage, but it is not ICT itself. Their research is the first one focusing on the ICT managerial skill as the ICT capability.

INDICES OF ICT DEVELOPMENT

ICT Use by SMEs

ICT utilization cannot be described with a single index, since various factors are involved, including size, industry, business practices, etc. For the surveys, the following indicators of ICT use by SMEs were selected: (i) number of PCs owned; (ii) number of PCs connected to networks such as LANs; (iii) the extent to which software that contributes to the efficient utilization of managerial resources has been implemented; and (iv) Internet use. No explanation is required for (i) and (ii), since these indices are simple quantitative proxies for ICT use: having more PCs is equivalent to using ICT more intensively. Items (iii) and (iv) are more qualitative measures of ICT use, since having a large number of computers does not necessarily mean using them efficiently.

Initially, software packages —for example, for accounting and marketing management— are introduced to promote efficiency in internal tasks. These applications are generally used independently on each PC. At more advanced stages of ICT, the various applications are no longer used separately but are interconnected and share databases. Item (iii) sheds more light on this. Subsequently, the PCs in one or several offices are connected to each other, generally with a groupware program. This use is covered by item (iv).

Index of Software Use

In the previous study, Tsuji et al. (2005), the index was constructed in such as way that 1 point is provided for question 1 to 8, and 10 points for questions 9 to 13. Questions 1 to 8 are quite different from 9 to 13 in their description of ICT use, since the latter deals with more complicated and integrated utilization than the former. This scoring may seem somewhat arbitrary. In this chapter, focus is placed on the usage of software and the Internet. The former is related to item (iii) in Q2 of our questionnaire, that is, SMEs were asked if they were using the software listed below:

1. Sales management (including POS and barcode)
2. Accounting
3. Payroll management
4. Purchases management
5. Inventories management
6. Design management (including CAD/CAM)
7. Production management

8. Logistics
9. Enterprise resource planning (EPR) packages
10. Customer Relations Management (CRM)
11. Groupware
12. Sales Force Automation (SFA)
13. Supply Chain Management (SCM)

It is reasonable to consider that the software which is used by large (small) number of SMEs is less (more) important so that it should have smaller (larger) point. The weight for the software is assigned according to the percentage of SMEs which provide affirmatives responses to questions 1-13: namely, the weight is a reciprocal number of the percentage. This index deals with more advanced and integrated uses, more points were assigned to them. The sum positive replies of these 13 questions weighted as indicated is a dependent variable referred to as software use.

Index of Internet Use

The index presented in (iv) above looks at Internet use in the same manner as does item (iii) of the questionnaire on software use. That is, the weight for the Internet use is assigned according to a reciprocal of the percentage of SMEs which provide affirmatives responses to questions 1-5 which are corresponding to Q3-3. Those are shown below:

1. Create and manage the company's homepage or related web pages
2. Employees' personal e-mail accounts (number of addresses)
3. Create and utilize electronic bulletin boards, and/or electronic meeting boards
4. Create and utilize mailing lists of customers and business partners
5. Establish a private domain name

The sum of a reciprocal of the percentage of positive replies in these 5 questions is a dependent variable referred to as Internet use. The following quantitative analyses are based on these indices.

Factors Affecting ICT Use

Here, variables which encourage ICT use are explained. The questionnaire asked SMEs about (i) company characteristics, (ii) management orientation, (iii) business environment and (iv) expected results from ICT use.

Company Characteristics

Company characteristics include variables such as industrial category, amount of capital, and number of employees (These six variables are listed in Table 2).

Managerial Orientation

Regarding managerial orientation as one variable, a detailed explanation is called for. The questionnaires contain ten items on managers' daily activities, shown in Table 1. Since there is some overlap between the ten questions, an attempt was made to isolate the variables through component analysis. In this manner, four variables, which account for 70.1% of the total responses, were isolated. The first of these includes questions to determine to what extent an SME is geared toward expansion, which is referred to as "orientation to expansion". The second category, "orientation to incentives," contains questions on management's performance vis-à-vis stakeholders and on any incentives it gives employees by relinquishing rights and responsibilities to them. The third variable includes questions on the extent to which firms learn from their mistakes and on whether top management considers employee suggestions. Since such courses of action are indicative of management's responsiveness, this factor is referred to as "orientation to adapting". The last variable, called "orientation to data use," contains questions on how firms make use of data

Table 1. Result of component analysis

Managerial Behavior	Common Factors			
	Expan-sion	Providing incentives	Adapting	Using data
There is employee training and rotation to utilize each employee's ability and knowledge.	**0.836**	**0.152**	**0.124**	**0.126**
The company offers ICT training to executives, managers and employees.	**0.813**	**0.056**	**0.074**	**0.210**
Employees are apprised of the company's plans for next 2-3 years.	**0.599**	**0.515**	**0.179**	**0.156**
New lines of business are constantly being sought and products developed.	**0.552**	**0.284**	**0.321**	**0.085**
Company's performance is disclosed to employees.	**0.200**	**0.824**	**-0.006**	**0.301**
Senior managers are given broad responsibility and authorities.	**0.112**	**0.567**	**0.488**	**0.194**
Company studies competitors' mistakes and learns from them.	**0.172**	**0.015**	**0.844**	**0.288**
Companies listen to any employee's opinion on how to improve management.	**0.281**	**0.538**	**0.587**	**0.064**
Past business data are extensively analyzed in company management.	**0.074**	**0.230**	**0.255**	**0.784**
Monthly business data are utilized to improve management.	**0.345**	**0.175**	**0.123**	**0.708**
Eigenvalue	**2.308**	**1.745**	**1.531**	**1.422**
Rotated Factor Pattern(%)	**44.8**	**10.7**	**7.3**	**7.2**
Cumulative Proportion(%)	**70.1**			

for decision-making. The results of the component analysis are summarized in Table 1.

Business Environment

As for business environment, seven variables were selected, including winning of new business partners, product characteristics and the effect of new entrants into the market. Finally, since the introduction and use of ICT depend on firms' expectations regarding their future business and management, nine variables were selected for the fourth category, including increased profits, promotion of higher productivity and timely decision-making.

ESTIMATION METHODS AND RESULTS

Estimation Model

The factors that determine the particular scores obtained by each SME will be examined below. To examine the validity of these factors, the following regression model was constructed:

$$Y_i = \beta_0 + \beta_1 X_{1i} + \beta_2 X_{2i} + \beta_3 X_{3i} + \ldots \ldots + \beta_n X_{ni} + e_i, \quad (1)$$

where Y_i is the index of ICT use; X_{ji} denotes variables such as the characteristics of the SMEs, amount of ICT investment, expectations for ICT use, etc.; β_i indicates the coefficients to be estimated; and e_i is the residual.

For the actual estimation, the following procedures were followed: (i) a stepwise method was adapted to select variables by making use of the Akaike Information Criterion [AIC]. The following two models were estimated, in accordance with the index selected: (i) the software utilization model; and (ii) the Internet utilization model. These indices were explained in detail in the preceding section. In addition to indices, two estimation methods are utilized so as to clear the verifiability of models; namely, OLS, and logit and probit models.

Table 2. Summary statistics

Variables		Average	Std Dev
ICT utilization *		0.151	0.120
Characteristics of firm	Capital (10 thousand Yen)	1,963.659	2,612.458
	The number of Enployees	20.491	31.078
	The number of Part-time job Employees	5.179	10.778
	Operation years	44.090	79.863
	CEO's generation	1.790	0.848
Managerial behavior **	Expansion type	0.000	1.000
	Incentive type	0.000	1.000
	Adaptiove type	0.000	1.000
	Data-using type	0.000	1.000
Business Environment	We obtain new business partners every year.	3.106	1.330
	The share of new products and services in our business is larger than before.	3.055	1.214
	Competition with rival companies has recently become more severe.	3.949	1.106
	New entrants from other business fields have recently increased in our market.	2.841	1.258
	Many purchase orders are repeatedly from the same business partners.	3.932	1.010
	We can price our own products.	3.323	1.260
	In recent years, we have not been able to employ younger (30-year-old or younger) workers.	2.938	1.590
Business problems ***	To secure orders and sales	0.707	0.455
	To secure positive profit and funds management	0.373	0.484
	To secure good employees and human resource management	0.503	0.500
	Development of ability for planning, R&D, and technology	0.398	0.490
	Company succession	0.208	0.406
Importance of the introduction of ICT in business management		3.974	1.122
Expectation of ICT usage	Increased profit	2.712	0.964
	Higher productivity of routine works, such as administrative works	3.292	0.828
	Higher productivity of non-routine business, such as project planning	2.536	0.956
	Higher speed of decision-making in management and business development	2.867	0.902
	Restructuring of the whole business process	2.598	0.900
	Active communication and accumulation sharing of information knowledge	3.012	0.895
	Close cooperation with customers and business partners	2.988	0.861
	Precise understanding of customer needs	2.733	0.910
	Better customer satisfaction by improvement in services and products	2.697	0.918
Company's ICT investment last Fiscal Year (10 thousand Yen)		292.735	1,646.981
notes: * indicates the result of AHP.			
** indicates four types of corporate management which were clarifed by the factor analysis.			
*** indicates dummy data.			

Table 3. OLS estimation of software utilization model

Variables		Coefficient	t-value	
	Capital	0.004439	1.66	*
Characteristics of firms	Wholesale	0.000001	2.7	***
	Company's ICT investment in preceding fiscal year	0.004306	4.6	***
Managerial orientation	Using data	0.001496	1.5	
Expectations from ICT use	Restructuring of the entire business process	0.002645	2.29	**
	R^2	0.096		

Note: *, **, and *** are significance at 10%, 5%, and 1%, respectively.

OLS Estimation I: Software Utilization Model

The index for this model measures software utilization. By using this index, two methods such as OLS, and logit and probit estimations are examined. The result of the estimation is given in Table 3. In this model, a variable related to SME size, such as amount of capital is significant. Belonging to the wholesale sector is also significant; the reason for this is that SME wholesalers need software to manage the large number of customers and suppliers they deal with. Another interesting result is found in variables such "restructuring of the entire business process", in the category of expectation from ICT use.

OLS Estimation II: Internet Utilization Model

Table 4 shows the results when the estimation of Internet use is the parameter. In this estimation, the size of the firm again affects Internet use. Managerial orientations such as "expansion" and "providing incentives" are also important for Internet use, while "adapting" has negative sign. Expectations from ICT use such as "higher productivity in non-routine tasks" and "restructuring of the entire business process" are the mostly significant. The Internet is aimed to introduce for new businesses activities or obtaining new business partners, which are not achieved by routine tasks but by non-routine or by restructuring whole businesses. "Higher productivity in routine tasks" has negative sign, but this is because SMEs which

Table 4. OLS estimation of internet utilization model

Variables		coefficient	t-value
Company Attribute	number of employees	0.0000242	2.58 **
	Company's ICT investment in preceding fiscal year	0.0006394	2.28 **
Managerial orientation	Expansion	0.0007315	2.64 ***
	providing incentive	0.0004788	1.77 *
	Adapting	-0.0010619	-2.05 **
Expectations from ICT use	higher productivity in routine tasks	-0.0006143	-1.71 *
	higher productivity in non-routine tasks	0.0008138	2.70 ***
	restructuring of the entire business process	0.0010619	3.16 ***
R2		0.123	

Note: *, **, and *** are significance at 10%, 5%, and 1%, respectively.

Table 5. Software utilization model

Variables	Logit			Probit		
	coefficient	p-value	marginal effect	coefficient	p-value	marginal effect
Capital	0.000076	0.060	0.000018	--	--	--
Years of Operation	0.184350	0.071	0.043998	0.097084	0.081	0.036240
Expansion	--	--	--	0.150280	0.007	0.056097
Incentive	--	--	--	0.150280	0.007	0.056097
Data Using	0.147771	0.127	0.035268	0.121742	0.022	0.045445
Obtain new business partners every year.	--	--	--	-0.083516	0.053	-0.031175
Development of ability for planning, R&D, and technology	0.358013	0.053	0.085556	--	--	--
To secure good employees and human resource management	0.313383	0.095	0.074392	0.209700	0.041	0.077959
Active communication & sharing of information knowledge	-0.271124	0.022	-0.064708	--	--	--
Restructuring of the whole business process	0.334408	0.005	0.079811	--	--	--
Company's ICT investment in preceding fiscal year	0.465844	0.000	0.111180	0.316854	0.000	0.118277
Log likelihood	-358.313			-427.485		

have higher ICT use had already experienced the reform of routine works. SMEs with the low level of Internet use still have higher expectation of improving productivity by ICT.

These two OLS estimations show that various factors significantly affect ICT use by SMEs. To shed light on the factors that most important of these factors, the results given in tables are summarized below: In two estimations, expectation on restructuring of the entire business process is perceived commonly as significant. This implies that SMEs tend to use ICT as a tool to seek new business through restructuring and to adjust to the transformation of the business environment. In addition to this, ICT investment in preceding fiscal year is also commonly significant in two estimations.

Logit and Probit Estimation I: Software Utilization Model

Here the results of logit and probit estimations are presented. The motivation of these two is that variables are constructed by the data obtained through mail survey usually take discrete value, and so that logit and probit estimations are better methods than OLS.

The result of estimations is indicated in Table 5. In these estimations, let us discuss the result obtained by the probit model. "Company's ICT investment in preceding fiscal year" is the most significant as in the OLS estimations. In addition, three variables in managerial orientation have also important influence, and this implies that managerial orientation is a key factor for software use by SME's.

Logit and Probit Estimation II: Internet Utilization Model

The result of this estimation is shown in Table 6. "Expansion" in managerial orientation and "restructuring of the whole business process" are the most significant. The amount of investment last year is also strong influence (at the 1% significance level). "Company's understanding of importance of ICT in business management" and "higher speed of decision-making in management and business" are also significant at the 5% level, in addition to "secure good employees and

Table 6. Result of estimation of internet utilization model

Variables	Logit			Probit		
	coefficient	p-value	marginal effect	coefficient	p-value	marginal effect
Information services	--	--	--	0.755127	0.093	0.2930451
Number of employee	--	--	--	0.043313	0.034	0.0017005
CEO's generation	0.2147792	0.011	0.0525628	--	--	--
Expansion	0.2529977	0.008	0.0619160	0.1823141	0.002	0.0715782
Incentive	0.2040279	0.028	0.0499317	0.1332995	0.019	0.0523346
Adapting	-0.2919589	0.002	-0.0714510	-0.1417308	0.015	-0.0556449
We are constantly developing new business and products.	0.1329419	0.090	0.0325348	--	--	--
To ecure good employees and human resource management	0.4388415	0.013	0.1067115	0.2357852	0.031	0.0921742
Company's understanding of importance of ICT in business management	0.2462921	0.018	0.0602750	0.1470214	0.020	0.0577220
Higher speed of decision-making in management and business development	-0.2498375	0.038	-0.0611426	-0.1729264	0.020	0.1059098
Restructuring of the whole business process	0.4335908	0.000	0.1061125	0.2697587	0.000	0.1059098
Company's ICT investment in preceding fiscal year	0.3357048	0.000	0.0821569	0.1507169	0.009	0.0591729
Log likelihood	-395.371			-376.657		

human resource management". The importance managerial orientation is the same as software utilization model.

PROBLEMS AND POLICY FOR ICT USE BASED ON ESTIMATIONS

Problems of ICT Use

Thus far, the analysis has focused on factors that encourage ICT use. This section examines the ICT-related issues that SMEs are facing, so as to identify problems and recommend policies that could be implemented to solve them.

According to replies to our questionnaires (Q9), obstacles faced by SMEs in each category of developed (developing) in ICT use were examined. The obstacles for the developed group were identified as related to security, coordination with purchasers and sellers, and funding for ICT investment, while those for the developing group were lack of leadership, difficulty in keeping up with technological change, lack of confidence regarding return on investment, and the length of time required to introduce new technologies. Here, by using OLS, the relationship between the indices of ICT use and the replies to questions related to problems of ICT use are analyzed. Variables utilized in estimation are selected by the stepwise method according to F values.

Let us examine first the software utilization model. The result of our estimation is indicated in Table 7. Among questions in Q9, the followings are identified to be positively related with the significance level:

16: "Concern with leakage of personal data through introduction of ICT"
12: "Attempt by business partners to adopt their own ICT systems"
6: "Employees' reluctance to use ICT"

Security and concern with leakage of personal data and employee's ability are common important issues for advanced companies, while question

Table 7. Problem of ICT use: software utilization model (OLS)

Variable	Coefficient	t-value
Employees' reluctance to use ICT	0.006131	2.57***
Company's inability to keep up with rapid development of ICT	-0.003759	-2.05**
Attempt by business partners to adopt their own ICT systems	0.003857	2.01**
Concern with compromising information through introduction of ICT	0.005501	2.94***
Constant	0.012477	14.36***
R^2	0.018	

Note: ***, **, and * indicate the significant at the 1, 5, and 10% level.

12 seems to be a common problem to all SMEs, since most of SMEs responded in such as way to in-depth interviews. The following question 11, on the other hand, has negative coefficient:

11: "Company's inability to keep up with rapid development of ICT"

The less developed SMEs in ICT use have this reaction than the more developed ones.

In sum, these can be interpreted as follows: Companies with higher software utilization index have strong desires to renovate their companies and restructure their whole business processes, and these desires lead them to maintain good relationships with business partners and employees through ICT use. Moreover, these companies do not think that rapid speed of technology development is an issue.

Second, the Internet utilization model is examined. The result is shown in Table 8. The following problems are positively related to the Internet use index:

15: "Concern with compromising information through introduction of ICT"
12: "Attempt by business partners to adapt their own ICT systems"
8: "Company's failure to instruct consultants on how to introduce ICT"
10: "Lack of software to meet needs of company's business and processes"
2: "Lack of concrete management objectives for ICT use"

The followings, on the other hand, are negatively related to the index:

1: "Lack of leadership regarding ICT use"
11: "Company's inability to keep up with rapid development of ICT"

These can be interpreted as follows: Companies with higher values of this index tend to have desires to promote higher productivity of non-routine works, to restructure their businesses, and adapt to changes in the business environment. These companies face problems regarding how to utilize the Internet or software.

Policies Advantageous to ICT Use as Suggested by Empirical Research

This section analyzes what kinds of policies are required to encourage the adaption of new technologies (Q12). According to replies, SMEs in the developed group focused on initiatives such as low-interest loans, tax exemptions and subsidies on ICT investment, along with a relaxing of several regulations; in other words, they advocated establishing an environment conducive to ICT investment. By contrast, the developing group tended to prefer initiatives such as ICT seminars and training in computer operation and

Table 8. Problem of ICT use: internet utilization model (OLS)

Variable	coefficient	t-value
Lack of leadership regarding ICT use	-0.0019571	-4.10***
Lack of concrete management objectives for ICT use	0.0010108	2.14**
Employees' lack of familiarity with ICT	0.0007472	1.69*
Company's failure to instruct consultants on how to introduce ICT	0.0019884	2.31**
Lack of software to meet needs of company's business and processes	0.0011081	2.24**
Company's inability to keep up with rapid development of ICT	-0.0014537	-2.66**
Attempt by business partners to adapt their own ICT systems	0.0014906	2.59**
Concern with compromising information through introduction of ICT	0.0013051	2.90***
Constant	0.0051617	14.66***
R^2	0.123	

Note: ***, **, and * indicate the significant at the 1, 5, and 10% level.

homepage construction; these proposals can be summarized as "human resource development to encourage ICT use".

In order to examine this problem, the same OLS model with the same indices is used. According to the results of our estimation of both software and Internet models, these two estimations identify commonly the following policies desired among others by SMEs:

5: Low-interest loans for ICT
7: Tax exemptions on ICT investment

The following policies are significant only in the software model.

8: Grants and other financial support for ICT investment-related projects

In the Internet model, the following policy is found to be desired:

9: Support for opening new portals
10: Deregulation

SMEs are financially weak so that they need policies promoting ICT investment through tax and subsidy schemes, in addition, further deregulations to create new business models by utilizing ICT, are requested by SMEs.

CONCLUSION

SMEs and Japanese Economic Development

Here, the role of SMEs in the Japanese economy is examined. The share of SME in production in term of value added is nearly half, a trend that has not changed greatly over time. The share of exports in the manufacturing sector is approximately half of that of large firms. But SMEs' shares are relatively larger in the sectors such as general machinery, electric machinery, and precision machinery, in which Japanese SMEs have technological advantage. The role of SMEs in investment indicates their share is about one-third, and has been increasing slightly in recent years. In data on numbers of firms, and the percentage SMEs is overwhelming.

In all sectors, SMEs occupy close to 100%. As for employment, the percentages are different from the industry data. The mining, construction, food stores, and real estate industries show SMEs with a high percentage of employment. On the other hand, in public inutilities such as electricity, gas, and water, SMEs occupy only 12.4%, and 13.9% in finance and insurance. These industries require huge amounts of investment in equipment and infrastructure so as to exploit economies of scale and network externalities. This inherent feature of these industries restricts entry to all but large firms. The average over all industries is about two thirds, showing that SMEs play a great role in employment.

In addition to the quantitative aspect of SMEs in Japanese economy, they also have been contributing qualitatively to the Japanese economic development. Japan's success is based on SMEs, which own vast reserves of accumulated technologies, skills and know-how, and have long been the foundation of Japan's manufacturing sector. As mentioned above, their contributions to the economic development are much larger than those of large companies.

But SMEs are not exempt from the requirements imposed by the development of ICT. These crucial firms are lagging behind in their ICT usage, and facing serious problems due not only to ICT but also to Japan's aging society. If Japan's economy is to once again exhibit the dynamic growth, innovation, and world leadership that it has in years past, the economy must bring its vast population of SMEs up to speed in the new world of ICT.

Factors Promoting ICT Use by SMEs

Based on the intensive mail survey in two Japanese major SME clusters such as Higashi-Osaka and Ohta ward, two indices of ICT use by SMEs are constructed, and then the factors promoting ICT use by SMEs are clarified. One of the most important factors found in our estimation is expectation from ICT use such as restructuring the whole business process, which is common to all four estimations. SMEs with intensive use of ICT believe in its effect and actually invest lots so as to renovate their businesses. It follows from this that the most important way to promote ICT use among SMEs is encourage them to be forward-looking. Once they adapt such an outlook, they can determine the exact ways in which they will introduce and use ICT, according to their specific goals.

In addition, the behaviour of CEO or the top management is also found to be important especially in the probit model. Since ICT use is a function of a business's management and strategy, the decisions made by senior managers are crucial. Even if SMEs operated under optimal conditions —if they had ICT specialists, sufficient money and government support— they would not be able to use new technologies to their advantage without correct decisions by their managers.

The empirical study identified the following types of management outlooks that affect ICT use: an orientation to expansion, to adapting, to using data and to providing incentives. Similar conclusions were reached by Tsuji and Choe (2004), who also tried to identify factors that encourage regional information policies, in the framework of an analysis of the demand for and supply of such policies. Using the same empirical methodology as the present study, these authors concluded that leadership shown by top local government officials is more crucial than the availability of funding.

The current study has sought to understand how top management determines what information technologies are to be used, and what kind of decision-making leads to greater ICT use. In the interviews, informants often said that ICT is "just a tool", by which they meant that it is useful only for promoting internal efficiency or productivity in routine tasks. In contrast, the authors believe that its prime function is to create entirely new business models. Ideally, ICT completely transforms businesses, and the economy itself, through Schumpeterian creative destruction. Most SMEs that successfully use ICT create new business models based on that more intensive use of technology.

DIRECTION OF FURTHER RESEARCH

Let us point out the direction of the further research. There is no definite single index to measure the degree of ICT use by firms. It should consist of quantitative as well as qualitative variables. The former includes the number of PC firm own or those connected to LAN, while the latter intensive use of software and the Internet, and security measure such as firewall. The construction of comprehensive measure is another task.

This chapter focuses on extracting factors promoting ICT use by SMEs. Once those are correctly grasp, then those are utilized for establishing suitable policy measures. They are so many policies implemented by various ministries of the government, which is listed in Tsuji *et al* (2005), Small and Medium Enterprise Agency (2001, 2002, 2003, 2004), but it hardly concludes that they seem to be are successful. Based on rigorous research, proper policy measure should be established.

REFERENCES

Barney, J. B. (1991a). Firm Resources and Sustained Competitive Advantage. *Journal of Management*, *17*(1), 99–120. doi:10.1177/014920639101700108

Barney, J. B. (1991b). Resource Based View. *Diamond Harvard Business Review*, *26*(5), 78–87.

Barney, J. B., & Clark, D. N. (2007). *Resource-Based Theory: Creating and Sustaining Competitive Advantage*. Oxford, UK: Oxford University Press.

Bharadwaj, A. S. (2000). A Resource-Based Perspective on Information Technology Capability and Firm Performance: An Empirical Investigation. *MIS Quarterly*, *24*(1), 169–196. doi:10.2307/3250983

Bunno, T., Idota, H., Tsuji, M., Miyoshi, H., Ogawa, M., & Nakanishi, M. (2006). An Empirical Analysis of Indices and Factors of ICT Use by SMall- and Medium-sized Enterprises in Japan. In *Proceedings of 16th ITS Biennial Conference* (CD-ROM), Beijing, China.

Giovannetti, E., Kagami, M., & Tsuji, M. (Eds.). (2003). *The Internet Revolution: A Global Perspective*. Cambridge, UK: Cambridge University Press.

Kuchiki, M., & Tsuji, M. (Eds.). (2005). *Industrial Clusters in Asia: Analyses of Their Competition and Cooperation*. Houndmills, UK: Palgrave Macmillan.

Mata, F. J., Fuest, W. L., & Barney, J. B. (1995). Information Technology and Sustained Competitive Advantage: A Resource-Based Analysis. *MIS Quarterly*, *19*(4), 487–505. doi:10.2307/249630

Small and Medium Enterprise Agency. (2001, 2002, 2003, 2004). *White Paper on Small and Medium Enterprises in Japan* (in Japanese). Tokyo: Ministry of Economy, Trade and Industry (METI).

Tsuji, M. (2005). ICT Use by SMEs in Japan: A Comparative Study of Higashi-Osaka and Ohta Ward, Tokyo. In M. Kuwayama, Y. Ueki, & Tsuji, M. (Eds.), *Information Technology for Development of Small and Medium-sized Exporters in Latin America and East Asia*. Santiago de Chili, Chili: ECLAC/IDE-JETRO/United Nations.

Tsuji, M., & Choe, I. (2004). An Ordered Probit Analysis of Factors Promoting a Regional Information Policy: The Case of Japanese Local Governments. *Mathematics and Computers in Simulation*, *64*(1), 203–212. doi:10.1016/S0378-4754(03)00133-2

Chapter 12
Telecommunications Capital Intensity and Aggregate Production Efficiency:
A Meta-Frontier Analysis

Alexandre Repkine
Korea University, Republic of Korea

ABSTRACT

This chapter explores the link between telecommunications capital intensity and aggregate production efficiency in the framework of meta-frontier analysis. The latter makes it possible to compare technical efficiency levels between countries operating under different technological frontiers. The author's analysis suggests that increasing per capita levels of telecommunication capital will push a country towards its local frontier, but it will not decrease much the technological gap with the global meta-frontier. In Africa policies providing incentives for firms and households to purchase more telecommunications equipment appear to be most justified in terms of efficiency gains, while this does not appear to be the case for the OECD countries. The author's general conjecture is, in order to avoid wasting productive resources on increasing the level of telecommunications capital intensity, it is advisable to keep a close eye on the location of a country's aggregate output with respect to both local and meta-frontiers.

INTRODUCTION

The focus of this study is on the link between telecommunications capital intensity and aggregate production efficiency in the global meta-frontier framework. Capital intensity in general is measured as a ratio of capital stock to labor. A greater extent of the telecommunications capital intensity is associated with the higher levels of labor productivity since better communication tools make workers and their management more efficient (Jorgenson & Stiroh, 2000). I attempt to estimate the effects of telecommunications capital intensity on the levels of aggregate production efficiency in a broad range of countries around the world, putting a specific emphasis on the difference between country group and global stochastic production frontiers.

There are several ways in which investments into telecommunications equipment, such as cables and switches, can render production more efficient.

DOI: 10.4018/978-1-61520-709-1.ch012

To a large extent, all of these channels are related to the strong network effects that characterize telecommunications capital goods (Creti, 2001). First, firms that are able to quickly gain access to and process large volumes of information on the prospective suppliers of their intermediate inputs are likely to end up with cheaper inputs of higher quality compared to their counterparts that do not have access to a developed information communications infrastructure. Second, such an exchange of information on inputs and outputs to the various production processes that can only be made possible by means of advanced telecommunications networks increases the extent of competitive pressure, which in turn boosts incentives for the firms to use their inputs more efficiently. Third, the existence of informational superhighways exerts a downward pressure on the time elapsing between conceiving and concluding the deal, urging businesses to act quickly and more efficiently, too.

The main contribution of this study is to employ the meta-frontier framework in order to analyze the link between telecommunications capital intensity as a measure of the informational network effects and aggregate productive efficiency in a worldwide setting. Meta-frontier analysis is different from the conventional stochastic frontier framework in that it allows one to make a distinction between the 'local' stochastic production frontier and the 'global' one (Battese & al., 2004.) The 'local' stochastic production frontiers in my study are defined for the four groups of countries formed according to their geographic proximity, while the 'global' stochastic production frontier is estimated for the whole sample. In contrast to the previous studies on the issue (e.g. Thompson & Garbacz, 2007), I am recognizing the fact that good performance in terms of a 'local' best-practice production frontier is not the same as good performance in terms of the 'global' best-practice benchmark. For that reason the impact of changes in the telecom capital intensity may be different depending on the type of productive efficiency.

I am opting for the telecom capital intensity to represent the extent of development of the telecommunications sector in order to better capture the network effects characterizing the latter. My basic reasoning is, a person who only has access to a land-line phone can communicate less efficiently (and therefore make less use of communication network effects) compared to the person who in addition can use cell phones, fax machines, satellite networks and the Internet. Thus, I believe that a higher level of telecommunications capital per person (higher levels of telecom capital intensity) makes it more possible to exploit the network effects provided by telecommunications networks. In contrast, the level of telecom capital *per se* (whose growth represents telecom capital widening) is hard to interpret without relating it to the number of people who have access to it. The importance of using the concept of capital intensity as opposed to capital widening has been recognized in e.g. Estevao (2004).

I find that higher levels of telecommunications capital intensity are associated with both higher country group efficiency scores and lower technological gap. However, the marginal effect of increased capital intensity is estimated to be far greater in case of increasing the country group efficiency levels as opposed to the case of reducing the technological gap with respect to the global meta-frontier. In terms of the country group differences in efficiency levels, quite expectedly I find the group of OECD countries to exhibit consistently higher local and meta-efficiency levels compared to countries in the Asian, African and Latin American region. Surprisingly, though, I estimate technological gap ratios to be very close to each other.

My policy implications strongly suggest pursuing economic policies to provide incentives for firms and households to purchase telecommunications equipment in the countries where inefficient production practices are not only manifestly present (low technical efficiency levels relative to the group production frontier), but where they also account for much of the deviation from the deterministic frontier (larger share of the inefficiency term variance in the total variance of the Solow residual). In addition, I would advise to pursue IT intensity-boosting policies in the countries with low technological gap ratio together with the policies that improve the technological level itself in order to avoid unnecessary waste of productive resources.

This study is organized as follows. Section 2 provides a review of the literature. Section 3 describes the estimation methodology and the dataset construction. Section 4 presents my empirical results. Section 5 summarizes the results and discusses policy implications.

LITERATURE REVIEW

Examining how the development of information and telecommunication technologies (IT) has affected the process of economic growth has been the subject of a significant number of studies including recent contributions by Oliner & Sichel (1994), Schreyer (2000), Dewan & Kraemer (2000), and Jorgenson & Stiroh (2000). Corroborating the initial claim made much earlier in the research by e.g. Jipp (1963) and Hardy (1980), the general conclusion of these studies is that the high extent of telecommunications infrastructure is generally conducive to the high level of economic development.

Recently the research emphasis has shifted away from assessing the direct contribution of IT sector to economic growth and performance and towards the estimation of telecommunications infrastructure on economic efficiency. In fact, given the relatively small contribution of the IT sector itself to the GDP and the variety of indirect (externality) effects outlined above, the key benefit of telecommunications investment is likely to be in the area of aggregate productivity and economic efficiency. Studies that have pursued this line of thinking such as Barry & Triplett (2000) have demonstrated that the indirect effects of IT investment on economic performance are by far no less important than the direct ones. For example, Jorgenson & Vu (2005) conduct a detailed growth accounting analysis in a cross-section of the world's countries and find that the IT investment produces a significant impact on economic growth not only as a traditional investment, but also as a factor contributing to economic efficiency.

Since Aigner & al. (1977) have formulated a technique for estimating stochastic production frontiers, several modifications have been put into place, especially in light of the fast increase in the available computing power. Thus, Battese & Coelli (1988) developed an econometric estimation procedure for the individual technical efficiencies given estimates of the stochastic production frontier within a panel data framework. Coelli (1992) provided for a practical way to estimate technical efficiency levels by releasing the Frontier computer program. The useful instrument provided by this program was that it allowed for the *simultaneous* estimation of the inefficiency effects' determinants and the underlying stochastic frontier. The usual practice before that program became available was to run an OLS regression of the estimated technical efficiency levels on a set of determinants. Since there was no way to test whether the estimated efficiency scores were independently distributed, the estimated standard errors for the inefficiency determinants were to be taken cautiously. The simultaneous estimation of efficiency scores *and* their determinants eliminated this problem.

Implicitly the assumption underlying the stochastic frontier estimation procedure (irrespectively of how efficiency scores' determinants were treated) was that the observed production units, be it the individual firms or countries, are rather homogenous in the sense that they are operating under the same (stochastic) production frontier. While that assumption worked well in many cases, it definitely did not hold when the task was to estimate production efficiency scores on the set of the production units that were very different. For example, one cannot seriously believe that the African countries are operating under the same production frontier as the Asian or Latin American countries do. In that case it would make sense to estimate individual production frontiers for every group of the observations and measure technical efficiency levels relative to those. However, the efficiency scores of the units belonging to *different* groups of observations were not directly comparable. For example, a 99% efficiency score of a firm (or country) is not necessarily an indicator of an extremely efficient organization of the production activity since it may well be the case that I am talking about a very 'low' production frontier itself for that group. Alternatively, an efficiency score of 70% in a group of very efficient countries is not necessarily a sign of inefficient production on a global scale.

Recognizing these shortcomings, Battese & al. (2004) have presented a practical way to solve the problem of efficiency scores comparability in a heterogeneous group of observations by estimating the *meta-frontier*. The meta-frontier is defined as an envelope of the country group stochastic frontiers estimated in the conventional way. Meta-frontiers are of the same functional form as the country group frontiers and, since they are envelopes of a group of the individual stochastic production frontiers, an efficiency score relative to the meta-frontier is greater or equal to the efficiency score relative to the individual frontier. In particular, the rankings of observational units within the group and the average efficiency rankings of those groups themselves may well change depending on whether the ranking procedure is based on efficiency scores measured against the individual or the meta-frontier.

The major method so far for estimating the meta-frontiers was to solve a constrained minimization problem with constraints making sure the meta-frontier is in fact an envelope. Battese & al. (2004) offer two ways to specify the objective function to be minimized—the sum of the absolute deviations of the output levels on group frontiers and the meta-frontier or the sum of these deviations' squares. In this paper I follow the approach based on the sum of absolute deviations.

To my knowledge, this is the first study that conducts a meta-frontier analysis of the link between telecommunications capital intensity and aggregate production efficiency. Comparison issues being one advantage of the meta-frontier approach, the identification of the difference between the technological gap and within-the-group inefficiency is another important exercise made possible by this methodology.

ESTIMATION METHODOLOGY AND THE DATASET CONSTRUCTION

In this section I explain how I arrived at my empirical results presented in Section 4. I start by describing the production function specification I employ and the way how I calculate technical efficiency levels relative to their respective country group stochastic frontiers. I then explain how I estimate the meta-frontier parameters and reduce the constraints number in the original minimization problem by exploiting the concept of segmented-frontier and by assuming the time-variant coefficients in the meta-frontier. By combining the results of the first two subsections, I show how the meta-frontier efficiency score can be decomposed into the product of country group efficiency score and the technology gap ratio. The final subsection describes the dataset with a special emphasis on the perpetual inventory method that I used to estimate stocks of conventional and telecommunications capital.

Estimation of Country Group Stochastic Frontiers and the Levels of Production Efficiency

For each one of the four geographical regions (OECD, Africa, Latin America and Asia) I estimate a separate country group production frontier. These estimates later serve as a basis for estimating the common meta-frontier. I postulate the basic Cobb-Douglas aggregate production function for each region $k = 1..4$: $Y_{it} = A_{kt} K_{it}^{\alpha_k} L_{it}^{\beta_k}$ where Y_{it} is output, K_{it} is capital and L_{it} is labor in country i in year t and $A_{kt} = A_0 D_k e^{\lambda_k t}$. Technology level A_{kt} is a function of global technological level A_0 geographical group-specific characteristic D_k and the technological time component $e^{\lambda_k t}$ that reflects the fact that the time dimension of my sample is large, especially considering the fast pace of advancements that had taken place in the area of telecommunications in the period between 1981 and 2004. Taking the logarithm of the above specification, I obtain the following expression for the aggregate production function:

$$\ln Y_{it} = \ln\left(A_0 D_k\right) + \alpha_k \ln K_{it} + \beta_k \ln L_{it} + \lambda_k t \tag{1}$$

The empirical stochastic frontier specification of (1) with the technical inefficiency component will assume the following form:

$$\ln Y_{it} = \ln\left(A_0 D_k\right) + \alpha_k \ln K_{it} + \beta_k \ln L_{it} + \lambda_k t + \varepsilon_{it} \tag{2}$$

where $\varepsilon_{it} = v_{it} - u_{it}$ is a stochastic term with v_{it} being standard i.i.d normal and $u_{it} > 0$ distributed as a truncated normal variable and representing the *inefficiency* of the (local) aggregate growth process in the sense that higher values of $u_{it} > 0$ represent *less* efficiency. The efficient production frontier corresponding to (2) will be then represented by

$$\ln Y_{it} = \ln\left(A_0 D_k\right) + \alpha_k \ln K_{it} + \beta_k \ln L_{it} + \lambda_k t + v_{it} \tag{3}$$

or, equivalently, (2) under the condition that $u_{it} = 0$. Technical efficiency of economic growth will then be given by the ratio of the right hand side of (2) to that of (3).

In this study I hypothesize that higher levels of per capita telecommunications capital stock increase technical efficiency of aggregate production relative to the efficient production frontier. In terms of specification (2) I am expecting to find a *negative* association between term u_{it} (representing technical *inefficiency* of aggregate production) and per capita telecommunications capital stock. Using the estimates of (3) I test the hypothesis that u_{it} is a decreasing function of $\frac{K_{IT}}{L}$ where K_{IT} is the real telecom capital stock.

I estimate the effects of telecommunications capital intensity on the *inefficiency* levels by maximizing the following likelihood function:

$$\begin{cases} \ln Y_{it} = \ln\left(A_0 D_k\right) + \alpha_k \ln K_{it} + \beta_k \ln L_{it} + \lambda_k t + v_{it} - u_{it}, u_{it} \geq 0 \\ \mu\left(u_{it}\right) = \delta_{k,1} + \delta_{k,2}\left(\frac{K_{IT,it}}{L_{it}}\right) + \delta_{k,3} t \end{cases} \tag{3a}$$

where $\mu\left(u_{it}\right)$ is the mean of inefficiency term u_{it} conditioned on the level of telecom capital intensity and the time trend term $\delta_{k,3} t$. I avoid running OLS regressions of inefficiency terms u_{it} on the levels of telecommunications capital intensity (the so-called two-stage approach) since it is not clear whether the estimated inefficiency terms in (5) are indeed independent. Denote the levels of technical efficiency estimated from (3a) as TE_{it}^k, where superscript k emphasizes the fact that I am talking about a technical efficiency level *relative to the country group, rather than to the meta-, frontier.* It is computed as $TE_{it}^k = e^{-\hat{u}_{it}}$ Since only one level of technical efficiency is computed for each observation, index k is not entering the right hand side of the expression for the level of technical efficiency.

Estimation of the Meta-Frontier

Meta-frontier is defined as an envelope of the individually estimated country group frontiers. The basic idea is to find the parameters of a production function $Y_{it} = A^*_t K_{it}^{\alpha^*} L_{it}^{\beta^*}$ such that the meta-frontier output level exceeds any of the country group output levels (given by the deterministic part of the estimated country group frontiers) for any combination of capital and labor in the sample. I can formalize this idea as follows:

$$\begin{cases} \underset{A_0^*,\lambda^*,\alpha^*,\beta^*}{Min} \; A_0^* e^{\lambda^* t} K_{it}^{\alpha^*} L_{it}^{\beta^*} \\ s.t. \\ A_0^* e^{\lambda^* t} K_{it}^{\alpha^*} L_{it}^{\beta^*} > A_0 D_k e^{\lambda_k t} K_{it}^{\alpha_k} L_{it}^{\beta_k}, \\ k = 1..K, t = 1..T, i = 1..N \end{cases} \quad (4)$$

where K is the number of geographical groups, T is the number of years, and N is the number of countries in the sample. Each one of the $K \times T \times N$ constraints in (4) guarantees that the meta-frontier level of output is greater than any output on any of the country group stochastic frontiers (of course, of their deterministic parts) corresponding to the same combination of capital and labor at any point in time.

Since the constraints' number in (4) is relatively large, I have simplified (4) in two ways. First, I notice that the constraints in (4) are satisfied whenever the meta-frontier output is greater than the *segmented-frontier* output. The latter is defined as the segmented envelope of the country group stochastic frontiers formally defined as $Y_{it}^s = \underset{k=1..K}{Max}\, A_0 D_k e^{\lambda_k t} K_{it}^{\alpha_k} L_{it}^{\beta_k}, i = 1..N, t = 1..T$ and s standing for segmented frontier. Each constraint in (4) then becomes $A_0^* e^{\lambda^* t} K_{it}^{\alpha^*} L_{it}^{\beta^*} > Y_{it}^s$ and their total number diminishes by four times.

The second way I simplify the constraints in (4) is by assuming that the meta-frontier may evolve over time, which is not unreasonable given the fact that my analysis spans the period of twenty-five years. This assumption modifies both the objective function and the constraints in (4). I am now solving several minimization problems with a smaller number of constraints rather than solving a single minimization problem with a great many constraints. In particular, I am solving a series of problems of the following type:

For each $t = 1..T$, solve:

$$\begin{cases} \underset{A_t^*}{Min} \; A_t^* K_{it}^{\alpha_t^*} L_{it}^{\beta_t^*} \\ s.t. \\ A_t^* K_{it}^{\alpha_t^*} L_{it}^{\beta_t^*} > Y_{it}^s \end{cases} \quad (5)$$

where α_t^* and β_t^* are the year-specific factor shares, A_t^* is the year-specific meta-frontier intercept and Y_{it}^s is the segmented-frontier output from (4). The number of constraints in (5) is equal to the number of countries in the sample, N.

I reduce (5) by taking logarithms of both the objective function and constraints, ending up with T linear programming problems of the following kind:

For each $t = 1..T$, solve:

$$\begin{cases} \underset{C_t^*,\alpha_t^*,\beta_t^*}{Min} \left[C_t^* + \alpha_t^* \left(\ln K_{it}\right) + \beta_t^* \left(\ln L_{it}\right)\right] \\ s.t. \\ C_t^* + \alpha_t^* K_{it} + \beta_t^* L_{it} > Y_{it}^s, i = 1..N \end{cases} \quad (6)$$

where $C_t^* = \ln A_t^*$. Denote $Y_{it}^* = A_t^* K_{it}^{\alpha_t^*} L_{it}^{\beta_t^*}$ to be country $i's$ meta-frontier output in year t.

Technology Gap Ratio and the Country Group Technical Efficiency Scores

Technology gap ratios measure how short the observed output levels fall of the meta-frontier. Denoting $Y_{it}^{eff} = \dfrac{Y_{it}}{TE_{it}^k}$ to be the efficient level of output for country i in year t relative to the *country group frontier* k, the technology gap ratio is defined as $TG_{it} = \frac{Y_{it}^{eff}}{Y_{it}^{*}}$. The product of the country group efficiency level TE_{it}^{k} and the corresponding technology gap ratio TG_{it} yields technical efficiency level relative to the meta-frontier TE_{it}^{*}:

$$TE_{it}^{*} = TE_{it}^{k} \times TG_{it} \quad (7)$$

In the right hand side o (7) index k is only serving as a reminder that I am talking about the level of technical efficiency relative to the country group, not meta-, frontier. This country group technical efficiency level is unique for each country in each period of time.

Construction of the Dataset

The data at my disposal come from two sources. The Penn World Table, version 6.2, provides data on real output, labor and investment flows. The International Telecommunications Union world telecommunications database provides us with the total annual investments in telecom defined as capital expenditure in the sector.

In either database I do not have the capital stock levels either for the conventional capital or for the telecom capital. For that reason, before estimating (3a) empirically, I need to estimate stocks of conventional and telecom capital K_{it} and $K_{IT,it}$, respectively.

I estimate the latter two stocks by employing the perpetual inventory method that allows one to estimate capital stocks as a sum of the past real investment flows weighted by the extent to which these investments depreciate over time. Assuming the finite useful lifetime of an investment equal to m (equivalent to saying that an asset becomes useless m years after purchase) and a yearly depreciation rate δ, I obtain the following expression for the value of a stock variable S_{it} that is characterized by investment flow I_{it}:

$$S_{it} = \sum_{\tau=0}^{m-1} \left(1 - \delta\right)^{\tau} I_{t-\tau} \quad (8)$$

To use (8) for the computational purposes, I assume the useful lifetime of conventional investment to be equal to thirty years, while that of the telecom investment to be equal to seven years (see Jorgenson and Vu, 2005). Depreciation rates δ that correspond to these values are 7.5% and 20%, respectively.

I obtain real values of investment flows into the conventional capital by combining the information on real GDP per capita (*rgdpl*), investment share of real GDP per capita (*ki*) and population (*pop*) provided by the Penn World table, version 6.2. Flows of investment into the telecommunications capital are defined by the ITU database as the total annual investment in telecom (including mobile service) for acquiring property and plant. Since the deflator for telecommunications investment is not explicitly provided by the ITU database, I employ the National Income and Product Account Tables provided by the U.S. Bureau of Economic Analysis (Table 1.1.4, price index for equipment and software under gross private fixed domestic investment). I then deflate the ITU data on telecom investments in the international U.S. dollars by this index.

To complete this section, a few remarks must be made on the scope of the countries and years covered by this study. As mentioned before, the Penn World Table provides the data on output, capital and labor, while the ITU provides the telecommunications investment data. The World Table data normally cover the period from 1950 through 2004, while the ITU data coverage is only from 1975 through 2004 for telecom investment. Since I take the useful lifetime for conventional capital stock to be thirty years, while that of the telecom capital stock to be seven years, the earliest year for which both conventional and telecom capital stocks could be constructed is 1981, which is the beginning year of the sample.

Since the statistical software I used in order to produce my estimations can deal with unbalanced panels, in principle it was possible to include those countries for which some observations were missing. However, in order to keep the panel reasonably balanced I did not include those countries where capital stocks could be calculated only for a few years such as the Eastern European countries and countries of the Former Soviet Union. For that reason, for example, Germany was not included in the sample. As a result, I ended up with forty-six countries listed below by their geographical location.

Table 2 presents summary statistics for my dataset:

Expectedly, Table 2 is demonstrating the well-known differences between the OECD and less developed countries. The OECD countries dominate in terms of the real GDP, accumulated conventional and the telecommunications capital. I also observe the mean accumulated real capital stock exceeding the value of mean GDP in all but the African region, the latter apparently being due to the low levels of investment activities in the African countries. The level of real telecommunications capital stock accumulated in all four regions is uniformly a relatively small fraction of the total conventional capital stock, ranging between one-half percent in Asia and a little over one percent in Africa. In per capita terms, I observe levels of telecommunications capital stock per person to be predominantly on the order of several hundred US dollars in the constant prices of 2000. In my view, such low estimates of the accumulated telecommunications capital per person is indicative of both the rapid depreciation rate of the telecom equipment, as well as of the fact that the latter's direct contribution to the economy is likely to be very small compared to the effect it has through its network and spillover effects.

Table 1. The geographical coverage

OECD	Asia	Latin America	Africa
1. Austria	1. China	1. Brazil	1. Egypt
2. Belgium	2.Hong Kong	2. Colombia	2. Kenya
3. Denmark	3. India	3. Costa Rica	3. Morocco
4. France	4. Indonesia	4. Ecuador	4.South Africa
5. Greece	5. Malaysia	5.El Salvador	5. Zambia
6. Iceland	6. Philippines	6. Paraguay	
7. Ireland	7. Singapore	7. Uruguay	
8. Italy	8. Taiwan	8. Venezuela	
9. Luxembourg	9.Thailand		
10. Netherlands	10. Korea		
11. Norway			
12. Portugal			
13. Spain			
14. Sweden			
15. Switzerland			
16. United Kingdom			
17. Australia			
18. Canada			
19. Japan			
20. New Zealand			
21. United States			
22. Turkey			
23. Mexico			

Note: Korea joined OECD only recently, so I consider it to be part of the Asian region

Table 2. Summary statistics

	Mean	SD	Min	Max
OECD (552 observations)				
Real GDP (billion USD, constant prices of 2000)	791	1610	4.41	10700
Real capital stock (billion USD, constant prices of 2000)	1640	3160	9.86	21202
Population (million persons)	38.23	57.66	0.23	295.41
Real telecom capital stock (billion USD, constant prices of 2000)	13.300	27.100	0.039	216.000
Real telecom capital stock per capita (USD, constant prices of 2000, per person)	411.16	539.07	16.70	8520.89
Africa (120 observations)				
Real GDP (billion USD, constant prices of 2000)	132	120	7.33	394
Real capital stock (billion USD, constant prices of 2000)	111	88	12.001	305
Population (million persons)	31.57	18.04	5.88	76.16
Real telecom capital stock (billion USD, constant prices of 2000)	1.210	1.540	0.026	6.940
Real telecom capital stock per capita (USD, constant prices of 2000, per person)	32.41	34.89	2.60	163.77
Latin America (216 observations)				
Real GDP (billion USD, constant prices of 2000)	176	331	8.49	1380
Real capital stock (billion USD, constant prices of 2000)	279	561	11.48	2234
Population (million persons)	26.82	47.49	2.26	184.55
Real telecom capital stock (billion USD, constant prices of 2000)	2.110	5.180	0.030	28.700
Real telecom capital stock per capita (USD, constant prices of 2000, per person)	70.99	59.83	6.62	300.93
Asia (210 observations)				
Real GDP (billion USD, constant prices of 2000)	787	1160	53.17	6910
Real capital stock (billion USD, constant prices of 2000)	1230	1950	131.89	13241
Population (million persons)	268.67	416.69	2.93	1294.85
Real telecom capital stock (billion USD, constant prices of 2000)	6.760	13.500	0.097	101.000
Real telecom capital stock per capita (USD, constant prices of 2000, per person)	145.14	187.02	0.32	763.24

EMPIRICAL META-FRONTIER ANALYSIS

In this section I am presenting my main empirical findings. I start by discussing the estimation results of the individual production frontiers for the four country groups. Subsection 4.2 continues with the discussion of the country group technical efficiency scores. The next two subsections deal with the meta-frontier estimation results and those of the meta-frontier efficiency scores. Subsection 4.5 analyzes the relative roles distances from the country group frontier and the technological gaps are playing in the determination of the overall meta-frontier efficiency level. The last subsection is dealing with the impact IT capital intensity is producing on both components of the meta-frontier efficiency.

Country Group Stochastic Production Frontiers

I estimate four country group stochastic production frontiers according to (3a) along with the pooled stochastic production frontier for the whole sample. As mentioned in the previous section, comparing technical efficiency levels obtained by estimating the pooled frontier may not be legitimate since different regions might operate under very different country group technologies. Table 3 details the results, the pooled sample estimates are provided for reference only.

As is evidenced by the pooled frontier estimation, the world on average is operating under constant returns to scale, but there are substantial country group differences with only the OECD countries following the CRS pattern with Africa, Asia and Latin America exhibiting either increasing or decreasing returns to scale. The generalized likelihood ratio test results strongly reject the hypothesis of the world operating under a single production frontier, corroborating the need for the meta-frontier analysis performed in this study.

The time trend is positive and significant at 1% level in all four regions, except for Asia, reflecting the technological progress. Expectedly, the country group frontier shifts out the most in case of the OECD countries, while in Africa it does not appear to do so with the course of time.

Technical Efficiency Estimates with Respect to the Country Group Frontiers

According to my estimates, production inefficiency appears to be strongly present in all four regions. The significance of production inefficiency effects is measured by parameter $\gamma = \frac{\sigma_u^2}{\sigma_u^2 + \sigma_v^2}$, which is essentially the share of the stochastic term's variance due to the inefficient production. Low values of γ make the interpretation of technical efficiency scores more difficult since in that case even the role of efficient behavior and organization on the overall performance is small compared to the exogenous random factors. In the context of this study the low values of γ would suggest a smaller extent, to which policy measures aimed at improving efficiency scores relative to the regional frontiers, are important.

My estimates suggest that in each region the inefficiency component is statistically significant, although its relative importance relative to the purely stochastic disturbance varies depending on geographical location. Specifically, in Africa almost all deviations from the country group stochastic frontiers are explained by the inefficient production rather than exogenous stochastic shocks (e.g. bad weather, world economic crisis, embargoes etc), while in the OECD countries inefficient production explains a much smaller part of these deviations. The average country group efficiency levels are the highest in the group of the OECD countries at 96.05%, followed by the Latin American, African and the Asian regions at 89.11%, 84.83% and 69.93%, respectively.

The time trend variable is either insignificant at the 5% significance level in case of Africa and Asia, or strongly significant at 1% in the OECD and Latin American regions. The sign of the time trend in those cases is positive suggesting that with the course of time production becomes more inefficient relative to the country group frontier. This is natural since, if a country is not aiming to increase its production efficiency levels (e.g. by promoting telecommunications capital intensity, discussed in the next subsection), it will 'relocate' further away from the country group efficient production frontier pushed upwards by the other countries in the group.

As suggested by my estimates, higher levels of telecommunications capital intensity are associated with the higher levels of technical efficiency (evidenced by the *negative* sign on the $\left(\frac{K_{IT,it}}{L_{it}}\right)$ variable (δ_2) in the estimated inefficiency function) in all four regions. The impact of telecommunications capital intensity is estimated to be significant at a 1% level in all regions except the OECD one where it is significant at the level of 2%. The size of telecom capital intensity impact is the highest in Latin America, while it appears to be the lowest in case of the OECD countries

Table 3. Local stochastic frontiers and technical efficiency levels

	OECD	Latin America	Developing Asia	Africa	World
Aggregate Production Function: Dependent Variable $Ln(Y_{it})$					
C	2.22 (0.000)	5.24 (0.000)	7.04 (0.000)	-3.97 (0.000)	2.89 (0.000)
$Ln(K_{it})$	0.69 (0.000)	0.44 (0.000)	0.36 (0.000)	0.84 (0.000)	0.66 (0.000)
$Ln(L_{it})$	0.31 (0.000)	0.49 (0.000)	0.49 (0.000)	0.68 (0.000)	0.33 (0.000)
Time Trend	0.01 (0.000)	0.005 (0.001)	0.009 (0.155)	0.002 (0.000)	0.005 (0.000)
Inefficiency Function: Dependent Variable U ($u_{it} = \delta_1 + \delta_2 \left(\frac{K_{ICT,it}}{L_{it}} \right) + \delta_3 t$)					
δ_1	-1.07 (0.000)	-0.97 (0.004)	0.96 (0.010)	0.5 (0.000)	-0.09 (0.529)
$\left(\frac{K_{ICT,it}}{L_{it}} \right)$	-0.004 (0.016)	-0.15 (0.000)	-0.03 (0.000)	-0.05 (0.000)	-0.014 (0.000)
Time Trend	0.025 (0.000)	0.036 (0.000)	-0.007 (0.300)	-0.007 (0.054)	0.009 (0.012)
γ	0.26 (0.09)	0.78 (0.11)	0.55 (0.24)	1.00 (0.000)	0.87 (0.02)
Average Efficiency	96.05% (3.61%)	89.11% (11.07%)	69.93% (18.41%)	84.83% (10.90%)	
Average Effic. in the World Sample					
# Obs	529	192	210	120	1194

Note: the coefficient for the $\frac{K_{ICT,it}}{L_{it}}$ variable is entering the ***inefficiency** function, so that the* **negative** *value for this coefficient corresponds to* ***increased** efficiency. P-values are in parentheses in all cases except for gamma and average efficiencies where in parentheses are their respective standard errors.*

with Africa and Asia impacts estimated to be inbetween.

In the absence of meta-frontier estimates I cannot directly compare average efficiency scores obtained for the four regions. For example, the average efficiency score of 89.11% for the Latin American region cannot be sensibly compared to the score of 69.93% for the Asian region since I do not know how the two regions are doing in terms of the distance from the world best-practice meta-frontier. The pooled-sample production frontier cannot substitute for the meta-frontier since it implicitly assumes every four regions are producing according to the same technology. If it turns out that the Asian countries' country group frontier is closer to the meta-frontier compared to the Latin American ones, the direct comparison of the two regions' technical efficiency levels estimated relative to the country group frontiers will be very misleading.

Meta-Frontier Production Function Estimates

I estimate twenty-five meta-frontiers for each year in the sample according to (6). Table 4 presents the results.

The intercept of the estimated meta-frontier is continuously growing over time, reflecting the ongoing technological progress in the world. My

Table 4. Meta-frontier estimates

Year	C	K	L
1984	2.132	0.680	0.499
1985	2.159	0.677	0.504
1986	2.191	0.673	0.508
1987	2.208	0.671	0.513
1988	2.228	0.668	0.518
1989	2.249	0.665	0.522
1990	2.267	0.663	0.525
1991	2.296	0.660	0.529
1992	2.334	0.657	0.534
1993	2.391	0.652	0.539
1994	2.451	0.647	0.545
1995	2.518	0.641	0.551
1996	2.564	0.636	0.558
1997	2.594	0.632	0.564
1998	2.591	0.630	0.569
1999	2.586	0.629	0.574
2000	2.57	0.62796	0.5786
2001	2.58	0.6258	0.584
2002	2.63	0.62	0.5904
2003	2.69	0.61	0.60
2004	2.72	0.609	0.606

estimates also suggest that the marginal product of capital has been decreasing, while the marginal product of labor has been increasing over time. These findings suggest that technological progress has been transforming the world production frontier in the way that was making labor more productive, while "allowing" the returns to capital to follow the path of diminishing returns.

Meta-Frontier Efficiency Scores Estimates

I now use the meta-frontier estimates above to infer the technological gap ratios (TGR) and meta-efficiency levels computed according to (7):

I do not observe a large amount of variation in the technological gap ratios between the four regions as I did in case of the country group technical efficiencies. OECD is the leader falling short by a little more than 5% of the meta-frontier on average, while the African region is 7% short of the meta-frontier. It is interesting to notice that the four regions' rankings are different with respect to the technical efficiency levels estimated relative to the country group benchmark frontiers and to the technological gap ratio. While the OECD and Latin American regions have the same rankings according to both measures, the African region ranks better according to the country group efficiency, while the Asian region is enjoying a narrower technological gap.

In principle, the fact that the Asian countries' country group frontier is 'closer' to the meta-frontier, is potentially conducive to the situation where the Asian meta-frontier efficiencies are on average higher than the African ones. I do not see this happening: the four regions rank in the same way according to both country group efficiencies and the technological gap ratios. However, the meta-frontier approach allows us to avoid the potential misinterpretation of the efficiency scores.

Table 6 below displays two rankings of the countries in my sample according to the average country group and meta-frontier efficiency levels. The richest country in the sample according to its GDP per capita is Luxembourg according to both types of ranking, while the Philippines, Thailand and China are the three poorest *and* inefficient countries according to both country group and meta-efficiency average scores. In general, however, the two rankings are different. Thus, the U.S. ranks number 5 in the OECD group of countries at 97.62% with respect to the country group frontier, while its global (meta-efficiency) ranking is number 15 at 90.65%. Similarly, Iceland ranks number 11 when measured against the OECD frontier, while its global ranking is number 2.

In general, countries in my sample rank differently according to which frontier their technical efficiency scores are measured against, which underscores the importance of estimating the

Table 5. Technological gap ratios, country group and meta-frontier technical efficiencies

	1981-1984	1985-1988	1989-1992	1993-1996	1997-2000	2001-2004	Sample Period
Technological Gap Ratios							
OECD	94.43% (1.08%)	94.46% (1.10%)	94.54% (1.16%)	94.53% (1.19%)	94.58% (1.28%)	94.72% (1.39%)	94.56% (1.22%)
Africa	93.57% (1.74%)	93.53% (1.66%)	93.45% (1.76%)	93.17% (1.88%)	92.97% (1.98%)	92.87% (2.03%)	93.22% (1.83%)
Latin America	94.30% (1.53%)	94.18% (1.47%)	94.00% (1.44%)	93.62% (1.36%)	93.33% (1.35%)	93.17% (1.36%)	93.69% (1.44%)
Asia	94.34% (1.07%)	94.07% (1.10%)	93.88% (1.14%)	93.35% (1.20%)	92.93% (1.27%)	92.76% (1.41%)	93.40% (1.32%)
Country Group Technical Efficiencies							
OECD	98.63% (0.34%)	98.16% (0.48%)	97.52% (0.87%)	96.11% (1.86%)	94.48% (3.46%)	92.06% (5.38%)	96.05% (3.61%)
Africa	81.06 (15.47%)	81.50% (12.03%)	86.06% (7.00%)	85.06% (6.76%)	86.42% (8.58%)	88.91% (11.99%)	84.83% (10.9%)
Latin America	88.78% (8.89%)	87.38% (9.93%)	87.08% (10.59%)	89.71% (10.55%)	91.24% (12.07%)	90.48% (13.92%)	89.11% (11.07%)
Asia	52.66% (9.22%)	57.66% (11.29%)	66.84% (15.80%)	74.35% (17.95%)	78.02% (18.08%)	80.71% (17.14%)	69.93% (18.41%)
Meta-Frontier Efficiencies							
OECD	93.03% (1.24%)	92.72 (1.23%)	92.20% (1.52%)	90.86% (2.42%)	89.38% (3.96%)	87.23% (5.75%)	90.60% (3.90%)
Africa	75.97% (13.96%)	76.33% (11.99%)	80.48% (7.39%)	79.33% (7.57%)	80.44% (9.11%)	82.62% (11.70%)	79.66% (9.95%)
Latin America	82.14% (8.97%)	82.14% (9.25%)	81.68% (9.79%)	83.83% (9.87%)	84.96% (11.23%)	84.11% (12.89%)	83.29% (10.53%)
Asia	51.42% (9.63%)	54.29% (10.90%)	62.83% (15.21%)	69.51% (17.27%)	72.62% (17.36%)	74.96% (16.43%)	66.94% (17.22%)

Note: standard deviations are in parentheses

meta-frontiers for the purpose of comparison of the (average) efficiency scores in the countries belonging to two or several different groups. It is also worthwhile noticing that there is a certain positive correlation between GDP per capita (Table 6, last column), and the average efficiency scores. The correlation coefficient is estimated to be greater in case of the meta-efficiency estimates (64% compared to 61% in case of the country group scores), suggesting richer countries use their productive resources more efficiently.

Decomposing Meta-Inefficiency Scores into the Country Group and Technological Gap Components

Taking logs of both sides of (7), I arrive at the following additive decomposition of the meta-frontier efficiency scores:

$$\ln\left(TE_{it}^{*}\right) = \ln\left(TE_{it}^{k}\right) + \ln\left(TG_{it}\right) \quad (8)$$

This decomposition allows us to infer the extent to which the ability to use productive resources efficiently given the available technology in a given country group and proximity to the world

Table 6. Rankings by average country group efficiency and meta-efficiency levels

Ranking	Country	Country Group Efficiency	Country	Meta-Efficiency	GDP per capita
1	Luxembourg	98.09%	Luxembourg	95.53%	$79 400
2	Norway	98.07%	Iceland	94.11%	$40 400
3	United Kingdom	97.89%	Norway	93.51%	$53 300
4	Switzerland	97.77%	Switzerland	92.92%	$40 100
5	United States	97.62%	Denmark	92.29%	$37 200
6	Australia	97.51%	Australia	91.92%	$37 300
7	Denmark	97.10%	Ireland	91.77%	$46 600
8	Sweden	96.94%	South Africa	91.76%	$9 700
9	South Africa	96.93%	Sweden	91.75%	$37 500
10	Austria	96.83%	Austria	91.74%	$39 300
11	Iceland	96.63%	Costa Rica	91.55%	$11 100
12	Japan	96.62%	United Kingdom	91.54%	$35 000
13	Netherlands	96.57%	Netherlands	91.06%	$39 000
14	Ireland	96.55%	Uruguay	90.93%	$10 800
15	Canada	96.40%	United States	90.65%	$45 800
16	Costa Rica	96.39%	Belgium	90.54%	$36 200
17	Uruguay	96.10%	Canada	90.49%	$38 600
18	Brazil	96.02%	New Zealand	90.36%	$27 200
19	Italy	95.89%	Portugal	90.31%	$21 800
20	Belgium	95.87%	Hong Kong	90.15%	$42 000
21	Portugal	95.82%	Japan	90.08%	$33 500
22	France	95.66%	Italy	89.59%	$30 900
23	Hong Kong	95.42%	France	89.36%	$32 600
24	Spain	95.18%	Spain	88.96%	$33 600
25	New Zealand	95.11%	Greece	87.59%	$30 600
26	Venezuela	93.79%	Brazil	87.46%	$9 500
27	Colombia	93.58%	Venezuela	86.93%	$12 800
28	Greece	93.16%	Colombia	86.81%	$7 400
29	Singapore	91.30%	Singapore	86.54%	$49 900
30	Mexico	91.10%	Taiwan	85.32%	$30 100
31	Turkey	90.84%	Mexico	84.03%	$12 400
32	Taiwan	87.53%	Turkey	83.68%	$12 000
33	El Salvador	86.83%	El Salvador	83.25%	$6 000
34	Paraguay	86.41%	Egypt	81.81%	$5 000
35	Morocco	86.16%	Paraguay	80.76%	$4 000
36	Egypt	84.77%	Korea	80.23%	$25 000
37	Korea	83.17%	Morocco	79.62%	$3 700
38	Kenya	79.19%	Kenya	72.81%	$1 700
39	Zambia	77.12%	Zambia	72.28%	$1 400

continued following page

Table 6. continued

Ranking	Country	Country Group Efficiency	Country	Meta-Efficiency	GDP per capita
40	Malaysia	73.43%	Malaysia	69.39%	$14 500
41	Ecuador	63.78%	Ecuador	58.65%	$7 200
42	Indonesia	58.32%	India	54.64%	$2 600
43	India	58.24%	Indonesia	54.03%	$3 600
44	China	55.25%	China	52.44%	$5 400
45	Thailand	54.67%	Thailand	52.31%	$8 000
46	Philippines	53.22%	Philippines	50.30%	$3 200

Source: own calculations and the CIA World Factbook, 2008; the GDP per capita is in U.S. dollars based on the PPP

technological best practice are contributing to the observed meta-efficiency score. The contribution of the first type is represented by $\frac{\ln\left(TE_{it}^{k}\right)}{\ln\left(TE_{it}^{*}\right)}$, while $\frac{\ln\left(TG_{it}\right)}{\ln\left(TE_{it}^{*}\right)}$ is representing the second-type contribution. Table 7 below presents the decomposition results by country.

According to my estimates, countries in question differ a lot in terms of the relative importance of the technological gap and distance to their country group frontier. In the United Kingdom and the United States (share of the technological gap ratio equal to 75.15% and 75.10%, respectively) most of the meta-efficiency is accounted for by close proximity to the world technological best practice frontier, while the ability to use resources efficiently given the available country group technology contributes the most to the meta-efficiency score in the Philippines and Thailand (share of the country group efficiency equal to 91.25% and 88.98%, respectively). Alternatively, in the Philippines and Thailand, the major source of aggregate production inefficiency is the low level of available technology, while in the U.S. and the U.K. the observed inefficiency is mostly due to the suboptimal usage of productive resources given the available technology in the OECD country group. Table 8 below summarizes the results by four broadly defined groups of countries.

Predictably, the problem of lack of technological knowledge is more of a problem in Africa and in the developing Asian countries where more than three-fifths of the average observed efficiency levels are due to the proximity to the countries' own country group, as opposed to the global, frontier. In the group of OECD countries, by contrast, proximity to the local frontier is only contributing around 40% to the observed average efficiency levels with the rest accounted for by the high extent of technological advancement. In all regions, however, there are countries where the predominant contributor to the observed level of productive efficiency is different from the group average. Thus, in South Africa most efficiency is due to the technological knowledge, while in Iceland around 60% of observed efficiency is caused by the efficient use of productive resources measured against the best practice OECD benchmark frontier.

The Impact of IT Capital Intensity on Technical Efficiency Levels and the Technological Gap Ratio

In order to identify the impact of IT capital intensity on the levels of technical efficiency relative to the country group frontiers and technological gap ratios, I observe that the estimated technical efficiency levels in the country groups $TE_{it}^{k} = e^{-u_{it}}$ can be transformed as

Table 7. Shares of country group efficiency & prox. to the global meta-frontier in the meta-efficiency scores

Country	Mean	Minimum	Maximum	Mean	Min.	Max.
	Share of country group efficiency			Share of the proximity to the global meta-frontier		
Australia	30.73% (7.33%)	18.31%	41.60%	69.27% (7.33%)	58.40%	81.69%
Austria	36.11% (14.52%)	20.85%	67.97%	63.89% (14.52%)	32.03%	79.15%
Belgium	41.58% (15.19%)	21.05%	66.38%	58.42% (15.19%)	33.62%	78.95%
Brazil	28.38% (9.64%)	14.82%	45.03%	71.62% (9.64%)	54.97%	85.18%
Canada	35.87% (14.67%)	16.54%	65.25%	64.13% (14.67%)	34.75%	83.46%
China	84.23% (6.74%)	69.90%	91.98%	15.77% (6.74%)	8.02%	30.10%
Colombia	42.73% (15.79%)	11.93%	58.89%	57.27% (15.79%)	41.11%	88.07%
Costa Rica	39.32% (16.79%)	15.35%	59.92%	60.68% (16.79%)	40.08%	84.65%
Denmark	37.32% (10.30%)	21.61%	57.54%	62.68% (10.30%)	42.46%	78.39%
Ecuador	86.93% (0.70%)	85.86%	88.34%	13.07% (0.70%)	11.66%	14.14%
Egypt	57.55% (31.52%)	0.00%	87.64%	42.45% (31.52%)	12.36%	100.00%
El Salvador	60.64% (27.59%)	13.02%	84.49%	39.36% (27.59%)	15.51%	86.98%
France	37.83% (16.23%)	17.03%	68.37%	62.17% (16.23%)	31.63%	82.97%
Greece	53.55% (14.33%)	28.20%	72.29%	46.45% (14.33%)	27.71%	71.80%
Hong Kong	35.31% (23.59%)	15.66%	79.89%	64.69% (23.59%)	20.11%	84.34%
Iceland	57.54% (18.23%)	11.89%	82.22%	42.46% (18.23%)	17.78%	88.11%
India	86.43% (2.80%)	81.20%	90.30%	13.57% (2.80%)	9.70%	18.80%
Indonesia	87.54% (1.52%)	85.22%	90.39%	12.46% (1.52%)	9.61%	14.78%
Ireland	41.65% (10.38%)	24.33%	65.82%	58.35% (10.38%)	34.18%	75.67%
Italy	36.98% (15.12%)	19.66%	62.09%	63.02% (15.12%)	37.91%	80.34%
Japan	32.49% (11.65%)	19.58%	61.47%	67.51% (11.65%)	38.53%	80.42%
Kenya	73.91% (4.66%)	66.84%	81.00%	26.09% (4.66%)	19.00%	33.16%
Korea, Republic of	52.61% (27.31%)	15.61%	87.83%	47.39% (27.31%)	12.17%	84.39%
Luxembourg	42.98% (8.87%)	33.01%	63.99%	57.02% (8.87%)	36.01%	66.99%
Malaysia	81.10% (10.57%)	66.92%	92.93%	18.90% (10.57%)	7.07%	33.08%
Mexico	51.21% (18.41%)	22.33%	76.88%	48.79% (18.41%)	23.12%	77.67%
Morocco	69.17% (10.27%)	45.82%	79.28%	30.83% (10.27%)	20.72%	54.18%
Netherlands	37.97% (9.70%)	23.04%	53.07%	62.03% (9.70%)	46.93%	76.96%
New Zealand	46.48% (17.96%)	24.26%	77.98%	53.52% (17.96%)	22.02%	75.74%
Norway	29.13% (8.10%)	14.75%	40.35%	70.87% (8.10%)	59.65%	85.25%
Paraguay	72.76% (6.06%)	59.91%	80.62%	27.24% (6.06%)	19.38%	40.09%
Philippines	91.25% (1.46%)	88.64%	93.16%	8.75% (1.46%)	6.84%	11.36%
Portugal	41.64% (13.24%)	24.41%	69.37%	58.36% (13.25%)	30.63%	75.59%
Singapore	50.84% (20.18%)	31.56%	90.60%	49.16% (20.18%)	9.40%	68.44%
South Africa	37.30% (17.61%)	0.00%	56.51%	62.70% (17.61%)	43.49%	100.00%
Spain	41.00% (16.00%)	21.33%	66.21%	59.00% (16.00%)	33.79%	78.67%

continued following page

Table 7. continued

Country	Mean	Minimum	Maximum	Mean	Min.	Max.
	Share of country group efficiency			Share of the proximity to the global meta-frontier		
Sweden	36.26% (12.04%)	20.31%	51.63%	63.74% (12.04%)	48.37%	79.69%
Switzerland	30.67% (11.24%)	19.74%	54.17%	69.33% (11.24%)	45.83%	80.26%
Taiwan	48.94% (25.51%)	17.13%	88.20%	51.06% (25.51%)	11.80%	82.87%
Thailand	88.98% (2.58%)	85.81%	93.10%	11.02% (2.58%)	6.90%	14.19%
Turkey	48.54% (22.72%)	17.75%	78.97%	51.46% (22.72%)	21.03%	82.25%
United Kingdom	24.85% (4.86%)	16.39%	31.05%	75.15% (4.86%)	68.95%	83.61%
United States	24.90% (8.98%)	12.86%	45.53%	75.10% (8.98%)	54.47%	87.14%
Uruguay	34.92% (14.24%)	21.30%	68.47%	65.08% (14.24%)	31.53%	78.70%
Venezuela	41.72% (13.10%)	21.18%	62.14%	58.28% (13.10%)	37.86%	78.82%
Zambia	62.40% (20.41%)	0.00%	84.17%	37.60% (20.41%)	15.83%	100.00%

Note: standard errors are in parentheses, measured in percentage point units

$\ln\left(TE_{it}^{k}\right) = \delta_{k,1} + \delta_{k,2}\left(\frac{K_{IT,it}}{L_{it}}\right) + \delta_{k,3}t$, where coefficients $\delta_{k,1}$, $\delta_{k,2}$ and $\delta_{k,3}$ are estimated from (3a). For the sake of consistency,

I am thus choosing to estimate the log-linear specification of the relationship between telecommunications capital intensity and the technological gap ratio. I use the fixed effects model in order to control for the unobserved country heterogeneity. Table 9 below is presenting the estimation results by four country groups. For comparison purposes I am reproducing the part of Table 3 that displays the estimates of the country group inefficiency function.

In all but one case the impact of telecommunications capital intensity on both technical efficiency with respect to the country group frontiers and the technological gap ratios is positive and significant at the 2% significance level. In the case of Latin American countries myestimates suggest that increased levels of telecom capital intensity are associated with a wider technological gap with the world benchmark meta-frontier. While I am puzzled by this finding, I have currently no ready explanation for that.

In the rest of the cases I estimate higher levels of the telecom capital intensity to be associated with both higher efficiency scores relative to the group frontier and a narrower technological gap between

Table 8. Shares of country group production efficiency and technology development level in the meta-efficiency scores by country group

Country group	Mean	Minimum	Maximum	Mean	Minimum	Maximum
	Share of country group efficiency			Share of the proximity to the global meta-frontier		
Africa	60.06% (22.76%)	0.00%	87.64%	39.94% (22.76%)	12.36%	100.00%
Asia	71.49% (25.05%)	15.61%	93.16%	28.51% (25.05%)	6.84%	84.39%
Latin America	50.93% (24.13%)	11.93%	88.34%	49.07% (24.13%)	11.66%	88.07%
OECD	39.01% (15.77%)	11.89%	82.22%	60.99% (15.77%)	17.78%	88.11%

Note: standard errors are in parentheses, measured in percentage point units

the latter and the meta-frontier. The magnitude of the telecom capital intensity's impact, however, varies a lot. Thus, in the OECD countries the impact is the lowest both in terms of increasing the country group technical efficiency score and of narrowing the technological gap. In Latin America increasing levels of the telecom capital intensity appears to have the most potential in terms of pushing the countries towards the Latin American best practice frontier, while in Africa the effect in terms of reducing the technological gap with the meta-frontier is estimated to be the largest.

In general the effect of telecom capital intensity on the size of the technological gap is much lower than its effect on the technical efficiency score measured against the country group frontier. This finding suggests that more overhead capital in terms of the telecommunications infrastructure works more in the direction of improving the process of managerial decision-making given the available state of technology, while the technology itself is affected much less.

DISCUSSION

General Results

The focus of this study is on the link between telecommunications capital intensity and the aggregate production efficiency in the meta-frontier framework. I analyzed forty-six countries over the period of twenty-four years. Countries in this study were divided into four groups according to their geographical location with the exception of the OECD countries. I applied meta-frontier analysis to the estimation of aggregate performance in order to make comparisons of technical efficiency scores between countries operating under different technologies meaningful.

I found that the division of countries in the sample into four groups was justified in the sense that the difference between the four estimated production frontiers is statistically significant. However, I did not find the distance between the four individual production frontiers and the global meta-frontier to be varying much across the four groups. In fact, the average technological gap ratio measuring this distance was estimated in the range between 93.22% for the African countries and

Table 9. Technological gap ratio and IT capital intensity, panel data regression analysis, fixed effects

	OECD		Africa		Latin America		Asia	
Dependent Variable	**Ln (TGR)**	**Ln (TE)**	**Ln (TGR)**	**Ln (TE)**	**Ln (TGR)**	**Ln (TE)**	**Ln (TGR)**	**Ln (TE)**
C	-0.06 (0.000)	1.07 (0.000)	-0.05 (0.000)	-0.5 (0.000)	-0.04 (0.000)	0.97 (0.004)	-0.02 (0.000)	-0.96 (0.01)
$\left(\frac{K_{IT,it}}{L_{it}}\right)$	0.00001 (0.002)	0.004 (0.016)	0.0006 (0.000)	0.05 (0.000)	-0.0001 (0.001)	0.15 (0.000)	0.00004 (0.016)	0.03 (0.000)
Time	0.0001 (0.000)	-0.025 (0.000)	-0.0006 (0.000)	0.007 (0.054)	-0.0006 (0.000)	-0.036 (0.000)	-0.001 (0.000)	0.007 (0.300)
R^2 within	31.58%		69.36%		89.56%		90.91%	
R^2 between	21.92%		43.62%		6.63%		0.17%	
R^2 overall	2.59%		20.91%		6.77%		19.55%	
Number of obs.	483		105		189		192	

Note: p-values are in parentheses

94.56% for the OECD. The difference between average technical efficiency scores relative to the group country frontiers was found to be much larger. Thus, the Asian countries scored 69.93% on average, while the OECD countries' average technical efficiency levels relative to the group frontier were estimated at 90.60%.

The empirical analysis has demonstrated that the extent to which telecommunications capital intensity affects the distance towards the global best-practice meta-frontier is different depending on the type of the distance and the region. Thus, while increases in the telecom capital intensity appear to be increasing both technical efficiency scores relative to the country group production frontiers and the technological gap ratios, the effect is much larger in the former case compared to the latter (note that an increase in the technological gap ratio means decreasing the technological gap itself!). Latin America seems to be able to benefit the most from increased levels of telecom capital intensity in terms of increasing its technical efficiency levels, followed by the African, Asian and the OECD countries. In the latter group, the size of the effect is on the order of one-tenth of that in the other three country groups, however, the OECD is the best performer both in case of the technical efficiency scores with respect to its country group frontier, and in terms of the proximity of the latter to the global meta-frontier.

According to the empirical estimates, increased levels of the telecommunications capital intensity are conducive to the reduction of the technological gap only to a minor extent compared to the effect on the country group frontier technical efficiency scores. I thus infer that an increased ability to communicate faster and over longer distances provided by more telecommunications capital per person is working in the direction of increasing productive efficiency and decision-making *using the existing technology* rather than in the direction of improving or advancing the technology itself.

Policy Implications for Sustainable Economic Development

The empirical findings in this study have confirmed and quantified the positive effects of increased levels of the telecommunications capital intensity on aggregate productive efficiency. However, one should be careful not to waste the country's productive resources by stimulating further investments into increases of the telecommunications capital stock per capita unless reasonable gains in production efficiency relative to the meta-frontier are to be reaped.

In particular, this study suggests that any policy measures increasing the rate of adoption of telecommunications equipment by firms and households will be most effective in the environment characterized by the following three characteristics *simultaneously*:

1. The existing technological knowledge is not employed to its fullest potential, corresponding to low technical efficiency scores measured against the local group frontier.
2. Deviations from the deterministic production frontier in a country group are mostly accounted for by the inefficient production practices rather than by stochastic disturbances (in terms of the discussion in subsection 4.2, $\gamma = \frac{\sigma_u^2}{\sigma_u^2 + \sigma_v^2}$ has to be closer to unity.)
3. The country group frontier is itself close to the global meta-frontier, or active policies are being implemented to improve the existing technological knowledge in the region.

The first two conditions guarantee that production inefficiency *is* a problem in the sense that more efforts by the management could push the country closer to its *group frontier*. The third condition makes sure productive resources are not wasted by pushing the country's firms towards

Table 10. Ranking of country regions according to the effectiveness of policies increasing IT capital intensity

Effectiveness of IT policy (1=most effective)	γ (efficiency versus stochastic deviation)		Technological gap ratio		Technical efficiency relative to group frontiers	
1	Africa	100%	Africa	93.22%	Asia	69.93%
2	Latin America	78%	Asia	93.40%	Africa	84.83%
3	Asia	55%	Latin America	93.69%	Latin America	89.11%
4	OECD	26%	OECD	94.56%	OECD	96.05%

the group frontier that is *inefficient with respect to the global meta-frontier*.

Table 10 below groups the countries in this study according to the three criteria listed above.

An interesting feature presented by Table 10 is that all of the four regions are characterized by similar levels of average technological gap ratios ranging from 93.22% in the case of African countries to 94.56% in the case of the OECD countries. That makes condition 3 (proximity of the group frontier to the meta-frontier) above rather less binding.

It is remarkable how the group of OECD countries is consistently placed in the end of the list. This should not be, however, erroneously interpreted as evidence of lack of importance of the telecommunications capital in these countries. Rather, due to the fact that this group of countries is already most advanced technologically, the relevance of the IT capital intensity-boosting policies is low compared to the other regions because most countries are producing efficiently already. In this case, channeling more investment resources into raising the levels of per capita telecommunications capital will undermine the prospects for sustainable economic growth since these resources can be used more productively elsewhere. One alternative, for example, would be to direct these investment funds into the R&D activities that would push the global frontier outwards since getting more efficient with respect to both local (OECD) and global (meta-) frontiers would only result in marginal benefits for the group of the most advanced countries.

Africa appears to be the region where policies providing incentives for firms and households to purchase more telecommunications equipment will produce the most sizeable effect. While the African countries' deviations from the African production frontier are overwhelmingly the result of the inefficient management and production practices, its technical efficiency levels relative to the group frontier are the second lowest in the sample, preceded by the Latin American countries. Thus, in the case of Africa it makes every sense to invest into raising per capita stocks of the telecommunications capital since such investments will both push it towards the African local production frontier, and are likely to decrease the role of the inefficient decision-making relative to that of the random factors.

With respect to Asia and Latin America, it is rather hard to compare the two regions since the Asian countries are estimated to be least efficient according to the country group frontier, while in the Asian countries the deviations from group frontier are less the result of the inefficient behavior compared to Latin American countries. Referring to the difference in the technological gap ratio does not help much since the two average values for the regions are very close to each other. I conclude thus that in both Latin America and in Asia the policies of increasing the level of IT capital intensity will produce an improvement in terms of achieving higher levels of aggregate production efficiency, although the size of this improvement is likely to be smaller than that in the African countries. Again, increasing the per capita telecommunications capital stocks in these two regions will not hamper the long-term economic growth and development by distracting resources into the unproductive uses.

My general conjecture is, in order to avoid wasting productive resources it is advisable to keep a close eye on the location of a country's aggregate output with respect to both local and meta-frontiers. While productivity gains due to increased levels of per capita telecommunications capital stock may be substantial in the countries whose output level falls far short of the local production frontier (the case of Africa in this study), such investments may be counterproductive if the local frontier itself is much below the global meta-frontier. Similarly, if the distances from both local and meta-frontier are small (the case of OECD countries), management and production practices are highly efficient both in the local and in the global sense. In that case further investment into the telecommunications capital stock will be less productive compared to investments into R&D so as to push the meta-frontier itself.

REFERENCES

Aigner, D., Lovell, C. A. K., & Schmidt, P. (1977). Formulation and estimation of stochastic frontier production function models. *Journal of Econometrics*, *6*, 21–37. doi:10.1016/0304-4076(77)90052-5

Barry, P. B., & Triplett, J. E. (2000). What's new about the new economy? IT, economic growth and productivity. *Brookings Economic Papers*.

Battese, G. E., & Coelli, T. J. (1988). Prediction of firm-level technical efficiencies with a generalized production function and panel data. *Journal of Econometrics*, *38*(3), 387–399. doi:10.1016/0304-4076(88)90053-X

Battese, G. E., & Coelli, T. J. (1995). A model for technical inefficiency effects in a stochastic frontier production function for panel data. *Empirical Economics*, *20*, 325–332. doi:10.1007/BF01205442

Battese, G. E., Rao, G. S. P., & O'Donnell, C. J. (2004). A metafrontier production function for estimation of technical efficiencies and technology gaps for firms operating under different technologies. *Journal of Productivity Analysis*, *21*(1), 91–103. doi:10.1023/B:PROD.0000012454.06094.29

Central Intelligence Agency. (2008). *The 2008 World Factbook*. Retrieved January 2, 2009, from https://www.cia.gov/library/publications/the-world-factbook/index.html

Coelli, T. J. (1992). A computer program for frontier production function estimation: Frontier version 2.0. *Economics Letters*, *39*(1), 29–32. doi:10.1016/0165-1765(92)90096-H

Creti, A. (2001). Network technologies, communication externalities and total factor productivity. *Structural Change and Economic Dynamics*, *12*(1), 1–28. doi:10.1016/S0954-349X(99)00029-6

Dewan, S., & Kraemer, K. L. (2000). Information technology and productivity: evidence from country-level data. *Management Science*, *46*(4), 548–562. doi:10.1287/mnsc.46.4.548.12057

Estevao, M. M. (2004). *Why is productivity growth in the euro area so sluggish?* (IMF working paper WP/04/200).

Hardy, A. P. (1980). The role of the telephone in economic development. *Telecommunications Policy*, *4*(4), 278–286. doi:10.1016/0308-5961(80)90044-0

Jipp, A. (1963). Wealth of nations and telephone density. *Telecommunications Journal*, 199-201.

Jorgenson, D. W., & Stiroh, K. J. (2000). Raising the speed limit: U.S. economic growth in the information age. *Brookings Papers on Economic Activity*, *1*, 125–211. doi:10.1353/eca.2000.0008

Jorgenson, D. W., & Vu, K. (2005). Information technology and the world economy. *The Scandinavian Journal of Economics*, *107*(4), 631–650. doi:10.1111/j.1467-9442.2005.00430.x

Oliner, S. D., & Sichel, D. E. (1994). Computers and output growth revisited: how big is the puzzle? *Brookings Papers on Economic Activity*, *2*, 273–317. doi:10.2307/2534658

Schreyer, P. (2000). *The contribution of information and communication technology to output growth: a study of the G7 countries* (STI Working Paper 2002/2).

Thompson, H. G., & Garbacz, Ch. (2007). Mobile, fixed line and internet service effects on global productive efficiency. *Information Economics and Policy*, *19*(2), 189–214. doi:10.1016/j.infoecopol.2007.03.002

Chapter 13
Evaluating the Internal Capabilities and External Linkages of the Philippine IT-Enabled Services (ITES) Industry

Clarissa Sales
University of Leipzig, Germany

Utz Dornberger
University of Leipzig, Germany

ABSTRACT

Over the past five years the Philippine IT-enabled services industry has grown tremendously, fuelled primarily by strong global demand. The main competitiveness drivers of the Philippines as an attractive location for offshore IT-enabled services are well documented: highly skilled, English proficient workforce; low labour costs; cultural affinity towards the United States; reliable telecommunications infrastructure; and business-friendly policies. It is this rare combination of resources that has attracted many FDIs to locate their outsourcing operations in the Philippines which has made the country a prime location for customer contact service centres and business process outsourcing. This chapter examines the internal capabilities and external linkages of the Philippine ITES industry based on an empirical study. It focuses on how these various capabilities and linkages play a significant role in facilitating the ITES industry's growth and long term sustainability.

INTRODUCTION

Globalization has enabled the seamless delivery of information technology and business process services across borders, through time zones, and over oceans. It has transformed our world into more of a global village than it has ever been. The demand for outsourced services, particularly in offshore destinations, is growing exponentially. In today's highly competitive global market, outsourcing is increasingly seen as a strategic management option to reduce costs while allowing the enterprise to focus on its core competencies, thereby achieving efficiency within the organization. McKinsey and Co. forecasts demand for outsourcing services to

DOI: 10.4018/978-1-61520-709-1.ch013

reach US$180 billion by 2010, with the customer contact services, finance and accounting, and human resource sub-sectors taking up the largest shares (Reloc8 Asia Pacific Group, 2007). Therefore, a fierce race in becoming a leading offshore destination has inevitably been set into play and driven by global competition.

Many countries are now starting to develop their IT-enabled services (ITES) and business process outsourcing (BPO) industries to cater to the growing demand in outsourced services. The market leaders in supplying services at present are India and Canada. India's early software services firms have been able to leverage their earlier head start in software services into capabilities for other ITES sectors such as BPO and call centres. Canada has historically been a significant outsourcer because a significant portion of the U.S., the largest client of BPO services at present, is a major trading partner. Ireland is also a big player in IT services exports. However, 2003 witnessed a significant growth in services exports in other countries such as China, Russia, and the Philippines. At the same time, countries such as the Czech Republic, Poland, Hungary, and Mexico emerged from relatively insignificant markets to legitimate contenders for market share in the growing ITES market (neoIT, 2004). In addition, many countries have had some success in attracting such work, or have the potential to do such work. These include Malaysia, Jamaica, South Africa, Ghana, and Costa Rica (Tschang, n.d.).

Over the past five years the Philippine IT-enabled services industry has grown tremendously, fuelled primarily by strong global demands. The rapid growth of the ITES industry can be attributed as a result of two forces: 1) the information revolution, which has made the movement of information fast and cheap; and 2) the dramatically lower costs of carrying out some business operations in developing countries due to relative abundance of cheap educated manpower. This enticed businesses in industrialized countries to outsource certain backroom operations in the Philippines, leading to the expansion of such service activities in the country like call centres for customer relations, medical and legal transcription, financial and personnel management, engineering design, animation, development of web and software programs, and other services powered by information and communications technology. The Philippine government has already identified the ITES industry as one of the ten industries that will bring in huge revenues for the country under the Philippine Export Development Plan (PEDP). In 2007, the sector has reached a size of about US$4.9 billion from just about US$350 million in 2001. The Philippine outsourcing industry is projected to generate US$12 billion in annual revenues and employ over 1 million workers by 2010 (Locsin, 2006). The Philippines is now increasingly being recognized as one of the locations that companies are seriously looking into as a major outsourcing destination. In 2005, the Philippines was voted by IT Executives around the world as one of the Top Four Leaders in the Outsourcing Market, next to India, China and Malaysia (Our Corporate Bureau, 2005). In July 2007, the International Data Corporation (IDC) released a report about the new Global Delivery Index (GDI) which compares cities in the Asia/Pacific as potential offshore delivery centres, based on a comprehensive set of criteria such as cost of labour, cost of rent, language skills, and turnover rate. In the report, Bangalore and Manila ranked numbers one and two respectively out of 35 Asia/Pacific cities studied ("China to topple India", 2007).

Indeed, the Philippine ITES industry has an opportunity to play a profound role in the Philippine's economic development directly and indirectly through spillovers. Evidently, the industry has done a lot to ease the country's unemployment problem because of the thousands of jobs it is generating. However, this industry is also a very dynamic sector that is growing by leaps and bounds. Inevitably, various challenges and issues emerge. At this point, the Philippine ITES industry's two greatest problems are: 1) the looming shortage in qualified, highly skilled workforce that may hold back the industry from sustaining its current growth rate and 2) strong competition from other low-cost countries. Add to these are the problems faced by the country in general, such as political and social instability, which have great potential to affect foreign investments in the long run. Although the Philippines has marked advantages in the field of offshore outsourcing, it must overcome significant obstacles in order to effectively compete with other outsourcing destinations. Therefore, the main questions which we would like to answer in this chapter are:

- *What are the key success factors in enhancing the competitive advantage of the Philippine IT-enabled services industry?*
- *How can the Philippines sustain its strong performance as a leading offshore outsourcing destination in the midst of strong competition in the global market?*

This research tries to elaborate answers to these questions by evaluating the internal capabilities and external linkages of Philippine ITES firms based on an empirical study. It focuses on how these various capabilities and linkages play a significant role in facilitating the ITES industry's growth and long term sustainability.

BACKGROUND

The rapidly globalizing economy has opened a huge door of opportunity for the Philippines in the form of IT-enabled services. Such strong industry development has caught the attention of many scholars, researchers, and academics during the past few years and has prompted many to write reports and research studies discussing the ITES industry in detail. Most of these reports and studies are based on government data and primary source materials but they generally just tend to describe what is happening in the industry or present its inherent advantages over other countries, such as the study made by E. Antonio and W. C. Padojinog who examined the profile of the IT-enabled services industry, its prospects and potential contributions to the Philippine economy (Antonio & Padojinog, 2003). Very few reports and studies actually analyses firm-level conditions and factors why Philippine ITES firms perform so well even in the international market. Thus, we would like to better understand the factors influencing the success of this service export industry and to assess future prospects as to how it can sustain its strong performance in the next few years. We used two broad bodies of literature to support this study: 1) the resource-based view of the firm (RBV) and 2) the social capital theories. Applying both the RBV and social capital theories, we will try to examine the firms' internal capabilities and external linkages.

Resource-Based View of the Firm (RBV)

Understanding sources of sustained competitive advantage for firms has become a major area of research in the field of strategic management. Since the 1960's, a single organizing framework has been used to structure much of this research. This framework suggests that firms obtain sustained competitive advantages by implementing strategies that exploit their internal strengths, through responding to environmental opportunities, while neutralizing external threats and avoiding internal weaknesses. Although both internal analyses of organizational strengths and weaknesses and external analyses of opportunities and threats have received some attention in the literature, recent work has tended to focus primarily on analyzing a firm's opportunities and threats in a competitive environment. As exemplified by research by Porter and his colleagues, this work has attempted to describe the environmental conditions that favour high levels of firm performance. Porter's

(1980) "five forces model" for example, describes the attributes of an attractive industry and thus suggests that opportunities will be greater, and threats less, in these kinds of industries.

However, much of this type of strategic research focus more on the analysis of the impact of a firm's environment on its competitive position and has placed little emphasis on the impact of firm attributes on a firm's competitive position. Instead of understanding the impact of a firm's environmental performance, the RBV examines the link between a firm's internal characteristics and its performance. The fundamental principle of the RBV is that the basis for competitive advantage of a firm lies primarily in the application of the bundle of valuable resources at the firm's disposal. Barney (1991) referring to Daft (1983) says: "...firm resources include all assets, capabilities, organizational processes, firm attributes, information, knowledge, etc; controlled by a firm that enable the firm to conceive and implement strategies that improve its efficiency and effectiveness".

A firm is said to have a sustained competitive advantage when it is implementing a value creating strategy not simultaneously being implemented by any current or potential competitors and when other firms are unable to duplicate the benefits of this strategy. Not all firm resources hold the potential of generating sustained competitive advantages. To have this potential, a firm resource must have four attributes. First, it must be valuable in the sense that it exploits opportunities and/or neutralizes threats in a firm's environment. Resources are valuable when they enable a firm to conceive or implement strategies that improve its efficiency and effectiveness. Second, it must be rare among a firm's current and potential competition. A firm enjoys a competitive advantage when it is implementing a value-creating strategy not simultaneously implemented by large numbers of other firms. Third, it must be imperfectly imitable. Valuable and rare organizational resources can only be sources of sustained competitive advantage if firms that do not possess these resources cannot obtain them. For firm resource to be imperfectly imitable, one condition could depend on the ability of the firm to obtain the resource based on unique historical conditions or circumstances. The RBV approach asserts that firms are not only intrinsically historical and social entities, but that their ability to acquire and exploit some resources depends upon their place in time and space. Once this particular unique time in history passes, firms that do not have space-dependent and time-dependent resources cannot obtain them, and thus these resources are imperfectly imitable. Another reason that a firm's resources may be imperfectly imitable is that they may be very complex social phenomena, beyond the ability of firms to systematically manage and influence. When competitive advantages are based in such complex social phenomena, the ability of other firms to imitate these resources is significantly constrained. A wide variety of firm resources may be socially complex. Examples include the interpersonal relations among managers in a firm, a firm's culture, a firm's reputation among suppliers, and customers. Fourth, the final requirement for a firm resource to be a source of sustained competitive advantage is that there must be no strategically equivalent valuable resources that are themselves either not rare or imitable (substitutability) (Barney, 1991).

Social Capital

Social capital, generally defined as the actual and potential resources embedded in relationships among actors, is increasingly seen as an important predictor of group and organizational performance. Social capital is an "umbrella concept" that acknowledges the inherent value of social structures such as relationships, networks and groups. It refers to the value of membership in a social group and the benefits individual actors derive from their social relationships. The central thesis of social capital theory is that "relationships matter" and that "social networks are valuable assets". Interaction enables people to build communities, to commit themselves to each other, and to knit the social fabric. A sense of belonging and the concrete experience of social networks (and the relationships of trust and tolerance that can be involved) can, it is argued, bring great benefits to people (Smith, 2007).

The concept of social capital has received considerable attention recently among sociologists, economists and political scientists. Irrespective of disciplinary focus, three thinkers that most commentators highlight in terms of developing a theoretical appreciation of social capital are Pierre Bourdieu, James Coleman and Robert Putnam. Pierre Bourdieu developed his concept of social capital during the 1970's and 1980's as one of the three forms of capital (economic, cultural, and social) present in the structure and dynamics of societies. For him, social capital represented an "aggregate of the actual or potential resources which are linked to possession of durable network". He stressed that access to social capital occurred via the development of durable relationships and networks of connections especially those among prestigious groups with considerable stocks of economic and cultural capital. James Coleman's contribution to the development of the notion of social capital was to develop a rational choice theory of social capital. According to Coleman, social capital is defined by its function. It is not a single entity, but a variety of different entities, having two characteristics in common: they all consist of some aspect of a social structure, and they facilitate certain actions of individuals who are within the structure. The structure of relations could help establish obligations between social actors, create a trustworthy social environment, open channels for information, and set norms and impose sanctions on forms of social behavior. In his book Bowling Alone, Robert Putnam argued that "the core idea of social capital is that social networks have value....social contacts affect the productivity of individuals and groups." He referred to social capital as "connections among individuals – social networks and the norms of reciprocity and trustworthiness that arise from them" (Putnam 2000).

The concept of "organizational social capital" points to a resource that is controlled by the collective, as opposed to a particular individual (Coleman, 1990; Leana and Van Buren, 1999). From an organizational point of view, social relationships function as valuable resources that enable individuals to act as groups and to undertake complex actions like joint knowledge work. Whereas human capital refers to the knowledge and capabilities of individuals, social capital takes into account the social fabric to empower individuals to collaborate effectively. The resources associated with organizational social capital consist of the relationships among employees within a firm ("internal social capital") as well as linkages between the firm and its external stakeholders, competitors and/or customers ("external social capital"). Organizations transact with suppliers and other partners in order to acquire external resources to produce products/services at competitive prices, so that they can attract and retain customers. Social capital can therefore explain the basis for the development of linkages and connections to enable firms to acquire resources from their external environment.

Linking the RBV and Social Capital Theories to the Philippine IT-Enabled Services Industry

The Resource-based view of the firm and Social capital theories have divergent concerns on the roots of firm performance, with the RBV stressing the internally accumulated resources or capabilities while social capital theory has underscored its relational characteristics with external entities. The two theories ought to be synthesized, since firms should develop specific assets while obtaining other critical resources through their social networks.

The main competitiveness drivers of the Philippines as an attractive location for offshore ITES services are well documented: its highly skilled workforce; low labour costs; cultural affinity towards the United States, its reliable telecommunications infrastructure; and business-friendly policies. It is this rare combination of resources that has attracted many FDIs to locate their outsourcing operations in the Philippines which has made the country a prime location for customer contact service centres and business process outsourcing. The country's English language proficiency can be traced back to its historical ties with the US. A former American colony for almost 50 years, English was made the medium of instruction in schools at all levels. It adopted a similar form of government structure, legal, and accounting systems. On top of that, Filipinos watched American TV shows and programs, enabling them to easily adopt a neutral American accent. Going back to the RBV theory, the country was able to accumulate a vast pool of English speaking professionals very much accustomed to Western culture and business processes not by its own choice but through its particular path in history. Adding to the country's overall competitive advantage is the Filipino people's innate customer service orientation, owing to the country's general culture of helpfulness and respectfulness, which gives the country an edge particularly in providing customer care services.

As to the quality and quantity of human resources, the Philippines is home to over 80 million Filipinos, more than half of whom are younger than 40 years old. Therefore, it has a young population that can contribute immensely to the global economy in terms of abundant labour supply. In the 2002 Global New Economy Index (GNEI) of the META Group, a US-based research firm, the Philippines was given the highest rating in Southeast Asia for "excellent availability" of skilled IT workers. The Philippines ranked fourth after India, Israel, and Ireland. In addition, a study on the competitiveness of the Philippines' IT sector conducted by Gartner Research in March 2002 showed that the Philippine workforce is technically proficient in computer science and programming, and many can achieve the desired level of expertise in US business processes (such as accounting and human resources) and knowledge specific to an industry (for example, medical terms for transcriptions). Investors will find that Filipinos are highly trainable, persevering, and resilient. Literacy rates are also among the highest in Southeast Asia.

The social capital theory stresses the importance of forging ties within and across communities. As the ITES industry continued to grow, representatives of the state, the corporate sector, and civil society created forums through which they can identify and pursue common goals. The government spearheaded the creation of an industry association which in turn created platforms for the dissemination of knowledge in the industry through its surveys and conferences. Drawing upon the success of India's IT/software industry, the government identified ITES/BPO as a key contributor to economic growth. It prioritized the attraction of FDI in this segment by establishing "IT Parks" and "Export Economic Zones". It offered benefits like tax-holidays and special tax rates for IT parks/Ecozone locators. It liberalized the telecommunications industry and opened up national, long distance, and international connectivity to competition (Tschang, n.d.).

RESEARCH METHODOLOGY

The Philippine ITES firms' internal capabilities and external linkages were measured using the following determinants and indicators:

The primary research for this study was conducted in Metro Manila, specifically in the central business districts (CBD's) of Makati, Pasig and Quezon City where a huge concentration of ITES firms, both domestic and multinational, have set base since the industry took off in 2001.

Table 1. Analytical framework

	Determinants	Indicators
Internal capabilities	Human resources and climate/institutional culture	Education Attrition rate Professional development and training
	Entrepreneurial orientation	Services offered to clients
	Technological capability	International certification R&D Market research
External linkages	Networking with other ITES/BPO firms	Existence of cooperation with other local or foreign ITES/BPO firms Areas of cooperation
	Participation in industry associations or informal association networks	Membership/affiliations in industry associations Benefits derived from membership in industry association
	Collaboration with universities or research institutions	Existence of collaboration with universities or research institutions
	Support from government institutions	Types of government support programs available for ITES/BPO firms

The main instrument used to gather primary data was electronic survey in the form of online questionnaire. The survey was conducted from November 2006 up to March 2007. A total of 226 executives representing a broad cross-section of the Philippine IT-enabled services and business process outsourcing industry (BPO) were invited to participate in the research study. Only one executive per company was asked to fill out the questionnaire. They were randomly selected from the 2005 ICT Directory provided by the Business Processing Association Philippines (BPA/P), a private sector-led organization representing the six distinct sectors of the Philippine BPO and ITES industry and their supporting industries (see table 2). Out of the 226 executives invited to participate, 60 completed questionnaires (27%) were gathered and used for data analysis.

Ninety percent of the respondents belong to the top executives and managers of the companies surveyed which means they are very knowledgeable about the company's operations and organizational characteristics. Forty-five respondents, or 75%, are male and the remaining fifteen, or 25%, are female. Although there are fewer female respondents, they nonetheless occupy very important positions in the industry such Chairman of the Board, CEO or President of the company.

Table 2. Philippine ITES industry – six distinct sectors

Sector	No. of Firms	No. of Employees	Est. Revenue	Growth Rate
1) Contact Centre (or Call Centre)	124	145,000	US$1.7 Billion	90%
2) Business Process Outsourcing (BPO)	62	30,500	US$180 Million	80%
3) Software Development and Maintenance	300	19,000	US$204 Million	40%
4) Medical Transcription & Legal Transcription	64 9	9,500 650	US$70 Million US$6 Million	80% 50%
5) Animation & Graphics	42	6,000	US$40 Million	25%
6) Engineering Design	24	3,800	US$48 Million	30%
TOTAL	**625**	**214,450**	**US$2.2 Billion**	

Note: Number of firms and employees are based on 2006 figures, while estimated revenue and growth rates are based on 2005 figures.

All sub-sectors of the ITES industry were represented among the 60 respondents. Many of the companies indicated that their core business operations encompass several of the six ITES sub-sectors simultaneously. For example, a call centre firm is also into the business of medical/legal transcription while a software development firm is also engaged in BPO. The most number of respondents came from the software and development sector with twenty three respondents (38%), followed by medical/legal transcription (27%) and contact centre services (23%).

Forty five companies, or 75% of the total number of companies interviewed, were established from 2001 up to 2006. As such, many of the companies that participated in the survey were barely five years old and are therefore relatively young in the business.

Forty six companies, or 76%, have 1-100 employees while nine companies, or 15%, have 101-500 employees. The Philippine Small and Medium Enterprise Development (SMED) Council defined small enterprises as having 10 – 99 employees and medium enterprises as having 100 – 199 employees. Therefore, a large number of the companies that participated in the survey are categorized as small and medium-sized enterprises (SMEs).

Fifty three companies, or 88%, are either 100% Filipino owned or Filipino companies that have tied up with a foreign company to run the business (joint venture). Only six out of the 60 companies surveyed (10%) are foreign-owned.

Forty seven companies, or 78%, export their services to other countries. The exporting firms indicated USA as the top destination of their export services. Second top export destination, though far behind the USA, was the United Kingdom while Canada and Australia tied in the third place. Because of close cultural ties, it is no wonder that the Philippines exports primarily most of its services to the United States. For US clients, having such closer cultural links help reduce some of the problems that result from teams working together but have different cultural backgrounds.

THE INTERNAL CAPABILITIES OF PHILIPPINE ITES FIRMS

The resource-based view highlighted the importance of a firm's resources and capabilities and helps explain why some firms perform better than others. Examining a firm's internal capabilities helps to determine its resources and likely sources of competitive advantage and to establish strategies that will exploit any sources of competitive advantage.

Human Resources

The Philippines continues to attract global companies to set up business process outsourcing facilities. Besides costs, other top considerations for many outsourcing firms include the education and language skills of workers, the availability of labour, and attrition risk in outsourcing destinations.

Education

Fifty six companies, or 94%, indicated that majority of their employees have bachelor's degree – implying that most of the employees in the industry went through a normal 4-year course at the university. Two companies have employees mostly holding Masters degree, while also two companies have employees mostly having non-degree or vocational training certificates. Foreign business have been attracted all along to the high number of college graduates in the work force and are impressed by the country's contemporary culture that values college degrees. Each year, the Philippine educational system produces around 400,000 graduates, 60 percent (240,000) of whom come from business administration and related courses, engineering and technology, fine and applied arts, law and jurisprudence, mathematics and computer science, medical and allied professions, and natural science (Llorito, 2005). These are the types of skills needed to man the growing non-voice BPO that is emerging. Filipino graduates' knowledge on liberal arts, or studies that provide general knowledge and intellectual skills, rather than more specialized occupational skills, gives the Philippines an advantage over other offshore destinations like India which are well-known for their technical skills. India is reported to have better technical universities but the Philippines is better in liberal arts, which is more appropriate for back-office processing.

Attrition Rate

One of the main drivers for the industry's success is the low attrition rate. Compared to India, Canada, and the United States where attrition rates go as high as 90 percent or even more, the Philippines have a much lower attrition rate at about 50 percent. Majority of the companies surveyed (66%) indicated that they do not have problems with high employee turnover.

Many Filipino graduates are lured to work for the ITES industry because it offers more attractive salary packages compared with other industries. But in reality, working in this industry is a very high pressure job that requires high level of commitment and skills. What's helping the country to maintain a low attrition rate is the fact that most contact centres now have implemented lifestyle programs, organizing and providing several activities like sports competitions, battle of the bands, and other recreational activities. Such programs aim to promote a healthy balance of life and work and help reduce or counter stress that goes with a call centre job.

Professional Development and Training

Fifty respondents, or 83%, indicated that their employees undergo professional development and training. This shows that the majority of the companies are investing in developing the skills and talents of their work force. Only nine companies do not have professional development programs for their employees.

For firms not showing professional development and training programs for employees, the most common cited reason for not having such kind of programs was hectic work schedule. As early as 2003, industry Executives say they already begun to notice shortages in English speakers which has somewhat caused an alarm for the Philippine outsourcing community. Many companies have since then established training programs at private universities and human resource consulting companies that train potential recruits. Sensing the potential loss in one of the few bright spots in the Philippine economy, the National government has also started to throw money at the problem. In 2006, President Gloria Macapagal-Arroyo earmarked US$9.8 million for outsourcing training, dubbed as "Training for Work" scholarship program. As part of that scheme, students interested in outsourcing jobs are given vouchers that may be used for tuition at government-accredited human resources institutions (Llorito, 2006). The President has also ordered the education department to make English the primary medium of instruction nationwide.

Entrepreneurial Orientation

The success of the Philippine ITES industry also depends in fostering an entrepreneurial environment that promotes the creation of new technologies, concepts, and processes. Results of the survey show that from 2004-2006, thirty seven companies, or 62%, have increased the number of their service offerings. Twenty companies, or 33%, said the number of services they offered for the past three years remained constant. No company indicated a decreasing trend for the same period. Thirty companies, or half of the total number of respondents, indicated that they offer new services to their clients "most of the time", while fourteen companies "always" offer new services to their clients. As already mentioned many of the companies indicated that their core business operations encompass several of the six ITES sub-sectors simultaneously. As such, it is normal for call centres which operate at night shift to also engage in BPO or software development during day-time to maximize office space and increase profitability. During the past few years, outsourcing has expanded beyond call centres into almost every conceivable business processes such as accounting, financial analysis, design engineering, software development, animation, medical and legal transcription services, etc. which exhibits a very entrepreneurial mindset among ITES/BPO companies.

Technological Capability

Aside from enhancing the language proficiency and technical skills of its human resources, another challenge that confronts the industry is the low level of technological capability of ITES/BPO firms. For instance, survey results revealed that few companies have certification in international quality standards or other internationally recognized qualification levels such as ISO, CMM, eSCM-SP, TQM, etc. Fewer companies also have R&D departments or conduct market research activities than companies that actually engage in such kind of activities.

International Certification

Forty three companies surveyed, or 71%, do not have certification in international quality standards or other internationally recognized qualification levels. Only sixteen companies indicated that they have international certification. Thus, majority of the ITES/BPO companies surveyed do not yet have international certification, which is a mark of excellence that assures consistent product and service quality. Such certifications are deemed very important especially to clients abroad.

Research and Development (R&D)

The key source of technological innovation is R&D. However, survey results revealed that more companies do not engage in R&D activities than companies that actually do. Twenty three companies, or 38%, have R&D department while thirty seven companies, or 62%, do not have such department. Majority of those that have R&D department are software companies. Out of the twenty three companies that have R&D department, only sixteen companies provided information that they spend in average 12.5% of their total revenue for R&D expenditure.

Market Research Activities

Market research is an essential part of any business that wants to offer products or services that are focused and well targeted. Business decisions that are based on good intelligence and good market research can minimize risk, identify opportunities, and create benchmark to help measure the company's progress. However, survey results revealed that not all Philippine ITES/BPO firms are actually engaging in such kind of activities. Only twenty six companies, or 43%, indicated that they conduct market research activities. This figure is slightly higher compared to the number of companies which conduct R&D activities.

Philippines ITES/BPO firms, which are predominantly SMEs in their early stages of growth, mostly rely on experience in understanding their customer needs. As such, marketing strategies are normally developed based on experience and not through systematic gathering and analyzing of data about their target market, competition, or market environment. However, market knowledge based on experience alone may not always be current and may become less relevant over time. Ultimately, these firms will need to have a better understanding of the market in which they operate – a market that is driven by globalization, stiff competition and more discriminating customers.

Thus, conducting market research activities will help these firms to maintain their advantage, reduce risk, and provide more room for innovation and growth in the long run.

Summary of Findings: Internal Capabilities

Based on survey results, it appears that Philippine ITES/BPO firms are quite strong in the quality of its human resources. A large percentage of employees have bachelor's degree. Aside from English language proficiency, the Philippines' contemporary culture that values college degrees also impresses many foreign businesses and helps to attract them to invest in the country. Attrition rate is also significantly lower compared with other countries, which is brought about by initiatives of some firms to implement "lifestyle programs" to improve employee satisfaction. A large percentage of the firms surveyed also invest in the professional development and training of their workforce. While there is indeed a looming shortage of highly skilled, English proficient workers due to the huge demand for outsourced services, firms are nonetheless taking initiatives to address the problem by partnering with universities and human resource consulting firms in establishing training programs for potential recruits. Likewise, the government is pouring money to develop the country's human capital.

Majority of the companies surveyed exhibited entrepreneurial orientation. As proof, many of them indicated that they have increased their new service offerings during the past three years (2004-2006). Not a single company reported a decreasing trend in new service offerings for the same period.

A big drawback for the industry is the low level of technological capability of ITES/BPO firms, a problem that is recognized by the industry association itself. Survey results revealed that fewer companies have certification in international quality standards or other internationally recognized qualification levels. More companies do not engage in R&D activities than companies that actually do while less than half of those surveyed conduct market research activities.

One explanation for this could be that the industry is still in its early stages of growth. Many of the respondents were just start-ups or young companies. Aside from their age, many of these companies are still categorized as SMEs. For Philippine SMEs, acquiring international certifications or investing in R&D and market research activities are normally very costly and are often not prioritized especially during the firm's early stages of growth. In contrast, the technological capability of the Indian ITES/BPO industry is undoubtedly more sophisticated and mature. However, more and more Philippine ITES/BPO firms are expected to build up their technological capability in the next few years to keep up with the growing demand and pressures of globalization.

THE EXTERNAL LINKAGES OF PHILIPPINE ITES FIRMS

Organizations, whether established ones or start-ups, cover only part of their value chain and depend critically on their environment. Firms have limited resources, outsource certain parts of the value chain, and transact with other economic actors having complementary assets. Networks are vital to the discovery of opportunities, to the testing of ideas, and to secure resources for the organization.

Networking with Other ITES/BPO Firms

Forty four companies, or 73%, indicated that they are able to cooperate or exchange information with other local or foreign ITES/BPO firms. On the other hand, only sixteen companies have no form of cooperation with other firms in the industry. Sales and marketing in the form of trade missions was cited as the top area where firms cooperate, followed by joint production and R&D.

For a long time now, the Philippines and India have been talking about collaboration to help boost their chances in the global outsourcing industry. This vision has finally turned into reality when the Business Processing Association of the Philippines (BPA/P) and India's National Association of Software and Service Companies (NASSCOM) signed an agreement in September 2006 to cooperate in seven "strategic" areas: strategic communications; geographic risk mitigation; shared best practices and adherence to international standards; data security and privacy; workforce development, collaboration and cooperation; and infrastructure improvement. Strategic communications involves joint lobbying to promote outsourcing in the global market, while geographic risk mitigation will mean both organizations selling the Philippines and India as one "geographic risk mitigation package". The two organizations will also work on data security and privacy standards for both countries, and share best practices in workforce management and infrastructure improvement.

By collaborating with India, the Philippines have the unique opportunity to learn from its Asian neighbour and at the same time create its own path to development. Thus, in the age of globalization, the Philippines and India need not be mere competitors in the ICT Outsourcing market. They could also be strategic partners who together can enlarge their respective shares in the global outsourcing market.

Participation in Industry Associations or Informal Networks

Forty seven companies surveyed, or 78%, are members of industry association. On the other hand, only twelve companies, or 20%, replied that they are not part of any association. Next to clients, the industry association was chosen by most respondents as source of information that influences the company's success. It ranked higher than universities or academic/research institutes and government agencies. Companies cited access to databases, studies and surveys as the top benefit they get from being a member of the association. This was closely followed by access to market opportunities as the association normally organizes trade missions abroad and performs business matching opportunities between its members and potential clients. Many of the companies surveyed are small in size and thus do not have enough capability to conduct such activities on their own. Hence, they turn to industry associations for support in order to further strengthen their market access and performance potential.

Collaboration with Universities or Research Institutions

It is a fact that some companies are now hard-pressed in finding enough skilled workers to manage their growing operations in the country. The problem is not really a shortage in people but a shortage in qualified, skilled and well-trained people. But the good news is that the industry, academe and government recognize the "education gap" problem and are taking concrete steps to address that gap. Since this industry is human resource-driven, there should be a steady supply of suitable talent and this can be achieved by establishing partnerships between the private sector and the academe. This has already happened to India and is similarly emerging in BPO locations in the Philippines such as Cebu, Bacolod and Dumaguete. Some specific examples of collaboration between firms and universities or research institutions aimed in addressing the "education gap" are:

- Etelecare, one of the leading call centres in the country, partnered with the Technical Education and Skills Development Authority (TESDA) to develop a courseware suited to call centre work.

- Exist Engineering, a Philippine-based software firm, is now working with local universities to design courses that will prepare fresh graduates for a software engineering job at the company.
- Sitel has partnered with the University of the Cordilleras (UC) for a five-year testing project to flesh out a curriculum designed for BPO firms. In 2007, the UC started a preparatory course in English proficiency, technical competency and customer relations designed by Sitel. The course gives college students a concrete idea what it is like to work in a call centre, where the final stretch of training will be an on-site, hands-on lesson at Sitel (Baguio City).

Support from Government Institutions

Thirty nine respondents, or 65%, indicated that there are no government programs helping their business to develop. On the other hand, eighteen companies or 30% have been beneficiary of several government support programs. Companies which indicated receiving government support for their businesses cited business matching activities as the most common form of government support program, followed by training and scholarship grants. Other forms of government support come in the form of tax breaks and subsidized trade missions.

Survey results revealed that despite the government's best efforts to carry out programs that will sustain the industry's long term competitiveness, very few companies actually benefit from such programs. It is not to say there are no government programs available, for clearly government support and commitment for this sector is as strong as ever. However, larger-scale programs meant to support the industry were only instituted beginning 2006 and may not have been fully implemented yet at the time of the survey. To prove the government's strong support for this industry, the Philippine President already announced in her annual State of the Nation Address (SONA) in July 2007 a promise to pour an unprecedented increase of investments in developing the country's human capital. Some US$642 Million more investments in education were allotted in 2007 compared to 2006, bringing the total spending on education to US$3.3 Billion - the highest in Philippine history.

Summary of Findings: External Linkages

73% of the companies are able to cooperate or exchange information with other local or foreign ITES/BPO firms. Sales and marketing in the form of trade missions was cited as the top area where firms cooperate, followed by production and R&D. The industry association plays a big role in raising the level of cooperation among ITES firms especially in marketing their service offerings to potential local and overseas clients. Next to clients, the industry association was chosen by most respondents as source of information that influences the company's success. It ranked higher than universities or academic/research institutes and government agencies.

The Philippine ITES industry also aims to strengthen its position in the global outsourcing market by creating strategic alliances with other leading outsourcing destinations. This resulted into forging an agreement with outsourcing leader, India, to cooperate in seven "strategic" areas.

In view of the looming shortage in skilled and well-trained manpower, firms are establishing partnerships with the academe through curriculum development and basic and applied research to ensure a steady supply of suitable talent.

65% of the respondents indicated that there are no government programs helping their business to develop, but one explanation could be that large-scale government programs intended to support the industry were only instituted in 2006 and may not have been fully implemented yet at the time of the survey. The Philippine government is supporting the vigorous growth of the ITES industry by pledging unprecedented increase of investments in developing the country's human capital.

CONCLUSION AND RECOMMENDATIONS

The medium-term outlook for the Philippines in the ITES industry remains to be very positive, particularly if the country is able to improve the maturity of its service providers and further develop the quality of its workforce. Leveraging on labour arbitrage alone will not take the industry to the next level. In order to improve the Philippines' competitive advantage, the country should continuously enhance the suitability of the labour supply through investments in English language proficiency; move up the value chain by focusing more on non-voice sector or services other than call centres; enhance its technological capability; improve the business environment; and focus on capturing more markets aside from the US.

Developing the Country's Human Capital Through Education

In the emerging knowledge-based economy, the sustainable competitive advantage of nations will reside in their ability to harness their countries' intellectual assets. The key to exploiting the opportunities lies in creating the kind of human resources that are needed for the global information economy. The Philippines' attractiveness as an outsourcing destination is no longer limited to low labour cost alone, but also to being able to provide global partners with a human resource possessing the "right skill sets and competencies supported by a sophisticated telecommunications infrastructure". The number one priority should be developing the country's human capital because investor's top concern now is whether the Philippines can actually supply the great demand for outsourced services. While political stability is important to their investment, investors are looking closely at how good the country's human resource base is. Particularly detrimental to the further development of the ITES industry is the declining English-language proficiency of the population, which could be addressed by a renewed emphasis on English-language teaching. Enhancing English proficiency is important as it is required in all six ITES sub-sectors.

The continued growth of the ITES labour force will require significant educational reform. One of the key issues in the education sector is to reform the curricula and learning objectives (e.g. types of skills to be acquired) in order to meet the challenges of ITES work. At a minimum the work appears to require improvements in the general quality of logical-analytical thinking skills as well as communication skills. A stronger focus on proper training could help, but rather than just training in IT, training involving a broader general education would be more beneficial. In Singapore for instance, universities and polytechnics have incorporated in their curricula programs for specific sectors such as animation and videogames, as well as IT-type programs that emphasize multidisciplinary work, new kinds of integrative thinking and problem-solving ability, and strong industry practicum. Thus, developing the country's human capital requires changes throughout the system including the curricula, content, and learning objectives.

Moving up the Value Chain

As the world becomes flatter with the outsourcing trend, Philippine ITES companies are becoming aware that to be able to compete in the global market they have to move up the value chain. With increasing competition from other low-cost countries, the imperative is for firms to shift their main activities to a higher level rather than just passive transactions like the Q&A type of call centre service or low level offshore programming. This is indeed a natural progression because companies initially just outsource low value functions offshore but soon start moving higher value processes when they are comfortable. Most of the clients of the call centres are now looking at what else the country can do apart from call centres. Back office business processes are considered more high value because they involve more than just answering queries from customers. One is actually doing process work and depending on the type of the business process, it could be a highly specialized business process like investment consulting. In the case of software development, maintenance and coding work are considered to be in the lower end of the value chain and higher value work is analysis and design.

While the offshore outsourcing industry has flourished by providing well-specified, structured and repeatable tasks, the ability to perform more value-added, knowledge-based activities like analytics, research, and credit analysis is opening up opportunities in Knowledge Process Outsourcing (KPO). This service requires significant area proficiency and the ultimate goal is to generate value for the client by providing business expertise rather than process expertise. Higher value work is what is perceived to give the industry a sustainable competitive advantage because it calls on creativity, domain expertise, and a reputation for quality.

Enhancing Technological Capability

Building competitive advantage based on low-cost service alone can't lead to sustainable growth. This is the oldest, harshest lesson of the global economy: If what you do can be done by anyone, there will always be someone willing to do it for less. Eventually, labour arbitrage will not be the major focus of outsourcing anymore. Within 7-10 years, when labour arbitrage has already ran its course and with prices always having a certain amount of difference, it will be those with deep process knowledge who will be successful. As such, prospects are good for those who can bring data security and have good knowledge of the complexity of the compliance environment that the U.S. and other potential markets have to live under. In a couple of years, companies should be able to move to the high-cost segment of the market and do more collaboration for bigger projects. Therefore, there is a need for companies to invest in the improvement of quality processes like getting certified and building domain expertise in light of the need to "demonstrate" competitiveness.

Likewise, the country should also invest more in R&D and promote local centres of innovation. R&D is the lifeblood especially of the software and BPO sub-sectors which are largely driven by cutting-edge technology. As such, it would be wise for Philippine firms to conduct "technology road map and R&D needs assessment" to ensure that they do not miss out on any trends. When society produces lots of scientists and talents, it would be easy to generate products, services and intellectual properties that entrepreneurs could sell to the rest of the world - and whose competitive advantage depends less on labour cost and more on knowledge content and other intangibles like branding.

Improving the Business Environment

As the ITES industry continues to shine, there are areas that need to be monitored in order for the country to preserve the country's position as a leading offshore service provider. The country still has a problem with perception as a risky location, both politically and economically. The general business condition should be improved, particularly by creating a stable political condition. The country's subpar business environment suffers from strict labour laws, high levels of corruption, and a surfeit of bureaucracy. Obtaining approval to open a call centre in the Philippines, for instance, takes twice as much time as it does in India or Malaysia. Another drawback is the lack of direct flights from the Philippines to important markets such as the United States.

A number of ITES/BPO locators have started to grumble about the relatively high costs of electricity in the Philippines. Among the countries in the Asia-Pacific region, the country has one of the highest per kilowatt-hour power rates. This oft-mentioned deterrent to Philippine economic development remains a disincentive for foreign investment, not only in the outsourcing sector, but also throughout the manufacturing, services and even agro-industrial sectors of the country. For certain outsourcing firms, energy charges have counted among their largest monthly expenditures, particularly for companies with 24-hour operations requiring 24-hour air-conditioning. The passage of legislation on the privatization and liberalization of the country's electricity industry was expected to significantly lower electricity charges nationwide. Unfortunately, the reforms in this sector have been hit by bureaucratic snags.

Looking Beyond the US Market

The success of the business also depends a lot on the country's ability to attract more markets for outsourced ITES services in the country. At the moment, the market is heavily skewed towards the U.S. so the country has to strengthen its ability to attract North American companies to outsource in the Philippines. But to further expand its market, the country must look beyond the United States and should reach out more to countries that are nearer to it like Japan, Taiwan, Korea, and other more developed countries in Asia. European countries also constitute a very attractive market for outsourced IT-enabled services. The Philippines is an important economic and trading partner of Europe. About 27 percent of the total foreign direct investments (FDI) in the Philippines came from the European Union (EU). United Kingdom is still the dominant market but outsourcing is gaining ground in Germany, the Netherlands, Spain and France. The relatively high cost of doing business in Europe is driving European companies to look at offshore outsourcing as a strategic alternative. The financial services sector is the largest consumer of BPO and IT-enabled services in Europe, followed by utilities and telecommunications, while human resources, finance and accounting are also showing notable growth.

The government must regularly organize trade missions to Europe such as business forums, business meetings with potential clients, and high-level networking receptions. It would be helpful for the Philippines to adopt a country-by-country strategy that will fit the service requirements of each market. As for marketing the Philippines to investors, the large population of Filipinos in US and Europe can be tapped as a "steady and continuous supply of ITES/BPO marketing advocates".

REFERENCES

Antonio, E. T., Jr., & Padojinog, W. C. (2003, February). *IT-Enabled Services in the Philippines: Prospects and Issues.* Paper presented at the AT10 Research Conference, Tokyo, Japan.

Barney, J. (1991). Firm Resources and Sustained Competitive Advantage. *Journal of Management, 17*(1), 99–120. doi:10.1177/014920639101700108

China to topple India as top offshoring center by '11. (2007). Retrieved September 1, 2007, from http://www.eetasia.com/ART_8800470999_480200_NT_e7abf55d.HTM

Coleman, J. S. (1990). *Foundations of Social Theory.* Cambridge, MA: Harvard University Press.

Leana, C. R., & Van Buren, H. J. (1999). Organizational Social Capital and Employment Practices. *Academy of Management Review, 24,* 538–555. doi:10.2307/259141

Llorito, D. L. (2005). *Prospects of Business Process Outsourcing in the Philippines.* Retrieved May 14, 2007, from http://davellorito111.wordpress.com/2005/12/25/prospects-of-business-process-outsourcing-in-the-philippines/

Llorito, D. L. (2006). *Help wanted for Philippines Outsourcing.* Retrieved June 19, 2007, from http://www.atimes.com/atimes/Southeast_Asia/HE10Ae02.html

Locsin, M. L. (2006). *Business Processing Association Philippines – Representing the Country's IT and IT-Enabled Services Industry.* Paper presented at the Business Processing Association Philippines (BPA/P) General Assembly, Manila, Philippines.
neoIT. (2004). Mapping Offshore Markets Update. *Offshore Insights White Paper, 2*(6,) 4. Retrieved August 27, 2007, from http://www.neoit.com/pdfs/whitepapers/OIv2i6_June_04_Mapping_Offshore_Markets.pdf

Our Corporate Bureau. (2005). *US among top locations for "offshore" work: AT Kearney.* Retrieved July 23, 2007, from http://www.domain-b.com/management/consulting/20051123_locations.html

Putnam, R. D. (2000). *Bowling Alone: The Collapse and Revival of American Community.* New York: Simon & Schuster.

Reloc8 Asia Pacific Group. (2007). Asia Pacific Updates. *Reloc8 – A Regional Relocation Resource, 1*(6), 8-9. Retrieved December 29, 2008, from http://www.reloc8asia.com/newsletters/Reloc8%20newsletter6%202007.pdf

Smith, M. K. (2007). Social capital. In *The encyclopedia of informal education.* Retrieved September 10, 2007, from http://www.infed.org/biblio/social_capital.htm

Tschang, T. (n.d.). *The Philippines' IT-Enabled Services Industry.* Singapore: Lee Kong Chian School of Business, Singapore Management University.

Section 5
Knowledge Society Transformation and Digital Divide

Chapter 14
The Potentials and Pitfalls of the Information Society Project in Turkey:
A Critical Assessment of Policy Paradigms Regarding E-Transformation and Digital Divide

M. Selcan Kaynak
Boğaziçi University, Turkey

ABSTRACT

This chapter aims to assess policies regarding information and communication technologies (ICTs) in Turkey within the last five years. The focus of the chapter will be on digital divide: Although, ICTs in general, and the Internet in particular, have become an essential part of everyday life in Turkey, access to the opportunities provided by these technologies has not been distributed equally. The divides with respect to social class, geographic location, gender and age cripple the potential benefits of these policies. In addition, the programs implemented so far have been highly influenced by the global policy agenda; in a sense, adapting the "information society" vision advanced globally to the local context. In order to actualize an equitable and sustainable transformation process, there is further need to understand the nuanced picture Turkey's social conditions present. This chapter will examine the ways in which information society project has been modeled in Turkey, the policy paradigms that shaped its direction and finally, where they fell short and where they offer potentials.

INTRODUCTION

Turkey's Information Society Project, launched in 2003, introduced its mission as transforming Turkey "to be a country that has become a focal point in the production of science and technology, that uses information and technology as an effective tool, that produces more value with information-based decision-making processes and that is successful in global competition, with a high level of welfare"[1].

DOI: 10.4018/978-1-61520-709-1.ch014

This and similar statements that explained the overall goal of this strategy were marked with confidence and optimism. Within the last six years since its inception and the bureaucratic unit established under the state planning agency to oversee and coordinate all policy initiatives that it involves, two main action plans have been executed; several policy and regulations have been instituted among which the newly opened e-state portal is one of the most comprehensive. Yet at the same time, the use of Information and Communication Technologies (ICTs) in Turkey is still not as wide as many other countries, generally located within the middle range of rankings, but more importantly, the use of such technologies is marked with divides—based on age, gender, and education level . Thus, one might ask, in which ways the Information Society Project has been on target and where it remains incomplete. To put it in other words, to what extent the State led initiative to transform Turkey into an information society set realistic, sustainable and efficient goals and along the process what kind of pitfalls it has experienced? The present chapter will address this question through focusing on the Information Society Department of the State Planning Organization, which was found to develop and oversee necessary action plans for the Information Society Project. Admittedly, assessing this Department's initiatives is a formidable task, requiring one to examine each of the new regulations that have been instituted -- covering quite diverse issues such as digital signature law and e-state services. In addition, such a policy assessment would require a test of their effectiveness through observing both executers and users; but the goal of this analysis is rather to focus on the overall framework under which this Unit has been operating; that is, the policy paradigms that appear to be guiding the so far initiated action plans. The reason to focus on the paradigms, instead of, say, how they are put in effect or the users' perspective, is to get at the heart of the transformation process: To understand what might be the motives to target certain policy areas, in which ways the policies here are inspired by global policy processes and how are they adopted at the local context.

The original impetus behind the Information Society Department (ISD) can be traced back to before 2003 when it was first launched. As documented by Christensen (2006), steps for instituting ICT related policies have been in the works for some time thanks to interested parties in the bureaucracy as well as those in the information technologies (IT) sector. But what marks 2003 as a turning point is the realization, on the part of the government, the necessity to systematize ICT related policies to be in alliance with the European Union's eEurope+ Initiative. Thus, it can be argued that, from the start, the e-transformation process to be analyzed in the rest of this chapter has been inspired by the global policy fora, in this specific case, the European Union (EU); and the discourse to promote the technologies themselves coupled with the policies regarding their use have also been stamped by these global trends.

Considering Turkey's quite young population, receptive to new technologies and quick to adopt them into their everyday lives, the use of the Internet and other interactive technologies expanded. Nevertheless, the expansion did not include all sectors of society, discrepancies in terms of basic access, let alone skills in using them, is striking: As will be further elaborated in this chapter, the existing statistics show that more men compared to women, young people compared to the elderly, those in urban areas rather than rural geographies are privileged[2]; a wide segment of society is still not part of the digital revolution; if this trend continues, it will likely have serious socio-political consequences. One can argue, then, that the reality on the ground provides a different picture compared to what has been projected in the policy initiatives; to assess the existing social processes regarding digital networks and their future, we need to pay attention to how and where the policies did not or do not meet the needs, conditions and wishes of their potential users.

Although there is a growing body of literature documenting studies on ICT policies in Turkey (e.g. Binark, 2003; Christensen, 2006 & 2008; Geray, 2000; Küçükçınar & Özcivelek, 2008; Törenli, 2006) there is still further need for a critical assessment of this issue. Turkey as a case study is thought to be worthwhile because as mentioned, with a fast growing ICT sector and a young population as enthusiastic consumers of its products and its candidacy to the EU, the drive toward an Information Society has been inevitable. Yet at the same time, the social divides regarding social class, geographic location, gender, and age cripple the potential benefits of these strategies. Thus, in observing Turkey, this study hopes to identify how in general we can begin to understand an equitable and sustainable transformation process can be possible.

The chapter will be composed to, first summarize the relevant literature, and then briefly introduce the current picture of the extent and range of ICT use in Turkey. Next, it will examine the Information Society Department through its policy documents and action plans executed since its inception in order to identify the main policy paradigms that shaped its direction. The overall goal in the analysis will be to identify which key policy areas have been emphasized, to what extent they have been executed and finally which stakeholders have been included in the process. Finally, in the conclusion section some future directions for concrete and sustainable strategies will be suggested.

ICTS and Globalization

The literature on ICTs and their connection to globalization is vast; these connections have been drawn on many levels, but probably the following three broad connections capture the essence of the long discussed nature of ICTs both as an instrument and subject of globalization: 1) The very nature of these technologies allowing global connections between social agents at many levels; evading the importance of geographical space in networks, 2) Their vapid diffusion to many parts of the world, and their range of use becoming an indicator of development, and thus, in effect wiping out the possibility to stay out of their reach, 3) The policies aimed to administer the process themselves as being influenced by global political agenda. To reiterate, ICTs own flow into different parts of the world has been set as a requirement for integration into the global political and economic structures, and at the same time, they reinforce globalizing tendencies in the contexts they are adopted, thus creating a process of reinforcing globalization in all its dimensions. Boyd-Barrett (2006) points to the multi-faceted nature of such processes: Intellectual property rights regimes required for recognition and funding by major global agents such as the World Trade Organization (WTO), International Monetary Fund (IMF) and World Bank (WB); global trade, finance and advertisements facilitated by ICT infrastructure and services; and finally and perhaps most potently, "global semiotic constructions" shaping "how globalization processes are perceived, accepted or contested." (Boyd-Barrett, 2006, p. 28). Boyd-Barrett argues that such an organic connection between media in general and ICTs in particular, with the way in which globalization takes place is not coincidental, it favors the major power holders within global economy, particularly the US based corporations. He further argues that such a dominance will continue to have effects on the content, form and perceptions of (and the related policies and regulations about) information and communication; thus, maintaining the hegemony of the US and other developed economies. He also states that Asian economies start to show presence and are likely to challenge the existing configurations; but the essence of his argument profoundly establishes the vital connection between globalization and ICTs. The Asian prominence is not marked with all glory as some of the recent critical accounts state: Lee (2008) argues that although South Korea has been launched as a global IT leader, its development into that role is marked with neo-liberal economic policies which leads to uneven development, favoring certain cities and leaving others completely out and at the same time allowing the state the means for controlling its citizens.

Furthermore, regarding the formation of a global information society regime, Cogburn (2004) stresses the weak presence of developing countries in decision making mechanisms.

The ambivalent role of the state within such complex layers of the global system has been addressed by many; although earlier accounts concluded that the ICTs and especially, the Internet, is not bound within the confines of the nation-state and further, will be a likely catalyst in its dissolution; later arguments such as Lee's, pointed to the nation state's still dominant role in controlling, shaping and regulating ICTs' use within their territories. In return, the role of non-state actors, such as grassroots organizations, civil association and social movements to respond to and engage in politics through ICTs has also been highlighted (e.g., Bentivegna, 2006). What emerges as an interesting pattern is that, as Drori reviews, through the last decade "diverse constituencies" all defined ICTs and their use as worthy of global attention. Particularly, the framing of digital divide as a global policy issue is telling; it simply points our attention again to the many corresponding features between ICTs and globalization. In her words, "the redirection of world society's attention towards this issue is related to the correspondence between the dimensions of globalization and those of the field of information and communications technologies" and thus, "the theme of information society was quickly defined as a global social problem because it corresponds to the themes of the era of globalization." (Drori, 2007, p. 297).

Digital Divide as a Global Problem

The World Summits on Information Society (WSIS) first in Geneva (2003) and in Tunis (2005) could be argued to be direct outputs of such a global concern, anticipated to incorporate multi-stakeholders' perspectives into the transnational debate sphere. Although as some have argued (e.g. Pickard, 2007) WSIS could also be seen as a platform to essentially continue the neo-liberal discourse toward ICTs, these summits drew attention to digital divide as an important concern for the global policy agenda.

Originally approached as referring to the gap between those who use ICTs and those who were not able, the concept of digital divide has been expanded: those comparing the US, Europe and developing countries of Latin America, Africa and Asia (Rogers, 2001); those involving disparities in access to not only the Internet but other communication technologies (Colby, 2001), and in a more critical fashion, examining digital divide as a multi-dimensional concept: Digital divides in access, in skills and in engaged citizenship and participation (Attewell, 2001, p. 253). In that regard, DiMaggio & Hargittai (2001) argue that attention should be drawn from digital divide to digital inequality, which involves inequalities in technical means, autonomy, skill, social support and purpose. Accordingly, some have argued that since digital divides in most societies were observed along with existing inequalities in terms of ethnicity, gender and socio-economic status, they could reinforce and further widen such gaps within and between nations (e.g. Attewell, 2001; Crenshaw & Robison, 2006; Drori & Jang, 2003; Guillén and Suárez, 2005; James, 2005; Mutula, 2005; Rogers, 2001). An ambivalence toward the Internet's contributions to social change is a constant theme, Drori and Jang (2003), for example, refer to a 'twin effect': The Internet as bringing both hope and despair to countries worldwide (p. 144). Thus, digital divide has been singled out as an obstacle on the path to realizing positive potentials of the Internet—as expressed by Castells (2001): "The heralding of the Internet's potential as a means of freedom, productivity, and communication comes hand in hand with the denunciation of the 'digital divide' induced by inequality on the Internet" (p. 247).

Regarding possible correlates of digital divides, socio-economic status, age, gender, education level, ethnicity, language, physical disability and rural-urban residence, and other socio-cultural factors such as attitudes toward new technologies, have been the most often explored variables (e.g. Bélanger & Carter, 2006; Drori & Jang, 2003; Korupp & Szydlik, 2005; Rogers, 2001). Policies need to take culture into account: A study conducted in Singapore (Cheong, 2007) finds that there are still significant differences between male and female users' access to new technologies. Although the island has one of the highest Internet penetration rates in the world and the government is rigorously engaged in maintaining this reputation, divides regarding effective utilization still exist. Thus, one needs to look beyond the overall statistics and address users' trust in the improvements new technologies will bring into their lives.

The global dimension of digital divide has also been examined; especially the more recent arguments point to the developing world's struggles toward becoming an information society: Mutula (2005) for example examines Botswana, and show that people living in rural areas prioritize essential needs such as water, electricity, health and sanitation, roads rather than ICTs (p. 593). Similarly, James (2005) argues that developing countries should not be analyzed with the same indicators used for developed countries, but instead the attitudinal and institutional issues specific to such cultures should be understood (p. 115). More critical perspectives question "ICT-induced" globalization as benefiting rich countries rather than the developing ones (Nwagwu, 2006) and particularly the disadvantaged groups within them, such as women (Mitter, 2004).

Global ICT Policies and Digital Divide

As mentioned earlier, globalizing dimensions of the Internet have been observed not only in material conditions but also in discourse; Shah (2008) states that the metaphors utilized to imagine or capture the global space reveal the larger discursive environment that not only shape Internet's potential as a globalizing force, but also legitimate the global political order that goes along with it. What is most striking in these discussions regarding the questions examined in this chapter is that global metaphors used to capture the Internet itself have concrete and discernible effects at the political level. Preston & Kerr (2001), for example, argue that the typical conceptualization of multimedia in expert discourse has informed actors in the policy field and industry; thus they add that, in order to benefit a more diverse and equitable new media environment, governments should play an active role in facilitating connections between progressive culture and policy. Most importantly, smaller nation states or groups utilizing creative digital spaces should be supported to challenge the hegemonic discourse dominating the technological space.

Although the EU in spirit aims such an Information Society Policy (Preston & Kerr, 2001), as Christensen (2008) elaborates, it is rather characterized by ambivalent tendencies: Emphasizing the efficiency of competition and self-regulation through market forces on the one hand, stressing the importance of media pluralism and freedom of speech on the other. In the end, Christensen argues, the current policies lean towards favoring the market, motivating member states to promote business interests and perhaps endanger the public sphere, which requires not only a diversity in opinions but also their protection. Stewart, Gil-Egui, Tian and Pileggi's (2006) analysis of policy documents from the EU and the US assess paradigms that appear to be operational in framing these policies. They find that while the US documents made references to the beneficiaries in terms of various demographic groups, the EU documents referred more to the public, citizens and society, thus reflecting the historical differences between the two political cultures (p. 744). However, despite such differences, the analysis of these documents over time show that there are important similarities as well: They both share a market-based approach with respect to dealing with digital divide. Concepts such as access, commerce and business can be traced in both sets of documents and interestingly, as the authors state "Their relationship started with their positioning very far away from each other and ended with their overlapping in 2002, both in A Nation Online and in eEurope, 2005". (p. 744). Thus, policymakers should reflect on the existing programs to realize how the market place biases them, because these trends could be an "indication of the gradual dominance that neo-liberal frames for policymaking are acquiring worldwide" (p. 746). Cogburn

ICT Policies in Turkey

As summarized in the previous section, digital divide as a social problem provides an arena in which one can observe how global policy agenda meet local concerns, needs and strategies for organized action. Törenli (2004) argues that in Turkey the adoption of ICT policies has been imposed by globalization which establishes transformation to an "information society" as an incontestable modernization project for the developing world. Consequently, in Turkey as elsewhere, such a transformation is perceived as essential for modernization and sustainable development.

Similarly, others earlier have also argued that dynamics that have shaped information and communication policies in Turkey have been pretty much brought in by global institutions such as the EU, IMF, WB and OECD (Başaran, 2003; Gencel Bek, 2003; Törenli 2004). Geray (1999) further argues that the US, EU and World Bank promote an idealistic model for ICTs in Turkey which mystifies these technologies as a cure for developing countries; however, such an idealism leaves investment in socio-economic development and thus dealing with access inequalities to deregulation and liberalization. Thus, these policies are bound to increase the digital divide within developing countries and between developed and developing ones (Geray, 2000). Similarly, Christensen (2006) provides a critical review of Turkey's telecommunications and information society policies from 1999, when it became a candidate to join the EU, to 2006 and argues that although the EU process provided an impetus to the earlier efforts, these policies are less then effective and result in an "exclusive" information society (p. 41). Both the analysis of the policy documents as well as her interviews with involved bureaucrats show that the reason for such an end result is not necessarily financial limits; but rather

"lack of better coordination between the projects prioritized in the Urgent Action Plan, lack of consistent policymaking, lack of accurate understanding of the stakes and failure to command concerted efforts both on the part of the state and private sector, institutional and personal rivalries, lack of a platform to bring together private sector actors and civil society actors to form lobbies to negotiate with policymakers were all pointed out as problem areas." (Christensen, 2006, p. 41)

The author also argues that the EU's information society policies by themselves are not sufficient to create an equitable media environment in each member state, especially in countries like Turkey where the economy is already on shaky grounds and several socio-economic divides already exist.

Digital Divide in Turkey

Although there are several descriptive reports about patterns of ICT use, scholarly attention

Table 1. Availability of ICT equipments in households (%), 2008

	Turkey	Urban	Rural
Mobile phone	87.2	89.8	82.2
Fixed line telephone	70.2	70.9	68.9
DVD, VCD, DivX player	40.5	48.5	25.3
Desktop computer	27.2	34.2	13.9
Digital camera/photography	18.9	24.0	9.3
Printer	11.8	15.0	5.8
Portable computer (Laptop, Tablet PC)	8.5	11.3	3.0
Scanner	4.4	5.5	2.3
Game console	3.6	4.4	2.2
Multi function device (including two or more functions like printer, scanner, fax, etc.)	1.1	1.4	0.5
Fax	1.1	1.5	0.3
Handheld computer	0.5	0.6	0.3
Other	0.9	0.4	1.9
None of above	3.0	2.2	4.5

Source: TSI, *ICT survey on households and individuals*, 2008.

on the topic especially concerning digital divide is recent and therefore the number of studies is limited. That is in a way understandable since the diffusion of the Internet and the emergence of divides in their use is a relatively recent phenomenon in Turkey. Turkish Statistical Institute (TSI) only started to measure Internet use in 2004. There are some earlier systematic reports, such as that by TUBITAK (Turkish Sciences and Technologies Research Institute, surveying trends between 1997 and 2000) and another by Geray (2000), a report submitted to OECD, summarizing the extent of digital divide at the time of its publication. Although these earlier works are not comprehensive in that they only focus on access and do not have such comparisons as rural-urban differences, they still provide a benchmark for observing changes in the last ten years. For example, Internet connectivity at home was 1.2% in 1997 (as reported in Geray, 2000) whereas it is 18.4% in 2007 (as reported by TSI).

Before moving onto further analysis of digital divide statistics, it must be mentioned that the available data from TSI for the last four years does not allow a continuum; categories for ICT use measures have been updated and expanded over time. Thus, only comparable categories among those that are most relevant to the discussion here will be presented.

According to the results of 2008 TSI survey, while 87.2% of those surveyed had mobile phones, 27.2% had personal computers and 8.5% had laptops as seen in Table 1. The mobile phone ownership percentage was 53.64%, personal computer ownership was 9.98% and laptops was 0.85% in 2004 (TSI, 2004). The percentage that had Internet access with any of the ICTs was listed as 8.66% a year later, in 2005 (TSI, 2005), in 2008 Internet connectivity reached 24.5%; thus on all these indicators there has been an increase in the last five years, the most notable being in mobile phones. The extensive use of mobile phones despite their high cost is often argued to be due to this technology's lack of requirement for literacy and special skills or training for its use. The percentage of Internet use is still quite low in comparison to many developed countries but the rate of increase is not negligible.

*Table 2. Computer and Internet use by gender, last time of use and geography (%), 2008**

		Computer			Internet		
		Total	Female	Male	Total	Female	Male
Within the last 3 months (January-March 2008)	Turkey	34.3	25.6	43.2	32.2	24.0	40.6
	Urban	42.6	33.0	52.3	40.6	31.4	50.0
	Rural	19.1	12.0	26.4	16.8	10.4	23.3
Between 3 months and a year ago	Turkey	1.8	1.4	2.2	2.2	1.7	2.8
	Urban	2.1	1.7	2.4	2.5	2.2	2.7
	Rural	1.2	0.8	1.7		0.7	2.9
More than one year	Turkey	2.0	2.1	2.0	1.4	1.4	1.5
	Urban	2.2	2.3	2.0	1.6	1.5	1.6
	Rural	1.8	1.7	1.9	1.1	1.0	1.2
Never used it	Turkey	61.9	70.9	52.7	64.2	73.0	55.2
	Urban	53.2	63.0	43.3	55.4	64.9	45.7
	Rural	77.9	85.6	70.0	80.3	87.9	72.6

Source: TSI, *ICT survey on households and individuals*, 2008.
*16-74 age group

Table 1 lists availability of all ICT related equipment in households. What is significant here is that except mobile and fixed line phones, the percentage for each equipment in urban areas is about double (or more) compared to the rural ones. The urban-rural divide in Turkey is persistent in all the following statistics; thus, one needs to exercise caution in examining Turkey's ranking in ICT related indices: The overall statistics hide (among others) the geographic divides; the more developed urban areas pull the total percentages up. Table 2 below reports patterns in computer and Internet use according to when they were last used, gender and, again, geographical context:

One can see that in total, 61.9% never used computers and 64.2% never used the Internet. These percentages are significant: If the majority of the population never used computers, let alone the Internet so far, there is a formidable task ahead for e-transformation. Furthermore, urban-rural divide is visible here and when coupled with gender divide, it becomes more striking: While almost 90% (87.9%) of women in rural areas never used the Internet, in urban areas this percentage is about 65 (64.9%). For men, 72.6% in rural areas and 45.7% in urban areas never used the Internet. Thus, for both men and women there is over a 20% difference between urban and rural residents. As just discussed, such a gap exists in all other social indicators as well, thus not necessarily unique to ICT patterns; nevertheless further research is urgent to understand possible infrastructure and social reasons behind the citizens' lack of access and/or use of ICTs in rural areas. Although TSI does not further distinguish geographical areas in ICT use surveys, it is quite likely that both the rural and urban area statistics will also show a further divide between the Eastern and Western regions; the already existing gaps between the relatively developed Western regions and the rest of the country most likely reflect on this indicator. Although we do not have any reliable information on that dimension so far, the findings from TSI's 2008 survey at least establish the rural areas' stark disadvantage regarding computer and Internet use.

*Table 3. Computer and Internet use by gender, age and education (%) 2008**

	Computer			Internet		
	Total	Female	Male	Total	Female	Male
Age group						
16 - 24	58.3	49.2	68.4	55.0	45.4	65.6
25 - 34	43.4	31.7	54.8	41.1	30.1	51.8
35 - 44	30.4	20.9	39.8	27.9	20.1	35.6
45 - 54	20.0	12.3	27.5	18.9	11.5	26.1
55 - 64	6.9	2.1	11.8	6.5	1.9	11.2
65 - 74	1.6	0.7	2.6	1.4	0.7	2.2
Education level						
Literate without a diploma	2.7	1.4	6.9	2.2	1.1	6.2
Primary school	11.6	7.0	16.4	9.6	5.9	13.6
Secondary and vocational secondary school	44.2	39.0	48.0	40.8	35.9	44.3
High and vocational high school	67.2	61.6	71.3	64.0	58.2	68.3
Higher education	87.9	86.9	88.5	87.2	86.2	87.9

Source: TSI, *ICT survey on households and individuals*, 2008.
*16-74 age group

The divide between men and women is most evident for regular users in urban areas: 50% of men and 31.4% of women report having used the Internet within the last three months. The difference drops to 13% (23.3% of men and 10.4% of women) in rural areas, but the reason is possibly not higher equality in access and use of technology: As just mentioned the Internet use is already quite low in rural areas, not allowing a big enough trend to observe gender divides. Gender divide can further be examined in the following table which lists computer and Internet use by gender, age and education level.

The age group with the highest percentage of computer and Internet use is 16-24 both for male and female respondents; percentages drop as age intervals increase. A similar pattern was observed in earlier surveys[3] and it seems to be consistent with findings from other countries: Younger generations have much more readily adopted new technologies. There is an increase in all age groups over the years, the youngest group (16-24) with the most significant increase; however when examined in terms of gender, the gap remains still in 2008: While 45.4% of females in this youngest group report to use the Internet, the percentage is 65.6 for male respondents. In fact, in all age groups, the female users are significantly less compared to male users. Obviously gender gaps exist in many realms of every day life in Turkey and one could argue that the Internet is just reflective of such existing patterns (such as in literacy, education levels, employment, income, and political representation); but as has been argued earlier, the access to and capacity to use information technologies is critical and inequality in that arena further leads to or at least reinforces inequality in opportunities for other ones.

Finally, when education level is taken into account, all Internet users are observed to reside in higher education levels[4]. The potential for education to equalize the opportunities for technology use is evident; these results reveal that first, as education level increases, the rate of computer and Internet use increases. Second, at the highest education levels, male and female respondents' percentages are almost the same. Quite possibly, higher levels of education correlate with higher socio-economic status; thus, a vicious cycle might be present: The underprivileged groups (such as women, those living in rural areas, and those in lower socio-economic status) are disadvantaged off the opportunity for having access to ICTs and getting trained in using them to enrich their everyday lives. Thus, as Torenli (2006) argues, unless state policies specifically target support for these groups (who are not very likely to have the opportunity to utilize ICTs in their everyday lives), this vicious cycle and the parallel digital divide will continue.

Turkey's Information Society Strategy

Information Society Department (ISD) was founded in 2003 as part of the "eTransformation Turkey Project" which was included in the 58th and 59th Government Urgent Action Plan. The Department, which operates as part of the State Planning Agency, was given the mission to coordinate studies being conducted and strategies developed by the state to execute the e-Transformation Turkey project. As described on ISD's website, this project aims "to carry out the process of transformation into an information society in a harmonious and integrated structure all over the society with all citizens, enterprises and public segments".

There are two executive councils to guide and shape the policies of the Department: The e-Transformation Turkey Executive Board which includes the State Minister and Deputy Prime Minister, Minister of Transportation, Ministry of Industry and Trade, some top-level bureaucrats and the Advisory Council including public and private sector and NGO representatives. The Executive Board appears more as a symbolic unit to show that top-level government officials are involved with the project; its overall guidance appears to be based on general policy principles. The Advisory Council reflects a multi-stake holder approach, however, when one examines its composition, the representatives are in one way or another related to the IT sector (consumer groups, business representatives, etc); even academic representation comes from engineering backgrounds. Thus, input in terms of the socio-political nature of Information Society Transformation appears to be almost non-existent for policy strategies.

The project and thus the Department's initial launching, as stated in the policy documents as well as on the website of the Department, was directly tied to Turkey's EU candidacy. Frequent references are made in various documents to the Lisbon Strategy whose mission is to make the EU to be the most competitive knowledge economy in the world by 2010. Similarly, Lisbon strategy's update, i2010 and eEurope+, policy program designed for EU candidate countries, are frequently referenced; it might be fair to state that these global policies not only initiated the Turkish strategy but also has been continually and directly utilized as legitimate reference points to frame the ongoing projects and goals.

Since the inception of the Department in 2003, two action plans have been developed. The first one was for the short term, covering the two years from 2003 to 2005. The second is a more extensive strategy plan covering the 2006-2010 period. The web site of the Department has detailed information about both of these plans; in addition it has an extensive range of posts which include but are not limited to the Executive Committee meeting agendas, various reports on Turkey's e-readiness and e-state (e.g. The Economist's, World Economic Forum's and the UN's), announcements on issues such as Internet crimes, e-government services and many others. In total, over 150 documents as either attachments or with links to other pages are presented. Although the English version of the site is not as extensive as its Turkish pages, one can locate the two action plans and some of the key policy announcements that particularly relate to international trade and/or governance. All in all, Information Society Department's website is comprehensive, includes information on almost all areas under its authority; it also provides a certain level of transparency to its executive process through announcing its meeting dates, participants, agendas and furthermore, internal assessments of the action plans' effectiveness. Having acknowledged this, however, when one evaluates this website as a portal for the general public to become familiar with all issues related to digitalization or e-transformation in Turkey, in other words, as a publicity vehicle for the overall project, it is not as efficient. It does not have any interactive features, its design is uninspiring, and most importantly is not inviting to those who are newly interested in the topic and are not familiar with the terminology or technical features of e-transformation. One of the most important aspects of a social project, such as e-transformation Turkey, is providing the public with the tools to become active participants in it; this website unfortunately does not fulfill such a task; it possibly would appeal to researchers or those already involved in the process; but not the lay public. Either through this website or a separate one, there is desperate need for a more interactive, informative and engaging public portal which would attract citizens to engage with e-transformation. Furthermore, with new services of e-state in Turkish people's everyday life, there is also an increasing concern about security of personal information, unauthorized release of personal information by one state agency to another, or simply acquiring basic skills to utilize such services—a public information campaign through the web but also traditional media by the Information Society Department would inform the public and address such concerns.

Before moving on to examining the paradigms underlying ISD's trajectory so far, it must be acknowledged that the policy documents, and particularly the 2006-2010 action plan, were reviewed in order to have a general understanding of the key references that framed the policies proposed. Since this study was aimed to be an exploratory analysis and didn't attempt to test hypotheses or employ quantitative measures, no systematic text analysis procedure was conducted. As past research show, computerized text analyses for revealing linguistic and conceptual patterns in policy texts could be quite helpful in mapping out how certain keywords are networked and what kind of clues they reveal to interpret the policies. Future research can further explore Information Society policy documents in Turkey through such a text analysis and report subtle patterns in the official discourse. The intention here is to review the more obvious, directly articulated reference points and thus the following summary will focus on them.

Overall, in the examined documents the most often repeated framework was economic competitiveness in the ICT sector as a remedy to most of the obstacles that stood on the way to the general goal. In many of the laws and regulations (whether they directly address economic issues and business-state relations or not) references to liberalization, privatization in the telecommunications services and competition as a panacea were often referenced.

The regulations to support business oriented services and the sector itself included (but are not limited to) the law on electronic signatures, the law reducing taxes for companies working on research and development in the ICT sector, other reductions in taxes for firms and employees in the ICT sector, law on online contracts. These laws and regulations mostly relate to either government's online services in the economic realm or its direct support to ICT businesses. The ironic situation in Turkey is that the taxes on ICT services such as those charged for mobile phones or Internet connections are among the highest in Europe. However, the emphasis on tax reductions for the sector itself does not necessarily involve the taxes users have to pay for access. Thus, although in these documents and as soon to be discussed, expressed in the interviews, there is a great deal of emphasis on support for ICT sector to boost the diffusion of such technologies, it is not very likely if these benefits are also extended to the users themselves either through reduction of service taxes and/or wide and easily available free public access services throughout the country.

A second common theme observed in the documents relates to state's efforts in enforcing the Internet as a safe space that can be easily used for various public services. Thus, information on online government services, regulations regarding integration and standardization of public service websites and most importantly the e-state portal are provided. The e-state portal itself is brand new, opened on December 18th of 2008; its reach and scope and efficiency are to be seen at least within the next few years. The portal provides entry to all online state services and information in three main areas: those involving the citizen, the business and the public sector. Although, most of what is offered through the portal existed earlier in each involved agencies' own website, this service provides one-step access to all available online services. It has been welcomed with both optimism and doubt, however, at this time it would be premature to conclude how effective it will function as a virtual state office; further research should assess its reach, user-friendliness and efficiency.

Confirming the arguments so far present in the literature (e.g. Stewart et. al. 2006, Christensen, 2006) the third often repeated policy area in the website of ISD concerned the objective to be part of global e-society initiatives such as those proposed by the EU and the UN. Accordingly, various reports on Turkey's ranking in terms of e-readiness are published: Thus, the focus on performance in terms of ranking is clear; this understandably is due to the importance of such indicators and each country's status with respect to them for global policy organizations. In a way, these lists present a universal and concrete reference point for where countries are on their path to information society. On the one hand, the advantage of comparison through these lists is to use concrete indicators for what constitutes an information society. In addition, they also reveal how extensive and wide ranging online services are and how diffused access is in those countries that are on top of the list. On the other hand, however, these ranks place focus on a linear projection of development, moving up and down in the list; and distract attention away from the complex nature of social transformation that goes along with such technologies. And as mentioned earlier, summary measures on such indices conceal the many divides within the country with respect to access and skills.

The main and most extensive policy document prepared by this Department is the 2006-2010 action plan. This document states the 4-year plan as involving the following goals:

- Sustainable growth and increasing competitive power
- Increasing quality of life
- Eliminating digital divide
- Increasing human resource competencies and employment
- Effective provision of citizen-focused public services in multi-channel environment
- Promoting e-commerce
- Ensuring standardization and security in information society applications
- Creating value by developing market-oriented R&D and innovation
- Making broadband communication infrastructure commonly available
- Enriching the content and information society applications
- Benefiting from convergence potential of technologies
- Leveraging media channels in the development of information society[5]

Understandably, all of these goals are quite general, as they constitute the mission statement. The rest of the document details particular strategies towards these goals in a more concrete fashion. Nevertheless, one could still observe the market-oriented approach; four of these goals make explicit references to encouraging competitiveness and business.

The strategy document is structured to address issues related to: Citizens, Businesses, and Government, ICT Sector and Research and Development innovation. In the first section of the document, strategic priorities as general goals are stated for each of these domains. These priorities mostly involve further penetration of ICTs into these areas; in the second section, more specific targets are set for 2010 and action plans to achieve these targets are listed. The most common theme that runs through the document is similar to the observations in other documents and in the general goals: Regardless of the particular social domain, there are often references to liberalization, privatization and competition as tools to bring out the maximum potential of ICTs for social transformation. Thus, overall a market-based approach is dominant here as well. This is hardly surprising since as others suggest, this is a global trend and the Turkish process fits into this pattern. In the last five years, this approach didn't help much with issues related to the unequal distribution of resources generated by ICTs; and the government's role in overseeing the process has been more on the side of hoping the incentives to the sector will boost the market, bring ICT costs down and thus, more and more people buying them. This cost and demand equation obviously has not been adequate to assess the needs and develop strategies to meet the needs of those who are excluded from market.

The document, although quite extensive in its scope, in its totality reflects an preliminary text that takes global Information Society policy statements and represents them to the local audience. General statements involving the importance of catching-up with developed industries, boosting creative research in technologies, expanding ICT sector, engaged citizenry are abundant and perhaps with all the good intentions, however, there are not many specific and direct references to the local context. The digital divide problem, in the documents, is approached as a diffusion issue, thus the remedies appear in the form of economic opportunities and access to public services. Under the principle of "ICTs available to all", the specific actions are listed as:

- Developing ICT infrastructure in schools
- Creating and improving ICTs usage for students at all levels
- Creating mechanism for life-long learning by ICT
- Preparing programs of occupational education and certification
- Increasing awareness of ICTs for all people

One cannot completely dismiss the plan in terms of its ignorance of digital divide; in fact, there are some actions suggested specifically for this issue. However, all in all, they constitute a not very significant section and more importantly, there are no assessments of the needs at the local level. In other words, Internet --without a substantial consideration of its particular uses and benefits for the local context-- is presented as an unquestionable social good. This issue is important, in that, the already existing social divides in Turkey, most notably in socio-economic status, gender, regions (urban-rural; east-west divides), make it absolutely essential to consider the specific needs of each segment. A one-size-fits-all approach is not likely to succeed especially when one considers information technologies and their use.

In order to have a more nuanced understanding of how these policies were developed and executed, key personnel in ISD who particularly work on digital divide were interviewed[6]. The most notable observation from these interviews is that executive officers themselves are aware of the problems in effective institution of the policies. They do not question the policies themselves;

that is, they did not reflect in our interviews on the paradigm behind the policies and how they were formulated; but rather, they expressed doubts about effective execution. They mostly stated that although their Department worked extensively on the background research and the actual preparation of the 2006-2010 action plan, they do not have much power for the execution of these goals. The goals are to be followed up with various ministries and their Department does not have any reinforcement power. Thus, the overall feeling through the interviews was a dose of disappointment and another of skepticism about whether or not politicians in respective ministries indeed cared about this strategy plan.

Related to the previous point, they also stated that such a plan needs higher-level political back up; and it was not that these politicians didn't support the overall goal of Information Society, but in their day-to-day political activities didn't prioritize this issue. A higher level enforcement and support for Information Society, in their view, would help their Department grow with more sanctioning power in the first place, and second, keep the process at a more urgent place in Turkey's political agenda.

A second theme that was often expressed in the interviews was skepticism towards other parties involved in the project. On the one hand, public administration system was argued to be not efficient, responsive or equipped to coordinate this ambitious project. The personnel in this Department argued that there was a lack of effective communication between different ministries and planning agencies. On the other hand, interestingly, they were also skeptical about the private sector input: They stated that (maybe not all, but some) representatives getting in touch with them, proposing projects for collaboration, mostly had their private interests/profit as a priority and not necessarily service to public as an overall goal. Thus, although the policy documents themselves and the overall strategy seem to be quite positive about the market, the bureaucrats have the awareness that market interests on their own might not necessarily be the right solution.

Finally, some interviewees, especially one who works on issues of digital divide, did discuss several possible projects that would address the inclusion of those who live in difficult to reach rural areas, who are in general also quite poor. One interviewee was in the process of preparing a report with concrete policy actions that specifically address basic, everyday services through ICTs. Although, she was not sure if her report would be immediately put in action, the fact that there is thoughtful consideration of the questions that were absent in the overall policy document is encouraging.

In conclusion, the overall mission of ISD and its personnel have to be acknowledged for their dedication in giving life to this project: For providing the country a road map in its journey of integrating new technologies into everyday lives, the potential to be recognized here is tremendous. However, the pitfalls emerge in materializing the positive intentions into concrete policies; the policies appear to have been entrapped by global political and economic forces. The neo-liberal discourse, as many others have argued earlier, shapes the policy paradigms of transnational institutions, which then are passed on to various locales. This has also been the case in Turkey for the last six years, but perhaps, the next phase will broaden its horizons to recognize and respond to the many needs, hopes and resources the users here offer.

CONCLUDING REMARKS

The observations of the extent of digital divide itself and related policies suggest the following conclusions:

1. The real and most urgent divide that seems to surface through this analysis is the one between strategizing/policy planning and

the actual conditions on the ground. Perhaps there is a complex set of factors that contribute to such a gap and most likely they are observed in other policy areas as well. However, in Information Society Project it is acutely visible.

The bureaucratic structure of the State Planning Agency, with not enough resources to invest in and research the "field", the imposition of global assessment and policy schemes to be taken in without major adjustments for the local conditions, and as the interviewees suggested, the lack of real importance placed on dealing with digital divide by high level politicians could be some of the reasons for this observation.

The danger in the ongoing gap between state policies and actual needs of the "digital have-nots" is first, the impotency and lack of applicability of the policies developed for certain segments of society (and thus further contributing to the digital divide) and second, the growing skepticism for the ever-achievability of the goals set. In other words, in time if the action plans continually fall short of being actualized, the belief in their importance and potential will be lost.

2. To balance the somewhat pessimistic tone in the previous conclusion, one also needs to acknowledge the gradual and in a way more basic achievements that have been and can be achieved through the Information Society Project. In Turkey, there has been a gradual increase in the use of ICTs, e-government services have been extended, a state-portal project is launched and primary school system is increasingly incorporating computers into their curriculum. Although quite broad, in the 2006-2010 action plan, there are policy actions suggested to bridge digital divides. The gradual effects of these actions are to be observed in the long term. However, an important consideration in evaluating the policies should be to what extent they take the local context into account. As discussed earlier, the documents published by the ISD sound and read like any other umbrella policy documents of the EU or UN. The global policy agendas are not necessarily and inherently a negative influence; in fact, the EU candidacy process initiated the Information Society Project in Turkey, and, the WSIS put the issue of digital divide on the local agenda. So, the global policies have had a stimulating effect for Turkey, but when they are adopted in an unquestioning fashion without taking geographical and demographic factors into account, the end result is sterile policies that do not have much potency in the "real world".
3. As related to the previous point, for a more grounded and realistic policy approach, there is urgent need for field work in the form of in-depth and qualitative studies to identify what kind of ICTs for which purposes could benefit various local contexts in Turkey. It is not suggested here to totally replace standardized indicators of ICT use and digital divide with qualitative studies. As mentioned earlier, existing indices are important for an overall and systematic assessment of these issues in a comparative manner. But these measures need to be backed-up with more detailed, qualitative and perhaps ethnographic studies that would examine and understand the local conditions to identify their needs and develop policy programs to meet such needs.

In addition, as suggested earlier, the indexes and the related performance have the overall effect of excessive focus on rankings. Such comparative lists published by global NGOs identify concrete evidence of performance, but they also distract attention away from more complex aspects of social transformation. Especially when one considers digital divide issues, the specific divides that could be observed differently from country to country (even in different contexts within each country) are lost in these lists.

The best strategy then would include quantitative measures contextualized with qualitative ones, which will together bring a complete understanding of digital divides and realistic policies to deal with them.

4. Finally, to develop such a nuanced and detailed approach, the state and civil society investment and involvement is absolutely necessary. In Törenli's words, if "*left purely to time or 'natural' market processes, the process of digital exclusion will continue to increase rapidly*" (Törenli, 2006, p. 436). The market approach, as other studies also suggested has not been and will not be a remedy for low ICT use rates, investment in difficult to reach segments of society requires a concentrated, vigorous and determined effort in social policy.

ACKNOWLEDGMENT

An earlier version of this study has been presented at the International Studies Association's 49th Annual Conference. The author would like to thank Sercan Gidişoğlu for his assistance in collection and analysis of data for that paper. The funding for the initial phase of this study has been provided by Boğaziçi University's Research Fund (Project 06C303).

REFERENCES

Attewell, P. (2001). The First and Second Digital Divides. *Sociology of Education*, *74*, 252–259. doi:10.2307/2673277

Basaran, F. (2003). Telekommunikasyon Politikaları: Avrupa Birliği ve Türkiye. In M. Gencel Bek (Ed.), *Küreselleşme, İletişim Endüstrileri ve Kimlikler: Avrupa Birliği ve Türkiye'de İletişim Politikaları* (pp. 165-204). Ankara, Turkey: Ümit Yay.

Bélanger, F., & Carter, L. (2006). The Effects of the Digital Divide on E-Government: An Empirical Evaluation. In *Proceedings of the 39th Hawaii International Conference on System Sciences*, Hawaii, USA.

Bentivegna, S. (2006). Rethinking Politics in the World of ICTs. *Global Media and Communication*, *2*(1), 21–41. doi:10.1177/1742766506061815

Binark, M. (2003). 'Avrupa Modeli Enformasyon Toplumu' Politikası ve Kadınların Bilgisayar ve İnternet Kullanmaları. In M. Gencel Bek (Ed.), *Küreselleşme, İletişim Endüstrileri ve Kimlikler: Avrupa Birliği ve Türkiye'de İletişim Politikaları* (pp. 135-161). Ankara, Turkey: Ümit Yay.

Boyd-Barrett, O. (2006). Cyberspace, globalization and empire. *Global Media and Communication*, *2*(21), 21–41. doi:10.1177/1742766506061815

Castells, M. (2001). *The Internet Galaxy*. Oxford, UK: Oxford University Press.

Cheong, P. H. (2007). Gender and Percieved Internet Efficacy: Examining Secondary Digital Divide Issues in Singapore. *Women's . Studies in Communications*, *30*(2), 205–230.

Christensen, M. (2006). EU Candidacy and Information Society Policies in Turkey: A Reality Check. *GMJ Mediterranean Edition*, *1*(1), 29–45.

Christensen, M. (2008). A Contentious Terrain in EU Information Society Policies: Media Pluralism and Freedom of Expression. *MedieKultur: Journal of Media and Communication Research*, *46*, 80–92.

Christou, G., & Simpson, S. (2007). Gaining a Stake in Global Internet Governance: The EU, ICANN and Strategic Norm Manipulation. *European Journal of Communication*, *22*(2), 147–164. doi:10.1177/0267323107076765

Cogburn, D. (2004). Elite Decision-making and Epistemic Communities: Implications for Global Information Policy. In S. Braman (Ed.), *The Emergent Information Regime* (pp. 155-178). New York: Palgrave.

Colby, D. (2001). Conceptualizing The "Digital Divide": Closing The "Gap" By Creating A Postmodern Network That Distributes The Productive Power Of Speech. *Communication Law and Policy*, *6*(1), 123–173. doi:10.1207/S15326926CLP0601_04

Crenshaw, E. M., & Robison, K. (2006). Globalization and the Digital Divide: The Roles of Structural Conduciveness and Global Connection in Internet Diffusion. *Social Science Quarterly*, *87*(1), 190–207. doi:10.1111/j.0038-4941.2006.00376.x

DiMaggio, P., & Hargittai, E. (2001). *From the 'Digital Divide' to 'Digital Inequality': Studying Internet Use as Penetration Increases* (Working Paper #15). Center for Arts and Cultural Policy Studies, Princeton University.

DPT. (2004, January). *Contributions of Turkey to e-Europe+ 2003 Progress Report.*

DPT. (2005, March). *e-Dönüşüm Türkiye Projesi 2005 Eylem Planı.*

DPT. (2008, February). *OECD IT Policy Questionnaire 2008.*

Drori, G. S. (2007). Information Society as a Global Policy Agenda: What Does it Tell Us About the Age of Globalization? *International Journal of Comparative Sociology*, *48*(4), 297–316. doi:10.1177/0020715207079532

Drori, G. S., & Jang, Y. S. (2003). The Global Digital Divide: A Sociological Assessments of Trends and Causes. *Social Science Computer Review*, *21*(2), 144–161. doi:10.1177/0894439303021002002

Gencel Bek, M. (2003). Küreselleşme, Ulus-Devlet ve İletişim: Avrupa Birliği'nin Türkiye'deki İletişim Politikalarına Etkisi Üzerine Bir Değerlendirme. In M. Gencel Bek (Ed.), *Küreselleşme, İletişim Endüstrileri ve Kimlikler: Avrupa Birliği ve Türkiye'de İletişim Politikaları* (pp. 237-286). Ankara, Turkey: Ümit Yay.

Geray, H. (1999). Network Policy Formation between Idealist and Strategic Models: a political economy perspective from Turkey. *Telecommunications Policy*, *23*, 495–511. doi:10.1016/S0308-5961(99)00033-6

Geray, H. (2000). *Extent and Scope of Digital Divide in Turkey: Policy Perspectives.* Paper presented at the OECD/DSTI, WPIE/TSIP Workshop, December 2000, OECD Paris.

Guillén, M. F., & Suárez, S. L. (2005). Explaining the Global Digital Divide: Economic, Political and Sociological Drivers of Cross-National Internet Use. *Social Forces*, *84*(2), 681–708. doi:10.1353/sof.2006.0015

Halavais, A. (2000). National Borders on the World Wide Web. *New Media & Society*, *2*(1), 7–28. doi:10.1177/14614440022225689

James, J. (2005). The Global Digital Divide İn The Internet: Developed Countries Constructs And Third World Realities. *Journal of Information Science*, *31*(2), 114–123. doi:10.1177/0165551505050788

Korupp, S. E., & Szydlik, M. (2005). Causes and Trends of the Digital Divide. *European Sociological Review*, *21*(4), 409–422. doi:10.1093/esr/jci030

Küçükçınar, A., & Özcivelek, R. (2008). Turkey. In G. Turlea & M. Bogdanowicz (Eds.), *EU Enlargement: Economic Development and the Information Society* (pp. 353-380). Brussels: VUB Press.

Lee, K. (2008). Globalization, Electronic Empire and the Virtual Geography of Korea's Information and Telecommunication Infrastructure. *The International Communication Gazette*, *70*(1), 3–20. doi:10.1177/1748048507084575

Mitter, S. (2004). Globalization, ICTs, and Economic Empowerment: A Feminist Critique. *Gender, Technology and Development*, *8*(1), 5–29. doi:10.1177/097185240400800102

Mutula, S. M. (2005). Bridging The Digital Divide Through E-Governance; A Proposal For Africa's Libraries And İnformation Centres. *The Electronic Library*, *23*(5), 591–602. doi:10.1108/02640470510631308

Nwagwu, W. E. (2006). Integrating ICTs into the Globalization of the Poor Developing Countries. *Information Development*, *22*(3), 167–179. doi:10.1177/0266666906069070

OECD e-Government Studies. (2003). *The E-Government Imperative*. OECD.

Pickard, V. (2007). From NWICO to Neoliberal Visions and Revisions in Global Communications Policy. *The Journal of Communication Inquiry*, *31*(2), 118–139. doi:10.1177/0196859906298162

Preston, P., & Kerr, A. (2001). Digital Media, Nation-States And Local Cultures: The Case Of Multimedia 'Content' Production. *Media Culture & Society*, *23*, 109–131. doi:10.1177/016344301023001006

Rogers, E. M. (2001). The Digital Divide . *Convergence*, *7*(4), 96–111. doi:10.1177/135485650100700406

Shah, N. (2008). From Global Village To Global Marketplace: Metaphorical Descriptions Of The Global Internet. *International Journal of Media and Cultural Politics*, *4*(1), 9–26. doi:10.1386/macp.4.1.9_1

Stewart, C., Gil-Egui, G., Tian, Y., & Pileggi, M. (2006). Framing The Digital Divide: A Comparison Of US And EU Policy Approaches. *New Media & Society*, *8*(5), 731–752. doi:10.1177/1461444806067585

Törenli, N. (2004). *Enformasyon Toplumu ve Küreselleşme Sürecinde Türkiye*. Bilim ve Sanat Yayınları, Ankara.

Törenli, N. (2006). The 'Other' Faces of Digital Exclusion: ICT Gender Divides in the Broader Community. *European Journal of Communication*, *21*, 435–455. doi:10.1177/0267323106070010

TSI. (2004). *ICT usage survey on households and individuals.*

TSI. (2005). *ICT usage survey on households and individuals.*

TSI. (2007). *ICT usage survey on households and individuals.*

TSI. (2008). *ICT usage survey on households and individuals.*

TUBITAK BILTEN. (2002, March). *Instruments to Combat Digital Divide: an evaluation based on Turkish experience*. Tübitak Bilten.

ENDNOTES

1 http://www.bilgitoplumu.gov.tr/eng/default.asp

2 http://www.bilgitoplumu.gov.tr/duyuru/2008_HanehalkiAnketi.pdf

3 Please see Table "Individuals using the computer and accessing the Internet in the last 3 months by age, education level and employment situation in the survey implementation period" at http://www.turkstat.gov.tr/VeriBilgi.do?tb_id=60&ust_id=2 for a full list of age, gender and education level statistics since 2004.

4 Although the data file published by TSI does not include any specific information on the percentages, those on education levels are most likely cumulative (i.e. higher education levels include lower categories).

5 (http://bilgitoplumu.gov.tr/BTStrateji.asp)

6 In-depth interviews conducted in February 2008.

Chapter 15
Sustainable Development and the Digital Divide Among OIC Countries:
Towards a Collaborative Digital Approach

Chamhuri Siwar
National University of Malaysia, Malaysia

Abdul-Mumin Abdulai
National University of Malaysia, Malaysia

ABSTRACT

Undoubtedly, digital technology (DT) has revolutionalised information and communications technology (ICT) base of the global economy, which has impacted tremendously the socio-economic, political, cultural and scientific development in the majority of the world's economies. The chapter examines "digital divide" in a broader perspective of information and communications technologies (ICTs) that encompass not only computers, but also telephone (line and cellular), television (TV), radio etc. It is an open secret that ICTs have played and will continue to play a pivotal role in sustaining economic development in the developed countries. Through ICTs, creating, storing and sharing enormous volume of information with relative ease in almost all the spheres of human endeavour have been made possible. The power inherent in ICT that can break up barriers and boundaries holding countries, continents and businesses miles apart can never be over-emphasized. Despite the attendant benefits of ICTs, there are still deep-seated ICT inequalities both within and among the Organization of the Islamic Conference (OIC) member countries. This chapter investigates the depth of the existing digital divide among the OIC member countries and to unearth the possible obstacles. Finally, some policy recommendations have been offered towards the end of the chapter.

DOI: 10.4018/978-1-61520-709-1.ch015

INTRODUCTION

It has long been acknowledged that the global economy has largely been sustained by the generation and transfer of varieties of innovative knowledge in the economic, scientific, social, cultural, spiritual and political arenas. The availability of, and the easy access to voluminous information, made possible through information and communications technologies (henceforth referred to as ICTs), facilitate knowledge transfer within and across countries. This scenario far too often aids sustainable development. As sustainability takes the form of resilience, the constant generation, storing and sharing of development-related information and knowledge can boost the resilience of development efforts in the majority of the world's economies.

Through ICTs, the impediments associated with time and space are increasingly becoming less noticeable. This achievement has in large part laid the foundation for the coming into being of the so-called "global village." Globalization owes its existence largely to ICTs that have successfully broken up barriers and boundaries that hither-to held countries, continents and businesses miles apart. The prime intention in revolutionalizing ICTs has been to scale up socio-economic, political, cultural and spiritual progress in the individual economies, and to enhance the overall global economic development. In spite of the attendant benefits of ICTs, there are still deep-seated ICT inequalities both within and among the world's economies and the Organization of the Islamic Conference (OIC) member countries are not immune to this saga. From equity perspective, the socio-economic development benefits associated with ICTs dictate that frantic efforts be mustered to bridge the existing digital divide.

Here, the OIC countries appear apt for study for the following three reasons. First, the majority of these countries is less developed or developing economies. Second, there has been a dire need to scale up social and economic development in these countries so as to improve livelihoods for the majority of the people in these countries. And third, the need for development cooperation among the Islamic countries has blossomed into forming the Organization of the Islamic Conference (OIC) about four decades ago. The development benefits that ICTs engender are known to all. Cooperation or collaboration has been in existence for the past three to four decades, yet there seems to be no much success story to tell about any progressive ICT development in the majority of the OIC countries. Furthermore, available literature shows that the digital divide is continuously widening with little sign of bridging among the Islamic countries; thereby forcefully bringing the so-called development cooperation or collaboration into disrepute. The questions arising from such digital scenario include the following:

1. What factors are exactly responsible for such an unfortunate digital scenario existing within and across the OIC countries? Lack of cooperation could be ruled out completely, as there won't be bodies such as OIC, Islamic Development Bank (IDB) etc.; and
2. Could it then be apathy on the part of member countries?

The chapter has explored the above raised questions and tried to locate the answers in the broader domain of (a) how accessible these ICT gargets are to the people, (b) their usage (i.e. the ability to use them), and (c) empowering the people with ICT expertise by integrating them into the mainstream of the knowledge-based economy.

BACKGROUND

ICTs are increasingly becoming a gigantic force underpinning sustainable global economic development. The immense role of ICTs in the successful development stories of the World's developed economies is a case in point. The principle of sustainable development requires that the means to achieving our cherished development goals (in terms of economic, social, political, scientific, cultural and spiritual progress) is made resilient. Networking and coordination through creating, storing and sharing of innovative and development-oriented knowledge are important elements in sustainable development. It therefore, appears convincing that effective development networking can be further enhanced by ICTs.

Perhaps this can be made feasible by the increasing power of ICTs to connect and bridge information gaps in knowledge generation, utilization and transfer across and within continents. Then again, the increasing power underpinning ICTs has been facilitated by 'digital technology.' Digital technology (DT) is believed to have revolutionalised ICTs; thereby impacting tremendously the social, economic, political, cultural and scientific development in the majority of the world's economies. What then is DT? .

DEFINING CONCEPTS

DT and ICT: The Link

On the one hand, DT refers to a "universal model" used to represent information through light and sound waves (Covell, 2000; Lallana with Margaret, 2003, p.6). DT is mostly seen as being contrary to analog technology (AT), as it "incorporates a combination of light and sound waves to get messages across"(Ibid.).The following features may throw more light on DT:

1. Data stored in digital format can withstand numerous copying without any deterioration in quality. However, data stored in analog format deteriorate in quality with the number of copies made;
2. DT has the ability to combine a number of media. For instance, one can only watch television with little interaction of the characters and can also only talk on telephone. However, "phones with video or interactive sound with pictures" are made possible through DT. This is referred to as "multimedia" (Ibid, p.8).

Computers are good example of DT that allows a wider spectrum of interactions. It also allows the creation, storing and sharing of mass volume of information through the internet. DT enables information and communication gadgets to be connected and function as single unit. On the other hand, ICT refers to the combination of telephones (both line and cellular), television, radio broadcasting and computers. From the preceding paragraphs, it appears that the link between DT and ICT has been nothing but complementary.

That being the case, the "digital divide" may be explained as lack of, or inadequate access to, ICT appliances and the skills to use them. According to the Organization for Economic Co-operation and Development, the digital divide is "the difference between individuals, households, businesses and geographic areas with regard to (a) their opportunities to access ICTs and (b) their use of the Internet for a wide variety of activities. It is the gap between those who have real access to information and communications technology and who are able to use it effectively, and those who don't have such access" (Bridges.org, 2000-2001; Lallana with Margaret, 2003, p.30).

At this juncture, it appears convincing that the examination of the "digital divide" and sustainable development must not be restricted to only computer divides, but also should encompass telephones, television, radio and other communications gadgets. Again, the examination of the "digital divide" should transcend accessibility to encompass:

1. Accessibility
2. Usage
3. Applicability or empowerment

Examining digital divide along these parameters is crucial, as merely providing the people with computers (to which conventional digital divide is mostly referred to) can bring only little impact on the economic and social life of the people. Usability or the ability to use these gargets is paramount in attaining the required heights in ICT in the OIC member countries. Improving the usage component will ensure tremendous success in the personal skills in ICTs. The missing link in the usage component of ICTs in the OIC countries needs urgent attention, which must be fixed to unleash the existing huge volume of development and productive information trapped in ICT ignorance. An equally important dimension has been the applicability of the skills acquired. Fulfilling the accessibility and usage requirements will fail to yield the expected development results if the supporting environment has not been created to put to use the skills and expertise acquired or better still the trained man power. By so doing, the people with ICT skills appear to be empowered to contribute to the development process.

Although access to ICTs still poses a problem in the poor and developing countries (Hudson, 2000, p.262), the accessibility dimension is increasingly becoming a non-issue because the price of computers is fast going down and in another five years to come, computers will be one-fourth their current price (Nielson, 2006, p.1). If that prediction becomes a reality when accessibility becomes less problematic, then much attention should then be given to usage and applicability or empowerment. However, other researchers are of the view that the digital divide is a reflection of the existing broader socio-economic inequalities, and the profound and long-standing economic and social divides within and between societies. The 'digital divide' and the broader social and economic divides reflect each other which the development process should address. This needs to be understood and addressed in the context of those broader divides (G8 DOT Force, 2001; Warris, 2004, p. 12).

From the above premise, addressing the digital divide will require effective and closed collaboration within and across countries and continents. It is the belief of this chapter that some countries, just like some poor individuals, cannot successfully contain the digital challenge by solely acting on their own. Against this backdrop, the authors then used OIC member countries to investigate:

1. The extent of the current digital divide existing among them
2. The collaborative efforts made to narrow this divide
3. The main obstacles that impede revolutionalizing ICT
4. To put forward a kind of collaborative model that policymakers in the OIC member countries may consider in their efforts to tackle the challenges that ICT poses

ISSUES IN ICTS AND SUSTAINABLE DEVELOPMENT

In the development literature, information has generally been considered as essential ingredient in the social and economic activities that comprise the development process (ILO, 2001; Warris, 2004, p.10). The significance of information in socio-economic development process has produced development-related jargons such as "information economy", "knowledge economy", e-governance", "e-commerce", etc. The information economy is used interchangeably with knowledge economy, and has been defined as the economy in which "the productivity and competitiveness of units or agents in the economy (be they firms, regions or nations) depend mainly on their capacity to generate, process, and apply efficiently knowledge-based information" (Castells, 1996; Lallana with Margaret, 2003, p.13). Again, it is simply referred to as an economy where information is both the currency and the product (Ibid.). The information or knowledge economy is believed by many in the development literature to be effective because of the following reasons:

1. It is global and the global economy has the capacity to work as a unit in real time on a planetary scale. For instance, it provides corporations and firms a worldwide base for skilled labour to tap. It also enables free capital flows between countries, which they can utilize in real time (Castells, 1996; Lallana with Margaret, 2003, p.13)
2. It is highly productive, as productivity growth has made a significant contribution to economy-wide productivity growth (Nordhaus, 2002; Lallana with Margaret, 2003, pp.13-14)

Now, if information has been viewed by many, though a few others have argued either wise, as crucial in the development process, then ICTs—the life wire of information processing and sharing— appear indispensable to socio-economic development drives.

However, many critics have downplayed the importance of ICTs in the development process. They argued that merely investing in ICTs with the aim of only increasing access had all too often failed to achieve any development goals. As noted by the International Labour Organisation (ILO), investments in ICTs alone are not sufficient for development to occur, although they can contribute significantly to socio-economic development (ILO, 2001; Warris, 2004, p.10). The argument continues that although ICTs are essential, they constitute insufficient condition for economic development (Schmandt et. al, 1990; Warris, 2004, p. 10). Going into specifics and with particular reference to the poor rural areas, Martin and McKeown (1993) concur that unless they fall in line with the principles of integrated rural development, ICTs are not sufficient to tackle the development problems of rural areas (quoted by Warris, 2004, p.10).

All these criticisms about the role of ICTs in socio-development process seem to be suggesting that if the right approach is adopted, the development-prowess of ICTs cannot be over-emphasised. Obviously, this is the case in all human endeavours. If the right approach is not taken, nothing goes right. However, Hudson (2000) observes that most researchers, since the 1960s, have established a close correlation between access to infrastructure (measured by teledensity) and economic growth (measured by per capita GDP). He is, however, not certain as to whether economic growth 'causes' infrastructural growth or the other way round (p.279). Making reference to a study conducted by Hardy (1980), Hudson (2000) notes that Hardy's study found causality as a two-way traffic between investing in infrastructure and economic growth. Thus investment increased as economies grew, but then telecommunications investment played a small yet crucial role in economic growth (Ibid.). Hudson (2000) argues further that ICTs, through accessing and sharing information, can be crucial in the development process by enhancing (a) *efficiency*, i.e., the ratio of output to cost; (b) *effectiveness*, i.e., the quality of products and services; and (c) *equity*, i.e., the distribution of development benefits throughout the society (p.264). More than one-third of the growth of real output in the US economy from 1995 to 1998 was contributed by the information technology (IT) industries (Henry et al., 1999; Hudson, 2000, p. 265).

A review of the development literature on the role of ICTs in sustainable socio-economic development lends much credence to the crucial role ICTs can play in all facets of socio-economic development. However, the right strategy needs to be pursued in order to reap the full development benefits of ICTs. The right strategy here may partly refer to pursuing the three-dimension approach, i.e., accessibility, usability/usage and empowerment or applicability.

OIC and the Digital Divide Literature

Previous studies conducted to investigate the extent of the digital divide among OIC member countries have revealed not much encouraging picture. In the investigation of the readiness of 17 OIC member countries to adopt ICTs, Lahkim, Barise & Boukhobzo (2004) found that a country's network readiness measured by the NRI (Networked Readiness Index) increased with increase in average per capita income of the country concerned. In other words, a little income difference of an Islamic country translates into much variation in the country's readiness and ability to use ICTs (p.402). The 17 countries used for the study were categorized into three income groups, i.e. Low income countries; Lower middle countries and Upper middle income countries. The countries in the low income group have been found to record the lowest NRI score.

This finding has underscored the impact of poverty on ICT adoption at both the macro and micro-levels. A part from income poverty, other factors such as illiteracy and the high percentage of rural population contribute to the low ICT adoption in the selected OIC countries. For the solutions, the study has recommended that much seriousness be attached to ICTs in the countries concerned, and the need to use widely ICTs in the formal education. Furthermore, Alam Khan (2004) found the main causes of the digital divide among countries to include widespread poverty, income disparities between the developed and less developed countries and communities and poor infrastructure. In some instances, political restriction of some groups of people constitutes an obstacle to accessing the internet. Khan's (2004) study was conducted to examine specifically the digital divide within Muslim communities. Unfortunately, he did not offer any solutions to the obstacles he has identified. However, one may classify the factors generally impacting digital divide in OIC countries to include socio-economic constraints, poor infrastructure, widespread illiteracy, and cultural values inimical to internet usage. As solutions, most researchers saw the need to intensify efforts to scale up ICT adoption in the OIC member countries, both within the individual countries and collectively across the member countries. In some studies, collaboration has been much favoured (Lahkim, Barise & Boukhobzo, 2004, p.402).

However, the majority of the studies recommending collaboration across the OIC member countries has failed to recommend the kind of collaboration that will yield results, as there has been collaboration among the OIC member countries for the past three to four decades with no much result. Hence, in this current chapter an attempt has been made to put forward a particular kind of collaborative approach that can bring wider impact to bear on ICTs within and across the OIC fraternity. And the collaborative model presented in this chapter can be as well extended to other areas of development within and across the OIC member countries.

DETERMINANTS OF SUSTAINABLE DEVELOPMENT AND THE ROLE OF ICTS

In this section, the authors examine the role of ICTs in sustainable socio-economic development by highlighting select determinants of socio-economic development. There are countless determinants of sustainable development in which ICT plays a pivotal role. However, a select of such determinants examined here include governance, education, health care, environment, business enterprises, and transportation.

Governance

Effective governance can lead to sound development management, as the role of the state is paramount in socio-economic development. The state is expected to play a leading role in charting the development path of the people while encouraging private sector involvement. For that reason, the effective governing of a nation is nothing short of efficiently managing socio-economic development. In that vein, good governance has come to be associated conventionally with sound socio-economic development management. The role of government in managing socio-economic development largely takes the form of policy support that is embedded in pragmatic policy decisions. (Chamhuri, 2005, p. 26.) The practice of good governance entails opened and enlightened development policy-making built upon accountability, participation and transparency. And the flow of information within the governance structures way down to the masses is an important determining factor in this direction. ICTs, by which information is processed, stored and shared, are so relevant in all facets of governance.

Four areas in which ICTs aid governance include: (a) information to support internal management, including staffing and budgeting accounts; (b) information to support policy and regulatory decision-making, including population, economic, financial, and other data; (c) information made publicly available, including laws, statistics, health information; and (d) information to support public services such as education, health, and transport (Heeks, 1998 ; Kenny, Navas-Sabater & Oiang, 2002, p. 411-2). In Morocco, for instance, ICTs have been instrumental in intermediary coordination, tax administration and auditing, public investment planning and monitoring, and spending management. As a result of using ICT gadgets, the time required to prepare the budgets has been reduced by half (World Bank, 1998; Kenny, Navas-Sabater & Oiang, 2002, p.413). The need to send information about government down to the grass-root level has induced the distribution, by government of Ghana, of 30,000 free-play radios in the rural areas for the rural folk to follow elections (Warris, 2004, p.13). The importance of ICTs in governance may be summed up under e-government. Thus, the use of ICTs to enhance the access and delivery of government services (Lallana, with Margaret, 2003, p. 28).

Education

Human capital development is essential to the overall development of the economy. Developing human capital is possible only through strong and efficient educational system. (Chamhuri, 2005; Abdulai & Chamhuri, 2008, p.7) The use of ICT appliances in teaching and learning process has tremendously enhanced educational system in the majority of countries. In most situations where teachers are inadequate, ICTs are known to have played effective teacher-role, particularly in deprived, poor rural areas.

The *Telesecundaria* program in Mexico has been designed to provide televised classes and a comprehensive curriculum through closed-circuit television, satellite transmissions, and teleconferencing between over 700,000 secondary school students and teachers in remote villages. It is found that, although the programme is only 16 percent more expensive per pupil served than normal urban secondary schools, students performed well in Maths just like their urban counter-parts, and then improved tremendously in their language score (1999de Moura and others 1999!; Kenny, Navas-Sabater & Oiang, 2002, pp.413-4). Educational radio has been used widely, perhaps because of its cost-effectiveness, in most literacy programmes.

Another area where ICTs appear crucial involves the processing and storing of large volumes of educational materials in electronic format. Electronic search engines have revolutionalised libraries the world over by pulling together huge amount of educational materials; thereby enhancing teaching and learning. Even people with disabilities are empowered through ICT-enabled education. (Kenny, Navas-Sabater & Oiang, 2002, p.414) Finally, students, who have acquired ICT skills, are opened to more chances than their ICT illiterate counter-parts. In conclusion, it is true that ICTs cannot fully substitute the role of teachers in the teacherand- learning process, but it aids tremendously the overall day-to-day administration of the educational section including teaching and learning.

Health Care

Information, just like the other development correlates, is essential in health care delivery. ICTs have worked to improve quality in health services. A study has revealed that a significant percentage of health workers in Uganda (54 percent) and Kenya (20 percent) have improved their knowledge, attitudes, and practices after undergoing radio-backed training courses. (Dodds 1999; Kenny, Navas-Sabater & Oiang, 2002, p.415) Also, networked computers are known to have played a vital role in controlling onchocerciasis, or river blindness, in many parts of the world. The use of ICT appliances, especially radio, can help enhance the health awareness of the people. This particularly is true in the wake of the HIV/AIDS pandemic.

Environment

The environment is so much important, as all development activities are planned and executed within the confines of the environment. And the impact of such development activities needs to be monitored so as to keep the environment supportive of our development needs and for those yet unborn. Environmental monitoring, therefore, is a data-intensive exercise. A large amount of the environment-monitoring inputs are ICT-enabled. For instance, Geographic Information Systems (GIS) use computer applications to process, store, and analyse data collected from remote imaging and other sources. These inputs are increasingly powerful tools that not only help to design sustainable management plans, but also to pre-empt environmental threats (Brodnig and Mayer-Schonberger, 1998; Kenny, Navas-Sabater & Oiang, 2002, p.416).

About disaster prevention management, for instance, the National Institute for Disaster Management in Mozambique used freeplay radios to broadcast to flood victims about the weather, health issues, land mines, etc (Ibid.). Then again, ICT-enabled devices are instrumental in the Tsunami-warning project. All with the sole aim to protect human lives alongside with the ecosystems. Undoubtedly,, long lifespan, healthy and literate citizens will boost socio-economic development.

Business Enterprises

Transactions in the corporate and financial sectors and the overall economy have been better enhanced now than ever before. This is so because ICTs beat down transaction costs significantly; thereby enabling large and diverse groups of people to have easier and cheaper access to the information they may need to make sound decisions and to effectively coordinate complex activities (Tapscott, Ticoll and Lowy, 2000; Lallana, with Margaret, 2003, p.16) . In the banking sector for instance, it has been acknowledged that "for the first time in 300 years the very nature of banking has changed" mainly due to easy access to information. Banks handle money, but it is believed that information, not money, is now the lifeblood of the banking industry (Ibid, p.14).

Term like "e-commence" is the direct acknowledgement of the influence of ICTs on businesses worldwide. E-commerce has been explained to mean the "buying and selling over the Internet or any transaction concluded through an information network" (Ibid, p.17). E-commerce is the use of electronic communications and digital information processing technology to create, transform and redefine relationships for purposes of enhancing the quality of business transactions. An example can be cited of the Automated Systems for Customs Data (Asycuda) developed by the United Nations Conference on Trade and Development to manage tariff collection and reduce frontier corruption. It is believed the system can speed up the movement of goods and reduce transport expenses (Kenny, Navas-Sabater & Oiang, 2002, p. 413).

Transport

Transport and communications are two sides of the same coin. These together are most often being merged to form an administration sector in most countries. For many in the development literature, the transport sector is a significant contributory factor in any country's ability to unleash its economic potential through an efficient transport system. This so because the transport sector forms an integral part of daily subsistence, economic and social activities (Gonnon et al, 2002, p. 235). This is true as the need to transport merchandise and people from one geographical location to another is concerned. If we understand the transport sector to involve something more than just the construction of roads, highways, ports etc, even in its narrow sense, ICTs are so helpful in efficiency enhancement in the transport sector. In a broader sense, ICTs are partly the lifeline of the aviation and maritime transport.

The improvement in transport by ICTs has reduced trade and investment costs. This is particularly true of imports and exports. An example has been given of Singapore, which has drastically reduced the costs of import and export through the networked information system called *Tradenet*, with estimated savings of about 1 percent of the city-state's GDP (World Bank 1998; Kenny, Navas-Sabater & Oiang, 2002, p. 411). If it is true that transport and communications are inseparable, then ICTs may constitute the bedrock.

OIC Member Countries in Perspective

The Millennium Declaration has recognised the crucial role ICTs can play to achieve the Millennium Development Goals (MDGs). Specifically and under Goal 8, target 18 urges all member countries to close their ranks with the private sector so as "to make available the benefits of new technologies, especially information and communications" (UNDP, 2003; Jingiu, 2008, p. 144). In that light, the following section examines briefly socio-economic development in the OIC member countries with respective to poverty alleviation—both human and income poverty. The nature of digital divide has also been examined here using some ICT access indicators like per capita internet usage, personal computer, telephone— line and celular pone subscription.

Socio-Economic Development Scenario

Poverty is rife among the OIC countries. The higher the prevalence rates of poverty and deprivation in a particular country, the higher the likelihood that the economy and its administrative apparatus are non-performing. Such scenario represents a non-performing economy underpinning an erratic development process. For this reason, poverty (both human and income poverty) has been taken in this chapter as one of the important measures of socio-economic development. The lower the incidence of poverty and other forms of deprivation, the better the living standards of the people. That is basically what development has sought to achieve. That is, economic growth with equitable distribution of the benefits accruing from growth.

Poverty is abhorred in its totality because it does not aid the course of development. Poverty hampers fully-fledged social and economic development of many a country, as the poor people would have been fully drawn into the mainstream economic activities from the peripheral areas where they are currently occupying; thereby contributing more effectively to economic growth. Pertaining to environmental sustainability—an important determinant of development—poverty renders the poor people poor environmental stewards (World Bank, 1992, p.19). Poor environmental stewardship is manifested in the clearance of valuable forest resources for purposes of farming and firewood. It also manifests in the over-cultivation of land leading to soil degradation and damaging the entire ecosystem. Again, maintaining overcrowded squatter, shanty and slum settlements is another example, which has debilitating health effects. As a consequence, the quality of the immediate environment of the poor, especially household environment, is deplorable, thereby creating frequent and widespread environmentally related health problems. Under such circumstances, livelihoods of the poor people are highly compromised. Spiritually and from religious standpoint, poverty and deprivations threaten an individual's religious faith.

Sustainable development in the OIC countries has best been captured in the UNDP Human Development Index (HDI). In the 2007 index, there was no OIC member country within the upper 10th quartile,that is, from 0.900 to 1. In the upper 20th quartile (i.e. 0.800-0.999) one could count only 10 OIC member countries. The first being Brunei with 0.894 placed as 30th in the world. This implies the first 29 best human-developed countries did not include any OIC member country. Does the OIC fraternity detest development? The answer will certainly be negative. Worst of all, eleven of the OIC member countries are among the least human-developed countries (UNDP, 2007). The importance of the HDI can never be overemphasized, as it incorporates measures that are crucial to sustainable livelihoods. These measures include literacy, education, life expectancy and standard of living measured by income inequality, poverty rate, real (i.e. inflation adjusted) income per person. All these measures underlie the poverty eradication and socio-economic development process in any countries.

The OIC member countries are not oblivious of the development benefits of ICTs. As a result, the need to tap the development benefits of ICTs has led to the formation of the Islamic States Telecommunications Union (ISTU) under the umbrella of OIC. Article 2 of the Union Stature contains 12 objectives of ISTU. Some of which have been listed below:

1. To promote Islamic solidarity in telecommunications field
2. To ensure self-sufficiency, integration and coordination among Member States in the telecommunications areas, as much as possible
3. To propose plans, undertake studies and pursue research with a view to develop and modernize telecommunications according to advanced technical and technological standards (this is objective 4 in the ISTU statute)
4. To extend all possible assistance to the Members for training manpower and establishing centres and institutes specialising in telecommunications (objective 5 in the ISTU stature)
5. To make the maximum possible use of the manpower, expert services and training facilities available in the Member States (objective 6)
6. To develop cooperation among members in establishing telephones, telegraph, telex, data and other telecommunications services and to enhance telecommunications services

Undoubtedly, all the 12 objectives identified in the main Stature are set to unleash the development capabilities of ICTs. Following the inception of ISTU, many people will be agitating to know the prevailing scenario of ICTs within and across the OIC countries. The intention in the following section dwells on that quest.

Measuring the Digital Divide in and across the OIC Member Countries

The factors underlying digital divide are not only numerous, but are also complex. This makes digital divide an issue that appears more difficult to measure in its entirety with a single method. Sontoyo (2003) corroborates this when he says that there is, currently, no precise measure of the digital divide.

Sontoyo (2003) has based his argument on the premise of the complexity and interdisciplinary nature of the problem, which makes it difficult to establish a set of parameters that include the major issues affecting the characteristics and evolution of the digital divide (p.21). However, the most basic indicator used to measure digital divide has been access to computers/ ICTs. In its simplicity, this indicator has been critiqued as being too simplistic a method to capture the true nature of the digital divide existing in the society. Barzilai-Nahon (2006) notes that the tendency to rely on easy-to-measure indicators like how many internet access points a place has presents a simplistic picture of today's digital divide. For that reason, there is the need for a more sophisticated approach to get an honest assessment of who is being left behind. She argues further that "Ten years ago, when someone had a connection, it was enough. Today, in some places it's nothing. The idea is what do you do with the content? Do you know how to use it?"

Inasmuch as Barzilai-Nahon(2003) could be right in her argument, this chapter contents that the need to have internet connection, though basic, constitutes the first step, which is as vital in many places of the world as the ability to use the internet has been in many other countries. This contention has been underscored by the definition of digital divide offered by Dewan and Riggins (2005) in which they referred to digital divide as: "The separation between those who have access to digital information and communications technology (ICT) and those who do not"(p.1). Here, an emphasis has been placed upon *access*. Furthermore, Dewan and Riggins (2005) analysed both the *first order effects* and the *second order effects* of the digital divide. And by first and second order effects, they meant *access* and inequality in *usage* respectively. Still on the access dimension, the US National Telecommunications and Information Administration acknowledges that people are the country's most important resource and "in a society that increasingly relies on computers and the internet to deliver information and enhance communication, we need to make sure that all Americans have access" (Schutz 2001, p.1).

To this far, it is clear that access to ICTs is as important as the ability to use the available technology. For this reason, the chapter measured the digital divide within and across the OIC member countries by using such access and usage indicators as: internet users per 100; PCs per 100; telephone lines per 100; and cellular subscribers per 100 of the population. The analysis assumes a regional pattern. OIC member countries are lumped into regions. And within each region the countries are further segregated into oil-producing and non-oil-producing member countries. These regional groups include: (a) The African region, (b) Middle East and Central Asia, and (c) East Asia, the Pacific and South American OIC Member Regions.

African Region

The access rate of ICTs in this region is not encouraging relative to the other regions. Thus, all the selected OIC member countries in this region have their number of internet users below 20 per 100 of their populations. Then again, there seems to be no much difference between the non-oil-producing member countries and some of the oil-producing countries in terms of internet users. Ironically, the sum of internet users in all the 10 selected oil-producing countries (70.74) is below that of, for instance, South Korea (71.11) taken from the same source. On average, the sum of the 16 members selected in this region amounts to 5.53 per 100. This is undoubtedly a dismal access rate, which, again although indirectly, reflects the extent of usage in this region. This is because one can talk of usage only when there is access. Without access there cannot be usage. With such dismal rate of access to internet, a further downward trend in personal computer rate is expected. However, there has been a relatively high access to telephone, but tends to be moving way from fixed lines to mobile or cellular phones. However, what is not

Figure 1. Access indicators of ICT in the selected African OIC member countries. Source: Compiled from UN, MDGs Export 2008

Country	Internet Users /100 Pop	PCs /100 Pop	Telephone Lines/100 Pop	Cellular Sub. /100 Pop.
Oil-Producing Countries				
Algeria	7.38	n/a	8.52	62.95
Cameroon	2.23	n/a	0.79	18.89
Chad	0.6	n/a	4.65	0.13
Cote d'Ivoire	1.63	n/a	1.41	22.03
Egypt	7.95	4.19	14.33	23.86
Libya	4.36	n/a	n/a	65.81
Morocco	19.85	2.99	4.12	52.07
Nigeria	5.95	n/a	1.26	24.05
Sudan	8.65	11.45	2.07	11.59
Tunisia	12.68	6.22	12.42	71.88
Non-oil Producing Countries				
Burkina Faso	0.59	0.66	0.7	7.46
Gambia	5.29	2.02	2.98	25.99
Mali	0.64	n/a	0.59	10.87
Niger	0.28	n/a	n/a	3.35
Senegal	5.45	n/a	2.37	24.99
Uganda	5.02	1.67	0.36	6.73

Source: UN, 2007. n/a = not available.

very vivid about this trend in cellular subscription in the Millennium Development Goals report is how much of such access rate contributes to socio-economic development process aside from what may be described as fashionable usage or people just being in vogue. There is the need for further research to ascertain the role of the high cellular subscription rate in the socio-economic development process. Table 1 below shows the various access indicators of ICTs in the African OIC member countries.

Middle East and Central Asian Region

Although the access and usability rates may not be as high in the Middle East and Central Asian (MECA) region as other developed economies like Japan, USA, etc, but across the OIC member regions MECA stands tall. Again, there has been no single country in this region having ratio above 40 per 100 of internet users. However, the internet usage in some oil-producing countries gives much hope. With much more efforts, ICTs will become part and parcel of the daily life of many countries in this region. Personal computer rate has been somewhat encouraging in a few countries. In the same manner, telephone usage is gaining grounds in the majority of these countries, which translates to making this region nearly the telephone hub of the OIC fraternity.

In terms of cellular subscription, countries like Bahrain, Qatar and U.A.E. tend to have rates that surpass those of Japan (79.32), USA (80.32), South Korea (83.77), and Singapore (109.34). Taking into account the levels of economic development and this particular access rate of cellular phones, one cannot but wonder if such high cellular telephone usage has been productive in such OIC countries. How much have cellular phones contributed in the socio-economic development process in countries posting high access rates? Are these high access rates being influenced merely by the relatively smaller population sizes of the countries concerned? Nonetheless on the whole, MECA carries the hope of the possibility to roll

Figure 2. Access indicators of ICT in the selected Middle East and Central Asian OIC member countries. Source: Compiled from UN, MDGs Export, 2008

Country	Internet Users /100 Pop	PCs /100 Pop	Telephone Lines/100 Pop	Cellular Sub. /100 Pop
Oil-Producing Countries				
Albania	14.98	3.81	n/a	60.38
Azerbaijan	9.79	n/a	14.03	39.23
Bahrain	28.44	18.28	26.3	122.88
Iran	25.54	10.53	32.11	23.92
Kazakhstan	8.71	n/a	19.77	52.86
Kuwait	28.93	n/a	18.7	91.49
Kyrgyzstan	12.21	n/a	8.62	23.7
Oman	11.1	6.89	10.32	69.59
Qatar	34.55	18.71	27.21	109.6
Saudi Arabia	18.66	13.89	15.68	78.05
Turkey	17.73	5.93	25.39	71
U.A.E	36.69	30.06	28.12	118.51
Uzbekistan	4.08	3.08	n/a	9.27
Yemen	1.25	2.77	4.47	13.76
Non-Oil-Producing Countries				
Lebanon	26.28	11.62	18.85	30.61
Jordan	13.65	6.34	10.52	74.4

Source: UN, 2007. n/a = not available.

up ICTs across the OIC member countries. Table 2 below further illustrates.

East Asia, the Pacific and South American Region

This region is hosting the first two leading countries with the highest rate of internet users among the 40 OIC member countries selected for this study. Specifically, Malaysia has the highest internet user ratio 54.23 per 100 among the entire 57 OIC countries, as of 2008. Brunei comes second with 41.69. However, personal computer rate is not as high as the user rate in these countries. Nevertheless, it is not very low. The non-oil producing countries are faring quite well. Bangladesh and Indonesia are the two countries in this region posting the lowest rates in all the indicators. In fact, Bangladesh has the lowest rate in all the indicators among all the three regions. There must be factors responsible for this ICT scenario in Bangladesh. Unfortunately, this current study has not been designed to tackle this about Bangladesh. Further research that seeks to investigate this unique ICT scenario in Bangladesh will yield productive results. Table 3 below further illustrates.

Access Indicators of ICT across the Regions

In Table 4 below, the intention has been to capture the trend of ICTs across the regions. In doing so we realise that there are more internet users in the EAPSAMC than in the MECAMC and AFMC. However, the combined figures of internet users per 100; PCs per 100; telephone line per 100 and cellular subscribers per 100 show the MECAMC to be in the lead, followed by EAPSAMC and the AFMC come third. By the individual ICT appliances, cellular subscribers appear to be the highest (130.61), internet users come next (42.19), telephone lines (33.62) and PCs (25.51). This trend reveals that the majority of the people of the OIC member countries cannot afford personal computers.

Figure 3. Access indicators of ICT in the selected East Asia, the Pacific and South American OIC member countries. Source: Compiled from UN, MDGs Export, 2008

Country	Internet Users /100 Pop	PCs /100 Pop	Telephone Lines/100 Pop	Cellular Sub. /100 Pop.
Oil-Producing Countries				
Bangladesh	0.31	2.42	0.79	13.25
Brunei	41.69	n/a	20.99	78.92
Indonesia	4.69	2	6.57	28.3
Malaysia	54.23	23.41	16.83	75.45
Pakistan	7.64	n/a	3.34	21.98
Suriname	8.41	n/a	18.03	70.8
Oil-Producing Countries				
Guyana	21.3	3.86	14.66	37.45
Maldives	8.97	20.08	10.88	87.88

Source: UN, 2007. n/a = not available

Assessing the Depth of the Digital Divide in the OIC Countries

There is still a deep-seated digital divide existing within and across the OIC member countries. To determine the depth of the existing digital divide, a proxy measure has been employed here in which the average sums of all the ICT indicators in all the three regions have been totalled and the figure appears to be slightly above average—57.98 per 100 *(i.e. 42.19+ 25.51+33.62+130.61= 231.93/4)*. Table 4 in the preceding section further illustrates. At the global level, the average sum of ICT penetration (measured by internet users per 100, personal computers per 100; telephone lines subscribers per 100 and cellular subscribers per 100) in the 40 OIC member countries sampled for this study as shown above (i.e., 57.98 per 100) appears to be far below the ICT penetration rates of individual countries such as USA *(71.41 per 100)*, South Korea *(64.79)*, and Singapore *(70.90)* measured by the same four indicators in Table 4 above. Obviously, there must be some factors that serve as obstacles to addressing this digital scenario in the OIC member countries. What are these obstacles? Some of which have been offered in the following section.

The Obstacles

The obstacles confronting the OIC member countries vary from one country to another based upon their economic and administrative capabilities. However and generally, the prime factors identified to be responsible for the dismal ICT scenario within and across the OIC member countries include the following:

a. **Widespread poverty:** Although the prices of computers and other ICT appliances have reduced substantially, the majority of people in many of the OIC member countries is so poor to afford computers and other ICT appliances
b. **High illiteracy rates:** The majority of the population cannot read and write in the English language— the main medium of ICTs, particularly the internet

The main obstacles at the macro-level include the following:

a. **Poor infrastructure:** Many OIC member countries have very poor infrastructure base that will boost the development of ICTs, especially the internet

Figure 4. Access indicators of ICT across the regions (averages). UN, MDGs Export, 2008

Access indicators	Internet Users/100	PCs/100	Telephone lines/100	Cellular Subscribers/100
AFMC	5.50	4.17	3.54	27.04
MECAMC	18.29	10.99	18.57	61.82
EAPSAMC	18.40	10.35	11.51	51.75
TOTAL	**42.19**	**25.51**	**33.62**	**130. 61**

Note: AFMC= African member countries; MECAMC= Middle East and Central Asian member countries; EAPSAMC= East Asia, the Pacific and South American member countries. *Source:* Authors' calculation based on data from UN, MDGs, Report, 2007.

b. **High cost:** The cost of providing such infrastructure is prohibitive for some member countries

TOWARD A COLLABORATIVE APPROACH OF SUSTAINABLE DEVELOPMENT AND DIGITAL DIVIDE WITHIN AND ACROSS OIC MEMBER COUNTRIES

Solutions and Recommendations

One way to roll up literacy effectively is through a collaborative, synergic work that will raise the levels of school enrolment in the member countries. Once the people are educated, to a very large extent, their chances of being employed will be enhanced, and member countries will at the same time attain high literacy heights. With high literacy rates, the possibility of acquiring ICT skills and usage will be as well high.

Another important measure has been to enhance the diffusion of technology across the OIC member countries. One way to do this can take the form of cross-transfer of ICT experts among the OIC member countries. This measure will require that the OIC member countries be classified along their levels of ICT penetration. Those member countries that appear to be better off should consider lending their expertise to the ICT-deficient OIC member countries. Alternatively, students from the poor OIC member countries can be given the opportunity to study in other member countries that are relatively advanced in ICTs. The establishment of community-based internet service centres where the benefits of ICTs can reach the poor rural people, particularly the peasant farmers is another vital measure to narrow the digital gap, and availing the rural folk, within and across OIC member countries, the benefits accompanying ICTs. This measure has been implemented in a good number of countries and it has proven to be effective and successful in efforts to diffuse ICT.

The most essential domain is the empowerment of the people, who have acquired ICT skills. The task associated with empowerment is enormous, which will require closed partnership between the public and private sectors in the individual countries, followed by closed collaboration among the OIC countries. This is a component that requires huge amount of capital investments to unleash the full development benefits of ICTs. It is the belief of the authors that these huge capital investments may be feasible only through the collective, collaborative and synergic resource pool of the OIC member countries. And by so doing the high ICT investment cost that denies some OIC member countries the chance to test the fruits of ICTs can be resolved largely.

The Collaboration Octagon Model

In terms of resource endowments and socio-economic development impacting ICT penetration in the OIC member countries, an attempt to rank these countries may produce an outlook as represented hypothetically in the following figure:

Figure 5. Development collaboration octagon. (Octagon model: multi-dimensional in nature)

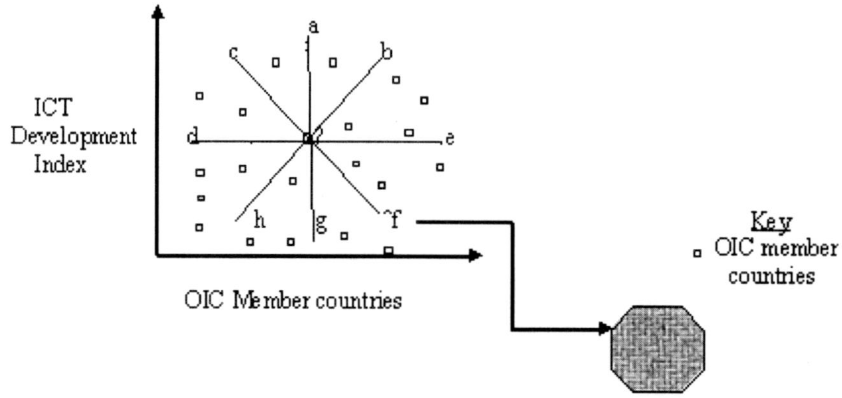

Figure 1: Development Collaboration Octagon
(Octagon Concept: Multi-Dimensional in nature)

In that perspective, effective, development-oriented collaboration in ICTs that can yield productive results should be multi-dimensional in nature. This in our case has been labelled ***Development Collaboration Octagon***. The Octagonal pattern reflects horizontal, vertical and lateral collaborations in the generation and utilization of development resources within and among the OIC countries. In the case of ICT, the level of ICT penetration utterly varies among the countries. This underscores the need for effective collaboration. In real life scenario, most bilateral and multilateral collaborations often assume heavily skewed dimensions that may have very little general impact as far as the huge number of poor countries is concerned. For instance, if a three-nation collaboration ensues among countries A,B, and C in the above diagram, such pattern of collaboration appears to be highly skewed, thereby excluding the average and least developed member countries. In our case and in terms of ICT penetration, these countries will include D, E,F, G and H. Again if collaboration develops horizontally among countries D, O and E, it is most likely that such pattern of collaboration cannot have any wider impact in the OIC fraternity, as these countries appear to have an above-average level of ICT penetration.

Nevertheless, a pattern of collaboration that appears to mirror in the least, the medium and the highest countries can assume vertical or lateral dimensions in our case, i.e., A,O, G; C,O,F and B, O, H. Such patterns of collaboration can yield great impact as the least- ICT-penetrated countries are paired with the medium and the relatively highest-penetrated countries. However, this kind of collaboration may still need other essential features to unleash greater and wider impact. To help minimise the pitfalls characterising most conventional bilateral and multi-lateral collaborations, the ***Octagonal Collaboration Model*** seeks to capture the horizontal, vertical and the lateral patterns of conventional collaboration. The Octagonal collaboration would include countries A, B, C, D, E, F, G and H in a group. Qualitatively ranked, each group of eight OIC member countries will then include the following:

A = Excellent penetration (relative standards)
B = Very Good penetration
C = Good penetration
D = Average penetration
E = Fair penetration
F = Poor penetration
G = Very poor penetration
H = Failed or No penetration

OIC member countries such as Somalia, Sierra Leone (often described as the dead economies) will fall within the Failed or No penetration zone. Such countries cannot be ignored in the efforts to scale up ICTs within and across the OIC fraternity. They should be incorporated into the mainstream of development collaboration. The development needs of the so-called "dead economies" would be much draining if left to similar or medium-level member countries. The Octagonal pattern of collaboration can be extended to other areas of development endeavours.

a. This pattern should be pursued within individual OIC member countries and across them
b. Resource generation among the OIC countries could assume the trend of intensifying trade and transfer of expertise in ICT resources within and across the OIC member countries

In reality and as golden rule of this concept, countries should have at least **8** other member countries in a comparative advantage kind of engagement that reliably and mutually reflects the development resource requirements, utilization needs and of course sustainable livelihoods aspirations, poverty alleviation targets and ICT development of member countries. This does not preclude trade in ICT resources emphasising the ICT needs of the poor and marginalised people in these countries.

FUTURE TRENDS

The importance of information in sustainable economic development has long been recognised. The questions of 'where, how, when to get what and for whom?' can only be addressed by reliable, cutting-edge information. Sustainable economic development process is replete with similar questions. Therefore, ICTs, the powerhouse of state-of-the-art information, will remain the backbone of global economic development. Again, ICTs will remain relevant in the foreseeable future in as much as information processing, storing and sharing remain part and parcel of knowledge generation and transfer. In that light, collaboration among nations will become more necessary in the years ahead, as many countries acting individually may not be that much successful in managing sustainable socio-economic development for obvious reasons. Resources will have to be pulled together to make up for the resource-deficits prevailing in many other resource-deficient developing countries.

FURTHER RESEARCH

Further research to empirically unearth the ICT capabilities of the individual OIC countries and the ICT requirements unique to each member country is worth undertaking. The findings of such research will facilitate the process of matching these countries for purposes of forging and pulling resources in the like-terms to scale up ICT endowments within and across the OIC fraternity.

CONCLUSION

The chapter has been designed to investigate: (a) the extent of the current digital divide existing within and among the OIC member countries in the broader perspective of ICTs, (b) the collaborative efforts made to narrow this divide in ICTs, (c) the main obstacles that impede revolutionalizing ICTs among these countries, and (d) to suggest some policy recommendations that policymakers in the OIC member countries may consider to forge a united front in tackling the challenges posed by the ICT divide.

To this end, the digital divide measured using indicators such as internet users per 100; PCs per100; telephone lines per 100 and cellular subscribers per 100 is still wide in individual member countries and across the regions. Abject poverty confronting the masses, high illiteracy rates, poor infrastructure in member countries to support ICTs and the high ICT investment cost are responsible for this ICT divide. The digital inequalities within and across the OIC countries may be contained significantly if much attention is paid to collaborative digital technology ventures. This is because collaborations and cooperation, in the years ahead, will become an effective mechanism to unleash capabilities and unearth hidden potentials within and across countries of the world, and the OIC is no exception.

REFERENCES

Abdulai, A. M., & Chamhuri, S. (2008, December). *Livelihoods sustainability experience in Malaysia: Implication for cooperation with West Asia.* A paper presented at an international conference on Malaysia-West Asia Relations: Prospects & Challenges, UKM, Bangi, Malaysia.

Barzilai-Nahon, K. (2006). *Better yardstick needed to measure digital divide.* Retrieved April 19, 2008, from http://www.govtech.com/dc/101673

Caneo, C. (2002, January). *Globalized and localized digital divides along the information highway: a fragile synthesis across bridges, ramps, cloverleaves, and ladders.* Paper presented at the 33rd Annual Sorokin Lecture, University of Saskatchewan.

Chamhuri, S. (2005). Poverty and governance: The role of the state, good governance, and an enabling policy framework in poverty alleviation in Malaysia. In J. Jabes (Ed.), *The role of public administration in alleviating poverty and improving governance* (pp. 22-41). Kuala Lumpur: Asian Development Bank.

Dewan, S., & Riggins, J. F. (2005). The digital divide: current research and future directions. *Journal of the Association of Information Systems*, 6(12), 298-337. Retrieved March 20, 2009, from http://misrc.umn.edu/workingpapers/fullpapers/2005/0524_120605.pdf

Gannon, C., et al. (2002). Transport. In K. Jeni (Ed.), *A source book for poverty reduction* (Vol. 2, pp. 232-369). Washington DC: World Bank. Retrieved October 21, 2008, from http://povlibrary.worldbank.org/files/13886_chap22.pdf

Hudson, H. E. (2000). Extending access to the digital economy to rural and developing regions. In E. Bryjoltsson & B. Kahin (Eds.), *Understanding the digital economy: Data, tools and research* (pp. 261-291). Cambridge, MA: MIT Press.

Jinqiu, Z. (2008). Information and communications technology for poverty reduction: Bringing technology to rural and disadvantaged communities in West China. In P. Steel, N. Fernandor, & M. Weddikkara (Eds.), *Poverty reduction that works: Experience of scaling up development success* (pp. 129-146). London: UNDP, Earthscan.

Kenny, C., Navas-Sabater, J., & Oiang, C. (2002). Information and communication technologies. In K. Jeni (Ed). *A source book for poverty reduction* (Vol. 2, pp. 405-438). Washington, DC: World Bank. Retrieved October 21, 2008, from http://povlibrary.worldbank.org/files/4430_chap17.pdf

Khan, M. A. (2004, December). Media globalization and the digital divide. In *Proceedings of an international conference on Poverty in the Muslim Countries and Communities: Causes and Solutions*, Kuala Lumpur, Malaysia.

Lajkim, M. B., Barise, A., & Boukhobza, I. (2004, December). Globalization and poverty alleviation in Islamic countries: The role of information communication technologies & science. In *Proceedings of an international conference on Poverty in the Muslim Countries and Communities: Causes and Solutions*, Kuala Lumpur, Malaysia.

Lallana, E. C., & Margaret, N. (2003). *The information age*. Manila and Kuala Lumpur: UNDP-APDIP.

Nielson, J. (2006). *Digital divide: The three stages*. Retrieved November 23, 2008, from http://useit.com

Santoyo, A. S. (2003). *Estimation and characterization of the digital divide*. Paper presented at a round table on developing countries access to scientific knowledge, the Abdus Salam ICTP, Trieste, Italy.

Schutz, L. (2001). Digital disconnect: Beyond the infrastructure. *Critical Issues. Minnesota*. Retrieved March 16, 2008, from http://www/mnplan.state.mn.us

UN. (2008). *Millennium development goals. Export*. Retrieved October 23, 2008, from http://MDG_Export_20080716_083055890

UNDP. (2007). Human Development Report. In *Making globalization work for all*. New York: UN.

Warris, R. W. (2004). *Information and communication technologies for poverty alleviation*. Kuala Lumpur: UNDP-APDIP.

World Bank. (1992). World development report. In *Development and the environment*. New York: Oxford University Press.

ADDITIONAL READING

Afele, J. S. C. (2003). *Digital bridges: Developing countries in the knowledge economy*. Hersheley PA: Idea Group Pub.

Akhtar, B., Surbuland, K., & Maria, G. (Eds.). (2005). *Connected for development: Information kiosks and sustainability*. New York: UN.

Corrochner, N., & Ordaninin, A. (2002). Measuring the digital divide. *Journal of Information Technology, 17*, 9–19. doi:10.1080/02683960210132061

Cullen, R. (2001). Addressing the digital divide. *Online Information Review, 5*, 311–320. doi:10.1108/14684520110410517

Erik, B., & Brian, K. (Eds.). (2000). *Understanding the digital economy: Data, tools and research*. Cambridge, MA: MIT Press.

Harbhajan, S. K., & Varinder, P. S. (Eds.). (2005). *Digital economy: Impacts, influences and challenges*. Hershey: Idea Group Pub.

Mitsuhiro, K., Masatsugu, T., & Emanuele, G. (Eds.). (2004). *Information technology policy and the digital divide: Lessons for developing countries*. Cheltenham, UK: Edward Elgar.

Murell, E. (2002). *Digital divide: Implications for developing countries*. London: Commonwealth Secretariat.

Osamu, S. (Ed.). (2005). *Digital economy and social design*. New York: Springer.

Parkinson, S. (2005). *Telecentres, access and development: Experience and lessons from Uganda and South Africa*. Ottawa, Canada: Ottawa International Development Research Centre.

Perrons, D. (2004). *Globalisation and social change: People, and places in a divided world*. London: Routledge.

Peter, D., & Douglas, S. (2004). *Community practice in the network society: Local action, global interaction*. London: Routledge.

Robert, D. G., Lynne, M. M., & Che, N. (Eds.). (2007). *Exploring information system research approaches, readings and reflections*. New York: Routledge.

Stewart, M., Wallace, T., & Xinghuo, Y. (Eds.). (2002). *Closing digital divide: Transforming regional economies and communities with information technology.* Westport, CT: Praeger.

Terry, K., & Irene, L. C. (Eds.). (2008). *Social information technology: Connecting society and cultural issues*. Hershey, PA: Information Science Reference.

Warschauer, M. (2003). *Technology and social inclusion: Rethinking the digital divide.* Cambridge, MA: MIT Press.

Chapter 16
Regional Innovation Strategies:
Europe and Turkey

Murad Tiryakioglu
Afyon Kocatepe University, Turkey

Sinan Alcin
Maltepe University, Turkey

ABSTRACT

Regional innovation strategies which emerged during the mid 90s and were implemented especially in the developing regions of the world are significant for the transformation of both the knowledge produced in the regional scale and the added value it created into competitive power in the national and global scale. These strategies which have successfully been implemented in different parts of the world are a great opportunity for a country like Turkey which has a large young population and stands out among the other developing countries with her strategic location and potentials for human resources, agriculture and commerce. Focusing on these strategies and exploring national and regional innovation systems, this chapter both investigates the leader implementations in Europe and examines the first implementations of regional innovation strategies in Turkey. This chapter suggests that by transforming her regional innovation skills into products and services that have added value, Turkey will have a potential to achieve rapid social and economic development and therefore increase her significance for the national and international innovative investors.

INTRODUCTION

Having become the major driving force of post-industry society, innovation processes emerge in all steps of production from production techniques to marketing. In the formation of an international industry zone, the combination of technology and innovation processes have formed the basis of competition superiority for the producers. Leaving behind collective consumption, individual preferences gained significance during the 1970s and this led to the development of flexible production systems to replace collective production. When the move away from Keynesian policies directed towards spending were combined with this process, it was inevitable for the producers to make constant

DOI: 10.4018/978-1-61520-709-1.ch016

technological innovations in the production systems and processes. The atmosphere of constant technological innovation have made the process of what Schumpeter (1942) called *"creative destruction"* more visible. Production systems that were renovated in every ten or fifteen years in the past are undergoing a transformation today challenging the time. The implications of this for the producer is on the one hand the rapid decrease of profitability and on the other the requirement of following and developing technological innovations to be able to survive economically in the prevalent competitive environment.

The creation of technological innovation within the production process itself is only possible with a qualified labor force not to mention the state policies supporting the development of such labor force. "National Innovation Systems" taking its frame of reference from List's (1841) teachings depend on governments' systematic implementation of long-term policies from education to economic incentives decisively.

With the onset of the competition among different countries in terms of technological innovation, the existing National Innovation Systems alone are not sufficient in addressing the needs. In order to catch up with the technological innovations faster and to spread the new production knowledge to the base, it has become a must for SMEs to be included in the innovation processes. As the global monopolies do not share the new production techniques and "knowledge goods" they produce under the intellectual and industrial property laws, SMEs have become weaker in the global competition. Even if SMEs, which have been highly affected by the global competition, increased their R&D activities individually, it would not help them in this competition process. That is why Regional Innovation Systems and Strategies which were developed as part of the National Innovation Systems are gaining importance. Thanks to the Regional Innovation Strategies, technological innovations and the potential to make innovations are diffused in the region.

First implementations of the development of Regional Innovation Strategies, which was set as an important target in the techno-economy policies of the European Union (EU), have also started in certain regions of Turkey. Since becoming an "associate member" of European Union, Turkey has been undergoing a process of harmonizing its national legislation with the EU acquis communautaire. Against this background, this study explores the development of Regional Innovation Strategies in Turkey in relation to the relevant EU policies.

In the first part of the study, Regional Innovation Systems and the Regional Innovation Strategy are investigated with respect to their primary characteristics. The second part of the study examines the emergence of Regional Innovation Strategies in Europe and the dynamics of development. In the third part, implementations in Turkey and the dynamics of development are inquired.

THE CONCEPT OF REGIONAL INNOVATION STRATEGIES

Since the awareness into the significance of knowledge[1] on the economic activities increases day by day, knowledge-based production factors are coming to the forefront getting ahead of the traditional factors. As the source of the innovation, knowledge is being produced by the firm and it diffuses from the firm to the industry, from the industry to the sector and from the sector to the national economy. The theoretical basis of the Innovation System approach (Freeman, 1987 and 1988; Lundvall, 1988 and 1992; Nelson, 1988 and 1993; Nelson 1993 and Rosenberg, 1993), the total of systematic efforts during the use and diffusion of this produced knowledge, lies back to Friedrich List (1841). In fact, the proposal of List for the development of Germany called "the national research development system" formed the basis of National Innovation System. While laying the foundations of national innovation system, List did not want to protect the "baby" industries[2], but to design a general series of policies, enabling and facilitating the economic growth and industrialization. As a matter of fact, many of these policies were concerned with learning and implementing the new technologies (Freeman and Soete, 1997, p. 295). As List (1841) puts it:

...The present state of the nations is the result of the accumulation of all discoveries, inventions, improvements, perfections and exertions off all generations which have lived before us: they form the intellectual capital of the present human race, and every separate nation is productive only in the proportion in which it has known how to appropriate those attainments of former generations and to increase them by its own acquirements...

... No progress, no new discoveries and inventions can be made in these sciences by which a hundred industries and processes could not be improved or altered. In the manufacturing State, therefore, sciences and arts must necessarily become popular...

It is obvious that in this study, List (1841)*gives importance to the function of state in implementing and coordinating the long-term economy and industry policies* (Freeman and Soete, 1997, p. 298). In other words, the result List inferred from his own theoretical analyses is in effect a long-term "national technology policy" dependent firmly on industry and education policies. As Freeman (1989, pp. 86-87) suggests, List writes about the fact that "in order for Germany to reach the technology level of Great Britain, it should lay the theoretical foundations of techno-economy policies to be implemented and that some patterns of List's teachings can be found in all implementations of almost all countries that caught up with the world technologies like Japan and South Korea."

Innovation, defined as "... *the implementation of a new or significantly improved product (good or service), or process, a new marketing method, or a new organizational method in business practices, workplace organization or external relations*" in the Oslo Guide book and originated from List's teachings and implementations reaching today, has started to be a major theme in the economy literature together with Schumpeter's notion of creative destruction. Having this notion, Schumpeter (1942) argues that innovation is produced by the capitalist system in order to survive. Schumpeter uses the notion of creative destruction in order to emphasize the essence of capitalism. For Schumpeter (1942 [2006], pp. 118-119):

...The fundamental impulse that sets and keeps the capitalist engine in motion comes from the new consumers' goods, the new methods of production or transportation the new markets, the new forms of industrial organization that capitalist enterprise creates...

...The opening up of new markets, foreign or domestic, and the organizational development from the craft shop and the factory to such concerns as US Steel illustrate the same process of industrial mutation –if I may use that biological term- that incessantly revolutionizes the economic structure from within incessantly destroying old one, incessantly creating a new one. This process Creative Destruction is the essential fact about capitalism. It is what capitalism consists in and what every capitalist concern has got to live in...

Schumpeter's ideas inspired Nelson and Winter (1982), who are regarded as the pioneers of evolutionist approach. Because the evolutionary theory essentially depends on the propositions of Schumpeter, this approach is called "Schumpeterian Approach." Although this approach stresses the importance of innovation in terms of sustainable economic activities, it was a neglected factor until the arrival of Internal Growth Theories. Solow (1957) included the technology factor among the factors influencing economic growth but considered it as an "external" factor. Internal Growth Theories developed by economists like Romer (1986, 1987, 1990) and Lucas (1988) in the second half of 1980s created a turning point as they argued that economic growth was determined internally by research and development, human capital and technological developments. Being one of the leading figures of Internal Growth theories, Lucas and his study (1988) have a distinct significance for the innovation process. Human capital modeled by Lucas (1988) and defined as "knowledge, skills and experience of an educated workforce essentially depending on labor" (Tiryakioglu, 2008, p. 310), can be activated within the innovation system as long as governments implement the long-term policies decisively and systematically.

National Innovation System, used to describe the institutional structure that ensures the operation of technological development process, was taken into consideration conceptually for the first time by Bengt-Ake Lundwall and Christopher Freeman. Freeman (1987, p.1) defines it as "*the network of institutions in the public and private sectors whose activities and interactions initiate, import, modify and diffuse new technologies*." As to Lundwall (1992), National Innovation System is "as much about research and discovery made by the economic structures and institutional entities as it is about their aspects and elements affecting education as well." Taymaz (2001, p. 27) argues that National Innovation System operates influencing all the other systems in the economy and divides it into two sub-branches as *"regional innovation systems"* and *"technological systems/ industry clusters."* Taymaz (2001, p. 27) also suggests a one step further system, namely *"global innovation systems"* for the places where the international flow of information and interaction are important.

With the National Innovation Systems developed to manage and direct the technological developments and changes, Regional Innovation Systems are also coming to the forefront to such an extent that the latter leaves the former behind. However, regional innovation system is not totally independent from the national innovation system (Lenger, 2006, p. 141). According to the Oslo Guidebook (2005, p. 39), regional innovation system can only develop in parallel with the national innovation system. The argument that the national innovation system's approach to provide solutions on the national level may in turn create certain problems (Lenger, 2006, p. 141) has attracted the attention to the regional innovation system. In fact, the roots of this attention go back to 1980s. The most important factor influential during the process is to transform the opportunities created by regional differences into competitive power.

In line with this view, Storper (2001, p. 148) gives a list of the reasons why regional policies are preferred to nation or EU-wide policies:

1. There are principal-agent problems at higher levels of territorial scale: implementing a policy over much larger groups of principals enhances the probability that governing agents will deviate from the desires of the principals
2. There are significant externalities of implementation at the higher level, enabling free-rider behavior in some places or incentive problems in others
3. There are excessively high transactions costs to centralized implementation, usually due to information impactedness; many forms of infrastructure development or environmental regulation
4. There are significant regional "asset specificities," such that these assets would be underutilized if not handled in a regionally-specific way. These specificities are generally relational (networks of people, the conventional content of their relations, the codes they use to communicate, the trust or methods of verification they use to carry out their relations); or informational (the

tacit or only partially-codified information, language, symbols they use for economic coordination)

Asheim and Coenen (2005, p. 1177) define regional innovation system that springs from regional learning as "the institutional infrastructure supporting innovation within the production structure of a region." Cooke et al. (2003, p. 367) argue that regional innovation systems have two subsystems related to the production and use of knowledge. Coordination between the producers of theoretical knowledge and those transforming the theoretical knowledge into economic value so as to ensure efficiency (METU-STPS, 1999) indicates the importance of these subsystems under regional innovation system. Activating the regional innovation system processes of knowledge production and transforming it to economic value, regional innovation strategies, whose implementations are diffused into larger areas day by day, are facilitating the development of innovative production factors. Regional innovation strategy is defined as the sum of methodological studies covering regional management, finance, production, trade, education and structuring and ensuring the optimization of regional innovation system with such expectations as the formation of competitive structures, improvement of social welfare and development of employment opportunities (Arıkan et al., 2003, p. 154). The aim of a Regional Innovation Strategy project is to develop an innovation strategy which, by taking into account the specific conditions of the region it covers, contributes to enhancing the region's innovation capabilities and competitiveness. In order for this to happen, the strategy needs to have political and institutional backing for its implementation, and be accompanied by an action plan with concrete measures to be launched in the region (IRE, 2005, p. 5).

Regional innovation strategies formed in accordance with these purposes are shaped in three steps:

- At the "**definition**" level, also referred to as stage 0, studies are shaped according to the following targets: (1) Securing a Relevant Project, (2) Securing a Good Project Delivery Organization and (3) Raising Awareness and Gaining Broad Commitment (IRE, 2005, p. 6)
- At the level of "**analysis**" or so-called Stage 1, the innovative potential and capacity of the region are evaluated. The objectives of Regional Innovation Strategy stage 1 are manifolds (1) To identify crucial issues to be addressed in the regional innovation strategy and action plan (2) To map the reality in the region from a system point of view (3) To understand the region's positioning in an international comparison, (4) To achieve consensus amongst the key players on the analysis results and their use and (5) To strengthen the commitment of the key players to the Regional Innovation Strategy Project (IRE, 2006, p. 6)
- Stage 2 is the stage of "**strategy definition, evaluation, monitoring and implementation mechanisms, pilot projects.**" Second stage of a Regional Innovation Strategy project involves the following activities: (1) To design a regional innovation strategy including priorities recommendations and measures/projects based on the analysis; (2) To elaborate an action plan for the implementation of the regional innovation strategy; (3) To define, select and test the Regional Innovation Strategy pilot actions based on the action plan; (4) To establish a monitoring system for the implementation of the regional innovation strategy; (5) To formulate recommendations for the further development of the regional innovation strategy beyond the completion of the Regional Innovation Strategy Project (IRE, 2007, p. 5)

Having the ability to discover the regional potential and to increase the competitive power with their structures, implementations and zones of influence, Regional Innovation Strategies are the pioneers of knowledge-based regional development. Since 1994, the number of regions whose regional innovation strategy, regional innovation and technology transfer strategies and infrastructure have been developed is over 150 (Elçi et al., 2008, p. 49). Developing countries which are able to realize and make use of this strategy, whose implementations are growing gradually, will be able to increase both national and international competitive power thanks to these kinds of regional moves.

IMPLEMENTATIONS OF REGIONAL INNOVATION STRATEGIES IN EUROPE

Regional research and technological development and innovation (RDTI) strategies have become one crucial and decisive (and perhaps unique) component of any "regional development policy". Thus regional development policies have seen their agenda very much occupied by objectives in terms of competitiveness, a significant departure from earlier periods when regional development policies used to be more concerned with equity (Barchter & Yuill, 2001).

Because of its co-evolution in academic as well as policy spheres, the concept of Regional Innovation Strategy has acquired a strong analytical and normative connotation simultaneously. In analytical terms, the Regional Innovation Strategy concept, in line with that of the learning region, is the outcome of an intellectual debate at the intersection of two bodies of work: the organization and systemness of innovation on the one hand, and spatial agglomeration on the other hand (Morgan, 1997).

In 1994 EU launched the Regional Innovation Strategies as the most active exercise in the promotion of R&D and innovation policies at the regional level with the aim of offering regional stakeholders a common platform to promote, design, implement, manage and evaluate the region's R&D and innovation policy (Zabala-Iturriagagoitia *et al.*, 2008). Regional Innovation Strategy initiative was introduced in 1994 as an instrument to promote STI policy implementation at the regional level aiming at "stimulating the development of clusters ... that combine industrial, technological and geographical advantages ... (which) requires the active involvement of all the actors concerned ... (and in which) the main emphasis should be on a horizontal, transsectoral and multidisciplinary approach" (European Commission, 1993).

The main aim of this Regional Innovation Strategy initiative was the design of an innovation oriented strategy for the regions (Oughton *et al.,* 2002). Other goals included (European Commission, 1998 and 19991999):

- to promote more open and consensus-based processes for developing regional policies
- to create an innovation culture
- to identify regional firms' needs in terms of innovation support services
- to target and strengthen identified small and medium-sized enterprise (SME) growth sectors and clusters
- to coordinate the actions of existing innovation support structures
- to increase inter-firm and public-private cooperation and networking
- to develop a horizontal, transectoral and multidisciplinary approach
- to identify new pilot innovation projects in firms and/or new innovation policy schemes
- to exploit the European dimension through engaging in interregional cooperation and benchmarking of policies and methods

Adoption of the Lisbon strategy at the EU summit in March 2000 has for its goal to present both the deep conviction of the Member States to start a principle reform of the social-economic system and to provide evidence to their ambition, optimism and faith that it is realizable. Thorough economic analysis establishes definite lagging behind of the EU in comparison with the development of the USA economy-slower rates and smaller opportunities for creation and implementation of new technologies, particularly in the field of information and communication innovations. The Lisbon strategy has an ambitiously defined target for the radical transformation of the European economy in 2010 as "the most competitive and the most dynamic knowledge-based economy in the world, capable of sustainable economic growth with more and better jobs and greater social cohesion". In order to achieve this objective, the following regulatory activities and the concentration of public finance are envisaged (Radev *at al,* 2007):

- Fast transition to knowledge-based economy including development of information society, R&D, qualification and skills improvement
- Liberalization and integration of these sectors and markets that have not been taken in by the common market: telecommunications, power engineering, transport, posts and financial services
- Development of entrepreneurship, deregulation and bigger support on the part of administration, easier access to funds and technologies, provision of conditions for real competition and restriction of possibilities for state subsidies
- Increasing the number of jobs and change in the social model: increase of professional activity, flexibility of labor market, improvement of education, modernization of the social insurance system, reduction of poverty and social isolation
- Protection of the environment: restriction of factors leading to climate changes and preservation of natural resources

Beneficiaries of the Lisbon strategy are all Member States of the EU. Its realization is carried out through open method of coordination, which includes:

- Coordination of common goals
- Including these goals in the national and regional programs taking into consideration the specific ways of attaining them
- Coordination of the common methods for evaluating the extent to which these goals are achieved (indicators, benchmarking)
- Monitoring, evaluation, comparison and exchange of good practices

In 2005 the EU analyzed the achievements of the Lisbon strategy and came to the conclusion that lagging behind was at hand in some of its basic parameters and that the differences between the EU and the leading innovative economies in the world were not overcome. When this lagging behind was combined with the realization of the new realities in the Community – enlargement of the EU with 10 new states and the accession of Bulgaria and Romania in 2007, the European Council was forced to adopt "A New Start for Lisbon Strategy (European Commission, 2005). With this document, the EU reforms the rules for the distribution of the resources in the Structural and Cohesive funds during the period of 2007-2013, by means of which the cohesive policy in support of growth and employment will be implemented. This policy is based on:

- priority for growth, employment and innovations
- decreasing financial instruments from 6 to 3 and the aims of intervention from 9 to 3
- improvement of cohesive policy management through
  - Elaboration of strategic guidelines of the EU
  - Elaboration of the national strategic referent framework for realization of cohesive policy on the national level

Table 1. Regions participating in regional innovation strategy pilot project by country and year

Country	Regional Technology Plans (RTP)	Regional Innovation Strategies (RISs)	Regional Innovation and Technology Transfer Strategies (RITTS)
Austria	1994 - 1996	1997 – 1999, Niederösterreich	1994-2000, Tirol, Salzburg, South Lower Austria
Belgium		Limburg	Flanders
Spain	Castilla y Leon	Aragon, Castilla la Mancha, Extremadura, Galicia, Pais Vasco	Asturias, Andalucia, Illes Balears Canarias, Cataluna, Madrid, Murcia, Valencia
Finland		Northern, Ostrobothnia Kainuu and Lapland	East Finland
France	Lorraine	Auvergne	Aquitaine, Ile de France, Nord-Pas de Calais, Rhone-Alpes
Germany	Halle-Leipzig-Dessau	Wesser Ems	Aachen, Berlin, Brandenburg, Bremen, Hamburg, Lüneburg,, Neubrandenburg-Greifswald, South Brandenburg, Reinland-Pfalz
Greece	Kentriki Makadonia	Dytiki Makadonia, Epirus, Sterea Elada, Thessalia	Crete, Eastern Makedonia and Thrace, North Aegean, Thessalia
Ireland		Shannon	Ireland
Italy		Abruzzo, Calabria, Puglia	East Lombardy, Marche, Milano, Sicily, Trento, Tuscany
The Nedherlands			Umbria, New Holland, North Brabant, Overijsel Rotterdam, Utrecht
Portugal		Norte	Lisbon and Tagus Valley
Sweden		Norbotten	East Sweden, North Sweden, South, Sweden, Stockholm, Uppsala, Western Sweden
UK	Wales	West Midlands, Western Scotland, Yorkshire & the Humber	East England, East Midlands, Highlands and Islands, Kent, London South, North London, Oxfordshire, South Coast Metropole

Source: *(Adapted from* Zabala *et al.*, 2008*)*

- Elaboration of operative programs (OP) for determining particular actions and measures in accordance with priorities and financial instruments
- Management and selection of projects financed according to different OP
- Annual monitoring, evaluation and actualization

Lisbon strategy is based on steady, homogeneous and one-way development of all regions of Europe on the knowledge-based economy. Some of the major instruments for attaining this goal are "Regional Innovation Strategy" projects. Their realization aims to increase the innovation potential of separate regions' economies giving an account of their specific conditions and strong sides.

Since 1996, many European regions have participated in Regional Innovation Strategy pilot projects. We can see these projects in Table 1.

In addition, Regional Innovation Strategy initiative counts on a very significant support structure from the European Commission. As a matter of fact, nowadays the IRE (Innovation Regions in Europe) Network constitutes one of the most relevant sources for carrying out bench-marking exercises on innovation policies in European regions, with more than 235 regions currently gathering the network. Its main target is to ease the exchange of experiences and good practices among those European regions enhancing their capacity to support innovation and competitiveness through the development and implementation of Regional Innovation Strategies and their schemes (Zabala *et al.*, 2008, pp. 1151).

LEADER IMPLEMENTATIONS OF REGIONAL INNOVATION STRATEGIES IN TURKEY

The fast transformation experienced with the 1990s has led to the evolution of regional development policies into knowledge-based development policies. This transformation requires development based on the "evaluation of the innovative capacities of the regions by determining their strengths and weaknesses, opportunities and threats." If this approach forming the basis of Regional Innovation Strategies is combined with applicable policies in an operating network, it will promote both regional and national competition. In other words, development to be achieved through transforming regions into learning regions will come to mean an increase in the competitive power.

The growing importance of regional development in recent years has become more prominent with the increase in efforts for minimizing the regional inequalities and discovering regional potentials. The results of the indicators showing regional differences suggest that Turkey needs to give priority to implementing regional development policies.

The inequality of income distribution[3] in different regions is regarded as the first indicator that shows the urgency and significance of regional development policies. According to year 2000 data, one forth of regional added value produced in Turkey belongs to Istanbul region alone. Aegean Region and the East Marmara region are in the second rank following Istanbul. North Eastern Anatolian region and Middle Eastern Anatolian region are the ones which produce the least added value. As the indicators show, there is a huge difference between the regions providing the most added value and those providing the least. This inequality is also valid for the relative added value per capita for the city, as could be seen in Table 2.

Claiming that the differences of income in different regions result from the differences in efficiency, Filiztekin (2008, p. 54) maintains that while the most efficient city was 9,5 times more efficient than the least efficient city in 1980, this gap became deeper in 2000 and the former became more than 11 times more efficient than the latter. If the pattern of inequality in the distribution of income in the last twenty years is tracked, it is seen that the "absolute convergence" hypothesis is not valid for Turkey[4].

The target of policies that will ensure both the regional development and the optimization of existing resources in accordance with the potential power of the region is to create regional specialization. The clusters that will be formed in this way will provide regional interaction and thus result in increased efficiency. Filiztekin (2008, p. 60) considers the importance of regional specialization as twofold and argues that regional specialization according to their factor intensity ensures regions to have comparative superiority over other regions. In this way regional growth and development will be faster. In addition, this growth process will result in the growth of other regions. On the other hand, with the specialization of different regions in different products, it will be possible to distribute the risks against the external shocks that the sector might face.

In a foresight study by Elçi et al. conducted in accordance with the results of the workshop organized by TURKONFED, the sectors that might have comparative superiority according to regional factor intensities are listed in Table 3.

When these foresights are considered according to the regional added value per capita indicators, it is seen that regions that produce relatively more added value (such as Istanbul, Western Anatolia and Central Anatolia) should specialize in knowledge-intensive sectors. On the other hand, the regions that produce less added value (like Eastern and Southeastern Anatolia) should specialize in labor and capital-intensive sectors. In this way, it would be relatively easier to design and implement policies in line with the regional resources. However, it is also possible to

Table 2. Regional added value and regional added value per capita (1980-2000)

	Rate in the total amount (%)	Rate in the total amount (%)	Relative Added Value Per Capita for the City (Turkey=1)	
	1980	2000	1980	2000
Istanbul	19,4	23,3	1,83	1,58
Western Marmara	5,8	4,9	1,15	1,15
Aegean Region	16,4	15,3	1,24	1,16
Eastern Marmara	10,5	12,6	1,36	1,49
Western Anatolia	10,2	10,6	1,03	1,11
Mediterranean	11,8	12,0	1,00	0,93
Central Anatolia	4,5	4,3	0,66	0,69
Western Black Sea	8,3	5,7	0,83	0,79
Eastern Black Sea	3,9	2,8	0,63	0,60
Northeastern Anatolia	2,0	1,4	0,42	0,37
Middleeastern Anatolia	2,9	2,4	0,50	0,43
Southeastern Anatolia	4,3	4,9	0,54	0,50

Resource: Filiztekin, A. (2008). Türkiye'de Bölgesel Farklar ve Politikalar, (Publication No.TÜSİAD-T/2008-09/471). Türkiye: TÜSİAD, pp. 46-47 [adapted from Table 1 and 2]

consider the influence of many other determining factors like the demographic structure, employment rates, the capacity and the quality of human capital, the potential of natural resources and the atmosphere in the design and implementation of the policies. It becomes difficult to determine the right policies and to construct innovation strategies for the regions with potential by optimizing all of these determining factors. For Turkey, there are two reasons in particular that make the discovery and transformation of regional potentials into actors of development more difficult (Filiztekin, 2008, p. 93):

1. Either not implementing the policies specified in written texts or implementing them inefficiently

Table 3. Sectoral foresights according to regional potentials

Region	Sectors
Western Anatolia	-Electronics and software,-Agriculture based technologies, -Eco Technologies
Marmara and Northern Anatolia	-Milk and Dairy Husbandry
Eastern Mediterranean	-Agriculture-Nourishment, -Logistics, -Textile
Eastern and Southeastern Anatolia	- Agriculture-Nourishment,- Natural stones, Tourism
Central Blacksea	- Agriculture-Nourishment, -Construction supplies
Eastern Blacksea	-Shipping Industry
Istanbul	-Package, - Elevator and Escalator, - Logistics - Chemistry/ Environment
Central Anatolia	-Machine and Appliance Industry, - Life and Science Technologies

***Resource**: (Adapted from*Elçi *et al.*, 2008*)*

2. Making policies that are far from being "creative" under the influence of international institutions

In addition to these two reasons, there are other factors that prevent the regional potentials to be realized such as economic and political instability, giving priority to the national policies rather than the regional ones, inadequate level of education offered to the young population and unemployment.

In order to realize her innovative potential and to make progress in this area, Turkey took her first step towards transforming the threats into opportunities by developing an Innovation Strategy for Mersin Region. Besides Mersin, Izmir and Eskisehir are making preliminary studies to have such a strategy. What is more, a study called "Innovation Valley" has been implemented in Gaziantep to raise consciousness.

IMPLEMENTATIONS OF REGIONAL INNOVATION STRATEGIES IN MERSIN

RIS-Mersin Project is a competitive example of a project that was implemented successfully in the process of modeling the regional development efforts of Mersin. This project, which was operated under the Sixth Framework Plan with the co-sponsoring of European Commission, enabled Mersin to become a member of the network of Innovative Regions of Europe (IRE). RIS-Mersin Project prepared for 2002-2016 term has been carried out under the leadership of Mersin Governorship with the coordination of METU Technopolis and the consultancy of Technopolis Group. Mersin Chamber of Commerce and Industry, Mersin-Tarsus Organized Industrial Zone, Mersin University and EPIRUS Region Business Development and Innovation Center (from Greece) are the partners of the project.

RIS-Mersin's basic elements were selected as the development of Mersin Innovation System and the culture of Mersin, increasing the innovative activities of the existing enterprises, realizing the regional potential in key sectors (such as agriculture, industry, logistics and tourism) and the development of knowledge producers. Among the linear targets of the project are building a culture of innovation and an agreement and confidence about innovation-based development among the actors of innovation system and the elimination of the obstacles caused by infrastructure, creation of an attractive image for the region and investment in the development of human resources.

According to Regional Innovation Strategy of Mersin, -Draft 1- the advantages to be gained are the following:

- Forming an urban consciousness by encouraging the stakeholders in the city to have shared beliefs and hopes about the "future"
- Establishing the tradition of working together among the stakeholders of the city
- Promoting the city both at home and in the world and bettering its image
- Starting the tradition of making projects
- Increasing the interest of the young people into entrepreneurship and innovation
- Increasing the interest of the firms into innovation
- Increase in the demands for the experience of Mersin's innovation strategy development all around Turkey
- Creating the opportunity to work with firms and institutions in Europe

Under RIS-Mersin, four different pilot projects were made: Entrepreneur 33, R&D 33, Export 33 and 1st Mersin Innovation Competition. In addition, steps were taken to build the necessary institutional structures for innovation in the region. "Regional Innovation Council," "Agriculture-Food Platform", "Tourism Platform", "Logistics Platform" and "Office of Technology Transfer" are some of the leading structures. The purpose of the pilot projects developed under the project was to formalize the attempts for innovation-based development (Elçi et al., 2008, p. 52).

The success of RISs-Mersin, which was the first example of *Regional Innovation Strategy* in Turkey, has supported and encouraged the implementations that started in Izmir, the biggest port city of the Aegean Region, and in Eskisehir, the industry city in Central Anatolia.

PRELIMINARY IMPLEMENTATIONS OF REGIONAL INNOVATION STRATEGIES IN IZMIR

Studies to form regional innovation strategies in Izmir, the largest port city of the Aegean Region, are conducted by Izmir Development Agency with the consultation of Technopolis Group. The studies made under this framework are not directly for determining a strategy, but to carry out a pre-study. Studies made by Izmir Development Agency are shaped so as to prepare a Regional Development Plan for 2009-2013. The results of the plan will provide an opportunity to develop an extensive strategy for the region.

As a result of a pilot project carried out by MEDIBTIKAR, a pre-study bringing together the general information concerning Izmir's innovation capacity and a Swot analysis were made. The target set for 2009 within this framework is to decide on Izmir's Innovation Strategy with the participation of regional actors in line with the Regional Development Plan and research results.

PRELIMINARY IMPLEMENTATIONS OF REGIONAL INNOVATION STRATEGIES IN ESKISEHIR

A similar study is being conducted in Eskisehir, which is one of the most powerful industrial cities of the Central Anatolian Region, under the leadership of Eskisehir Chamber of Industry. This study which started with the attempt, direction and contribution of the regional actors in order to form a Regional Innovation Strategy, which is called the Project of Capacity Building for Innovation Strategies in Eskisehir, is operated in collaboration with Eskisehir Chamber of Industry and Turkey Technology Development Foundation. This Project, which started in the beginning of 2008, was designed for a year. The steps taken in this timeframe are as follows (ESİNKAP; 2009):

- **Step 0:** Formation of Direction Council
- **Step 1:** Consciousness Raising
- **Step 2:** Technological and Environmental Competency Evaluation
- **Step 3:** Needs Analysis
- **Step 4:** Evaluation of Technology/ Environmental Needs/Talents
- **Step 5:** Training for Preparing Projects
- **Step 6:** Project Market
- **Step 7:** Evaluation and Follow-up
- **Step 8:** Forming Regional Interface

The basic purpose of "R&D Project Market", designed as the last step of the project as a two-day activity to be the first activity of year 2009, was to bring together representatives from universities, research and industry institutions and to ensure the active participation of the parties so that they can present each other the concrete R&D project proposals in order to seek opportunities for cooperation. This activity which was a success shows that Eskisehir took the first steps effectively in forming a regional innovation strategy.

TURKEY'S ADAPTATION TO REGIONAL INNOVATIVE STRATEGIES

As the developing countries give priority to national developments, the formation and thus the implementation of the regional development policies and strategies have been delayed. Like most other developing countries, Turkey was not able to reach the optimum level in terms of regional development policies partly because already existing regional strategies and policies were not implemented. Another reason why this process was postponed is the make up of the bureaucracy which prevented the production and implementation of policies that would underline the regional differences. Turkey's attempts focusing on Southeastern Anatolian Project in 1990s helped her gain experience both at the national and local level (Dulupçu, 2006). Yet, due to the losses resulting from the economic instabilities of the time, it was not possible to transform these experiences into regional innovation policies.

Turkey's becoming an EU candidate on equal footing with the Helsinki Summit in 1999 was a turning point for the regional innovation strategies among others. The importance given to regional development by the EU and the significant budget allocation for the projects aiming to eliminate the regional differences have urged Turkey to take action. The fact that regional development was given an important place in Turkey's 8th and 9th Five-Year Development Plans (SPO, 2000 and SPO, 2006) is an indicator of the awareness on the issue. Still, according to Dulupçu (2004), for this awareness to turn into a process producing added value and to create successful projects, Turkey needs to answer the following questions immediately:

1. How were the regional economies that have risen by synthesizing the innovation with regional proximity able to achieve this high performance?
2. Which tools should be activated and used in order to achieve success in the regional scale as it becomes more and more appropriate in terms of policy implementation?

Regions in Europe that have developed Regional Innovation Strategy and regional innovation and technology transfer strategies and infrastructure (RITTS) with the support of European Commission since 1994 set examples for Turkey. In this process, the fact that Turkey's first Regional Innovation Strategy implementation, namely Mersin was implemented with the support and methodology of the European Commission under the European Union's 6th Framework Program makes it easy to find the answers for both of the questions. In addition, EU's support and supervision of the projects implemented in Turkey has provided a great opportunity for the success of the adaptation processes. What needs to be considered in this process is the question whether the cultural and social differences determined via analyses during the first steps of the strategy will turn into elements of resistance or not. In other words, carrying out a thorough study rather than making a technical adaptation will ensure the success and sustainability of the strategies.

Ensuring the regional development carries a great significance for Turkey which has a large young population and stands out among the other developing countries with her strategic location and potentials for human resources, agriculture and commerce. One of the -most important- ways of transforming Turkey's opportunities into strengths is the discovery and activation of regional potentials. Departing from this frame of reference, Regional Innovation Strategies, whose implementations started in three different cities in Turkey, are important attempts to activate regional dynamics in Turkey.

CONCLUSION

Regional innovation strategies which emerged during the mid 90s and were implemented especially in the developing regions of the world are significant for the transformation of both the knowledge produced in the regional scale and the added value it created into competitive power in the national and global scale. To put it another way, regional policies and strategies gain more significance day by day so as to have global competitive power. Regional and local innovation systems not only ensure efficiency in themselves but also make national innovation systems more efficient with the synergy they create. Cooperations and networks developed in this way make the collaboration between those that produce knowledge (universities, research institutes, etc.) and those that transform knowledge into economic value (such as innovative firms) and thus enable the diffusion of knowledge into the base. This diffusion sets the ground for the innovative local firms to become global firms or trademarks. The operation of this process depends on the design and more importantly on the implementation of the regional policies and strategies so that they support the national innovation strategies.

Coming into being thanks to the cooperation of public sector, private sector and university, these strategies have been realized via RIS-Mersin in Turkey. They could be considered something new for Turkey. However, Turkey's relatively new encounter with these strategies creates a great many opportunities. The raised consciousness into regional economies reflected in the last two development plans, the support of European Commission for the leader implications and Turkey's profile which is full of potentials standing out among the other developing countries are the factors that will ensure Turkey's success in the implementation of these strategies. The more Turkey moves away from the obstruction of the bureaucracy and traditional management policies, the closer she will be to transforming these strategies into a process creating added value. When Turkey starts realizing these strategies, regional potentials will come to the forefront. Thus by turning her regional innovation skills into products and services that have added value, Turkey will have a potential to achieve rapid social and economic development and therefore increase her significance for the national and international (innovative) investors.

REFERENCES

Arıkan, C., Akyos, M., Durgut, M., & Göker, A. (2003). *Ulusal İnovasyon Sistemi, Kavramsal Çerçeve, Türkiye İncelemesi ve Ülke Örnekleri* (Publication No: TÜSİAD-T/2003/10/362). Türkiye: TÜSİAD.

Asheim, B. T., & Coenen, L. (2005). Knowledge Bases and Regional Innovation Systems: Comparing Nordic Clusters. *Research Policy, 34*(8), 1173–1190. doi:10.1016/j.respol.2005.03.013

Bachtler, J., & Yuill, D. (2001). *Policies and Strategies for Regional Development: A Shift Paradigm*? (No. 46 EPRC) [*Regional and Industrial Policy Research Paper*]. University of Strathclydee.

CEC. (2000). *Presidency Conclusions of the Lisbon European Council, March 23/24*. Brussels, Belgium: Commission of the European Communities.

CEC. (2001). *The Regional Dimension of the European Research Area*. Brussels, Belgium: Commission of the European Communities.

Cooke, P., Roper, S., & Wylie, P. (2003). The Golden Thread of Innovation and Northern Ireland's Evolving Regional Innovation System. *Regional Studies, 37*(4), 365–379. doi:10.1080/0034340032000074406

Dulupçu, M. A. (2004). *Bolognese Yenilik (İnovasyon) Stratejileri: Türkiye'de Bölgesel Gelişme İçin Alternatif Olabilir mi? 4*. İzmir İktisat Kongresi, Ankara: SPO.

Dulupçu, M. A. (2006). Bölgesel Politikalar Kopyalanabilir Mi? Bölgeselleş(tir)me (Yönetim) Karşısında (Yeni) Bölge(sel)cilik (Yönetişim). In *Bölgesel Yönetişim Sempozyumu*. Ankara, Türkiye: METU-TEPAV.

Elçi, S., Karataylı, İ., & Karaata, S. (2008). *Bölgesel İnovasyon Merkezleri: Türkiye İçin Bir Model Önerisi* (Publication No. TÜSİAD-T/2008-12/477). Türkiye: TÜSİAD.

ESİNKAP. (2009). *Eskişehir İli İnovasyon Stratejileri İçin Kapasite Oluşturma Projesi*. Türkiye Teknoloji Geliştirme Vakfı.

European Commission. (1993). *White Paper on Growth, Competitiveness, and Employment. The Challenges and Ways Forward into the 21st Century*. Brussels, Belgium: European Commission.

European Commission. (1997). *Methodology Guides for RIS Projects: Guidelines for Project Managers*. Brussels, Belgium: European Commission.

European Commission. (1998). *Regional Innovation Strategy Pilot Projects. Article 10 of the European Regional Development Fund*. Brussels, Belgium: European Commission.

European Commission. (1999). *A Guide to Regional Innovation Strategies*. Brussels, Belgium: European Commission.

European Commission. (2005). *Working Together for Growth and Jobs: A New Start for the Lisbon Strategy*. Brussels, Belgium: European Commission.

Filiztekin, A. (1998). *Convergence Across Industries and Provinces in Turkey* (No. 1998/08). İstanbul, Türkiye: Koç University.

Filiztekin, A. (2008). *Türkiye'de Bölgesel Farklar ve Politikalar* (Publication No.TÜSİAD-T/2008-09/471). Türkiye: TÜSİAD.

Freeman, C. (1987). *Technology Policy and Economic Performance: Lessons from Japan*. London: Frances Pinter.

Freeman, C. (1988). Japan: A New Institutional System of Innovation? In G. Dosi, C. Freeman, R. Nelson, G. Silverberg, & L. Soete (Eds.), *Technical Change and Economic Theory*. London: Pinter.

Freeman, C. (1989). New Technology and Catching Up. *European Journal of Development Research*, *1*(1), 85–93. doi:10.1080/09578818908426503

Freeman, C., & Soete, L. (1997). *The Economics of Industrial Innovation*. London: Pinter.

Gezici, F., & Hewings, G. J. D. (2004). Regional Convergence and the Economic Performance of Peripheral Areas in Turkey. *Review of Urban and Regional Development Studies*, *16*(2), 113–132. doi:10.1111/j.1467-940X.2004.00082.x

Gürak, H. (2006). *Ekonomik Büyüme ve Küresel Ekonomi*. Bursa, Türkiye: Ekin Yayınevi.

Innovating Regions in Europe Network-IRE. (2005). *RIS Methodological Guide Stage Zero*. IRE Secretariat.

Innovating Regions in Europe Network-IRE. (2006). *RIS Methodological Guide Stage One*. IRE Secretariat.

Innovating Regions in Europe Network-IRE. (2007). *RIS Methodological Guide Stage Two*, IRE Secretariat.

Karaca, O. (2004). *Türkiye'de Bölgelerarası Gelir Farklılıkları: Yakınsama var mı?* (Discussion Paper, No.: 2004/7). Ankara, Türkiye: Turkish Economic Association.

Lenger, A. (2006). Bölgesel Yenilik Sistemleri ve Devletin Rolü: Türkiye'deki Kurumsal Yapı ve Devlet Üniversiteleri . *Egean Academic Review*, *6*(2), 141–155.

List, F. (1841). *The National System of Political Economy* (S. S. Lloyd, Trans.). London: Longmans, Green and Co.

Lucas, R. E. (1988). On The Mechanics of Economic Development. *Journal of Monetary Economics*, *22*(2), 2–42.

Lundvall, B.-Å. (1988). Innovation as an Interactive Process: From User-Producer Interaction to National Systems of Innovation. In G. Dosi, C. Freeman, R. Nelson, G. Silverberg, & L. Soete (Eds.), *Technological Change and Economic Theory.* London: Pinter.

Lundvall, B.-Å. (1992). Introduction. In B. A. Lundvall (Ed.), *National Systems of Innovation: towards a theory of innovation and interactive learning.* London: Pinter.

Lundvall, B.-Å., Johnson, B., Andersen, E. S., & Dalum, B. (2002). National Systems of Production, Innovation and Competence Building. *Research Policy, 31*(2), 213–231. doi:10.1016/S0048-7333(01)00137-8

Mersin-RIS. (2008). *Mersin Bölgesel İnovasyon Stratejisi 2006-2016.* Ankara, Türkiye: MetuTechnopolis.

Middle East Technical University, Science and Technology Policies Reserarch Center (METU-STPS). (1999). *İnovasyonun Değişen Ortam ve Şartları, Hükümetlerin/Devletin Yeni Rolü, Aykut Göker (Derl.), METU-STPS Seminar Note.* Ankara, Türkiye: METU-STPS.

Morgan, K. (1997). The Learning Region: Institutions, Innovation and Regional Renewal. *Regional Studies, 31*(5), 491–503. doi:10.1080/00343409750132289

Nelson, R. (1988). Institutions Supporting Technical Change in the United States. In G. Dosi, C. Freeman, R. Nelson, G. Silverberg, & L. Soete (Eds.), *Technological Change and Economic Theory.* London: Pinter.

Nelson, R. (1993). *National Innovation Systems: A Comparative Analysis.* New York: Oxford University Press.

Nelson, R. R., & Rosenberg, N. (1993). Technical Innovation and National Systems. In R. Nelson (Ed.), *National Innovation Systems: A Comparative Analysis.* New York: Oxford University Press.

Nelson, R. R., & Winter, S. (1982). *An Evolutionary Theory of Economic Change.* Cambridge, MA: The Belknap Press.

OECD. (2005). *Oslo Manual: Proposed Guidelines for Collecting and Interpreting Technological Innovation Data.* Paris: OECD.

Oughton, C., Landabaso, M., & Morgan, K. (2002). The Regional Innovation Paradox: Innovation Policy and Industrial Policy. *The Journal of Technology Transfer, 27*(1), 97–110. doi:10.1023/A:1013104805703

Radev, D., Angelov, A., & Stamenov, S. (2007). Regional Innovation Strategy of the North-East Planning Region. *Advances in Bulgarian Science, 3*, 32–40.

Romer, P. (1986). Increasing Returns and Long-Run Growth. *The Journal of Political Economy, 94*(5), 1003–1037. doi:10.1086/261420

Romer, P. (1987). Growth Based on Increasing Returns Due to Specialization. *The American Economic Review, 77*(2), 56–62.

Romer, P. (1990). Endogenous Technological Change. *The Journal of Political Economy, 98*(5), 71–102. doi:10.1086/261725

Schumpeter, J. A. (1942). *Capitalism, Socialism and Democracy.* New York: Harper Torchbooks.

Solow, R. (1957). Technical Change and the Aggregate Production Function. *The Review of Economics and Statistics, 39*(3), 312–320. doi:10.2307/1926047

State Planning Organization (SPO). Türkiye. (2000). *Sekizinci Beş Yıllık Kalkınma Planı.* Ankara: SPO.

State Planning Organization (SPO). Türkiye. (2006). *Dokuzuncu Beş Yıllık Kalkınma Planı.* Ankara: SPO.

Storper, M. (2001). Regional Technology Policies in Europe: TSER1 Research Projects, 1998-2000, The Regional Level of Implementation of Innovation Policies. In *Proceedings of a Workshop held in Brussels.*

Taymaz, E. (2001). *Ulusal Yenilik Sistemi: Turkiye İmalat Sanayiinde Teknolojik Değişim ve Yenilik Süreçleri.* Ankara, Türkiye: TÜBİTAK/TTGV/DİE.

Temel, T., Tansel, A., & Albersen, P. J. (1999). Convergence and Spatial Patterns in Labor Productivity: Nonparametric Estimations for Turkey. *Journal of Regional Analysis and Policy, 29*(1), 3–19.

Tiryakioğlu, M. (2008). Beşeri Sermaye Yoksulluğu. *Egean Academic Review, 8*(1), 321–339.

Zabala-Iturriagagoitia, J. M., Jimenez-Saez, F., & Castro-Martnez, E. (2008). Evaluating European Regional Innovation. *Strategies . European Planning Studies, 16*(8), 1145–1160. doi:10.1080/09654310802315849

ENDNOTES

1 According to Gürak (2006, p.7), *"knowledge is the finding gathered and mentally evaluated by training, observation and experience to recognize understand and explain the facts and events."* Information is, however, "descriptive expressions that help eliminating the ambiguity about a certain topic."

2 Thesis of baby industry argues that industries that might have comparative superiority when developed should be protected from international competition temporarily until they reach the level of optimum production level. In this way, new established industries will be able to compete with the foreign producers thanks to the internal and external economies when they reach the optimum production volume.

3 The study from which the data is taken (Filiztekin, 2008) uses "Value Added for City" as income.

4 Some of the studies that have found such findings are Filiztekin (1998), Temel et al. (1999), Karaca (2004), Gezici and Hewings (2004).

Chapter 17
Governance-Based Regional Development and E-Government:
The Turkish Case

Mehmet Zahid Sobaci
Uludag University, Turkey

Bekir Parlak
Uludag University, Turkey

ABSTRACT

The notion of new regional development is built on the model of governance in Turkey. E-government has some serious potential of contributing to the implementation of this new notion of regional development. In this context, the aim of this chapter is to discuss the current state of the concept of regional development in Turkey and to analyze the contributions of e-government to the notion and applications of new regional development. Within this framework, initially, paradigmatic shift in regional development is analyzed. And then, the role and effect of e-government is explicated within the triangular relationship between development, good governance and e-government in socio-economic development. Subsequently, the notion of regional development in Turkey and its application is introduced from a historical perspective and the very recently adopted notion of new regional development is explained. Finally, the potential contributions of the e-government applications to this new notion of regional development in Turkey are analyzed.

INTRODUCTION

Development lies in the very heart of the trio of a strong state, strong economy and strong society. The critical value of development has taken on an essential and significant meaning in the new century in a way that it has never happened before. The most important trump that the countries possess in their race of development is the human resource, and the most important instrument is the efficiency and functionality of public administration. In fact, it is not a coincidence that those countries where public administration works effective, efficient and dynamic stick out in the race of development.

DOI: 10.4018/978-1-61520-709-1.ch017

Especially since 1950s, public administration is considered to be the most important instrument of development and the facilitating and stabilizing impact of an efficiently functioning public administration on development is welcome. In fact, even though development administration, considered to be a branch of public administration (Hossain, 2007; Siffin, 2001), has lagged a little behind since 1980s, it has today once again gained importance through studies and researches done on economic globalization, governance, decentralization, and information and communication technologies, and even become more important.

As a result of the perception of the significance of an efficiently and rationally functioning public administration in terms of social and economic development, especially the last quarter of the twentieth century has become a restructuring period of public administration. One of the primary developments that has led the public administration into reform is the improvements experienced in information and communication technologies (Heeks, 1999). In this context, one of the most prominent elements of the administrative reforms performed is the e-government applications.

In the process of globalization, the notion and applications of development are currently undergoing a transformation. The new development model is based on a multi-agent, participatory, dynamic and efficient notion of development shaped around the concept of "good governance". In this development model, a "multi-agent structure" in which such structures as local governments, regional organizations, public sector, NGOs and direct public support exist holds true. Central government is to function as a coordinator and catalyst in accordance with new public management in new development model. Therefore, "cooperation, coordination and monitoring" become all the more important. At this point, "the e-government facilities" have some serious potential in terms of facilitating the coordination and optimizing the cooperation. While e-government acts as "an integrator" among policies and their applications of the agents to take a role in development, it, on the other hand, may contribute significantly to resource optimization and efficient resource utilization that are primarily important for the notion of development.

Within this framework, aim of this study is to analyze the current state of the concept of regional development in Turkey and to discuss the contributions that the e-government can make to the applications in this field. The basic hypothesis of this study is the idea that the new notion of region-focused development can help countries to materialize their development in a more dynamic, economical and democratic fashion and e-government can contribute to this. The facilitating potential of e-government in this development model has the capacity of offering functional possibilities that no other instrument possesses.

In this context, initially, the change in the paradigm of regional development is analyzed in this study. And then, the role and effect of e-government is explicated within the triangular relationship between development-good governance-e-government in socio-economic development. Subsequently, the notion of regional development in Turkey and its application is introduced from a historical perspective, and the problems regarding the existing structure are clarified. Then, the very recently adopted notion of new regional development is explained. Finally, the potential contributions of the e-government applications to this new notion of regional development in Turkey are analyzed.

PARADIGMATIC SHIFT IN REGIONAL DEVELOPMENT: FROM TOP-DOWN TO BOTTOM-UP

The notion of development is ambiguous one and varies from region to region or from country to country. The concept of development can only be identified with an economically-focused notion

(Beer et al., 2003; Press, 1996). In this framework, the fact of local and regional development has historically been dominated by "economic issues" such as growth, revenue and employment (Pike et al., 2007).

However, since the criticism of the orthodox neo-classical economy in 1960s and 1970s and dissatisfaction with the current approaches, "alternative approaches" started to question the predominant economic focus regarding the local and regional development (Geddes & Newman, 1999; Vazquez-Barquero, 2002). The predominant economic focus regarding the local and regional development was enlarged to include social, ecological, political and cultural issues as well (Madon, 2000; Morgan, 2004). Within the framework of enlarged local and regional development, minimization of social inequality, promotion of environmental sustainability, instigation of a comprehensive state and governance and acceptance of cultural variability were emphasized (Pike et al., 2007). In this connection, in accordance with the perception of UNDP, the notion of development together with its economic and social dimensions should be perceived within a larger perspective to include efficiency and productivity, education, health, sustainability, human rights and the quality of democracy. In fact, the sustainable development that was accepted in the 1992 World Summit in Rio reflects such a large perspective and the latest phase of development reached today.

Today, in order for development to be materialized in a specific region together with its social and economic dimensions and to increase the living standards, a new approach regarding regional development has come up: the Bottom-Up Approach. Essentially, this approach comprises the theoretical framework of the mentality that a development starts at the bottom. In fact, it is stated that in the globalization era, local communities and regions are called to play a front line role in mobilizing internal and external assets to establish economical development initiatives to be materialized in a bottom-up fashion (Squazzino, in press) In parallel to this, the international aid organizations, since mid-1990s, have supported and advocated decentralized and participatory programs as an instrument of improving the provision of services and promoting the participation of local communities to their own development (Babajanian, 2005).

In parallel to a changing perception in development theory, there has been a substantial increase in the literature related to local and regional development since 1980s (Armstrong & Taylor, 2000; Blair & Reese, 1999; Blakely & Bradshow, 2002; Dudek, 2001; Dulupcu & Ozgur, 2006; Hudson, 2007; Pike et al., 2006; Pinder & Aldcroft, 1983; Stöhr & Taylor, 1981; Vazquez-Barquero, 2002). The bottom-up approach, endogenous development and community economic development in the literature can be regarded as concepts pointing towards a similar notion of policy regarding local and regional development (McCall, 2003; Polése & Shearmur, 2006). According to bottom-up approach, structural characteristics of regions have an important role to play in its development level.

In contrast to the top-down paradigm in which the decisions regarding regional development are taken by central governments without consulting the locals, the bottom-up approach basically envisages the mobilization of potentials in the region and materializing regional development within the framework of cooperation between public sector, private sector and NGOs. With such a notion of development, the local-regional agents are highlighted. In this context, the local governments, private sector representatives, NGOs and the regional agents are anticipated to take part in the process of decision making regarding regional development.

The new notion of regional development is basically built upon the model of governance. The bottom-up approach in whose heart lies such semi-autonomous institutions such as regional development agencies (RDAs), emerge as the application of regional governance. In fact, the RDAs are regarded as an instrument of governance model (Beer & Maude, 2005; Brown, 2005; Sobaci, 2008; Webb & Collis, 2000). For instance, governance at regional level was intended to be strengthened and one of the most important consequences of this purpose turned out to be the establishment of RDAs (Ayres & Pearce, 2004; Jeffery & Reilly, 2003; Jeffery & Mawson, 2002; Tomaney, 2002).

In order for new model of regional development to be better understood, it will be useful to comparatively review the traditional notion of development and governance-based new regional development. As a basis to this comparison one can make use of the criteria determined by Danson and colleagues (Danson et al., 2002). The authors characterize the notions of traditional and new-model ways of development under five headings being Organization, Operational Freedom, Economic Objectives, Mode of Operation, and Policy Instruments.

In this context, it is clear that there are some obvious differences between the traditional and new notion of development. The traditional notion of top-down development offers a model that is predicated on the national level, under the liability of government departments, single-agent and put into practice within the bureaucratic structure. The traditional notion that highlights national economic growth and interregional equalities puts on a nonselective and reactive appearance. Moreover, the traditional notion of development envisages realizing the specified targets especially through bureaucratic arrangements and financial instruments.

The bottom-up approach, on the other hand offers a model that is predicated on the regional level, takes the semi-autonomous institutions as the main agent and adopts a business-like management style. The new notion of development emphasizes a move towards from government to governance, from public administration to private sector, from centralization to decentralization and offers for national and local governments a development method, within this perspective, that is based on participation, autonomy, decentralization, efficiency and competency. The new model that has especially specified interregional competition and the growth of regional economy as an economic target, adopts a selective and proactive style of operation. On the base line of contemporary development approach, there lies the utilization of financial incentives substituting the bureaucratic regulation.

RDAs, in the implementation of the new notion of development, are gradually becoming widespread all over the world as structurally and operationally the most optimum organization proposed by this model. While the RDAs that have, on the one hand, spread over the developing countries, ensure the organization of development on the local and regional level, they, on the other hand, represent effectuating of the governance structure through its qualities of multi-agency and participation.

THE INDISPENSABLE DUO OF THE NEW NOTION OF DEVELOPMENT: GOOD GOVERNANCE AND E-GOVERNMENT

In the age of competition, an efficiently and rationally operating public administration is one of the most important leading factors in terms of fast and balanced development of countries and regions. Such as mechanism of public administration today is discussed within the framework of good governance. In other words, the elements inherent in the concept of good governance characterize a public administration believed to be today a prerequisite in terms of socio-economic development of countries. In this context, there is a universal consensus that good governance is a crucial instrument in the fulfilling of a sustainable development (AusAID, 2000; Ciborra & Navara, 2005; United Nations, 2003a; 2003b; UNDP, 1997).

The information and communication technologies, on the other hand, are instruments that will significantly contribute to the development of countries (DOI, 2001; Marker et al., 2002; Misuraca, 2007; UNDP, 2001). Given the utilization of the information and communication technologies in public administration, the very first application that springs to mind and is the most common one is in no doubt the e-government activities. E-government offers an unprecedented capacity and ability to the administrations at all levels in the implementation of efficient, transparent, dynamic and participatory public administration. In this context, e-government proves to be the most important and safest instrument for the implementation of good governance.

In fact, the discussion over good governance and e-government are closely related to one other. It is simply because it has common goals such as administrative efficiency, the quality of the public services and democratic participation (Haldenwang, 2004). In short, today the fact of e-government is very crucial for the countries to implement the fact of good governance and good governance itself in terms of sustainable development.

The notion of governance has been supported by international organizations (such as WB, UN, OECD, EU) after especially 1990s and has evolved and developed through the reports consecutively issued by the WB (World Bank, 1992; 1994; 1997). The notion of governance with its current implication was used for the first time in 1989 in report on Africa's development by the Word Bank and was defined as "the exercise of political power to manage a nation's affairs" (World Bank, 1989, p. 60). The UN also defined the concept of governance in a similar fashion. Governance according to UNDP (1997) is "the exercise of political, economic and administrative authority to manage a nation's affairs. It is the complex mechanisms, processes, relationships and institutions through which citizens and groups articulate their interests, exercise their rights and obligations and mediate their differences" (p. 9). Governance signifies multilateral relations instead of unilateral ones. It refers an interactive policy formation process at a multi-agent structure comprising central government, local governments, NGOs and private sector. In fact, Rhodes (1996) stated that we live in centreless society in polycentric state characterized by multiple centres and central government is not supreme.

Good governance is an expression of a concept that signifies the current state of governance model. Good governance means the management of the resources and internal affairs of a country in an open, transparent, accountable, equitable fashion and responsive to the needs of the public (AusAID, 2000). In this sense, participation, consensus-oriented, accountability, transparency, responsiveness, effectiveness and efficiency, equality and inclusiveness, and the rule of law emerge as the qualities of good governance (UNESCAP, 2008). Good governance with such qualities is stated to be indispensable for the building of peaceful, prosperous and democratic societies (Kim et al., 2005). This particular perspective of good governance is also adopted by the EU and good governance with the qualities mentioned above is regarded as one of the most crucial factor to achieve sustainable development (Council of the European Union, 2005). In other words, it is possible to talk about a similar vision regarding good governance by the international organizations.

However, it is rather difficult for the underdeveloped and developing countries to implement good governance. The fundamental reason behind this is the governments in developing countries that agree on the modernization of particular institutions, but are reluctant to question the traditional and elitist character and functioning of the political process itself (Haldenwang, 2004). In this context, there are even points of view implying that the notion of good governance has declined as a policy metaphor (Doornbos, 2001). Despite these concerns, in order for the implementation of good governance that is very crucial for the social-economic development of countries, e-government is regarded as an essential instrument and all the attention and interest are drawn on it. In fact, Haldenwang (2004) stated that there was a considerable increase in the use of e-government applications in public administration and formation of public policies and with the OECD countries leading the way, the governments in the developed countries and in most of the other countries first and foremost determined their national e-government strategies.

E-government has a critical power in the formation of a new notion of public services for the public institutions to offer their citizens modernized and comprehensive public services (Silcock, 2001). Within the framework of an emerging new notion of development with its multi-agent, cooperative and participatory characteristics, the power of e-government becomes all the more important. In order to be able to better understand the contributions that the fact of e-government can make to development, e-government has to be considered within a larger perspective.

In fact, in addition to the internet and websites; it is stated that information and communication technologies utilized by the public administration comprise a large spectrum of items from *software* that assists the public decision makers in urban planning to *geographic information systems and decision support systems* that enhance the institutional performance and efficiency, and positively contribute to the decision-making process and the quality of public services offered; *from wireless palmtop pilot systems to pagers, facsimiles and other devices for accessing information* (Chen et al., 2004; Hughes, 2003; Kelly, 1995; Rocheleau, 2005; Snellen, 2005). The use of these instruments in an efficient way for regional development will be useful on many issues from the rationality of the decisions made to the implementation of the projects regarding development in a healthy fashion.

E-government has a potential of making contributions to the implementation of good governance targets by both having an impact on the internal operation of the public institutions and the processes, and redefining the relationship of the government with the citizens, NGOs and the private sector. For the achieving of development goals adopted at the Millennium Summit of the UN, only the efforts of the government will not be sufficient. Today, in addition to the government, both NGOs and the private sector have to act and take certain roles in the process of development. At this point, e-government that offers new opportunities and channels for the maintenance of the relationships between the sectors in question, will greatly contribute to sustainable development of countries.

Within the framework of publish, interact and transact phases of e-government (infoDEV, 2002), various activities regarding regional development are implemented in an efficient and productive fashion through the opportunities provided by e-government practices. As is clear to see, e-government deeply transforms public administration's relationship with the other partners. In other words, in addition to the fact that e-government is an alternative and complementary approach regarding provision of services, e-government also has to be regarded as an instrument that redefines the relationships between the government and citizens (G2C), between the government and the business (G2B) and within the government itself (G2G) and ensures the realization of these relationships in an more transparent, closer, more appropriate and convenient and more economical fashion (Misuraca, 2007).

It is possible to explain the contributions that e-government applications can make, by offering opportunities to achieve the good governance, to the socio-economic development of a country in the following way:

a. **Efficiency and Productivity in Public Services:** E-government capacity offers opportunities that no other administrative instrument and medium has in terms of the provision of public services at more economical conditions. While the provision of services in the medium of e-government functions in a fast and practical fashion, it is also possible for the cost of services to be at a minimum level. In such developing countries as Turkey where the resources available are relatively insufficient, it is the main criterion of the public services to be provided to the citizens at a minimum level. E-government applications would lead to the provision of public services at a minimum cost and the resources to be used more rationally, thus providing savings. The savings obtained, on the other hand, can be transferred to the state's preferential areas or to new programs.

b. **Political and Administrative Participation:** "Participation" in today's democracies has turned out to be a critical fact that has come to be discussed again and interpreted differently. Participatory democracy stands as both an opportunity and a necessity for the political systems. The criterion of participation to be accomplished imminently and easily reflects the mentality today's political and administrative participation. It is possible for e-government to take on the responsibility of achieving such participation just at this point. It is because e-government with its capacity to transform the citizen's participation into direct democracy and full participation seems to have already occupied a privileged place in the new democracy theory.

c. **Accountability:** Accountability has become an administrative concept that political and administrative institutions have to primarily consider due to such reasons as the new pursuits for the inspection of administration, the need to utilize the public resources more productively and cautiously on the basis of rising service necessities, the rise of the general social consciousness, rise in education level, for the notion of participatory administration to become more widespread. As e-government offers the most appropriate ground for administration and officials to fulfill their duties and responsibilities in a manner that is accountable, it occupies an indispensable place in today's modern administration systems. Thus e-government strengths transparency and openness level of public institutions.

d. **Cooperation and Coordination:** E-government in terms of achieving coordination, harmony and cooperation among the administrative levels, and building up partnerships across sectors, is the most efficient instrument for the governors and for the governed through networks. In fact, Heeks (2001) argue that computer networks create new digital connections within government, between government and citizens, between government and business, between government and NGOs, between and within NGOs, and within and between communities. The provision of fast, uninterrupted and interactive communication among the individuals with very different abilities and capacities in different geographical situations and different institutions, among the administrative units, between the administration and citizens, between the public administration and private sector can be achieved through e-government applications. Cooperation and coordination in administration is an undeniable necessity in terms of increasing administrative efficiency and offering more efficient services. In this context, e-government is an important instrument in the implementation of the facts of cooperation and participation in the new notion of regional development.

THE NEW NOTION OF REGIONAL DEVELOPMENT IN TURKEY AND E-GOVERNMENT

The Historical Perspective of the Regional Development Approach and Applications in Turkey

Regional development and regional planning that has so far had a rather fluctuating progress, has not sufficiently improved conceptually and in terms of application. The very first regional planning action started late 1950s and especially picked up speed in the "First" and "Seventh" Five-Year Development Plan periods (SPO, 2000).

The notion of regional development and applications in Turkey can essentially be analyzed in two main periods under the Republican government. The first one (1923-1960) is the pre 1960s period during which various ways and methods were followed in development. The second one (1960-2008) is the post 1960s period during which "Planned Development" was commenced. In the first period, predominantly statist industrialization and development policies were implemented, but a systematic and regular strategy of development failed to be applied. Nevertheless, it was observed that some industrial plans were applied and search for new development models commenced. It is possible to say that the notion of "regional development" almost did not exist in the development applications in this period. Since the whole country had traces of underdevelopment, Turkey fundamentally favored for a public policy for the establishment and improvement of infrastructures and public enterprises all over the country.

After the military coup in 1960, the political and administrative structure and operation of the country underwent a change. In parallel to this, there was also a fundamental chance in the policy of development. The new period was called the period of "planned development" and a new central unit was established to undertake the duties and responsibilities in development area. In the new Constitution (the 1961 Constitution), a passage that mandated the establishment of an organization to undertake the duty of the State's planning placed and based on this order, the "State Planning Organization" was established with the Law No 91 on the 30th of June, 1960. In parallel to this perception, according to Article 166 of 1982 Constitution still valid today, planning the economic, social and cultural development; speedy improvement of industry and agriculture all over the country in a balanced and consistent fashion; and the utilization of the resources of the country by itemizing and assessing them is duty of state and state has to establish an organization to fulfill this duty.

Essentially, the perspective of "the improvement of the development of industry and agriculture all over the country in a balanced and consistent fashion" as stated in the 1982 Constitution represents a perception considering "regional balances" and focusing on "regional development". Removing the existing imbalances across the regions and maintaining the socio-economic development across the country in a balanced fashion, points toward a new policy of development occupying a specific place in the development plans and government programs in recent years.

The policies of regional development and regional planning in Turkey came to order in the country with the First Five-Year Development Plan (1963-1967) coming into force in 1963. In the Second (1968-1972), Third (1973-1977) and Fourth (1979-1983) Five-Year Development Plans, regional development and planning were considered through concepts such as "Environmental Development", "Undeveloped Region", "Balanced Distribution of Public Services", "Region Planning", "Priority Regions for Development-PRD", "Regional Development", "Provincial Planning" and "Spatial Organization". In the planning periods mentioned, some works and studies were undertaken under the framework of "Region Planning".

Regional development used as a more important argument in economic development especially as of the mid 1980s became the indispensable topic of the Fifth Five-Year Development Plan and the following Five-Year Development Plans in Turkey. "Region Development Plan" together with "Provincial Development Plan" became the common point of the Fifth, Sixth, Seventh and Eighth Five-Year Development Plans and the PRD project proceeded in these periods.

As of 1985 within the framework of "Region and Sub Region Plan", the development potentials of regions started to be taken into account in public investments to increase the welfare in a balanced fashion. Notion of sustainable development based on arguments of the minimization of developmental differences between rural and urban regions, fast development of the undeveloped regions, points of growth, specialization of settlings, region centers has left their mark on the last thirty years of Turkish development planning.

Regional planning experiences in Turkey emerged as studies of regional planning in few pilot regions. Each of these studies has focused on a different problem. Concrete planning projects applied for the development of regions can be listed as in the following:

- The Eastern Marmara Planning Project
- The Zonguldak Project
- The Antalya Project
- The Çukurova Region Project
- The Zonguldak-Karabük-Bartın Regional Development Project
- The Eastern Anatolian Project
- The Eastern Black Sea Regional Development Project
- The Yeşilırmak Basin Development Project
- The Southeast Anatolian Project (SAP)

While the regional planning projects mentioned above are regarded as concrete steps taken for regional development, it is not possible to say that the expected results have been achieved from these projects except the Southeast Anatolian Project respectively (Dulupcu, 2006; Kayasü & Yaşar, 2006).

The developments in the theory and applications regarding the concepts of "regionalization" and "region" that seem like an irony in this age of globalization have an impact on all the nation states. Due to such factors as Turkey's EU harmonization, interregional imbalances, the impacts caused by the natural disasters, redistribution of economic activities, accomplishment of income justice, strengthening the domestic safety and economic and social development projects built up against terrorism, increase in consciousness for the environment and abnormal population build up in metropolitan cities, regional development in Turkey has become all the more important compared to the past.

THE PROBLEMS REGARDING REGIONAL DEVELOPMENT IN TURKEY

Turkey has still been unable to solve the three critical problems regarding planned development in general and regional development in specific. These critical problem areas are as in the following (SPO, 2007):

- The differences between the most and least developed regions
- Inability to mobilize the local potential
- Non realization of mental and institutional transformation

These three main headings simply sum up the problems that complicate regional development and region planning, and weaken the success of the applications in this particular area. The problems explicated in detail under specific headings below should be regarded as difficulties Turkey has to overcome regarding regional development.

It is possible to explicate those difficulties as in the following:

As demographic difficulties; fast increase of population, imbalanced distribution of the population across regions, the ongoing internal migration, imbalanced mobility of population within the provincial areas as well as between the rural and provincial areas can be indicated.

The difficulties regarding planning and policy formation can be classified as in the following; the fact that not desirable results were obtained from the project of PRD, insufficiency of financial incentives and misapplications, the fact that the notion of region and region planning were not sufficiently adopted by the political and administrative decision makers, the fact that the spatial dimension was not well adopted in the plans, the fact that political interests and populist policies caused irrational distribution of the resources across the regions, misuse of regional incentives and financial aids, inability to consider region planning within the country as a whole and with the system approach, insufficient importance attached to planning on the provincial level.

Given the difficulties regarding the institutional capacity insufficiency; problems such as inconsistent politics and failure to ensure permanence in administration, the powerful centralism dominant in the administrative system, problems regarding the distribution of functions and powers across the administrative units, failure to establish regional units within the State Planning Agency, insufficiency of the specialist staff are the first ones to come to one's mind.

Other difficulties are the facts regarding the national geographic and economic structure. Leading the problems are those such as disadvantages regarding regional economic, geographical and human resources, insufficiencies and difficulties in transport, natural risks, sharp twists and turns in capital movements and concentration of capital in the west.

Finally, it is necessary to talk about the difficulties stemming from characteristics of the socio-psychological and general cognitive level of the society. In this framework, factor such as the fact that local egoism complicates cooperation and division of labor, insufficiency of the reflex and consciousness of protecting the historical, cultural and natural environment, insufficient level of scientific studies and production of information on this particular subject, imbalanced and insufficient level of equality of opportunities, failure to accomplish a consensus on regional development can be pointed out.

As can be calculated, some of the difficulties regarding regional development in Turkey are of general and some others are of more specific. While the effect and importance of those difficulties may vary, almost all of them prove to be the problems that more or less either negatively impact or have the capacity to negatively impact regional development in Turkey. To achieve improvement in regional development and therefore accomplish a whole balanced country-wide development will be realized through the proportion to overcome those difficulties. The consensus emerged on this issue may convert the current period of Ninth Five-Year Development Plan (2007-2013) into a period in which brand-new and appropriate steps in the field of regional development will be taken, and regional imbalances will commence to be resolved. In fact, a new notion of regional development have adopted in Turkey in order to overcome three main problems mentioned above.

THE NEW NOTION OF REGIONAL DEVELOPMENT IN TURKEY

The new notion of development in whose heart lies the RDAs has started in Turkey. The change of perception regarding the regional development in Turkey can be considered within the context of external and internal factors. Given the external factors, one of the fundamental reasons behind this change of perception in Turkey is the transition in the whole world from fordizm to post-fordizm in the economic field and from centralization to decentralization in the administrative field. A transition from a fordist notion based on massive and standard production to a post-fordist production notion in which the production process was defragmented and localized took place. This particular state of affair intrinsically started the process of local and regional specialization.

Throughout the process of global competition, the localities/regions which are specialized in certain sectors may comparatively have an advantage. The competition among the countries in this day and age is now on among the cities and regions now. In this context, in order for the regional economies to keep up with the unbearable conditions of competition and take the necessary precautions, there is a need for flexible and dynamic local and regional institutions which can take quick decisions and put them into practice immediately. Therefore, the local and regional governments come to the fore and the central administration transfer most of its duties and responsibilities to local and regional governments. Turkey was also influenced by those changes experienced in the economic and administrative fields.

Given another reason within the context of external factors, Turkey is now a candidate country for EU. The fact that Turkey started to welcome a supra-national organization like EU and is attempting to harmonize to the regional policy is a significant element of the change experienced in the notion of regional development (Reeves, 2006; Sobaci, 2009). The local government's reform and the process of establishing RDAs since 2005 can be regarded as the most concrete indications of this impact in Turkey.

The problems related to Turkey's failure to remove the inequalities across regions and immobilize the local resources and the difficulties mentioned above can also be illustrated as the internal reasons for the transition to the new notion of regional development in Turkey. The search for solutions to the problems mentioned has been influential for Turkey to adopt a new notion of bottom-up regional development. Thus, traditional top-down model regarding regional development was abandoned in Turkey.

The new notion of regional development in Turkey also implies divergence from the established regional development policies. These policies were centrally determined and didn't take into account local advantages and disadvantages. The new notion of regional development envisages expediting the regional development and removing interregional imbalances within the framework of cooperation between public sector, private sector and NGOs.

This new notion of regional development in Turkey has been built up model of governance. In fact, in the general justification of the proposal regarding the Law No 5449 that established the development agencies in Turkey, it is clearly explicated that governance is the fundamental principle. In this framework, the local government, development agencies, provincial units, local NGOs and local entrepreneurs are influential in determining the regional development policies.

In the heart of the new notion of regional development in Turkey lie the development agencies. In fact, the development agencies were established in order to expedite regional development in harmonious to the principles and policies envisaged in the national development plan and program, to ensure sustainability and to minimize the developmental interregional as well as intraregional differences, by improving the cooperation among public sector, private sector and NGOs, ensuring the appropriate and efficient use of the resources and mobilizing the local potential. Following the period in which the Law No 5449 that came into force by it publication in the Official Gazette on the 28th of February, firstly "Izmir Development Agency" and "Çukurova Development Agency" covering the Provinces of Adana and Içel were established in Turkey by the Turkish Council of Ministers' Decree No. 2006/10550, dated the 6th of July, 2006.

Afterwards, a new step for the establishment of development agency for the specific case of Istanbul was taken. The Istanbul Development Agency established by the Turkish Council of Ministers' Decree published in the Official Gazette dated 22nd of November 2008, would to be a milestone in Turkey's practices of regional development.

The development agencies have been structured in accordance with the governance model emphasizing the participation, transparency and cooperation among the participating sides. For the partnership and participation, the development agencies, create new opportunities and areas at the regional level in Turkey and include various agents within the decision making process of regional development. Consequently, they also have the potential to contribute for the establishment of a more transparent and accountable regional development policy. In addition, through a decision making mechanism based on the representation of the agents and their points of view in the region, the development agencies have the potential to take more rational decisions and based on these decision to produce more efficient and productive services for the region concerned (Sobaci, 2008). Moreover, in accordance with the rationale of enabling the other agents and guiding them in the society that governance possesses, the development agencies in Turkey will function as a catalyst and coordinator in regional development. The development agencies will act as a coordinator both between the sectors and among the administrative levels.

In this context, for the implementation of such concepts as the inter sector cooperation, the harmony among the administrative levels, coordination, participation, transparency and accountability, the opportunities presented by e-government can be used. These concepts and principles are essential for new notion of regional development in Turkey. Therefore, e-government applications in Turkey have the potential of contributing to the socio-economic development at the national level in general and to the regional development in specific.

THE POTENTIAL CONTRIBUTIONS OF E-GOVERNMENT TO THE NOTION OF REGIONAL DEVELOPMENT IN TURKEY

E-government makes direct and effective contributions to the new notion of regional development with its connecting and unifying functions. The implementation of governance-based development at either national or regional level necessitates an efficient cooperation and coordination. Ensuring cross administrative harmony and integrity is crucially important for the successful provision of public services and activities as well as public investment projects. Within the framework of efficient public administration notion, the time, resources and efforts in every kind of administrative transaction have to be utilized in the most efficient manner. The capacity of e-government to ensure communication, interactivity, sharing and harmony in the most optimum way, in no doubt, is the most powerful trump that Turkey has, just like the other states do in today's competition for development.

The contributions of e-government to the new notion of regional development in Turkey can be explicated from the perspective of development agencies and the projects run by public institutions.

From the perspective of development agencies:

The size of the geography and the number of the participating actors in regional development applications require at least similar level of cooperation and coordination. When we look at the basic duties of development agencies in Turkey, it is easily observed that the fulfillment of these duties can be possible on the basis of a very dynamic cooperation. In fact, in the general justification of the proposal of the Law No 5449, it was stated that the development agencies were to support the executive agencies and the local actors, and act as a coordinator, organizer and catalyst among these actors. Therefore, for the development agencies not to replace the regional and local actors operating for regional improvement and development, not to have a direct application, to support its partners with the resources and technical know-how and guide their projects in a complementary fashion were envisaged.

Providing support for the preparation of regional strategy and plans, supporting the rural and local development attempts, improving the cooperation between public, private sectors and NGOs, supporting entrepreneurship, one-stop pursuit and finalization of transaction of permissions and authorizations of the investors, promoting the business and investment opportunities of the region, realizing the function of mediation and coordination for the utilization of EU and international funds, establishing research and database, supporting the planning efforts of the local governments and the functions of inspection and assessment necessitates a constant interaction between the parties concerned. In addition, many of these duties require more or less e-government applications to be performed.

Development agencies are to take on a crucial role in transferring the local information to the centre, in maintaining a constant interaction between the SPA leading the way, central administrative institutions and organizations (such as the Ministry of Finance, the Treasury, Undersecretariat of Foreign Trade, the Ministry of Internal Affairs, the Ministry of Industry and Trade, the Department of Development and Support for the Small and Large Scale Industries, the Scientific and Technological Research Council of Turkey, the Development Bank) that operate in the field of regional improvement and development, and the local agents in the region. In this role that it undertakes, the unifying potential and the capacity to harmonize between administrative levels of e-government become all the more important.

In this context, one point that development agencies have to focus on is, in no doubt, the development of an advanced network and efficient operation of this network structure. The fact that the development agencies have a well prepared website and operate it in a way to meet for all kinds of needs and demands, by building up a operational bridge between the agents, will prove to be an indispensable instrument of governance-based regional development.

When we have a look at the organizational structure of development agencies, we can see that they have three main organs: Development Committee, Management Board and Investment Support Offices. Development Committee is an advisory body. It has been formed in the format of a body whereby participation, the main phenomena of new notion of governance-based regional development, can be put into practice. The public institutions regarding regional development such as governorship, the local governments with municipalities leading the way; private sector organizations; the trade associations; the representatives of non-governmental organizations; the universities; and State Planning Agency come together for a collective work within the development agencies. As can be observed, these new institutions in which participation is effectively exercised are regarded as successful examples of governance.

In addition, while the functions of election, advice, monitoring and assessment of the Development Committee are the institutional outputs relevant agents; the reports of plan, annual and inspection are regarded as the feedbacks given to the Committee. The instruments of the e-government are indispensable for the provision of this feedback.

The Management Board is decision making body of development agencies. It has built on the phenomena of participation and accountability. The Management Board is a senior management level undertaking the responsibility of accountability and formed with a notion different from the traditional public institution. According to the article 10 of the Law No 5449, the management board of the development agencies is composed of the governor, the mayor of the metropolitan municipality, the president of the general provincial council, the director of the chamber of industry, the director of the chamber of commerce and the representatives of private sector and NGOs.

The most possible way of announcement of the operations and decisions of the management board and response of the parts concerned to the announcements is the e-government services. It is thus possible for the development agency to make the inter actors interaction sustainable in an efficient fashion through website. Some important e-participation applications such as watching the management board meetings, having direct e-mail communication with the board members or discussing the decisions virtually made and the policies determined to be realized with board members at kiosks can be implemented through the websites owned by the development agencies. This particular state of affairs is likely to put the responsibility of accountability of the management board into practice by mobilizing the public inspection.

The Investment Support Offices affiliated with the Secretariat General are executive body of development agencies in Turkey. The websites and the other e-government applications are the most important instruments for the operation of these offices. In the process of choosing projects for the regional development, in the phase of applying the projects and carrying out the functions of monitoring-assessment, all sorts of wishes, complaints, suggestions, exchange of information and execution of collective works of the participants are accomplished in a fast and economical manner through the websites.

From the perspective of regional development-related public projects and programs:

Regional development and other local-scale planning initiatives in Turkey within the framework of new notion of development are now considered differently with a new perspective. Within the framework of modernization of public administration, some projects and programs related to regional development in Turkey gives a hint about this new perspective. E-government contributes these projects and programs.

One of the central projects is the *ILEMOD Project* that means the modernization project of the provincial inventory in the provinces and the application and monitoring project of rural infrastructure services, is a e-government centered project that is implemented with the aim of contributing to local-regional development. The project is implemented by the Ministry of Internal Affairs and some units and government officials have been commissioned in the provinces within the framework of this project.

Another project is the *Decision Support System of Civilian Administration Directors (DSSCAD)*. DSSCAD is an original project ran by the Ministry of Internal Affairs and based on the fact of e-government. Another project aimed at realizing the public services and investments in the most efficient way on provincial scale and related to the project mentioned above is the *Developing the System of Provincial Inventory and Decision Support System*. It was launched in 2007. This study proves to be a participation-centered framework on local and regional development. With this project, the data which is collected within framework of ILEMOD will be expanded to include the innovations in the provinces, and the provincial planning and investment decisions will be activated with the decision support and reporting to be built on a database. Moreover, the data available in the ILEMOD system will be transferred to the electronic media and electronic data sharing will take place with the other systems collecting data on local governments. In addition to this, an inventory of natural, historical and cultural values will be prepared in provinces and content will be provided for the Portal of Turkish Culture (see for detail, http://www.ilemod.gov.tr/index.asp).

Another project related the new notion of regional development in Turkey is the *Restoration of the Planning Process Project* ran by the Ministry of Public Works and Settlement. This project was carried out between October 2006 and February 2007. In this work that will run with information systems, the web based e-government services are the indispensable instruments of the new planning concept. Especially, this work that is based on the use of the "Geographic Information Systems-GIS" throughout the planning process and the real data method is likely to bring about some expansions for the regional development in Turkey (The Ministry of Public Works and Settlement, 2008).

Moreover, there are some certain programs underway that aim to minimize regional socio-economic development differences and promote social welfare in Turkey. Leading those programs are the "Regional Competitiveness Operational Programme" that is implemented by the Ministry of Trade and Industry, "Social Support Program" run by State Planning Organization, "12 Priority Level 2 Region Determined in the Preliminary National Development Plan" run within the framework of Turkey-EU Co-Finance Development Programs by State Planning Organization. Implementation of these programs requires an intensive interaction and communication between the parts concerned. In addition, within the framework of these programs, the public is asked to propose their own projects. In terms of both maintaining the interaction and communication and of the process of accepting, assessing and monitoring the projects, e-government opportunities can be utilized.

The practical works explained so far illustrate us how the governance-based new notion of regional development, on the one hand, is nested with the fact of e-government and how much growing importance, on the other hand, is attached day by day to this subject and how much progress has been made.

CONCLUSION AND SUGGESTIONS

Within the framework of those explicated above, in order to overcome the existing difficulties and problems regarding the implementation of the new notion of regional development in Turkey, the following suggestions can be proposed in the context of e-government applications:

- Since the success of the new notion is dependent on the applications of governance and e-government, it is imperative that the applications of governance and e-government be made more effective. Therefore, some steps have to be taken to get the public involved in administration and make it more widespread; and new ways and methods have to be implemented and the existing organizations (such as City Council, Local Agenda 21 Programs, and Urban Volunteers' Houses) have to be made more efficient and operative.
- While taking investment decisions at regional and local levels, and preparing the annual investment programs, the thoughts, ideas and suggestions of the public have to be regularly and systematically asked especially through e-government. Appropriate mechanisms have to be implemented in order for the public inspection to take place. Moreover, the necessary aid and support channels have to be established in order to obtain the local participation for the implementation of investments and projects as well as to obtain in an increasing manner the materialistic or non materialistic contributions of the NGOs and individuals.
- The e-government projects ran by the public administration should be completed as soon as possible regarding and the new projects should be introduced. It should be proved efficient operation of the E-government Gateway. These are crucially important for the successful implementation of the new notion of development.

- One of the principal conditions of efficiency in e-government applications is the accessibility. In order to increase the level of accessibility of e-government services, internet subscription has to be simplified and made cheaper; in addition, necessary steps have to be taken to increase PC ownership and it has to be financed and supported by the public budget.
- Since lifting the effectiveness of regional and local governments regarding e-government services is a priority, financing and supporting the services in question of those governments, providing incentives, subjecting them to performance inspection and increasing the awareness of the public on this subject is one of the fundamental issues.
- Asking about the preferences and the opinions of the local groups, informing the public about the investments and projects regularly and timely, and ensuring the maximum contribution of the citizens to the local and regional development through direct participation of the public to the public decision-making process have to be ensured and e-government services have to be utilized to accomplish it.
- Considering the regional development applications on a nationwide scale, macro decisions and strategies have to be determined and put into practice in a consistent and determined way. The e-government opportunities should be efficiently used during process of the establishment and operation of development agencies.
- The division of functions and powers across the administrations has to be accomplished in a rational and efficiently operative manner and the service and investment needs at local level have to be met by the most appropriate institutions in the most economical way. In addition to necessary legal arrangements, the optimum utilization of the e-government opportunities has paramount importance.
- By collecting the investments and projects as well as strategic and performance plans of the local governments with the municipalities and special provincial administrations leading the way under one umbrella, an environment of efficiently operating e-government has to be implemented in order to ensure maximum level of coordination and interaction.
- For the preparation of the master building development schemes, provincial landscaping plans and building development schemes which are important and guiding instruments in regional and local development geographic information systems and software have to be used, and those plans have definitely to be put into practice with the participation of the citizens and all the agents concerned by using the opportunities offered by e-government.

In Turkey, where the regional imbalances have reached some crucial levels and created some serious social, political and cultural problems, it is vital that regional development be accomplished in a fast and efficient way. The governance-based the notion of regional development has potential to pave the way for Turkey on this subject. However, there are still some problems and difficulties to be tackled and resolved. It is imperative for Turkey to overcome them. The new notion of regional development which is considered as a prescription for problems regarding development in Turkey can be implemented in a more efficient and permanent way through the use of the e-government instruments.

The recommendations listed for Turkey above are true to a great extent for "developing countries" as well. The economical, social, political, cultural, administrative and technological characteristics of Turkey correspond in general to those of developing countries. Such characteristics as the formation and functionality of political and administrative structures in those countries, their democratic culture, the content of their economic policies, the economic indicators, interregional imbalances, level of income and its distribution, their capacity of technology and e-government possibilities are encountered as the common determiners in the success of many projects and practices to be maintained.

It is commonly accepted that regional development is a vital necessity in developing countries. It is simply because the regions that lagged in terms of socio-economic development in those countries present themselves as a common problem. In an attempt to overcome this problem, cooperative and participatory political and administrative instruments should be used in developing countries. And leading those instruments is the concept of "governance" and "e-government" practices that represent the main thesis of this manuscript.

Due to the decay of the political mechanisms that have not been very open to participation, the problem of legitimacy and crisis of credibility, it is indispensable to ensure the involvement and participation of the citizens in public issues such as development that will have a direct and deep impact on them. The way to achieve it is to convert the political and administrative structures into "governance" which is based on the concept of "collaborative governing". The most efficient method of achieving governance and sustain it, by all means, is "e-government". In developing countries, focusing on these two concepts in efforts of political and administrative restructuring and making the e-government possibilities easily available and functional will contribute to regional development more than any other instrument would make. Therefore, in developing countries in general and in Turkey in specific, the concept of governance-based regional development will be more efficiently and permanently implemented through the practices of the e-government. In developing countries, policy makers and administrators can contribute the sustainable development by implementing the phenomenon of good governance through e-government.

REFERENCES

Armstrong, H., & Taylor, J. (2000). *Regional economics and policy*. Oxford, UK: Blackwell Publishers.

AusAID (Australian Agency for International Development). (2000). *Good governance: Guiding principles for implementation*. Canberra, Australia: AusAID Publication.

Ayres, S., & Pearce, G. (2004). Central government responses to governance change in the English regions. *Regional & Federal Studies*, *14*(2), 255–280. doi:10.1080/1359756042000247474

Babajanian, B. V. (2005). Bottom up and top down? Community development in post-soviet Armenia: The social fund model. *Social Policy and Administration*, *39*(4), 448–462. doi:10.1111/j.1467-9515.2005.00449.x

Beer, A., Haughton, G., & Maude, A. (2003). *Developing locally*. Bristol, UK: Policy Press.

Beer, A., & Maude, A. (2005). Governance and the performance of regional development agencies in Australia. In R. Eversole & J. Martin (Eds.), *Participation and governance in regional development: Global trends in an Australian context* (pp. 61-78). Aldershot, UK: Ashgate Publishing.

Blair, J. P., & Reese, L. A. (Eds.). (1999). *Approaches to economic development: Readings from economic development quarterly*. Thousand Oaks, CA: Sage Publications.

Blakely, E. J., & Bradshow, T. K. (2002). *Planning local economic development: Theory and practice*. Thousand Oaks, CA: Sage Publication.

Brown, A. J. (2005). Regional governance and regionalism in Australia. In R. Eversole & J. Martin (Eds.), *Participation and governance in regional development: Global trends in an Australian context* (pp. 17-42). Aldershot, UK: Ashgate Publishing.

Chen, Y., Huang, W., Li, D., Zhang, P., Shen, H. Z., & Klamo, L. (2004). A comparative study of strategic issue of digital government implementations between developed and developing countries. In W. Huang, K. Siau, & K. K. Wei (Eds.), *Electronic government strategies and implementation* (pp. 191-213). Hershey, PA: Idea Group Publishing.

Ciborra, C., & Navarra, D. D. (2005). Good governance, development theory, and aid policy: Risks and challenges of e-government in Jordan. *Information Technology for Development, 11*(2), 141–159. doi:10.1002/itdj.20008

Council of European Union. (2005). *The European consensus on development* (Brussels 14820/05).

Danson, M., Halkier, H., & Damborg, C. (2002). Regional development agencies in Europe: An introduction and framework for analysis. In H. Halkier, M. Danson, & C. Damborg (Eds.), *Regional development agencies in Europe* (pp. 13-25). London: Routledge.

DOI (Digital Opportunity Initiative). (2001). *Creating a development dynamic*. New York: Digital Opportunity Initiative.

Doornbos, M. (2001). Good governance: The rise and decline of a policy metaphor? *The Journal of Development Studies, 37*(6), 93–108. doi:10.1080/713601084

Dudek, C. M. (2001). European Union's effect upon regional economic development and regional government's policy making ability. *Regional & Federal Studies, 11*(1), 101–125.

Dulupcu, M. A. (2006, Eylül). *Bölgesel politikalar kopyalanabilir mi? Bölgeselleş(tir)me (yönetim) karşısında (yeni) bölge(sel)cilik (yönetişim)*. Paper presented at the Bölgesel Kalkınma ve Yönetişim Sempozyumu, Ankara.

Dulupcu, M. A., & Ozgur, H. (2006). Yerel ekonomik gelişmede yerel yönetimlerin rolü. In H. Ozgur & B. Parlak (Eds.), *Avrupa perspektifinde yerel yönetimler* (pp. 171-202). Bursa, Turkey: Alfa Aktüel.

Geddes, M., & Newman, I. (1999). Evolution and conflict in local economic development. *Local Economy, 14*(1), 12–26. doi:10.1080/02690949908726472

Haldenwang, C. V. (2004). Electronic government (e-government) and development. *European Journal of Development Research, 16*(2), 417–432. doi:10.1080/0957881042000220886

Heeks, R. (1999). Reinventing government in the information age. In R. Heeks (Ed.), *Reinventing government in the information age: International practice in IT-enabled public sector reform* (pp. 9-21). London: Routledge.

Heeks, R. (2001). *Understanding e-governance for development* (Working Paper, No: 11). Manchester, UK: University of Manchester, Institute for Development Policy and Management.

Hossain, F. (2007). *What has happened to development administration? Some critical reflections* (Working Paper, No: 72). Manchester, UK: University of Manchester, Institute for Development Policy and Management.

Hudson, R. (2007). Regions and regional uneven development forever? Some reflective comments upon theory and practice. *Regional Studies, 41*(9), 1149–1160. doi:10.1080/00343400701291617

Hughes, O. (2003). *Public management and administration: An introduction*. New York: Palgrave Macmillan. infoDEV (Information for Development Programme). (2002). *The e-government handbook for developing countries*. Washington, DC.: infoDEV and Center for Democracy and Technology.

Jeffrey, C., & Mawson, J. (2002). Introduction: Beyond the white paper on the English regions. *Regional Studies, 36*(7), 715–720. doi:10.1080/0034340022000006033

Jeffrey, C., & Reilly, A. (2003). *Devolution to the regions (executive summary)*. London: LGA Publication.

Kayasü, S., & Yaşar, S. (2006, Eylül). *Avrupa Birliği'ne üyelik sürecinde kalkınma politikaları: Yasal ve kurumsal dönüşümler*. Paper presented at the Bölgesel Kalkınma ve Yönetişim Sempozyumu, Ankara.

Kelly, K. (1995). *A framework for evaluating public sector geographic information systems*. Albany, NY: University of Albany, Centre for Technology in Government.

Kim, P. S., Halligan, J., Cho, N., Oh, C. H., & Eikenberry, A. M. (2005). Toward participatory and transparent government: Report on the global forum on reinventing government. *Public Administration Review, 65*(6), 646–654. doi:10.1111/j.1540-6210.2005.00494.x

Madon, S. (2000). The internet and socio-economic development: Exploring the interaction. *Information Technology & People, 13*(2), 85–101. doi:10.1108/09593840010339835

Marker, P., McNamara, K., & Wallace, L. (2002). *The significance of information and communication technologies for reducing poverty*. London: Department for International Development.

McCall, T. (2003). Institutional design for community economic development models: Issues of opportunity and capacity. *Community Development Journal, 38*(2), 96–108. doi:10.1093/cdj/38.2.96

Ministery of Puclic Work and Settlement. (2008). *Planlama sürecinin yenilenmesi projesi*. Ankara, Turkey: Mattek Basım Yayın.

Misuraca, G. C. (2007). *E-governance in Africa from theory and practice: A handbook on ICTs for local governance*. NJ: African World Press and International Development Research Center.

Morgan, K. (2004). Sustainable regions: Governance, innovation and scale. *European Planning Studies, 12*(6), 871–889. doi:10.1080/0965431042000251909

Pike, A., Rodriguez-Pose, A., & Tomaney, J. (2006). *Local and regional development*. London: Routledge.

Pike, A., Rodriguez-Pose, A., & Tomaney, J. (2007). What kind of local and regional development and for whom? *Regional Studies, 41*(9), 1253–1269. doi:10.1080/00343400701543355

Pinder, D., & Aldcroft, D. H. (1983). *Regional economic development and policy: Theory and practice in European Community*. London: Allen & Unwin.

Polése, M., & Shearmur, R. (2006). Why some regions will decline: A Canadian case study with thoughts on local development strategies. *Papers in Regional Science, 85*(1), 23–46. doi:10.1111/j.1435-5957.2006.00024.x

Press, L. (1996). The role of computer networks in development. *Communications of the ACM, 39*(2), 23–29. doi:10.1145/230798.230800

Reeves, T. (2006, Eylül). *Regional development in the EU and Turkey*. Paper presented at the Bölgesel Kalkınma ve Yönetişim Sempozyumu, Ankara.

Rhodes, R. A. W. (1996). The new governance: Governing without government. *Political Studies*, *XLIV*, 652–667. doi:10.1111/j.1467-9248.1996.tb01747.x

Rocheleau, B. (2005). *Public management information systems*. Hershey, PA: Idea Group Publishing.

Siffin, W. J. (1991). The problem of development administration. In A. Farazmand (Ed.), *Handbook of comparative and development public administration* (pp. 1-8). New York: CRC Press.

Silcock, R. (2001). What is e-government? *Parliamentary Affairs*, *54*(1), 88–101. doi:10.1093/pa/54.1.88

Snellen, I. (2005). Technology and public administration: Conditions for successful e-government development. In G. Petroni & F. Cloete (Eds.), *New technologies in public administration* (pp. 5-19). Amsterdam: IOS Press.

Sobaci, M. Z. (2008). Türkiye'de bölgesel yönetişimin kurumsal yansıması: Kalkınma ajansları. *Finans Politik & Ekonomik Yorumlar*, *45*(519), 61–74.

Sobaci, Z. (2009). Regional development agencies in Turkey: Are they examples of obligated policy transfer. *Public Organization Review*, *9*(1), 51–65. doi:10.1007/s11115-008-0069-0

SPO (State Planning Organization). (2000). *Bölgesel gelişme: Özel ihtisas komisyonu raporu*. Ankara, Turkey: SPO.

SPO (State Planning Organization). (2007). *Kalkınma ajansları*. Ankara, Turkey: SPO.

Squazzino, F. (in press). Local economic development initiatives from the bottom-up: the role of community development corporations. *Community Development Journal*.

Stöhr, W. B., & Taylor, D. R. F. (Eds.). (1981). *Development from above or below?: The dialectics of regional planning in developing countries*. New York: Wiley.

Tomaney, J. (2002). The evolution of regionalism in England. *Regional Studies*, *36*(7), 721–731. doi:10.1080/0034340022000006042

UNDP (United Nations Development Programme). (1997). *Reconceptualising governance*. New York: UNDP Publication.

UNDP (United Nations Development Programme). (2001). *Human development report 2001: Making new technologies work for human development*. New York: Oxford University Press.

UNESCAP (United Nations Economic and Social Commission for Asia and the Pacific). (2008). *What is Good Governance?* Retrieved October 20, 2008, from http://www.unescap.org/pdd/prs/ProjectActivities/Ongoing/gg/governance.asp

United Nations. (2003a). *World public sector report 2003: E-government at the crossroads*. New York: United Nations Publication.

United Nations. (2003b). *Monterrey Consensus on financing for development*. New York: United Nations Publication.

Vazquez-Barquero, A. (2002). *Endogenous development: Networking, innovation, institutions and cities*. London: Routledge.

Webb, D., & Collis, C. (2000). Regional development agencies and the 'new regionalism' in England. *Regional Studies, 34*(9), 2000, 857-864.

World Bank. (1989). *Sub-Saharan Africa: From crisis to sustainable development*. Washington, DC: World Bank.

World Bank. (1992). *Governance and development*. Washington, DC: World Bank.

World Bank. (1994). *Governance: The World Bank's experience*. Washington, DC: World Bank.

World Bank. (1997). *World development report 1997: The state in changing world*. Oxford, UK: Oxford University Press.

ADDITIONAL READING

Alexei, P., & Garson, D. (Eds.). (2003). *Digital government: Principles and best practices*. Hershey, PA: Idea Group Publishing.

Ciborra, C. (2005). Interpreting e-government and development: Efficiency, transparency or governance at a distance? *Information Technology & People*, *18*(3), 260–279. doi:10.1108/09593840510615879

Davidson, J., & Lockwood, M. (2008). Partnerships as instruments of good regional governance: Innovation for sustainability in Tasmania. *Regional Studies*, *42*(5), 641–656. doi:10.1080/00343400701543165

Ferry, M. (2007). From government to governance: Polish regional development agencies in a changing regional context. *Eastern European Politics and Societies*, *21*(3), 447–474. doi:10.1177/0888325407303706

Graham, J., Amos, B., & Plumptre, T. (2003). *Principles for good governance in the 21st century* (Policy Brief No. 15). Ottawa, Canada: Institute on Governance.

Halkier, H. (2006, Eylül). *Regional development agencies and multi-level governance: European perspectives*. Paper presented at the Bölgesel Kalkınma ve Yönetişim Sempozyumu, Ankara.

Halkier, H., & Danson, M. (1997). Regional development agencies in western Europe: A survey of key characteristics and trends. *European Urban and Regional Studies*, *4*(3), 243–256. doi:10.1177/096977649700400304

Heeks, R. (2001). *Building e-governance for development: A framework for national and donor action* (Working Paper, No: 12). Manchester, UK: University of Manchester, Institute for Development Policy and Management.

infoDEV (Information for Development Programme). (2003). *Information and communication technologies, poverty and development: Learning from experience*. Washington, DC: World Bank.

Jessop, B. (1998). The rise of governance and the risk of failure: The case of economic development. *International Social Science Journal*, *50*(155), 29–45. doi:10.1111/1468-2451.00107

John, P. (2001). *Local governance in western Europe*. London: Sage Publication.

Khosrow-Pour, M. (Ed.). (2005). *Practicing e-government: A global perspective*. Hershey, PA: Idea Group Publishing.

Lai, O. (1994). Promoting health and welfare: The challenge for information technology? *Information Technology & People*, *7*(1), 81–99. doi:10.1108/09593849410074043

Liou, K. T. (2000). Linking administrative reform to economic development: Issue and the national experience. In K. T. Liou (Ed.), *Administrative Reform and National Economic Development* (pp. 1-18). Aldershot, UK: Ashgate Publishing.

OECD (Organisation for Economic Co-operation and Development). (1995). *Participatory development and good governance*. Paris: OECD.

OECD (Organisation for Economic Co-operation and Development). (2003). *The e-government imperative*. Paris: OECD.

Olatokun, W. M. (2007). ICTs and governance in Africa. In A. Anttiroiko & M. Malkia (Eds.), *Encyclopedia of digital government* (pp. 978-983). Hershey, PA: Idea Group Inc.

Roy, K. C., & Tisdell, C. A. (1998). Good governance in sustainable development: The impact of institutions. *International Journal of Social Economics*, *25*(6-8), 1310–1325. doi:10.1108/03068299810212775

Scott, A. J., & Storper, M. (2003). Regions, globalization and development. *Regional Studies, 37*(6-7), 549–578.

Silcock, R. (2001). What is e-government? *Parliamentary Affairs, 54*(1), 88–101. doi:10.1093/pa/54.1.88

Stoker, G. (1998). Governance as theory: Five propositions. *International Social Science Journal, 50*(155), 17–28. doi:10.1111/1468-2451.00106

United Nations. (2007). *Good governance Practices for the Protection of Human Rights*. New York: United Nations.

Walburn, D. (2006, Eylül). *Regional development agencies: The tool to stimulate economic development in regions*. Paper presented at the Bölgesel Kalkınma ve Yönetişim Sempozyumu, Ankara.

Werlin, H. (2003). Poor nations, rich nations: A theory of governance. *Public Administration Review, 63*(3), 329–342. doi:10.1111/1540-6210.00293

Young-Hyman, T. (2008). The potential for effective regional development agencies in Turkey: A comparative analysis. *Regional & Federal Studies, 18*(4), 375–402. doi:10.1080/13597560802223953

KEY TERMS AND DEFINITIONS

Bottom-Up: New regional development model which starts development from local and focuses on activation of local potential and rational and efficient usage of local resources.

E-Government: A strategic use of ICT in public administration in order to improve the quality of service provided to public, simplify and facilitate administrative procedures, achieve coordination among public institutions and enhance citizen participation and democracy.

Good Governance: Good governance refers to the process of decision-making and implementation of such decisions in participatory, transparent, responsive, equitable and effective manner.

Regional Development Agencies: Institutions established to facilitate regional development and make it sustainable through achieving cooperation among public, private and civilian sectors and activating local potential.

Regional Development: Regional development is a phenomenon, which aims to facilitate development in a region in terms of economic, social and cultural dimensions and remove socio-economic imbalances among the regions in a country. Thus, it includes a set of principles, policies, strategies, means and applications regarding development in regional level.

Sustainable Development: A concept which aims to make development sustainable, considering also future generations, through balanced and efficient use of resources that will achive development.

Top-Down: Traditional approach prioritizing central actors rather than local players and means in regional development.

Compilation of References

Abdulai, A. M., & Chamhuri, S. (2008, December). *Livelihoods sustainability experience in Malaysia: Implication for cooperation with West Asia.* A paper presented at an international conference on Malaysia-West Asia Relations: Prospects & Challenges, UKM, Bangi, Malaysia.

Addison, T., & Heshmati, A. (2002). *Democratization and New Communication Technologies as Determinants of Foreign Direct Investment in Developing Countries.* Paper Presented at the Conference on "New Economy in Development". Helsinki: UNU/WIDER.

Adger, W. N., Brown, K., Fairbrass, J., Jordan, A., Paavola, J., Rosendo, S., & Seyfang, G. (2003). Governance for sustainability: towards a 'thick' analysis of environmental decision making. *Environment & Planning A, 35*, 1095–1110. doi:10.1068/a35289

Ahluwalia, M. S. (2002). Economic Reforms in India Since 1991: Has Gradualism Worked? *The Journal of Economic Perspectives, 16*(3), 67–88. doi:10.1257/089533002760278721

Ahmad, Y. J., et al. (Eds.). (1989). *Environmental Accounting for Sustainable Development.* Washington, DC: World Bank.

Aigner, D., Lovell, C. A. K., & Schmidt, P. (1977). Formulation and estimation of stochastic frontier production function models. *Journal of Econometrics, 6*, 21–37. doi:10.1016/0304-4076(77)90052-5

Akpınar, A. (2008). Kur'an'a Gore Calısmanın Cok Yonlulugu ve Ibadet Boyutu. In *Islam ve Calısma Hayatı Ulusal Sempozyumu* (pp. 23-37). Izmir, Turkey: Faculty of Divinity Publishing.

Alexei, P., & Garson, D. (Eds.). (2003). *Digital government: Principles and best practices.* Hershey, PA: Idea Group Publishing.

All about Shanghai and environs: A standard guide book. (1936). Shanghai: University Press.

Al-Yousif, Y. K. (2002). Financial Development and Economic Growth: Another Look at the Evidence from Developing Countries. *Review of Financial Economics, 11*, 131–150. doi:10.1016/S1058-3300(02)00039-3

Andersen, T., & Tarp, F. (2003). Financial Liberalization, Financial Development and Economic Growth in LDCs. *Journal of International Development, 15*, 189–209. doi:10.1002/jid.971

Angus, J. B. (2008). A Survey of Recent Developments in the Literature of Finance and Growth. *Journal of Economic Surveys, 22*, 536–576. doi:10.1111/j.1467-6419.2007.00542.x

Ansari, M. I. (1998). Financial Development and Economic Growth: The South Asian Experience. *Journal of Asian Economics, 9*, 503–517. doi:10.1016/S1049-0078(99)80100-6

Ansari, M. I. (2002). The Impact of Financial Development, Money, and Public Spending on Malaysia National Income: An Econometric Study. *Journal of Asian Economics, 13*, 72–93. doi:10.1016/S1049-0078(01)00113-0

Antonio, E. T., Jr., & Padojinog, W. C. (2003, February). *IT-Enabled Services in the Philippines: Prospects and Issues.* Paper presented at the AT10 Research Conference, Tokyo, Japan.

Arellano, M. (2003). *Panel data econometrics.* New York: Oxford University Press.

Arellano, M., & Bond, S. (1991). Some tests of specification for panel data: Monte Carlo evidence and an application to employment equations. *The Review of Economic Studies, 58*, 277–297. doi:10.2307/2297968

Arestis, P., Demetriades, P. O., & Luintel, K. B. (2001). Financial Development and Economic Growth: The Role of Stock Markets. *Journal of Money . Credit and Banking, 33*, 16–41. doi:10.2307/2673870

Arıkan, C., Akyos, M., Durgut, M., & Göker, A. (2003). *Ulusal İnovasyon Sistemi, Kavramsal Çerçeve, Türkiye İncelemesi ve Ülke Örnekleri* (Publication No: TÜSİAD-T/2003/10/362). Türkiye: TÜSİAD.

Aristotle. (1941). Politics. In R. McKeon (Ed.), *The Basic Works of Aristotle* (pp. 1127-1325). New York: Random House.

Aristotle. (2007). *Nikomakhos'a Etik* (S. Babur, Trans.). Ankara, Turkey: BilgeSu Press.

Armstrong, H., & Taylor, J. (2000). *Regional economics and policy.* Oxford, UK: Blackwell Publishers.

Arnone, M., & Bandiera, L. (2004). *Monetary Policy, Monetary Areas, and Financial Development with Electronic Money* (Working Paper, 04/122). International Monetary Fund.

Arslan, A. (2002). *Ibni Haldun'un Ilim ve Fikir Dunyası.* Ankara, Turkey: Vadi Publishing.

Asheim, B. T., & Coenen, L. (2005). Knowledge Bases and Regional Innovation Systems: Comparing Nordic Clusters. *Research Policy, 34*(8), 1173–1190. doi:10.1016/j.respol.2005.03.013

Asian Development Bank. (2005). The Role of Credit Rating Agencies in Asia's Emerging Bond Markets. In *38th Annual Meeting Seminar*, Istanbul, Turkey.

Atiyas, S. W., Dutz, M., & Frischtak, C. (1992). *Fundamental Issues and Policy Approaches in Industrial Restructuring* (Industry and Energy Department Working Paper, World Bank Industry Series Paper, No. 56).

Atje, R., & Jovanovic, B. (1993). *Finance and Development.* Mimeo, New York University.

Attewell, P. (2001). The First and Second Digital Divides. *Sociology of Education, 74*, 252–259. doi:10.2307/2673277

Aulakh, P. S. (2007). Emerging Multinationals from Developing Economies: Motivations, Paths and Performance. *Journal of International Management, 13*(3), 235–240. doi:10.1016/j.intman.2007.05.001

AusAID (Australian Agency for International Development). (2000). *Good governance: Guiding principles for implementation.* Canberra, Australia: AusAID Publication.

Avgerou, C. (1998). How can IT enable economic growth in developing countries? *Information Technology for Development, 8*(1), 15–29.

Ayres, S., & Pearce, G. (2004). Central government responses to governance change in the English regions. *Regional & Federal Studies, 14*(2), 255–280. doi:10.1080/1359756042000247474

Babajanian, B. V. (2005). Bottom up and top down? Community development in post-soviet Armenia: The social fund model. *Social Policy and Administration, 39*(4), 448–462. doi:10.1111/j.1467-9515.2005.00449.x

Bachtler, J., & Yuill, D. (2001). *Policies and Strategies for Regional Development: A Shift Paradigm?* (No. 46 EPRC) [*Regional and Industrial Policy Research Paper*]. University of Strathclydee.

Bagehot, W. (1783). *Lombard Street.* Homewood, IL: Irwin.

Baggiani, L. (2007). *Il Bene (e il Male) della Moneta Elettronica.* Retrieved April 2, 2007, from http://ideashaveconsequences.org/il-bene-e-il-male-della-moneta-elettronica/jacopo

Balassa, B. (1971). *The Structure of Protections in Developing countries.* Baltimore, MD: Johns Hopkins University Press.

Balassa, B. (1978). Exports and Economic Growth: Further Evidence. *Journal of Development Economics, 5*(2), 181–189. doi:10.1016/0304-3878(78)90006-8

Balassa, B. (1985). Exports, Policy Choices and Economic Growth in Developing Countries after the 1973 Oil Shock. *Journal of Development Economics, 18*, 23–35. doi:10.1016/0304-3878(85)90004-5

Balassa, B. (1989). Outward Orientation. In H. Chenery & T.N. Srinivasan (Eds.), *Handbook of Development Economics* (pp. 1645-1690). New York: North Holland.

Baldwin, R. (1989). Exporting the Capital Markets: Comparative advantage and Market Imperfections. In D. Audretsch, L. Sleuwaegen, & H. Yamawaki (Eds.), *The Convergence of International and Domestic Markets.* Amsterdam: North-Holland.

Baltagi, B. H. (2008). *Econometric analysis of panel data.* West Sussex, UK: John Wiley&Sons Ltd.

Banerjee, A., Dolado, J. J., Galbraith, J. W., & Hendry, D. F. (1993). *Coitegration, Error-Correction and the Econometric Analysis of Non-stationary Data.* Oxford, UK: Oxford University Press.

Barber, N. (1979). *The fall of Shanghai.* New York: Coward, McCann and Geoghegan.

Barney, J. B. (1991a). Firm Resources and Sustained Competitive Advantage. *Journal of Management, 17*(1), 99–120. doi:10.1177/014920639101700108

Barney, J. B. (1991b). Resource Based View. *Diamond Harvard Business Review, 26*(5), 78–87.

Barney, J. B., & Clark, D. N. (2007). *Resource-Based Theory: Creating and Sustaining Competitive Advantage.* Oxford, UK: Oxford University Press.

Barry, P. B., & Triplett, J. E. (2000). What's new about the new economy? IT, economic growth and productivity. *Brookings Economic Papers.*

Barzilai-Nahon, K. (2006). *Better yardstick needed to measure digital divide.* Retrieved April 19, 2008, from http://www.govtech.com/dc/101673

Basaran, F. (2003). Telekommunikasyon Politikaları: Avrupa Birliği ve Türkiye. In M. Gencel Bek (Ed.), *Küreselleşme, İletişim Endüstrileri ve Kimlikler: Avrupa Birliği ve Türkiye'de İletişim Politikaları* (pp. 165-204). Ankara, Turkey: Ümit Yay.

Bassani, A., & Scarpetta, S. (2002). Growth, technological change, and ICT diffusion: Recent evidence from OECD countries. *Oxford Review of Economic Policy, 18*(3), 324–344. doi:10.1093/oxrep/18.3.324

Battese, G. E., & Coelli, T. J. (1988). Prediction of firm-level technical efficiencies with a generalized production function and panel data. *Journal of Econometrics, 38*(3), 387–399. doi:10.1016/0304-4076(88)90053-X

Battese, G. E., & Coelli, T. J. (1995). A model for technical inefficiency effects in a stochastic frontier production function for panel data. *Empirical Economics, 20*, 325–332. doi:10.1007/BF01205442

Battese, G. E., Rao, G. S. P., & O'Donnell, C. J. (2004). A metafrontier production function for estimation of technical efficiencies and technology gaps for firms operating under different technologies. *Journal of Productivity Analysis, 21*(1), 91–103. doi:10.1023/B:PROD.0000012454.06094.29

Beck, T. (2003). Financial Dependence and International Trade. *Review of International Economics, 11*, 396–316. doi:10.1111/1467-9396.00384

Beck, T., Levine, R., & Loyaza, N. (2000). Finance and the Sources of Growth. *Journal of Financial Economics, 58*, 261–300. doi:10.1016/S0304-405X(00)00072-6

Beer, A., & Maude, A. (2005). Governance and the performance of regional development agencies in Australia. In R. Eversole & J. Martin (Eds.), *Participation and governance in regional development: Global trends in an Australian context* (pp. 61-78). Aldershot, UK: Ashgate Publishing.

Beer, A., Haughton, G., & Maude, A. (2003). *Developing locally.* Bristol, UK: Policy Press.

Bélanger, F., & Carter, L. (2006). The Effects of the Digital Divide on E-Government: An Empirical Evaluation. In

Proceedings of the 39th Hawaii International Conference on System Sciences, Hawaii, USA.

Belke, A., & Fehn, R. (2001). *Institutions and structural unemployment: Do capital-market imperfections matter?* (CESifo Working Paper, 504).

Bencivenga, V. R., & Smith, B. D. (1991). Financial Intermediation and Endogenous Growth. *The Review of Economic Studies*, *58*(2), 195–209. doi:10.2307/2297964

Bentham, J. (1843). Of the Mode of Warming the Building. In J. Bowring (Ed.), *The Works of Jeremy Bentham* (Vol. 4). Edinburgh, UK: W. Tait.

Bentivegna, S. (2006). Rethinking Politics in the World of ICTs. *Global Media and Communication*, *2*(1), 21–41. doi:10.1177/1742766506061815

Berg, V. (2001). *Economic Growth and Development*. New York: Mc-Graw-Hill.

Bergère, M. (1981). The other China: Shanghai from 1919 to 1949. In C. Howe (Ed.), *Shanghai: revolution and development in an Asian metropolis* (pp. 1-34). New York: Cambridge University Press.

Bergère, M. (2002). *Histoire de Shanghai*. Paris: Fayard.

Berthelemy, J. C., & Varoudakis, A. (1998). Financial Development, Financial Reforms and Growth: A Panel Data Approach. *Revue-Economique*, *49*(1), 195–206. doi:10.2307/3502501

Bertoni, F., Elia, S., & Rabbiosi, L. (2008). *Drivers of Acquisitions from BRICs to Advanced Countries: Firm-Level Evidence*. Paper presented in the conference on Emerging Multinationals: Outward FDI from Emerging and Developing Economies, Copenhagen Business School, Copenhagen, Denmark.

Bhagwati, J. N. (1978). *Foreign Trade Regime and Economic Development: Anatomy and Consequences of Exchange Control Regimes*. Cambridge, UK: Ballinger.

Bhagwati, J. N. (1988). Re-examining Export-Led Growth Hypothesis: A Multivariate Cointegration Analysis. *Applied Economics*, *31*, 525–530.

Bhagwati, J. N., & Srinivasan, T. N. (1979). Trade Policy and Development. In R. Dornbusch & J. A. Frenkel (Eds.), *International Economic Policy: Theory and Evidence* (pp. 1-38). Baltimore, MD: John Hopkins University Press.

Blackburn, K., & Hung, V. T. Y. (1998). A Theory of Growth, Financial Development and Trade. *Economica*, *65*, 107-124.

Bharadwaj, A. S. (2000). A Resource-Based Perspective on Information Technology Capability and Firm Performance: An Empirical Investigation. *MIS Quarterly*, *24*(1), 169–196. doi:10.2307/3250983

Binark, M. (2003). 'Avrupa Modeli Enformasyon Toplumu' Politikası ve Kadınların Bilgisayar ve İnternet Kullanmaları. In M. Gencel Bek (Ed.), *Küreselleşme, İletişim Endüstrileri ve Kimlikler: Avrupa Birliği ve Türkiye'de İletişim Politikaları* (pp. 135-161). Ankara, Turkey: Ümit Yay.

Birkenholtz, T. (2008). Contesting expertise: the politics of environmental knowledge in northern Indian groundwater practices. *Geoforum*, *39*, 466–482. doi:10.1016/j.geoforum.2007.09.008

Blair, J. P., & Reese, L. A. (Eds.). (1999). *Approaches to economic development: Readings from economic development quarterly*. Thousand Oaks, CA: Sage Publications.

Blakely, E. J., & Bradshow, T. K. (2002). *Planning local economic development: Theory and practice*. Thousand Oaks, CA: Sage Publication.

Bordo, M. D., & Schwartz, A. J. (2004). IS-LM and Monetarism. *History of Political Economy*, *36*(Supplement), 217–239. doi:10.1215/00182702-36-Suppl_1-217

Bossone, B., & Promisel, L. (1999). *The Role of Financial Self-Regulation in Developing Economies, Financial Sector* (Web Note). Washington, DC: The World Bank.

Bosworth, B., & Collins, S. (2003). The empirics of growth: An update. *Brookings Papers on Economic Activity*, *2*(xx), 113–206. doi:10.1353/eca.2004.0002

Bowen, J. R., & Rose, D. C. (1998). On the absence of privately owned, publicly traded corporations in China:

The Kirby Puzzle. *The Journal of Asian Studies*, *57*(2), 442–452. doi:10.2307/2658832

Boyd-Barrett, O. (2006). Cyberspace, globalization and empire. *Global Media and Communication*, *2*(21), 21–41. doi:10.1177/1742766506061815

Brandon, C., & Hommann, K. (1995). *The cost of inaction: Valuating the economy-wide costs of environmental degradation in India*. Washington, DC: The World Bank, Asia Environment Division.

Brandt, L. (1989). *Commercialization and agricultural development: Central and eastern China, 1870–1937*. New York: Cambridge University Press.

Bresnahan, T., & Trajtenberg, M. (1995). General purpose technologies. *Journal of Econometrics*, *65*, 83–108. doi:10.1016/0304-4076(94)01598-T

Brown, A. J. (2005). Regional governance and regionalism in Australia. In R. Eversole & J. Martin (Eds.), *Participation and governance in regional development: Global trends in an Australian context* (pp. 17-42). Aldershot, UK: Ashgate Publishing.

Bunno, T., Idota, H., Tsuji, M., Miyoshi, H., Ogawa, M., & Nakanishi, M. (2006). An Empirical Analysis of Indices and Factors of ICT Use by SMall- and Medium-sized Enterprises in Japan. In *Proceedings of 16th ITS Biennial Conference* (CD-ROM), Beijing, China.

Campanella, T. (2003). The City of the Sun. In *The New Atlantis and the City of Sun: Two Classic Utopias*. New York: Dower Publications.

Caneo, C. (2002, January). *Globalized and localized digital divides along the information highway: a fragile synthesis across bridges, ramps, cloverleaves, and ladders*. Paper presented at the 33rd Annual Sorokin Lecture, University of Saskatchewan.

Castells, M. (2001). *The Internet Galaxy*. Oxford, UK: Oxford University Press.

CEC. (2000). *Presidency Conclusions of the Lisbon European Council, March 23/24*. Brussels, Belgium: Commission of the European Communities.

CEC. (2001). *The Regional Dimension of the European Research Area*. Brussels, Belgium: Commission of the European Communities.

Central Intelligence Agency. (2008). *The 2008 World Factbook*. Retrieved January 2, 2009, from https://www.cia.gov/library/publications/the-world-factbook/index.html

Central Pollution Control Board. (1992). *Basin/Sub-Basin Inventory of Water Pollution - The Ganga Basin, Part One: The Yamuna sub-basin*. New Delhi, India: Central Pollution Control Board.

Central Statistical Organisation. (1997). *National Accounts Statistics*. New Delhi, India: Government of India.

Cevdet, A. (2002). Preface by the Translator (M. Sukru Hanioglu, Trans.). In C. Kurzman (Ed.), *Modernist Islam, 1840-1940: A Sourcebook* (pp. 172-175). New York: Oxford University Press.

Chamhuri, S. (2005). Poverty and governance: The role of the state, good governance, and an enabling policy framework in poverty alleviation in Malaysia. In J. Jabes (Ed.), *The role of public administration in alleviating poverty and improving governance* (pp. 22-41). Kuala Lumpur: Asian Development Bank.

Chandavarkar, A. (1992). Of Finance and Development: Neglected and Unsettled Questions. *World Development*, *22*, 133–142. doi:10.1016/0305-750X(92)90142-I

Chang, T., & Ho, Y.-H. (2002). Financial Development and Economic Growth in South Korea: A Note on Testing Demand-Following or Supply Leading Hypothesis. *The Indian Economic Journal*, *77*(2), 153–160.

Chataway, J., & Smith, J. (2007). Participation, communication and innovation: thinking about the international AIDS vaccine initiative. *IDS Bulletin*, *38*(5), 74–82. doi:10.1111/j.1759-5436.2005.tb00410.x

Chaurey, A., Ranganathan, M., & Mohanty, P. (2004). Electricity access for geographically disadvantaged rural communities – technology and policy insights. *Energy Policy*, *32*, 1693–1705. doi:10.1016/S0301-4215(03)00160-5

Chen, Y., Huang, W., Li, D., Zhang, P., Shen, H. Z., & Klamo, L. (2004). A comparative study of strategic issue of digital government implementations between developed and developing countries. In W. Huang, K. Siau, & K. K. Wei (Eds.), *Electronic government strategies and implementation* (pp. 191-213). Hershey, PA: Idea Group Publishing.

Chen, Z. W. (2006). *The stock market in China's modernization process: Its past, present and future prospects*. Yale School of Management - Unpublished Paper Working Paper.

Cheong, P. H. (2007). Gender and Percieved Internet Efficacy: Examining Secondary Digital Divide Issues in Singapore. *Women's . Studies in Communications*, *30*(2), 205–230.

Cheung, P. T. Y. *(1996). The political context of Shanghai's economic development. In Y. M. Yeung & Y. W. Sung (Eds.),* Shanghai: Transformation and modernization under China's open door *(pp. 49-92). Hong Kong: Chinese University Press.*

China to topple India as top offshoring center by '11. (2007). Retrieved September 1, 2007, from http://www.eetasia.com/ART_8800470999_480200_NT_e7abf55d.HTM

Christensen, M. (2006). EU Candidacy and Information Society Policies in Turkey: A Reality Check. *GMJ Mediterranean Edition*, *1*(1), 29–45.

Christensen, M. (2008). A Contentious Terrain in EU Information Society Policies: Media Pluralism and Freedom of Expression. *MedieKultur: Journal of Media and Communication Research*, *46*, 80–92.

Christopoulos, D. K., & Tsionas, E. G. (2004). Financial Development and Economic Growth: Evidence from Panel Unit Root and Cointegration Tests. *Journal of Development Economics*, *73*, 55–74. doi:10.1016/j.jdeveco.2003.03.002

Christou, G., & Simpson, S. (2007). Gaining a Stake in Global Internet Governance: The EU, ICANN and Strategic Norm Manipulation. *European Journal of Communication*, *22*(2), 147–164. doi:10.1177/0267323107076765

Ciborra, C. (2005). Interpreting e-government and development: Efficiency, transparency or governance at a distance? *Information Technology & People*, *18*(3), 260–279. doi:10.1108/09593840510615879

Ciborra, C., & Navarra, D. D. (2005). Good governance, development theory, and aid policy: Risks and challenges of e-government in Jordan. *Information Technology for Development*, *11*(2), 141–159. doi:10.1002/itdj.20008

Clarke, R. (1996). Equilibrium Interest Rates and Financial Liberalization in Developing Countries. *The Journal of Development Studies*, *32*(3), 391–413. doi:10.1080/00220389608422421

Cleaver, F. (2002). Reinventing institutions: bricolage and the social embeddedness of natural resource management. *European Journal of Development Research*, *14*, 11–30. doi:10.1080/714000425

Cleaver, F., & Frank, T. (2005). *Water Governance and Poverty: What Works for the Poor?* Bradford Centre for International Development, University of Bradford.

CMIE. (2007). *Mergers and Acquisitions*. Mumbai, India: Centre for Monitoring the Indian Economy.

Coe, D. T., & Helpman, E. (1995). International R&D Spillovers. *European Economic Review*, *39*(5), 859–887. doi:10.1016/0014-2921(94)00100-E

Coelli, T. J. (1992). A computer program for frontier production function estimation: Frontier version 2.0. *Economics Letters*, *39*(1), 29–32. doi:10.1016/0165-1765(92)90096-H

Cogburn, D. (2004). Elite Decision-making and Epistemic Communities: Implications for Global Information Policy. In S. Braman (Ed.), *The Emergent Information Regime* (pp. 155-178). New York: Palgrave.

Colby, D. (2001). Conceptualizing The "Digital Divide": Closing The "Gap" By Creating A Postmodern Network That Distributes The Productive Power Of Speech. *Communication Law and Policy*, *6*(1), 123–173. doi:10.1207/S15326926CLP0601_04

Coleman, J. S. (1990). *Foundations of Social Theory*. Cambridge, MA: Harvard University Press.

Commission of the European Communities. (2008). *Proposal for a Regulation of the European Parliament and of the Council on Credit Rating Agencies* (COD/2008/0217), Brussels.

Cooke, P., Roper, S., & Wylie, P. (2003). The Golden Thread of Innovation and Northern Ireland's Evolving Regional Innovation System. *Regional Studies, 37*(4), 365–379. doi:10.1080/0034340032000074406

Council of European Union. (2005). *The European consensus on development* (Brussels 14820/05).

Crenshaw, E. M., & Robison, K. (2006). Globalization and the Digital Divide: The Roles of Structural Conduciveness and Global Connection in Internet Diffusion. *Social Science Quarterly, 87*(1), 190–207. doi:10.1111/j.0038-4941.2006.00376.x

Creti, A. (2001). Network technologies, communication externalities and total factor productivity. *Structural Change and Economic Dynamics, 12*(1), 1–28. doi:10.1016/S0954-349X(99)00029-6

Dadaro, S. (1993). Exports and Economic Growth: A Reconsideration of Causality. *Journal of Developing Areas, 27*, 227–244.

Danson, M., Halkier, H., & Damborg, C. (2002). Regional development agencies in Europe: An introduction and framework for analysis. In H. Halkier, M. Danson, & C. Damborg (Eds.), *Regional development agencies in Europe* (pp. 13-25). London: Routledge.

Darrat, A. F. (1999). Are Financial Deepening and Economic Growth Causality Related? Another Look at the Evidence. *International Economic Journal, 13*(3), 19–35. doi:10.1080/10168739900080018

Das, R. K., & Kumar, R. (2007). Export-led Growth in South Asia: A Panel Evidence. *The Indian Economic Journal, 55*(3), 132–146.

David, P. (1990). The dynamo and the computer: A historical perspective on the modern productivity paradox. *The American Economic Review, 80*(2), 355–361.

Davidson, J., & Lockwood, M. (2008). Partnerships as instruments of good regional governance: Innovation for sustainability in Tasmania. *Regional Studies, 42*(5), 641–656. doi:10.1080/00343400701543165

Dawar, N., & Frost, T. (1999). Competing with Giants: Survival Strategies for Local Companies in Emerging Markets. *Harvard Business Review, 77*(2), 119–129.

De Gregorio, J., & Guidotti, P. E. (1995). Financial Development and Economic Growth. *World Development, 23*(3), 433–448. doi:10.1016/0305-750X(94)00132-I

de Janvry, A., & Sadoulet, E. (2002). World poverty and the role of agricultural technology: direct and indirect effects. *The Journal of Development Studies, 38*(4), 1–26. doi:10.1080/00220380412331322401

De La Fuente, A., & Marin, J. M. (1994). *Innovations, Bank Monitoring and Endogenous Financial Development* (Universitat Pompeu Fabra Working Paper, No. 59).

Deardorff, A. (1984). The General Validity of the Law of Comparative Advantage. *The Journal of Political Economy, 88*, 941–957. doi:10.1086/260915

Deme, M. (2002). An Examination of the Trade-Led Growth Hypothesis in Nigeria: AS Cointegration, Causality, and Impulse Response Analysis. *Journal of Developing Areas, 36*(1), 1–15.

Demetriades, P. O., & Hussein, A. K. (1996). Does Financial Development Cause Economic Growth? Time Series Evidence from 16 Countries. *Journal of Development Economics, 51*, 387–411. doi:10.1016/S0304-3878(96)00421-X

Demetriades, P. O., & Luintel, K. B. (1996). Financial Development, Economic Growth and Banking Sector Controls: Evidence from India. *The Economic Journal, 106*, 359–374. doi:10.2307/2235252

Denton, F. (2002). Climate change vulnerability, impacts, and adaptation: why does gender matter? *Gender and Development, 10*(2), 10–20. doi:10.1080/13552070215903

Dewan, S., & Kraemer, K. L. (2000). Information technology and productivity: evidence from country-level data. *Management Science, 46*(4), 548–562. doi:10.1287/mnsc.46.4.548.12057

Dewan, S., & Riggins, J. F. (2005). The digital divide: current research and future directions. *Journal of the Association of Information Systems*, 6(12), 298-337. Retrieved March 20, 2009, from http://misrc.umn.edu/workingpapers/fullpapers/2005/0524_120605.pdf

Dewey, J. (1920). *Reconstruction in Philosophy*. New York: Henry Holt and Company.

Dewey, J. (1957). *Outlines of A Critical Theory of Ethics*. New York: Hillary House.

Dewey, J. (1967). The Public and Its Problems. In J. Boydston (Ed.), *The Early Works, 1882-1898* (Vol. 2). Carbondale, IL: Southern Illinois University Press.

Dewey, J. (1969). The Ethics of Democracy, In J. Boydston (Ed.), *The Early Works, 1882-1898* (Vol. 1). Carbondale, IL: Southern Illinois University Press.

Dewey, J., & Tufts, J. H. (1959). *Ethics*. New York: Henry Holt and Company.

Dikito-Wachtmeister, M. (2000). *Women's participation in decision-making processes in rural water projects, Makoni district, Zimbabwe*. Unpublished doctoral dissertation, University of Bradford, UK.

DiMaggio, P., & Hargittai, E. (2001). *From the 'Digital Divide' to 'Digital Inequality': Studying Internet Use as Penetration Increases* (Working Paper #15). Center for Arts and Cultural Policy Studies, Princeton University.

Din, M.-u. (2004). Exports, Imports, and Economic Growth in South Asia: Evidence Using a Multivariate Time Series Framework. *Pakistan Development Review*, *43*(2), 105–124.

Din, M.-u., Ghani, E., & Siddique, O. (2003). Openness and Economic Growth in Pakistan. *Pakistan Development Review*, *42*(4), 795–807.

DOI (Digital Opportunity Initiative). (2001). *Creating a development dynamic*. New York: Digital Opportunity Initiative.

Dollar, D. (1992). Outward-Oriented Developing Economies Really Do Grow More Rapidly: Evidence from 95 LDCs, 1976-85. *Economic Development and Cultural Change*, *40*(3), 553–544. doi:10.1086/451959

Doornbos, M. (2001). Good governance: The rise and decline of a policy metaphor? *The Journal of Development Studies*, *37*(6), 93–108. doi:10.1080/713601084

Dornbusch, R. (1992). The Case for Trade Liberalization in Developing Countries. *The Journal of Economic Perspectives*, *6*(1), 69–85.

DPT. (2004, January). *Contributions of Turkey to e-Europe+ 2003 Progress Report*.

DPT. (2005, March). *e-Dönüşüm Türkiye Projesi 2005 Eylem Planı*.

DPT. (2008, February). *OECD IT Policy Questionnaire 2008*.

Drori, G. S. (2007). Information Society as a Global Policy Agenda: What Does it Tell Us About the Age of Globalization? *International Journal of Comparative Sociology*, *48*(4), 297–316. doi:10.1177/0020715207079532

Drori, G. S., & Jang, Y. S. (2003). The Global Digital Divide: A Sociological Assessments of Trends and Causes. *Social Science Computer Review*, *21*(2), 144–161. doi:10.1177/0894439303021002002

Dudek, C. M. (2001). European Union's effect upon regional economic development and regional government's policy making ability. *Regional & Federal Studies*, *11*(1), 101–125.

Dulupçu, M. A. (2004). *Bolognese Yenilik (İnovasyon) Stratejileri: Türkiye'de Bölgesel Gelişme İçin Alternatif Olabilir mi? 4*. İzmir İktisat Kongresi, Ankara: SPO.

Dulupçu, M. A. (2006). Bölgesel Politikalar Kopyalanabilir Mi? Bölgeselleş(tir)me (Yönetim) Karşısında (Yeni) Bölge(sel)cilik (Yönetişim). In *Bölgesel Yönetişim Sempozyumu*. Ankara, Türkiye: METU-TEPAV.

Dulupcu, M. A., & Ozgur, H. (2006). Yerel ekonomik gelişmede yerel yönetimlerin rolü. In H. Ozgur & B. Parlak (Eds.), *Avrupa perspektifinde yerel yönetimler* (pp. 171-202). Bursa, Turkey: Alfa Aktüel.

Dunning, J. H. (2000). The Eclectic Paradigm as an Envelope for Economic and Business Theories of MNE Activity. *International Business Review*, (2): 163–190. doi:10.1016/S0969-5931(99)00035-9

Dunning, J. H., et al. (1998). Third World Multinationals Revisited: New Developments and Theoretical Implications. In J.H. Dunning (Ed.), *Globalization, Trade and Foreign Direct Investment*. Oxford, UK: Pergamon.

Durlauf, S., Johnson, P., & Temple, J. (2005). Empirics of growth and development. In P. Aghion & S. N. Durlauf (Eds.), *Handbook of Economic Growth*. Amsterdam: North-Holland.

Durlauf, S., Kourtellos, A., & Tan, C. (2008). Are Any Growth Theories Robust? *The Economic Journal*, *118*(527), 329–346. doi:10.1111/j.1468-0297.2007.02123.x

Easterly, W., Levine, R., & Roodman, D. (2004). Aid, policies and growth [Comment]. *The American Economic Review*, *94*(3), 774–780. doi:10.1257/0002828041464560

Economist intelligence unit. (2008). Country profile – China. London: The Economist.

Edwards, S. (1992). Trade Orientation, Distortions, and Growth in Developing Countries. *Journal of Development Economics*, *39*, 31–57. doi:10.1016/0304-3878(92)90056-F

Edwards, S. (1998). Openness, Productivity and Growth: What Do we Really Know? *The Economic Journal*, *108*(447), 383–398. doi:10.1111/1468-0297.00293

El Serafy, S. (1989). The proper calculation of income from depletable natural resources. In Y. J. Ahmad et al. (Eds.), *Environmental Accounting for Sustainable Development*. Washington, DC: World Bank.

Elçi, S., Karataylı, İ., & Karaata, S. (2008). *Bölgesel İnovasyon Merkezleri: Türkiye İçin Bir Model Önerisi* (Publication No. TÜSİAD-T/2008-12/477). Türkiye: TÜSİAD.

Elkhoury, M. (2008). Credit Rating Agencies and Their Potential Impact on Developing Countries. In *United Nations Conference on Trade and Development, Discussion Paper No. 186,* (UNCTAD/OSG/DP/2008/1), United Nations.

Engle, R. F., & Granger, C. W. J. (1987). Cointegration and Error Correction: Representation, Estimation and Testing. *Econometrica*, *55*(2), 251–276. doi:10.2307/1913236

ESİNKAP. (2009). *Eskişehir İli İnovasyon Stratejileri İçin Kapasite Oluşturma Projesi*. Türkiye Teknoloji Geliştirme Vakfı.

Estevao, M. M. (2004). *Why is productivity growth in the euro area so sluggish?* (IMF working paper WP/04/200).

European Commission. (1993). *White Paper on Growth, Competitiveness, and Employment. The Challenges and Ways Forward into the 21st Century*. Brussels, Belgium: European Commission.

European Commission. (1997). *Methodology Guides for RIS Projects: Guidelines for Project Managers*. Brussels, Belgium: European Commission.

European Commission. (1998). *Regional Innovation Strategy Pilot Projects. Article 10 of the European Regional Development Fund*. Brussels, Belgium: European Commission.

European Commission. (1999). *A Guide to Regional Innovation Strategies*. Brussels, Belgium: European Commission.

European Commission. (2005). *Working Together for Growth and Jobs: A New Start for the Lisbon Strategy*. Brussels, Belgium: European Commission.

Fama, E. (1970). Efficient Capital Markets: A Review of Theory and Empirical Work. *The Journal of Finance*, *25*, 383–417. doi:10.2307/2325486

Fanelli, J. M., & Medhora, R. (2002). Finance and Competitiveness: Framework and Synthesis. In J. M. Fanelli & R. Medhora (Eds.), *Finance and Competition in Developing Countries* (pp. 1-19). Ottawa, Canada: International Development Research Centre.

Fase, M., & Abma, R. (2003). Financial Environment and Economic Growth in Selected Asian Countries.

Journal of Asian Economics, 12, 11–21. doi:10.1016/S1049-0078(02)00237-3

Feder, G. (1983). On Export and Economic Growth. *Journal of Development Economics, 12*, 59–74. doi:10.1016/0304-3878(83)90031-7

Feenberg, A. (1999). *Questioning technology*. London: Routledge

Feldstein, M. (2003). Why is Productivity Growing Faster? *Journal of Policy Modeling, 25*(5), 445–451. doi:10.1016/S0161-8938(03)00039-5

Feng, H. Y., Froud, J., & Johal, S. (2001, November). A new business model? The capital market and the new economy. *Economy and Society, 30*(4), 467–503. doi:10.1080/03085140120089063

Ferreira da Silva, G. (2002). The Impact of Financial System Development on Business Cycle Volatility: Cross-Country Evidence. *Journal of Macroeconomics, 24*, 233–253. doi:10.1016/S0164-0704(02)00021-6

Ferry, M. (2007). From government to governance: Polish regional development agencies in a changing regional context. *Eastern European Politics and Societies, 21*(3), 447–474. doi:10.1177/0888325407303706

Filiztekin, A. (1998). *Convergence Across Industries and Provinces in Turkey* (No. 1998/08). İstanbul, Türkiye: Koç University.

Filiztekin, A. (2008). *Türkiye'de Bölgesel Farklar ve Politikalar* (Publication No.TÜSİAD-T/2008-09/471). Türkiye: TÜSİAD.

Fitch Ratings. (2005, February 8). *Statement of Stephen W. Joynt, President and Chief Executive Officer, Fitch Ratings, in the Hearing of the U.S. Senate Committee on Banking, Housing and Urban Affairs on Examining the Role of Credit Rating Agencies in the Capital Markets*. European Union. (2006, March 11). Communication from the Commission on Credit Rating Agencies (2006/C 59/02). *Official Journal of the European Union, C*(59/02).

Fitch Ratings. (2009, March 3). *Coercive Debt Exchange Criteria*.

Fontana, G. (2006). *The "New Consensus" View of Monetary Policy: A New Wicksellian Connection?* (Working Paper, 476). The Levy Economics Institute.

Forstater, M., & Randall, L. W. (2007). *The General Theory after 70 Years*. Houndsmills, UK: Palgrave Publishing.

Frankel, J. A., & Romer, D. (1999). Does Trade Causes Growth? *The American Economic Review, 89*, 379–399.

Frasheri, S. S. (2002). Transferring the New Civilization to the Islamic Peoples (M. Sukru Hanioğlu, Trans.). In C. Kurzman (Ed.), *Modernist Islam, 1840-1940: A Sourcebook* (pp. 149-151). New York: Oxford University Press.

Freeman, C. (1987). *Technology Policy and Economic Performance: Lessons from Japan*. London: Frances Pinter.

Freeman, C. (1988). Japan: A New Institutional System of Innovation? In G. Dosi, C. Freeman, R. Nelson, G. Silverberg, & L. Soete (Eds.), *Technical Change and Economic Theory*. London: Pinter.

Freeman, C. (1989). New Technology and Catching Up. *European Journal of Development Research, 1*(1), 85–93. doi:10.1080/09578818908426503

Freeman, C., & Soete, L. (1997). *The Economics of Industrial Innovation*. London: Pinter.

Frees, E. W. (2004). *Longitudinal and Panel Data: Analysis and Applications in the Social Sciences*. West Nyack, NY, USA: Cambridge University Press.

Friedman, M. (1956). The Quantity Theory of Money: A Restatement. In M. Friedman (Ed.), *Studies in the Quantity Theory of Money*. Chicago, IL: University of Chicago Press.

Friedman, M. (1968). The Role of Monetary Policy. *The American Economic Review, 58*, 1–7.

Fry, M. J. (1988). *Money, Interest, and Banking in Economic Development*. Baltimore, MD: Johns Hopkins University Press.

Fry, M. J. (1995). *Money, Interest Rate, and Banking in Economic Development* (2nd ed.). Baltimore, MD: The Johns Hopkins University Press.

Fry, M. J. (1997). In Favour of Financial Liberalization. *The Economic Journal*, *107*, 754–770. doi:10.1111/1468-0297.00191

Gammeltoft, P. (2008). Emerging Multinationals: Outward FDI from the BRICS Countries. *International Journal of Technology and Globalisation*, *4*(1), 5–22. doi:10.1504/IJTG.2008.016184

Gannon, C., et al. (2002). Transport. In K. Jeni (Ed.), *A source book for poverty reduction* (Vol. 2, pp. 232-369). Washington DC: World Bank. Retrieved October 21, 2008, from http://povlibrary.worldbank.org/files/13886_chap22.pdf

Garrison, R. W. (2005). *Time and Money. The Macroeconomics of Capital Structure*. London, UK: Routledge.

Geddes, M., & Newman, I. (1999). Evolution and conflict in local economic development. *Local Economy*, *14*(1), 12–26. doi:10.1080/02690949908726472

Gencel Bek, M. (2003). Küreselleşme, Ulus-Devlet ve İletişim: Avrupa Birliği'nin Türkiye'deki İletişim Politikalarına Etkisi Üzerine Bir Değerlendirme. In M. Gencel Bek (Ed.), *Küreselleşme, İletişim Endüstrileri ve Kimlikler: Avrupa Birliği ve Türkiye'de İletişim Politikaları* (pp. 237-286). Ankara, Turkey: Ümit Yay.

Geray, H. (1999). Network Policy Formation between Idealist and Strategic Models: a political economy perspective from Turkey. *Telecommunications Policy*, *23*, 495–511. doi:10.1016/S0308-5961(99)00033-6

Geray, H. (2000). *Extent and Scope of Digital Divide in Turkey: Policy Perspectives*. Paper presented at the OECD/DSTI, WPIE/TSIP Workshop, December 2000, OECD Paris.

Gezici, F., & Hewings, G. J. D. (2004). Regional Convergence and the Economic Performance of Peripheral Areas in Turkey. *Review of Urban and Regional Development Studies*, *16*(2), 113–132. doi:10.1111/j.1467-940X.2004.00082.x

Ghatak, S. (1997). Financial Liberalization: The Case of Sri Lanka. *Empirical Economics*, *22*(1), 117–131. doi:10.1007/BF01188173

Ghazanfar, S. M. (2003). The Economic Thought of Abu Hamid Al-Ghazali and St. Thomas Aquinas: Some comparative parallels and links. In S. M. Ghazanfar (Ed.), *Medieval Islamic Economic Thought: Filling the Great Gap in European Economics* (pp. 184-208). New York: Routledge, Curzon.

Ghazzali, A. H. (1873). *The Alchemy of Happiness* (Henry A. Homes, Trans.). Albany, New York: Munsell.

Ghazzali, A. H. (1921). *Some Religious and Moral Teachings of Al-Ghazzali* (S. N. Ali, Trans.). Baroda, India: Lakshmi Vilas P. Press.

Giovannetti, E., Kagami, M., & Tsuji, M. (Eds.). (2003). *The Internet Revolution: A Global Perspective*. Cambridge, UK: Cambridge University Press.

Godø, H. (2008). Technological evolution, innovation and human agency. In E. G. Carayannis, A. Kaloudis, & A. Mariussen (Eds.), *Diversity in the knowledge economy and society* (pp. 18-34). Cheltenham, UK: Edward Elgar.

Gokalp, Z. (2002). Islam and Modern Civilization (N. Berkes, Trans.). In C. Kurzman (Ed.), *Modernist Islam, 1840-1940: A Sourcebook* (pp. 192-197). New York: Oxford University Press.

Golami, R., Sang-Yong, T. L., & Almas, H. (2003). *The Casual Relationship between Information and Communication Technology and Foreign Direct Investment* (WIDER Discussion Paper, No. WDP 2003/30).

Goldsmith, R. W. (1969). *Financial Structure and Development*. New Haven, CT: Yale University Press.

Graham, J., Amos, B., & Plumptre, T. (2003). *Principles for good governance in the 21st century* (Policy Brief No. 15). Ottawa, Canada: Institute on Governance.

Granger, C. (1988). Some recent developments in a concept of causality. *Journal of Econometrics*, *39*(2), 199–211. doi:10.1016/0304-4076(88)90045-0

Greenaway, D., Morgan, W., & Wright, P. (2002). Trade Liberalization and Growth in Developing Countries. *Journal of Development Economics, 67*, 229–244. doi:10.1016/S0304-3878(01)00185-7

Greenwood, J., & Jovanovic, B. (1990). Financial Development, Growth and the Distribution of Income. *The Journal of Political Economy, 98*(5), 1076–1107. doi:10.1086/261720

Greenwood, J., & Smith, B. (1997). Financial Markets in Development and the Development of Financial Markets. *Journal of Economic Dynamics & Control, 21*, 145–181. doi:10.1016/0165-1889(95)00928-0

Greiner, A., Semler, W., & Gong, G. (2004). *The Forces of Economic Growth: A Time Series Perspective*. Princeton, NJ: Princeton University Press.

Guillén, M. F., & Suárez, S. L. (2005). Explaining the Global Digital Divide: Economic, Political and Sociological Drivers of Cross-National Internet Use. *Social Forces, 84*(2), 681–708. doi:10.1353/sof.2006.0015

Gupta, K. L. (1984). *Finance and Economic Growth in Developing Countries*. London: Croom Helm.

Gürak, H. (2006). *Ekonomik Büyüme ve Küresel Ekonomi*. Bursa, Türkiye: Ekin Yayınevi.

Halavais, A. (2000). National Borders on the World Wide Web. *New Media & Society, 2*(1), 7–28. doi:10.1177/14614440022225689

Haldenwang, C. V. (2004). Electronic government (e-government) and development. *European Journal of Development Research, 16*(2), 417–432. doi:10.1080/0957881042000220886

Halkier, H. (2006, Eylül). *Regional development agencies and multi-level governance: European perspectives*. Paper presented at the Bölgesel Kalkınma ve Yönetişim Sempozyumu, Ankara.

Halkier, H., & Danson, M. (1997). Regional development agencies in western Europe: A survey of key characteristics and trends. *European Urban and Regional Studies, 4*(3), 243–256. doi:10.1177/096977649700400304

Hand, J. R., Holthausen, R. W., & Leftwich, R. W. (1992). The Effect Of Bond Rating Agency Announcements On Bond And Stock Prices. *The Journal of Finance, 47*(2), 733–752. doi:10.2307/2329121

Hannon, B. M. (1991). Accounting in Ecological Systems. In R. Costanza (Ed.), *Ecological Economics: The Science and Management of Sustainability* (pp. 234-252). New York: Columbia University Press.

Harchaoui, T., Tarkhani, F., Jackson, C., & Armstrong, P. (2002). Information technology and economic growth in Canada & the US. *Monthly Labour Review*. Retrieved from http://www.bls.gov/opub/mlr/2002

Hardy, A. (1980). The Role of the Telephone in Economic Development. *Telecommunications Policy, 4*(4), 278–286. doi:10.1016/0308-5961(80)90044-0

Haripriya, G. S. (2000). Integrating forest resources into the system of national accounts in Maharashtra. *Environment and Development Economics, 5*, 143–156. doi:10.1017/S1355770X00000103

Harwit, E. (2005). Telecommunications and the internet in Shanghai: Political and economic factors shaping the network in a Chinese city. *Urban Studies (Edinburgh, Scotland), 42*(10), 1837–1858. doi:10.1080/00420980500231738

Has Hacib, Y. (2006). *Kutadgu Bilig* (R. R. Arat, Trans.). Istanbul, Turkey: Kabalcı Publishing.

Hayami, Y., & Godo, Y. (2005). *Development Economics: From the Poverty to the Wealth of Nations*. Oxford, UK: Oxford University Press.

Heeks, R. (1999). Reinventing government in the information age. In R. Heeks (Ed.), *Reinventing government in the information age: International practice in IT-enabled public sector reform* (pp. 9-21). London: Routledge.

Heeks, R. (2001). *Building e-governance for development: A framework for national and donor action* (Working Paper, No: 12). Manchester, UK: University of Manchester, Institute for Development Policy and Management.

Heeks, R. (2001). *Understanding e-governance for development* (Working Paper, No: 11). Manchester, UK:

University of Manchester, Institute for Development Policy and Management.

Helpman, E. (1984). The Factor Content of Foreign Trade. *The Economic Journal*, *94*, 84–94. doi:10.2307/2232217

Helpman, E. (Ed.). (1998). *General purpose technologies and economic growth*. Cambridge, MA: MIT Press

Helpman, E., & Krugman, P. R. (1985). *Market Structure and Foreign Trade: Increasing Returns, Imperfect Competition and the International Economy*. Bridgton, ME: Wheatsheaf Books.

Hendry, D., & Krolxig, H. (2005). The properties of automatic GETS modeling. *The Economic Journal*, *115*(20), C32–C31. doi:10.1111/j.0013-0133.2005.00979.x

Hendry, D., Pagan, A., & Saragan, J. (1984). Dynamic Specification In Z. Grilliches & M. D. Intriligator (Eds.), *Handbook of Econometrics* (Vol. 2, pp. 1023-1100). Amsterdam: North-Holland.

Heyd, U. (1950). *Foundations ofTurkish Nationalism: The Life and Teachings of Ziya Gokalp*. London: Luzac.

Hicks, J. (1969). *A Theory of Economic History*. Oxford, UK: Clarendon Press.

Horesh, N. (2007). The bund and beyond: Re-thinking the sino-foreign financial grid in pre-war Shanghai. *China Review*, *7*(1), 1–26.

Hossain, F. (2007). *What has happened to development administration? Some critical reflections* (Working Paper, No: 72). Manchester, UK: University of Manchester, Institute for Development Policy and Management.

Houben, A., & Kakes, J. (2002). ICT innovation and economic performance: The role of financial intermediation. *Kyklos*, *55*(4), 543–562. doi:10.1111/1467-6435.00201

Howe, C. (1981). Industrialization under conditions of long-run population stability: Shanghai's achievement and prospect. In C. Howe (Ed.), *Shanghai: Revolution and development in an Asian metropolis* (pp. 153-187). Cambridge, UK: Cambridge University Press.

Hsiao, C. (2002). *Analysis of panel data*. Cambridge, UK: Cambridge University Press.

Huang, C. (2002). *How do endogenous models explain the Asian growth experience? A time series study of eleven Asian economies* (Working paper 2002). Department of Economics, National Tsing Hua University.

Huang, Y. S. (2008). *Capitalism with Chinese characteristics: Entrepreneurship and the state*. Cambridge, UK: Cambridge University Press.

Hudson, H. E. (2000). Extending access to the digital economy to rural and developing regions. In E. Bryjoltsson & B. Kahin (Eds.), *Understanding the digital economy: Data, tools and research* (pp. 261-291). Cambridge, MA: MIT Press.

Hudson, R. (2007). Regions and regional uneven development forever? Some reflective comments upon theory and practice. *Regional Studies*, *41*(9), 1149–1160. doi:10.1080/00343400701291617

Huerta De Soto, J. (1998). *Dinero, Crédito bancario y Ciclos Económicos*. Madrid, Spain: Unión Editorial. Galì, J. (2000). *New Perspectives on Monetary Policy, Inflation, and the Business Cycle*. Paper presented at the 2000 World Congress of the Econometric Society, Seattle.

Hughes, O. (2003). *Public management and administration: An introduction*. New York: Palgrave Macmillan. infoDEV (Information for Development Programme). (2002). *The e-government handbook for developing countries*. Washington, DC.: infoDEV and Center for Democracy and Technology.

Hume, D. (1960). *An Enquiry Concerning the Principles of Morals*. La Salle, IL: Open Court Publishing.

Hur, J., Raj, M., & Riyanto, Y. E. (2006). Finance and Trade: A Cross-Country Empirical Analysis on the Impact of Financial Development and Asset Tangibility on International Trade. *World Development*, *34*, 1728–1741. doi:10.1016/j.worlddev.2006.02.003

Hymer, S. (1976). *The International Operation ofNational Firms*. Cambridge, MA: MIT Press.

Ibn Haldun. (1989). *Mukaddime (volume I-III)* (Z. K. Ugan, Trans.). Istanbul, Turkey: Milli Egitim Bakanlıgı Press.

Ibn Khaldun. (1950). *An Arab Philosophy of History: Selections from the Prolegomena of Ibn Khaldun of Tunis (1332-1406)* (C. Issawi, Trans.) (1st ed.). London: John Murray.

Iimi, A. (2004). Banking Sector Reforms in Pakistan: Economies of Scale and Scope, and Cost Complementarities. *Journal of Asian Economics*, *15*, 507–528.

Imai, K. (2006). Culture, Civilization or Economy? Test of the Clash of Civilizations Thesis. *International Journal on World Peace*, *23*(3). Retrieved January 1, 2009, from http://findarticles.com/p/articles/mi_hb6428/is_3_23/ai_n29321324

infoDEV (Information for Development Programme). (2003). *Information and communication technologies, poverty and development: Learning from experience*. Washington, DC: World Bank.

Innovating Regions in Europe Network-IRE. (2005). *RIS Methodological Guide Stage Zero.* IRE Secretariat.

Innovating Regions in Europe Network-IRE. (2006). *RIS Methodological Guide Stage One.* IRE Secretariat.

Innovating Regions in Europe Network-IRE. (2007). *RIS Methodological Guide Stage Two,* IRE Secretariat.

International Monetary Fund. (1999). Emerging Markets in the New Financial System: Nonstandard Responses to External Pressure and the Role of the Major Credit Rating Agencies in Global Financial Markets. In *World Economic and Financial Surveys, International Capital Markets: Developments, Prospects, and Key Policy Issues*. Washington DC: International Monetary Fund.

International Organization of Securities Commissions. (2003, September 25). *IOSCO Statement of Principles Regarding the Activities of Credit Rating Agencies: A Statement of the Technical Committee of the International Organization of Securities Commissions.*

Iqbal, Z., & Zahid, G. M. (1998). Macroeconomic Determinants of Economic Growth in Pakistan. *Pakistan Development Review*, *37*(2), 125–148.

Irwin, A. D., & Tervio, M. (2002). Does Trade Raise Income? Evidence from the Twentieth Century. *Journal of Development Economics*, *58*(1), 1–18.

Jackson, T. (2005). *Motivating sustainable behaviour: a review of evidence on consumer behaviour and behavioural change*. University of Surrey, Centre for Environmental Strategy.

James, J. (2005). The Global Digital Divide İn The Internet: Developed Countries Constructs And Third World Realities. *Journal of Information Science*, *31*(2), 114–123. doi:10.1177/0165551505050788

Jayaratne, J., & Strahan, P. (1996). The Finance-Growth Nexus: Evidence from Bank Branch Deregulation. *The Quarterly Journal of Economics*, *111*(3), 639–670. doi:10.2307/2946668

Jeffrey, C., & Mawson, J. (2002). Introduction: Beyond the white paper on the English regions. *Regional Studies*, *36*(7), 715–720. doi:10.1080/0034340022000006033

Jeffrey, C., & Reilly, A. (2003). *Devolution to the regions (executive summary)*. London: LGA Publication.

Jessop, B. (1998). The rise of governance and the risk of failure: The case of economic development. *International Social Science Journal*, *50*(155), 29–45. doi:10.1111/1468-2451.00107

Jha, R. (2006). Outward Foreign Direct Investment from India. In *2006 Global Meeting.* VA: Emerging Markets Forum.

Jin, J. C. (2000). Openness and Growth: An Interpretation of Empirical Evidence from East Asian Countries. *The Journal of International Trade & Economic Development*, *9*(1), 5–17. doi:10.1080/096381900362517

Jinqiu, Z. (2008). Information and communications technology for poverty reduction: Bringing technology to rural and disadvantaged communities in West China. In P. Steel, N. Fernandor, & M. Weddikkara (Eds.), *Poverty reduction that works: Experience of scaling up development success* (pp. 129-146). London: UNDP, Earthscan.

Jipp, A. (1963). Wealth of nations and telephone density. *Telecommunications Journal*, 199-201.

Johansen, S. (1988). Statistical Analysis of Cointegrating Vectors. *Journal of Economic Dynamics & Control*, *12*, 231–254. doi:10.1016/0165-1889(88)90041-3

Johansen, S. (1991). Estimation and Hypothesis Testing of Cointegrating Vectors in Gaussian Vector Autoregressive Models. *Econometrics*, *55*, 251–276.

Johansen, S., & Juselius, K. (1990). Maximum Likelihood Estimation and Inference on Cointegration-with Application to the Demand for Money. *Oxford Bulletin of Economics and Statistics*, *52*(2), 169–210.

John, P. (2001). *Local governance in western Europe*. London: Sage Publication.

Jones, C. (1995). Time series tests of endogenous growth models. *The Quarterly Journal of Economics*, *110*(2), 495–525. doi:10.2307/2118448

Jorgenson, D. W., & Stiroh, K. J. (2000). Raising the speed limit: U.S. economic growth in the information age. *Brookings Papers on Economic Activity*, *1*, 125–211. doi:10.1353/eca.2000.0008

Jorgenson, D. W., & Vu, K. (2005). Information technology and the world economy. *The Scandinavian Journal of Economics*, *107*(4), 631–650. doi:10.1111/j.1467-9442.2005.00430.x

Kabir, S. H., & Hoque, H. A. A. B. (2007). Financial Liberalization, Financial Development and Economic Growth: Evidence from Bangladesh. *Savings and Development*, *31*, 431–448.

Karaca, O. (2004). *Türkiye'de Bölgelerarası Gelir Farklılıkları: Yakınsama var mı?* (Discussion Paper, No.: 2004/7). Ankara, Türkiye: Turkish Economic Association.

Kateja, A., & Jha, D. (2008). Exploring the Casual Relationship between Telecommunication and GDP Growth in India, 1988-2007. *Artha Vijnana*, *L*(3), 195–208.

Kayasü, S., & Yaşar, S. (2006, Eylül). *Avrupa Birliği'ne üyelik sürecinde kalkınma politikaları: Yasal ve kurumsal dönüşümler*. Paper presented at the Bölgesel Kalkınma ve Yönetişim Sempozyumu, Ankara.

Keely, C., & Quah, T. (1998). *Technology in Growth* (CEP discussion paper no. 391).

Keesing, D. B. (1967). Outward-looking Policies and Economic Development. *The Economic Journal*, *77*(306), 303–320. doi:10.2307/2229306

Keesing, D. B. (1979, August). Trade Policies for Developing Countries (World Bank Staff Working Paper, 353).

Kelly, K. (1995). *A framework for evaluating public sector geographic information systems*. Albany, NY: University of Albany, Centre for Technology in Government.

Kemal, A. R., Din, M.-u., Qardir, U., Fernando, L., & Colombage, S. (2002). *Exports and Economic Growth in South Asia*. A Study Prepared for the South Asia Network of Economic Research Institutes.

Kenny, C., Navas-Sabater, J., & Oiang, C. (2002). Information and communication technologies. In K. Jeni (Ed). *A source book for poverty reduction* (Vol. 2, pp. 405-438). Washington, DC: World Bank. Retrieved October 21, 2008, from http://povlibrary.worldbank.org/files/4430_chap17.pdf

Keynes, J. M. (1936). *The General Theory of Employment, Interest, and Money*. London, UK: MacMillan.

Khalid, A., & Cheng, B. T. (1997). Imports, Exports and Economic Growth: Cointegration and Causality Tests for Singapore. *The Singapore Economic Review*, *42*(2), 32–39.

Khan, A. H., & Hasan, L. (1998). Financial Liberalization, Savings, and Economic Development in Pakistan. *Economic Development and Cultural Change*, *46*(3), 581–597. doi:10.1086/452359

Khan, A. H., Malik, A., & Hasan, L. (1995). Exports, Growth and Causality: An Application of Cointegration and Error-Correction Modelling. *Pakistan Development Review*, *34*(4), 1001–1012.

Khan, M. A. (2004, December). Media globalization and the digital divide. In *Proceedings of an international conference on Poverty in the Muslim Countries and Communities: Causes and Solutions*, Kuala Lumpur, Malaysia.

Khan, M. A. (2007). *Foreign Direct Investment and Economic Growth: The Role of Domestic Financial Sector* (PIDE Working Papers 2007:18).

Khan, M. A. (2008). Financial Development and Economic Growth in Pakistan: Evidence Based on Autoregressive Distributed Lag (ARDL) Approach. *South Asia Economic Journal*, *9*(2), 375–391. doi:10.1177/139156140800900206

Khan, M. A., & Qayyum, A. (2006). Trade Liberalization Financial Sector Reforms, and Growth. *Pakistan Development Review*, *45*(4), 711–731.

Khan, M. A., Qayyum, A., & Sheikh, S. A. (2005). Financial Development and Economic Growth: The Case of Pakistan. *Pakistan Development Review*, *44*(4), 819–837.

Khan, M. S., & Senhadji, A. S. (2000). *Financial Development and Economic Growth: An Overview* (IMF Working Paper 00/209). Washington, DC: International Monetary Fund.

Khan, M. S., & Zahler, R. (1985). Trade and Financial Liberalization Given External Shocks and Inconsistent Domestic Policies. *IMF Staff Papers*, *32*, 22–55.

Khana, T., & Palepu, K. (2006). Emerging Giants: Building World-Class Companies in Developing Countries. *Harvard Business Review*, *84*(10), 60–70.

Khosrow-Pour, M. (Ed.). (2005). *Practicing e-government: A global perspective*. Hershey, PA: Idea Group Publishing.

Kılıc, R. (2008). Calısma Hayatımızın Problemleri Uzerine. In *Islam ve Calısma Hayatı Ulusal Sempozyumu* (pp. 360-366). Izmir, Turkey: Faculty of Divinity Publishing.

Kim, P. S., Halligan, J., Cho, N., Oh, C. H., & Eikenberry, A. M. (2005). Toward participatory and transparent government: Report on the global forum on reinventing government. *Public Administration Review*, *65*(6), 646–654. doi:10.1111/j.1540-6210.2005.00494.x

King, F. H. H. (1965). *Research guide to China-coast newspapers, 1822-1911*. Cambridge, MA: Harvard University Press.

King, R. G., & Levine, R. (1992). *Financial Indicators and Growth in Cross-Section of Countries* (World Bank Working Paper No. 819).

King, R. G., & Levine, R. (1993a). Finance and Growth: Schumpeter Might be Right. *The Quarterly Journal of Economics*, *108*, 717–737. doi:10.2307/2118406

King, R. G., & Levine, R. (1993b). Finance, Entrepreneurship and Growth. *Journal of Monetary Economics*, *32*, 30–71.

Kleinknecht, A. (1987). *Innovation Patterns in Crisis and Prosperity: Schumpeter's Long Cycle Reconsidered*. London: Macmillan Press.

Kletzer, K., & Bardhan, P. (1985). Credit Markets and International Trade. *Journal of Economic Development*, *27*(1-2), 57–70. doi:10.1016/0304-3878(87)90006-X

Kohcerlakota, N., & Yi, K. (1996). A simple time series test of endogenous vs. exogenous growth models: An application to the United States. *The Review of Economics and Statistics*, *78*(1), 126–134. doi:10.2307/2109852

Kondratieff, N.D. (1926). Die Langen Wellen der Konjunktur. *Archiv fur Sozialwissenschaft und Sozialpolitik*, *56*, 573ff.

Korupp, S. E., & Szydlik, M. (2005). Causes and Trends of the Digital Divide. *European Sociological Review*, *21*(4), 409–422. doi:10.1093/esr/jci030

Kowalski, P. (2003, May 8). *Challenges Facing Rating Agencies In Emerging Markets*. Bucharest: Fitch Ratings.

Kozak, I. E. (1984). *Ibn Haldun'a Gore Insan-Toplum-Iktisat*. Istanbul, Turkey: Pınar Publishing.

Krueger, A. O. (1978). *Foreign Trade Regime and Economic Development, Liberalization Attempts and Consequences*. Cambridge, MA: Ballinger.

Krueger, A. O. (1988). *The Experience and Lesson of Asia's Super-Exporters*. In V. Corbo, A. Krueger, & F. Ossa (Eds.), *Export-Oriented Development Strategies: The Success of Five Newly Industrializing Countries*. Boulder, CO: West View Press.

Krueger, A. O. (1998). Why Trade Liberalization is Good for Growth. *The Economic Journal, 108*, 1513–1522. doi:10.1111/1468-0297.00358

Krugman, P. R. (1990). *Rethinking International Trade*. Cambridge, MA: MIT Press.

Krugman, P. R. (1998). *What Happened in Asia?* (Mimeograph). Cambridge, MA: MIT. Retrieved from http://www.web.mit.edu/krugman/www/DISINTER.html

Kuchiki, M., & Tsuji, M. (Eds.). (2005). *Industrial Clusters in Asia: Analyses of Their Competition and Cooperation*. Houndmills, UK: Palgrave Macmillan.

Küçükçınar, A., & Özcivelek, R. (2008). Turkey. In G. Turlea & M. Bogdanowicz (Eds.), *EU Enlargement: Economic Development and the Information Society* (pp. 353-380). Brussels: VUB Press.

Kuilman, J. *(2007). Institutional change, diversity and competition: foreign banks in Shanghai, 1847-2004. In B. Krug & H. Hans (Eds.),* The Chinese economy in the 21st century: Enterprise and business behaviour *(pp. 21-41). Cheltenham, UK: Edward Elgar.*

Kumar, N. (1995). *Industrialization, Liberalization and Two Way Flows of Foreign Direct Investments: The Case of India* (Discussion Paper No. 9504). Institute for New Technologies, Maastricht: United Nations University.

Kumar, P. C., & Tsetsekos, G. P. (1992). Securities Market Development and Economic Growth. In K. P. Fischer & G. J. Papaioannou (Eds.), *Business Finance In Less Developed Capital Markets* (pp. 55-65). London: Greenwood Press.

Kumar, P. C., & Tsetsekos, G. P. (1993). Managerial Ownership and Stock Price Reaction to Bond Downgrades. *Applied Financial Economics, 3*(1), 357–364. doi:10.1080/758534950

Kwan, A. C., Wu, Y., & Zhang, J. (1998). An Exogeneity Analysis of Financial Deepening and Economic Growth: Evidence from Hong Kong, South Korea, and Taiwan. *The Journal of International Trade & Economic Development, 7*(3), 339–354. doi:10.1080/09638199800000018

Lai, H. C., Chiu, Y. C., & Leu, H. D. (2005). Innovation capacity comparison of China's information technology industrial clusters: The case of Shanghai, Kunshan, Shenzhen and Dongguan. *Technology Analysis and Strategic Management, 17*(3), 293–315. doi:10.1080/09537320500211284

Lai, O. (1994). Promoting health and welfare: The challenge for information technology? *Information Technology & People, 7*(1), 81–99. doi:10.1108/09593849410074043

Lajkim, M. B., Barise, A., & Boukhobza, I. (2004, December). Globalization and poverty alleviation in Islamic countries: The role of information communication technologies & science. In *Proceedings of an international conference on Poverty in the Muslim Countries and Communities: Causes and Solutions*, Kuala Lumpur, Malaysia.

Lall, S. (1983). *The New Multinationals: the Spread of third World Enterprises*. New York: John Wiley.

Lallana, E. C., & Margaret, N. (2003). *The information age*. Manila and Kuala Lumpur: UNDP-APDIP.

Lau, S. (2008). Using an error correction model to test whether endogenous long run growth exists. *Journal of Economic Dynamics & Control, 32*(10), 648–676. doi:10.1016/j.jedc.2007.06.004

Laurenceson, J., & Chai, J. C. H. (2003). *Financial Reforms and Economic Development in China*. Cheltenham, UK: Edward Elgar.

Leana, C. R., & Van Buren, H. J. (1999). Organizational Social Capital and Employment Practices. *Academy of Management Review, 24*, 538–555. doi:10.2307/259141

Lee, J.-W. (1993). International Trade Distortions and Long-run Economic Growth. *IMF Staff Papers*, 299-328.

Lee, K. (2008). Globalization, Electronic Empire and the Virtual Geography of Korea's Information and Telecommunication Infrastructure. *The International Communication Gazette, 70*(1), 3–20. doi:10.1177/1748048507084575

Lenger, A. (2006). Bölgesel Yenilik Sistemleri ve Devletin Rolü: Türkiye'deki Kurumsal Yapı ve Devlet Üniversiteleri . *Egean Academic Review*, *6*(2), 141–155.

Levine, R. (1997). Financial Development and Economic Growth: Views and Agenda. *Journal of Economic Literature*, *35*, 688–726.

Levine, R. (1998). The Legal Environment, Banks, and Long-run Economic Growth. *Journal of Money . Credit and Banking*, *30*, 596–613. doi:10.2307/2601259

Levine, R. (2002). Bank-Based or Market-Based Financial Systems: Which is Better? *Journal of Financial Intermediation*, *11*, 398–428. doi:10.1006/jfin.2002.0341

Levine, R. (2004). *Finance and Growth: Theory and Evidence* (NBER Working Paper No. 10766).

Levine, R., & Renelt, D. (1992). A Sensitivity Analysis of Cross-Country Growth Regressions. *The American Economic Review*, *82*, 942–963.

Levine, R., & Zervos, S. (1998). Stock Markets, Banks, and Economic Growth. *The American Economic Review*, *88*, 537–558.

Levine, R., Loayza, N., & Beck, T. (2000). Financial Intermediation and Economic Growth: Causality and Causes. *Journal of Monetary Economics*, *46*, 31–77. doi:10.1016/S0304-3932(00)00017-9

Lewer, J. J., & Van den Berg, H. (2003). How Large is International Trade's Effect on Economic Growth? *Journal of Economic Surveys*, *17*(3), 363–396. doi:10.1111/1467-6419.00198

Liou, K. T. (2000). Linking administrative reform to economic development: Issue and the national experience. In K. T. Liou (Ed.), *Administrative Reform and National Economic Development* (pp. 1-18). Aldershot, UK: Ashgate Publishing.

List, F. (1841). *The National System of Political Economy* (S. S. Lloyd, Trans.). London: Longmans, Green and Co.

Llorito, D. L. (2005). *Prospects of Business Process Outsourcing in the Philippines*. Retrieved May 14, 2007, from http://davelloritol11.wordpress.com/2005/12/25/prospects-of-business-process-outsourcing-in-the-philippines/

Llorito, D. L. (2006). *Help wanted for Philippines Outsourcing*. Retrieved June 19, 2007, from http://www.atimes.com/atimes/Southeast_Asia/HE10Ae02.html

Locke, J. (1824). Of Civil Government. In *The Works of John Locke* (Vol. 4) (12th ed.). London: C. Baldwin, Printer.

Locsin, M. L. (2006). *Business Processing Association Philippines – Representing the Country's IT and IT-Enabled Services Industry*. Paper presented at the Business Processing Association Philippines (BPA/P) General Assembly, Manila, Philippines. neoIT. (2004). Mapping Offshore Markets Update. *Offshore Insights White Paper*, *2*(6,) 4. Retrieved August 27, 2007, from http://www.neoit.com/pdfs/whitepapers/OIv2i6_June_04_Mapping_Offshore_Markets.pdf

Lucas, R. E. Jr. (1988). On the Mechanics of Economic Development. *Journal of Monetary Economics*, *22*, 3–42. doi:10.1016/0304-3932(88)90168-7

Lundvall, B.-Å. (1988). Innovation as an Interactive Process: From User-Producer Interaction to National Systems of Innovation. In G. Dosi, C. Freeman, R. Nelson, G. Silverberg, & L. Soete (Eds.), *Technological Change and Economic Theory*. London: Pinter.

Lundvall, B.-Å. (1992). Introduction. In B. A. Lundvall (Ed.), *National Systems of Innovation: towards a theory of innovation and interactive learning*. London: Pinter.

Lundvall, B.-Å., Johnson, B., Andersen, E. S., & Dalum, B. (2002). National Systems of Production, Innovation and Competence Building. *Research Policy*, *31*(2), 213–231. doi:10.1016/S0048-7333(01)00137-8

Ma, D. B. (2008). Economic growth in the lower Yangzi region of China in 1911–1937: A quantitative and historical analysis. *The Journal of Economic History*, *68*(2), 355–392. doi:10.1017/S002205070800034X

Ma, Z. D. (2001). Shanghai guoji qianyi biandong chutan (Preliminary survey of Shanghai international arrivals and departures). *Journal of Shanghai Public Security Academy, 11*(3), 42–45.

MacPherson, K. L. (1996). The Shanghai model in historical perspective. In Y.M. Yeung & Y.W. Sung (Eds.), *Shanghai: Transformation and modernization under China's open door* (pp. 493-527). Hong Kong: Chinese University Press.

Madon, S. (2000). The internet and socio-economic development: Exploring the interaction. *Information Technology & People, 13*(2), 85–101. doi:10.1108/09593840010339835

Madrick, J. G. (1995). *The end of affluence*. New York: Random House.

Majid, M. S. A., & Mahirizal. (2007). Does Financial Development Cause Economic Growth in the ASEAN-4 Countries? *Savings and Development, 31*(4), 369–398.

Mak, G. C. L., & Lo, L. N. K. (1996). Education. In Y.M. Yeung & Y.W. Sung (Eds.), *Shanghai: Transformation and modernization under China's open door* (pp. 375-398). Hong Kong: The Chinese University Press.

Mallick, H., & Agarwal, S. (2007). Impact of Real Interest rates on Real Output Growth in India: A Long-run Analysis in a Liberalized Financial Regime. *The Singapore Economic Review, 52*, 215–231. doi:10.1142/S021759080700266X

Mani, S. (2007). Revolution in India's Telecommunication Industry. *Economic and Political Weekly, 42*(7), 578–580.

Mankiw, N. G., Romer, D., & Weil, D. N. (1992). A contribution to the empirics of economic growth. *The Quarterly Journal of Economics, 107*(2), 407–437. doi:10.2307/2118477

Mansell, R., & When, U. (Eds.). (1998). *Information technology for sustainable development*. Oxford, UK: Oxford University Press.

Mao, G. P., & Higano, Y. (1996). A Study of the labor input in Shanghai: Effects of information development and employment policy. *Hitotsubashi Journal of Economics*, (37): 155–173.

Marker, P., McNamara, K., & Wallace, L. (2002). *The significance of information and communication technologies for reducing poverty*. London: Department for International Development.

Marx, C. (1887). *Capital* (Moore & Aveling, Trans.). London, UK: Engels.

Mata, F. J., Fuest, W. L., & Barney, J. B. (1995). Information Technology and Sustained Competitive Advantage: A Resource-Based Analysis. *MIS Quarterly, 19*(4), 487–505. doi:10.2307/249630

Matambalya, F., & Wolf, S. (2001). *Performance of SMEs in East Africa: Case Studies from Kenya and Tanzania*. Bonn, Germany: Centre for Development Research (ZEF).

Mathews, J. A. (2006). Dragon Multinationals: New Players in 21st Century Globalization. *Asia Pacific Journal of Management, 23*(1), 5–27. doi:10.1007/s10490-006-6113-0

Matteucci, N., O'Mahony, M., Robinson, C., & Zwick, T. (2005). Productivity, workplace performance and ICT: Industry and firm-level evidence for Europe and the US. *Scottish Journal of Political Economy, 521*(3), 359–386. doi:10.1111/j.0036-9292.2005.00349.x

McCall, T. (2003). Institutional design for community economic development models: Issues of opportunity and capacity. *Community Development Journal, 38*(2), 96–108. doi:10.1093/cdj/38.2.96

Mckinnon, R. I. (1973). *Money and Capital in Economic Development*. Washington, DC: Brooking Institution.

Mckinnon, R. I. (1982). The Order of Economic Liberalization: Lessons from Chile and Argentina. In K. Brunner & A. Metzler (Eds.), *Economic Policy in a World of Change: Carnegie-Rochester Conference Series on Public Policy* (Vol. 17). Amsterdam: North Holland

Mehta, L. (2005). *The politics and poetics of water: naturalising scarcity in Western India*. New Delhi, India: Orient Longman.

Menger, C. (1871). *The Principles of Economics*. New York, NY: New York University Press.

Mensch, G. (1979). *Stalemate in technology: Innovations overcome depression.* Cambridge, MA: Ballinger Publishing Company.

Mersin-RIS. (2008). *Mersin Bölgesel İnovasyon Stratejisi 2006-2016.* Ankara, Türkiye: MetuTechnopolis.

Mevlana, C. R. (1960). *Mesnevi* (V. Izbudak, Trans.). Istanbul, Turkey: Milli Egitim Press.

Michaelpoulos, C., & Jay, K. (1973). *Growth of Exports and Income in Developing World: A Neoclassical View* (AID Paper No. 28).

Michaely, M. (1973). Exports and Economic Growth: An Empirical Investigation. *Journal of Development Economics, 18*, 49–54.

Middle East Technical University, Science and Technology Policies Reserarch Center (METU-STPS). (1999). *İnovasyonun Değişen Ortam ve Şartları, Hükümetlerin/ Devletin Yeni Rolü, Aykut Göker (Derl.), METU-STPS Seminar Note.* Ankara, Türkiye: METU-STPS.

Mill, J. S. (1965). Principles of Political Economy. In J.M. Robson (Ed.), *The Collected Works of John Stuart Mill* (Vol. 3). Canada: University of Toronto Press.

Mill, J. S. (1967). Essays on Economics and Society: 1824-1845. In J.M. Robson (Ed.), *The Collected Works of John Stuart Mill* (Vol. 4). Canada: University of Toronto Press.

Minami, R. (1994). *The economic development of China: A comparison with the Japanese experience.* London: Macmillan.

Ministery of Puclic Work and Settlement. (2008). *Planlama sürecinin yenilenmesi projesi.* Ankara, Turkey: Mattek Basım Yayın.

Misuraca, G. C. (2007). *E-governance in Africa from theory and practice: A handbook on ICTs for local governance.* NJ: African World Press and International Development Research Center.

Mitter, S. (2004). Globalization, ICTs, and Economic Empowerment: A Feminist Critique. *Gender, Technology and Development, 8*(1), 5–29. doi:10.1177/097185240400800102

Mittler, B. (2004). *A newspaper for China?: Power, identity, and change in Shanghai's news media, 1872-1912.* Cambridge, MA: Harvard University Press.

Mohsin, M. H., Kemal, M. A., & Qadir, U. (2001). *Impact of Trade Reforms on Poverty.* Pakistan Institute of Development Economics, 16th Annual General Meeting: Islamabad.

Mokyr, J. (1990). *The lever of riches.* Oxford, UK: Oxford University Press.

Monsurrò, P. (2007). *Beni Capitali Submarginali e Non-Neutralità della Moneta.* Retrieved April 24, 2007, from http://ideashaveconsequences.org/beni-capitali-submarginali-e-non-neutralita-della-moneta/jacopo

Moody's Investors Service. (2002, November 21). *Written Statement of Raymond W. McDaniel, President, Moody's Investors Service, Before the United States Securities and Exchange Commission on Credit Rating Agencies.*

Moody's Investors Service. (2009, March). *Approach to Evaluating Distress Exchanges.*

Morgan, K. (1997). The Learning Region: Institutions, Innovation and Regional Renewal. *Regional Studies, 31*(5), 491–503. doi:10.1080/00343409750132289

Morgan, K. (2004). Sustainable regions: Governance, innovation and scale. *European Planning Studies, 12*(6), 871–889. doi:10.1080/0965431042000251909

Murphey, R. (1953). *Shanghai: Key to modern China.* Cambridge, MA: Harvard University Press.

Murphey, R. (1977). *The outsiders: The western experience in India and China.* Ann Arbor, MI: Michigan University Press.

Murty, M. N. (2001). Environmentally Sustainable Income and Shadow Price of Natural Resources. In *Environmentally Corrected GDP: Valuation and Accounting for Industrial Pollution in India.* New Delhi, India: Institute of Economic Growth.

Muter, N. B., & Gokbunar, R. (2003). Devletin Etkinligi ile Ilgili Ekonomik, Politik, Kulturel Teoriler. *Celal Bayar Universitesi Sosyal Bilimler Dergisi, 1*(1), 53–70.

Mutula, S. M. (2005). Bridging The Digital Divide Through E-Governance; A Proposal For Africa's Libraries And İnformation Centres. *The Electronic Library*, *23*(5), 591–602. doi:10.1108/02640470510631308

Nagraj, R. (2006). Indian Investments Abroad: What Explains the Boom? *Economic and Political Weekly*, *41*(46), 4716–4717.

Nair-Reichert, U., & Weinhold, D. (2001). Causality Tests for Cross-Country Panels: A New Look at FDI and Economic Growth in Developing Countries. *Oxford Bulletin of Economics and Statistics*, *63*, 153–171. doi:10.1111/1468-0084.00214

National Bureau of Soil Survey and Land use Planning. (1994). *Soil degradation in India: Status and Impact* (NBSSLUP Publication No. 38). New Delhi, India: Oxford & IBH Publishers.

Nayyar, D. (2008). *Internationalization of Firms From India: Investment, Mergers and Acquisitions. Trade and Globalization*. New Delhi, India: Oxford University Press.

Negroponte, N. (1998). The Third Shall be First: The Net Leverages Latecomers in the Developing Worlds. *Wired Magazine*.

Nelson, E., & Schwartz, A. J. (2007). *The Impact of Milton Friedman on Modern Monetary Economics: Setting the Record Straight on Paul Krugman's "Who Was Milton Friedman?"* (Working Paper, 2007-048D). Federal Reserve Bank of St. Louis.

Nelson, R. (1988). Institutions Supporting Technical Change in the United States. In G. Dosi, C. Freeman, R. Nelson, G. Silverberg, & L. Soete (Eds.), *Technological Change and Economic Theory*. London: Pinter.

Nelson, R. (1993). *National Innovation Systems: A Comparative Analysis*. New York: Oxford University Press.

Nelson, R. R., & Rosenberg, N. (1993). Technical Innovation and National Systems. In R. Nelson (Ed.), *National Innovation Systems: A Comparative Analysis*. New York: Oxford University Press.

Nelson, R. R., & Winter, S. (1982). *An Evolutionary Theory of Economic Change*. Cambridge, MA: The Belknap Press.

Nielson, J. (2006). *Digital divide: The three stages*. Retrieved November 23, 2008, from http://useit.com

Ning, L. (2007). Economic Liberalization for High-Tech Industry Development? Lesson from China's Response in Developing the ICT Manufacturing Sector Compared with the Strategies of Korea and Taiwan. *The Journal of Development Studies*, *43*(3), 562–587. doi:10.1080/00220380701204547

Nobutaka, I. (1954). The pattern of railway development in Japan. *The Far Eastern Quarterly*, *14*(1), 217–229.

Noda Masaho. (1980). *Nihon shōken shijō seiritsu* [History of the Japanese securities markets]. Tokyo: Yūhikaku.

Norton, S. W. (1992). Transaction costs, telecommunications, and the microeconomics of macroeconomic growth. *Economic Development and Cultural Change*, *41*(1), 175–196. doi:10.1086/452002

Nwagwu, W. E. (2006). Integrating ICTs into the Globalization of the Poor Developing Countries. *Information Development*, *22*(3), 167–179. doi:10.1177/0266666906069070

Odedokun, M. O. (1998). Financial Intermediation and Economic Growth in Developing Countries. *Journal of Economic Studies (Glasgow, Scotland)*, *25*, 203–224. doi:10.1108/01443589810215351

OECD (Organisation for Economic Co-operation and Development). (1995). *Participatory development and good governance*. Paris: OECD.

OECD e-Government Studies. (2003). *The E-Government Imperative*. OECD.

OECD. (2000). *Policy Brief: Science, Technology and Innovation in the New Economy*. Retrieved from http://www.oecd.org/publication/pol_brief/

OECD. (2003). *OECD Science, Technology and Industry Scoreboard 2003: Towards a Knowledge-Based Econo-*

my. Retrieved from http://www1.oecd.org/publications/e-book/92-2003-04-1-7294/

OECD. (2004). *Science and Innovation Policy: Key Challenges and Opportunities*. Retrieved from http://www.oecd.org/publications/pol-brief/

OECD. (2005). *Oslo Manual: Proposed Guidelines for Collecting and Interpreting Technological Innovation Data*. Paris: OECD.

Oguzname. (2009). (critical ed. Ali Haydar Bayat). Ankara, Turkey: Ataturk Kultur, Dil ve Tarih Yuksek Kurumu Press.

Okumus, E. (2008). *Osmanlı'nın Gozuyle Ibn Haldun*. Istanbul, Turkey: Iz Publishing.

Olatokun, W. M. (2007). ICTs and governance in Africa. In A. Anttiroiko & M. Malkia (Eds.), *Encyclopedia of digital government* (pp. 978-983). Hershey, PA: Idea Group Inc.

Oliner, S. D., & Sichel, D. E. (1994). Computers and output growth revisited: how big is the puzzle? *Brookings Papers on Economic Activity*, *2*, 273–317. doi:10.2307/2534658

Opper, S. E. (2002). *The Austrian Theory of Business Cycle: Old Lessons for Modern Economic Policy?* (Working Paper, 02/2). International Monetary Fund.

Ouattara, B. (2004). *Foreign Aid and Fiscal Policy in Senegal*. Mimeo, University of Manchester.

Oughton, C., Landabaso, M., & Morgan, K. (2002). The Regional Innovation Paradox: Innovation Policy and Industrial Policy. *The Journal of Technology Transfer*, *27*(1), 97–110. doi:10.1023/A:1013104805703

Our Corporate Bureau. (2005). *US among top locations for "offshore" work: AT Kearney*. Retrieved July 23, 2007, from http://www.domain-b.com/management/consulting/20051123_locations.html

Papadopoulos, G. (2007). *Electronic Money and the Possibility of a Cashless Society* (Working Paper, 18.02.2007). EIPE.

Papaioannou, M. G., & Duke, L. K. (1993). The Internationalization of Emerging Equity Markets. *Finance & Development*, *30*(3), 36–39.

Papaioannou, M. G., & Tsetsekos, G. P. (1994, February 15). *Developing the Financial Infrastructure in Greece: The Role of Rating Agencies* (Drexel University College of Business and Administration Faculty Working Paper Series, WP72-93).

Parikh, J. K., & Parikh, K. S. (Eds.). (1997a). *Accounting and Valuation of Environment – Volume I: A Primer for Developing Countries*. Bangkok, Thailand: Economic and Social Commission for Asia and Pacific.

Parikh, J. K., & Parikh, K. S. (Eds.). (1997b). *Accounting and Valuation of Environment – Volume II: Case Studies from the ESCAP Region*. Bangkok, Thailand: Economic and Social Commission for Asia and Pacific.

Parikh, K. S., Parikh, J. K., Sharma, V. K., & Painuly, J. P. (1992). *Natural Resource Accounting: A Framework for India*. Report prepared for Ministry of Environment and Forests. Mumbai, India: Indira Gandhi Institute of Development Research.

Pauli, G. (1999).*Towards a technology strategy for sustainable livelihoods*. UNDP programme.

Pearce, D., Markandya, A., & Barbier, E. B. (1989). *Blueprint for a Green Economy* (A report prepared for the UK Department of Environment). London: Earthscan Publishers Ltd.

Pesaran, M. H., & Pesaran, B. (1997). *Working with Microfit 4.0: An Interactive Approach*. Oxford, UK: Oxford University Press.

Pesaran, M. H., Shin, Y., & Smith, R. J. (1999, February). *Bounds Testing Approaches to the Analysis of Long Run Relationships* (Working Paper).

Pesaran, M. H., Shin, Y., & Smith, R. J. (2001). Bounds Testing Approaches to the Analysis of Level Relationships. *Journal of Applied Econometrics*, *16*, 289–326. doi:10.1002/jae.616

Pickard, V. (2007). From NWICO to Neoliberal Visions and Revisions in Global Communications Policy. *The Journal of Communication Inquiry*, *31*(2), 118–139. doi:10.1177/0196859906298162

Pike, A., Rodriguez-Pose, A., & Tomaney, J. (2006). *Local and regional development*. London: Routledge.

Pike, A., Rodriguez-Pose, A., & Tomaney, J. (2007). What kind of local and regional development and for whom? *Regional Studies, 41*(9), 1253–1269. doi:10.1080/00343400701543355

Pinder, D., & Aldcroft, D. H. (1983). *Regional economic development and policy: Theory and practice in European Community*. London: Allen & Unwin.

Plato. (1961). Republic. In E. Hamilton & H. Cairns (Ed.), *The Collected Dialogues of Plato, Including the Letters* (pp. 575-844). New York: Pantheon Books.

Pohjola, M. (2002). The new economy in growth and development. *Oxford Review of Economic Policy, 18*(3), 380–396. doi:10.1093/oxrep/18.3.380

Polése, M., & Shearmur, R. (2006). Why some regions will decline: A Canadian case study with thoughts on local development strategies. *Papers in Regional Science, 85*(1), 23–46. doi:10.1111/j.1435-5957.2006.00024.x

Prasad, A., & Ghosh, S. (2007). Competition in Indian Banking: An Empirical Evaluation. *South Asia Economic Journal, 8*, 265–284. doi:10.1177/139156140700800205

Press, L. (1996). The role of computer networks in development. *Communications of the ACM, 39*(2), 23–29. doi:10.1145/230798.230800

Preston, P., & Kerr, A. (2001). Digital Media, Nation-States And Local Cultures: The Case Of Multimedia 'Content' Production. *Media Culture & Society, 23*, 109–131. doi:10.1177/016344301023001006

Pritchett, L. (2006). The Quest Continues. *Finance and Development, 43*(1). Retrieved from http//www.imf.org/external/pubs/ft/fandd/2006/03/pritchet.htm

Putnam, R. D. (2000). *Bowling Alone: The Collapse and Revival of American Community*. New York: Simon & Schuster.

Qian, Y. Y. (2002). *How the reform worked in China* (William Davidson Institute Working Paper, 473).

Quibria, M. G., Ahmed, S. N., Tschang, T., & Reyes-Macasaquit, M.-L. (2003). Digital Divide: Determinants and Policies with Special Reference to Asia. *Journal of Asian Economics, 13*, 811–825. doi:10.1016/S1049-0078(02)00186-0

Radev, D., Angelov, A., & Stamenov, S. (2007). Regional Innovation Strategy of the North-East Planning Region. *Advances in Bulgarian Science, 3*, 32–40.

Rajan, R. G., & Zingalas, L. (1998). Financial Dependence and Growth. *The American Economic Review, 88*, 559–586.

Rajan, R. G., & Zingalas, L. (2003). The Great Reversals: The Politics of Financial Development in the Twentieth Century. *Journal of Financial Economics, 69*, 5–50. doi:10.1016/S0304-405X(03)00125-9

Ram, R. (1985). Exports and Economic Growth: Some Additional Evidence. *Economic Development and Cultural Change, 33*, 415–425. doi:10.1086/451468

Ram, R. (1999). Financial Development and Economic Growth: Additional Evidence. *The Journal of Development Studies, 35*(4), 164–174. doi:10.1080/00220389908422585

Ramakrishna, N. (2005). Resource Accounting for Regional Water Management: A Case Study of Yamuna River Sub-basin. *South Asian Journal of Management, 11*(2), 95–110.

Ramakrishna, N., Balakameswari, K., Srinivas Rao, M., & Ram Babu, P. (2007). Integrated Environmental Economic Accounting for Sustainable Development: A Case of NCT-Delhi. *ICFAI Journal of Environmental Economics, 5*(3), 54–68.

Ramamurti, R. (2008). *What Have We Learned About Emerging-Market MNEs? Insights from a Multi-Country Research Project*. Paper Presented in the Conference on Emerging Multinationals: Outward FDI from Emerging and Developing Economies, Copenhagen Business School, Copenhagen, Denmark.

Rao, B., & Cooray, A. (2008a). *How useful is the theoretical and the empirical growth literature for policies in the developing countries*. EERI Research paper Series (9/2008), Belgium.

Rao, B., & Singh, R. (2007). *Effects of trade openness on the steady state growth rates of selected Asian countries with an extended exogenous growth model* (MPRA Paper 8605). University Library of Munich, Germany.

Rao, B., & Tamazian, A. (2008b). A model of growth and finance: FIML estimates for India (MPRA Paper 8763). University Library of Munich, Germany.

Rawski, T. G. (1989). *Economic growth in prewar China*. Berkeley, CA: University of California Press.

RBI. (2005-06). *Annual Report*. Mumbai, India: Reserve Bank of India.

RBI. (2007-08). *Annual Report*. Mumbai, India: Reserve Bank of India.

RBI. (2009, January). Indian Investment Abroad in Joint Ventures and Wholly Owned Subsidiaries: 2008-09. *Monthly Bulletin*. Mumbai, India: Reserve Bank of India.

Reed, C. (2004). *Gutenberg in Shanghai: Chinese print capitalism, 1876-1937*. Honolulu, HI: University of Hawai'i Press.

Reeves, T. (2006, Eylül). *Regional development in the EU and Turkey*. Paper presented at the Bölgesel Kalkınma ve Yönetişim Sempozyumu, Ankara.

Reloc8 Asia Pacific Group. (2007). Asia Pacific Updates. *Reloc8 – A Regional Relocation Resource, 1*(6), 8-9. Retrieved December 29, 2008, from http://www.reloc8asia.com/newsletters/Reloc8%20newsletter6%202007.pdf

Repetto, R., McGrath, W., Wells, M., Beer, C., & Rossini, F. (1991). *Wasting Assets: Natural Resources in the National Income Accounts*. Washington, DC: World Resource Institute.

Research and Information System (RIS) for the Non-aligned and Other Countries. (2004). *South Asia Development and Cooperation Report 2004*.

Rhodes, R. A. W. (1996). The new governance: Governing without government. *Political Studies, XLIV*, 652–667. doi:10.1111/j.1467-9248.1996.tb01747.x

Richards, P. (2005). Plant biotechnology and the rights of the poor: a technographic approach. In M. Leach, I. Scoones, & B. Wynne (Eds.), *Science and Citizens* (pp. 199-214). London: Zed Books.

Robins, S. (2005). AIDS, science and citizenship after apartheid. In M. Leach, I. Scoones, & B. Wynne (Eds.), *Science and citizens* (pp. 113-129). London: Zed Book.

Robinson, J. (1952). *The Rate of Interests and Other Easys*. London: Macmillan.

Rocheleau, B. (2005). *Public management information systems*. Hershey, PA: Idea Group Publishing.

Rogers, E. M. (2001). The Digital Divide. *Convergence, 7*(4), 96–111. doi:10.1177/135485650100700406

Röller, L.-H., & Waverman, L. (2001). Telecommunications infrastructure and economic development: A simultaneous approach. *The American Economic Review, 91*(4), 909–923.

Romer, P. (1986). Increasing returns and long run growth. *The Journal of Political Economy, 94*(October), 1002–1037. doi:10.1086/261420

Romer, P. (1987). Growth Based on Increasing Returns Due to Specialization. *The American Economic Review, 77*(2), 56–62.

Romer, P. (1990). Endogenous Technological Change. *The Journal of Political Economy, 98*(5), 71–102. doi:10.1086/261725

Romer, P. M. (1993). Idea Gaps and Object Gaps in Economic Development. *Journal of Monetary Economics, 32*(3), 543–573. doi:10.1016/0304-3932(93)90029-F

Romer, P. M. (1994). The Origin of Endogenous Growth. *The Journal of Economic Perspectives, 8*(1), 3–22.

Rosenthal, E. I. J. (1968). *Political Thought in Medieval Islam: An Introductory Outline*. Cambridge, UK: Cambridge University Press.

Rothbard, M. N. (2001). *The Case for a 100 Percent Golden Dollar*. Auburn, AL: The Ludwig von Mises Institute.

Roubini, N., & Sala-i-Martin, X. (1991). *Financial Development, the Trade Regime and Economic Growth* (NBER Working Paper No. 3876).

Rousseau, P. L., & Vuthipadadorn, D. (2005). Finance, Investment, and Growth: Time Series Evidence from 10 Asian Economies. *Journal of Macroeconomics, 27*, 87–106. doi:10.1016/j.jmacro.2003.09.004

Rousseau, P. L., & Wachtel, P. (1998). Financial Intermediation and Economic Performance: Historical Evidence from Five Industrialized Countries. *Journal of Money . Credit and Banking, 30*(4), 657–678. doi:10.2307/2601123

Roy, K. C., & Tisdell, C. A. (1998). Good governance in sustainable development: The impact of institutions. *International Journal of Social Economics, 25*(6-8), 1310–1325. doi:10.1108/03068299810212775

Roy, M., & Venema, H. (2002). Reducing risk and vulnerability to climate change in India: the capabilities approach. *Gender and Development, 10*(2), 78–83. doi:10.1080/13552070215904

Sachs, J. D., & Warner, A. (1995). Economic Reforms and Process of Global Integration. *Brookings Papers on Economic Activity, 1*, 1–118. doi:10.2307/2534573

Sala-i-Martin, X. (1997). I just ran two million regressions. *The American Economic Review, 87*(2), 178–183.

Sala-i-Martin, X., & Barro, R. J. (1995). *Economic Growth.* New York: McGraw-Hill.

Santos-Paulino, A., & Thirwall, A. P. (2004). The Impact of Trade Liberalization on Exports, Imports and the Balance of Payments of Developing Countries. *The Economic Journal, 114*, F50–F72. doi:10.1111/j.0013-0133.2004.00187.x

Santoyo, A. S. (2003). *Estimation and characterization of the digital divide.* Paper presented at a round table on developing countries access to scientific knowledge, the Abdus Salam ICTP, Trieste, Italy.

Sarı Mehmet Pasha, D. (1969). *Devlet Adamlarına Ogutler* (H. R. Ugural, Trans.). Ankara, Turkey: Turk Tarih Kurumu Press.

Saxton, J. (2001). Information technology and the new economy. A Joint Economic Committee Study, United States Congress, Washington.

Schreyer, P. (2000). *The contribution of information and communication technology to output growth: a study of the G7 countries* (STI Working Paper 2002/2).

Schumacher, E. F. (1974). *Small is beautiful: a study of economics as if people mattered.* London: Abacus.

Schumpeter, J. A. (1911). *Theorie der Wirtschaftlichen Entwicklung* [The Theory of Economic Development] (Opie, R. Trans.). Leipzig, Germany: Dunker & Humblot.

Schumpeter, J. A. (1939). *Business cycles: A theoretical, historical, and statistical analysis of the capitalist process.* New York: McGraw-Hill.

Schumpeter, J. A. (1942). *Capitalism, Socialism and Democracy.* New York: Harper Torchbooks.

Schutz, L. (2001). Digital disconnect: Beyond the infrastructure. *Critical Issues. Minnesota.* Retrieved March 16, 2008, from http://www/mnplan.state.mn.us

Schwentker, W. (2005). The Spirit of Modernity: Max Weber's Protestant Ethics and Japanese Social Sciences. *Journal of Classical Sociology, 5*(1), 73–92. doi:10.1177/1468795X05050039

Scott, A. J., & Storper, M. (2003). Regions, globalization and development. *Regional Studies, 37*(6-7), 549–578.

Senhadji, A. (2000). Sources of economic growth: An extensive growth accounting exercise. *IMF Staff Papers, 47*(1).

Shah, N. (2008). From Global Village To Global Marketplace: Metaphorical Descriptions Of The Global Internet. *International Journal of Media and Cultural Politics, 4*(1), 9–26. doi:10.1386/macp.4.1.9_1

Shankarnarayan, K. A., Harsh, L. N., & Kathju, S. (1987). Agroforestry in the arid zones of India. *Agroforestry Systems, 5*, 66–88. doi:10.1007/BF00046414

Shaw, E. S. (1973). *Financial Deepening in Economic Development.* Cambridge, MA: Harvard University Press.

Siddiki, J. U. (2002). Trade and Financial Liberalization and Endogenous Growth in Bangladesh. *International Economic Journal*, *16*, 23–37. doi:10.1080/10168730200080019

Siffin, W. J. (1991). The problem of development administration. In A. Farazmand (Ed.), *Handbook of comparative and development public administration* (pp. 1-8). New York: CRC Press.

Silcock, R. (2001). What is e-government? *Parliamentary Affairs*, *54*(1), 88–101. doi:10.1093/pa/54.1.88

Singh, A., & Weisse, B. A. (1998). Emerging Stock Markets, Portfolio Capital Flows and Long-Term Economic Growth: Micro and Macroeconomic Perspectives. *World Development*, *26*(4), 607–622. doi:10.1016/S0305-750X(98)00003-5

Sinha, D., & Macri, J. (2001). Financial Development and Economic Growth: The Case of Eight Asian Countries. *Economia Internazionale*, *54*(2), 218–234.

Small and Medium Enterprise Agency. (2001, 2002, 2003, 2004). *White Paper on Small and Medium Enterprises in Japan* (in Japanese). Tokyo: Ministry of Economy, Trade and Industry (METI).

Smith, A. (1776). *An Inquiry into the Nature and Causes of the Wealth of Nations*. New York, NY: Oxford University Press.

Smith, A. (1981). *An Inquiry into the Nature and Causes of the Wealth of Nations* (Volume I & II). Indianapolis, IN: Liberty Press.

Smith, A. (1984). *The Theory of Moral Sentiments*. (Ed. D.D. Raphael & A.L. Macfie). Indianapolis, IN: Liberty Press.

Smith, M. K. (2007). Social capital. In *The encyclopedia of informal education*. Retrieved September 10, 2007, from http://www.infed.org/biblio/social_capital.htm

Snellen, I. (2005). Technology and public administration: Conditions for successful e-government development. In G. Petroni & F. Cloete (Eds.), *New technologies in public administration* (pp. 5-19). Amsterdam: IOS Press.

Sobaci, M. Z. (2008). Türkiye'de bölgesel yönetişimin kurumsal yansıması: Kalkınma ajansları. *Finans Politik & Ekonomik Yorumlar*, *45*(519), 61–74.

Sobaci, Z. (2009). Regional development agencies in Turkey: Are they examples of obligated policy transfer. *Public Organization Review*, *9*(1), 51–65. doi:10.1007/s11115-008-0069-0

Solow, R. (1956). A contribution to the theory of economic growth. *The Quarterly Journal of Economics*, *71*(1), 65–94. doi:10.2307/1884513

Solow, R. (1957). Technical Change and Aggregate Production Function. *The Review of Economics and Statistics*, *39*(August), 312–320. doi:10.2307/1926047

Solow, R. (2008). The last 50 years in growth theory and the next 10. *Oxford Review of Economic Policy*, *23*(1), 3–14. doi:10.1093/oxrep/grm004

Spears, A. (1992). The Role of Financial Intermediation in Economic Growth in Sub-Saharan Africa. *Canadian Journal of Development Studies*, *13*(3), 361–380.

SPO (State Planning Organization). (2000). *Bölgesel gelişme: Özel ihtisas komisyonu raporu*. Ankara, Turkey: SPO.

SPO (State Planning Organization). (2007). *Kalkınma ajansları*. Ankara, Turkey: SPO.

Squazzino, F. (in press). Local economic development initiatives from the bottom-up: the role of community development corporations. *Community Development Journal*.

Standard and Poor's. (2009a, January 28). *Ratings Implications of Exchange Offers and Similar Restructurings*.

Standard and Poor's. (2009b, April 10). An Examination of How Investor Needs are Served by Various Ratings Business Models: Ensuring Analytical Independence and Freedom from Conflicts of Interest of Credit Rating Firms [White Paper].

State Bank of Pakistan. (2007). *Annual Report for 2006-07* (Vol. 1).

State Planning Organization (SPO). Türkiye. (2000). *Sekizinci Beş Yıllık Kalkınma Planı.* Ankara: SPO.

State Planning Organization (SPO). Türkiye. (2006). *Dokuzuncu Beş Yıllık Kalkınma Planı.* Ankara: SPO.

Stewart, C., Gil-Egui, G., Tian, Y., & Pileggi, M. (2006). Framing The Digital Divide: A Comparison Of US And EU Policy Approaches. *New Media & Society, 8*(5), 731–752. doi:10.1177/1461444806067585

Stöhr, W. B., & Taylor, D. R. F. (Eds.). (1981). *Development from above or below?: The dialectics of regional planning in developing countries.* New York: Wiley.

Stoker, G. (1998). Governance as theory: Five propositions. *International Social Science Journal, 50*(155), 17–28. doi:10.1111/1468-2451.00106

Storper, M. (2001). Regional Technology Policies in Europe: TSER1 Research Projects, 1998-2000, The Regional Level of Implementation of Innovation Policies. In *Proceedings of a Workshop held in Brussels.*

Stringer, L., & Reed, M. (2007). Land degradation assessment in Southern Africa: integrating local and scientific knowledge bases. *Land Degradation and Development, 18*, 99–116. doi:10.1002/ldr.760

Suikidi. (2006). Max Weber's Remarks on Islam: The Protestant Ethic Among Muslim Puritans. *Islam and Christian Muslim Relations, 17*(2), 195-205.

Svaleryd, H., & Vlachos, J. (2005). Financial Markets, the Pattern of Specialization and Comparative Advantage. *European Economic Review, 49*, 113–144. doi:10.1016/S0014-2921(03)00030-8

Tadesse, S. (2002). Financial Architecture and Economic Performance: International Evidence. *Journal of Financial Intermediation, 11*, 429–454. doi:10.1006/jfin.2002.0352

Taylor, J. B. (1993). Discretion versus Policy Rules in Practice. *Carnegie-Rochester Conference Series on Public Policy, 39.*

Taymaz, E. (2001). *Ulusal Yenilik Sistemi:Turkiye İmalat Sanayiinde Teknolojik Değişim ve Yenilik Süreçleri.* Ankara, Türkiye: TÜBİTAK/TTGV/DİE.

Temel, T., Tansel, A., & Albersen, P. J. (1999). Convergence and Spatial Patterns in Labor Productivity: Nonparametric Estimations for Turkey. *Journal of Regional Analysis and Policy, 29*(1), 3–19.

Temple, J. (1999). The New Growth Evidence. *Journal of Economic Literature, 37*, 112–156.

TERI. (2006). *Looking back to Change Track: Green India 2047.* New Delhi, India: The Energy and Resources Institute (TERI) Press.

Thompson, H. G., & Garbacz, Ch. (2007). Mobile, fixed line and internet service effects on global productive efficiency. *Information Economics and Policy, 19*(2), 189–214. doi:10.1016/j.infoecopol.2007.03.002

Thornton, J. (1996). Financial Deepening and Economic Growth in Developing Economies. *Applied Economics Letters, 3*(4), 243–246. doi:10.1080/758520872

Tiryakioğlu, M. (2008). Beşeri Sermaye Yoksulluğu. *Egean Academic Review, 8*(1), 321–339.

Tomaney, J. (2002). The evolution of regionalism in England. *Regional Studies, 36*(7), 721–731. doi:10.1080/0034340022000006042

Törenli, N. (2004). *Enformasyon Toplumu ve Küreselleşme Sürecinde Türkiye.* Bilim ve Sanat Yayınları, Ankara.

Törenli, N. (2006). The 'Other' Faces of Digital Exclusion: ICT Gender Divides in the Broader Community. *European Journal of Communication, 21*, 435–455. doi:10.1177/0267323106070010

Torero, M., Choudhary, S., & Bedi, A. S. (2005). Telecommunication and Economic Growth: Implications for India. In A. Saith & M. Vijayabaskar (Eds.), *ICT's and Indian Economic Development* (pp. 231-264). New Delhi, India: Sage Publications.

Tschang, T. (n.d.). *The Philippines' IT-Enabled Services Industry.* Singapore: Lee Kong Chian School of Business, Singapore Management University.

TSI. (2004). *ICT usage survey on households and individuals.*

TSI. (2005). *ICT usage survey on households and individuals.*

TSI. (2007). *ICT usage survey on households and individuals.*

TSI. (2008). *ICT usage survey on households and individuals.*

Tsuji, M. (2005). ICT Use by SMEs in Japan: A Comparative Study of Higashi-Osaka and Ohta Ward, Tokyo. In M. Kuwayama, Y. Ueki, & Tsuji, M. (Eds.), *Information Technology for Development of Small and Medium-sized Exporters in Latin America and East Asia.* Santiago de Chili, Chili: ECLAC/IDE-JETRO/United Nations.

Tsuji, M., & Choe, I. (2004). An Ordered Probit Analysis of Factors Promoting a Regional Information Policy: The Case of Japanese Local Governments. *Mathematics and Computers in Simulation, 64*(1), 203–212. doi:10.1016/S0378-4754(03)00133-2

TUBITAK BILTEN. (2002, March). *Instruments to Combat Digital Divide: an evaluation based on Turkish experience.* Tübitak Bilten.

Tyler, W. (1981). Growth and Export Expansion in Developing Countries. *Journal of Development Economics, 9*, 121–130. doi:10.1016/0304-3878(81)90007-9

U.S. Securities and Exchange Commission. (1992-1993). *International Institute of Securities Market Development: Notes On Developing Capital Markets.* Mimeo.

U.S. Securities and Exchange Commission. (2003, January). *Report on the Role and Function of Credit Rating Agencies in the Operation of Securities Markets.*

UN. (2008). *Millennium development goals. Export.* Retrieved October 23, 2008, from http://MDG_Export_20080716_083055890

UNCTAD. (2006). FDI from Developing and Transition Countries: Implications for Development. In *World Investment Report 2006.* New York: United Nations.

UNCTAD. (2008). Transnational Corporations and the Infrastructure Challenge. In *World Investment Report 2008.* New York: United Nations.

UNDP (United Nations Development Programme). (1997). *Reconceptualising governance.* New York: UNDP Publication.

UNDP (United Nations Development Programme). (2001). *Human development report 2001: Making new technologies work for human development.* New York: Oxford University Press.

UNDP. (2007). Human Development Report. In *Making globalization work for all.* New York: UN.

UNEP (United Nations Environment Programme). (2008). *Global green new deal – environmentally-focused investment historic opportunity for 21st century prosperity and job generation.*

UNESCAP (United Nations Economic and Social Commission for Asia and the Pacific). (2008). *What is Good Governance?* Retrieved October 20, 2008, from http://www.unescap.org/pdd/prs/ProjectActivities/Ongoing/gg/governance.asp

United Nations. (1993). *Integrated Environmental and Economic Accounting, Interim version* (Studies in Methods Series (UNSEE) F. No. 61). New York: Department of Economics and Social Information and Policy analysis.

United Nations. (2003a). *World public sector report 2003: E-government at the crossroads.* New York: United Nations Publication.

United Nations. (2003b). *Monterrey Consensus on financing for development.* New York: United Nations Publication.

United Nations. (2007). *Good governance Practices for the Protection of Human Rights.* New York: United Nations.

van Ark, B., Inklaar, R., & McGuckin, R. H. (2003). ICT and productivity in Europe and the United States: Where do the differences come from? *CESifo Economic Studies, 49*(3), 295–318. doi:10.1093/cesifo/49.3.295

van Duijn, J. J. (1983). *The Long Wave in Economic Life.* London: George Allen & Unwin.

Vazquez-Barquero, A. (2002). *Endogenous development: Networking, innovation, institutions and cities*. London: Routledge.

Veblen, T. (2007). *The Theory of the Leisure Class*. New York: Cosimo, Inc.

von Böhm-Bawerk, E. (1891). *The Positive Theory of Capital*. London, UK: MacMillan.

von Hayek, F. A. (1931). *Prices and Production*. London, UK: Routledge and Sons.

von Hayek, F. A. (1933). *Monetary Theory and Trade Cycle*. London, UK: Jonathan Crape.

von Mises, L. E. (1931). The Causes of the Economic Crisis. In Greaves B.B. (Ed.), *On the Manipulation of Money and Credit*. Dobbs Ferry, NY: Free Market Books.

von Mises, L. E. (1934). *The Theory of Money and Credit* (Batson, Trans.). Oxford, UK: Alden.

Wakeman, F. J. (1995). *Policing Shanghai, 1927-1937*. Berkeley, CA: University of California Press.

Walburn, D. (2006, Eylül). *Regional development agencies: The tool to stimulate economic development in regions*. Paper presented at the Bölgesel Kalkınma ve Yönetişim Sempozyumu, Ankara.

Waller, S. A. (2000). *Theories of economic growth and the new economy*. University of Missouri Working paper.

Warris, R. W. (2004). *Information and communication technologies for poverty alleviation*. Kuala Lumpur: UNDP-APDIP.

Warschauer, M. (2003). *Technology and social inclusion: Rethinking the digital divide*. Cambridge, MA: MIT Press.

Wasserstrom, J. (2000). Locating old Shanghai: Having fits about where it fits. In J. W. Esherick (Ed.), *Remaking the Chinese city: Modernity and national identity, 1900-1950*. Honolulu, HI: University of Hawai'i Press.

WCED. (1987). *Our Common Future*. New Delhi, India: Oxford University Press.

Webb, D., & Collis, C. (2000). Regional development agencies and the 'new regionalism' in England. *Regional Studies, 34*(9), 2000, 857-864.

Weber, M. (2008). *Protestan Ahlakı ve Kapitalizmin Ruhu* (Z. Gurata, Trans.). Ankara, Turkey: Ayrac Kitabevi Publishing.

Werlin, H. (2003). Poor nations, rich nations: A theory of governance. *Public Administration Review, 63*(3), 329–342. doi:10.1111/1540-6210.00293

Wicksell, K. (1965). *Interest and Prices: A Study of the Causes Regulating the Value of Money*. London, UK: MacMillan.

WITSA. (2008). *Digital planet 2008*. Retrieved from http://www.witsa.org/

Wong, S. (2009). Climate change and sustainable technology: re-linking nature, governance and gender. *Gender and Development, 17*(1), 95–108. doi:10.1080/13552070802696953

Wong, S. L. (1996). The entrepreneurial spirit: Shanghai and Hong Kong compared. In Y.M. Yeung & Y. W. Sung (Eds.), *Shanghai: Transformation and modernization under China's open door* (pp. 25-48). Hong Kong: Chinese University Press.

Wong, S., & Sharp, L. (2009). Making power explicit in sustainable water innovation: re-thinking subjectivity, institution and structure through environmental citizenship. *Environmental Politics, 18*(1), 37–57. doi:10.1080/09644010802624785

Woodford, M. (2007). *How Important is Money in the Conduct of Monetary Policy?* (Manuscript). Columbia University.

World Bank. (1987). *World Development Report*. Oxford, UK: Oxford University Press.

World Bank. (1989). *Sub-Saharan Africa: From crisis to sustainable development*. Washington, DC: World Bank.

World Bank. (1989). *World Development Report 1989*. Oxford, UK: Oxford University Press.

World Bank. (1992). *Governance and development.* Washington, DC: World Bank.

World Bank. (1992). World development report. In *Development and the environment.* New York: Oxford University Press.

World Bank. (1994). *Governance: The World Bank's experience.* Washington, DC: World Bank.

World Bank. (1997). *World development report 1997: The state in changing world.* Oxford, UK: Oxford University Press.

World Bank. (2004). *Water resources sector strategy. Strategic directions for World Bank engagement.* Washington, DC: World Bank.

Yang, Y., & Haung, Y. (1997). *Impact of Trade Liberalization on Income Distribution in China* (Economic Division Working Paper No. 1).

Yanikkaya, H. (2003). Trade Openness and Economic Growth: A Cross-Country Empirical Investigation. *Journal of Development Economics, 72*(1), 57–89. doi:10.1016/S0304-3878(03)00068-3

Yeung, Y. M. (1996). Introduction. In Y. M. Yeung and Y. W. Sung (Eds.), *Shanghai: transformation and modernization under China's open door* (pp. 1-23). Hong Kong: Chinese University Press.

Yin, R. (1994). *Case study research: design and methods.* London: Sage.

Yoo, S.-H. (2003). Does information technology contribute to economic growth in developing countries? A cross-country analysis. *Applied Economics Letters, 10,* 679–682. doi:10.1080/1350485032000138971

Young-Hyman, T. (2008). The potential for effective regional development agencies in Turkey: A comparative analysis. *Regional & Federal Studies, 18*(4), 375–402. doi:10.1080/13597560802223953

Yusof, R. M., & Majid, M. S. A. (2007). Macroeconomic Variables and Stock Returns in Malaysia: An Application of the ARDL Bound Testing Approach. *Savings and Development, 31*(4), 449–469.

Zabala-Iturriagagoitia, J. M., Jimenez-Saez, F., & Castro-Martnez, E. (2008). Evaluating European Regional Innovation. *Strategies . European Planning Studies, 16*(8), 1145–1160. doi:10.1080/09654310802315849

About the Contributors

Muhammed Karatas received his Ph.D. from Mugla University, Turkey. He is currently working as an associate professor at Mugla University. His main areas of interests are economic development, socioeconomic development, human capital, natural resources and the economy of the environment, the European Union, and innovation and technology. He teaches on the topics of natural resources and the economy of the environment, economic development and growth, economics, international economic integration and the European Union, international institutions, and the economics of innovation. He has published a number of papers and book chapters in various subjects.

Mustafa Zihni Tunca is an associate professor at Suleyman Demirel University, Turkey. He is the director of e-MBA Program at SDU. He earned his Ph.D. degree from Lancaster University, UK. His research interests include e-commerce, ICTs, and supply chain management. He has published several papers, book chapters and conferance papers. He is the editor of two books.

* * *

Abdul Mumin Abdulai holds a Bachelor's degree in Geography & Resource Development with Sociology from the University of Ghana, Legon-Accra, and Master's degree in Sociology & Anthropology from the International Islamic University Malaysia (IIUM). Currently, he is in the final year of his PhD programme in Environment & Development at the Institute for Environment & Development (LESTARI), National University of Malaysia. His research interests include Livelihoods Sustainability, Poverty Alleviation, Resource Use and Enhancement, & Environmental Governance.

Sinan Alcin received his PhD from the Department of Economics at Marmara University, Institute of Social Sciences. He is an Assistant Professor of Economics at Maltepe University. His research areas are labor economics and economics of technology.

Leonardo Baggiani was born in 1974 near Pisa (Italy). He got graduate in Economics at the University of Pisa in 1998 with a discussion on Inflation Targeting and the new-born European Central Bank. In 2003, after a short working period in the credit/financial sector, he got a Master Grade in Finance and Risk Management at the Bicocca University in Milan. Since few years he is working as derivatives trader and analyst for a bank in Florence. He has published some papers on Jensen's Social Sciences Research Network site about modeling the euro-dollar exchange-rate and a simple economy affected by money-illusion. He manages an Italian blog to expose sketches of his economic insights mainly on business cycle theories. He collaborates with an important Italian on-line journal as economic columnist. He collaborates with some associations and economists to develop and spread new business-cycle theoretical perspectives.

Chamhuri Siwar: Professor Siwar has more than 35 years experience as lecturer and researcher at Universiti Kebangsaan Malaysia (UKM). Presently, he is a Principal Research Fellow at the Institute for Environment and Development (LESTARI), UKM. He has served as lecturer at the Faculty of Economic at UKM, where he once served as Head, Department of Agriculture and Resource Economics. His area of research specialisation includes: Agricultural and Resource Economics, Rural Economics, Environmental Economics, Poverty and Income Distribution, Sustainable Economies, Socioeconomics and Impact Studies, sustainable livelihood and sustainability evaluation, corporate social responsibility, trade and environment. He has successfully supervised 10 PhDs and 12 Masters, and has served as external examiners to graduate students of Universiti Malaya, Universiti Sains Malaysia, Universiti Putra Malaysia, Universiti Malaysia Sabah, Wageningan University (Neatherlands), Bharathidasan University(India).

Teruyuki Bunno, Professor of Business Management, Faculty of Business Administration, Kinki University. Major areas of specialty include Innovation Theory, Lifecycle of Firms and New Business Creations. Current research focuses on the roles of human resources in order to grow up a firm. Publications include Business Issues of Venture Business to overcome (ed. R. Takada, H. Ueno, T. Murakoso and K. Maeda), Doyuukan 2009, in Japanese, Venture Business Theory (ed. with K. Ota and K. Ikeda), Jikkyo Shuppan 2007, in Japanese. He is a board member of Japan Academy of small Business Studies and The Kansai Association for Venture and Entrepreneur Studies.

Utz Dornberger is a Professor and the Director of the 'International SEPT (Small Enterprise Promotion and Training) Program' at University of Leipzig, Germany. His research interest includes firm internationalization and international entrepreneurship, innovation management and entrepreneurship. He holds a MSc. in Biology and an MBA in SME Development. He manages the entrepreneurship promotion programme SMILE and the MBA programme in SME Development at the University of Leipzig which belongs to the Top International Master Programme in Germany. He is CEO of the consulting company INNOWAYS Inc. managing several promotion programmes for high-tech SMEs in developing countries.

Erkan Erdil (Ankara, 1968) studied Political Science and Public Administration at Middle East Technical University (METU) in Ankara. He received Bachelor of Science degree in 1990. He received Master of Science degree in 1994. He further received Ph.D. in Economics from University of Maastricht in 2001 and another Ph.D. from METU in 2004. He was appointed as instructor in 1997 and as the vice-chairman of the Department of Economics at METU. He was, then appointed as assistant professor in 2001 and associate professor in 2005. He is also the director of Science and Technology Policy Research Center (METU-TEKPOL) since 2002. His main areas of interest are labor economics, economics of technology, applied econometrics, economics of information and uncertainty. He has been author/co-author, and referee of articles in Applied Economics, Applied Economics Letters, Agricultural Economics, METU Studies in Development and presented papers to various international conferences.

Hakan Gundogdu is an assistant professor at the Department of Philosophy of the Faculty of Arts and Sciences, Gazi University in Ankara, Turkey. He was educated at Dokuz Eylul University in Izmir, Turkey, where he graduated in 1992 with a BA in divinity. He also received his M.A. (1995) and Ph.D. degrees (2003) in Philosophy and Religious Sciences from the Institute of Social Sciences at Dokuz Eylul University. He worked as a teacher at public schools between 1992 and 1996. He became research assistant in 1996 and assistant professor in 2004 at the chair of History of Philosophy at the same University. In 2009, he joined the Department of Philosophy at the Faculty of Arts and Sciences, Gazi University in Ankara. While his doctoral thesis was about contemporary humanism and atheism, since 2004, Dr. Gundogdu has generally been working on social, moral and political philosophy. His recent academic publications are about multiculturalism, globalization, toleration, critical thinking, free will debate and existentialism. In addition to his own writings, he translated some articles and books on general philosophy, thinking straight, understanding history and Michel Foucault. Since 2004, he has taught both graduate and undergraduate courses on philosophy of history, philosophy of education, reading and writing skills in philosophy, history of philosophy, modern philosophy, ancient philosophy, introduction to philosophy, logic, philosophy of religion, Islamic philosophy, philosophical texts, and ethics.

Niv Horesh is Lecturer in Chinese Studies at UNSW, Sydney, Australia. He worked as Business Development Manager with one of China's largest security-system integrators between 2000-2003. Dr. Horesh's academic research focuses on the economic history of Shanghai, and depictions of China in 18th century classic European literature.

Hiroki Idota, Associate Professor of Management Information, Faculty of Management, Otemon Gakuin University. Major areas of specialty include Management Information System, Management Administration. Board of Director of the Japan Society for Management Information and the Japan Society for Information and Management. Current research focuses on the transformation of the ICT capability and Industry cluster. Publications include The Information Quality Management in Organizations, Journal of Japan Society for Information and Management, Vol. 23, No. 4 in Japanese, The Factors to Promote the Practical Use of Customer's Personal Information in the Japanese firms, Otemon Economic Studies, Vol. 41, 2008, The Theory and Practical Use of Information Security Management, Hakuto Shobou, 2004, in Japanese.

Varinder Jain is a Doctoral Fellow at the Centre for Development Studies, Thiruvananthapuram, Kerala (INDIA). He has obtained his M. Phil degree from Jawaharlal Nehru University, New Delhi. He has published a few research papers in prestigious journals and edited books. His research interests are varied. These include political economy issues, vulnerability, informal sector, social security and foreign direct investment.

M. Selcan Kaynak is an Assistant Professor at the Political Science and International Relations Department of Bogazici University, Turkey. Her research focuses on digital divide policies, cultural globalization, and political socialization and mass media. She obtained her Ph.D. from the Mass Media and Communication Program at Temple University.

Muhammad Arshad Khan is currently working as Senior Research Economist, Pakistan Institute of Development Economics (PIDE), Islamabad (Pakistan). He has received his Master degree in Economics from University of Azad Jammu & Kashmir Muzaffarabad (Azad Kashmir), M.Phil form Quaid-i-

Azam University Islamabad (Pakistan) and Ph.D. from Pakistan Institute of Development Economics (PIDE) Islamabad. Mr. Khan has more than 16 years of teaching experience, and has worked in various capacities including Lecturer in Economics, University of Azad Jammu & Kashmir Muzaffarabad, Principal, Government College Kotli (Azad Kashmir) and Head Department of Economics, Government Post-graduate College Muzaffarabad (Azad Kashmir) before he joined PIDE. He has more than 20 publications so far that include book chapters, refereed articles in the International and National Journals in the areas of exchange rate, Finance and Growth, Banking Sector Reforms, Energy Issues and Trade and Finance. His area of interest is macroeconomics, macroeconometric modelling, monetary economics and international trade and finance.

Israfil Kurtcephe is the rector of Akdeniz University in Antalya, Turkey. He is a member of Department of History since 1999. He has taken several administrative, consultive, editorial tasks. He has published several books, chapters, papers and delivered a number of conferances along with documentary consultancies and TV/Radio programmes.

Hiroaki Miyoshi, Professor of Graduate School of Policy and Management, Doshisha University, Kyoto and director at its Institute for Technology, Enterprise and Competitiveness (ITEC). He worked at a major private sector think tank for 10 years, conducting research and making policy recommendations on a broad range of issue as a senior researcher and joined Doshisha University in 2003. His research interests include public economics and organizational economics. His recent publications include Knowledge Asset Management and Organizational Performance (ed. with Y. Shouzugawa), Hakuto-Shobo Publishing Company, 2009; Technological Innovation in the Automotive Industry and Economic Welfare (ed. with M. Tanashita), Hakuto-Shobo Publishing Company, 2008; 'Factors Associated with Safety of Passenger Cars' (with M. Tanashita), IATSS Research, 2008; and 'Japanese Corporate Governance: Structural Change and Financial Performance' (with A. M. Colpan, T. Yoshikawa, and T. Hikino), Asian Business & Management, 2007.

Ramakrishna Nallathiga is an Urban Environmental Planner and holds a Master's degree of Philosophy in Land Economy (UK). His work experience spanning over ten years concerns with urban and regional development planning, urban and environmental policy as well as environmental planning, assessment and management. During his career, he was associated with national academic and research institutes of repute like NEERI – Nagpur, IGIDR – Mumbai, IIT – Bombay and Bombay First. Currently, he is affiliated to the Centre for Good Governance, Hyderabad. He has presented papers in a dozen international conferences, both in India as well as abroad. He has more than a dozen publications in international and national journals to his credit.

Masaru Ogawa, Associate Professor of Economics, Department of Business Management, Kobe Gakuin University. Major areas of specialty include Operations Research and Business Management. Current research focuses on application of DEA (Data Envelopment of Analysis) to Japanese information industries such as telecommunications and broadcasting. Publications include "Benchmarking Method Considering Complementary Network Externality, Scientiae Mathematicae Japonicae, (Japanese Association of Mathematical Sciences) Vol. 58, No. 3, 2002, and "The Total Ranking Method from Multi-categorized Voting Data Based on AHP, Industrial Engineering and Management Systems, Vol. 1, No. 1, 2003. Received B.A. in Engineering from Osaka University; M.A. from Osaka School of International

Public Policy, Osaka University; and Ph.D. in Engineering from Osaka University. He served as a core member of Social Implications of Technology and Information Ethics Committee, Network Operation Guideline Working Group, and Technology and Ethics Examination Working Group, the Institute of Electronics, Information and Communication Engineers (IEICE).

Bekir Parlak is a professor in the Department of Public Administration at the University of Uludag in Turkey. He received his Ph. D. degree in Province Administration and Local Governments from the University of Cumhuriyet. His research interests are regional development, e-government, local e-government, theory of democracy, administrative history and administrative reforms. He teaches courses on Public Administration, Local Governments, Governance and E-Government, Comparative Government Systems, Personnel Management, Modern Management Techniques, Administrative Reforms in Turkey and Turkish Administrative History.

Michael G. Papaioannou is a senior economist in the IMF's Monetary and Capital Markets Department. Previously, he was a senior economist in three other IMF Departments. While at the Fund, he served as a Special Adviser to the Governing Board of the Bank of Greece. Prior to his employment with the IMF, he was a Senior Vice President and Director of the Foreign Exchange Service of The WEFA Group (Wharton Econometrics Forecasting Associates). He has also served as Chief Economist of the Council of Economic Advisors of Greece. He taught at Temple University as an Adjunct Associate Professor of Finance. He was a Principal Research Fellow at the University of Pennsylvania, Department of Economics, LINK Central, and a Summer Intern in the World Bank. He holds a Ph.D. in economics from the University of Pennsylvania, and an M.A. in economics from Georgetown University (full distinction). He has co-edited a book, published numerous articles in the area of international finance, and is an associate editor of a finance journal.

Alexandre Repkine graduated with B.Sc. in mathematics from the Moscow State University in 1993, Alexandre Repkine studied at the New Economic School in Russia in a Master of Economics program, where he obtained the M.Sc. in Economics degree in 1995. At that time his research interests were mostly focusing on the process of economic transition that his native country was going through at that time. Alexandre Repkine received his Ph.D. in Economics from the Catholic University of Leuven, Belgium, in 2000. Over the years, his research covered topics of economic transition, productive efficiency, spatial econometrics and consumer choice theory. He has been working and teaching economics at Korean universities since 2001. He is currently an assistant professor with the department of Economics at Korea University.

Clarissa Sales was born in Malolos City, Bulacan, Philippines. For five years she worked as Project Manager for the Development Academy of the Philippines, an institution that is focused on approaches to national development. She was tasked to manage various productivity and quality improvement programs for small and medium sized exporting firms. In 2005 Ms. Sales was awarded full scholarship by the German Academic Exchange Service (DAAD) to pursue post-graduate studies in Germany. She completed her MBA in Small and Medium-Sized Enterprise Development from the University of Leipzig in 2007. Currently she works as Project Manager for Cygnific B.V., the call centre of Air-France KLM for Northern and Western Europe. She is a certified Lean Belt and trained in Lean Six Sigma methodology.

Lakhwinder Singh is presently serving as Professor of Economics at Punjabi University, Patiala, Punjab (INDIA). He has been Visiting Fellow at the School of Economics, Seoul National University, South Korea and Post-Doctoral Fellow at Yale University, USA. He has been awarded the Ford Foundation Fellowship in Economics and Asia Fellowship by the Institute of International Education. His teaching and research initiatives focus on the areas of industrial organisation, development economics, international technology transfer and knowledge spillovers, innovations and high-tech. trade, globalisation and comparative development experience of South and South East Asian Countries.

Rup Singh is a lecturer in Economics at the University of the South Pacific, Suva (Fiji). He teaches Macroeconomics and Applied Econometrics. His doctorate study (in progress) is on growth models and policy. He has jointly published on growth topics particularly with an emphasis on growth policy, see http://ideas.repec.org. Currently his research is focused on the extension and the use of the exogenous neo-classical model of Solow for policy in newly industrialized economies of East Asia.

Mehmet Zahid Sobaci is a research assistant in the Department of Public Administration at the University of Uludag in Turkey. His research interests are e-government, policy transfer, governance, independent regulatory agencies, new public management and administrative reforms. He is author of many articles.

Murad Tiryakioglu received his MA from Business Administration in Afyon Kocatepe University, the Institute of Social Sciences. He also has an MA in Economics from the same university. Currently he is doing his PhD in Economics and working at Afyon Kocatepe University as a lecturer. His research areas are industrial organization, economics of technology and micro-based economic growth.

Masatsugu Tsuji, Professor of Economics, Graduate School of Applied Informatics, University of Hyogo, and Professor Emeritus of Osaka University. Major areas of specialty include Economic Theory, Economics of Information and Telecommunications. Current research focuses on the transformation of the ICT industry. Publications include The Flowchart Approach to Industrial Cluster Policy (ed. with A. Kuchiki), Palgrave Macmillan 2008, Industrial Agglomeration and New Technology (ed. with E. Giovannetti and M. Kagami), Edward Elgar 2007, The Internet Revolution: A Global Perspective, (ed. with E. Giovannetti and M. Kagami), Cambridge University Press, 2003. He was honored by the Minister of Internal Affairs and Communications for his contributions to telecommunications policy. Received B.A. in Economics from Kyoto University; M.A. in Economics from Osaka University; and Ph.D. in Economics from Stanford University. He also served as visiting professor of Carnegie Mellon University, Board of Director, International Telecommunications Society (ITS) and Council of International Society for Telemedicine.

Burcu Turkcan, graduated from Ege University with Bachelor's degree on Economics in 2005. In 2008, she completed her master's degree in the same university. Her thesis was on the relationship between FDI and economic growth. Between 2007-08, she worked as a research asistant in Izmir University of Economics. She began her PhD. in Ege University in 2008 and became research assistant in the same university. She involved in several research projects in the last three years. Her interest areas are macroeconomics and econometrics.

George P. Tsetsekos holds the R. John Chapel, Jr., Dean's Chair in Leadership Drexel University's LeBow College of Business. He has served as Dean of the LeBow College of Business since August 2001. Prior to his appointment as Dean, he served as Drexel's vice president for Academic Administration and served as a member of the team that achieved the merger between Drexel and MCP Hahnemann Universities. Dr. Tsetsekos joined LeBow College's finance faculty in 1988 and directed its Risk Management Center. His research covers the areas of corporate finance, investments, banking and international finance. He serves on the boards of the Federal Reserve Bank of Philadelphia (Economic Advisory Board), The PENJERDEL Council, Pennsylvania Economic League, The Conference Board, World Trade Center of Greater Philadelphia, Global Interdependence Center, and the editorial boards of academic finance journals. He holds a Ph.D. in Finance from the University of Tennessee, an MBA in Finance and a B.S. in Electrical and Mechanical Engineering from the National Technical University of Athens, Greece.

Yasushi Ueki, Research Fellow, Bangkok Research Center, Institute of Developing Economies, Japan External Trade Organization, Thailand. His research interests include development economics, new technologies for development, and Asian and Latin American economies. Current researches focus on agglomeration, production and logistics networks, and industrial upgrading and innovation. Publications include Information Technology for Development of Small and Medium-sized Exporters in Latin America and East Asia (ed. with M. Kuwayama and M. Tsuji), United Nations Economic Commission for Latin America and the Caribbean (ECLAC), 2005, and "Electronic Industry in Asia: Changing Supply Chain and the Effects," in The Internet Revolution: A Global Perspective (ed. Giovannetti, E., M.Kagami and M. Tsuji), Cambridge University Press, 2003. Received B.A. in Economics from Waseda University, M.A. in Economics from Tokyo University, and Ph.D. from Graduate School of International Public Policy, Osaka University. He also served for U.N. ECLAC.

Sam Wong: Previously worked as a journalist in Hong Kong, Sam Wong is lecturer in the School of Earth and Environment at the University of Leeds, UK. His research interests lie in sustainable technology, climate change, sustainable livelihoods and gender. He is the author of the book Exploring Unseen Social Capital in Community Participation (Amsterdam University Press, 2007). He also has publications in Environmental Politics, Gender and Development, and Urban Studies. He has obtained grants from the EPSRC, British Academy, British Council and NESTA. His research areas include India, Bangladesh, Ghana, Burkina Faso, China, England and Wales. He is experienced in inter-disciplinary research. He was recently interviewed by the BBC about this research in sustainable development.

I. Hakan Yetkiner has received his B.Sc. in Management from Middle East Technical University (METU), Ankara, Turkey. He has two master's degree. One is M.S. in Economics from METU, Ankara, Turkey and the second one is M.Sc. in Economics from London School of Economics, England. He holds two Ph.D.s: one from METU, Ankara, Turkey and another from the University of Groningen, the Netherlands. He is currently faculty member of Izmir University of Economics. He is also director of Vocational School in the same university. His publications appeared in Applied Economics, Resource and Energy Economics, Kyklos, and METU Studies in Development. His research interests are economic growth and scientific communication.

Index

D

E

F

G

H

I

J

K

L

M

U

V

W

Y